Global Activism Reader

GLOBAL ACTIVISM READER

Edited by

Luc Reydams

continuum

NEW YORK • LONDON

2011

The Continuum International Publishing Group
80 Maiden Lane, New York, NY 10038
The Tower Building, 11 York Road, London SE1 7NX

www.continuumbooks.com

Library of Congress Cataloging-in-Publication Data
Global activism reader / edited by Luc Reydams.
  p. cm.
Includes bibliographical references and index.
ISBN-13: 978-1-4411-1650-5 (hardcover : alk. paper)
ISBN-10: 1-4411-1650-8 (hardcover : alk. paper)
ISBN-13: 978-1-4411-7955-5 (pbk. : alk. paper)
ISBN-10: 1-4411-7955-0 (pbk. : alk. paper) 1. Civil society. 2. Transnationalism.
3. Social movements–International cooperation. 4. Social action–International cooperation.
I. Reydams, Luc. II. Title.

JZ1318.G5544 2011
322.4–dc22

                                                                                            2010022594

ISBN: HB: 978-1-4411-1650-5
       PB: 978-1-4411-7955-5

Typeset by Newgen Imaging Systems Pvt Ltd, Chennai, India
Printed in the United States of America by Sheridan Books, Inc

Contents

Preface   ix

Acknowledgments   xiii

PART I SOCIAL MOVEMENTS, NGOs, NETWORKS, AND
THE IDEA OF A GLOBAL CIVIL SOCIETY

Chapter One
Social Movements, NGOs, and Networks   3
Mary Kaldor

Chapter Two
Transnational Advocacy Networks in the Movement Society   24
Margaret E. Keck and Kathryn Sikkink

Chapter Three
The Rise and Fall of Transnational Civil Society: The Evolution
of International Non-Governmental Organizations
since the Mid-Nineteenth Century   35
Thomas Richard Davies

PART II ANTI-SLAVERY AND CONGO REFORM

Chapter Four
Transatlantic Activism in the Eighteenth Century:
the Anti-Slavery Movement   47
Huw T. David

Chapter Five
Transnational Humanitarian Heroes in the Early Twentieth Century:
The Congo Reform Movement   59
William E. DeMars

PART III GLOBAL LABOR

Chapter Six
Transnational Pioneers: The International Labor Movement   73
Dan Gallin

Chapter Seven
Labor Rights as Human Rights: Regulation in the Context of
a "Thinned" National State   81
Gay W. Seidman

PART IV HUMAN RIGHTS

Chapter Eight
The Power of Norms versus the Norms of Power: Transnational
Civil Society and Human Rights   115
Thomas Risse

Chapter Nine
Civil Society and the International Criminal Court   134
Johan D. van der Vyver

Chapter Ten
Human Rights NGOs: A Critical Evaluation   149
Makau Mutua

PART V WOMEN'S RIGHTS

Chapter Eleven
The Global Women's Movement: Origins, Issues and Strategies   163
Peggy Antrobus

Chapter Twelve
Contesting Women's Rights: Charting the Emergence
of a Transnational Conservative Counter-network   190
Louise Chappell

PART VI ENVIRONMENT

Chapter Thirteen
Spinning the Green Web: Transnational Environmentalism   221
Wendy E. F. Torrance and Andrew W. Torrance

Chapter Fourteen
Transnational Policy Networks and the Role of Advocacy Scientists:
From Ozone Layer Protection to Climate Change   236
Reiner Grundmann

Chapter Fifteen
Challenging Global Warming as a Social Problem: An Analysis
of the Conservative Movement's Counter-Claims   251
Aaron M. McCright and Riley E. Dunlap

PART VII PEACE AND DISARMAMENT

Chapter Sixteen
Banning the Bomb   273
David Cortright

Chapter Seventeen
The Ottawa Process: Nine-Day Wonder or a New Model for
Disarmament Negotiations? 291
Maurice Bleicher

Chapter Eighteen
Assessing the Small Arms Movement: The Trials and Tribulations
of a Transnational Network 300
Suzette R. Grillot, Craig S. Stapley, and Molly E. Hanna

PART VIII SOCIAL JUSTICE AND DEMOCRACY
Chapter Nineteen
Before Seattle: The Historical Roots of the Current Movement against
Corporate-led Globalization 327
Robin Broad and Zahara Heckscher

Chapter Twenty
Reclaiming the Commons 341
Naomi Klein

Chapter Twenty-One
Creating Spaces for Global Democracy: The World Social Forum Process 347
Jackie Smith

Chapter Twenty-Two
Is Another World Possible? Problems and Shortcomings
of the World Social Forum 376
Owen Worth and Karen Buckley

Notes on Authors 388
Index 391

Preface

Take Action Now! The idea for this Reader grew out of an undergraduate writing seminar I have taught for almost ten years in the Political Science Department at the University of Notre Dame. All this time I struggled with the question what to call the course. After considering names such as Transnational Advocacy Networks and Global Social Movements, I settled on the clear and simple Global Activism. The term "activism" encompasses both actors and action in the transnational sociopolitical space. Student feedback suggests that it is the activism that draws them to the seminar, and the whole range of it: progressive and conservative, elite and mass, civic and "direct," in the streets and on the internet, professional and volunteer, etc. I also observed an eagerness among my students to explore the principle issue areas (or causes) of transnational activism and then, as the semester progresses, to research a campaign or movement of their choice. In the course of the years I further became convinced of the usefulness of movies and documentaries for teaching global activism. They are important activist tools, and watching them together in the classroom helps create a seminar identity. Finally, and as the cover of this book suggests, the internet in no time has become an indispensable organizing and mobilizing medium. Countless activist websites compete for attention and call on visitors to "take action now!" Thus I set out to create a Reader that would respond to these expectations and to the latest developments in global activism. My top concerns all along were the "5Cs": coherence, comprehensiveness, complementarity, continued relevance, and controversy. Realizing and reconciling these objectives in one volume took years of puzzling with hundreds of worthy written pieces. My students were instrumental in helping me solve the puzzle, and most of the time I deferred to their judgment as to whether a text "works" and "fits". So the final product is the result of much trial and error, lively discussion, and inevitable compromise—and I am confident that it works for students and instructors.

Coherence. The Reader starts with two by-now classical texts from the social movements/ advocacy networks/civil society literature. They provide the conceptual and analytical framework for the rest of the volume. Subsequent chapters refer to and build on them—and sometimes challenge them. This is already evident in the third text in the introductory part, which tempers the optimism about an emerging transnational civil society. Thus the tone is set and the foundation laid for the rest of the volume: parts and chapters build on, complement, and criticize one another. A dialectical tension runs through each part and, therefore, through the entire Reader.

Comprehensiveness. The Reader aims to be comprehensive in two respects. Historically by going back to the earliest instance of transnational activism (the anti-slave trade campaign in the late eighteenth century) and by ending with a movement that emerged on the eve of the twenty-first century (social justice and democracy); and thematically, by covering the principal issue areas of transnational activism: labor, human rights, women's rights, the environment, peace and disarmament, and social justice and democracy. The fact that these issue areas correspond with the major contemporary social movements, however, does not make this volume a "social movements reader." The book's focus is more on campaigns (e.g. climate change, small arms, international criminal justice) than on the movements that wage them. The Reader situates itself therefore more in political history and international relations than in (political) sociology.

Complementarity. Texts were selected and edited in order to ensure maximum flow and minimum overlap, but some gaps and repetition remain. The theoretical framework, for instance, returns regularly, and deliberately so, for it helps structure and deepen class discussions. Gaps in the readings, on the other hand, result from space constraints and have been filled as much as possible by suggesting selected further readings.

Continued relevance. Within any given issue area numerous topical campaigns are waged simultaneously. Campaigns come and go, catch on or falter, succeed or go dormant. The challenge was to choose campaigns to which the current generation of students can relate and which will remain relevant in the foreseeable future. Global warming, international criminal justice, small arms control, and the World Social Forum, for example, will remain high on the activist and political agenda in the coming years. The inclusion of these issues should make the Reader useful to the next generations of students as well.

Controversy. The Reader puts itself in the middle of the battle of ideas without taking sides. Some articles (or documentaries) challenge the conventional wisdom about activists and their causes. The controversy built into each set of readings hopefully draws even the most indifferent student into the discussion.

Overview. The Reader consists of 22 chapters arranged in eight parts and a companion website with further readings and resources. Parts I and II are introductory, Parts III to VIII cover the principal issue areas in transnational activism. Authors hail from around the world and various academic disciplines, viz. international relations, sociology, law, history, political economy, and peace studies. Some are scholar-activists or scholar-sympathizers, others are distinctively more critical. Three authors come from outside academia: writer Naomi Klein, diplomat Maurice Bleicher, and former international trade union leader Dan Gallin.

Part I provides the conceptual and analytical framework and consists of three chapters. The first two are by grandes dames in their respective fields: Mary Kaldor, Margaret Keck, and Kathryn Sikkink. Chapter One, taken from Mary Kaldor's noted book *Global Civil Society—An Answer to War*, introduces the various nongovernmental actors in global politics. Chapter Two by Margaret Keck and Kathryn Sikkink is an article version of their groundbreaking *Activist Beyond Borders. Transnational Advocacy Networks in International Politics.* Published in 1998, the book quickly became the cornerstone of transnational activism studies. Chapter Three is an original contribution by political historian Thomas Richard Davies. Davies challenges the conventional wisdom that transnational civil society progresses linearly.

Part II consists of two historical studies. In Chapter Four, historian Huw David chronicles and analyzes what is believed to be the earliest instance of transnational activism: the campaign against the international slave trade in the late eighteenth century. Chapter Five is an original contribution by international relations scholar William DeMars who recounts the "NGO war" over Congo in the early twentieth century and draws interesting parallels with the Save Darfur campaign in the period 2005–2010.

Part III, titled Global Labor, consists of two chapters. Chapter Six by Dan Gallin, former secretary-general of the International Federation of Food, Agriculture, Hotel and Catering and Tobacco Workers' Union, is an historical overview of the international labor movement from the late nineteenth century up to the beginning of the twenty-first century. In Chapter Seven, sociologist Gay Seidman discusses some of the issues that are raised as labor activism moves from a national to a transnational arena, and labor rights are redefined as human rights.

Part IV on the international human rights movement consists of three chapters. International relations scholar Thomas Risse describes in Chapter Eight the origins of the movement and its ascendency in the 1990s. Then follow two articles by legal scholars. Johan van der Vyver in Chapter Nine tells the story of one movement's greatest political victories: the adoption in the 1998 of the treaty establishing the International Criminal Court. Chapter Ten by Makau Mutua is a rare critical note on human rights NGOs.

Part V on women's rights begins with excerpts from *The Global Women's Movement: Origins, Issues and Strategies* by eminent women's rights activist and scholar Peggy Antrobus (Chapter Eleven). In Chapter Twelve, feminist scholar Louise Chappell charts the emergence over the past two decades of a powerful transnational conservative counter-movement.

Part VI on environmental activism comprises three chapters. In Chapter Thirteen, political scientist Wendy Torrance and lawyer-biologist Andrew Torrance narrate the spinning over the years of a dense web of transnational environmentalism. Political scientist Reiner Grundmann, in Chapter Fourteen, zooms in on the role of scientists ("epistemic communities") in the campaigns against ozone depletion and climate change. In Chapter Fifteen, sociologists Aaron McCright and Riley Dunlap investigate the counter-claims of the conservative movement in the climate change "war."

Part VII on peace and disarmament also consists of three chapters. Chapter Sixteen, 'Banning the Bomb', is an excerpt from *Peace: A History of Movements and Ideas* (2008) by David Cortright. Cortright was executive director in the 1980s of the largest disarmament organization in the United States. Chapter Seventeen is taken from *Disarmament Forum*, a publication of the United Nations Institute for Disarmament. Maurice Bleicher, a French official, critically reflects therein on the "Ottawa Process" leading to the adoption in 1997 of the convention on the prohibition of anti-personnel mines. In Chapter Eighteen, political scientists Suzette Grillot, Craig Stapley, and Molly Hanna discuss the trials and tribulations of the campaign against small arms and light weapons.

Part VIII deals with mobilization against the neo-liberal international economic order and consists of four chapters. Chapter Nineteen, by Robin Broad and Zahara Heckscher, draws on an article first published in Robin Broad (ed.) *Global Backlash: Citizen Initiatives for a Just World Economy* (2002). Broad and Heckscher explore the historical roots of the current movement against corporate-led globalization. "Reclaiming the Commons" (Chapter Twenty) by Canadian writer-activist-journalist Naomi Klein is the transcript of an influential speech she gave in 2001 and can be considered the movement's manifesto. Chapter Twenty-one on the World Social Forum is an excerpt from *Social Movements for Global Democracy* (2007) by my Notre Dame colleague, sociologist Jackie Smith. The Reader ends on a critical note. Political scientists Owen Worth and Karen Buckly analyze in Chapter Twenty-two the problems and shortcomings of the World Social Forum.

A Companion Website contains for each chapter further (annotated) readings and resources, such as companion video documentaries, links to activist websites, timelines, etc. The book is the basic menu; the site is the à-la-carte part.

Good Luck! To the instructor user of the Reader: with the exception of the first two chapters, none of the texts should take more than two hours to read, and several require significantly less time. It should be possible, therefore, to go through the entire volume in a thirteen or fifteen week semester – without losing momentum and without overburdening its users. After three or four weeks the class or seminar should 'run itself.' Students can find ample up-to-date additional resources in the Reader for individual research. Instructors may want to view in advance a number of the suggested movies and documentaries. They are easily available and make great classes. A most useful complement for writing assignments is *They Say/I Say: The Moves That Matter in Academic Writing* by Gerald Graff and Cathy Birkenstein (2006).

To the student user of the Reader: Part I, like most introductions of academic books, is fairly dense, and it is therefore quite normal to feel overwhelmed, especially if you are a freshman. Concepts, categories, and acronyms may start to blur and, on top of that, you may start to doubt some priorly held beliefs. But don't panic, after Part I the readings only get lighter. They become less theoretical and definitely more empirical, and you will be able to relate to most of them through personal experience. It is important, however, to go back every now and then to Part I and the first two chapters in particular. They are the platform and framework of this volume that should prevent you from getting lost in the complex world of global activism.

Good luck!

Luc Reydams
Associate Professional Specialist, Department of Political Science,
University of Notre Dame and Fellow,
Center for Global Governance Studies,
University of Leuven

Acknowledgments

As said in the preface, the idea for this Reader grew out of an undergraduate writing seminar I have taught for almost ten years in the Political Science Department at the University of Notre Dame. I thank my students for their contributions to the seminar and their feedback on earlier versions of the Reader. I owe special thanks to my research assistants Mark Bond, Michael Lucien, and Michelle Schmit. Mark was a great help in organizing the bibliography and Michael and Michelle were instrumental in making the final cut. At Notre Dame, I further thank Jackie Smith for her collegiality, and the Institute for Scholarship in the Liberal Arts (College for Arts and Letters) for a grant to defray copyright costs, and Gina Pellouchoud of DCL-Services for securing reproduction permissions.

I wrote the proposal for the Reader during a research stay at the Center for Global Governance Studies at the University of Leuven. I sincerely thank its director Jan Wouters for his friendship and support. Thank you also to my "virtual" colleague, Clifford Bob from Duquesne University, for years of correspondence and exchanges by email. I hope that we will meet soon.

It has been a great pleasure working with Marie-Claire Antoine at Continuum Publishing. My warmest thanks to her for her guidance—and patience. Sincere thanks also to the three anonymous reviewers for valuable comments on the proposal and to William DeMars, Thomas Richard Davies, Owen Worth, and Karen Buckly for contributing original pieces.

Finally, pursuing my academic dreams would not have been possible without the unconditional love and support of my wife Griet.

PART I

SOCIAL MOVEMENTS, NGOs, NETWORKS, AND THE IDEA OF A GLOBAL CIVIL SOCIETY

CHAPTER ONE

Social Movements, NGOs, and Networks

Mary Kaldor

Source: Mary Kaldor *Global Civil Society: An Answer to War* (2003) 8–108 © 2003 Polity Press Ltd—Reproduced with permission.

Terms like 'global politics' or global civil society signify the domestication of the international. We are accustomed to think of the international as the realm of diplomacy, high level meetings and military strategy and the domestic, at least in democratic societies, as the realm of debate, discussion, and public pressure—in short, the realm of politics; that is the meaning of the Great Divide. The 'global scene' says Bauman was traditionally 'the theatre of *inter-state*' relations. Then after the Second World War, the development of '*supra-state* integration', the emergence of blocs, not just East and West but also the non-aligned bloc, meant that the '"global scene" was increasingly seen as the theatre of co-existence and competition between *groups of states*, rather than between states themselves.'[1]

The salient characteristic of the world after 1989 is the advent of politics in the 'global scene'. By global politics, I mean the interaction between the institutions of global governance (international institutions and states) and global civil society—the groups, networks and movements who comprise the mechanisms through which individuals negotiate and renegotiate social contracts or political bargains at a global level. In other words, a system of relations between states or groups of states, characterised by a process of bargaining based on collective interest, in which the threat of armed conflict was an ever-present characteristic of the bargaining, has been supplanted by a much more complex world of politics, involving a range of institutions and individuals and in which there is a place, perhaps small, for individual reason and sentiment, and not just state or bloc interest.

This development is the outcome of changes both from above and from below. On the one hand, 1989 marked the end of global conflict, the disintegration of blocs, and the end of the prevalent use of ideology to suppress critical voices or even just good-tempered conversation at the international level. This made it possible for states and international institutions to deal with each other in new co-operative and discursive ways that were more receptive to individuals and citizens groups outside the corridors of power. On the other hand, the movements and groups who had struggled for peace and democracy or for human rights and environmental responsibility during the Cold War years were able to take advantage of this new openness as well as the ways in which the new language of global civil society legitimised their activities.

A theme of this chapter is that this process involved what I call the 'taming' of the social movements of the pre-1989 period. Their successors, I argue, are what are known as NGOs. The growing dominance of NGOs, together with the rise of new nationalist and religious movements and the decline of many older civic associations like trades unions, has tempered the initial enthusiasm for the language of civil society, at least among activists.

There is, to day, a proliferation of language used to describe the non-state actors in global politics: global social movements[2]; international NGOs (INGOs); transnational advocacy networks[3]; civil society organisations; global public policy networks[4]; to name but a few. I use the term global civil society [. . .] to describe the global process through which individuals debate, influence and negotiate an ongoing social contract or set of contracts with the centres of political and economic authority. In other words, global civil society includes all those organisations, formal and informal, which individuals can join and through which their voices can be heard by decision-makers. In this chapter, I develop a typology of the main ways, in which global civil society is organised, which is summarised in Table 1.1. These are in effect, ideal types; it is always possible to identify organisations which do not fit neatly into one category or which has overlapping characteristics.

In elaborating this typology, I do not draw a strict distinction between what is 'national' and what is 'global'; indeed the central thrust of my argument is that those distinctions no longer make sense. Although it is possible, for example, to focus on International NGOs (INGOs), that is to say NGOs registered as international organisations, and I do provide some data about their growth, this does not, by a long way, cover all the NGOs that have some form of global connection. Indeed almost all social movements and NGOs, including parochially minded nationalist and religious groups, have some kind of transnational relations. Precisely because these groups inhabit a political space outside formal national politics (parties and elections), they address a range of institutions (local, global and national), they operate through links with a range of international institutions (NGOs, inter-governmental organisations, foreign states, Diaspora groups) and they often receive funding from abroad.

'Old' and 'New' Social Movements

The first two types of actor are what are called 'old' and 'new' social movements. Like civil society, there are a range of definitions of social movements but it is generally agreed that social movements are organisations, groups of people, and individuals, who act together to bring about transformation in society. They are contrasted with, for example, more tightly organised NGOs or political parties. Tarrow says that social movements are an 'invention of the modern age and an accompaniment to the rise of the modern state.'[5] At the base of all social movements are what he calls 'contentious politics'—action, which is 'used by people who lack regular access to institutions, who act in the name of new or unaccepted claims and who behave in ways that fundamentally challenge others or authorities.'[6] There has always been contentious politics but social movements can be described as the modern form of contentious politics. Tilly talks about the contrast in repertoires between traditional and modern protests.[7] He uses the term 'repertoire' to resolve the tension between structure and agency, between protest as a deterministic response to structural conflict or malfunctions in society, and protest as a conscious individualistic act. Protests are an expression of human agency, of the will of the participants, but they are constrained by frameworks inherited from the past. Thus the repertoire of social movements can be distinguished from earlier forms of protest, according to Tilly, in three respects:

1. They are 'cosmopolitan' rather than parochial, that is to say, they are concerned with issues and principles that apply to human beings in general and not just to their own interests in a particular locality. Tarrow cites the amazement of the Jamaican sugar lobby when the first great petition against slavery was circulated in 1788: 'these abolitionists had neither been

Table 1.1 A Typology of Global Civil Society Actors

	'Old' Social Movements pre-1970	'New' Social Movements c. 1970s and 1980s	NGOs, Think-tanks and Commissions c. Late 1980s and 1990s	Transnational Civic Networks c. Late 1980s and 1990s	'New' Nationalist and Fundamentalist Movements 1990s	'New' Anti-Capitalist Movement c. Late 1990s and 2000s
Issues	Redistribution, employment, and welfare Self-determination and anti-colonialism	Human rights Peace Women Environment Third world solidarity	Human rights development and poverty reduction humanitarianism conflict resolution	Women Dams Land mines International criminal court Global climate change	Identity politics	Solidarity with victims of globalisation Abolition or reform of global institutions
Social composition	Workers and intellectuals	Students, new information class, caring professions	Professionals and experts	Professionals, experts, and activists	Workers, small entrepreneurs, farmers, informal sector	Students, workers and peasants
Forms of organisation	Vertical, hierarchical	Loose, horizontal coalitions	Ranges from bureaucratic and corporate to small-scale and informal	Networks of NGOs, Social Movements and grass roots groups	Vertical and horizontal, charismatic leadership	Networks of NGOs, social movements, and grass roots groups
Forms of action	Petition, demonstration, strike, lobbying	Use of media Direct action	Service Provision Advocacy Expert knowledge Use of media	Parallel summits Use of media Use of local and expert knowledge Advocacy	Media, mass rallies, violence	Parallel Summits Direct action, use of media Mobilisation through internet
Funding	Membership	Individual supporters, events like concerts	Governments International institutions Private foundations	Individual supporters Private foundations INGOs	Diaspora Criminal activities	Individual supporters Churches Private foundations
Relation to power	Capturing state power	Changing state/ society relations	Influencing civil society, the state and international institutions	Pressure on states and international institutions	Capturing state power	Confrontation with states, international institutions and transnational corporations

injured by slavery nor would they personally benefit from its end; what right had they to petition for its abolition?'[8]

2. They are 'autonomous' rather than bifurcated; that is to say individuals form organisations through which they can directly address the relevant authorities, in contrast to pre-modern or early modern forms of protest where individuals addressed a local patron or authority even where the issues were of more than local significance.

3. They are 'modular' rather than particular, that is to say, they develop routines of protest, like the petition, the strike or the demonstration, that are easily transferable to different situations, in contrast to traditional protests like grain seizures or rick burnings that varied from issue to issue and locality to locality.

One might add a further difference. Traditional protests were often violent. The rise of social movements involves a 'civilising' of protest.[9] Even though social movements may break the law, through various forms of direct action or civil disobedience, non-violence has become a dominant commitment of contemporary social movements, at least until the recent anti-capitalist actions.

Social movements rise and fall. Their success depends both on their capacity to mobilise and on the responsiveness of authorities. To the extent that authorities permit protest and take seriously the demands of the protestors, then social movements are 'tamed', integrated into the political process and institutionalised. 'Taming' is not just about access; it is about adaptation on both sides. The authorities accept part of the agenda of protest; the movements modify their goals and become respectable. To the extent that authorities repress protest and reject demands, social movements are marginalised and may turn to violence. Tarrow talks about cycles of contention; although the endings may differ, social movements do always come to an end:

> Each time they appear, the world seems to be turning upside down. But just as regularly, the erosion of mobilisation, the polarisation between sectors of the movements, the splits between institutionalisation and violence, and elites selective use of incentives and repression combine to bring the cycle to an end. At its height, the movement is electric and seems irresistible, but it is eroded and integrated through the political process.[10]

Or, as Rob Walker argues, the point of social movements is that they move:

> They come and go, rise and decline, provoke a fuss and wither the vine. They take the familiar path from charisma to regularised routine, from inventiveness and passion to bureaucracy, hierarchy and instrumental reason. Or alternatively, they fracture, mutate, dissipate, gather no moss. To be in motion is to be at odds with many of the criteria on which serious politics has come to be judged.[11]

The literature on social movements tends to distinguish between 'old' and 'new' social movements, as in Table 1.1. 'Old' movements tend to be labour movements or movements for self-determination, as in the case of nineteenth century national movements or anti-colonial movements. They were mass membership movements that addressed the state and were organised hierarchically, with executive committees and Chairmen and Secretary-Generals. They used the modern repertoire of protest—petitions, demonstrations and strikes. 'New' social movements are generally considered to be the offspring of the 1968 student revolutions. They are concerned with new issues—human rights, gender, the environment or peace. They express the political frustrations of a new educated middle class or brain workers—ICT specialists or the caring professions (doctors, lecturers, social workers) generated by post-industrialism and the welfare state.[12] They pioneer new forms of horizontal organisation and new forms of protest, making use of the media, especially television. Whereas the 'old' movements aimed at persuading states to act and in the process helped to strengthen them, the 'new' movements are much more concerned about individual autonomy, about resisting the state's intrusion into everyday life.[13] Claus Offe has argued that the 'new' movements represent a demand for radical democracy. 'Among the principal innovations of the new movements, in contrast with the workers' movement, are a critical ideology in relation to modernism and progress; decentralised and participatory organisational structures; defence of interpersonal solidarity against the great bureaucracies; and the reclamation of autonomous spaces rather than material advantages.'[14]

The new social movements, from the beginning, have been a global phenomenon. The 1970s and 1980s witnessed the emergence of human rights groups, environmental groups, or women's groups in Latin America, Asia, and Africa as well.[15] Rajni Kothari, writing in the late 1980s described this new phenomenon of the 'non-party political process'—the 'churning of civic consciousness'—in India. The response of spontaneous citizens' initiatives to the Bhopal disaster, to the anti-Sikh pogroms after the assassination of Mrs Gandhi, or the support for struggles like those of people in the Narmada Valley or the Chipko movement, are all examples of what he calls 'islands of hope'. 'The new social groups and movements' writes Kothari, in words that would be familiar to East and West Europeans as well as to Latin Americans and Africans, 'whether of peasants or environmentalists, or the new breed of human rights and civil liberties movements, or the ethnic movements among the minorities, or the whole new upsurge of women—this is a whole new space. It is a different space, which is essentially a non-party space. Its role is to deepen the democratic process in response to the State that has not only ditched the poor and oppressed but has itself turned oppressive and violent. It is to highlight dimensions that were not hitherto considered political and make them part of the political process.'[16]

It is sometimes also argued that the 'old' movements are 'national' in contrast to the cosmopolitan character of the 'new' social movements.[17] But Tilly is right to characterise the modern repertoire as 'cosmopolitan'. The 'old' movements were not originally national. The various movements that pressed for the achievement of individual rights were always universalistic in their aspirations, as I discussed in Chapter 2. Likewise, the labour movement was always an international movement. The first international of labour was held in 1864; workers travelled to different countries to express solidarity with their fellow workers from the late nineteenth century onwards; the International Federation of Trades Unions was founded in 1901. The identification of 'old' movements as national is the consequence of the cycle of contention. 'Old' movements did primarily address the state, although not exclusively, but it was through the state that 'old' movements were 'tamed'. This was true both of workers movements, which became left political parties and trades unions, and anti-colonial struggles, which were transformed into new ruling parties, as was the case for the Congress Party in India or is the case for the African National Congress in South Africa to-day. These movements were transformed into political parties and, in the case of trades unions, into negotiating partners for states and employers at a national level. The mass character of the 'old' movements, their vertical and hierarchical forms of organisation, are all perhaps explainable in terms of the organisational norms of industrial, bureaucratic and military society.

NGOs

It can be argued that the third type of global civil society actor represents the 'taming' of the 'new' social movements. In contrast to 'old' social movements, the 'new' social movements were 'tamed' not within a national framework but within the framework of global governance. Compared with social movements, NGOs are institutional and generally professional; they include voluntary associations, charities, foundations, or professional societies and they are usually formally registered. Organisations can be defined as 'purposeful, role-bound social units'.[18] NGOs are organisations, which are voluntary, in contrast to compulsory organisations like the state or some traditional, religious organisations, and do not make profits, like corporations. It is sometimes said that they are 'value-driven' organisations.[19] In fact, values like public service, for example, or wealth creation, are also important for states and for corporations. Rather, it could be said that, in any organisation, both internal relationships and relations with external actors are regulated through a combination of coercion, monetary incentives, and altruism (or values). In the case of NGOs, the latter is relatively more important.

NGOs are not new although the term is relatively recent; non-governmental organisations are mentioned in Article 71 of the UN Charter, where the Economic and Social Committee is empowered 'to make suitable arrangements for consultation with non-governmental organisations which are concerned with matters in its competence.'[20] Already, international NGOs (INGOs) were established in the nineteenth century. The most famous examples are probably the Anti-Slavery Society (1839) and the International Red Cross (1864). By 1874, there were 32 registered INGOs and this had increased to 1083 by 1914 although not all survived.[21] INGOs were instrumental in setting up international institutions, during this period, many of which began as non-governmental institutions.[22] They also influenced treaty making, particularly in the case of anti-slavery and many of the techniques that INGOs use today were pioneered during this period, particularly parallel fora at inter-governmental conferences. The Hague Peace Conferences of 1899 and 1907 were particularly significant in this respect where NGOs organised parallel sessions and even published an unofficial newspaper.[23]

In the inter-war period, INGOs were very active in the League of Nations up to 1935 and in the International Labour Organisation, which even today includes delegates from trades unions, employer organisations and women's groups in its formal structures, alongside governmental organisations. According to Charnowitz, the two most influential groups were the Women's International League for Peace and Freedom (WILPF), founded in World War I, which moved its headquarters to Geneva, and the International Chamber of Commerce.[24]

The number of INGOs increased during the post-war period not only under the stimulation of new social movements but also as former missionaries and colonial administrators sought new occupations. In the 1950s and 1960s, however, their influence was constrained by the Cold War and the statist character of many of the post-war international institutions. It was not until the 1970s that the opening up of access for 'new' social movements to local and international institutions led to the proliferation of both NGOs in general and INGOs in particular. Initially, this opening up applied mainly to 'soft' issues that did not seem to engage directly with the ideological conflict, mainly the environment and women. The Stockholm Conference on Environment and Development in 1972 marked the beginning of the parallel summit as a way of organising global civil society organisations on particular issues. Likewise, a series of world conferences on women helped to galvanise women's groups—Mexico City 1975, Copenhagen 1980, Nairobi 1985 and Beijing 1995.[25] By the 1980s, development and humanitarian INGOs also began to be seen as partners for governments and international institutions for a variety of reasons; their local knowledge, the need to bypass ineffective or authoritarian governments, and the need to find ways to implement structural adjustment packages.

The end of the Cold War accelerated these tendencies. It was no longer possible to ally with authoritarian governments in the context of a wave of support for democratisation and human rights. As the ideological conflict dissolved, governments and international institutions became more responsive to peace and human rights groups. A number of writers stress the importance of the 'New Policy Agenda', which came to prominence after the end of the Cold War. The 'new policy agenda' combined neo-liberal economic strategy with an emphasis on parliamentary democracy. Already in the 1980s, the World Bank had established an NGO-World Bank Committee. Markets plus elections became the ideological formula of the 1990s. NGOs were seen as an important mechanism for implementing this agenda. They can provide a social safety net without extending the role of the government. They can provide training in democracy and citizenship. They can check abuses of the state and poor governmental practises. And they can push corporations towards an agenda of social responsibility. Concepts like 'social capital' (Putnam) or 'trust' (Fukuyama) contributed to the new found enthusiasm for NGOs both by development institutions like the World Bank and in the peace and human rights field.

Moreover, in the second half of the 1990s, 'third way' politicians came to power in Western Europe, who accepted the neo-liberal orthodoxy, but nevertheless had learned their politics through the experience of new social movements and were ready to pursue new issues and to open up the corridors of power to 'tamed' social movements. Finally, as the immediate post-Cold War neo-liberal triumphalism was blunted, even the hard core international institutions like the IMF began a dialogue with INGOs.[26]

These openings have encouraged institutionalisation and professionalisation, the transformation of social movements into NGOs or INGOs. Lester Salamon has described the dramatic growth of NGOs in the 1980s and 1990s as the 'global associational revolution'. The Johns Hopkins Survey of the non-profit sector in 22 countries showed that this sector had contributed significantly to employment growth in the 1980s and 1990s. The sector accounted for some 5.1% of total employment in the countries surveyed and some 10.4 million volunteers, bringing the total to 7.1% of total employment.[27] The same rapid increase can be found among NGOs registered as international organisations. During the 1990s, registered INGOS increased by one third, from 10,292 to 13,206 and their memberships increased from 155,000 to 263,000 over the same period.[28] A major factor in the growth of NGOs has been the increase in official funding. OECD figures show that, by the end of the 1990s, some 5% of all official aid were channelled through NGOs, with differing shares for different countries. Some 85% of Swedish aid is channelled through NGOs and some 10% of UK aid.[29]

These overall figures conceal the very wide differences between NGOs and the changing composition of NGOs. The term NGO includes those organisations that are typically considered NGOs, international NGOs (INGOs) like Oxfam, Amnesty International or Greenpeace, that are organised around a particular cause—poverty, human rights, or protection of the environment. But it also includes professional societies and self-help groups, like trades unions, sporting groups, or refugee organisations. And it includes those organisations that are sometimes called community building groups (CBOs) or grass roots organisations (GROs) that may be informal and local. Some organisations are very big and similar to large companies; in the development and humanitarian field, for example, there are some eight market leaders, each with a budget of roughly $500 million a year; they include famous names like Oxfam, Médecins Sans Frontières, Save the Children or CARE.[30] Others may be small, self-organised and spontaneous.

As a consequence of their 'tamed' character, NGOs are able to act as interlocutors on issues with which new social movements are concerned. In addition, many have built up expert knowledge on particular policy areas, which enables them to challenge the official experts. This is why I have included think tanks and international Commissions in this category as well as NGOs. Like many of the NGOs, think tanks are a source of alternative expert knowledge. International Commissions are another 'taming' device in which independent groups of prominent individuals and experts are brought together to produce reports on issues of global significance. The Brandt, Palme and Brundlandt Commissions pioneered this approach on development, security and the environment respectively. In the 1990s, this type of commission has proliferated—for example, the World Commission on Dams (WCD), the Kosovo Commission, or the two Carnegie Commissions on the Balkans and on Deadly Conflicts.

A subset of this category, which is rarely mentioned in the literature on global civil society but which is nevertheless extremely powerful, are the think-tanks, like the American Enterprise Institute or the Centre for Civil Society in India, and lobbying organisations allied to transnational business. These groups have a much longer history of access to official agencies and, have been much more successful than other INGOs in getting their proposals on to the global policy agenda.[31]

It is possible to identify four main differences among NGOs, which have affected the overall composition of NGOs. These are:

Northern versus Southern NGOs. Since many Northern NGOs are set up to assist people in the South, a distinction is often drawn between Northern and Southern NGOs and often equated with the distinction between NGOs and GROs (grass roots organisations) or CBOs (community building organisations). In fact some Southern NGOs are extremely large like the Bangladesh Rural Advancement Committee (BRAC) and there are many local community groups in advanced industrial countries, which could be categorised as CBOs and GROs. The point of the distinction, however, is primarily about the contrast between NGOs who are outsiders and, at the same time, are closer to the policy-making community as well as to the sources of funds, and those NGOs more rooted in the local environment.

Advocacy versus Service Provision. NGOs undertake a wide variety of tasks, not of all of which are captured by the headings 'advocacy' and 'service provision'. Service provision includes relief in emergencies, primary health care, non-formal education, housing and legal services, and provision of micro-credit as well as training to other service providers. Advocacy includes lobbying as well as public mobilisation and campaigning around particular issues like debt relief or the Tobin tax or protection of forests. And then there are a range of activities, which can be included under both headings like monitoring compliance with international treaties, particularly in the human rights field, conflict resolution and reconciliation, public education and the provision of alternative expert knowledge. Service provision and the middle range of activities have become more important in the 1990s as donors have contracted or encouraged NGOs to fill the gaps created by the withdrawal of the state from many public services.

Solidarity versus Mutual Benefit. Some NGOs are established to express solidarity with others. Thus Oxfam was established to help poor people in the third world; Amnesty International was established to help political prisoners. Typically solidaristic NGOs are organisations, dependent on outside funding, whose members are committed individuals, often from the middle classes. They do not represent the poor and the deprived although their staff and members care about the poor and the deprived. Mutual benefit NGOs are formed for the mutual benefit of the members like, for example SEWA, the Self-employed Women's Association in India. Professional societies are typical mutual benefit organisations. The composition of mutual benefit NGOs tends to reflect the structure of society and it changes as society changes. The period of the 1990s has been a period of rapid structural change both because of globalisation and IMF policies, and because of rapid technological change especially the introduction of ICT. Many of the traditional mutual benefit organisations have been eroded and their political links broken; this is especially true of trades' unions and farmers organisations. On the other hand, new organisations have been developing to defend the rights of the victims of rapid structural change, although these, of course, are as yet weak. Such groups include movements of people in areas threatened by dam construction, like the Narmada valley, new organisations of informal workers, organisations of refugees and displaced persons like the Srebrenica women.

Organisational Forms. There are wide differences among NGOs concerning their forms of organisation—formal versus informal, hierarchy versus participation, networks versus federations, centralised versus decentralisation, not to mention differences of organisational culture. Some NGOs are membership organisations; others are governed by boards or trustees. Moreover, the meaning of membership varies. In Amnesty International, for example, the members are the 'owners' of the organisation and determine its decision-making. By contrast, the members of Greenpeace are more like supporters passively donating money and numbers. Some NGOs organise themselves on bureaucratic principles; others are more corporate in management style. Transnationalisation and the growing use of ICT does tend to favour decentralised, network type organisations. There is some evidence that NGOs are currently going through a rapid period of experimentation with organisational forms; the statistics seem to suggest a growing share of NGOs whose organisational forms cannot be classified.[32]

The growing use of the term 'NGO' reflects what has been described as the 'NGOisation' of public space. Effectively, what this means is that those NGOs, who are Northern and therefore close to the centres of power and funding, whose emphasis is service provision, who are solidaristic rather than mutual benefit, and whose organisation tends to be more formal and hierarchical have come to dominate the NGO scene. This is, in part, a consequence of the growing support of Northern governments towards NGOs: they tend to favour service provision and may be nervous about advocacy; they are biased towards NGOs from their own countries and also prefer to deal with formally organised professional NGOs. And it is partly a consequence of rapid structural change, which has eroded traditional mutual benefit organisations as well as the kind of local community ties, which help to foster GROs and CBOs.

The growth of this type of NGOs has given rise to widespread criticism of NGOs especially in Africa, Latin America and South Asia. First of all, it is argued that growing dependence on particular donors may distort the priorities or mission of NGOs. Dependence on government funding has, in some cases, transformed NGOs into parastatal organisations, or government subcontractors. In some cases, they have become substitutes for the state; since NGOs can bypass formal mechanisms of democratic accountability, they may reduce rather than enhance the power of citizens. Bangladesh, where NGOs have become such important actors, has been described as the 'Franchise State.'[33] It can also lead to a damping down of the advocacy role of NGOs since NGOs are fearful of losing their sources of income; in Afghanistan, for example, no American NGO even questioned the official air drop of humanitarian supplies, although European NGOs did so. Advocacy may also be weakened because powerful government funded NGOs may displace local GROs and CBOs, as has been observed in Latin America and India.[34] In extreme cases, it is argued that NGOs are merely the 'handmaidens of capitalist change', with little serious concern for effective poverty alleviation strategies. They are seen as the 'modernisers and destroyers of local economies', introducing Western values and bringing about 'economicide'.[35]

This problem is exacerbated by the decline of many traditional mutual benefit organisations, like professional associations as a consequence of structural change. In the case of Africa, Gymah-Boadi has argued that: 'Civil associations of all kinds have seen their material bases of support eroded, first by the protracted economic crisis that gripped Africa starting in the 1980s and then by stringent neo-liberal adjustment measures intended to resolve it. Many associations have lost so much self-confidence and organisational capacity that they seem but shadows of what they were a decade ago. Neopatrimonial leaders, meanwhile, find them easy targets for co-option. Faced with the prospect of penury, many leaders of middle-class and professional groups find it hard to resist making personally advantageous deals with incumbent autocratic regimes, even if such deals undermine pro-democracy movements and shore up authoritarian rule.'[36] Patrick Chabal suggests that, in the context of patrimonial states, NGOs created by Western donors 'are often nothing other than the new "structures" with which Africans can seek to establish an instrumentally profitable position within the existing system of patrimonialism.'[37] And in much of the post-Communist world, NGOs provide a fund-raising channel for impoverished professionals or aspiring politicians.

A parallel argument is made about newly emerging relation between NGOs and companies. As part of the new commitment to social responsibility, companies undertake social and environmental programmes through subcontracting NGOs. It is sometimes argued that NGOs who implement this type of programme are contributing to what is essentially a public relations exercise where 'good works' conceal the longer-term strategic damage inflicted by the companies. According to this line of argument, oil companies in Nigeria and Angola, for example, undertake this type of programme, while, at the same time, oil revenues are fuelling conflict and oil exploitation, however well managed, is contributing to environmental degradation.

Another criticism levelled at NGOs is that the growth of the predominant type of Northern NGO has led to an intense competition—an emerging 'marketplace of ideas, funders, backers and supporters'.[38] To sustain themselves financially, NGOs need to identify a market niche, and to distinguish the NGOs brand name from others. This contradicts the co-operative practises, which ought to and often do take place as a consequence of the normative character of the mission, the value-driven nature of NGOs. As Fowler puts it:

> Increasing market profile and income share is now a common concern of Northern NGDOs [non-governmental development organisations] fundraising; overstating impact is widespread; distortions in fund-raising images are a frequent complaint of NGDOs from the South and East; and the lack of transparency is a source of disquiet in development circles and the media.[39]

In the NGO marketplace, media coverage is all important. A particular problem arises from the dependence of NGOs on media coverage. There is a tendency to exaggerate crises in order to mobilise public support, as in the case of Greenpeace and Brent Spa or the crisis in Eastern Zaire in 1995 or in some cases of GM crops.[40] And this is often encouraged by the media in search of newsworthy stories. As George Alagiah of the BBC put it:

> Relief agencies depend upon us for publicity and we need them to tell us where the stories are. There's an unspoken understanding between us, a sort of code. We try not to ask the question too bluntly: 'Where are the starving babies'. And they never answer explicitly. But we get the pictures all the same.[41]

In short, NGOs can be considered to be the 'tamed' successors of the 'new' social movements of the 1970s and 1980s. 'Taming' can range from co-option to autonomy. Perhaps NGOs could be described as a new sort of intermediary organisation, an expression of the blurred boundaries between state and non-state, public and private. One way to describe them is in terms of the emergence of a flexible state, a mechanism through which states can adjust more rapidly to changes in society than is possible within the traditional bureaucratic model of the state. Another way to describe them is in terms of the extension of market principles throughout society, with the emphasis on competition and the idea of public-private partnerships. Nevertheless, they still remain 'value-driven' organisations and, even if they do not live up to expectations, they continue to be organised around humanistic missions. Even though they work with states and companies, most NGOs do retain a strong sense of their original mission and past practise, and many continue to provide an infrastructure, which can be used by a range of social movements and grass roots organisations.

Transnational Civic Networks

The fourth category in my typology is global civic networks. These are networks that connect INGOs, social movements and grass roots organisations, as well as individuals on specific issues and campaigns. 'Détente from Below' described in the last chapter can be understood as the construction of a transnational civic network. Likewise, campaigns about human rights, violence against women, or the environment, during the 1980s pioneered the contemporary form of network, although the precedents had been set much earlier.[42] Keck and Sikkink use the term 'transnational advocacy network' and their networks include states and international organisations as well.

Networks, says Castells, are the 'new social morphology' of the contemporary era.[43] They are flexible, fluid, and they provide an opportunity for the voices of grass roots groups to be heard. They are forms of communication and information exchange; mutual discussion and debate transform the way issues are understood and the language within which they are expressed. They represent a kind of two-way street between Southern groups and individuals, or rather the groups and individuals who directly represent victims, whether it the victims of human rights violations, poverty or environmental degradation, with the so-called Northern solidaristic 'outsiders'. The former provide testimony, stories and information about their situation and they confer legitimacy on those who campaign on their behalf. The latter provide access to global institutions, funders or global media as well as 'interpretations' more suited to the global context. Another way of describing this collaboration is in terms of the link between 'tamed' organisations and more activist groups; the latter tend to be more innovative and agenda-setting, while the former can professionalise and institutionalise campaigns.

Keck and Sikkink have coined the term, the 'boomerang effect', whereby local groups blocked at a national level can use the network to influence other states and international organisations to unblock the national situation.[44] Thus the AIDs/HIV network has been successful in pressing for cheaper drugs as a result of a global campaign against (and sometimes in co-operation with) states, international organisations and pharmaceutical companies. A particularly important form of the 'boomerang effect' lies in the existence of international rules, to which states have subscribed like the 1975 Helsinki Agreement or the US Congressional legislation on human rights violations in Latin America in the 1970s, which can be used by local groups as an instrument in their campaigns. Also important are inspirational events like the Nairobi and Beijing women's' conferences. In Sierra Leone, for example, women's groups had always been active in the Churches, local communities or Descendants groups. But it was not until 1994 that they came together to establish the Women's Forum, in order to prepare for the United Nations' Women's Conference in Beijing, with international support. This was the moment they became aware of their potential power and some of the women argued for a more political stance and in particular, the need for women to play a role in securing peace. As a result the Sierra Leonean women's peace movement was formed, which was to have a decisive influence on the democratisation process in 1995.[45]

It might be more appropriate to talk about a 'double boomerang' effect since the consequences of these local actions are often to strengthen international instruments as well, which can then be used to enhance local campaigns. Particularly important in the 1990s, for example, has been the influence of networks on international treaty making: Land Mines, the International Criminal Court or Global Climate Change. What has been new since the end of the Second World War has been the development of humanitarian or cosmopolitan law that applies to individuals and not just states and is about setting norm in global affairs. Pressure from civic networks organised specifically for the purpose has been critical to this development.[46]

Transnational civic networks are not necessarily harmonious, democratic or effective. They represent a space for interchange which is often acrimonious and sometimes disillusioning. Southern NGOs often complain of being steamrollered. Indigenous peoples groups are uncomfortable with the individualistic assumptions of Northern groups, while the latter are often concerned about the patriarchal communitarian tendencies of Southern groups. Focus and effectiveness in campaigning often overrides democratic and participatory ways of working. Nevertheless, especially in the last decade, such networks have had a considerable impact in transforming the normative content of global politics.

'New' Nationalist and Fundamentalist Movements

Just as the new social movements were being tamed and as transnational civic networks were learning to act in the global arena, however, a new family of social movement developed—the 'new' nationalist or fundamentalist movements. These include exclusive nationalist movements in the Balkans and much of the post-Communist world, religious communalism (both Islamic and Hindu) in the Middle East and Asia, millennial or 'new age' movements in Africa and the United States, or the growing anti-migrant movements in Western Europe.

In some respects, these movements are similar to 'old' social movements, in that they are often mass movements, which include workers and peasants; they are organised, at least in part, in traditional hierarchical ways, often with a charismatic leaders; and their aim is most often to capture state power. But they differ from 'old' nationalist, labour and anti-colonial movements, in several respects. First, they tend to be about the claim to power on the basis of labels rather than ideas. In the case of ethnic nationalist movements, this means that they make claims to political power on the basis of an ethnic label, which excludes and is indeed hostile towards others with a different label. Or in the case of religious fundamentalist movements, they make claims to political power on the basis of religious practise, which also excludes others with different or non religious practises.

Earlier nationalisms were typically about defining a nation as the basis for citizenship and, in the case of civic nationalisms, citizenship was a matter of residency not cultural background or language even though these had to be learned. In particular, self-determination or anti-colonial movements were about democracy, participation and rights not about ethnicity or religion; they tended to be about a vision of nation building. There have, of course, been ethnic nationalist movements in the past, like Zionism or Greek nationalism and these movements have shared many of the characteristics of contemporary movements although they also had their progressive forward-looking projects about democracy and nation building. Likewise, earlier religious struggles were about new visions of society—the role of the individual or the power of institutionalised religion. In Northern Ireland or the former Yugoslavia, religious struggles have little to do with beliefs; they are about access to political power.

There are many similarities between extreme ethnic chauvinism and religious fundamentalism. Both tend to be backward looking; they appeal to those disaffected with materialism and corruption. They conjure up an idea of a pure traditional way of life—nostalgia for a past where supposedly this existed. Both emphasise violent forms of struggle and celebrate histories of bloody battles lost or won. Both are forms of identity politics, by which I mean the claim to power on the basis of identity, i.e. labels. Fundamentalist or extremist identity politics involve exclusive claims to power in the name of identity, i.e. the denial of the claims of other identities.

Some religious groups may also have a missionary character. By missionary character, I mean the effort to convert others and the insistence on the application of religious rules.

Different Islamic groups, for example, distinguish themselves in terms of the way they interpret scriptures and Islamic Law. Thus Al-Quaeda, bases its ideology on Wahabi—an austere branch of Sunni, practised in Saudi Arabia and also Chechnya, in which non-Wahabi are equated with non-believers. They distinguish themselves from other Sunni groups, as well, of course, from Shias. Nevertheless, the primary goal, as with other Islamic groups, is power not the spread of religion. Al Quaeda is linked to disaffected members of Saudi royal family. The stated goal is a Muslim caliphate (state) in the whole of the Middle East but undoubtedly, there is an underlying interest in power in Saudi Arabia. As Fred Halliday puts it:

> Religious fundamentalism in all societies has . . . one goal; this goes for the *haredim* in Israel, the ranting bible-thumpers of America, Islamic fundamentalists in the Middle east and Hindu chauvinists in India. The goal is not to convert other people to their beliefs, but to seize power, political, social and gendered, within their own societies.[47]

The 'new' nationalist and religious movements tend to represent themselves as a reaction against modernity, as opposed to 'old' nationalist movements that saw themselves as agents of progress, building the modern state. Indeed, the new nationalism and religious fundamentalism are ways of mobilising *against* democracy and openness.

A second difference has to do with social composition. The new nationalist and fundamentalist movements have a capacity to mobilise workers and peasants, as was the case for 'old' social movements. But these groups are shrinking as a proportion of society as a consequence of the dramatic structural changes that have taken place as a consequence of globalisation. Instead, an important constituency for these movements are those people have been forced to migrate to urban conglomerations all over the world and who make a living in low-paid service jobs or on the margins of the formal economy in the growing 'grey' activities that are associated with globalisation. These are uprooted people living with the frustrations both of insecurity and, especially important for the new generation of restless young men who join these movements, forced inactivity and loss of self-worth as a consequence of unemployment.

A third difference has to do with forms of organisation. Many nationalist and religious political movements organise themselves on the model of former left political parties. This is the case for the post-Communist nationalists in Eastern Europe and the Balkans and for Islamic parties or the BJP in India. However, these movements also characteristically combine this form with the construction of networks. Ethnicity like religion is now transnational. Both religious and nationalist movements have constituencies that cross borders. For nationalist movements, both Diaspora groups and kin-based organisations are important elements in the support infrastructure, providing funds and other forms of assistance, and acting as global lobbying groups. Likewise, religious institutions in different countries—mosques, synagogues, Churches or temples—provide similar support to religious movements. Just as civic networks make use of the 'boomerang effect' so Croatians in Germany or Irish Americans, London-based mosques or North American 'new age' groups have a major role in enhancing the effectiveness of these movements through lobbying, raising public awareness or through financial and technical assistance. Nor are the networks merely transnational, they are also functional as well. Whereas, 'old' movements were largely funded through membership and engaged in traditional forms of political action, the 'new' movements make a range of connections with criminal groups, mercenaries, security services, enterprises and banks, both as a form of funding and because of the way in which they engage in violent and coercive activities.

A fourth difference has to do with the way the 'new' nationalist and fundamentalist movements have adapted some of the repertoire of the 'new' social movements. In particular, they engage in symbolic politics of a destructive and powerful kind, like the destruction of the Ayodha

Mosque in India in 1992, or the Taliban's destruction of the stone sculptures of Buddha. Like the 'new' social movements, they place considerable emphasis on media impact, making use of television, radio, websites, and videos. Videocassettes of Bin Laden's speeches circulate throughout the Middle East. The attacks on the World Trade Towers and the Pentagon on September 11 represent a devastating example of symbolic, media conscious, public, and deliberately nihilistic, action.[48]

The weakness of both 'new' social movements and NGOs is that although they have widespread moral authority, they are largely composed of an educated minority and they lack the capacity for popular mobilisation. They are often part of the class of informational 'haves'— they have credit cards and access to Internet and satellite television, they can afford to travel and meet each other. The 'new' nationalist movements appear to fill the gap left by the 'taming' of 'old' social movements and their virtual demise after the end of the Cold War. They can appeal to the 'ontological insecurity' of the 'have-nots'—those who are excluded from the new global class built upon global financial transactions, global communication and air travel, but nevertheless are deeply affected by the changes wrought by these developments. It is the nationalist and fundamentalist movements, not the democratic movements that seem better able to capture popular sentiment, at least in some parts of the world.

Not all nationalist and religious groups, of course, are exclusivist and extremist. I have focussed on this type of movement because of its current importance. Apart from movements concerned with cultural or religious freedoms, or streams of religious thinking, like liberal Islam or liberation theology, which have contributed to the development of humanistic norms, an important category of organisation are the neo-traditional groups that provide welfare, religious instruction or even some form of security in many part of the world. They are often the main support networks and mobilising mechanisms in, for example, newly urbanised poor neighbourhoods. These groups are often compulsory and communalist but they do not necessarily subscribe to nationalist and fundamentalist ideologies. They are often characterised by tolerance towards other parts of society and even engaged in struggles for democratisation, social advancement or environmental protection. It is these groups that have occasioned debate among the theorists of civil society, reflecting a real tension and ambivalence in their relationship to other civil society agents. Pearce and Howell describe these tensions between radical cultural and radical popular groups in relation to the Mayan people of Guatemala, who played such a key role in the democratisation struggle under the banner of 'civil society'. 'On the one hand, civil society holds out a promise of freedom as it does for the popular sectors, on the other hand, it is not clear how associations now visibly trying to influence the state in the public political sphere relate to communal structures of indigenous villages.'[49]

The New Anti-Capitalist Movement

The last category of global civil society actor is the 'new' anti-capitalist movement that burst into the streets of Seattle and Prague at the end of the decade. It is usually described as the anti-globalisation movement but this is a misnomer as groups like 'globalise the resistance' or slogans like the 'world-wide movement against globalisation' make clear. The term anti-capitalism is a more apt description since most of those engaged in the movement oppose the unregulated spread of capitalism and the growing power of the market over every aspect of life, and since it represents, in some respects, a revival of the great anti-capitalist movements of the late nineteenth century and early twentieth century.[50] At the World Social Forum in Porto Alegre in 2002, the activists defined themselves as a 'global movement for social justice and democracy'.[51]

The new anti-capitalist movement is similar in form to the global civic networks. But instead of being organised around a specific issue, it is a social movement in terms of its transformative goals. It is inspired by movements in poor countries like the Zapatistas, the landless peasant movement in Brazil, or the East Asian Third World Network. It brings together elements of the 'new' social movements and their 'tamed' successors—INGOs, networks and movements concerned with women's issues, the environment, or indigenous people's rights. But it also embraces the new mutual benefit organisations that are beginning to emerge in response to structural change—informal workers, refugees and displaced persons and so on, as well as what might be called the 'new' labour movement. The 'new' labour movement includes: international trade union federations, who have been forced to reform after the Cold War when their activities were hamstrung by ideological divisions; new social movement unions in Brazil, South Africa or Korea; new forms of labour organisations like homeworkers in India or African township traders; as well as labour oriented grass roots groups and NGOs in various parts of the world. There has been a sea-change in labour movement attitudes; the functions of unions have been reconceptualised away from an economistic preoccupation with wages towards new notions of labour rights; and methods of organising have become more like 'new' social movements. The Liverpool Dockers strike is one example of the changing character of the labour movement. As Munck puts it, Labour is coming to be seen as just another movement or NGO.[52]

The 'new' anti-capitalist movement does include rejectionists and fundamentalists, who want to reverse globalisation and return to the world of nation-states; an important tendency is the 'localisers' who want to return to small territorial communities.[53] It includes reformers, who want to 'civilise' and 'democratise' globalisation and offer concrete proposals like debt relief (Jubilee 2000) or a Tobin tax (ATTAC) to make this possible. And it includes those who want to abolish current global institutions and construct alternatives, like the Zapatistas 'Declaration for Humanity and Against Neo-Liberalism'[54]. The opening offered by the Third Way politicians and, gingerly, by the international economic institutions at the end of the 1990s provided an opportunity to mobilise a movement whose demands go far beyond what any of the officials expected. The transformatory character of the movement's discourse, the involvement of women, workers and peasants in many parts of the world, and the inclusion of social and economic rights in addition to the non-material concerns of the new social movements all mean that it has the potential to construct a genuinely popular form of action.

The demonstrations at the G8 summit in Genoa in 2001 seem to have marked a turning point. The demonstrations were marred by horrific violence, in which the anti-capitalist movement experienced its first martyr—a young man killed in the riots. The violence was partly initiated by a group, known as the Black Box anarchists, and was partly a result of the aggressive behaviour of the Italian police, which was comparable, according to some of the protestors to the behaviour of the police in Pinochet's Chile, who appeared to be in cahoots with the anarchists. But the Genoa Social forum as it was called did come up with more concrete, sophisticated and better formulated demands than many of the earlier 'parallel summits' and its seems to have provokes a serious response from global institutions and political elites. After Genoa, the IMF and World Bank responded to an invitation by Global Exchange, Jobs with Justice, 50 Years is Enough and Essential Action to engage in a public debate, writing that they were prepared to do so in principle, provided that it was a non-violent dialogue, conducted with respect for different views[55] and Guy Verhofstadt, Prime Minister of Belgium and President of the European Union at the time, wrote an open letter to the so-called anti-globalisation movement, published in many major newspapers around the world, and collected the responses in a book.[56] In France, the health Minister, Bernard Kouchner described the events at Genoa as a 'global kind of May 1968'. He anticipates a Tobin tax and global ethical investment. And the French Prime Minister,

Lionel Jospin, welcomed 'the emergence of a citizens movement at the planetary level' and put forward an official proposal for a Tobin tax.[57]

The events of September 11, however, seemed to overwhelm the anti-capitalist movements and many planned activities were curtailed or postponed. But by early 2002, the movement had recovered. Some 50,000 people attended the World Social Forum in Porto Allegre in February, of which some 30,000 came from within Latin America, and some 300,000 demonstrated at the European Summit in Barcelona including parliamentarians and local officials. Some governments and international organisations have responded more positively to the anti-capitalist movement, out of a conviction that global redistribution may be an important factor in dealing with the causes of terrorism.

The Role of the Media

All the literature on social movements emphasises the importance of forms of communication. The invention of the printing press is part of the explanation for the emergence of modern forms of protest. They were cosmopolitan because people became aware through newspapers of a wider community of people; they could relate not only to those they knew personally but also to fellow readers. Their protests were modular because others could easily learn their techniques and understand their demands through newspaper reports and the circulation of leaflets and petitions. They were autonomous because any individual could sign a petition or write to a newspaper. The 'imagined community' of nations was created by printing—the availability of novels and newspapers in the vernacular language, which allowed writers and readers to see themselves as part of a shared discourse.

The development of new forms of communication, based on the revolution in information technology as well as the spread of television and radio has created quite new 'imagined communities'. New social movements have capitalised on the possibility of what the French call mediatique events; something pioneered by Médecins sans Frontières. Both symbolic politics and information politics depend on instant news and images, especially through television, which makes possible the consciousness of a global community: 'Global political space is skimmed twenty-four hours a day and produced as a stream of televisual images featuring a terrorist attack here, a currency crisis there, and a natural disaster elsewhere. Global space becomes political space. Being there live is everything. The local is instantly global, the distant immediately closes. Place-specific struggles become global televisual experiences.'[58] One of the reasons why globalisation makes closed totalitarian societies so difficult to sustain is the difficulty of insulating airwaves; thus East Europeans could watch West European television during the 1980s.

All the same, global networks like CNN and the BBC are only accessed by an English speaking elite. Moreover, they do not only spread humanistic consciousness; they also spread awareness of the global consumer culture. State-run television or even radio in vernacular languages, on the other hand, can be used as a powerful propaganda tool for the 'new' nationalists, as was the case in the former Yugoslavia or 'hate radio' in Rwanda, which incited the genocide against Tutsis. Whereas newspapers mobilised a reading public, generally urban-based, television, radio and the circulation of videos operates as a form of rapid mobilisation in remote areas where people do not have the reading habit, creating new 'imagined' communities based on fear and hate and reconstructions or reinventions of past grievances. Visual images and even voices are a much more powerful way to bring the past to life and to impose on the present real or imagined injustices of the past than history books and newspapers, although that happens too.

One of the positive developments of the 1990s has been the way in which democratisation has led to the break-up of state monopolies in broadcasting. However, public service broadcasting has been difficult to foster and many of the new television and radio stations are largely entertainment driven. These private entertainment media can also provide mechanisms for the spread of particular versions of exclusive culture; in South Asia, the new satellite stations Zee TV and Star TV generate a kind of homogenised Hindu culture, based on Bollywood (Bombay based Hindi films) and often expressing nationalistic bias in news reporting.

Nevertheless, the new openings have offered space to community groups, social movements and NGOs. A recent development has been the spread of community radio stations in Africa and especially in Latin America, often financed from abroad. The network of local independent radio stations, set up by radio B92 in Serbia, and financed by western donors, is often considered the key factor in the fall of Milosevic. The importance of community radio in Latin America may well explain the high density of global civil society activity as shown by statistics on numbers of INGOs and participation in parallel summits.[59] Another recent development has been the growing importance of talk shows, which it claimed, is reinvigorating Africa's oral traditions.[60]

A fascinating phenomenon in the wake of September 11 is the Al Jazeera (the peninsular) TV station set in Qatar and broadcasting in Arabic throughout the Middle East. Outspoken and independent, the station claims 35 million viewers and has been banned from Tunisia, Saudi Arabia and Morocco because of its criticisms of their regimes. Libya recalled its ambassador to Qatar and Jordan closed down its station bureau in Amman after criticism of the government.

Finally, of course, Internet and e-mail have become essential tools for organising in the 1990s. Petitions are circulated through e-mails; networks are sustained through e-mail lists; websites mobilise global demonstrations. And these are important tools for all categories of actors. Web sites are as important for Diaspora groups as for INGOs.

Who is Global Civil Society?

The different contemporary definitions of global civil society outlined in the first chapter tend to correspond to different categories of actors. Thus the neo-liberal version of global civil society, where civil society is seen as a substitute for the state, a sort of laissez-faire politics, corresponds to the idea of a civil society composed of a market of NGOs. The very term NGO seems to imply 'not' or 'instead of' the state. The activist model of civil society corresponds to a civil society composed of social movements and civic networks, while the post-modern version would include the nationalist and fundamentalists as well.

At the end of the 1980s, the energies of the 'new' social movements culminated in the wave of democratisation that affected not only Eastern Europe but Africa, Asia and Latin American as well. I have described the dramatic growth of NGOs in part as the 'taming' of the new social movements in the aftermath of democratisation and in response to new opportunities offered by international institutions, governments and even global companies. This was also a period when earlier social organisations and civic associations, often the legacy of 'old' social movements, were eroded and undermined by economic crisis and structural change. Thus in the 1990s, the sphere of informal politics came to be dominated, on the one hand, by NGOs and, on the other, by 'new' nationalist and fundamentalist movements.

This explains the growing disaffection with the term 'civil society', the criticism that has been increasingly levelled at the language of 'civil society' as being too Euro-centric and, indeed 'imperialistic'. Neera Chandhoke says that 'civil society' has become a hurrah word, emptied of content and 'flattened out'. 'Witness the tragedy that has visited proponents of the concept: people struggling against authoritarian regimes demanded civil society, what they got were NGOs . . . If everyone from trades unions, social movements, the UN, the IMF, lending agencies, to states both chauvinistic and democratic hail civil society as the most recent elixir to the ills of the contemporary world, there must be something wrong.'[61]

But that is perhaps precisely the advantage of the term. In the late 1990s, new grass roots groups and social organisations and the new anti-capitalist movement began to emerge offering some renewed hope for creating an emancipatory economic and social agenda. If we think of global civil society, not as NGOs, but as a process, through which contracts or agreements are negotiated at global, national and local levels, then it has to include all the various mechanisms through which individual voices can be heard. Civil society provides a legitimising platform for discordant and radical demands—a name, which explains why authorities have to take these demands seriously. Moreover, there are peace and human rights groups still struggling in oppressive regimes like Burma or Zimbabwe or in conflict zones like the Middle East, Kashmir, or the Caucasus, for whom the term 'global civil society' holds out some promise of being heard.

Global civil society includes the INGOs and the networks that are the 'tamed' successors to the new social movements of the 1970s and 1980s. It also includes the allies of transnational business who promote a market framework at a global level. It includes a new radical anti-capitalist movement, which combines both the successors of the new social movements and a new type of labour movements. And to the extent that nationalist and fundamentalist movements are voluntary and participatory, i.e. they provide a mechanism through which individuals can gain access to centres of authority, then they have to be included as well; although in practise as I have argued, in actually existing civil society, such distinctions may be difficult to draw. The array of organisations and groups, through which individuals have a voice at global levels of decision-making, represents a new form of global politics that parallels and supplements formal democracy at the national level. These new actors do not take decisions. Nor should they have a formal role in decision-making since they are voluntarily constituted and represent nobody but their own opinions. The point is rather that through access, openness and debate, policy-makers are more likely to act as a Hegelian universal class, in the interests of the human community.

The differentiated character of global civil society can be understood in terms of the complexity of the contemporary world. New Social Movement theorists sometimes talk about a 'movement society'.[62] The salient feature of globalisation is the rapidity of technological and social change. The modern state, in its twentieth century form is too top heavy, slow and rigid to find ways of adapting to the myriad of unintended consequences of change. Civil society, a combination of different movements, NGOs and networks, is a way of expressing the reflexivity of contemporary world

It is the contestation between these different types of actors as well as states, international institutions and transnational corporations that will determine the future direction of globalisation. Will it be a 'civilising' process in which global politics becomes the normal form of relations at a global level, or can we expect a return to inter-state relations, or, perhaps worse, a wild anarchic process involving inequality and violence?

[. . .]

Notes

1. Zygmunt Bauman *Globalisation: The Human Consequences* Polity Press, Cambridge, 1998, pp. 62–3.
2. Robin Cohen and Shirin M. Rai *Global Social Movements* Athlone Press, London and New Brunswick, 2000; see also Jackie Smith et al. (eds), *Transnational Social Movements and Global Politics*, (Syracuse University Press, Syracuse, NY, 1997).

3. Margaret Keck and Kathryn Sikkink *Activists Beyond Borders*, Cornell University Press, Cornell, 1998; see also Ann M. Florini *The Third Force: The Rise of Transnational Civil Society* Japan Center for International Exchange and Carnegie Endowment for International Peace, Tokyo and Washington, 2000.

4. Wolfgang Deckers.

5. Sydney Tarrow *Power in Movements: Social Movements and Contentious Politics* Cambridge University Press, 2nd edition, 1998, p. 3.

6. Ibid. p. 3.

7. Charles Tilly *Popular Contention in Great Britain 1758–1834* Oxford University Press, Oxford, 1995.

8. Ibid. p. 38.

9. Tarrow, *Power in Movements*.

10. Ibid. p. 175.

11. R.B.J. Walker, 'Social Movements/World Politics?' *Millennium: Journal of International Studies*, 23, 3 (1994), p. 677.

12. Alain Touraine *The Voice and the Eye: An Analysis of Social Movements* Cambridge University Press, Cambridge, 1981.

13. Alberto Melucci *Nomads of the Present: Social Movements and Individual Needs in Contemporary Society* Hutchinson, London, 1988; *Challenging Codes: Collective Action in the Information Age* Cambridge University Press, Cambridge, 1996.

14. Donatella Della Porta and Mario Diani *Social Movements: An Introduction* Blackwell, Oxford, 1999, p. 12.

15. See *Towards a Liberating Peace* United Nations University.

16. Rajni Kothari *Politics and the People: In search of a Humane India*, Volume II, Ajanta Publications, Delhi, 1989, pp. 429–430.

17. Cohen and Rai, *Global Social Movements*.

18. Alan Fowler *Striking a Balance: A Guide to Enhancing the Effectiveness of NON-Governmental Organisations in International Development* Earthscan, London, 1997, p. 20.

19. E.A. Brett 'Voluntary Agencies as Development Organisations: Theorising the Problem of Efficiency and Accountability' *Development and Change* Vol. 24, 1993, pp. 269–303.

20. Leon Gordenker and Thomas E. Weiss (eds) *NGOs, the UN and Global Governance*, 24, 9 (1993), p. 22.

21. Charles Chatfield, 'Inter-governmental and Non-governmental Associations to 1945', in Jackie Smith, Charles Chatfield and Ron Pagnucco (eds), *Transnational Social Movements and Global Politics* (Syracuse University Press, Syracuse, NY, 1997).

22. Thus for example, the International Bureau of Weights and Measures (1875), the International Council for the Exploration of the Sea (1902) or the International Meteorological Office (1891) all began as non-governmental institutions. See Steve Charnowitz 'Two Centuries of Participation: NGOs and International Governance' *Michigan Journal of International Law* Winter 1997.

23. At the 1907 Peace Conference, Baroness Bertha von Suttner welcomed conference delegates and INGOs to tea and lectures every afternoon. Charnowitz, 'Two Centuries'.

24. Ibid.

25. Martha Alter Chen 'Engendering World Conferences: The International Women's Movement and the UN' in Gordenker and Weiss, *NGOs, the UN and Global Governance*.

26. Robert O'Brien et al., *Contesting Global Governance: Multilateral Economic Institutions and Global Social Movements* (Cambridge University Press: Cambridge, 2000).

27. Helmut K. Anheier 'Managing Non-profit Organisations: Towards a New Approach' in *Civil Society Working Papers*, Number 1, Centre for Civil Society, LSE, London (January 2000).

28. See Helmut Anheier, Marlies Glasius and Mary Kaldor, *Global Civil Society 2001* (Oxford University Press, Oxford, 2001).
29. Ibid.
30. See David Hulme and Michael Edwards *NGOs, States and Donors: Too close for Comfort?* (Macmillan in association with Save the Children, Basingstoke, 1997).
31. See Leslie Sklair, *The Transnational Capitalist Class* (Blackwell: Oxford, 2000).
32. Helmut Anheier and Nuno Themudo 'Organisational Forms in Global Civil Society' *Global Civil Society 2002* Oxford University Press, 2002
33. G.D. Wood 'States without citizens: the problem of the franchise state' in David Hulme and Michael Edwards *NGOs, States and Donors: Too close for Comfort?* (Macmillan in association with Save the Children, Basingstoke, 1997).
34. S. Arllano-Lopez and J.F. Petras 'Non-governmental organisations and Poverty Alleviation in Bolivia' *Development and Change,* 25, 1995, pp. 555–568.
35. For a discussion of this perspective, see David Lewis *The Management of Non-Governmental Development Organisations: An Introduction* Routledge, London and New York, 2001, p. 32.
36. E.Gymah-Boadi 'Civil Society in Africa: The good, the bad, the ugly' *civnet.org/journal* May 1997.
37. Patrick Chabal and Jean-Pascal Daloz *Africa Works: Disorder as a Political Instrument* The International African Institute, James Currey and Indiana University Press, Oxford, Bloomington and Indianapolis, p. 22.
38. Lewis, *Management,* p. 199.
39. Fowler, *Striking a Balance,* p. 30.
40. See Diane Osgood 'Dig it Up: Global Civil Society's Responses to Plant Biotechnology' *Global Civil Society 2001.*
41. Alex de Waal , A. Famine Crimes: Politics & the Disaster Relief Industry in Africa, *James Currey/Indiana University Press, Oxford and Indiana, 1997,* p. 83.
42. See Margaret E. Keck and Kathryn Sikkink, *op. cit.* for an insightful analysis and survey of what they call transnational advocacy networks.
43. Manuel Castells *The Rise of the Network Society: Volume I of The Information Age: Economy, Society and Culture* Basil Blackwell, 1998.
44. Keck and Sikkink, *Activists Beyond Borders,* for an insightful analysis and survey of what they call transnational advocacy networks.
45. Yasmin Jusu-Sheriff 'The Women's Movement in Sierra Leone' *Conciliation Resources,* Issue 9, 2000.
46. See, for example, Marlies Glasius *Global Civil Society 2002.*
47. Fred Halliday *Two Hours that Shook the World: September 11, 2001: Causes and Consequences* Saqi Books, London, 2002, p. 47.
48. See Navid Kermani 'A Dynamite of the Spirit—Why Nietzsche, not the Koran, is the dangerous inspiration of the suicide bombers' *Times Literary Supplement* March 29 2002.
49. Jude Howell and Jenny Pearce, *Civil Society and Development: A Critical Exploration* (Lynne Rienner, Boulder, Colo., 2001), p. 151.
50. See Meghnad Desai and Yahia Said 'The new Anti-Capitalist Movement: Money and Global Civil Society' *Global Civil Society 2001.*
51. Mario Pianta, 'Box 1.2. World Social Forum in Porto Alegre', in Glasius, Kaldor and Anheier, *Global Civil Society 2001.*
52. Roland Munck 'Labour in the Global' and Sarah Ashwin 'International Labour Solidarity after the Cold War' in Cohen and Rai.
53. See Colin Hines *Localisation: A Global Manifesto* Earthscan, London, 2000.
54. See Desai and Said, 'The New Anti-Capitalist Movement'.

55. World Bank Group 'An Open Letter'. http://www.worldbank.org/html/extdr/openletter. htm 17 Aug 2001.

56. Verhofstadt, Guy 'Open Letter: The Paradox of Anti-Globalisation', in *Open Letter on Globalisation: The Debate*. Laeken: European Council, 2001.

57. Graham, Robert, and Haig Simonian 'Jospin Sees France as the Pilot of the G8 Protests'. *Financial Times*. 24 July, 2001.

58. O'Tuathail, quoted in Roland Bleiker, *Popular Dissent, Human Agency and Global* Politics (Cambridge University Press: Cambridge, 2001), p. 31.

59. See *Global Civil Society 2002*.

60. James Deane 'The Other Information Revolution: media and Empowerment in Developing Countries' *Ibid*.

61. 'A Cautionary Note on Civil Society, paper at Expert Seminar, Meaning and Value of Civil Society in Different Cultural Contexts, LSE, 28–9 Sept. 2001.

62. Della Porta and Diani, *Social Movements*.

CHAPTER TWO

Transnational Advocacy Networks in the Movement Society

Margaret E. Keck and Kathryn Sikkink

Source: David S. Meyer and Sidney Tarrow (eds) *The Social Movement Society: Contentious Politics for a New Century* (1998) 217–238 © 1998 Rowman & Littlefield Publishing Group—Reproduced with permission.

Advocacy networks are one of the main vehicles for transnational activity around rights and social justice issues. Like activists in social movement organizations, activists in transnational advocacy networks seek to make the demands, claims, or rights of the less powerful win out over the purported interests of the more powerful. They do this by presenting issues in new ways (framing), seeking the most favorable arenas in which to fight their battles (paying attention to political opportunity structure), confounding expectations (disruption), and broadening the network's scope and density to maximize its access to necessary information (mobilizing social networks). Although they often include activists who are part of social movements, transnational advocacy networks are not themselves transnational "movements." If we define social movements as sustained, organized, contentious collective action around grievances or claims, these networks depart from the definition in various ways.[1] The clearest of these is in the mobilizational dimension: although advocacy networks may at times stimulate mobilized collective action, more commonly they are alternatives to mass action. This is especially true when the groups on whose behalf advocates organize are blocked from making demands at home—either because the rights violator is the state itself or because their voices are too weak to be heard domestically.

Transnational advocacy networks include those relevant actors working internationally on an issue, who are bound together by shared values, a common discourse, and dense exchanges of information and services.[2] They are *communicative structures* for political exchange. Network nodes (individuals and organizations) vary enormously in nature, density of organization, resources, and domestic standing; their main collective currency is information. Besides nongovernmental actors, networks may include individual officeholders in states or multilateral organizations or even whole agencies.

The conceptual apparatus developed to study domestic social movements remains extremely valuable for understanding transnational advocacy networks. In this essay we discuss the relevance of concepts of mobilizing structures, political opportunity structure, and framing for our discussion of transnational advocacy networks, and we consider why they travel so well.

In distinguishing between social movements and advocacy networks, we are trying to separate an analysis of what activists in advocacy networks do from an account of the biographies of network members. We recognize that this is a purely heuristic exercise—in real life they are inseparable. As in social movements, activism in advocacy networks occurs "at the intersection of biography and history" in a special way—"as biographies and identities are modified in accordance with the newly perceived historical imperatives" (McAdam 1988, p. 11). Advocacy network activists often have a history of involvement with social movements; some social movement organizations are part of networks, and networks can provide crucial resources for movements. Or, conversely, movements and advocacy networks may compete for legitimacy in the same terrain. Some members of advocacy networks conceive of themselves as part of a transnational social movement; others most decidedly do not.

Core activists in advocacy networks most often work for nongovernmental organizations (NGOs), in the United States, frequently called public interest groups or nonprofits. They are, in other words, career activists. These NGOs may be wholly devoted to international activities (e.g., human rights groups) or barely at all (most environmental organizations). Activists involved in an advocacy network may therefore be speaking for their organizations or may be using the organization as a platform on which to stand. In either case organizational affiliation matters, but the solidity of organizational linkages may affect the resources on which a network can draw.

A brief note on the subject of NGOs is in order. We use the term to refer to professionalized nonprofit organizations (with paid staff, fund-raising capabilities, and, except in highly repressive situations, juridical recognition). In developing countries, NGOs may be involved in service provision or in advocacy and social promotion; many do both. Some are highly politicized, ranging from quasi-governmental fronts to vehicles for radical opposition; others are less so. The origin of the NGO sector varies widely from country to country. In advocacy networks NGOs involved tend most often to be run either by people with histories of activism in other areas (social movements, political parties) or by professionals (e.g., lawyers, ecologists, agronomists) seeking more engaged alternatives to traditional employment. Although NGOs can be involved in a wide range of activities, the ones we discuss in our work are devoted to social change issues.

Social Networks

Social movement theorists have repeatedly stressed the importance of social networks—concrete linkages that derive from locality, shared experience, kinship, and the like—as foundations on which movements are built. In recent explorations, Tarrow (1996a) questions whether or how the functional equivalent of these could be mobilized transnationally. But in fact, many social networks that nourish the creation of transnational advocacy networks and support their work reveal histories of personal relationships and shared experiences that parallel those found in domestic movements.

Just as domestic public interest groups often grow out of social movement struggles, many professional advocacy NGOs involved in transnational activity derive sustenance from earlier movements. Funding from private foundations and religious organizations has similarly played an important role. The Ford Foundation program in public interest law aided in the establishment of U.S. consumer and environmental groups (Berry 1993, pp. 30–33; Ingram and Mann

1989, p. 137); Ford, with NOVIB (the Dutch affiliate of the international Oxfam organisation) and other European funders also played a key role in financing human rights groups and Third World environmental advocacy. In developing countries, advocacy NGOs have appeared in response to the push of a particular movement or the pull of funding opportunities that coalesced with strongly held beliefs. During the recent democratic transitions in Latin America, activists involved in popular education or grassroots organizing established new institutes as "private organizations fulfilling public functions" in campaigns against violence and promoting rights of women, racial minorities, indigenous peoples, workers and the landless, the environment, human rights, and so forth (Fernandes 1994; Landim 1993). These professionalized groups, in turn, are linked through social networks forged in past struggles to other activists (Doimo 1995). In countries lacking a history of freedom of association, mobilizing networks of trusted activists for particular campaigns is a more familiar mode of organization than establishing institutions.

Repressive regimes in Latin America (and elsewhere) have spurred the transnationalization of advocacy networks in two ways. Repression forces the externalization of domestic rights struggles. Unable to address issues like human rights, disappearances, and labor rights in situations in which the chief violators of rights were state institutions, activists formed alliances with their counterparts abroad. Together, they sought recourse either by approaching international institutions or by mobilizing foreign pressure to change the behavior of their governments.

Repression also generated diasporas. The thousands of Latin American political exiles who spent part of the 1970s in Europe and the United States inspired a generation of young people, already socialized into movement politics by the events of the late 1960s, with their stories. The exiles developed lasting friendships, political ties, and relations of trust. They also developed relationships with organizations in their host countries—universities, churches, foundations, and research institutes—that became key resources for them when they returned home. Some individuals gained international reputations. Thus, at the onset of democratization, former exiles played an important role in creating new NGOs in Latin America, securing funding, and acting as go-betweens for other initiatives. Some became active in new international NGOs (e.g., Amnesty International, Americas Watch) or other international organizations. Other kinds of international experience became more common as well. In the United States, networks appealed to a public socialized into more cosmopolitan worldviews through participation in student exchange programs, government programs like the Peace Corps, and lay missionary programs that sent thousands of young people to live and work in the developing world.

Social networks forged in earlier social or political struggles are not the only ones relevant to the formation of advocacy networks. Professional networks are also important, and increasingly so. Human rights and environmental lawyers, anthropologists, forensic and environmental scientists, health specialists, agronomists, all may become involved through professional activities in advocacy work. Besides NGO activists, crucial parts of advocacy networks are individuals in governmental agencies or intergovernmental organizations who share the activists' values and try to further their goals within organizations.

International conferences proliferated beginning in the 1970s, bringing activists from around the world together to discuss common concerns. Such meetings led to visits and exchanges. The precipitous fall in airfares that made international travel accessible for more and more people was followed in the 1980s by a revolution in telecommunications. Fax and computer technology made almost instantaneous flows of information that could have taken weeks or never arrived at all. These transnational contacts built the social networks on which advocacy networks were founded; information was the currency by which they gained influence.

Although frequently undertaken by people with strong principled motivations, running effective organizations involves learned techniques and transferrable expertise. NGO or non-profit management has increasingly become a profession. Transnational networking also involves skills taught by more experienced networkers to newer ones, just as more experienced movement organizers pass on the tools of campaigning to the next generation of campaigners.

Finally, networks have spawned networks (McAdam and Rucht 1993; Meyer and Whittier 1994). Connections forged in the mid-1970s among activists committed to working for a more equitable international economic order, campaigning around food and increasing corporate monopolies of plant germplasm in the International Coalition for Development Action, fed the organization of the International Baby Food Action Network, the Pesticides Action Network, and Health Action International. These in turn were important models for the creation of subsequent generations of health, environmental, and development action networks.

Political Opportunity Structure

Advocacy networks have been the most visible in situations in which domestic access of claimants is blocked or those making claims are too weak politically for their voices to be heard. In such instances, network activists have sought international or foreign venues in which to present claims, effectively transforming the power relationships involved by shifting the political context. Human rights activists brought the "dirty war" in Argentina to the U.S. Congress, producing significant reverberations in Buenos Aires; environmental activists took the problems of rubber tappers in the western Amazon to the multilateral development banks, producing (among other things) the creation of extractive reserves as a legal category.

We call the feedback that comes from this kind of venue shifting "the boomerang effect," and producing it is one of the most common strategic activities of advocacy networks. When the links between state and domestic actors are severed, it initiates the "boomerang": domestic NGOs bypass their state and directly search out international allies to try to bring pressure on their states from outside. Linkages are important for both sides: for the less powerful Third World actors, networks provide access, leverage, information, and material resources they could not expect to have on their own; for northern groups, they make credible the assertion that they are struggling with, and not only "for" their southern partners. Not surprisingly, such relationships can produce considerable tensions. Nonetheless, the practical activity they occasion helps to build the kinds of shared understandings that can form the basis for future work (Calhoun 1995a, pp. 173–76).

Transnational advocacy networks strategize by mapping relationships among a variety of domestic and international institutions. Their ability to get things done frequently depends on their ability to exert leverage over more powerful actors, mainly officials of states (their own or others) or international organizations. Environmentalists and indigenous rights activists lobby members of the U.S. Congress and Treasury Department to influence officials of the World Bank to put pressure on Brazil regarding indigenous land policy. NGO activists in Brasilia provide information to mid-level European diplomats tasked with updating their governments on environmental issues, so that their governments, in turn, raise questions in international fora or with the Brazilian government. Mexican pro-democracy and human rights advocates brought Mexican electoral abuses before the Inter-American Commission on Human Rights. These moves involve strategic choices of activity predicated on an assessment of relations among governments and among national and international institutions. These "opportunities" are dynamic; the political opportunity structure relevant for this kind of activity has to do as much with political relations as with political institutions (Tarrow 1996b).[3]

Network members actively seek ways to bring issues to the public agenda, both by framing them in innovative ways and by seeking hospitable venues. Transnational networks normally involve a small number of activists from the organizations and institutions involved in a given campaign or advocacy role. The kinds of pressure and agenda politics in which advocacy net-works engage rarely involve mass activism. Boycott strategies are a partial exception. Instead, network activists engage in what Baumgartner and Jones (1991), borrowing from law, call venue shopping. "This strategy relies less on mass mobilization and more on the dual strategy of the presentation of image and the search for a more receptive political venue" (p. 1050). Very occasionally, groups become such integral parts of policy networks that they spend very little effort trying to influence public opinion; this kind of purely insider strategy is comparatively rare in transnational advocacy network politics (Walker 1991, p. 12).

[. . .]

Framing

Building cognitive frames is an essential component of networks' political strategies. David Snow and his colleagues have called this strategic activity *frame alignment*—"by rendering events or occurrences meaningful, frames function to organize experience and guide action, whether individual or collective" (Snow et al. 1986, pp. 464–465; Snow and Benford 1988, 1992). *Frame resonance* concerns the relationship between a movement organization's interpretive work and its ability to influence broader public understandings. Although initially new frames must be laboriously put into place, over time, "a given collective action frame becomes part of the political culture—which is to say, part of the reservoir of symbols from which future move-ment entrepreneurs can choose" (Tarrow 1992, p. 197).

The ability of transnational advocacy networks to frame issues successfully is especially problematic, because unlike domestic social movements, different parts of advocacy networks need to appeal to belief systems, life worlds, and stories, myths, and folk tales in many different countries and cultures. This is even more problematic when networks link activists from highly industrialized and less developed countries. We argue that one of the kinds of issues most characteristic of issue networks—involving bodily harm to vulnerable individuals—speaks to aspects of belief systems or life worlds that transcend a specific cultural or political context.

Why do these issues appear so prominently in international campaigns? Although the issue of bodily harm resonates with the liberal ideological traditions in the United States and Western Europe, it is also a component of basic ideas of human dignity. Not all cultures have beliefs about human rights (as individualistic, universal, and indivisible), but most do contain ideas of human dignity (Donnelly 1989, pp. 49–50). Of course, defining bodily harm, and claims about who is vulnerable or innocent, may be highly contested. Nevertheless, we argue that campaigns against practices involving bodily harm to populations perceived as vulnerable or innocent are most likely to be effective transnationally, especially where there is a short and clear causal chain or story assigning responsibility. Issues involving bodily harm also lend themselves to dramatic portrayal and personal testimony that are such an important part of network tactics. Finally, the stark immediacy of the power relationship implied by physical violence against vulnerable individuals relegates the kinds of power asymmetries that frequently divide networks to the background, making possible the development of shared practice that can contribute to a com-mon frame.[4]

The adoption of new frames frequently involves the imagination of political entrepreneurs. The recent coupling of indigenous rights and environmental struggles is a good example of strategic reframing by indigenista activists, who found the environmental arena more receptive to their claims than human rights venues were. Although initially the argument that preserving forest peoples' livelihoods and conserving forests were inseparable provoked resistance from some conservationists, this frame very rapidly entered the accepted repertoire of environmentalist discourse (Keck 1995; Conklin and Graham 1995).

Information flows in advocacy networks provide not only hard data but also *testimony*—stories told by people whose lives have been affected. Moreover, they interpret facts and testimony: activist groups frame issues simply, as right or wrong, because their purpose is to stimulate people to take action. An effective frame must show that a given state of affairs is neither natural nor accidental, identify the responsible party or parties, and propose credible solutions. This requires clear, powerful messages that appeal to shared principles and often have more impact on state policy than advice from technical experts An important part of the political struggle over environmental issues, for example, is precisely the degree to which they are defined primarily as technical questions, subject to consideration by "qualified" experts, or as questions that are properly the concern of a much broader global constituency.

Networks call attention to issues or even "create issues" by using language that dramatizes and draws attention to their concerns. A good example is the recent campaign against the practice of female genital mutilation. Before 1976, the widespread practice of female circumcision in many African and a few Asian and Middle Eastern countries was known outside these regions mainly among medical experts and anthropologists (World Bank 1993, p. 50). A controversial campaign, initiated in 1974 by a network of women's and human rights organizations, began to draw attention to these issues.

One of the main ways the campaign drew attention to the issue was to "reframe" it by *renaming the problem*. Previously the practice was referred to by more technical and "neutral" terms like female circumcision, clitoridectomy, or infibulation. The campaign around female genital mutilation raised its salience, literally creating the issue as a matter of public international concern. By renaming the practice, the network broke the linkage with male circumcision (seen as a personal medical or cultural decision), implied a linkage with the more feared procedure—castration—and reframed the issue as one of violence against women. It thus resituated the problem as a human rights violation. The campaign generated action against female genital mutilation in many countries, including France and the United Kingdom; the United Nations studied the problem and made a series of recommendations for eradicating certain traditional practices (Kouba and Muasher 1985; Slack 1988; Sochart 1988; United Nations 1986).

The tropical forest issue is fraught with scientific uncertainty about forests' role in climate regulation, their regenerative capacity, and the value of undiscovered or untapped biological resources. By reframing the issue, calling attention to the impact of tropical forest destruction on particular populations, environmentalists have made a call for action independent of the scientific status of the issue. Human rights activists, baby food campaigners, and women's groups play a similar role. By dramatizing the situations of the victims, they turn the cold facts into human stories, intended to motivate people to action. For example, the baby food campaign that began in the early 1970s relied heavily on public health studies that proved that improper bottle feeding contributed to infant malnutrition and mortality and that corporate sales promotion was leading to a decline in breast-feeding (Jellife and Jellife 1978; Ambulatory Pediatrics Association 1981). Network activists repackaged and interpreted this information in dramatic ways designed to promote action. The British development organization War on Want published a pamphlet entitled The Baby Killers, which the Swiss Third World Action Group translated into German and retitled Nestle Kills Babies. Nestle inadvertently gave activists a prominent public forum when it sued the Third World Action Group for defamation and libel. In 1977, U.S. campaigners initiated the boycott of Nestle that made the corporation increasingly a focus of controversy and brought more attention and resources to the issue.

Information Politics

Information binds network members together and is essential for network effectiveness. The main activity of advocacy networks is collecting credible information and deploying it strategically at carefully selected sites. Many information exchanges are informal: telephone calls, E-mail and fax communications, and the circulation of small newsletters, pamphlets, and bulletins. They provide information that would not otherwise be available, from sources that might not otherwise be heard, and they must make this information comprehensible and useful to activists and publics who may be geographically and/or socially distant.

Networks strive to uncover and investigate problems and alert the press and policy makers. One activist described this as the "human rights methodology—promoting change by reporting facts" (Thomas 1993, p. 83; also Lumsdaine 1993, pp. 187–88, 211–13). To be credible, the information of networks must be reliable and well documented. To gain attention it must be timely and dramatic. Sometimes these multiple goals of information politics conflict. The notion of reporting facts does not fully capture the way networks strategically use information and testimony to frame issues.

Testimony by people affected by the abuse being protested serves two informational functions: besides making a problem real to distant publics, it attests to the credibility and reach of the network. Thus, when indigenous rights advocates sponsor international tours for indigenous leaders and environmentalists do so for forest people's leaders, it shows their connection to the people on whose behalf they make claims. The indigenous and forest people's leaders in turn show their compatriots that their claims are recognized abroad.

Even as we highlight the importance of testimony, however, we have to recognize the mediations involved. The process by which testimony is discovered and presented normally involves several layers of prior translation. Transnational actors may identify what kinds of testimony would be valuable, then ask an NGO in the area to seek out people who could tell those stories. They may filter through expatriates, through traveling scholars like ourselves, and through the media. A huge gap often exists between the story's telling and its retelling—in sociocultural context, in instrumental meaning, and even in language. Successful frames become stylized; conflicts told as morality tales may lose the specificity of their local construction as local actors are cast in roles written for them elsewhere. Local people, in other words, normally lose control over their stories in a transnational campaign. How this process of mediation/translation occurs is a particularly interesting facet of network politics.

Nongovernmental networks link testimonial information with technical and statistical information. Without the individual cases, activists cannot motivate people to seek change policies. Increasingly, international campaigns by networks take this two-level approach to information. In the 1980s even Greenpeace, which initially had eschewed rigorous research in favor of splashy media events, began to pay more attention to getting the facts right. While testimony does not avoid the need to manage technical information, it helps to make the need for action more real for ordinary citizens.

A dense web of north-south exchange, aided by computer and fax communication, means that governments can no longer monopolize information flows as they could a mere half-decade ago. These technologies have had an enormous impact on moving information to and from Third World countries, where mail service has often been both slow and precarious. We should note, however, that this gives special advantages to organizations that have access to such technologies. A good example of the new informational role of networks occurred when U.S. environmentalists pressured President George Bush to raise gold miners' ongoing invasions of the Yanomami indigenous reserve when Brazilian president Fernando Collor de Mello was in Washington in 1991. Collor believed that he had squelched protest over the Yanomami question by creating major media events out of the dynamiting of airstrips used by gold miners, and a decade earlier he would have succeeded. However, since network members had current information faxed from Brazil, they could counter his claims with evidence that miners had rebuilt the airstrips and were still invading the Yanomami area.

The central role of information in all these issues helps to explain the drive to create networks. Information in these issue areas is both essential and dispersed. Nongovernmental actors depend on their access to information to help make them legitimate players. Contact with like-minded groups at home and abroad provides access to information necessary to their work, broadens their legitimacy, and helps to mobilize information around particular policy targets. Most nongovernmental organizations cannot afford to maintain staff people in a variety of countries. In exceptional cases, they send staff members on investigation missions, but this is not practical for keeping informed on routine developments. Forging links with local organizations allows groups to receive and monitor information from many countries at a low cost. Local groups, in turn, depend on international contacts to get their information out and help to protect them in their work.

Finally, the media plays an essential role in network information politics. To reach a broader audience, networks strive to attract press attention. Sympathetic journalists may become part of the network, but more often network activists cultivate a reputation for credibility with the press and package their information in a timely and dramatic way to draw press attention.

Campaigns

Advocacy networks organize around campaigns. For our purposes, campaigns are sets of strategically linked activities in which members of a diffuse principled network develop explicit, visible ties and mutually recognized roles toward a common goal (and generally against a common target). In a campaign, core (usually experienced) network actors mobilize others, initiating the tasks of structural integration and cultural negotiation among the groups in the network. Just as in domestic campaigns, they connect groups to each other, seek out resources, propose and prepare activities, and do public relations. They must also consciously seek to develop a "common frame of meaning," a task complicated by cultural diversity within transnational networks (Gerhards and Rucht 1992, pp. 558–59). Activist groups have long used the language of campaigning to talk about focused, strategically planned efforts. International campaigns by environmental and conservation organizations, for example, traditionally had a topical focus (saving furry animals, whales, tropical forests), while human rights campaigns had either a country (the Argentina campaign) or issue focus (the campaign against torture) (Schiotz 1983, pp. 120–22).

Focusing on campaigns provides a window on transnational relations as an arena of struggles in ways that a focus on networks themselves or on the institutions they try to affect does not. This focus highlights relationships—connections among network actors and between activists and their allies and opponents. We can identify the kinds of resources that make a campaign possible—information, leadership, symbolic or material capital (McCarthy and Zald 1977). And we must consider the kinds of institutional structures—both domestic and international—that encourage or impede particular kinds of transnational activism. Finally, a focus on campaigning lets us explore negotiation of meaning while we look at the evolution of tactics; we can recognize that cultural differences, different conceptions of the stakes in a campaign, and resource inequalities among network actors exist, while we identify critical roles that different actors fill. Campaigns are processes of issue construction constrained by the action context in which they are to be carried out: activists identify a problem, specify a cause, and propose a solution, all with an eye toward producing procedural, substantive, and normative change in their area of concern. In networked campaigns, this process of "strategic portrayal" (Stone 1988, p. 6) must work for the different actors in the network and for target audiences.

The process we describe is interactive: nongovernmental organizations pressure for international events, such as declarations, treaties, theme years, theme decades, and conferences, which in turn serve as arenas for network formation. In the baby food campaign, network pressures motivated U.S. Senator Edward Kennedy to hold hearings on the issue in 1978. Kennedy in turn called on WHO/UNICEF to hold consultative meetings on the issue of the marketing of infant formula, a move favored by industry representatives, who believed that moving to an international venue would help to depoliticize the issue. Industry's expectations were frustrated when these meetings included not only representatives from governments, international organizations, industry, and academia but also NGO and consumer activists. This was the first time NGO activists were full participants alongside industry and government representatives in a United Nations consultation. At the conclusion of the 1979 consultative meeting, NGO activists present formed the International Baby Food Action Network (IBFAN), which eventually brought together a hundred groups working in sixty-five countries on issues of infant nutrition. Network members played a crucial role in helping draft and lobbying government to vote for the WHO/UNICEF Code of Marketing for Breast-milk Substitutes, an innovative effort to regulate transnational business activities in the interest of infant health (Sikkink 1986).

[. . .]

Notes

1. This is similar to their definition by Sidney Tarrow (1996a, pp. 13–14) as "sustained sequences of collective action mounted by organized collective actors in interaction with elites, authorities and other actors in the name of their claims or the claims of those they represent."
2. This discussion of transnational advocacy networks draws heavily on our book, *Activists Beyond Borders*, though this chapter takes steps beyond the book in relating our argument more explicitly to debates in social movement theory.
3. By political opportunity structure, Tarrow (1996b, p. 54) means "consistent—but not necessarily formal, permanent, or national—signals to social or political actors which either encourage or discourage them to use their internal resources to form social movements . . . The most salient kinds of signals are four: the opening up of access to power, shifting alignments, the availability of influential allies, and cleavages within and among elites" (italics in original).
4. We concur with Craig Calhoun (1995, p. 173) in his stress on practice as a basis for the development of shared understandings. He writes, "Indeed, both the translation and metadiscourse models [of shared understandings] are too static, too inattentive to the extent to which our mutual understandings are in fact constructed through processes of historical change, and too exclusively individualistic. . . . [We need to grasp] the historical and political processes by which people come to shared understandings without translations or metadiscourses."

References

Ambulatory Pediatrics Association. 1981. "Statement by the Board of Directors on the WHO Code of Marketing of Breast-Milk Substitutes." *Pediatrics* 68 (September).

Baumgartner, Frank R., and Bryan D. Jones. 1991. "Agenda Dynamics and Policy Subsystems." *Journal of Politic* 53: 1044–74.

Berry, Jeffrey. 1993. "Citizen Groups and the Changing Nature of Interest Group Politics in America." *Annals of the American Academy of Political and Social Science* 528: 30–41.

Calhoun, Craig. 1995a. *Critical Social Theory.* Oxford: Blackwell.

Conklin, Beth, and Laura R. Graham. 1995. "The Shifting Middle Ground: Amazonian Indians and Eco-Politics." *American Anthropologist* 97(4) (December): 695–710.

Doimo, Ana Maria. 1995. *A Vez e a Voz do Popular: Movimentos Sociais e Participacab politica no Brasil pos-70.* Rio de Janeiro: ANPOCS/Relume Dumara.

Donnelly, Jack. 1989. *Human Rights in Theory and Practice.* Ithaca, NY: Cornell University Press.

Fernandes, Rubem Cesar. 1994. *Privado porem Pablico: 0 Terceiro Setor na America Latina.* Rio de Janeiro: CIVICUS/Relume Dumara.

Gerhards, Jurgen, and Dieter Rucht. 1992. "Mesomobilization: Organizing and Framing in Two Protest Campaigns in West Germany." *American Journal of Sociology* 98(3): 555–95.

Ingram, Helen M., and Dean E. Mann. 1989. "Interest Groups and Environmental Policy," Pp. 135–57 in James P. Lester, ed., *Environmental Politics and Policy: Theories and Evidence.* Durham, NC: Duke University Press.

Jager, Thomas. 1993. *Betriebsschlief3ung and Protest: Kollektive Handlungschancen gegen die Stillegung des Hiittenwerkes Duisburg-Rheinhausen.* Marburg: Schtiren.

Jellife, D., and Jellife, E. P. 1978. *Human Milk in the Modern World.* Oxford: Oxford University Press.

Keck, Margaret E. 1995. "Social Equity and Environmental Politics in Brazil: Lessons from the Rubber Tappers of Acre." *Comparative Politics* 27: 409–24.

Kouba, Leonard J., and Judith Mausher. 1985. "Female Circumcision in Africa: An Overview." *African Studies Review* 28 (March): 95–110.

Landim Assumpcao, Leilah. 1993. *A Invencgo das ONGs: Do servicv invisivel a profissao sem name.* Unpublished Ph.D. dissertation, Universidade Federal do Rio de Janeiro, Museu Nacional, Programa de Pos-Graduagao em Antropologia Social.

Lumsdaine, David. 1993. *Moral Vision in International Politics: The Foreign Aid Regime, 1949–1989.* Princeton, NJ: Princeton University Press.

McAdam, Doug. 1988. Freedom Summer. Chicago: University of Chicago Press.

McAdam, Doug, and Dieter Rucht. 1993. "Cross-National Diffusion of Social Movement Ideas and Tactics." *Annals of the American Academy of Political and Social Sciences* 528 (July): 56–74.

McCarthy, John D., and Mayer N. Zald. 1973. *The Trend of Social Movements in America: Professionalization and Resource Mobilization.* Morristown, NJ: General Learning Press.

—. 1977. "Resource Mobilization and Social Movements: A Partial Theory." *American Journal of Sociology* 82: 1212–41.

Meyer, David S., and Nancy Whittier. 1994. "Social Movement Spillover." *Social Problems* 41: 277–98.

Schiotz, Arne. 1983. "A Campaign Is Born." *IUCN Bulletin* 14 (October—December): 120–22.

Slack, Alison T. 1988. "Female Circumcision: A Critical Appraisal." *Human Rights Quarterly* 10: 437–86.

Snow, David A., and Robert D. Benford. 1988. "Ideology, Frame Resonance, and Participant Mobilization." Pp. 197–217 in Bert Klandermans, Hanspeter Kriesi, and Sidney Tarrow, eds., *From Structure to Action: Comparing Social Movement Research across Cultures.* Greenwich, CT: JAI.

—. 1992. "Master Frames and Cycles of Protest." Pp. 133–55 in Aldon D. Morris and Carol McClurg Mueller, eds., *Frontiers in Social Movement Theory.* New Haven, CT: Yale University Press.

Snow, David, E. Burke Rochford, Steven K. Worden, and Robert D. Benford. 1986. "Frame Alignment Processes, Micromobilization, and Movement Participation." *American Sociological Review* 51: 464–81.

Sochart, Elise A. 1988. "Agenda Setting, The Role of Groups and the Legislative Process: The Prohibition of Female Circumcision in Britain." *Parliamentary Affairs* 41(4) (October): 508–26.

Stone, Deborah A. 1988. *Policy Paradox and Political Reason.* New York: Harper-Collins.

Tarrow, Sidney. 1992. "Mentalities, Political Cultures, and Collective Action Frames: Constructing Meanings through Action." Pp. 174–202 in Aldon D. Morris and Carol McClurg Mueller, eds., *Frontiers in Social Movement Theory.* New Haven, CT: Yale University Press.

—. 1996a. "Fishnets, Internets and Catnets: Globalization and Transnational Collective Action." Working Paper 78 (March). Madrid; Institutio Juan March de Estudios e Investigaciones.

—. 1996b. "States and Opportunities: The Political Structuring of Social Movements." Pp. 41–61 in Doug McAdam, John D. McCarthy, and Mayer Zald, eds., *Comparative Perspectives on Social Movements.* Cambridge: Cambridge University Press.

United Nations. 1986. "Report of the Working Group on Traditional Practices Affecting the Health of Women and Children." UN Doc. E/CN.4/1986/42.

Walker, Jack L., Jr. 1991. *Mobilizing Interest Groups in America: Patrons, Professions, and Social Movements.* Ann Arbor: University of Michigan Press.

World Bank. 1993. *World Bank Development Report 1993: Investing in Health.* Washington, D.C.: World Bank.

CHAPTER THREE

The Rise and Fall of Transnational Civil Society: The Evolution of International Non-Governmental Organizations since the Mid-Nineteenth Century

Thomas Richard Davies

Source: http://www.city.ac.uk/intpol/dps/WorkingPapers/T_Davies%20The%20Rise%20and%20Fall%20 of%20Transnational%20Civil%20Society.pdf

Three years before the outbreak of the First World War, a prominent American academic and diplomat, Paul S. Reinsch, claimed that 'the barren ideal of no war, no patriotism, no local interest, has given way to a potent centripetal force . . . cosmopolitanism is no longer a castle in the air, but it has become incorporated in numerous associations and unions world-wide in their co-operation.'[1] Similarly, in the post-Cold War era it has been claimed that transnational (or global) civil society may provide 'an answer to war'.[2] Much of the evidence provided in this chapter suggests that there are reasons to be as cautious about such claims today as a century ago.

This chapter is an early step in an endeavour to explore the history of transnational civil society. Contrary to conventional wisdom, it will suggest that transnational civil society may not have developed following a course of linear progress. Instead, this chapter will offer an outline history that suggests that transnational civil society rises and falls in waves.

The first part of this chapter introduces the concept of transnational civil society and discusses the possible ways of tracing its historical evolution. This is followed by an assessment of the principal factors that have affected the development of transnational civil society. Thirdly, an outline history of transnational civil society is suggested, highlighting the different ways in which it has arguably 'risen' and 'fallen' over time. The conclusion provides a brief assessment of arguments surrounding the future trajectory of transnational civil society.

1. Defining and Measuring 'Transnational Civil Society'

It is only recently—in the period since the end of the Cold War—that the term 'transnational civil society' and the bolder term 'global civil society' have entered popular usage in academic literature on international politics. As Helmut Anheier, Marlies Glasius and Mary Kaldor have argued, the meaning of these terms is 'subject to widely differing interpretations'.[3] Nevertheless, most definitions refer to 'uncoerced collective action around shared interests, purposes and values'[4] that is non-governmental and not for profit.[5] Whereas *'global* civil society' involves activities that 'straddle the whole earth, and . . . have complex effects that are felt in its four corners',[6] the less ambitious concept of *'transnational* civil society' (which is the focus of this chapter) refers to non-governmental non-profit collective action that *transcends national boundaries* but does not necessarily have global reach. The key actors in transnational civil society are international non-governmental organizations (INGOs), i.e. international organizations that are neither profit-making nor instruments of government,[7] as well as internationally-orientated national non-governmental organizations. A distinction is often made between international non-governmental organizations that exist simply to provide services to their members and issue-oriented international non-governmental organizations, which are the principal foci in studies of transnational civil society and therefore this chapter too.

In order to gain an understanding of how transnational civil society has evolved, it is necessary to think about how the phenomenon can be measured. The task of measuring transnational civil society is as problematic as the issue of definition, since the variety of factors that potentially need to be taken into account is considerable. Much of the existing literature on transnational civil society has focused on one major unit of assessment: the number of (issue-oriented) international non-governmental organizations that exist.[8] This unit of assessment appears to support the proposition that transnational civil society has been following a path of linear progress. According to one source, whereas up to 1854 only six INGOs had been founded, by the turn of the century this figure had reached 163, and by 1945 over a thousand INGOs had been established.[9] By the end of the twentieth century it was claimed that there were over 20,000 INGOs in the world.[10]

Beyond pointing out the increasing number of international non-governmental organizations that have been founded, those who claim that transnational civil society has been following a path of linear progress also highlight its apparent contribution towards significant recent international developments. For instance, transnational civil society is said to have played an important role in bringing the Cold War to an end, has contributed towards the redefinition of development and security to include humanitarian concerns, and has helped facilitate international agreements such as the 1987 Montreal Protocol and the 1997 Ottawa Landmines Convention.

Although INGO numbers and the apparent impact of transnational civil society are the two principal means of gauging transnational civil society cited in the existing literature, both measures may be misleading. For instance, an expansion in the number of international non-governmental organizations may represent fragmentation of transnational civil society into smaller INGOs rather than growth. As for the apparent impact of transnational civil society on recent developments, the relative contribution to these developments of transnational civil society compared with other factors is very difficult to ascertain. Furthermore, transnational civil society's influence on major developments in world politics is far from new: for instance transnational non-governmental activism contributed to the abolition of the slave trade in the nineteenth century and to the foundation of the League of Nations and the United Nations Organization in the first half of the twentieth century.

An examination of alternative methods of evaluating the evolution of transnational civil society reveals that the development of this phenomenon may be more complex than has traditionally been portrayed. One alternative method of evaluating the development of transnational civil society is to assess the number of INGO foundations and dissolutions per annum. As John Boli and George Thomas have noted, although the total number of INGOs has increased overall since the nineteenth century, the number of INGOs founded each year dropped considerably at the time of the First World War, and after recovering in the 1920s dropped again at the time of the Great Depression and Second World War. In the case of the number of INGO dissolutions per annum, there were sharp increases during the two World Wars and the Great Depression.[11]

Further methods of evaluating the development of transnational civil society reveal a still more complex evolutionary path. A much-neglected but important consideration is the extent of popular participation in transnational civil society. There are many different ways that popular participation in transnational civil society may be assessed. One option is to examine the proportion of the world's population represented in global campaigns, for instance through membership of an organization in a campaigning coalition or through signing a transnational petition. In the case of both of these measures, participation in the main transnational civil society campaigns in the present era is arguably less substantial than in campaigns that took place more than seventy years ago.[12] The argument that transnational civil society has been following a path of linear progress must therefore be called into question.

2. Explaining the Evolution of Transnational Civil Society

The third section of this chapter will provide a narrative of how transnational civil society has arguably risen and fallen in waves since the mid-nineteenth century. This section of the chapter will briefly introduce some of the main factors that help to explain why transnational civil society may have evolved in this way. These factors can be split into five categories: technological; economic; social; external political; and internal political. As will become apparent from the next section of this chapter, many of the factors that have in some ways contributed towards the expansion of transnational civil society have in other ways contributed also towards its decline.

Technological developments are amongst the most commonly cited reasons for the alleged expansion of transnational civil society in the post-Cold War era: cheap air travel and tele-communications, mobile telephones, and the internet are all said to be making the post-Cold War world a smaller place. Similarly the emergence of transnational civil society in the mid-nineteenth century was facilitated by innovations such as the steamship and electrical telegraphy.

The global economy is another factor influencing the development of transnational civil society: periods of economic globalization such as the late nineteenth century and the present era appear to correlate with periods of an expanding transnational civil society. Conversely, periods of global economic decline, such as the Great Depression, coincide with a downturn in transnational civil society activities. As for social factors, demographic changes such as urbanization, and psychological changes such as the development of 'global consciousness', are said to facilitate the growth of transnational civil society.

The political influences on the evolution of transnational civil society may be divided into external and internal factors. External political factors such as democratization, interstate peace, the emergence of transnational political issues, the growth of intergovernmental organizations, and the development of international law and norms have arguably facilitated the expansion of transnational civil society. Other external political factors such as nationalism, on the other hand, have arguably had the reverse effect.

Amongst the most interesting of the factors influencing the development of transnational civil society are the characteristics of transnational civil society itself. The degree of unity and co-ordination of civic associations, the nature of their objectives, and the consequences of their actions can all contribute in different ways both towards the expansion of and towards the decline of transnational civil society. The contribution of these 'internal political' factors to the development of transnational civil society will be central to the examination of the phenomenon's evolution in the next section of this chapter.

3. The Evolution of Transnational Civil Society

Although transnational civil society arguably has a very long history,[13] this suggested outline of its development will begin in the nineteenth century, when the first international non-governmental organizations of the modern era were founded. One of the earliest modern INGOs is said to be Anti-Slavery International, established as the British and Foreign Anti-Slavery

Society in 1839, and one of the most significant early transnational civic campaigns is the transnational network that, according to Margaret Keck and Kathryn Sikkink, 'succeeded first in helping create abolition as a pressing political issue in the United States, and then, when the issue ultimately contributed to war, became a critical factor in preventing British recognition of the South'.[14]

By the turn of the century, transnational civil society had expanded beyond the anti-slavery movement to include temperance (the International Order of Good Templars was founded in 1852), labour rights (the International Workingmen's Association was established in 1864), peace (the International Peace Bureau was created in 1891), and women's suffrage (the International Alliance of Women was formed in 1902). A peak of activity was arguably reached at the time of the Hague conferences of 1899 and 1907, at which the technique of lobbying intergovernmental conferences was pioneered.

As the previous section of this chapter outlined, a variety of technological, economic and social developments in the nineteenth century facilitated the emergence of transnational civil society in this period. Together, these factors contributed towards what Akira Iriye has described as a nascent 'global consciousness'.[15] As Paul Reinsch argued in 1911:

> The most important fact of which we have become conscious in our generation is that the unity of the world is real. The most remote regions are being made accessible. The great economic and financial system by which the resources of the Earth are being developed is centralized. The psychological unity of the world is being prepared by the service of news and printed discussions, by which in the space of one day or week the same events are reported to all the readers from Buenos Aires to Tokyo, from Cape Town to San Francisco. The same political dramas evoke our interest, the same catastrophes compel our sympathy, the same scientific achievements make us rejoice, and the same great public figures people our imagination. That such a unity of thought and feeling is drawing after it a unity of action is plainly apparent. Our destiny is a common one.[16]

At the same time, the emergence of intergovernmental organizations and the increasing number of intergovernmental conferences provided greater political opportunities for transnational civic action. National-level developments also facilitated transnational associational activity: for example the consolidation of the nation-state in Europe provided the infrastructure for the development of national branches of transnational civic organizations.

However, to portray the development of transnational civil society in the nineteenth century as following a path of continuous progress would be misleading. For instance, there were peaks of such activity at the time of the anti-slavery campaign and at the Hague conferences. More significantly, by the end of this period, transnational civic activity was greatly disrupted by the onset of the First World War. INGO foundations and the volume of transnational non-governmental meetings diminished considerably after 1913, while INGO dissolutions rose sharply. Some of the factors that had previously worked to facilitate transnational civil society acted on this occasion in the opposite direction. The rise of the nation-state, for instance, had not only provided the context within which domestic civil society could flourish, it also provided a locus for the nationalistic forces that contributed towards the First World War. More interestingly, transnational civil society itself arguably contributed towards its own demise at this time. For instance, Michael Howard in his classic work on *War and the Liberal Conscience* states:

> [H]ypnotised by the apparent transformation of warmongering capitalists into a strong force for peace, liberals and socialists in 1914 underestimated the true dangers: those arising from

forces inherent in the states-system of the balance of power which they had for so long denounced, and those new forces of militant nationalism which they themselves had done so much to encourage. It was these which combined to destroy the transnational community they had laboured to create . . . [17]

Following the First World War, transnational civil society recovered and expanded at an unprecedented pace. The number of international non-governmental organizations founded in the 1920s was twice the number founded in the entire nineteenth century. The breadth of transnational civil society expanded, too: for example, a new international organization explicitly devoted to human rights was founded in 1922: the International League for the Rights of Man; and new humanitarian assistance organizations were created, such as the Save the Children International Union, established in 1920. Many INGOs acquired considerable mass memberships in this period: for instance, two of the principal new INGOs founded after World War I, the Interallied Federation of Ex-Servicemen and the International Federation of Trade Unions, had memberships of eight million and twenty million respectively. At the beginning of this period there is also considerable evidence for the impact of transnational civil society campaigns on major political developments such as women's suffrage and the establishment of the League of Nations.

The scale of transnational mobilization that became achievable after the First World War is particularly well illustrated by the campaign for disarmament that took place in the 1920s and early 1930s. This campaign mobilized a uniquely broad spectrum of civil society groups (from Rotary International to the Communist International!), including the world's principal labour, humanitarian, religious, students', women's and peace organizations of the period. The campaign peaked during the World Disarmament Conference convened by the League of Nations in 1932–3, at which INGOs with a combined membership estimated to have been between two hundred million and a billion people lobbied delegates for a general disarmament convention. The scale of the activities that these organizations undertook is illustrated by the disarmament petition circulated by women's international organizations from 1930 to 1932, which remains the world's largest international petition in terms of the proportion of the world's population that signed it.[18]

Transnational activism on this scale was facilitated by many of the types of factors cited in the previous section of this chapter. The factors include post-war economic recovery, technological developments such as the first commercial transatlantic telephone calls, and the establishment of the League of Nations, which assisted INGOs by publishing data on their activities, sending representatives to observe INGO gatherings, giving INGOs the opportunity to participate in League of Nations meetings and conferences, and printing INGO petitions in its official publications.[19] The role of the First World War was especially notable: although it had contributed towards the collapse of many of the most significant elements of pre-war transnational civil society, its brutal consequences provided a need for the creation of new humanitarian and ex-servicemen's organizations, while the wish for prevention of recurrence of such a conflict revitalized the peace movement.

From 1933 onwards, however, transnational civil society again began to decline. The Great Depression was responsible for a dramatic reduction in INGO revenues, and many organizations had to cut back on their conferences, publications and other activities. Although the rise of far right regimes in some countries provided a strong reason for anti-fascist campaigners elsewhere to increase their activities, in countries such as Germany, Japan, Austria, Italy, Spain and Portugal many social change INGOs were forced to close their branches. INGO membership consequently declined, and by the second half of the 1930s the rate of INGO foundations was about half that of the late 1920s, a rate that halved again with the onset of the

Second World War. With the spectacular failure of large-scale transnational activism at the World Disarmament Conference (which collapsed in 1933), INGO influence in world political affairs was also diminished.

Central to explaining this decline are three significant developments: the Great Depression, the rise of fascist governments, and the onset of the Second World War. Factors that had previously contributed towards the rise of transnational civil society were important in precipitating these developments. For instance, the League of Nations, in its attempt to implement collective security in respect of Italy's invasion of Abyssinia, disrupted efforts effectively to balance the growing power of Nazi Germany: a key moment in what Michael Howard has called the 'melancholy story of the efforts of good men to abolish war but only succeeding to make it more terrible'.[20]

As with the decline of transnational civil society at the onset of the First World War, the role of transnational civil society itself in contributing towards its own demise in the 1930s is highly significant. The transnational disarmament campaign described above, for instance, may not have succeeded in its objective of a convention for general and comprehensive disarmament, but—as Winston Churchill argued—disarmament activism in the liberal countries made them 'an easy prey' in the run-up to the Second World War.[21]

There is considerable evidence to support the argument that transnational civil society has recovered impressively since the end of World War Two. According to Kathryn Sikkink and Jackie Smith, the number of INGOs promoting social change goals sextupled between 1953 and 1993.[22] At the same time, the geographical spread of transnational civil society has expanded, with a doubling in the proportion of INGO headquarters located outside Europe. The breadth of INGO activities has also increased, with the emergence of the transnational environmentalist movement from the late 1960s and the rapid growth of the development aid sector from the 1980s onwards. As for the impact of transnational civil society, the Cold War era witnessed the success of the European federalist movement, and transnational social movements played a role in bringing the Cold War to an end.[23] Successful transnational campaigns in the post-Cold War era include those for the banning of landmines, for developing countries' debt reduction (Jubilee 2000), and against the Multilateral Agreement on Investment.

The many factors that help to explain this recovery of transnational civil society since 1945 include technological developments such as jet aeroplane travel, cheap global telecommunications, and the internet. Economic developments have also been important, such as globalization and the increasing number of transnational corporations, which have provided new targets for transnational activism. As for political developments, one of the most significant is the foundation of the United Nations, which—like the League of Nations—was to work closely with INGOs and granted many of them 'consultative status'. Another influential political development is decolonization, which facilitated the growth of domestic civil society in formerly suppressed parts of the world and which brought to the fore 'Third World issues' such as economic development. Further important issues that have emerged in the post-war era include climate change, HIV and increasing migration flows, which governments are unable to tackle on their own and which transnational non-governmental organizations have made a focus of their activities. The spread of democratic institutions in the post-war era has also been important, and even the Cold War arguably helped transnational civil society by contributing towards the 'long peace' after 1945 and by creating global challenges such as the threat of nuclear annihilation. Conversely, the end of Cold War is said to have been the critical event in facilitating the accelerated growth of transnational civil society in the last two decades.[24]

However, it should be noted that—just as in the period leading up to the First World War— transnational civil society activities in the post-Second World War era have arguably developed in waves, with periods of particularly concentrated activity such as in the years 1945, 1968 and 1989.[25]

More importantly, and contrary to conventional opinion, it can be argued that in some respects transnational civil society has failed fully to recover from the mid-century shocks of the Great Depression, Second World War and Cold War. For instance, popular participation in post-Cold War campaigns such as Jubilee 2000 and the Global Call to Action against Poverty has arguably been less substantial as a proportion of the world's population than was participation in the campaign for disarmament of the 1920s and 1930s.[26] In addition, transnational civil society today suffers from splits that were absent prior to the Cold War, such as the division of the international trade union movement between the International Trade Union Confederation and the World Federation of Trade Unions.

4. The Future Trajectory of Transnational Civil Society

It has become commonplace in the contemporary literature on transnational civil society to assume that the apparent growth of the phenomenon in the present era will continue. Transnational communications are faster and cheaper than they have ever been before; the process of economic globalization has continued apace; and transnational problems requiring global solutions such as climate change have become increasingly apparent. All of these factors seem to suggest that there will be a greater role for transnational civil society in the future than at present.

However, there are also many reasons not to be so optimistic. For instance, many of the factors that have arguably contributed towards transnational civil society's post-World War Two revival may also have the reverse effect. For example, decolonization has not only provided the opportunity for transnational civil society to spread all over the world, in so doing it has also stimulated the creation of transnational associational organizations at a purely regional level and enabled the perception of a North-South divide. Another development—the growth of national civil society in parts of the world where it was previously insignificant—not only provides the building blocks for transnational associational activity in these places, it may also contribute towards nationalism, just as it had in Europe in the nineteenth century.

Nationalism in some countries today may be far more powerful than transnational civil society: for instance, whereas the global efforts of the Jubilee 2000 coalition succeeded in acquiring just 24 million signatures to its anti-debt petition, the names of 44 million people were obtained for a Chinese petition opposing Japan's membership of the Security Council in 2005. It is possible to argue that a similar situation may exist today to the situation in the 1930s, when nationalism in Germany and Japan and the isolation of these countries from transnational civil society undermined that phenomenon. Today, nationalism in China and Islamic fundamentalism in parts of the Arab world is combined with a relatively low level of liberal internationalist civic activity in both regions, and this may pose a considerable challenge to contemporary liberal internationalist sections of transnational civil society.

Another factor that has contributed towards the apparent growth of transnational civil society but which may also have the reverse effect is globalization. As Geir Lundestad has argued, globalization and fragmentation 'exist in a dialectical relationship with each other . . . when globalization is strengthened, so is fragmentation'.[27] Thus, arguably, the growth of transnational communications technology and transport has, by bringing different peoples into closer contact with one another, made them also more aware of their differences. And economic globalization—with its negative consequences for those unable effectively to compete in the world economy—has provoked nationalistic reactions that have considerable potential to undermine transnational civil society.

More interestingly, transnational civil society itself may, as it has done before, contribute towards its own demise. For example, transnational civil society may contribute towards the fragmentary trends noted in the last two paragraphs: the growth of xenophobic and fundamentalist groups is arguably partly a defensive reaction to a perceived threat to local cultures posed by the apparently 'Western' ideals promoted by many of the predominant liberal elements of contemporary transnational civil society. INGOs that focus on the civic and political rights of individuals, which arguably conflict with possibly more communitarian so-called 'Asian values', are especially likely to provoke such a reaction.

This ideational clash is exacerbated by a number of further problematic features of contemporary transnational civil society, such as the tendency for INGOs to be 'unelected and accountable only to their funders', who are located primarily in the rich nations.[28] This problem is particularly significant in the case of humanitarian assistance organizations, where there is a very clear social divide between those on whom the organizations depend for funding and those whom the organizations claim to serve. International non-governmental organizations concerned with aid distribution have also been susceptible to accusations of being more expensive and less effective than local actors in performing the same tasks.

A further way in which transnational civil society can contribute towards its own demise is poor policy. For instance, even though one of the key factors enabling transnational civil society to reach its current position has been the process of economic globalization, numerous transnational campaigns have been undertaken by transnational civic coalitions to undermine this process despite the knock-on effect for the campaigners.

Elements of transnational civil society may also make claims to be able to achieve unattainably ambitious objectives, such as the World Social Forum's claim that 'Another World is Possible.' Claims such as this have the potential to raise to an excessive degree expectations as to what transnational civil society has the capacity to achieve, and even thereby to reverse the development of transnational civil society. The evidence of the last century indicates that transcendence of capitalism and of the state system is an unattainable ideal, as anti-capitalist idealists found after the 1917 revolution in Russia and as pacificist and pacifist idealists found in the periods preceding the two World Wars. In each of these cases, there is a strong case for arguing that the already unpleasant externalities of the normal functioning of the capitalist world economy and of the state system were made worse by the attempts of elements of transnational civil society to transcend them, and this worsening in turn set back transnational civil society.

In conclusion, transnational civil society has not followed a course of linear progress as much of the existing literature assumes. Instead, this chapter has provided evidence to support the argument that it has risen and fallen in waves over the course of the last two centuries. The rise and fall of transnational civil society may even be a cyclical process: the factors that promote its rise are often the same as those that promote its decline, and transnational civil society itself has in the past and could in the future contribute towards its own demise.

Notes

1. Paul S. Reinsch, *Public International Unions: Their Work and Organization: A Study In International Administrative Law* (Boston: Ginn and Company, 1911), pp. 2, 4.
2. Mary Kaldor, *Global Civil Society: An Answer to War* (Cambridge: Polity Press, 2003).
3. Helmut Anheier, Marlies Glasius and Mary Kaldor, 'Introducing Global Civil Society', in Helmut Anheier, Marlies Glasius and Mary Kaldor (eds.), *Global Civil Society 2001* (Oxford: Oxford University Press, 2001), p. 3.

4. London School of Economics and Political Science Centre for Civil Society, 'What is Civil Society?', http://www.lse.ac.uk/collections/CCS/what_is_civil_society.htm (last accessed on 15 December 2006).
5. Jan Aart Scholte, *Global Civil Society: Changing the World?* (Coventry: Centre for the Study of Globalization and Regionalization (CSGR), University of Warwick, 1999), pp. 2–3.
6. John Keane, *Global Civil Society?* (Cambridge: Cambridge University Press, 2003), p. 8.
7. Lester M. Salamon and Helmut K. Anheier, *Defining the Nonprofit Sector: A Cross-National Analysis* (Manchester: Manchester University Press, 1997). The original definition of an international non-governmental organization adopted by the Economic and Social Council of the United Nations was much broader: 'any international organization which is not established by intergovernmental agreement'.
8. See, for example, Kathryn Sikkink and Jackie Smith, 'Infrastructures for Change: Transnational Organizations, 1953–93', in Sanjeev Khagram, James Riker and Kathryn Sikkink (eds.), *Restructuring World Politics: Transnational Social Movements, Networks and Norms* (Minneapolis: University of Minnesota Press, 2002), 24–44.
9. G. P. Speeckaert, *Les 1978 Organisations Internationales Fondées depuis le Congrès de Vienne* (Brussels: Union of International Associations, 1957), viii.
10. Source: Union of International Associations.
11. John Boli and George Thomas, *Constructing World Culture: International Nongovernmental Organizations Since 1875* (Stanford, CA: Stanford University Press, 1999), 23–4.
12. For a comparison of the scale of participation in contemporary campaigns with those that took place between the two World Wars, see section 3 of this chapter and Thomas Richard Davies, *The Possibilities of Transnational Activism: The Campaign for Disarmament between the Two World Wars* (Leiden and Boston: Martinus Nijhoff, 2007), 159–60.
13. Transnational religious organizations such as the Quakers, for instance, pre-date the analysis in this chapter.
14. Margaret Keck and Kathryn Sikkink, *Activists Beyond Borders: Advocacy Networks in International Politics* (Ithaca, NY: Cornell University Press, 1998), 45, 51.
15. Akira Iriye, *Global Community: The Role of International Organizations in the Making of the Contemporary World* (Berkeley, CA: University of California Press, 2002), 9.
16. Reinsch, *Public International Unions*, 3.
17. Michael Howard, *War and the Liberal Conscience* (Oxford: Oxford University Press, 1978), 72.
18. For further information on this campaign, see Davies, *Possibilities of Transnational Activism*.
19. Steve Charnovitz, 'Two Centuries of Participation: NGOs and International Governance', *Michigan Journal of International Law*, 18:2 (1997), 220–37.
20. Howard, *War and the Liberal Conscience*, 130.
21. For the argument that disarmament activism contributed to slowness in anti-fascist rearmament, see Martin Gilbert, *Winston S. Churchill*, vol. 5 (London: Heinemann, 1976), 696.
22. Sikkink and Smith, 'Infrastructures for Change', 30.
23. Disarmament campaigners arguably helped bring the Cold War to an end from above, while anti-Communist movements in central and eastern Europe arguably helped bring the Cold War to an end from below.
24. Kaldor, *Global Civil Society*, 114.
25. On these peak periods, see Gerd-Rainer Horn and Padraic Kelly (eds.), *Transnational Moments of Change: Europe 1945, 1968, 1989* (Lanham, MD: Rowman and Littlefield, 2004).
26. See Davies, *Possibilities of Transnational Activism*, part five.

27. Geir Lundestad, 'Why does Globalization Encourage Fragmentation?', *International Politics*, 41 (2004), 1.

28. Sandra Halperin and Gordon Laxer, *Global Civil Society and its Limits* (Basingstoke: Palgrave Macmillan, 2003) p. 10, citing James Petras and Henry Veltmeyer, *Globalization Unmasked: Imperialism in the 21st Century* (Halifax, Nova Scotia: Fernwood, 2001).

PART II

ANTI-SLAVERY AND CONGO REFORM

CHAPTER FOUR

Transatlantic Activism in the Eighteenth Century: the Anti-Slavery Movement

Huw T. David

Source: Huw T. David 'Transnational Advocacy in the Eighteenth Century: Transatlantic Activism and the Anti-Slavery Movement' *Global Networks* (2007) 7:3, 367–382 © 2007 Huw T. David—Reprinted with permission.

Transnational activism in its different forms has provoked a wealth of recent literature and debate. Covering patterns of interaction and types of activity that stretch across country borders, from *transnational advocacy networks* to *transnational coalitions* to *transnational social movements*, it has been characterized as a powerful modern phenomenon, albeit one with distinct historical precursors. The growth of transnational activism has been seen to mirror, and has been facilitated by, developments in technology and the ever greater ease of communication and travel between countries. As such, transnationalism can be portrayed as being both enabled by and constitutive of the processes of 'globalization'. Writers have studied the influence of transnationalism on international and domestic politics, arguing that transnational activism is supplanting domestic political opportunity structures (Tarrow 1998: 180–2), or even 'restructuring world politics' (Khagram et al. 2002: 3). To provide a structure for the different modes of transnational activity, Khagram et al. suggest three ascending levels of transnational collective action: transnational advocacy networks, transnational coalitions and transnational social movements.

Transnational advocacy networks are the least formal grouping of actors, linked across country boundaries and distinguished and united by shared values or concerns and by a common discourse. Most networks arise from informal contacts, though some are more formal in their internal discourse. Unlike the more structured transnational coalitions or social movements, the networks do not involve the tactical co-ordination or mobilization of people and resources to attain their ends: the dense exchange and use of information is the essential characteristic of network activity. *Transnational coalitions* involve a greater degree of transnational coordination, sharing tactics and strategies to influence social change. Coalitions operate through transnational campaigns and, because of this, involve a greater degree of interaction between actors, who meet each other and strategize on how to implement a campaign. *Transnational social movements* are a culmination of the previous two stages. They have, or aim to have, the capacity to publicly influence social change in more than one country through sustained and coordinated social mobilization. Collective action, often through protest or disruptive action, is their dominant mode of operation (Khagram et al. 2002).

Some writers have suggested that transnational activism is a specifically modern phenomenon, 'a powerful new force in international politics . . . transforming global norms and practices' (Khagram et al. 2002: 4). Historical precursors to transnational activism have, however, been observed in transnationalism literature, suggesting it is less modern than sometimes assumed. In his work on transnational social movements, Tarrow (1998: 182) notes the close connections in the late eighteenth century between the American Revolution, the Dutch Patriot movement and the French Revolution. Networks theorists have also scrutinized later transnational network activism. Keck and Sikkink provide perhaps the best known study of historical precedents to modern transnationalism. Among several case studies, they analyse the international campaign for the abolition of slavery in the United States between 1833 and 1865, a campaign which operated as 'a nascent transnational advocacy network, mobilizing around a moral issue, using some tactics similar to modern networks' (1998: 51). They also note the 'tradition of transatlantic networking and information exchange that had flourished during the last decades before American independence' (1998: 44) and acknowledge Quaker anti-slave trade activism in the eighteenth century.

Keck and Sikkink's focus, however, is on the more structured *anti-slavery* campaign of the mid-nineteenth century, as opposed to its less formal precursor, the *anti-slave trade* network which operated in the mid-to-late eighteenth century. Like the nineteenth century campaign, but more than half a century earlier, transatlantic cooperation and the dissemination of ideas marked anti-slave trade activism in Britain and its American colonies. In this article, I suggest that we can trace the historical precedents to modern transnationalism back to this point, beyond the historical treatments of transnationalism offered in existing studies. I also use an historical perspective to interrogate the process of how transnational advocacy develops through the stages of network, coalition and social movement, as modelled by Khagram, Riker and Sikkink. As the eighteenth century campaign against the slave trade moved from coalition to movement, its transnational dimension diminished. When the campaign became embedded in British society and began to utilize the political opportunity structure the British state afforded, opportunities for transatlantic activism and influence receded. It therefore highlights that, while the process of network development that Khagram et al. modelled is persuasive, the development of transnationalism within this is neither linear nor inevitable.

In Britain, little over four decades elapsed between the first serious public questioning of the moral and ethical basis of slavery and the legal abolition of the slave trade. Until the 1760s, what John Wesley would call 'that execrable sum of all villainies' (quoted in Anstey 1975: 232) had been largely accepted as a given element of the British maritime economy, underpinning the country's global political and economic rise. Only in that decade were the first stirrings of abolitionist sentiment popularly aired on both sides of the Atlantic. The retrospective words of a prominent Boston resident encapsulate the mood of the time in the American colonies— but it is a judgment which could equally be applied to contemporary Britain. 'About the time of the Stamp Act [1765], what were before only slight scruples in the minds of conscientious persons became serious doubts and, with a considerable number, ripened into a firm persuasion that the slave trade was *malum in se* [evil in itself]' (cited in Thomas 1997: 458). Yet by 1807, the slave trade had become so odious in the eyes of both the public and legislators in Britain that Parliament, despite the pressure of vested interest, was compelled to abolish it.

A 40-year process of changing attitudes and reform brought about this transformation, roughly divisible into two distinct periods. The first is one of ideational formation and informal network activism, the second of collective protest and legislative attempts at reform. The latter period, running from the mid-1780s to 1807 and beyond—Parliament did not pass the Slave Abolition Act, emancipating slaves in British colonies, until 1833—has arguably been the focus for greater historical attention, and is certainly better known popularly. Greater emphasis on the mass social and legislative campaigns is understandable: popular protest was the most dramatic manifestation of anti-slavery activism and organization in the abolitionist movement. Moreover, as activists recognized at the time, the power to abolish the slave trade necessarily rested in the hands of the state. Network and social movement theorists also recognize the central importance of the state in social protest. If they are to realize their claims, social movements must direct their energies towards the state, and interact with it in some form. 'The state is simultaneously target, sponsor and antagonist for social movements, as well as the organiser of the political system and the arbiter of victory . . . Social movements that aim to alter social institutions and practices have to come into contact with the state, if only to consolidate their claims' (Jenkins and Klandermans 1995: 3).

Here I shall focus on the earlier period of abolitionist activism, which lasted from the mid-1750s to the mid-1780s and was characterized by transnational activity. The relationship between Britain and America changed fundamentally during this period when the 1776–82 War of Independence turned Britain's American colonies into the independent United States. Nonetheless, the political realignment had little bearing on transatlantic anti-slavery activism, for it did little to disrupt the patterns of personal and organizational interaction between abolitionists across the Atlantic. Because of this, and to stay within the recognised vocabulary of transnationalism, I treat what might strictly be termed the 'metro-colonial' activism of the pre-Revolutionary period and the more literal 'transnational' activism after American independence as a single process of *transnational* activity. I examine how the seeds of abolitionist sentiment were planted and agitation nurtured; by focusing on the seminal role of Quakers within this, I show how the distinct network structure of Quakerism engendered a wider denominational coalition against the slave trade and laid the foundations for the campaign's development into a powerful social and political movement.

Quakerism in Britain and America

The nascent anti-slavery network was firmly rooted in Quakerism. The leading figures of the early anti-slavery movement, including men such as John Woolman and Anthony Benezet, were almost all members of the Society of Friends (or Quakers) and residents of the American middle colonies, Pennsylvania and New Jersey, where America's Quakers were concentrated. They inherited the Quaker tradition of transatlantic itinerancy, making lengthy trips to visit Quaker communities on both sides of the Atlantic and to spread and reaffirm the Society's doctrines. Quakerism not only imbued their actions with theological and moral conviction, but it also provided an informal network structure through which to propagate their opposition to slavery. Through their literature, their network of personal contacts and frequent personal visits to British shores, these campaigners were uniquely influential. They galvanized British anti-slavery activism and then broadened this Quaker-led network into a wider, inter-denominational campaign. Allied to the strength of their abolitionist arguments, it was the network characteristics inherent in Quakerism that would allow their campaign to spread, laying the foundations for the popular campaign against slavery and the slave trade that developed in Britain in the 1780s and 1790s, and putting abolition on the legislative agenda.

In the late eighteenth century, Quakerism numbered around 50,000 Friends in Britain and 40,000 in the American colonies. This 'Atlantic community' (Anstey 1975: 200) was notable for the high level of association between its two branches; indeed, the transatlantic bonds in the Society of Friends were appreciably stronger than in other denominations at the time. Presbyterianism, rapidly growing Methodism and Anglicanism, despite its episcopal structure and emphasis on the communion of the faith, all failed to approach it in terms of how frequently their adherents ventured across the Atlantic or communicated with transatlantic brethren. The strength of transatlantic connections within the Society stemmed in part from the marginalization of Quakers in both colonial and British society. Shared experiences formed and cemented Quaker self-identity: from the prejudice and hostility faced by each branch grew a common sense of purpose and moral conviction.

Within the Society of Friends, organizational structures on either side of the Atlantic were analogous. When Quakers first moved to Pennsylvania in the late seventeenth century, establishing the colony as a refuge from persecution, they brought with them the structure introduced by the Society's founder, George Fox. Parallel structures remained in place on either side of the Atlantic throughout the eighteenth century. Without a formal head or a written creed, meetings and assemblies were the primary forum for discussion. In the hierarchy of meetings, the *monthly meetings for business*, composed of Friends from several local worship meetings, were the basic level of association. Issues deemed worthy of wider discourse—namely disciplinary matters or minor theological points—were referred to *quarterly meetings*; from these, issues relevant for debate at the highest level were sent to the Society's *yearly meetings* (Soderlund 1985: 192). The foremost deliberative bodies on either side of the Atlantic were the yearly meetings in Philadelphia, the administrative centre and largest city in Pennsylvania, and in London. The two meetings had equal status within Quakerism.

The parallel structures and common social position of Quakers on either side of the Atlantic helps explain the resilience of the network through the political upheavals of American independence. Despite the severing of political ties between Britain and America, made formal in the Treaty of Paris in 1783, Quakers continued to correspond, travel and consult one another as before. In America, their detachment from the revolutionary struggle insulated them from the social upheavals of the post-revolutionary years, particularly the backlash felt by loyalists to Britain. In both Britain and America, Quakers' abstention from politics left them to concentrate on doctrinal and theological matters and social causes, manifested most clearly in their opposition to slavery. Quakerism counted a similar number of adherents on either side of the Atlantic, giving neither branch numerical superiority. These reasons, and the well established parity between congregations and meetings on either side of the Atlantic, meant that the structure of transatlantic Quakerism had never mirrored the parent–child dynamic of political relations between Britain and the American colonies. Quakers on both sides of the Atlantic continued after American independence to interact as one community, separated geographically but not politically.

Transatlantic Customs and Traditions

Frequent correspondence between *yearly meetings* and between individual Friends on issues of faith and conscience, and on administrative matters, had long played an important role in sustaining transatlantic linkages and rapport. Trade between Quaker merchants in Philadelphia, New York and Newport, Rhode Island and their counterparts in London, Bristol and Plymouth cemented informal links between the two communities into more formal business relationships (Tolles 1960: 19). Most significant in maintaining and reinforcing inter-personal bonds was the constant travel by Friends between the continents, evangelizing journeys undertaken to re-imbue Quaker spirituality and spread the faith. In tours lasting several months, itinerant preachers addressed meetings and local groups on both sides of the Atlantic, from established communities to isolated farms. 'The travelling ministry—the most potent force for cohesion—became a reciprocal force,' notes Tolles.

This itinerant tradition dated back to the earliest Quakers: George Fox, the Society's founder, had travelled extensively in Britain, the North American colonies and the West Indies. The custom was not unique to Quakerism—it was a feature of mid-eighteenth century revivalism. John Wesley and George Whitefield travelled widely in their evangelizing missions; both spent time in the southern colonies in the 1730s and Whitefield spent much of his life travelling between Britain and America. Similarly, the leading American preachers of the Great Awakening, the resurgence in popular religion in the mid-18th century colonies, led peripatetic lives. In no other denomination, however, was itinerancy such an established or common activity among ordinary members of the faith. While precise figures are hard to determine, estimates suggest that the number of Quakers making transatlantic tours in the eighteenth century comfortably exceeded that of other groups (Tolles 1960: 14).

Quakers and Slavery

In their attitude towards slavery, however, most Quakers until the mid-eighteenth century were more conventional, reflecting contemporary ambivalence: slavery was thus accepted within Quakerism as 'part of the natural order of things' (Fogel 1989: 210). Fox himself sought converts among the slaveholders in the West Indies, lodging with wealthy sugar planters and slaveholders who had converted to Quakerism (Davis 1969: 333). He established, however, in the structures and traditions of Quakerism, an organization better suited than perhaps any other contemporary network, religious or secular, to the dissemination and transmission of ideas internally. Thus, when the institution of slavery came to trouble Quaker consciences, the close transatlantic bonds, cemented through the itinerant tradition, regular correspondence and— inadvertently—the shared experience of social marginalization, allowed for abolitionist sentiment to be widely and rapidly conveyed.

Early Quaker anti-slavery agitation was intra-mural in nature, confined to persuading Quakers themselves—often on an individual basis—of the evils of the practice. Only later did the structure and character of Quakerism, allied to the determination of its members, prove to be equally well suited to extending the network into a wider coalition. Early Quaker abolitionist calls had addressed the inconsistency of slave trading and ownership among Friends. Even with the limited objective of persuading Friends of the wrongs of the practice, however, the calls fell largely on deaf ears. In 1676, William Edmundson, a close friend of George Fox and leading figure in early Quakerism, sent a letter from Rhode Island to Quakers in all slave-owning places theorizing that the practice was 'an oppression on the mind', unacceptable to all Christians (Thomas 1997: 456). The first organized Quaker protest was recorded twelve years later, among Friends in Germantown, Pennsylvania in 1688, where a petition was offered to the Philadelphia Yearly Meeting condemning slave ownership (Soderlund 1985: 18). The Philadelphia Yearly Meeting itself advised its members to end their participation in the slave trade in 1696 and 1711 (Moulton 1971: 12). Like the occasional advocates of reform in other denominations, however, these calls were isolated and went unheeded.

This was because, for most Quakers in the early eighteenth century, slavery was a matter of fact. Many Quakers prospered from the institution; besides Quaker slave ownership in the West Indies, many Friends in the American colonies owned slaves or actively participated in the slave trade. Leading Quaker families in Philadelphia, in the 1730s, and as late as the 1760s in Rhode Island, whose largest town, Newport, was an important North American port in the slave trade, were involved in the trade (Davis 1969: 305). In the early eighteenth century there was even a slave ship owned by Friends which was named, ironically, 'the Society' (Thomas 1997: 457). In the southern colonies, where Quakerism had spread during the eighteenth century, slave ownership among Friends—as in wider southern society—was still more entrenched. Qualms concerning the moral and theological basis of the slave trade and slavery itself were thus confined to a minority before the 1750s. It was not until 1758 that the Philadelphia Yearly Meeting adopted a formal minute urging Quakers to free their slaves, arranged for visits to be made to slaveholders and decreed that any recalcitrant Friends who bought or sold slaves would be excluded from Quaker business meetings and from making financial contributions to the Society.

The genesis of this change can be identified in the events of the 1750s. Successive calamities provoked soul-searching among the Quakers of the middle-colonies. The end of their dominance of Pennsylvanian public office emphasized the decline in their influence within the former bastion of Quakerism. The traumas of fierce Indian raids, the popular hostility generated by their anti-war stance and an earthquake in Philadelphia in 1754 seemed to point to divine judgment upon them. Quakers had apparently lost their way, with the series of disasters which befell their community in the 1750s interpreted by many as retribution for recent sinfulness (Soderlund 1985: 8–10; Fogel 1989: 210–1). In the ensuing moral introspection, Quakers assigned particular significance to the general tolerance of slavery in their communities. Alongside the greater spirituality and sobriety of dress, manners and speech promoted by preachers such as Samuel Fothergill, withdrawal from the slave trade was a self-denying and conscientious step.

Over the next two decades, the Society's branches in the various colonies gradually disowned Friends involved in the slave trade. New York Friends took this step in 1770; Rhode Island disowned slave-holding members in 1773 (Aptheker 1940: 349). It was only around the close of the War of Independence in the early 1780s, however, that Quaker slave-ownership— and only north of the Mason-Dixon line at that—seems to have finally ended (Aptheker 1940: 352). Steps to curtail slavery within Quakerism took place in the context of more significant political moves against the slave trade in the American colonies. Rhode Island had ruled in 1774 that slaves imported into the colony would automatically become free; Connecticut and Delaware had also prohibited importation, while Pennsylvania taxed the trade out of existence. Spurred by the actions of individual colonies and the exigencies of warfare, the Continental Congress voted in 1776 to stop the importation of slaves into any of the thirteen colonies. Yet slavery remained a central feature of economic and social fabric in several colonies, particularly south of the Mason-Dixon line in Virginia, the Carolinas and Georgia. In this context, with Quakers both buoyed by the congressional ban on the slave trade but facing limited prospects for wider abolition in America, transatlantic advocacy offered a propitious outlet for abolitionist activism. American Friends would, as they had done since the mid-eighteenth century, continue to look to shape British attitudes and activities on slavery, and the slave trade in particular, through the distinctive network characteristics of transatlantic Quakerism.

Stirrings of Abolitionism in Britain

In England, as in the American colonies, the disquiet about the slave trade, which featured in the Society's early-eighteenth century discussions, had abated by the 1750s. The London Yearly Meeting of 1727 had advised Friends to cease participation in the slave trade but no further action was taken and the issue was disregarded at the annual meeting for the next 30 years. In 1757, however, the question of slavery and the slave trade resurfaced. Evidence for the re-emergence of abolitionism into mainstream Quaker discussion at this moment points strongly to the influence of colonial Friends. Through correspondence, widely circulated pamphlets and tracts, and personal visits to Britain, North American Quakers reignited anti-slavery feelings among their British counterparts. Capitalizing on prevailing Enlightenment questioning of the moral legitimacy of slavery, their transatlantic influence put anti-slavery issues on, first, the Society's own agenda, and then into wider British social and political debates.

A parallel contemporary influence can be found in Enlightenment philosophy, which provided an ideational backdrop to the Quaker activism. By the 1750s, Enlightenment philosophy, mostly emanating from France, had begun to question the moral legitimacy of slavery. In his *Discours sur l'origine et les fondements de l'inégalité* in 1754, Rousseau denounced slavery as the final manifestation of the degrading and idiotic principle of authority. More influential was Montesquieu's juridical questioning of slavery. His *Esprit des Lois* in 1748 argued that slavery was bad for both master and servant. The 1765 edition of the *Enclopédie* developed his arguments. Its article on slavery asserted that slavery and the slave trade violated religion, morality, natural law and all human rights, and that all slaves should have the right to freedom. In Britain, the influence of these *philosophes* fostered an intellectual climate more receptive to abolitionist endeavours, helping anti-slavery activism metamorphose from a predominantly Quaker campaign into a wider political and social movement. Philosophical, legal and economic arguments—by the late eighteenth century, the economic logic of slavery was being questioned in Britain, America and France—appealed strongly to the political and legal classes whose support for abolitionism would be vital in bringing the issue into the political mainstream.

That Quaker anti-slavery activists such as John Woolman and Anthony Benezet increasingly turned their attention to England in this climate was not accidental. The network structure of contemporary Quakerism fostered close links on both an inter-personal and inter-organizational level between England and the American colonies, facilitating their activism. Strong evidence suggests that Samuel Fothergill, who had recently returned from an exhaustive tour of the American colonies, raised the issue of slavery at the London Yearly Meeting in 1757 (Drake 1950: 60). Alongside Fothergill's first-hand testimony of the horrors of slavery, the first colonial abolitionist tracts had recently become available to English Friends. In 1746, John Woolman, a New Jersey tailor, had visited the plantations of Virginia and North Carolina in a three month and 1,500 mile tour (Moulton 1971:17). He later—prophetically—recorded his experiences in his diary: 'I saw in those southern provinces so many vices and corruptions increased by the [slave] trade and this way of life that it appeared to me as a dark gloominess hanging over the land; and though many now willingly run into it, yet in future the consequence will be grievous to posterity' (Moulton 1971: 38). Woolman's account of what he witnessed informed a pamphlet, *Some considerations on the keeping of negroes*, which was published and widely distributed in 1754 and which established him as the pre-eminent Quaker abolitionist writer of the day. The tract had almost certainly been read by the time of the London Yearly Meeting in 1757 by a number of English Friends (Anstey 1975: 220). After slavery was re-introduced onto the English Quakers' agenda, colonial influence began to be exerted through more formal channels. The issue of slavery became increasingly prominent in the frequent correspondence between the Philadelphia and London meetings. Advice on the matter was passed in both directions, from the American colonies to England and vice versa. An injunction in the annual epistle of the London meeting in 1758 advised Friends everywhere to 'be careful to avoid being in any way concerned in reaping the unrighteous profits arising from the iniquitous practice [of slave trading]' and was widely reprinted in the colonies by the American Quaker and publisher, Anthony Benezet (Drake 1950: 62). In London, the landmark decision by the 1761 Yearly Meeting to disown Quakers participating in the slave trade has been attributed to 'quiet pressure from Philadelphia Friends' (Anstey 1975: 220).

Correspondence between meetings would continue to play a formative role in abolitionist advocacy, and might be characterized as the formal side of transatlantic activism. Allied to this was the wider dissemination of abolitionist literature through letter-writing. In 1743, John Fothergill, brother of Samuel, and a leading Quaker in his own right, was made the designated correspondent from the London Yearly Meeting to its Philadelphia equivalent. He became a well regarded adviser, particularly on political and administrative matters, to the colonial body. In 1767 Fothergill brought to the London Meeting for Sufferings, an offshoot of the London Yearly Meeting, a letter from the equivalent body in Pennsylvania. It suggested that copies of Benezet's pamphlet *Observations on the enslaving, importing and purchasing of negroes* should be reprinted and distributed. This was duly undertaken, with 1,500 copies circulated, including to every member of the House of Commons (Anstey 1975: 222). As Benezet's publication of the 1758 London epistle has suggested, transatlantic activism of this form was a two-way process. In 1773, London Friends wrote to their counterparts in Maryland praising the decision by Virginia's House of Burgesses to petition King George III against the slave-trade. Stirred into action, the Maryland Quakers sent copies of the London Friends' letter to both houses of their colonial legislature (Drake 1950: 86–7).

Close cooperation on an inter-organizational level, between North American and English meetings, continued after American independence, even though the War of Independence between 1775 and 1782 had hindered the nascent anti-slavery organizations in the colonies. American Quakers were sidelined in society, just as they had been during the Seven Years War (1756–63), by their refusal to endorse violence, let alone participate. The launch of the Pennsylvania anti-slavery society in 1775 could not have come at a more inauspicious time, and it lapsed into inactivity, only revived in 1784 as the *Society for the Relief of Free Negroes Unlawfully Held in Bondage* (Fogel 1989: 247). The split between colonies and motherland had little bearing on the network of transatlantic Quakerism, however. The closure of channels for advocacy in the colonies may even have cemented transatlantic advocacy, strengthening the focus of North American Quakers on the campaign in Britain. The network remained strong and active, with correspondence continuing unabated, reflecting the close bonds that remained between Britain and America on an inter-personal and social, if no longer administrative, level. One work in particular exemplifies this. In 1783, the appeal presented to Parliament on behalf of London Quakers, *The case of our fellow creatures, the oppressed Africans*, was one of Benezet's tracts (Drake 1950: 94). When it was reprinted the following year in America by the Philadelphia Yearly Meeting and sent to members of the new Congress, the tract had come full circle. If any single piece of literature symbolizes transatlantic Quaker abolitionist cooperation, this might be it: of American origin, the British campaign had co-opted the tract for propaganda purposes before it was recycled as part of the American campaign.

Its author similarly epitomized Anglo-American Quaker abolitionism, particularly its inter-personal dimension. Born in St. Quentin, northern France, and educated in England before emigrating to America at the age of 18 and settling in Philadelphia, Anthony Benezet had a cosmopolitan background (Thomas 1997: 469). A former merchant before becoming a school-master, Benezet brought together a persuasive blend of Quaker theology and Enlightenment moral philosophy in his tracts. Through his prodigious literary output, personal connections and numerous visits to Britain, Benezet became the outstanding figure of late-eighteenth century Quaker abolitionism. His background and the content of his writings meant he was 'not only a link between the writings of moral philosophers, such as Montesquieu, and the Quakers, but also one between America and Britain; and indeed between the Anglo-Saxons and the French' (Thomas 1997: 471). Between 1759 and 1771, Benezet wrote numerous tracts against the injustice of slavery. His pamphlets were essentially compilations of notes, quotations and extracts on African culture and the barbarity of the slave trade, his reverence for the former serving to emphasize the injustice of the latter, and lending them an anthropological dimension rare in the literature of the time. It was a tactic which carried distinct echoes of what modern social movement theorists have termed the 'information politics' methodology of human rights campaigners two centuries later. The tactic employs dramatic testimonies to bring evidence—whether of the eighteenth-century slave trade or of modern human rights abuses—to public attention. Network activism is thus promoted, public awareness raised, and the first moves towards political action set in motion (Keck and Sikkink 1998: 45).

Broadening the Denominational Base of Abolitionism

Interaction with evangelical Anglicans would widen the denominational foundations of transatlantic anti-slavery activism from a specifically Quaker network to a broader coalition. More significant still was the co-option of Methodism to the burgeoning anti-slavery campaign. In February 1772, John Wesley found Benezet's *Some historical account of Guinea*. He noted the discovery in his journal: 'I read a very different book, published by an honest Quaker, on that execrable sum of all villainies, commonly called the Slave Trade. I have read nothing like it in the heathen world, whether ancient or modern' (quoted in Walvin 1986: 103). Wesley was clearly impressed: his own *Thoughts upon slavery*, published in 1774, drew heavily—indeed, frequently verbatim—from the tract. Slavery was condemned as a 'pagan abomination', 'murder . . . by thousands' and the most heinous crime in all English history. Given the public attention received by all Wesley's works, the pamphlet constituted the most formidable attack yet on the slave trade (Thomas 1997: 475). Wesley's own latent revulsion to slavery, drawn from first-hand testimony of the practice on his visit forty years earlier to Georgia, had been rekindled. While Benezet cannot be solely credited with this, the influence of his literature on Wesley and, through Wesley, on awakening Methodist abolitionist sentiment is clear.

The first religious figure of national prominence to join the protest against slavery, Wesley would devote considerable time and energy between 1772 and his death in 1791 to writing and sermonizing against the practice. Copies of *Thoughts upon slavery* were distributed to all Methodist chapels in the country, using Methodism's own distinct network structure to spread abolitionism. It is hard to overstate the significance of Wesley's contribution to the anti-slavery movement, lending it, through his personal reputation, an authority that the likes of Woolman, Benezet and Granville Sharp, an evangelical Anglican strongly influenced by Benezet's tracts and who became a leading figure in British abolitionism, could never have bestowed. In harnessing the growing popular and institutional force of Methodism to the anti-slavery cause, moreover, abolitionism underwent an important transformation. Though its appeal to the urban and working classes, Methodism helped attach a mass social base to the anti-slavery campaign. As an inter-denominational coalition, the campaign would be capable of exerting far greater political influence than the socially marginal and still disenfranchised Quakers could bring to bear alone. Abolition could less easily be dismissed by its opponents as the utopian goal of a marginal and radical sect; at the same time, Wesley's personal standing in Britain helped legitimize its political aspirations, bringing abolitionism towards mainstream politics. Together, these factors fashioned the political opportunity essential for advocacy groups to develop into broader social movements. Social movement theorists—notably Jenkins and Klandermans—have asserted that social movements must interact with the state in some form for their claims to be realized (1995: 3–7). The broadening of the abolitionist network into a wider coalition was an essential step towards this interaction and towards its attaining political legitimacy and influence.

Interaction with the State

Recognition that legislative action at Westminster was the only means to achieve change pre-dated abolitionism's association with Methodism, however. Once again, transatlantic influence was instrumental, with American Friends providing the impulse to move the campaign into the political sphere. In a series of letters to prominent English Quakers in 1772, Benezet had sug-gested 'whether it might not be the duty of our Friends . . . to lay the iniquity and dreadful consequence of the slave trade before Parliament, desiring a stop may be put to it' (quoted in Anstey 1975: 223). A similar proposal, made through Benezet the same year on behalf of the Virginia Yearly Meeting, was that London Friends 'use their endeavours with those in authority' (Anstey 1975: 224) in support of a Virginian motion to George III to end the trade. Although neither proposal was successful, American Friends persisted in encouraging their English coun-terparts to apply parliamentary pressure.

The influence of American Quakers on British abolitionism, especially on efforts at legisla-tive reform, remained strong into the 1780s. The Quaker petition to Parliament in June 1783, marking the beginning in earnest of legislative attempts at reform, was put forward on the insistence of American Friends present at that year's London Yearly Meeting. When it was rejected by Parliament on the grounds of economic expediency, it was to American literature that London reformers again turned, reprinting Benezet's *The case of our fellow creatures, the oppressed Africans* and sending copies directly to the King, Queen and Prince of Wales. Some 11,000 copies were printed and distributed to members of both Houses of Parliament, mer-chants and clergymen, representing a new level of organization in the campaign (Anstey 1975: 229). Direct political lobbying would become a central tactic of the abolitionist campaign, with American Quaker influence again at the fore. Benjamin West, a friend of Benezet and one time leading member of the Pennsylvania Society, was able to use his connections as a court painter to present Queen Charlotte with a number of Benezet's pamphlets in 1783; four years later Patience Brayton, another of the many American Quakers to undertake British tours, person-ally entreated George III to end slavery in his realms (Drake 1950: 92).

By the late 1780s, the anti-slavery campaign had begun to adopt a more direct political approach, presaging the more highly organized advocacy of the parliamentary phase of reform. In 1787, the Society for the Abolition of the Slave Trade was formed. Although its committee was dominated by Quakers, the fact that it was headed by an Anglican, Granville Sharp (Walvin 1986: 105–6), gives further evidence that abolitionists appreciated their cause had to encompass a broader denominational section. The Abolition Society would give organization to a growing popular clamour against slavery, which would be manifested in mass protests and petitions in the early 1790s. The first organization of its type in Britain explicitly dedicated to abolition, its creation formalized the changing character of anti-slavery advocacy. The campaign had already metamorphosed from the loose, specifically Quaker, transatlantic advocacy network of the 1760s into a broader coalition in the 1770s, through the co-option of Methodists and evangelical Anglicans to the cause. By the final decade of the eighteenth century, anti-slavery activism had, to borrow the terminology of Khagram et al., undergone a full transition from *transnational advocacy network* to *transnational social movement*, capable of exerting significant political pres-sure and interacting with the state to achieve this (Khagram et al. 2002: 4–8). In so doing, how-ever, its basis and means of operation was similarly transformed from transnational to distinctly domestic.

As the Quaker influence in the campaign became diluted by the late-1780s, so the cam-paign's transnational dimension diminished. This was not due to the severing of imperial ties between Britain and America—the network of transatlantic Quakerism survived the revo-lution unscathed—but to the broadening abolitionist consensus and the opportunities for the campaign's political advancement in Britain. Abolitionism was fast becoming an inter-denominational coalition. It had gained critical mass, ensuring it no longer relied upon promptings from America Quakers to urge the campaign forward or to suggest new tactics or opportunities to explore. Equally, interaction with the political opportunity structure of the state, focusing activists' attention on legislative prospects at Westminster, brought British, and especially parliamentary, abolitionists to the fore, further helping to nationalize the campaign. Benezet's death in 1784 coincided with the rise in prominence of British, non-Quaker abolitionists, most notably Thomas Clarkson and William Wilberforce, who would lead parliamentary attempts to ban the slave trade. The abolitionist movement in Britain had been aroused by Quaker activism, largely of American origin, and its influence continued to be strong into the early 1780s, with the first attempts at legislative reform. By the later 1780s and 1790s, however, the British anti-slavery campaign had gathered a domestic momentum of its own.

Conclusion

Anti-slavery activism had evolved by the 1780s through the ascending stages of collective action, from *transnational advocacy network* to *coalition*. As the coalition attracted a mass popular base from the 1780s and 1790s onwards, it began to exert significant political pressure and was, ultimately, able to publicly influence social change, thus assuming the essential characteristics of *social movements* as defined by Khagram, Riker and Sikkink (2002). The Abolition Act of 1807, outlawing the slave trade, marked the successful culmination of the anti-slave trade campaign, although abolitionists would have to wait a further 26 years for the passing of the Slavery Abolition Act and the emancipation of slaves in British colonies. Narrating and scrutinizing the later, *social movement* phase of the abolitionist campaign is beyond the scope of this article. Instead, I have intended to show the process of transition and evolution between the first and second stages (*network* and *coalition*) of the eighteenth-century abolitionist campaign and suggest the organizational and ideational bases from which the more popular and public third stage (*movement*) developed. In so doing, I buttress the work on historical transnationalism developed most notably by Keck and Sikkink and extend the focus on transnationalism back in time, examining events not hitherto addressed in transnationalism literature. I show that the transnational dimension to the anti-slavery movement in the mid nineteenth century which Keck and Sikkink note (1998)—predominantly one of British activism in support of a domestic American campaign—was preceded by a transnational campaign of similar conscience and vigour more than half a century earlier. Moreover, eighteenth-century transatlantic abolitionism exhibited the key features which denote later transnational activism. Information exchange, the sharing of methods and tactics, and a recognition of the importance of interacting with the state were all central to its operation.

The article broadly confirms the applicability of Khagram et al.'s model of transnational network development within a historical context. However, it also reveals that the development of transnational collective action through its ascending levels cannot be assumed: transnational networks (and coalitions) do not necessarily become transnational social movements. In the case of anti-slavery activism, as shown by this chapter, a transnational network morphed into a transnational coalition, but became a largely national or domestic social movement. As the campaign against the slave trade assumed the characteristics of a social movement from the 1780s onwards, it became increasingly British dominated—in its principal actors, its tactics and in its growing interaction with the British state. American influence, which had played such a significant role in the early phases of abolitionism's development, diminished in proportion to the movement becoming more rooted in British society and politics. Further study of whether other campaigns have followed a similar—from transnational to national—trajectory, the circumstances in which this has taken place, and the processes involved would make a valuable addition to transnationalism literature.

References

Anstey, R. (1975) *The Atlantic slave trade and British abolition 1760–1810*, London: Macmillan.
Aptheker, H. (1940) 'The Quakers and Negro Slavery', *Journal of Negro History*, 25, 331–62.
Benezet, A. (1784) *The case of our fellow creatures, the oppressed Africans*, London: James Phillips.
Cadbury, H. (1971) *John Woolman in England, 1772*, London: Friends Historical Society.
Davis, D. B. (1969) *The problem of slavery in Western culture*, Ithaca, NY: Cornell University Press.
Davis, D. B. (1971) 'New sidelights on early antislavery radicalism', *William and Mary Quarterly*, 3rd series, 28, 585–94.
Drake, T. (1950) *Quakers and slavery in America*, Gloucester, Mass.: Yale University Press.
Fogel, R. (1989) *Without consent or contract: the rise and fall of American slavery*, New York: Norton.
James, S.V. (1963) *A people among peoples: Quaker benevolence in 18th century America*, Cambridge, Mass.: Harvard University Press.
Jenkins, J. C. and B. Klandermans (eds) (1995) *The politics of social protest: comparative perspectives on states and social movements*, London: UCL Press.
Keck, M. and K. Sikkink (1998) *Activists beyond borders: advocacy networks in international politics*, Ithaca, NY: Cornell University Press.
Khagram, S., J. V. Riker, and K. Sikkink (eds) (2002) *Restructuring world politics: transnational social movements, networks and norms*, Minneapolis: Minnesota University Press.
Moulton, P. (ed.) (1971) *The journal and major essays of John Woolman*, Oxford: Oxford University Press.
Soderlund, J. R. (1985) *Quakers and slavery: a divided spirit*, Princeton, NJ: Princeton University Press.
Tarrow, S. (1998) *Power in movement: social movements, collective action and politics*, Cambridge: Cambridge University Press, 2nd edition.
Thomas, H. (1997) *The slave trade: the history of the Atlantic slave trade 1440–1870*, London: Picador.
Tolles, F. (1960) *Quakers and the Atlantic culture*, New York: Macmillan.
Walvin, J. (1986) *England, slaves and freedom, 1776–1838*, London: Macmillan.

CHAPTER FIVE

Transnational Humanitarian Heroes in the Early Twentieth Century: The Congo Reform Movement

William E. DeMars

Source: Adapted from "NGOs and Transnational Networks: Wild Cards in World Politics", William E. DeMars, 2005, Pluto Press, London and Ann Harbor, MI

The historical roots of contemporary single-issue advocacy campaigns date back to the eighteenth and nineteenth centuries when great universalistic movements emerged from among British dissenting Protestant in England and the United States. From this cultural base emerged a series of historic reform agendas for the abolition of slavery, temperance, women's suffrage, universal public education, and urban reform, among others.[1]

When these campaigns focus on Sub-Saharan Africa, a strong historical pattern has emerged in which the region is mediated to the West through larger-than-life humanitarian heroes. The Western public, particularly in the English-speaking world, seeks out such celebrity advocates to explain and enact our relationship with the African other. Inevitably, the reality of Africa is both represented and distorted by the dynamics of that relationship, even when the humanitarian heroes proceed with the best of motives. This chapter explores an early expression of this pattern in the Congo Reform Movement of the early twentieth century, and concludes with some remarkable parallels in the early twenty-first century.

The series of anti-slavery campaigns were the first to garner widespread support for a single, bounded issue based on universal moral principles. From the formation of the Society for the Abolition of the Slave Trade in London in 1787, it was only two decades until Britain and the United States withdrew from involvement in the international slave trade (1807), and three more decades until Britain abolished slavery in all its colonies (1838). By 1888, a century after the beginning of the movement, slavery was formally abolished in its last stronghold of Brazil.[2] In light of this history, the Society for the Abolition of the Slave Trade and its successor, the British Anti-Slavery Society, may be the most effective NGOs ever launched.[3]

The antislavery movements bequeathed to all later campaigns and movements several deep assumptions about the relationship between society and state.[4] In brief, they held three foundational convictions as a matter of both faith and practical organization. First, they believed in the moral and political autonomy of society from the state. Second, using this autonomy they confidently asserted supranational moral authority above all states. Third, they employed their autonomy and supranational moral authority in the service of advocacy projects for collective moral progress that were both moral and secular.

By the later 1860s, after a string of successes, the antislavery movement turned its sights on the Arab slave trade in Africa and other Islamic regions.[5] In this struggle, several prominent Europeans struck a humanitarian pose on the public stage by their proclaimed opposition to Arab slavery—David Livingstone, Henry Morgan Stanley, King Leopold, and E. D. Morel. Each of these men reflected the contradictions of the age. Each was profoundly dedicated to improving himself, and all four projected into Africa their wildly divergent notions of self-improvement. King Leopold and Morel finally faced off, each having established a formal NGO modeled on the British Antislavery Society, and fought a war of public relations and humanitarian advocacy in which the lives of millions of Africans and billions of francs were at stake. This was perhaps the first "NGO war" in which apparently principled advocacy organizations took positions on opposite sides of a high stakes political dispute and used sophisticated public relations techniques to promote their messages.[6]

New technologies vastly extended the reach of business, politics, and culture in the late nineteenth century. It was culture, surprisingly, that reached first and farthest. The steamship, railroad, telegraph, and mass publication of newspapers and books provided the infrastructure upon which a bridge of the imagination was built. The British and American publics in particular saw themselves in sub-Saharan Africa through the writings of correspondents and explorers well before their business and political classes established themselves there. The leaders of this process were entrepreneurs of the imagination, intrepid explorers with mass audiences for their articles and books.

Born of poor, devoutly Calvinist parents in Scotland in 1813, David Livingstone was zealous to improve both himself and the world. He responded to a call by British and American churches for medical missionaries, and when the Opium War frustrated his dream to go to China, he turned instead to sub-Saharan Africa. For 30 years he traversed the continent—from 1841 when he landed at Cape Town at the southern tip, to 1871 when he was famously met and resupplied by Henry Morton Stanley on the shore of Lake Tanganyika. He died two years later in what is now Zambia, frustrated in his search for the source of the Nile, and his body was returned to Britain for a magnificent funeral and burial in Westminster Abbey.[7]

From the start, Livingstone's dreams of progress for Africa had embraced the components of Christianity, commerce, and civilization in a seamless vision. His quest to discover trade routes that would link central Africa to the Atlantic Ocean, the Pacific Ocean, and the Nile River sprung from a belief that legitimate commerce eventually would displace the Arab slave trade. He trusted that enlightened British politics and science would bring great improvement over Arab, Boer, or Portuguese hegemony, a belief that his own observations confirmed.

A missionary—but not only for the Christian Gospels—Livingstone no longer had to rely on support from the London Missionary Society after his first book, *Missionary Travels and Researches in Southern Africa*, made publication history in 1857 by selling more than 70,000 copies. In addition to religious and publishing affiliations, Livingstone maintained an association with the Royal Geographical Society for nearly a quarter century. His estimates of the prospects for profitable commerce and benevolent politics in Africa proved overly optimistic. Nevertheless, more than perhaps any other single person, David Livingstone helped the English speaking public imagine itself in Africa.

The merger of cultural, economic, and political agendas was characteristic of the European attitude toward Africa in the late nineteenth century. In an atmosphere of pervasive faith in human progress, Europeans saw themselves in the mirror of the undeveloped African continent. It appeared that anything was possible, for themselves and for Africa. The earlier antislavery movement had banned the trade in slaves taken from Africa, and was in the process of liberating African slaves worldwide. Livingstone's earnest goal was to bring an analogous collective moral progress to Africans living in Africa itself. The European readers of Livingstone's books could identify personally with this mission of moral progress.

In 1841 the boy who would call himself Henry Morton Stanley, and thirty years later rescue Livingstone at Lake Tanganyika, was born in Wales, the bastard child of housemaid Elizabeth Parry and local drunkard John Rowlands.[8] Shuffled from relatives to workhouse, he made his way as a cabin boy to New Orleans in 1859, where he took on the name of his employer. In America, Stanley managed to fight on both sides of the Civil War, and made a living reporting from the frontier of the American West to the big city newspapers of the East. As a reporter, Stanley learned that the drama of the story was far more important than the accuracy of the facts.

Stanley's overblown tales on the dwindling Indian wars in the American West led the publisher of the *New York Herald* to assign him in 1868 to cover the wars and explorations on the yet larger and more dramatic African frontier. As Livingstone had preached more than the Gospel, Stanley reported more than the news. From their encounter at Lake Tanganyika, Stanley wove the myth that sealed his reputation ("Dr. Livingstone I presume?"). Stanley assumed the mantle of heroic explorer, anti-slavery moralist, and herald of progress from the aging missionary. However, while Stanley easily aped the conventional ideology of progress, he had no personal sense of mission beyond maintaining his own celebrity. Given a mission, and funding, Stanley would be a formidable force indeed.

In the conventional ideology that Stanley had inherited from Livingstone, African exploration by western Europeans was considered progressive in and of itself. The logic seemed plausible: By exploring and mapping a new area, and publicizing the expedition, the European would "open" it simultaneously to several progressive and mutually supportive forces. Since Europe had renounced slavery, legitimate trade could only undercut the Arab slave trade. Christianity would prepare peoples to shoulder the responsibilities of civilization, which could be transferred in discrete sets of practices—scientific medicine, advanced agriculture, parliamentary politics— and "reassembled" in Africa. Among its many problems, this ideology gave presumptive legitimacy to all actions by Europeans in Africa, with no structure of accountability in Africa itself, and little or none in Europe. Such an arrangement could avoid disaster only so long as the Europeans involved were all of the highest moral character and most sound judgment.

In other words, the apparently innocent assumption inherited from the antislavery movement that society is morally and politically autonomous from the state quickly turned pernicious when applied to the European "opening" of Africa in the late nineteenth century. The idea of societal autonomy led Europeans to assume that unregulated societal relationships between Europe and Africa would be civil and not predatory. Prospective predators were only too willing to use that cultural naïveté to cover their bloody tracks.

When King Leopold II assumed the throne of Belgium in 1865, he was 30 years old and bitterly frustrated. He had inherited a small people and a small country, which possessed no colonies and was already outgrowing the monarchy to rule through parliamentary elections. The longing for material progress and personal improvement that pervaded Europe took the ironic form, in the young king, of an unquenchable lust for the wealth and power of a sovereign who stood above the world. Like David Livingstone and the son of John Rowlands, Leopold wanted to "better" himself. The nominal king sought the social status bestowed by the external trappings of sovereignty—on the scale of the palaces of Louis XIV. Before his twentieth year, Leopold had known that he needed a colony of his own to achieve these goals.

Before he located and gained control of a colony, and well before he found a profitable product to be exploited, Leopold identified the method that would make him rich. He pored over archives of the Spanish colonial empire in Seville, and studied the finances of the Dutch East Indies. By 1864, a year before being crowned, Leopold had concluded that the level of profit he desired could only be met by forced labor. He was not deterred by the expectation that forced labor might be difficult to institutionalize or conceal after the antislavery campaign had abolished slavery in European colonies and America.

For years Leopold searched the world for a colony that could be bought—perhaps a part of Argentina, Fiji, Abyssinia, the Philippines, or some drained lakes in the Nile Delta. Finally, his eye settled on the vast unexplored and unclaimed regions of Africa. While Stanley was traversing Africa, out of contact with Europe, following the Congo River to its source, Leopold meticulously planned a Geographical Conference to be held in his royal palace in downtown Brussels. When it convened in September 1876 Leopold had assembled an unprecedented gathering of explorers, geographers, businessmen, military heroes, and humanitarians, including the president of the British Anti-Slavery Society. Renouncing any ambition for himself or Belgium, Leopold in his opening speech charged the participants to decide on the "location of routes to be successively opened into the interior, of hospitable, scientific, and pacification bases to be set up as a means of abolishing the slave trade, establishing peace among the chiefs, and procuring them just and impartial arbitration."[9] As imagined by the participants, each base would combine a school for the natives, a hospitality station for explorers, and an infirmary. For Leopold only two things really mattered: that the proposed string of bases must traverse the unclaimed Congo River basin, and that the actual establishment of bases by any European must be given presumptive legitimacy under the norms of the conference. He achieved both goals. Indeed, the meeting voted to establish the International African Association and elected Leopold chairman. This was essentially a shell NGO that attracted favorable publicity and even financial contributions across Europe, but which had no specific responsibilities and would operate under no supervision. In practice, the International African Association became a symbolic umbrella under which any action by Leopold in Africa would take on a humanitarian hue.

Leopold, by convening a humanitarian conference which founded a humanitarian NGO, had performed a profoundly political act. According to Adam Hochschild,

> He had learned from his many attempts to buy a colony that none were for sale; he would have to conquer it. Doing this openly, however, was certain to upset both the Belgian people and the major powers of Europe. If he was to seize anything in Africa, he could do so only if he convinced everyone that his interest was purely altruistic. In this aim, thanks to the International African Association, he succeeded brilliantly. Viscount de Lesseps, for one, declared Leopold's plans "the greatest humanitarian work of this time."[10]

The progressive ideology of Livingstone and Stanley had already conflated economic, political, and humanitarian goals. Leopold's Geographical Conference had magnified the normative authority of that ideology, and had endowed the act of establishing bases anywhere near the planned routes with the full weight of that progressive, humanitarian, normative authority.

It is important to fully appreciate the intricacy of Leopold's political legerdemain at the 1876 conference. As King, he served nominally as the head of the Belgian government. He used the residual prestige of his office to convene an international conference, which invoked supranational authority—located nominally above all governments—to confer upon himself the identity of the leading humanitarian of European society. He was only nominally humanitarian of course, for this was the cover he needed to be the real government of the Congo. Nominally governmental, nominally supragovernmental, and nominally non-governmental, and all in service of predatory rule—such was the scale of Leopold's trick at the 1876 international conference. Such was his pernicious use of the idea of supranational authority inherited from the antislavery movement.

Leopold had defined a mission. He needed only a man with an iron will to carry it out. When Henry Morton Stanley reappeared in August 1877 at the Atlantic mouth of the Congo River after having spent four years traversing the waist of Africa from east to west, all of Europe and North America were prepared to lionize him for his Herculean achievements of exploration. King Leopold was prepared to offer him a contract. After recuperating in Europe and writing his third book, Stanley finally agreed.

Working for Leopold from 1879 to 1884, Stanley built the physical and legal infrastructure for the King's personal colony in the Congo Basin. According to plan, Stanley constructed a base at the mouth of the Congo River, took two years to carve a rough road 220 miles around the string of cataracts that was Livingstone Falls, and then hauled a couple of small steamships in pieces around the falls to be reassembled upriver. From these steamships, Stanley built a string of stations along 1,000 miles of navigable river. Equally important, he negotiated preposterously asymmetric "treaties" between Leopold's International Association of the Congo and tribal chiefs along the route. In the treaties, unreadable to the chiefs who signed their "X," the Association exchanged cloth and baubles for a monopoly on trade, large tracts of land, sovereign governing rights, and the chiefs' commitment "to assist by labour or otherwise, any works, improvements or expeditions which the said Association shall cause to be carried out in any part of these territories."[11] This clause formed the pseudo-legal basis for forced labor.

Parallel to Stanley's projects on the ground, Leopold mounted a bold campaign of international diplomacy to secure his exclusive right to sovereignty over the Congo Basin. No major power actively sought the expense and trouble of colonizing the Congo basin; but each desired to exclude the others. By delicately playing major powers against each other, Leopold gained formal recognition from the United States, Germany, and finally the entire Berlin Conference of 1884.[12] His agents misrepresented the new entity as a confederation of "free negroe republics" that would grant free trade to individuals from all other states. Moreover, he used the vaguely interchangeable titles of "International African Association," and "International Association of the Congo," which had earlier passed for humanitarian NGOs, as receptacles for recognition of a sovereign state with himself as its only government.

Leopold had successfully carried the humanitarian pose to the extremity of absolute power.

And he got away with it for 23 years, until 1908, barely a year before his death, when he was finally pressured to sell the colony to Belgium for 200 million francs. During that period, Leopold presided over a regime of forced labor that inflicted violence against Africans on a massive scale. In the early years the main product had been ivory, which, despite the high demand in Europe, failed to fully repay Leopold's expenses.

The 1890s brought a boom in the rubber market to feed emerging auto and electrical industries. The jungles of the Congo were full of wild rubber trees, but extracting, drying, and transporting the sap to steamships was backbreaking work that natives shunned. Leopold's agents and concessionary companies perfected the use of violence to enforce labor. A typical operation would begin by assaulting a village and taking the women hostage, where they were subject to harsh treatment and rape. To gain their release, the village chief had to deliver a quota of rubber. Alternately, Leopold's police would massacre all the people in one village to gain the cooperation of its neighbors; the police having to account for each bullet used by returning the severed right hand of the man, woman, or child who had received it. The population loss in the Congo under the years of Leopold's rule—from murder, starvation, exhaustion, disease, and plummeting birth rate—amounted to ten million people.[13]

Presiding over all this, and reaping its profits, Leopold never set foot in the Congo.

Public opposition to Leopold's misrule was sporadic and isolated for many years. Protestant missionaries from Britain and America took the lead in denouncing the violence through speeches and articles, but no organized opposition emerged until 1898. E.D. Morel was a young businessman in the Liverpool shipping company that held a monopoly on cargo shipped to and from the Congo Free State. Fluent in French, Morel was sent to supervise the company's dock operations in Antwerp. He observed that his company's ships arrived filled with rubber and ivory, but departed for the Congo with little more than arms and ammunition. As a businessman, and a member of the dissident Protestant Clapham Sect that had produced the antislavery leader William Wilberforce, Morel recognized that there was no real *trade* with the Congo since nothing of value was sent back in return for rubber and ivory.[14] The evidence before his eyes pointed to a regime of forced labor. Morel confirmed this conclusion by examining the financial and shipping records of his company and those of the Congo Free State.

In 1901 Morel quit his job and dedicated himself to writing and organizing. In 1903 he founded the *West African Mail*, a publication to serve as the organ for a new organization, the Congo Reform Association. Reluctant at first to establish an organization focused on campaigning for change exclusively in the Congo, when well-established groups like the Aborigines Protection Society and Anti-Slavery Society had intermittently addressed the region, Morel was persuaded by Roger Casement, a member of the British consular service in Africa who served as a covert channel of detailed information to Morel. Moreover, Morel was convinced that the Congo was a unique case of a state founded and sustained on slave labor, and so should be treated *sui generis* rather than as part of a larger category. Thus, Morel's Congo Reform Association in the early twentieth century was a forerunner of contemporary NGO country campaigns.

The Congo Reform Association was really a working NGO that served as the nucleus for a growing movement against Leopold's personal colony. Morel brought great advocacy skill to the movement. His *West African Mail* provided a magnet for information from all sources and a measure for the accumulation of evidence against Leopold. Morel held mass rallies and recruited prominent individuals, always emphasizing the unique evil institutionalized in the Congo Free State.

Faced with the growing moral authority of Morel's Congo Reform Association, Leopold retaliated by creating a series of shell NGOs and international commissions to fight on his side: the Commission for the Protection of the Natives, the Committee for the Protection of Interests in Africa, the West African Missionary Association.[15] To counter the information in Morel's *West African Mail*, Leopold bribed editors and journalists across Europe and sponsored books to argue his cause. In perhaps the most significant foreshadowing of the contemporary NGO scene, Leopold and Morel conducted an "NGO war" in which ostensibly principled organizations on opposing sides of a political conflict mobilized international norms and information. Both men struck the pose of a humanitarian hero who was saving Africa. Five years after the inauguration of the Congo Reform Association, Leopold gave up control of the Congo.

As a model of moral integrity and dedication to a just cause, E.D. Morel has few rivals. With King Leopold well cast as the personification of evil, the characters form a morality play that projects a satisfying clarity on the gulf between good and evil. Morel was a real humanitarian hero; Leopold a criminal villain. And yet, ironies emerge around the edges. In fact, Leopold's Congo colony was not unique in its reliance on forced labor, which pervaded a broader region of central Africa where wild rubber thrived. In addition, forced labor persisted in the Belgian Congo under modified forms through World War II.[16] Morel was wrong in the factual claim that the Congo Free State was a singular case, and in the causal theory that the use of forced labor would end when Leopold was no longer involved in Africa.

Also intriguing are the curious parallels between the lead characters in our morality play, Leopold and Morel. Neither man ever set foot in the Congo. Yet from their vantage points in Brussels and London, they vied with each other like titans to shape human lives and commodities there. Each man arrived at the same crucial insight concerning the economics of colonies— the centrality of forced labor in a profitable colonial enterprise. Leopold grasped this in 1862 by studying the archives of the Spanish empire and the financial history of the Dutch East Indies.

Morel made the same inference in 1898 on the docks of Antwerp. Equipped with the same causal insight, the major difference between the two men was that Morel applied his personal moral compass to correct what Leopold's distinctly amoral compass had wrought.

Both Leopold and Morel were bilingual in French and English, and both were masters of public relations, often playing on the same humanitarian themes to influence their audiences. Ironically, both built on the prior success of the antislavery movement to garner broad public allegiance: Leopold posed falsely as an opponent of the Arab slave trade, and Morel honestly condemned Leopold's forced labor, but both appealed to the same diffuse longing in the European public for moral progress in their relations with Africa. Neither man had ever seen Africa. Nevertheless, each was taken seriously when he appointed himself as a humanitarian hero representing African society.

Why was the public so easily fooled by Leopold's lies, and also so readily mobilized by Morel's accurate facts but partly illusory notions of the cause and cure for forced labor? Given the distance between Europe and Africa and the few channels of information, a resourceful individual could powerfully shape the flow of apparently authoritative stories about the continent. In addition, the European and American publics cared far more about the image of themselves in Africa than they did about what was really happening in Africa. For the public, to celebrate any combination of the achievements of exploration, the spread of Christianity, the suppression of the Arab slave trade, or the expansion of free trade was to project themselves onto the empty canvas of the imaginary future of Africa. It is difficult to avoid the conclusion that the cultural narcissism of the middle class plays a role in this tragedy, even when the best men were leading the NGOs.

Today, in the early twenty-first century, the historical pattern of humanitarian heroes representing Africa to the West remains remarkably strong, and celebrity advocates attract both ardent admirers and bitter critics. The Harvard economist Jeffrey Sachs has championed implementation of the UN's Millennium Development Goals to reduce poverty and disease in Africa.[17] With crucial leadership from Dr. Paul Farmer, the HIV/AIDS network has mushroomed since 2000 to generate more than 60,000 NGOs spending $20 billion a year mostly in sub-Saharan Africa.[18] The Carter Center and the Bill and Melinda Gates Foundation have mobilized funding and the moral authority of their founders to spearhead a network for eradication of tropical diseases that strike Africans the hardest.[19] Irish rocker Bono has lobbied world leaders, founded several NGOs including the ONE Campaign to attack extreme poverty in Africa, and even edited a special Africa issue of *Vanity Fair* in July, 2007.[20]

However, no African issue has provoked such recent attention in the West as genocide in the Darfur region of Sudan. In 2004, U.S. Secretary of State Colin Powell and President George W. Bush both publicly denounced "genocide" in Darfur. President Bush sought to distinguish himself from his predecessor Bill Clinton, whose administration had failed to acknowledge genocide in Rwanda in 1994. Indeed, the tenth anniversary of the Rwanda genocide profoundly shaped both governmental and societal responses to Darfur. In the dominant narrative, the United States had failed to save Rwanda in 1994, and 800,000 people had died. Only a year later in 1995 the United States had acted decisively in Bosnia, after several years of dallying, to stop an ongoing genocide. It is no exaggeration to observe that thousands of American policymakers, journalists, activists, and scholars were seared with the guilt of Rwanda and galvanized in the determination to do better next time. Such guilt can be politically useful if skillfully mobilized. In 2004 and after, this guilt, and the sharp contrast between the Rwanda analogy and the Bosnia analogy, energized the movement to save Darfur when President Bush's timid actions did not match his decisive speech.[21]

Samantha Power's book, *A Problem from Hell: America and the Age of Genocide*, became the "veritable bible for the anti-genocide movement."[22] From its 600 pages, the lesson for activists was condensed into an oft cited paragraph on page 509:

> With foreign policy crises all over the world affecting more traditional U.S. interests, genocide has never secured top-level attention on its own merits. It takes political pressure to put genocide on the map in Washington. When Alison Des Forges of Human Rights Watch met with National Security Advisor Anthony Lake two weeks into the Rwanda genocide, he informed her that the phones were not ringing. "Make more noise!" he urged. Because so little noise has been made about genocide, U.S. decision-makers have opposed U.S. intervention, telling themselves that they were doing all they could—and most important, all they should—in light of competing American interests and a highly circumscribed understanding of what was domestically "possible" for the United States to do.[23]

The moral and political clarity of Anthony Lake's three word analysis in 1994, "Make more noise!" has guided the entire save Darfur movement since 2004 (whether or not it was an accurate analysis of the Rwandan genocide). The response to Darfur in America has been strategically committed to avoiding "another Rwanda" by mobilizing pressure on the U.S. government.[24]

In the dialectic between 1994 and 2004, there are clear echoes of David Livingstone. Once again the English speaking West is cast in the role of savior to Africa. And once again, humanitarian heroes arise to articulate the moral clarity of good and evil, and to enact the narrative of rescue. These heroic advocates emerge from the ranks of journalists and scholars (Nicholas Kristof, Samantha Power, Michael Barnett), United Nations officials (Romeo Dallaire, Mukesh Kapila, Kofi Annan), activists and policymakers (John Prendergast, Susan Rice, Brian Steidle), and, inevitably, actors and entertainers (George Clooney, Mia Farrow, Don Cheadle).[25] And once again, the organizational form of choice for heroic advocacy is the humble NGO (Save Darfur Coalition, STAND, Genocide Intervention Network, Enough!, Justice Africa, International Crisis Group, Human Rights Watch, and more).[26] In the ultimate celebrity partnership, veteran humanitarian advocate John Prendergast teamed up with actor Don Cheadle to write a primer for young Darfur activists.[27]

However, in a significant shift in the historical pattern, there is no longer presumptive legitimacy granted for the actions of outsiders in Africa. In fact, the very controversy and criticism that have accompanied the save Darfur movement provides strong evidence of an increasingly dense network of accountability for activists.[28] To the extent this exists, it is largely informal—the activists, NGOs, journalists, policymakers and scholars watch and criticize each other. Mahmood Mamdani, for example, has accused the save Darfur movement of outright neocolonialism.[29] More plausibly, Alex de Waal, experienced scholar and advocate for Africa and active participant in the Darfur network, has charged his fellow activists with promoting a narrative of exaggerated Arab evil and African innocence, and thereby privileging policies of forceful interventionism over mediation and negotiation to end the war.[30]

Nicholas Kristof, whose *New York Times* columns had sounded an early clarion call on Darfur during 2004, acknowledged in 2009 that the movement was stalled. "We got what we hoped for," Kristof affirmed, in the International Criminal Court indictment for genocide of Sudanese President Omar al-Bashir.[31] However, he admitted, the situation on the ground for Darfuris may have worsened as a result, and the other war between north and south in Sudan could reignite at any time to engulf the country in much greater violence. In addition, the movement was fragmenting. John Prendergast and Alex de Waal exchanged bitter criticisms in *Newsweek* of their contrasting strategies for responding to Darfur.[32]

The movement accomplished much in pressuring both the United States and Sudan's patron China to take significant action through the UN Security Council by sending peacekeeping troops, imposing mild sanctions, and referring the conflict to the ICC. Chastened by his realization of the mixed and inadvertent consequences of the Darfur movement, Kristof still savors the transnational solidarity it engendered:

> For all the failures, there is something inspiring about how hundreds of thousands of university students around America have marched, fasted, and donated money on behalf of people of a different race and religion who live halfway around the world, in a land they had never heard of five years ago, and who rarely appear on their television screens.[33]

Anyone who attempts to mobilize, or educate, the Western public in response to Africa inevitably steps into the shoes of David Livingstone and E.D. Morel. Mediating between the expectations of the West and the realities of Africa, and assuming to some degree the mantle of humanitarian hero, is fraught with personal and policy ambiguities. If members of the Save Darfur movement have lost some moral clarity and political clout, they may have gained a more seasoned idealism about the complexity of African conflicts, the agency of Africans in those conflicts, and the limits of outside intervention.

Notes

1. Robert William Fogel, *The Fourth Great Awakening and the Future of Egalitarianism* (Chicago, IL: University of Chicago Press, 2000).
2. Ethan A. Nadelman, "Global Prohibition Regimes: The Evolution of Norms in International Society," *International Organization*, Vol. 44, No. 4 (1990).
3. David Brion Davis, *Slavery and Human Progress* (Oxford University Press, 1984).
4. For an extended treatment of these themes, see William E. DeMars, Chapter 3, "Ironic Origins of Transnational Organizing," in William E. DeMars, *NGOs and Transnational Networks: Wild Cards in World Politics* (London: Pluto Press, 2005).
5. Suzanne Miers and Richard Roberts, eds, *The End of Slavery in Africa* (Madison, WI: University of Wisconsin Press, 1988).
6. DeMars, *NGOs and Transnational Networks,* "Early NGO Wars Over Africa," pp. 70–9.
7. Tim Jeal, *Livingstone* (New York: G. P. Putnam's Sons, 1973).
8. Much of this section relies on the gripping and exhaustively researched book by Adam Hochschild, *King Leopold's Ghost* (New York: Houghton Mifflin, 1998).
9. Hochschild, *King Leopold's Ghost,* p. 45.
10. Hochschild, *King Leopold's Ghost,* p. 46.
11. Quoted in Hochschild, *King Leopold's Ghost,* p. 72.
12. Hochschild, *King Leopold's Ghost,* Chapter 5, "From Florida to Berlin."
13. Hochschild, *King Leopold's Ghost,* Chapter 15, "A Reckoning."
14. Hochschild, *King Leopold's Ghost,* p. 211.
15. Hochschild, *King Leopold's Ghost,* pp. 174, 239, 251.
16. Hochschild, *King Leopold's Ghost,* pp. 275–83; David Northrup, "The Ending of Slavery in the Eastern Belgian Congo," in Miers and Roberts, eds, *The End of Slavery in Africa.*
17. Nina Munk, "Jeffrey Sach's $200 Billion Dream," *Vanity Fair* (July, 2007); Jeffrey D. Sachs, *The End of Poverty: Economic Possibilities for Our Time* (New York: Penguin, 2005).
18. Laurie Garrett, "The Challenge of Global Health," *Foreign Affairs,* Vol. 86, No. 1 (Jan-Feb, 2007), 14–38; Tracy Kidder, *Mountains Beyond Mountains: The Quest of Dr. Paul Farmer, A Man Who Would Cure the World* (New York: Random House, 2004).

19. "Diseases On the Brink," series of seven articles by Donald G. McNeil, Jr. and Celia W. Dugger, *The New York Times,* March 31 to December 22, 2006, [www.nytimes.com/ref/health/2006_BRINK_SERIES.html] (accessed on March 11, 2010).
20. Andrew F. Cooper, *Celebrity Diplomacy* (Boulder, CO: Paradigm, 2008); Sridhar Pappu, "Bono's Calling," *Washington Post,* November 26, 2007; Bono as Guest Editor of "Special Issue: Africa," *Vanity Fair* (July, 2007), [www.vanityfair.com/magazine/toc/2007/toc200707] (accessed on March 11, 2010). On the "aid celebrity trinity" of Bono, Jeffrey Sachs and Paul Farmer, see Lisa Ann Richey and Stefano Ponte: *Brand Aid, Celebrities, Consumption and Development* (University of Minnesota Press and Zed Books, forthcoming).
21. Kenneth A. Rodman, "Darfur and the Limits of Legal Deterrence," *Human Rights Quarterly* (2008), Vol. 30, pp. 529–560; Colin Thomas-Jensen and Julia Spiegel, "Activism and Darfur: Slowly Driving Policy Change," *Fordham International Law Journal* (2008), Vol. 31, pp. 843–58.
22. Rebecca Hamilton and Chad Hazlett, " 'Not On Our Watch': The Emergence of the American Movement for Darfur," Chapter 14 in Alex de Waal, ed., *War in Darfur and the Search for Peace* (Global Equity Initiative, Harvard University, 2007), p. 346.
23. Samantha Power, *"A Problem from Hell" America and the Age of Genocide* (New York: Basic Books, 2002), p. 509.
24. This is abundantly substantiated in Deborah Murphy, "Narrating Darfur: Darfur in the U.S. Press, March—September 2004," Chapter 13 in Alex de Waal, ed., *War in Darfur and the Search for Peace* (Global Equity Initiative, Harvard University, 2007).
25. Nicholas Kristof, columns in *The New York Times,* [http://topics.nytimes.com/top/opinion] (accessed on March 11, 2010), and articles in the *New York Review of Books,* [www.nybooks.com/authors/10534] (accessed on March 11, 2010); Michael Barnett, *Eyewitness to Genocide: The United Nations and Rwanda* (Ithaca, NY: Cornell University Press, 2002); Romeo Dallaire, *Shake Hands With the Devil: The Failure of Humanity in Rwanda* (Toronto: Random House Canada, 2003); Zachary D. Kaufman, "Justice in Jeopardy: Accountability for the Darfur Atrocities," *Criminal Law Forum* (2005), Vol. 16, pp. 343–360; James Traub, *The Best Intentions: Kofi Annan and the UN in the Era of American World Power* (New York: Farrar, Straus and Giroux, 2006); Brian Steidle and Gretchen Steidle Wallace, *The Devil Came on Horseback: Bearing Witness to the Genocide in Darfur* (New York: PublicAffairs, 2007); Susan E. Rice, "Dithering on Darfur: U.S. Inaction in the Face of Genocide," Testimony before the U.S. Senate Foreign Relations Committee April 11, 2007, The Brookings Institution, [www.brookings.edu/~/media/Files/rc/testimonies/2007/0411africa_rice/20070411.pdf] (accessed on March 11, 2010); Alex de Waal, "The Humanitarian Carnival: A Celebrity Vogue," *World Affairs Journal* (Fall, 2008), [www.worldaffairsjournal.org/2008%20-%20Fall/full-DeWaal.html] (accessed on March 11, 2010).
26. International Crisis Group, "Crisis in Darfur: International and local NGOs working on Darfur," [www.crisisgroup.org/home/index.cfm?id=6509&l=1#C6] (accessed on March 11, 2010).
27. Don Cheadle and John Prendergast, *Not On Our Watch: The Mission to end Genocide in Darfur and Beyond* (New York: Hyperion, 2007).
28. David Lanz, "Save Darfur: A Movement and Its Discontents," *African Affairs* (2009), Vol. 108, No. 433, pp. 669–677.
29. Mahmood Mamdani, *Saviors and Survivors: Darfur, Politics, and the War on Terror* (Pantheon, 2009).
30. Julie Flint and Alex de Waal, *Darfur: A New History of a Long War,* 2nd Edition (London: Zed Books, 2008).

31. Nicholas D. Kristof, "What to Do about Darfur," *New York Review of Books* (July 2, 2009), Vol. 56, No. 11, [www.nybooks.com/articles/22771] (accessed on March 11, 2010).

32. Alex de Waal and John Prendergast, "Dueling Over Darfur," *Newsweek,* Nov. 8, 2007, [www.newsweek.com/id/69004] (accessed on March 11, 2010).

33. Kristof, "What to Do about Darfur."

PART III

GLOBAL LABOR

CHAPTER SIX

Transnational Pioneers: The International Labor Movement

Dan Gallin

Source: Srilatha Batliwala and L. David Brown (eds) *Transnational Civil Society: An Introduction* (2006) 84–100 © 2006 Kumarian Press—Reproduced with permission.

Introduction

In the most common acceptance of the term, especially in the United States, the labor movement refers primarily to the trade union movement. It is actually far more than that. Historically, it also comprises the political parties created by workers to defend their interests, such as labor, socialist, and social-democratic parties, as well as the many institutions created for specific purposes: workers' cooperatives (both of producers and of consumers), workers' banks, educational associations, schools and colleges, health and welfare institutions, cultural institutions (theaters, libraries, chorales, brass bands, book clubs), leisure activities (sports and hiking clubs), women's organizations, youth organizations, solidarity and defense organizations (including armed militias), radio and television stations, newspapers and review magazines, publishing houses, and bookshops. All of these, taken together, constitute the historical labor movement.

The full range of such institutions and organizations rarely exists all at the same time in any one country. The important point is that all these institutions taken together are not only meant to support workers in all aspects of their lives but also to constitute an alternative society and a counterculture. The labor movement is thus a multifaceted social movement with a cause and a vision of society.

The trade union movement is the most important component of the labor movement in its wider sense. It is the first, and often the last, line of resistance that workers have to defend themselves, and without it none of the other institutions of the labor movement would survive. It is also the most representative part of the labor movement; it exists in every country in the world except in those with the most extreme dictatorships.

From the very beginning, the labor movement has been inspired and organized by many different ideologies: Marxism in various (sometimes contradictory) interpretations, revolutionary and conservative syndicalism, Christian social doctrines, radical liberation movements, and others. Each ideology derives its values and objectives from its own traditions, but they share a common cause, which by now constitutes the culture of the mainstream labor movement. The basic elements of this culture are reflected in the movement's values and goals.

The labor movement is the oldest social movement seeking to transform society in the name of universal values, with the objective of creating a society that meets the needs and aspirations of all human beings. The fundamental value, from which all others are derived, is a sense of dignity of the human being—a value stronger than even survival, since people are prepared to die for it. A related value is that of equality; all human beings are of equal worth, and therefore should have equal rights. From this derives the value of justice; it is unacceptable that, because of the way power is distributed in society, some should enjoy wealth and privilege while others, the greater number, should be circumscribed by poverty, starvation, and early death. Finally, all human beings aspire to freedom—freedom from exploitation and oppression. These values have driven every movement of resistance throughout history, and they are driving the modern labor movement.

What differentiates the modern labor movement from the many earlier liberation movements is that it is international in nature. The transnationality of the labor movement is rooted in the perception that workers constitute a class with a common cause. Because it has a vital interest in the abolition of exploitation for all people, the labor movement is not only a self-help movement of workers but also a liberation movement for all humanity.

The values of the labor movement explain its concept of democracy as a process and method, not just as an ultimate goal. This concept is based on the understanding that ends and means are closely linked: for example, undemocratic means cannot lead to democratic outcomes. Therefore, democracy is a living process and a continuous work in progress.

The goals of the labor movement naturally derive from its values. They are several, and include:

- The defense of the immediate interests of its members on the job: decent wages, security of employment, working conditions that are not threatening to the mental and physical health of the workers, and basic social protection;
- Socially progressive legislation in the interests of all workers and, indeed, for humanity as a whole;
- A political society where the rights of workers and of all citizens are guaranteed;[1]
- International solidarity, since its achievements are under threat as long as injustice and oppression exist anywhere.

The enduring strength of the solidarity principle is demonstrated by the resilience of the international labor movement, which survived the wars and totalitarian dictatorships of the twentieth century. Dictatorships establish themselves by breaking unions; churches and businesses have survived and flourished in dictatorships where labor activists have been sent to jail, concentration camps, and death.

This chapter first outlines the history of the birth and growth of the labor movement, from its optimistic beginnings in Europe in the mid-nineteenth century to a powerful entity worldwide a century later. It then analyzes the setbacks to the movement, stressing particularly the ideological, and subsequently the economic, factors that have challenged it in the last fifty years.

History

[...]

The Social-Democratic and Communist Labor Movement

Origins to World War I

The modern labor movement began in Europe at the turn of the nineteenth century with the rise of the Industrial Revolution, the emergence of capitalist mass production, and the formation of an impoverished working class. The brutal injustice of the emergent society inspired social reformers to propose a more rational and fairer social order. By the end of the

1830s, small groups of trade unionists, socialists, and democrats in Britain and France were planning for an "international association for the emancipation of the working class."[2]

However, it was not until 1847 that a group of workers and political exiles living in London organized a meeting, at which a declaration and a program authored by Karl Marx and Friedrich Engels was adopted. This document, which came to be known as the Communist Manifesto, eventually emerged as the basic statement of the Marxist version of socialism, and the theoretical basis of the modern mainstream labor movement.

In 1864, a meeting in London that was attended by local and national workers' societies as well as many other forms of workers' organizations (political parties and propaganda groups, unions, cooperatives, mutual-aid societies, etc.) led to the establishment of an organization that came to be called the First International. The first congress of the International met in Geneva in 1866, and for the next ten years the organization grew rapidly as unions formed in many countries and allied themselves to it. Despite its evident relevance and popularity, however, the First International was short-lived. Struggles between the Marxists and the anarchists within the organization led to several splits, and eventually contributed to its demise in 1876. As an international labor organization, the First International had an obvious weakness: geographically limited to Europe, it was supported by a thin layer of politically conscious workers in essentially conservative societies. Severe financial constraints were part of the problem as income from dues was never enough to carry out even basic tasks such as publishing a bulletin or conducting research. Despite this, its achievements were remarkable. It gave the first practical expression to labor internationalism and established the first regular contacts between labor organizations in different countries; those contacts survived its dissolution and became the basis of its successor organizations. The First International was the first to formulate general demands (such as the eight-hour day), which became common demands of unions internationally, and it provided a theoretical and political framework for later international action.

Several attempts to re-create an international labor organization in the following decade led to the establishment of the Second International in Paris in 1889. On the last day of its deliberations, the congress declared May 1 as an international day of struggle for the eight-hour day. The first May Day in 1890 turned out to be a more forceful and impressive demonstration than its organizers had anticipated. May Day immediately became the official day of remembrance of workers' struggles, and of celebration of the international labor movement.

The Second International was an umbrella organization that included political parties, trade unions, and other workers' organizations. It was soon recognized, however, that a clearer division of labor was necessary. After 1900, the Second International evolved into an association of socialist parties and other organizations developed for other functions. Some members of the International founded international organizations of workers in the same trade or industry. These became known as the international trade secretariats (ITS), the first permanently organized form of international trade union solidarity. Twenty-eight ITSs had been formed by 1911, with a total membership of about 6.3 million. Their main activities were centered on organizing worker solidarity during strikes, and exchanging information on trade and labor legislation. When in 1903 the national trade union centers in some countries felt the need for an independent international organization, they founded what became in 1913 the International Federation of Trade Unions (IFTU). In that year, the IFTU had members in twenty countries with a total membership of approximately 7.7 million.

The Interwar Years

The first phase of the movement came to an abrupt end with the outbreak of World War I in August 1914. Neither the Second International nor the IFTU survived the war intact. In the preceding decade, the socialist labor movement had developed into a mass movement with strong positions against militarism and war. Nevertheless, when war broke out, the tidal wave of nationalism and patriotic fervor swept all before it. The socialist parties largely supported the governments in most European countries and voted for the war.

After one year of hostilities, the labor movement split into the parties and unions that supported the Allies, those that supported the Central Powers, and those of the neutral countries. Only a minority of revolutionary socialists and syndicalists opposed the war in all European countries, but this opposition gained in strength as the war dragged on and revulsion against the mass slaughter on the battlefield spread throughout Europe.

In 1917, revolution broke out in Russia; the czar was overthrown and replaced, first by a center-left Constituent Assembly and later by a coalition government of revolutionary socialists (led and eventually taken over by the Bolsheviks). They established a government based on Councils (Soviets) and took Russia out of the war. They nationalized the land and the main industries, created a Red Army, and in the ensuing civil war repressed political opposition through terror. The impact of the Bolshevik revolution on the labor movement was twofold: it greatly strengthened the agitation for peace and for political, social, and economic reforms, but it also caused a deep rift in the socialist movement. Most socialist parties and unions rejected the Bolshevik concept of political dictatorship supported by terror, and stressed political democracy as an inseparable part of socialism.

In March 1919, the Bolsheviks convened an international conference in Moscow to establish the Communist or Third International. The conference, called in haste to preempt the reconstitution of the Second International, was hardly representative of the wider movement, but it adopted provisional statutes and elected a provisional executive committee. In its sessions it called on workers to rise and establish Soviet republics on the Russian model, and for an uncompromising struggle against socialist parties and movements that did not accept their leadership. Two years later a congress of trade unionists in Moscow established the Red International of Labor Unions (RILU), an international coalition of communist and syndicalist unions, with a close connection to the Communist International.

Meanwhile, the IFTU had been revived at a congress in Amsterdam in 1919, and had a representation of 23 million members in twenty-two countries. The Second International was reconstituted in 1923 as the Labor and Socialist International. Also in 1919, the Allies constituted the International Labor Organization (ILO) as a part of the Treaty of Versailles. It was initially intended to be a reformist alternative to the revolutionary threat from Russia. The ILO, a tripartite institution with representation from government, employers, and workers, survived World War II and is now part of the United Nations system. It prepares social legislation in the form of conventions that are then ratified by the member states to form the basis of national legislation.

The period from the 1920s to the outbreak of World War II in 1939 was dominated by the bitter and increasingly irreconcilable split between the social-democratic and communist movements. Antifascist and popular-front "unity" policies promoted by the communist parties proved to be tactical foreign policy maneuvers of the USSR, as Russia was now known. Stalin's intervention in the Spanish civil war demonstrated that the communist parties would accept unity only on their terms, involving total control.

These political struggles formed part of a historical catastrophe of huge proportions. Fascism had wiped out the labor movement in Italy, Germany, Austria, Portugal, and Spain, and then in most of Europe as the German armies occupied nearly the entire continent.[3] Hundreds of thousands of socialists, anarchists, and communists in Russia and later in Eastern and Central Europe perished in the Stalinist forced-labor camps. In the three decades following the Russian revolution, two generations of labor activists and leaders disappeared. In 1939, as a result of the

USSR and Nazi Germany signing a treaty of nonaggression, the communist parties had denounced Britain and France for declaring war on Germany. In 1941, however, Germany attacked the USSR, and the communist parties now declared that this was no longer an imperialist struggle but a war for democracy and freedom. The USSR joined the war on the side of the Allies, and in May 1943, the Communist International was dissolved to reassure the Allied powers that the USSR no longer harbored revolutionary ambitions.

The Cold War Period

The social-democratic labor movement emerged from the war in a strong political position but actually greatly weakened by its losses and far more dependent on the State than in the past. This dependence grew from its wartime alliance with the Allied governments, the weakened state of economies devastated by the war, and the fact that many postwar governments were now ready to support the legislative agenda of the labor movement.

Although the Socialist International was reconstituted in 1951 it gradually lost its relevance, evolving over time into an open forum with weak links to the trade union movement. Attempts to broaden its constituency beyond Europe reduced its political substance, and by the end of the twentieth century it had ceased to exercise a significant influence in international labor politics. At the end of the war, there was a widespread assumption that the wartime alliance of the Allies could be reflected in trade union terms, and that a united international trade union organization could include the Soviet as well as the Western social-democratic unions. After several exploratory international meetings, the World Federation of Trade Unions (WFTU) was established in 1945, and the IFTU was formally dissolved by its General Council. Soon, however, differences developed between the social-democratic and communist unions. In Eastern Europe the social-democratic, independent left, and dissident communist cadres quickly disappeared into jails and labor camps. Trade unions were replaced by State organizations for labor administration on the Soviet model. In Western Europe, the European Recovery Program was welcomed by the social-democratic unions and opposed by the communist unions. The ITSs broke off relations with the WFTU. By 1949, escalating tensions led to the noncommunist unions leaving the WFTU and establishing the International Confederation of Free Trade Unions (ICFTU) by the end of that year.

The Cold War, which began in 1949, cast its shadow over the trade union movement, but many factors in the split were a result of earlier tensions over issues such as whether "bourgeois democracy" was preferable to no democracy at all; whether unions should be accountable to their members or to a State; and whether this State represented a new class exercising control over society, including the working class, by means of terror. The beginning of the Cold War meant that the antifascist alliance that had briefly held together organizations with fundamentally opposed views, could no longer bridge these divisions.

The newly formed ICFTU was less grounded in the socialist tradition than the IFTU had been. Anticommunism was a far stronger driving force, even though this sometimes limited its agenda for workers' and human rights. The main achievement of the ICFTU was to become a truly worldwide organization, whereas all previous international labor organizations had been essentially Eurocentric, in practice if not in intent.

[. . .]

Labor Unions in Other Parts of the World

Since the labor movement originated in the workers' revolt against exploitation in the early capitalist economies, it first developed in Europe and North America, where the capitalist economy was most advanced. The First and Second Internationals and the IFTU were essentially European organizations. It was easy to establish and maintain international organizations in a relatively small, densely populated area. Maintaining regular contact with organizations that could be reached only after weeks of travel was a different matter. The early labor internationals were worldwide in intent, but remained largely (with some US participation) European in practice.

In the United States, unions developed at the same time as in Europe. The first lasting federation of national unions, the American Federation of Labor (AFofL), was established in 1886. Massive immigration from Europe radicalized American unions, creating socialist organizations. Socialist ideals greatly influenced the US labor movement in the first decades of the twentieth century: Eugene Victor Debs, founder of the American Railway Union, gained 6 percent of the popular vote as Socialist Party candidate for president in 1912. The Industrial Workers of the World (IWW), a revolutionary trade union federation founded in 1905, had close to two hundred thousand members in the United States, and branches in Australia, Britain, Canada, Chile, Germany, Mexico, New Zealand, Norway, and South Africa at its peak. In the 1930s, the mass-production industries were organized under the leadership of the Congress of Industrial Organizations (CIO). (The AFofL and the CIO eventually merged in 1955.)

Although the labor movement began in response to the capitalist economies of the West, its ideas spread rapidly to other parts of the world, often through seamen or immigrants. This was particularly so in the colonies of the European countries; unions as well as workers' parties and other labor movement institutions formed in Latin America and Asia in the second half of the nineteenth century, and in Africa a few decades later.

In Latin America, anarcho-syndicalist unionism from Spain, Portugal, and Italy was predominant. Social struggles were often violent, with military repression by employers and conservative governments a common response to strikes in most countries. In the 1940s, other powerful actors intervened. In Argentina, for example, General Peron combined an authoritarian ideology with pro-labor policies (while suppressing socialist, communist, and syndicalist unions) to create a unionism that survived the second Peron presidency and a military dictatorship to remain the dominant force in the Argentine labor movement. In Brazil, the trade union movement linked to a socialist mass party emerged as a strong social and political force in the 1990s, with a former union organizer gaining the presidency in 2003.

[. . .]

In the British colonies, however, labor movements were often closely linked to political struggles. In India, for example, organized strikes were frequent at the end of the nineteenth century, particularly in the textile industry and the railways, even in the absence of unions. The arrest in 1908 of Bal Gangadhar Tilak, a prominent nationalist leader, resulted in a six-day general strike by the Bombay textile-mill workers, the first politically motivated mass strike in Indian history. The All India Trade Union Congress was founded in 1920; following independence in 1947, however, the trade union movement began to fragment as different groups formed alliances with the various political parties.

Labor organizations in the African colonies of the United Kingdom also took on critical political roles. The movement often first came into being in those areas that were closely linked with the plundering activities of the colonizers: mining and plantations, railways, harbors, and administration. The mineworkers in the copper belt in Zambia, for example, struck in 1935, 1940, and again in 1957, finally winning a wage increase. In many countries the labor movement became a training ground for national leaders, since it provided opportunities for building leadership skills and learning ways to prevail upon the colonialists via economic pressure. In South Africa, discrimination against blacks created race-based unions that became major political actors in the struggle against apartheid.

In the French colonies, the trade union movement started as branches of the French trade unions, especially after 1944, when the freedom to organize trade unions was extended to the colonial territories. Here as elsewhere, the trade unions were soon linked to nationalist movements. In 1952, the unions in French West Africa called a general strike for the enactment of a forty-hour week, with a 20 percent increase in the hourly wage rates. The strike was totally effective throughout the colony, an unprecedented event, and it forced the French government to pass the bill. In 1955–56, the African unions severed their links with the French trade unions and constituted themselves as independent, African organizations.

In Asia, European immigration and colonization played a lesser role in the rise of the labor movement, although contacts between the Asian intelligentsia and European and American radicals influenced the direction of the early Asian labor movements. In Japan, the trade union movement emerged from radical intellectuals concerned with challenging an authoritarian regime, though the organizers of the early Japanese unions had gained their expertise by organizing Japanese workers in San Francisco with the AFofL. Sun Yat Sen, the leader of the Chinese democratic revolution of 1911, and other progressive Chinese intellectuals maintained friendly relations with the Second International. Chinese anarchist groups were in touch with their counterparts in Paris and Tokyo in the same period. Indonesian labor leaders learned their trade from Dutch unionists, while progressive Filipino intellectuals discovered socialism and anarcho-syndicalism in Spain in the late nineteenth century.

[...]

By the end of World War II, most European powers had given up their colonial empires, sometimes with destructive military rear-guard actions (France in Indochina and Algeria, the Netherlands in Indonesia, later Portugal in its African colonies). The labor movement in this "Third World" was initially strong, benefiting from its alliance with the liberation movements that formed the first postcolonial governments. In the 1950s and 1960s, however, the Cold War became the new global political reality. Each of the two superpowers deployed tremendous financial and political resources to control the labor movement in support of their respective blocs. The movement thus became polarized, and the position of those who tried to maintain an independent trade union movement based on class interest became very difficult. The contending blocs in the Cold War were trying to buy allies, thereby introducing widespread corruption.

Other factors contributed to the gradual erosion of the labor movement's position of strength. In Africa and Asia particularly, regimes that were initially democratic became tyrannical and authoritarian, confronting the labor movement in their countries with the choice of submission or repression. From the 1980s onward, the structural adjustment policies imposed by the international financial institutions all over the world undermined the public sector, and therefore an important membership base of the trade union movement.

Many Third World unions tried to maintain solidarity by forming regional organizations such as the Organization of African Trade Union Unity (OATUU), but because their member unions had for the most part become State-controlled, these regional organizations served mainly the political purposes of the governments that financed and controlled them. Much the same can be said for the European Trade Union Confederation (ETUC), which is largely dependent on the European Union for its budget.[4] The ideological basis of this new regional organization was a strong sense of European identity, which some perceived as European nationalism. This new, inward-looking orientation of many European unions strained relations between the ETUC, the ICFTU, and the GUFs. The ETUC includes the European Trade Union Federations (ETUF), which correspond largely to the GUFs in their jurisdictional scope. In some cases, two competing organizations reflecting internationalist or Europeanist priorities existed side by side and only unified after several years of protracted conflict.

European separatism also affected trade union positions when the European works councils (EWC) were formed by EU directive in 1994, wherein transnational corporations (TNC) are obliged to establish works councils in which workers are represented. Although hailed by unions as enforcing that corporations meet with representative bodies of their employees at least once a year, the directive is greatly inhibiting in that it only covers EU countries; defines the purpose of the EWCs as "information and consultation" (not negotiation); and does not refer to unions but to "workers' representatives" (who could be handpicked by management). The directive, however, also provides that the management and the workers can together negotiate changes.[5]

Thus, by the end of the twentieth century, the labor movement the world over had clearly been weakened by a series of political factors. However, the worst was yet to come, in the form of economic compulsions that were as devastating to workers' interests as they were widespread. The labor movement now had to face the onslaught of globalization.

[...]

Notes

1. The earliest battles of the labor movement were conducted to achieve universal suffrage as well as universal and free education, freedom of association, and a free press—in most countries via political power exercised through its own parties.
2. Lewis Lorwin, *The International Labor Movement: History, Policies, Outlook* (New York: Harper, 1953), 4.
3. The Jewish Labor Bund was destroyed as its entire membership (the Jewish working class in Poland, the occupied part of the USSR and in other Eastern European countries) was terminated.
4. Corinne Gobin, L'Europe Syndicale (Brussels: Editions Labor, 1997), 186.
5. European Trade Union Information Bulletin, no. 4/1994.

A longer version of this paper is available (or has appeared) on the website of the Global Labour Institute (www.global-labour.org), under 'International Labour Movement.

CHAPTER SEVEN

Labor Rights as Human Rights: Regulation in the Context of a "Thinned" National State

Gay W. Seidman

Source: Gay W. Seidman *Beyond the Boycott: Labor Rights, Human Rights, and Transnational Activism* (2007) 15–46 © 2007 American Sociological Association and Russell Sage Foundation—Reproduced with permission.

What does it mean to redefine labor rights as human rights? Transnational campaigns often try to mobilize global support by invoking universal standards rather than locally enforced labor law. But in the process, labor activists often abandon older labor strategies, which tended to focus on expanding definitions of citizenship and national regulation. In this chapter, I contrast an approach based on the human rights model—using consumer boycotts and privatized, voluntary regulatory schemes to raise labor standards—to the older, more state-centric approach, which emphasizes the construction of national labor law and industrial relations frameworks. What assumptions about power, voice, or targets are embedded in global campaigns to "name and shame" corporate violators, and how do these assumptions change the dynamics of local labor struggles? What has propelled the shift, and to what extent does it redefine the very content of labor campaigns?

These questions underlie a growing discussion among transnational activists about global governance and the construction of independent monitoring processes. In recent decades, scholars, policymakers, and activists have increasingly focused on voluntary regulatory schemes to protect labor rights, but they rarely stop to think through the assumptions involved in the strategy. What are the links between transnational campaigns, consumer boycotts, and new visions of global governance? Why have so many activists turned to stateless regulatory mechanisms rather than seeking to strengthen the national legal frameworks that have historically been the primary mechanism providing protection for citizens at work? What happens when activists turn their attention away from workplace negotiation to focus instead on mobilizing consumers to punish or reward multinational employers?

In an era when most national governments seem weaker than footloose multinational corporations, the international human rights movement and past examples of transnational consumer-based pressure on corporations seem to offer promising new directions for transnational campaigns. In this chapter, I interrogate this promise, hoping not to undermine efforts by transnational activists to find new approaches to organizing workers, but to provoke discussion: in the effort to create new support for workers' struggles, why do so many activists neglect or bypass local institutions designed to protect citizens, and what might be gained or lost as a result?

The "Thinned" National State

By the early twenty-first century, the state's centrality in discussions of labor rights seemed to have been blurred. In an increasingly integrated global economy, many labor activists and policymakers viewed states with skepticism and distrust. When increased capital mobility threatens economic stability and growth, when businesses can realistically threaten to pack up and move to a lower-wage site, and when politicians routinely express the fear that workplace intervention will undermine growth, how can states be relied on to protect citizens at work? This is the puzzle that confronts transnational labor activists: in a competitive global environment, when corporations can move or outsource production and states cannot be counted on, what regulatory mechanisms can be put in place to enforce labor protections?

Since the early 1980s, rapidly changing international economic policies and an increasingly competitive global market have altered the relationship between states, business, and labor, apparently undermining states' willingness to intervene in the workplace. Even in already industrialized countries, these pressures have eroded workers' protections (Bronfenbrenner and Hickey 2004; Golden and Pontusson 1992). In developing countries—where states were notoriously weak and corrupt and politicians viewed labor rights as balanced in a precarious trade-off with job creation and economic growth—what hope could labor activists place in a thinned national state?

From the mid-1970s, changing technologies, changing trade rules, and changing economic orthodoxies transformed corporate strategies, and global supply chains became the hallmark of transnational production. Corporate managers discovered that a more flexible approach to production could cut costs. Instead of owning a subsidiary outright and producing for a single national market, multinational corporations increasingly moved production toward a global assembly line: components of the final product might be made in one region, brought together for final assembly in another, and sold to consumers in still a third. At the same time, corporate managers began to restructure managerial relationships, relying increasingly on buying components from independently owned factories through subcontracting relationships that left the multinationals to emphasize design, advertising, and branding.

The flip side of the global supply chain was brutal competition on the shop floor. Viewing contracts with major multinationals as a way to gain access to wealthy global markets, small firms from Mauritius to Vietnam competed for contracts from big multinational labels—especially in relatively low-skilled manufacturing industries, such as apparel and toys, but increasingly in higher-skilled industries like automobiles and electronics as well (Gereffi and Korzeniewicz 1994; Herod 2001; Kaplinsky 2005; Kapstein 1999; Ruggie 1998; World Bank 1996). Relationships between multinationals, subcontractors, and the workers who actually produced the goods became increasingly attenuated (Collins 2003; Gereffi and Korzeniewicz 1994; Juárez Núñez and Babson 1998; Rosen 2002; Ross 2004). The "runaway shop"—a term originally coined to refer to garment factories that abandoned New York City's heavily unionized garment district for the more pliable non-unionized workers in small-town Pennsylvania (Wolensky, Wolensky, and Wolensky 2002)—now came to refer to factories that moved across international borders, beyond the reach of either union contracts or regulatory pressures.

This pattern was exacerbated by new economic theories and international institutions, which insisted that states in developing countries should seek to attract foreign investors as a strategy for increasing exports. By the mid-1990s, most economists and global policymakers agreed that economic growth required increased exports, and they urged developing countries to liberalize their economies. In the effort to expand exports, many states concentrated on attracting more investment, hoping that increased production would bring more jobs and economic growth (Babb 2001; Biersteker 1995; Evans 1997, 2000; Kapstein 1999; McMichael 2000; Stallings 1995; Stiglitz 2003; World Bank 1996).

The neoliberal "Washington Consensus" of the 1980s and 1990s constrained national governments—especially national governments in developing countries—in ways that have greatly diminished their capacity to regulate and control investment capital or provide social services to their citizens. Threats of capital flight and job loss often persuaded governments to back away from efforts to regulate business and also persuaded workers to accept more "flexible" labor regulations—giving employers greater flexibility to hire and fire workers, which makes any effort to demand collective bargaining rights at work even more risky for individual workers (Cook 2006). Even governments that had developed an institutional capacity to enforce domestic labor law—a capacity lacking in many developing countries—often explicitly waived labor laws for new investors, fearing that the threat of law enforcement might scare away the investors.

This pattern is most clearly visible in export-processing zones around the world, but it can even be seen in advanced industrialized countries. Writing about the United States, Human Rights Watch (2000, 10) concluded that, in the face of global competitive pressures, "workers' freedom of association is under sustained attack and the government is often failing its responsibility under international human rights standards . . . to protect workers' rights."

Of course, increased global trade holds some promise for developing countries as well as dangers. Optimists argue that in the long run the benefits will outweigh the cost: by spreading industrial growth around the world, globalization brings new jobs and skills and ultimately will benefit workers. An increasingly liberalized trade regime, it is argued, will push everyone to adopt more efficient, cheaper production processes; the combined effects of new trade rules and new production possibilities will stimulate countries to be more productive and to seek niches in which they may have a comparative advantage, creating greater economic growth around the globe. Countries that manage to attract new industrial investment may gain jobs for more skilled workers, with new opportunities for high-wage industrial employment and job creation. From this perspective, rigid labor laws could undermine economic growth by limiting countries' abilities to exploit their "comparative advantage"; the "high road" could lead to prosperity as skilled workers join with management to find new productive niches—new efficient production processes, new products, and new international markets. Optimists suggest that skilled and efficient workers will be able to demand higher wages, since employers depend on workers' participation in production, and that gradually the benefits will trickle out to the entire economy (Kapstein 1999; Moran 2002; World Bank 1996).

More skeptical analysts fear, however, that international competition narrows governments' and workers' options. First, economic restructuring—particularly the restructuring resulting from pressure on developing countries to open their markets and increase exports—has routinely involved massive layoffs in the large, often state-owned companies that served as the basis of industrial expansion for most late industrializers, undermining the relatively privileged core of many developing country labor movements (Candland and Sil 2001; Webster and Adler 2000). But even beyond the cold shock of restructuring, globalization could lead to a "race to the bottom" as companies search for cheap and acquiescent labor and developing countries compete for new investments by promising low wages and a stable, cheap workforce (Greider 1997; Lipietz 1987). Industrialized countries may be able to draw on historical assets to retain high-wage jobs—educated workforces, developed infrastructures and labor markets, and easy access to the world's wealthier consumers—but developing countries may have little choice but to offer low wages, low taxes, and limited regulation if they want to create jobs in the private sector (Moody 1997).

How do these new patterns of industrialization change workers' ability to demand better working conditions? New technologies have reorganized the geography of industrial production; they may involve new skills, and they certainly permit new managerial strategies. New technologies have allowed the spread of industrial production to new sites, stimulated the production of nontraditional commodities and products for export, and promoted increasing international competition. But even optimists acknowledge that new, sophisticated technologies have not always strengthened workers' ability to negotiate with employers. Workplaces may be organized to reduce the possibility that even skilled workers could disrupt production, and technologies that in the context of tight labor markets seem linked to greater trust and cooperation—in what is often called "post-Fordism"—may look meaner rather than leaner when embedded in authoritarian and hierarchical workplaces where there is abundant labor available (Juarez Núñez and Babson 1998; Kaplinsky 1995; McKay 2006; Posthuma 1995; Shaiken 1995). Even more importantly, most foreign investment does not involve sophisticated new technology or require skilled workers. Many export-processing zones simply bring old equipment to new, cheaper workers, especially in labor-intensive industries (Cowie 1999; Freeman 2000; Kaplinsky 1993); employers are often more interested in cutting labor costs than in finding cooperative workers.

When national governments are constrained by the threat of capital flight, labor cannot expect much support for expanding the enforcement of local labor law. Global competition seems to "thin" the national state, limiting states' ability to tax corporate profits, regulate corporate behavior, or protect workers from unfair labor practices. High tax rates could chase away investments, while higher wage bills undermine international competitiveness; indeed, global competition may erode state revenues in countries that already lack social services or infrastructures—further undermining any possibility that developing countries will educate workers to give them skills that might increase their bargaining power with employers or create any of the social security programs that characterize what Marshall calls "social" citizenship. When large multinational companies hold out a country's best hope for investment capital or technology transfer, even democratic states find it difficult to set terms or restrictions.

In a competitive environment, governments are often tempted to strike what Judith Tendler (2002) calls the "devil's deal," waiving basic health, safety, and labor rules in the hope that businesses will create jobs for more citizens—a tension especially obvious in thousands of export-processing zones, where government incentives range from tax breaks or export subsidies to explicit waivers of national labor laws and minimum wage levels (International Labor Organization 1997, 2003, 2006). Indeed, many governments put more resources into publishing brochures advertising their citizens' "nimble fingers" than into monitoring health and safety protections at work (see, for example, Lee 1998; Ong 1987; Ross 2003). From El Salvador to the Dominican Republic to the Philippines to China, governments have found themselves weighing labor law enforcement and corporate tax revenues against their desire to attract new jobs and new industries, repeatedly choosing to promote growth rather than protect citizens (Lee 1998; London 2003; Marmon 2003; McKay 2006; Ross 1997).

Needless to say, this "thinning" of the state's regulatory capacity is not what Karl Marx had in mind when he predicted the withering away of the state. But neoliberal development strategies have undermined state capacity for intervention at the workplace by creating a sense that states must choose between job creation and labor law enforcement or tax collection. Fearing that labor law enforcement might frighten away potential investors, states often choose jobs over regulation, leaving workers with few protections. Labor rights, though often written into law, are seldom enforced; inspectors rarely visit worksites and even more rarely impose fines or sanctions against abusive employers. Measuring the impact of increased global trade, Nita Rudra (2005, 30) concludes that while workers in poor countries "are experiencing greater economic gains (greater employment opportunities), they are not necessarily increasing their bargaining power with employers, [much less] with their government. The repercussions may be significant: labor-friendly policies (e.g., higher wages, national welfare programs, employment benefits, political freedoms, etc.) will be inconceivable in poor nations undergoing globalization."

How should organized labor respond? If an increasingly competitive global economy has transformed management strategies and limited state capacity for enforcement of national laws, it has also created new dilemmas for unions. If labor militancy might frighten away investors and reduce employment levels, how should unions define or defend their members' interests? Even well-established labor movements have struggled to find new bases of solidarity or support to sustain union efforts, responding to the threat of capital flight by urging members to cooperate with employers to meet the global challenge (Adler and Webster 2000; Candland and Sil 2001; Clawson 2003; Golden and Pontusson 1992; Gupta 1998; Heller 1999; Milkman 1997; Moody 1997; Silver 2003; von Holdt 2000).

In a context where states back away from protecting citizens and unions worry that strikes might drive away investors and jobs, what can transnational labor activists do? During the 1990s, many labor activists turned away from traditional strategies, looking for new vulnerabilities created by the logic of the global market. In the late 1990s more and more transnational activists turned to nonstate actors in the search for new nodes of pressure.

Boycotts: A Global Strategy

Might a changing global environment offer possibilities as well as constraints? While national states and organized labor may everywhere be weaker than they were in the middle of the twentieth century, the human rights movement offers an inspiring example of how global activism can change national and international policies. In the absence of both international and national mechanisms to prevent abusive work conditions, could a global labor movement imitate the successes of recent human rights campaigns, linking consumers separated by borders and oceans—as well as barriers of language and culture—to those who work in export-processing zones, using consumer pressure to reward companies that comply with basic labor standards and punishing those that fail?

To many labor sympathizers, the underlying problem—global corporate pressure and weak states—suggests an obvious alternative. By the late 1990s, labor activists had begun to explore strategies based in the dynamics of market-driven globalization. Rather than emphasizing citizenship, these transnational strategies sought to find points of entry in the structure of global production, using international consumer pressure to target global supply chains—the complicated networks of suppliers, subcontractors, producers, and retailers through which goods are made, assembled, and sold. Instead of trying to fight global integration, this strategy involves trying to understand—and redefine—the dynamics of globalization itself.

It is worth noting that stateless strategies differ more than many activists recognize from the strategies deployed by international human rights groups. Human rights activists do frequently work outside state systems, mobilizing networks of concerned individuals to provide evidence and write to abusive governments, but states are always crucially involved, both as targets and as instruments of transnational activism. Human rights activists seek to apply direct pressure to authoritarian states through the "naming and shaming" process, and they view democratic states as potential allies, asking these governments to use whatever diplomatic leverage they can muster to put pressure on authoritarian states. In less egregious cases, campaigns to protect human rights on the ground almost inevitably work through national states, seeking to construct democratic national institutions that will protect citizens rather than permit abuse. Although the human rights movement may draw its inspiration and energy from networks of principled individuals, those networks almost invariably work with, and through, national states.

By contrast, transnational labor activists often treat national states, especially in developing economies, as irrelevant and weak, focusing instead on corporations as the key actors of globalization. These activists argue that as production and consumption become geographically divided, and as governments lose any capacity to regulate powerful multinationals, global activism needs to find new points of vulnerability and new sources of pressure.

For many activists, global consumer boycotts appear the most logical way to force companies to respect workers' rights. Consumer boycotts, of course, predate corporate globalization: campaigns to build solidarity beyond the workplace through consumer campaigns have a long history. As proponents argue, successful consumer boycotts have helped make distant grievances visible to broad audiences, creating a community of concern far beyond the local workplace. In the 1790s, British antislavery activists refused to take sugar in their tea while slaves worked on sugar plantations, and perhaps as many as half a million people in England stopped drinking "the blood-sweetened beverage" (Hochschild 2005, 193; Robert Southey, quoted in Hochschild 2005, 194). Some two hundred years later, the United Farm Workers publicized the conditions of migrant workers in California's fields through a national boycott of table grapes; the boycott mobilized widespread support for labor law reform, and American laws were rewritten to give farmworkers basic collective bargaining rights. If the sugar boycott "caught people's imagination because it brought [hidden] ties to light, laying bare the dramatic, direct connection between British daily life and that of slaves" (Hochschild 2005, 194), the grape boycott vividly reminded middle-class Americans of how agricultural workers lived and worked, giving sympathizers across the country an easy way to demonstrate their support with the striking farmworkers.

Appeals to consumers resonate, too, with the history of national labor relations frameworks. Around the world, striking workers have appealed for support from a moral community on the basis of a shared humanity—as, for instance, when a community of Irish peasants refused to pay their rent to an abusive landlord named Charles Cunningham Boycott, giving rise to the noun. Today transnational activists seek to build a broader sense of community, forcing consumers to consider the conditions under which goods are produced, no matter how far away. In an increasingly global market, consumers may need reminding that they share a community with workers spread across the globe. Just as distance allows corporate decisionmakers to ignore the human consequences of cost-cutting policies, it permits consumers to overlook the conditions under which goods are produced. Jane Collins (2003) suggests that transnational activists need to build a sense of "moral accountability" by reminding consumers to consider the lives of the people who produce the goods they consume. By publicizing accounts of unacceptable conditions in far-off factories and appealing to consumers to boycott products made under inhumane conditions, activists hope to make the problem visible. If globalization has stretched the distances between workers and consumers, boycotts can publicize grievances and pressure corporations, helping build new transnational awareness and a sense of shared humanity across borders.

Historically, even famously successful consumer boycotts constitute only one tactic within larger campaigns. Thus, for example, middle-class women called on fellow American consumers in the mid-twentieth century to support workers' efforts to organize, arguing that they had a moral responsibility to help improve the conditions under which the clothes for their families were sewn; organizers were more concerned, however, with raising awareness than with actually enforcing codes of conduct (Boris 2003; Cohen 2003; Frank 1999).

By contrast, many transnational campaigns of the early twenty-first century seem more focused on forcing companies to comply with corporate codes of conduct by exploiting corporate sensitivity to threats to "their most valuable asset: their carefully cultivated brand image" (Rodriguez-Garavito 2005b, 74). Oddly enough, there is surprisingly little concrete evidence that even widely publicized campaigns have a significant impact on corporate profits. For example, because companies refuse to comment publicly, there is no public information about the extent to which sales were affected by either the widely publicized Nestle boycott of the 1970s (provoked by the company's advertising tactics for its baby formula, which were seen as undermining poor mothers' commitment to breast-feeding) or the 1990s campaign against Nike shoes (provoked by the labor and environmental practices of the company's subcontractors). As Dana Frank (1999) shows in her insightful history of "buy American" campaigns, even active efforts by retailers to attract ethical consumers seem rarely to have altered spending habits.

Most activists recognize that while consumer boycotts place some pressure on corporations, the impact on sales is hard to determine. Some go so far as to suggest that the privatized nature of consumption choices does not lend itself to public acts of protest. James Jasper (1997, 264) writes that consumer boycotts "can express a moral stance. But they never do so very articulately or forcefully. *A silent choice, made alone, in the aisle of a crowded supermarket, is a poor way to sustain a sense of injustice and indignation*" (emphasis in original).

Consumer boycotts are clearly a complicated strategy, one limited in scope and fraught with risks. Consumer pressure tends to be most effective when applied to well-known logos, easily identifiable products, or goods produced in specific countries. Most goods produced in export-processing zones are not easily identifiable and thus are not vulnerable to transnational boycotts. Even ethical consumers—certainly a small part of the global market—balk at boycotts of goods they consider necessities; it is much easier to persuade consumers to support a boycott if the goods involved are luxuries, or ones for which there are easy substitutes, than to ask them to engage in real sacrifice.

Boycotts across borders may be even more complicated. Not only are most goods not vulnerable to transnational consumer pressure, but developing country unionists have repeatedly warned that transnational consumer boycotts could reinforce global hierarchies. Global boycotts work only for some products; most goods—especially those produced in rural areas for domestic markets—are never exported and thus are not subject to transnational campaigns, no matter how bad the conditions under which they are produced. Further, as many developing country activists note, a strategy that puts decisionmaking power in the hands of wealthy consumers in North America and Europe carries the risk that those consumers, rather than workers in developing countries, will make key decisions about which labor rights matter and which factories will be targeted (Ali 1996). Consumer campaigns carry other risks for workers too: wealthy consumers lose nothing if a company goes bankrupt, but workers risk losing their jobs (Ali 1996; Bickham Mendez 2005; Brooks 2007; Esbenshade 2004). Just as corporate executives often worry that a badly researched activist campaign might unfairly punish companies that are energetically trying to improve conditions at a problematic factory, labor activists around the world discuss their fear that a successful consumer campaign might lead to a factory's closing just when workers are on the verge of winning trade union recognition. And, even if international consumers respond to workers' concerns, activists frequently debate when to end a campaign; who should decide whether a situation has improved enough to call off consumer pressure (Bullert 2000)?

Nevertheless, transnational consumer campaigns clearly threaten corporate images—to such an extent that policymakers and scholars have begun to incorporate these campaigns into their thinking about the long-term effects of global economic integration. Most importantly, transnational campaigns can increase global awareness of the conditions under which goods are produced. Campaigns by groups like Oxfam, Global Exchange, and the Ethical Trading Initiative have clearly raised consumers' awareness of the impact of global competition on the daily lives of workers, their families, and their communities. Even economists who firmly insist that increased trade will eventually benefit all regions of the world recognize that transnational campaigns matter. Economist Pietra Rivoli (2005, 214–15), for example, argues that the "moral case for trade [is] even more compelling [than] the economic one," but she ends her discussion of how trade helps by urging an imaginary student activist to continue to publicize corporate exploitation because "Nike, Adidas, and GAP need her to keep watching, and so do Wal-Mart and the Chinese government . . . Future generations of sweatshop workers and cotton farmers need her as well."

Transnational activists seek to create a sense of moral accountability in order to create global pressure on corporations. In response, some major corporations have made sincere efforts to improve working conditions, either because they fear that transnational campaigns may tarnish their image and hurt their sales, or because they recognize the validity of activists' concerns. But before turning to activist efforts to deploy consumer boycotts as a means to regulate multinational corporations, I want to examine the issues that have attracted transnational consumer attention and compare them to the kinds of issues that have motivated more traditional labor campaigns.

Labor Rights as Human Rights

What rights do transnational activists hope to protect through consumer pressure, and which rights matter most? Through the 1990s, much as feminist activists since about 1980 have viewed international treaties as tools for changing national state obligations toward their citizens (Brown-Thomson 2002), many transnational labor activists viewed campaigns against corporations as a starting point for raising global awareness and sought to redefine international norms against which to measure local conditions. But appeals to international audiences also often involved a subtle shift in the kinds of grievances stressed. To mobilize international audiences, activists cannot emphasize the mundane or prosaic. Dramatic images of child workers and wretched working conditions are meant to provoke sympathy and outrage, persuading consumers that they would prefer to pay more for goods produced in safer, more dignified, more humane conditions.

The appeal for protection of innocent victims has deep roots. From the eighteenth century, David Brion Davis (1992, 23) writes, Western writers popularized "an ethic of benevolence" in which "the man of sensibility needed to objectify his virtue by relieving the sufferings of innocent victims." This ethic required, of course, that beneficiaries of altruistic acts be conceived as victims. Early antislavery activists offered as the iconic image of their campaign a kneeling black man asking plaintively, "Am I not a man and a brother?", evoking sympathy for an injured innocent, Adam Hochschild (2005, 128) notes, rather than offering a figure of heroic resistance or even an African on his home soil. Similarly, Keck and Sikkink (1998, 27) point out that the images that have inspired some of the most outstanding transnational campaigns revolve around the protection of innocent, vulnerable victims, usually from egregious physical harm:

> As we look at the issues around which transnational advocacy networks have organized most effectively, we find two issue characteristics that appear most frequently: (1) issues involving bodily harm to vulnerable individuals, especially when there is a short and clear causal chain (or story) assigning responsibility; and (2) issues involving legal equality of opportunity.

Transnational activists tend to frame appeals in terms of helplessness and vulnerability, insisting that only international intervention can prevent abuses so extreme that any decent human being would accept the need for social change. Most successful transnational labor campaigns of the late twentieth century—the anti-apartheid campaign, the Nestle campaigns, the campaigns against child labor and against forced or prison labor—have been framed in terms that fit more easily within a discourse of human rights violations and victimization than one that stresses workers' labor rights or making workers' voices more audible. Apparently, appeals to broad universal concerns—often based on vivid, dramatic images of bodily harm to workers or violent repression—evoke far more international response than appeals based on the kind of procedural or detailed grievances that arise in most workplaces over issues like low wages or forced overtime.

By the late 1990s, labor activists seeking to confront globalization responded to the apparent success of the international human rights movement by adopting both its rhetoric and its strategies; activists and policymakers began to talk about "labor rights as human rights," framing labor rights within a human rights paradigm. To most transnational activists this shift is logical and easy, since they view labor rights as fundamental to human rights and see workers' exploitation as egregious. But in seeking to appeal to broader audiences, activists frequently offer workers' "testimonials" bearing witness to egregious violations. Accounts of suffering or deprivation stemming from abuse or the neglect of basic human needs, like hunger, exhaustion, or exploitation in an authoritarian workplace, are far more likely to provoke international support than a dry discussion of labor laws (see, for example, Featherstone and United Students Against Sweatshops 2002; Ross 1997). Seeking international support, transnational campaigns regularly frame appeals in terms that are instantly recognizable: physical violation, discrimination, and coercion are all linked to violations of basic human rights. Such claims demand redress; international intervention in such circumstances has been legitimized by several decades of changing attitudes toward universal norms.

Campaigns seeking to mobilize transnational networks of sympathetic consumers who are willing to act on information about corporate misdeeds by boycotting products often emphasize workers' victimization rather than the construction of channels for negotiation or bargaining. In her examination of several transnational labor campaigns in the 1990s, Ethel Brooks (2003) argues that reframing workers as victims can become itself a victimizing process, turning activist workers into international symbols for solidarity campaigns. In a more detailed case study, Brooks (2005) suggests that activists in a transnational campaign against child labor in Bangladesh's garment industry recognized that a focus on child workers would appeal to a broad audience; such a focus united diverse interests in a coalition that included people concerned about the exploitation of innocent victims and American activists seeking to protect jobs for adults in the United States; the use of images of child workers avoided some of the thornier problems that plague international labor solidarity.

Does the search for images that evoke international sympathy shift labor's focus from the effort to strengthen workers' voices to the creation of images that demand sympathy? Historically, labor campaigns emphasized workers' dignity and strength; unions have sought to create channels through which workers could articulate their own grievances. By contrast, in the effort to gain international audiences' sympathy for victims, most transnational campaigns present workers as victims who are vulnerable to "global pillage" and dependent on outside support—much as international human rights campaigns have done. Only visible, egregious violations of labor rights are likely to evoke international sympathy or mobilize international audiences. As Brooks (2005) points out, appeals based on protecting victims tend to avoid issues of empowerment; these campaigns often appeal on behalf of the voiceless, claiming protection for victims rather than insisting on the right of citizens and workers to negotiate on their own behalf.

To put it bluntly, in the effort to reach transnational consumers, these campaigns may be more likely to help workers "bear witness" and gain international sympathy than to negotiate with managers on their own behalf. Indeed, many business ethicists view codes in precisely this light—as a way to protect the voiceless. For example, Lisa Nelson (2000, 277) suggests that codes should embody a corporate commitment to protecting the "mute victims—the refugee, the tribesman, and the land itself"; echoing Dr. Seuss's repentant capitalist, the lorax, she asks, "Who will speak for the trees?" It is, of course, easier to imagine intervening on behalf of help-less victims than designing a strategy for creating new collective bargaining processes in far-off regions of the world, but is there a tension between creating a voice for workers and creating global sympathy for their cause? Does speaking out to protect local workers impede the creation of new channels through which they could speak on their own behalf?

In the mid-1990s, the ILO displayed a version of this tension in its decision to focus on "core labor rights," a set of universal labor principles designed to attract global attention to egregious violations of labor rights. For most of the twentieth century, the ILO sought to persuade member states to incorporate labor rights into their legal codes and asked them to ratify the conventions drawn up by international conferences (Charnovitz 2000; Gould 2003; Leary 1996; Weisband 2000). In 1998, however, the ILO turned to a new strategy: constructing a global standard for labor rights that would be simple and universal rather than specific, multifaceted, or enforced through national legal institutions (see, for example, ILO 1997, 1998a, 2001, 2003). Apparently, the ILO's shift came in direct response to concerns that global integration was undermining local labor law enforcement: when a ministerial meeting of the World Trade Organization (WTO) in 1996 refused to include labor standards in trade rules, arguing that labor standards could be used for "protectionist purposes" and insisting "that the comparative advantage of countries, particularly low-wage developing countries, must in no way be put into question" (World Trade Organization 1996), the WTO asked the ILO to develop core labor standards to prevent a race to the bottom.

Thus, the ILO began to develop an internationally recognized, easily understandable set of core labor rights: freedom of association and recognition of a right of collective bargaining; elimination of all forms of forced or compulsory labor; effective abolition of child labor; and elimination of employment and occupation discrimination (ILO 1998a; see also Howse 1999; Langille 1999). In 1998 the ILO conference approved a new "Declaration on Fundamental Principles and Rights at Work," describing the core obligations meant to be binding on all member governments. Imitating a human rights approach that holds national governments up to a universal standard, the ILO also moved away from stressing national ratification of ILO conventions. Because the new declaration suggests that ILO membership entails obligations regarding core labor principles, most international legal analysts agree that the new approach "represents in itself a very significant, if not revolutionary, step" (Francis Maupain, cited in Charnovitz 2000, 8; see also Alston 2006).

Yet the ILO's shift to core labor principles may redirect the attention of labor activists to the kinds of labor violations most likely to appeal to transnational audiences, so as to evoke sympathy and concern beyond the small networks of principled individuals already committed to publicizing labor grievances (Compa 2000). Coerced labor, discrimination, and child labor all involve immediate physical harm to relatively powerless victims. The ordinary workplace grievances experienced more frequently in workplaces around the world are less dramatic and perhaps demand less immediate attention. While the ILO's shift to core principles may strengthen its ability to intervene in extreme cases—such as the 2002 ILO call for global sanctions against Myanmar 's military government for its widespread use of forced labor (Olsen 2002; ILO 1998b)—it may also prompt the "international community" to overlook more commonplace labor grievances.

Even where this discursive shift—reframing labor rights as human rights and focusing on egregious bodily harm—does not reduce real workers to victims, it may narrow the definition of labor violations, especially by undermining a historic emphasis on strengthening workers' voices. While the ILO's core labor principles include the right to free association—a right that, if honored, empowers workers to organize their own unions or staff associations, through which they can raise ordinary grievances—the principle remains somewhat ambiguous.

The right to free association is almost as difficult to define and implement as it is to police. Most common violations of collective bargaining rights are relatively invisible and hard to prove: for instance, workers blacklisted for union organizing attempts, employers' failure to permit union elections, or employers declaring bankruptcy (while reopening next door under a different name) to forestall union recognition. None of these violations involve the kind of egregious bodily harm that might attract global attention. Transnational activists acknowledge that the most serious obstacles to collective bargaining generally involve unfair dismissals, especially among employers who blacklist or fire union activists. But when transnational movements seek to mobilize international support, their first step is usually to look for more visible indications of harm, with physical markers of exploitation and abuse. Most workers who are brought to speak to international audiences generally tell stories reflecting more immediate, physical concerns—those revolving around underage workers, coercion, or physical harm. Indeed, it is no exaggeration to suggest that these testimonies often come closer to "bearing witness" to violations of human rights than to discussing strategies for organizing workers in export-processing zones. Just as private corporate codes of conduct are far more likely to mention the ILO's other core standards than to include consideration of collective bargaining rights (Jenkins 2002), labor activists appealing to global audiences may be tempted to stress traumatic violations of the ILO's more human rights-based core principles—bans on child labor, forced labor, and discriminatory practices—than more complicated, less visible violations (see Blanpain 2000).

Finally, transnational pressures sometimes overlook local concerns. most transnational labor activists are committed to the goals of empowering local workers and forcing multinational corporations to recognize and negotiate with local unions, yet those goals remain remarkably elusive. Examples of transnational campaigns that have successfully strengthened local unions are hard to find. Around the world, local trade unionists express strong suspicions of transnational campaigns, viewing consumer boycotts as potentially undermining local efforts to organize workers. Although this hostility may simply reflect local jealousies and turf battles, the recurrent pattern suggests that something more important is at stake: transnational campaigns may find it difficult to construct viable channels for workers' voices. Indeed, workers' voices are frequently absent from monitoring schemes, and nongovernmental groups rarely create processes through which transnational activists might become accountable to workers (Bandy and Bickham Mendez 2003; Bickham Mendez 2005; Esbenshade 2004, 145–77; Frundt 2005).

Even with the best of intentions, the international community is ill equipped to ascertain the legitimacy of workers' organizations or to distinguish unions that provide real avenues of expression for workers' concerns from authoritarian corporatist bodies that restrict workers' participation; the history of international efforts to support unions across borders is replete with manipulation, tainted by national governments' foreign policy concerns and protectionist impulses (Bergquist 1996; Gordon 2000; Herod 2001). Union-to-union cross-border labor alliances have been complicated by outsiders' multiple agendas: transnational labor alliances often reflect domestic agendas rather than responses to workers' immediate concerns (Khor 1994; see also Ali 1996).

And of course, transnational campaigns become especially complicated when they try to intercede in complex negotiations between employers, unions, and local government officials.

All too frequently, when transnational campaigns pressure a single factory or company to recognize a union, the employer simply closes up shop; sometimes the company reopens under a new name, but the original workers are left unemployed. As Heather Williams (2003, 527) concludes, "While much optimism remained among labor and human rights activists about the potential of transnational networks to meet the labor challenges presented by the rapid relocation of manufacturing to ever lower wage markets, a number of stunning and brutal defeats in recent years have served as cautionary notes in drawing conclusions about the direction of citizen action."

Global Governance

Once global attention has been mobilized, how well can it be deployed in support of international labor standards? Can consumer pressure really be used to enforce voluntary codes of conduct? In discussions of global governance, success tends to be defined in terms of enforcement: how can activists construct regulatory schemes that would persuade "bad" companies as well as "good" ones to improve work conditions? What kinds of enforcement across borders might prompt heedless employers to provide better conditions, pay higher wages, or permit workers to organize unions or engage in collective bargaining?

The need for enforcement mechanisms is almost self-evident. Activists, scholars, and policymakers agree that while voluntary systems of compliance may persuade some companies to meet high standards, corporate actors facing a competitive environment are tempted to cut corners. An entirely voluntary enforcement system permits free-riding, and market pressures almost inevitably push corporations to "play for the gray," appearing to comply with standards while effectively avoiding them (Braithwaite 2002). Studies of voluntary regulatory frameworks across companies, industries, and countries have repeatedly demonstrated the limits of persuasion (Ayres and Braithwaite 1992; Esbenshade 2004; Guthman 2004; Mamic 2004). Even if well-intentioned companies adopt and implement voluntary corporate codes of conduct (see, for example, Mamic 2004), there are always some managers for whom voluntary codes are little more than a public relations exercise, a strategy for staving off public pressure. Without some mechanism to monitor compliance, and without some threat that violations will be noticed and punished, actors in a market environment have strong incentives to evade compliance (Compa 2001; Compa and Darricarrere 1996; Posner and Nolan 2003; Schoenberger 2000; Wells 1998).

But who should monitor compliance, and how? Again, most discussions of transnational labor monitoring in the early twenty-first century embrace a vision of workplace regulation that bypasses the national state. Distrusting the contradictory motives of states in a competitive global economy, many scholars and activists assume that mobilized consumers and nongovernmental groups make more reliable allies than governments. If the world is viewed in terms of a dichotomous distinction between states and civil society, the underlying problem—weak states—suggests an obvious alternative. Michael Santoro (2003, 102) summarizes the broad consensus that emerged at the turn of the century among activists, policymakers, and scholars:

> In developing countries the competition to attract foreign capital and corruption both contribute to lax enforcement of local labor laws in a phenomenon that some have called a "race to the bottom." At the same time that national governments have failed to regulate global labor practices of [multinational enterprises, or MNEs], international institutions have yet to acquire sufficient power and global support to do so . . .

NGOs, along with labor unions, have stepped into the power vacuum to become the most conspicuous and vociferous critics of MNEs on labor and human rights. NGOs, by default, are the primary channel for exerting pressure on MNEs to meet this moral obligation.

Activists argue that as production and consumption become geographically divided, and as governments in developing countries fail to control powerful multinationals, global activism needs to identify new points of vulnerability and new sources of pressure. Especially since the collapse of the statist regimes of Eastern Europe, social movement activists have embraced "civil society" (defined largely by the absence of state involvement) as the primary sphere for citizens' interaction, and they have come to view nongovernmental groups and privatized, market-based programs as more credible, more reliable, and often more effective than governmental institutions (Somers 1999). NGOs gather information and publicize local conditions, holding local behavior accountable to global norms of environmental protection, women's rights, and human rights (Bandy and Smith 2003; della Porta, Kriesi, and Rucht 1999; Guidry, Kennedy, and Zald 2000 ; Khagram, Riker, and Sikkink 2002; Sikkink 2002; Smith and Johnston 2002; Tarrow 2005); transnational activists often assume that protecting global labor rights should be similarly built on nongovernmental processes (see, for example, Hartman, Arnold, and Wokutch 2003; Kidder 2002). Tim Bartley (2003, 441) writes, "As NGOs experienced repeated defeats in international arenas, they put more energy and resources into developing nongovernmental programs"—a shift that dovetailed with "government [support for] private programs that were immune to rules about international trade."

This nonstate approach has attracted prominent critics, of course. Transnational activists frequently note NGOs' limited capacity for monitoring or enforcement, as well as their limited accountability to workers and governments. Labor law experts remind activists that states have historically been central to enforcement of rights at work (Arthurs 2004; Murray 2003), while many activists recognize that non-state actors have trouble gaining access to work sites. Scott Nova, the widely respected founding executive director of the Workers' Rights Consortium (WRC), suggests that a nongovernmental group Like the WRC is better positioned to publicize workers' grievances through international networks than to try to mount a regular monitoring program (Scott Nova interview, 2004). In contrast to many global campaigns, the WRC has taken what is sometimes described as a "fire-alarm" approach: using publicity to raise consumer awareness about abuses rather than claiming to certify that specific manufacturers have complied with global codes (O'Rourke 2003, 19).

Yet in discussions of transnational strategies, the turn away from the state remains a persistent theme. Since the mid-1990s, a series of global initiatives have claimed to provide credible information about global manufacturing conditions. Despite their many differences in standards, reporting, funding, and corporate sponsorship, all these groups—including the Fair Labor Association (FLA), Social Accountability International (SA8000), Worldwide Responsible Apparel Production (WRAP), the Ethical Trading Initiative (ETI), the Clean Clothes Campaign, and the Fair Wear Foundation—reflect deep suspicion of state willingness or capacity to protect workers. Dara O'Rourke (2003, 5) notes the irony:

> Many transnational activists have historically been extremely suspicious of market mechanisms, weakening state roles, and privatized regulation. However, for groups interested in strengthening the enforcement of labor standards, nongovernmental regulation is attractive as a supplemental system of monitoring and enforcement. Increasingly influential NGOs are thus advancing market-oriented, nongovernmental standards and monitoring systems as a supplement to state regulation in countries where it is ineffective and as a new point of leverage over firms operating globally, The turn to "voluntary private initiatives" reflects, in large

measure, the realities of international power: lacking a set of global institutions through which to design and enforce new rules, most policy-makers and activists emphasize cooperation rather than coercion.

Certainly, many activists and policymakers turn to market-based approaches to labor rights more out of desperation than out of any conviction that consumer-based campaigns offer an easy alternative.

Like social movement activists, many distinguished scholars began in the 1990s to rethink strategies through which businesses might be regulated, even in already industrialized countries. Partly in response to political discussions of deregulation and privatization throughout the industrialized world, a new approach to regulation emerged, stressing the importance of cooperation between "stakeholders" rather than punitive sanctions and coercion. Hoping to avoid the authoritarian excesses that often marred state oversight in the past, while also hoping that regulatory frameworks might be more responsive to rapidly changing conditions, many policymakers sought to replace coercive rules with privatized monitoring frameworks built on flexibility, learning, and responsive regulation rather than punitive measures (Picciotto 2002).

Many of these schemes rested on the participation of nongovernmental groups and private agencies, often viewed as the expression of "global civil society" and vaguely assumed to be acting on more credible information, propelled by more altruistic motives, and holding actors accountable to more universalistic standards than more self-interested national states. Thoughtful analysts regularly remind their readers that "soft" regulatory processes can coexist with more state-centric enforcement processes, but this vision—involving horizontal networks of policymakers, bureaucrats, and transnational activists developing new rules that would transcend national borders and gaining compliance through monitoring and transnational campaigns—became increasingly accepted as basic to a "new world order" (Sikkink 2002; Slaughter 2004). Nonstate transnational networks seemed especially appropriate for regulating cross-border problems, from pollution and deforestation to water rights and agricultural change (Bartley 2003; Commission on Global Governance 1995; Slaughter 2004).

This vision of "soft" regulation-by-monitoring first emerged in discussions of domestic regulation: legal and business scholars suggested that policymakers seek to promote voluntary compliance through a framework that stressed mutual learning and efforts to attain mutually desirable goals. Acknowledging that corporate self-regulation alone has often failed to produce socially responsible behavior, Ian Ayres and John Braithwaite (1992, 101–32) proposed what they called "enforced self-regulation": by enlisting management to write rules, they argued, states could create regulatory systems that would enlist managers' participation to ensure compliance and be more responsive to a rapidly changing business environment.

It is important to note, however, that most discussions of regulation-by-monitoring assume that voluntary self-regulation will be backed by state enforcement in domestic settings. Ayres and Braithwaite (1992, 129), for example, noted that small and medium-sized businesses—more fly-by-night, more vulnerable to competitive pressures, or less visible to consumers—would always have to be policed by national government inspectors, since their low profit margins are likely to tempt them to cut corners. Yet when these schemes are proposed as a mechanism for international regulation, enforcement is left entirely to ethical consumers overseas. When Ayres and Braithwaite propose flexible monitoring for international corporate regulation, their discussion of enforcement seems based on faith rather than evidence. Taking as their model the transnational campaign against Nestle marketing practices, monitored by transnational activists and enforced by a consumer boycott, they suggest, "With an international regulatory problem and in the absence of an international regulatory agency, [public-interest groups] acted as a proxy for the state to give effect to enforced regulation" (Ayres and Braithwaite 1992, 132).

Like Ayres and Braithwaite, other scholars in the 1990s viewed transnational consumer-based campaigns as the basis for new forms of global regulation. Often citing as positive examples the Sullivan Principles in South Africa or the Rugmark Foundation in India (see, for example, Braithwaite and Drahos 2000, 254–55; Sethi and Steidlmeier 1991; Waddock 2002; Williams 2000a, 2000b), most of these proposals linked corporate self-regulation, independent monitoring by civil society groups, and international consumer pressure. Proponents of this new form of business regulation laid a new stress on corporate social responsibility as business leaders and ethicists began to argue that corporations do best when they incorporate ethical concerns into their business practices.

In the mid-1960s, corporate leaders had frequently insisted that their only concern should be profits and that their only goal should be raising shareholders' dividends. By the late 1990s, in part because of experiences with transnational campaigns like the anti-apartheid movement and the Nestle campaign, business leaders were much more likely to accept some level of social responsibility in the communities where they did business. That shift in business discourse opened new avenues for cooperation—if managers were more willing to police themselves, and if public pressure could ensure that violations carried real costs, then privatized, voluntary regulatory schemes began to seem more plausible. Further, these proposals reflected a larger epistemological shift, suggesting a prominent role for civil society and nongovernmental organizations rather than a state-centered vision.

Thus, for example, Archon Fung, Dara O'Rourke, and Charles Sabe (2001) suggest that corporate codes of conduct and consumer campaigns could provide the basis for "ratcheting labor standards" upwards by combining independent monitors and international consumer pressure to enforce corporate social responsibility. While major corporations could begin to "benchmark" best practices, they suggest, alert consumers could demand ever more stringent monitors. It is worth quoting from their conclusion at length to give the full flavor of their approach:

Even as contemporary globalization makes us complicit in terrible abuses of workers, it opens up new possibilities for public action to mitigate these wrongs. These possibilities come from the increasing capabilities of corporations—under the pressure of public revulsion at their social practices—to improve workplace conditions through the same sophisticated management strategies that make them champions of the current globalization in the first place.

We have argued that the best way to exploit these possibilities is through a new kind of labor regulations—Ratcheting Labor Standards—that relies on information, competition, and the participation of not only regulators and firms but also workers, consumers, journalists, investors, NGOs, and the public at large. RLS promises labor standards that are feasible because they are based on actual best practices, and non-protectionist because they take into account differences in contexts of economic development. These labor standards, moreover, join the limited enforcement power of government to the potentially great disciplinary forces of social pressure and market competition. They aim, finally, not at establishing a minimum fixed set of core workplace rights, but rather at creating a process that makes workplaces as good as they can be and better over time, as companies become more capable and nations more developed. (Fung et al. 2001, 38–39)

Proposals such as this are not simply academic exercises. Searching for new systems of global governance, key international institutions have begun to try to enlist corporate managers and transnational consumers to prevent the race to the bottom. In 1999 Kofi Annan launched a United Nations initiative called the "Global Compact," building on principles much like those embodied in the "ratcheting labor standards" scheme: by bringing together major multinational corporations, trade unions, and nongovernmental groups, the Global Compact hopes "to generate consensus-based understandings of how a company's commitment to [human rights and labor and environmental principles] can be translated effectively into corporate management practices" (Ruggie 2003, 111). These multinationals would teach by example; John Ruggie (2003, 108), a distinguished scholar and active participant in the Compact, suggests optimistically "the adoption of good practices by major firms may exert an upward pull on the performance of local enterprises in the same sector."

Like the Global Compact, international proposals for voluntary regulatory schemes tend to rely far more heavily on social pressure, including monitoring by nongovernmental organizations, than on sanctions or enforcement through external regulatory agencies. Where discussions of regulation within national borders generally assume that internal monitoring schemes will be backed by national state enforcement, that question is left hanging in international proposals. Fung, O'Rourke, and Sabel (2001) point vaguely to large international institutions (primarily the World Bank, with a nod to the International Labor Organization) as potential repositories of information about monitors and corporations; similarly, Braithwaite and Drahos (2000, 255) suggest that corporate monitoring capacities could be linked to the ILO's reporting capacities, but the only concrete enforcement mechanism they suggest involves "taking corporate abuses to mass publics." The UN's Global Compact is perhaps even more voluntaristic; Ruggie (2003, 108) notes that it has thus far depended entirely on consumer pressure, since firms' decisions to engage with the compact are "driven . . . above all by the sensitivity of their corporate brands to consumer attitudes." Ruggie adds: "The Compact is not a code of conduct but a social learning network. It operates on the premise that socially legitimated good practices will help drive out bad ones through the power of transparency and competition" (113).

This stateless vision is echoed in activists' proposals, which regularly invoke independent monitoring as the basis for alerting consumers to corporate misconduct. The call for independent monitoring is reflected, for example, in the campaign against Nike's global production practices. Typically, activists considered the giant footwear corporation's agreement to "include non-governmental organizations in its factory monitoring" and make those monitors' reports available to the public "the most important of [Nike CEO Philip] Knight's promises" in 1998—although some concluded three years later that the company's subsequent monitoring efforts were in fact woefully inadequate (Connor 2001, 2, 44–51). Similarly, in 2004 Oxfam urged consumers to buy fair trade-labeled products, but it also urged consumers to demand that brand names "ensure adequate monitoring and independent verification" (Oxfam 2004, 89).

At the heart of most activist proposals lies active monitoring by civil society; independent NGOs, perhaps working in cooperation with corporate headquarters, would monitor conditions in corporate factories and the facilities of their suppliers, providing information that would allow consumers and activists to "name and shame" abusers and focusing on transnational campaigns as the most realistic source of pressure on multinationals.

Most proposals recognize the limits of voluntarism, but few see any viable alternative. Thus, for example, Fung, O'Rourke, and Sabel (2001, 36) suggest in an aside that perhaps national states could be persuaded to incorporate elements of the "ratcheting labor standards" into their domestic legal systems, but they fail to pursue their own logic. Similarly, Jill Esbenshade (2004) is keenly aware of the flaws of purely U.S.-based voluntary monitoring schemes in the American apparel industry, but at an international level she views independent monitoring as the only option. The best workplace monitors, she notes, are workers themselves, at least in situations where they feel protected enough from victimization to assert their concerns and secure enough in their employment to ignore threats of capital flight. In developing countries, however, where states are weak, unions are repressed, and employers can threaten to move at a moment's notice, are corporate codes of conduct, transnational consumer pressure, and nongovernmental monitoring groups the best route to improving working conditions? Like most analysts who discuss transnational regulatory schemes, she ends by calling for what she considers a second-best option: since states are weak and unions weaker, perhaps voluntary regulation involving corporate codes and independent monitors offers the only realistic approach to protecting workers.

Conclusion

Over the past twenty years, a rapidly integrated global economy has changed the relationship between national governments, businesses, and labor, raising fears that governments may engage in a race to the bottom as they trade away worker protections in the hope of attracting investors and creating jobs. In response, policymakers, academics, and activists have sought new ways to regulate transnational corporations. Modeling their approach on the international human rights movement, activists have targeted logos and regions instead of governments; campaigns have sought to mobilize international sympathy by "bearing witness" to egregious violations and creating nonstate monitoring systems instead of focusing on creating new channels of negotiation and union representation.

The shift is not, perhaps, quite as simple as it appears. As I have tried to show, transnational labor campaigns may redirect attention away from labor's traditional strategies and toward those core labor principles that look most like universal human rights; sometimes this approach emphasizes the protection of victims rather than the strengthening of workers' voices.

But in an era of global economic integration, when governments and international institutions view international investors as their best hope for economic growth and employment creation, the appeal of labor strategies that deploy the logic of global markets to improve working conditions is obvious. If national states lack the capacity, even the will, to enforce labor laws, transnational consumer pressure offers an alternative form of sanction on abusive employers. Most proponents of this approach recognize that transnational labor campaigns are limited, but they hope that even localized or industry-specific interventions will gradually lead to other, more systematic improvements in working conditions around the world by "ratcheting up" labor standards.

References

Adams, Julia, Elisabeth Clemens, and Ann Shola Orloff, eds. 2005. *Remaking Modernity: Politics, History, and Sociology.* Durham, N.C.: Duke University Press.

Adler, Genn, and Eddie Webster, eds. 2000. *Trade Unions and Democratization in South Africa, 1985–1997.* New York: St. Martin's Press.

Agnivesh, Swami. 1999a. "A Critique of Selective Western Interventions and WTO." In *Against Child Labor: Indian and International Dimensions and Strategies,* edited by Klaus Voll. New Delhi: Mosaic Books.

—. 1999b. "Indian Child Labor: Historical-Contemporary Review and Worsening Civilizational Crisis." In *Against Child Labour: Indian and International Dimensions and Strategies,* edited by Klaus Voll. New Delhi: Mosaic Books.

Ali, Karamat. 1996. "Social Clauses and Workers in Pakistan." *New Political Economy* 1(2): 269–73.

Ally, Shireen. 2006. "'Maid' with Rights: The Contradictory Citizenship of Domestic Workers in Post-Apartheid South Africa." PhD diss., University of Wisconsin at Madison.

Alperson, Myra. 1995. *Foundations for a New Democracy: Corporate Social Investment in South Africa: How It Works, Why It Works, Who Makes It Work, and How It's Making a Difference.* Johannesburg: Ravan Press.

Alston, Phillip. 2006. "'Core Labor Standards' and the Transformation of the International Labor Rights Regime." In *Social Issues, Globalization and International Instiutions,* edited by Virgina A. Leary and Daniel Warner. Boston, Mass.: Martinus Nuhoff Publications.

Amnesty International. 1987. *Guatemala: The Human Rights Record.* London: Amnesty International Publications.

Anner, Mark. 2000. "Local and Transnational Campaigns to End Sweatshop Practices." In *Transnational Cooperation Among Labor Unions,* edited by Michael Gordon and Lowell Turner. Ithaca, N.Y.: Cornell University/ILR Press.

Antony, Piush, and V. Gayathri. 2002. "Child Labor: A Perspective of Locale and Context." *Economic and Political Weekly* (December 28): 5186–9.

Aries, Phillippe. 1962. *Centuries of Childhood.* Translated by Robert Baldick. New York: Vintage Books.

Armbruster-Sandoval, Ralph. 2003. "Globalization and Transnational Labor Organizing: The Honduran Maquiladora Industry and the Kimi Campaign." *Social Science History* 27(4): 551–76.

—. 2005. *Globalization and Cross-Border Solidarity in the Americas: The Anti Sweatshop Movement and the Struggle for Social Justice.* New York: Routledge Press.

Arthurs, Harry. 2004. "Private Ordering and Workers' Rights in the Global Economy: Corporate Codes of Conduct as a Regime of Labor Market Regulation." In *Labor Law in an Era of Globalization: Transformative Practices and Possibilities,* edited by Joanne Conaghan, Richard Fischl, and Karl Klare. Oxford: Oxford University Press.

Ayres, Ian, and John Braithwaite. 1992. *Responsive Regulation: Transcending the Deregulation Debate.* Oxford: Oxford University Press.

Babb, Sarah L. 2001. *Managing Mexico: Economists from Nationalism to Neoliberalism.* Princeton, N.J.: Princeton University Press.

Bain, Carmen. 2006. "Standards for Whom? Standards for What? The Regulation of Agricultural Labor in Chile and Its Gendered Effects." Paper presented to the American Sociological Association Meetings. Montreal, Quebec, August 2006.

Bair, Jennifer, and Gary Gereffi. 2002. "NAFTA and the Apparel Commodity Chain: Corporate Strategies, Interfirm Networks, and Industrial Upgrading." In *Free Trade and Uneven Development: The North American Apparel Industry After NAFTA,* edited by Gary Gereffi, David Spener, and Jennifer Bair. Philadelphia, Pa.: Temple University Press.

Bandy, Joe, and Jennifer Bickham Mendez. 2003. "A Place of Their Own? Women Organizers in the Maquilas of Nicaragua and Mexico." *Mobilization: An International Journal* 8(2, June): 173–88.

Bandy, Joe, and Jackie Smith, editors. 2003. *Coalitions Across Borders: Transnational Protest and the Neoliberal Order.* Lanham, Md.: Rowman and Littlefield.

Baquele, Assefa, and Jo Boyden. 1988. "Child Labor: Problems, Policies, and Programs." In *Combating Child Labor,* edited by Assefa Baquele and Jo Boyden. Geneva: International Labor Organization.

Bartley, Tim. 2003. "Certifying Forests and Factories: States, Social Movements, and the Rise of Private Regulation in the Apparel and Forest Products Fields." *Politics and Society* 31(3, September): 433–64.

Basu, Kaushik. 2003. "International Labor Standards and Child Labor." In *Child Labor and the Right to Education in South Asia: Needs Versus Rights?* edited by Naila Kabeer, Geetha B. Namissan, and Ramya Subrahmanian. New Delhi: Sage Publications.

Battista, Andrew. 2002. "Unions and Cold War Foreign Policy in the 1980s: The National Labor Committee, the AFL-CIO, and Central America." *Diplomatic History* 26(3, Summer): 429–51.

Becker, Elizabeth. 2005. "Low Cost and Sweatshop Free." *New York Times,* May 12.

Beckman, Marc. 1999. "Success and Limitations of Social Labeling Against Child Labor in the Carpet Industry." In *Against Child Labor: Indian and International Dimensions and Strategies,* edited by Klaus Voll. New Delhi: Mosaic Books.

Bender, Daniel, and Richard Greenwald, editors. 2003. *Sweatshop USA: The American Sweatshop in Historical and Global Perspective.* New York: Routledge. Bender, Thomas, editor. 1992. *The Anti-Slavery Debate: Capitalism and Abolitionism as a Problem in Historical Interpretation.* Berkeley, Calif.: University of California Press.

Bergquist, Charles. 1996. *Labor and the Course of American Democracy.* London: Verso Press.

Bernasek, Alexandra, and Richard C. Porter. 1990. *Private Pressure for Social Change in South Africa: The Impact of the Sullivan Principles.* Discussion paper 125. Ann Arbor, Mich.: University of Michigan, Center for Research on Economic Development (August).

Bhargava, Pramila. 2003. *The Elimination of Child Labour: Whose Responsibility?* New Delhi: Sage Publications.

Bhattacharyya, B., and L. Sahoo, editors. 1996a. *The Indian Carpet Industry: Evolving Concerns, Prospects, and Strategies*. New Delhi: Indian Institute of Foreign Trade/Global Business Press.

—. 1996b. *Carpet Industry: Prospects and Perspectives*. New Delhi: Indian Institute of Foreign Trade.

Bickham Mendez, Jennifer. 2005. *From the Revolution to the Maquiladoras: Gender, Labor, and Globalization in Nicaragua*. Durham, N.C.: Duke University Press.

Biersteker, Thomas J. 1995. "The 'Triumph' of Liberal Economic Ideas in the Developing World." In *Global Change, Regional Response: The New International Context of Development*, edited by Barbara Stallings. Cambridge: Cambridge University Press.

Bissell, Susan. 2003. "The Social Construction of Childhood: A Perspective from Bangladesh." In *Child Labor and the Right to Education in South Asia: Needs Versus Rights?* edited by Naila Kabeer, Geetha B. Namissan, and Ramya Subrahmanian. New Delhi: Sage Publications.

Blanpain, Roger, editor. 2000. *Multinational Enterprises and the Social Challenges of the Twenty-first Century: The ILO Declaration on Fundamental Principles at Work, Public and Private Corporate Codes of Conduct*. The Hague and Boston: Kluwer Law International.

Blashill, John. 1972. "Proper Role of U.S. Corporations in South Africa." *Fortune* (July): 49.

Blowfield, Mick. 1999. "Ethical Trade: A Review of Developments and Issues." *Third World Quarterly* 20 (4, August): 753–70.

Bonacich, Edna, and Richard Appelbaum. 2000. *Behind the Label: Inequality in the Los Angeles Garment Industry*. Berkeley, Calif.: University of California Press.

Boris, Eileen. 2003. "Consumers of the World Unite! Campaigns Against Sweating, Past and Present." In *Sweatshop USA: The American Sweatshop in Historical and Global Perspective*, edited by Daniel Bender and Richard Greenwald. New York: Routledge Press.

Bose, Tarun. 1997. Untitled study of child labor and social labeling in the carpet industry. New Delhi: Center for Education and Communication. Braithwaite, John. 2002. "Rewards and Regulation." *Journal of Law and Society* 29(1, March): 12–26.

Braithwaite, John, and Peter Drahos. 2000. *Global Business Regulation*. Cambridge: Cambridge University Press.

Brobowsky, David. n.d. "Creating a Global Public Policy Network in the Apparel Industry: The Apparel Industry Partnership." Case study for UN Vision Project on Global Public Policy Networks. Accessed at www.globalpublic policy.net, January 18,2007.

Bronfenbrenner, Kate, and Robert Hickey. 2004. "Changing to Organize: A National Assessment of Union Strategies." In *Rebuilding Labor: Organizing and Organizers in the New Union Movement*, edited by Ruth Milkman and Kim Voss. Ithaca, N.Y.: Cornell University/ILR Press.

Brooks, Ethel. 2003. "The Ideal Sweatshop: Transnational and Gender Protest." In *Sweatshop USA: The American Sweatshop in Historical and Global Perspective*, edited by Daniel Bender and Richard Greenwald. New York: Routledge Press.

—. 2005. "Transnational Campaigns Against Child Labor: The Garment Industry in Bangladesh." In *Coalitions Across Borders: Transnational Protest and the Neoliberal Order*, edited by Joe Bandy and Jackie Smith. Lanham, Md.: Rowman and Littlefield.

—. 2007. *Unraveling the Garment Industry: Transnational Organizing and Women's Work*. Minneapolis, Minn.: University of Minnesota Press.

Brown-Thomson, Karen. 2002. "Women's Rights Are Human Rights." In *Restructuring World Politics: Transnational Social Movements, Networks, and Norms*, edited by Sanjeev Khagram, James V. Riker, and Kathryn Sikkink. Minneapolis, Minn.: University of Minnesota Press.

Brysk, Alyson, and Gershon Shafir, eds. 2004. *People Out of Place*. New York: Routledge Press.

Bullert, B. J. 2000. "Progressive Public Relations, Sweatshops, and the Net." *Political Communication* 17: 403–7.

Burra, Neera. 2003. "Rights Versus Needs: Is It in the 'Best Interest of the Child'?" In *Child Labor and the Right to Education in South Asia: Needs Versus Rights?* edited by Naila Kabeer, Geetha B. Namissan, and Ramya Subrahmanian. New Delhi: Sage Publications.

Candland, Chris, and Rudra Sil. 2001. "The Politics of Labor in Late-Industrializing and Post-Socialist Economies: New Challenges in a Global Age." In *The Politics of Labor in a Global Age*, edited by Chris Candland and Rudra Sil. Oxford: Oxford University Press.

Carmack, Robert M., ed. 1988. *Harvest of Violence: The Maya Indians and the Guatemalan Crisis*. Norman, Okla.: Oklahoma University Press.

Charnovitz, Steve. 2000. "The International Labor Organization in Its Second Century." In *Max Planck Yearbook of United Nations Law*, vol. 4, edited by Armin von Bogdandy and Rudiger Wolfrum, with Christianne Phillip. Leiden, Netherlands: Martinus Nuhoff Publications. Accessed at http://www.mpil. de/shared/data/pdf/pdfmpunyb/charnovitz_4.pdf.

Chowdhry, Geeta, and Mark Beeman. 2001. "Challenging Child Labor: Transnational Activism and India's Carpet Industry." *Annals of the American Academy of Political and Social Sciences* 575(May): 158–75.

Clawson, Dan. 2003. *The Next Upsurge: Labor and the New Social Movements*. Ithaca, N.Y.: Cornell University/ ILR Press.

Cohen, Lizabeth. 2003. *A Consumers' Republic: The Politics of Mass Consumption in Postwar America*. New York: Alfred A. Knopf.

Collins, Jane. 2003. *Threads: Gender, Labor, and Power in the Global Apparel Industry*. Chicago, Ill.: University of Chicago Press.

Commission on Global Governance. 1995. *Our Global Neighborhood*. Report of the Commission on Global Governance. Oxford: Oxford University Press.

Committee on Monitoring International Labor Standards, National Research Council, National Academy of Science. 2004. *Monitoring International Labor Standards*. Washington: The National Academies Press.

Compa, Lance. 2000. "The Promise and Perils of 'Core' Labor Rights in Global Trade and Investment." Unpublished paper, Cornell University.

— 2001. "Wary Allies." *The American Prospect* 12(12, July): 181–97.

Compa, Lance, and Tashia Hinchliffe Darricarrere. 1996. "Private Labor Rights Enforcement Through Corporate Codes of Conduct." In *Human Rights, Labor Rights, and International Trade*, edited by Lance Compa and Stephen Diamond. Philadelphia, Pa.: University of Pennsylvania Press.

Compa, Lance, and Stephen Diamond, editors. 1996. *Human Rights, Labor Rights, and International Trade*. Philadelphia, Pa.: University of Pennsylvania Press.

Connor, Tim. 2001. *Still Waiting for Nike to Do It: Nike's Labor Practices in the Three Years Since CEO Phil Knight's Speech to the National Press Club*. San Francisco, Calif.: Global Exchange.

Cook, Maria Lorena. 2006. *The Politics of Labor Reform in Latin America: Between Flexibility and Rights*. University Park, Pa.: Pennsylvania State University Press.

Cooper, Frederic. 1996. *Decolonization and African Society: The Labor Question in French and British Africa*. New York: Cambridge University Press.

Cortright, David, and George Lopez, eds. 1995. *Economic Sanctions: Panacea or Peacebuilding in a Post-Cold War World?* Boulder, Colo.: Westview Press. COVERCO. 2005. "Mission Statement." Accessed at http://www.coverco.org.gt/eng/about_us/#History, April 20,2007.

Cowie, Jefferson. 1999. *Capital Moves: RCA's Seventy-Year Quest for Cheap Labor*. Ithaca, N.Y.: Cornell University/ILR Press.

Danaher, Kevin. 1984. *In Whose Interest? A Guide to U.S.-South Africa Relations*. Washington: Institute for Policy Studies.

Davis, David Brion. 1992. "What the Abolitionists Were Up Against." In *The Anti-Slavery Debate: Capitalism and Abolitionism as a Problem in Historical Interpretation*, edited by Thomas Bender. Berkeley, Calif.: University of California Press.

Davis, Jennifer. 1995. "Sanctions and Apartheid: The Economic Challenge to Discrimination." In *Economic Sanctions: Panacea or Peacebuilding in a Post-Cold War World?* edited by David Cortright and George Lopez. Boulder, Colo.: Westview Press.

Davis, Shelton. 1988. "Sowing the Seeds of Violence." In *Harvest of Violence: The Maya Indians and the Guatemalan Crisis*, edited by Robert Carmack. Norman, Okla.: Oklahoma University Press.

Della Porta, Donatella, Hanspeter Kriesi, and Dieter Rucht, eds. 1999. *Social Movements in a Globalizing World*. New York: St. Martin's Press.

Dhawan, R. K. 1996. "Export Promotion Policies and Programs for Carpet Industry." In *Carpet Industry: Prospects and Perspectives*, edited by B. Bhattacharyya and L. Sahoo. New Delhi: Indian Institute of Foreign Trade/Global Business Press.

Dion, Douglas. 1998. "Evidence and Inference in the Comparative Case Study." *Comparative Politics* 30 (2, January): 127–45.

Erwin, Alec. 1989. "Why COSATU Has Supported Sanctions." In *Sanctions Against Apartheid*, edited by Mark Orkin. Cape Town, South Africa: David Phillips.

Esbenshade, Jill. 2003. "Leveraging Neo-Liberal 'Reforms': How Garment Workers Capitalize on Monitoring." Paper presented to the American Sociological Association meetings. Atlanta, Ga., August 2003.

——. 2004. *Monitoring Sweatshops: Workers, Consumers, and the Global Apparel Industry*. Philadelphia, Pa.: Temple University Press.

Evans, Peter. 1997. "The Eclipse of the State? Reflections on Stateness in an Era of Globalization." *World Politics* 50(1): 62–87.

——. 2000. "Counter-Hegemonic Globalization: Transnational Networks as Political Tools for Fighting Marginalization." *Contemporary Sociology* 294(January): 230–41.

Fantasia, Rick, and Kim Voss. 2004. *Hard Work: Remaking the American Labor Movement*. Berkeley, Calif.: University of California Press.

Featherstone, Liza, and United Students Against Sweatshops. 2002. *Students Against Sweatshops*. London: Verso Press.

Feld, Werner J. 1980. *Multinational Corporations and UN Politics: The Quest for Codes of Conduct*. New York: Pergamon Press.

Flanagan, Robert J., and William B. Gould IV, editors. 2003. *International Labor Standards: Globalization, Trade, and Public Policy*. Stanford, Calif.: Stanford University Press.

Forster, Cindy. 1998. "Reforging National Revolution: Campesino Labor Struggles in Guatemala, 1944–1954." In *Identity and Struggle at the Margins of the Nation-State*, edited by Aviva Chomsky and Aldo Lauria-Santiago. Durham, N.C.: Duke University Press.

Frank, Dana. 1999. *Buy American: The Untold Story of Economic Nationalism*. Boston, Mass.: Beacon Press.

Freeman, Carla. 2000. *High Tech and High Heels in the Global Economy: Women, Work, and Pink-Collar Identities in the Caribbean*. Durham, N.C.: Duke University Press.

Frundt, Henry. 1987. *Refreshing Pauses: Coca-Cola and Human Rights in Guatemala*. New York: Praeger.

——. 1998. *Trade Conditions and Labor Rights: U.S. Initiatives, Dominican and Central American Responses*. Gainesville, Fla.: University Press of Florida.

——. 1999. "Cross-Border Organizing in the Apparel Industry: Lessons from Central America and the Caribbean." *Labor Studies Journal* 24(1, Spring): 89–106.

——. 2005. "Movement Theory and International Labor Solidarity." *Labor Studies Journal* 30(2): 19–40.

Fuchs, Frieda. 2005. "The Effects of Protective Labor Legislation on Women's Wages and Welfare: Lessons from Britain and France." *Politics and Society* (December): 595–635.

Fung, Archon, Dara O'Rourke, and Charles Sabel. 2001. *Can We Put an End to Sweatshops?* Boston, Mass.: Beacon Press.

Gay, Kathlyn. 1998. *Child Labor: A Global Crisis*. Brookfield, Conn.: Millbrook Press.

Gereffi, Gary. 1994. "The Organization of Buyer-Driven Commodity Chains." In *Commodity Chains and Global Capitalism*, edited by Gary Gereffi and Miguel Korzeniewicz. Westport, Conn.: Greenwood Press.

Gereffi, Gary, and Miguel Korzeniewicz, editors. 1994. *Commodity Chains and Global Capitalism*. New York: Praeger.

Gereffi, Gary, David Spener, and Jennifer Bair, eds. 2002. *Free Trade and Uneven Development: The North American Apparel Industry After NAFTA*. Philadelphia, Pa.: Temple University Press.

Global March Against Child Labor. 2006. "World Cup Campaign 2006." Accessed at http://www.globalmarch.org/campaigns/worldcupcampaign/ worldcup2006.php3.

Goldberg, Chad. 2007. *Citizens and Paupers: Relief, Rights, and Race, from the Freedmen's Bureau to Workfare*. Chicago, Ill.: University of Chicago Press.

Golden, Miriam, and Jonas Pontusson, eds. 1992. *Bargaining for Change: Union Politics in North America and Europe*. Ithaca, N.Y.: Cornell University/ILR Press.

Goldin, Liliana. 2005. "Labor Ideologies in the International Factories of Rural Guatemala." *Latin American Perspectives* 32(5): 59–79.

Golodner, Linda F. 2000. "The Apparel Industry Code of Conduct: A Consumer Perspective on Social Responsibility." In *Global Codes of Conduct*, edited by Oliver Williams. Notre Dame, Ind.: University of Notre Dame Press.

Gordon, Jennifer. 2005. *Suburban Sweatshops: The Fight for Immigrant Rights.* Cambridge, Mass.: Belknap Press of Harvard University Press.

Gordon, Michael. 2000. "The International Confederation of Trade Unions: Bread, Freedom, and Peace." In *Transnational Cooperation Among Labor Unions,* edited by Michael Gordon and Lowell Turner. Ithaca, N.Y.: Cornell University /ILR Press.

Gordon, Michael, and Lowell Turner, eds. 2000. *Transnational Cooperation Among Labor Unions.* Ithaca, N.Y.: Cornell University /ILR Press.

Gosh, Ruma. 2000. "Child Labor: Issues and Concerns." Reprinted in National Resource Center on Child Labor, *Child Labor in India: An Overview,* rev. 2nd ed. New Delhi: V. V. Girl National Labor Institute/ ILO-IPEC (International Program on the Elimination of Child Labor), 2001.

Gould, William B., IV. 2003. "Labor Law for a Global Economy: The Uneasy Case for International Labor Standards." In *International Labor Standards: Globalization, Trade, and Public Policy,* edited by Robert Flanagan and William B. Gould IV. Stanford, Calif.: Stanford University Press.

Grandin, Greg. 2000. *The Blood of Guatemala: A History of Race and Nation.* Durham, N.C.: Duke University Press.

Greenwald, Richard. 2005. *The Triangle Fire, the Protocols of Peace, and Industrial Democracy in Progressive-Era New York.* Philadelphia, Pa.: Temple University Press.

Greider, William 1997. *One World, Ready or Not: The Maniac Logic of Global Capitalism.* New York: Simon & Schuster.

Guidry, John, Michael Kennedy, and Mayer Zald. 2000. *Globalizations and Social Movements: Culture, Power, and the Transnational Public Sphere.* Ann Arbor, Mich.: University of Michigan Press.

Gupta, Ahkil. 1998. *Postcolonial Developments: Agriculture in the Making of Modern India.* Durham, N.C.: Duke University Press.

Guthman, Julie. 2004. *Agrarian Dreams: The Paradox of Organic Farming in California.* Berkeley, Calif.: University of California Press.

Hale, Charles. 2002. "Does Multiculturalism Menace? Governance, Cultural Rights, and the Politics of Identity in Guatemala." *Journal of Latin American Studies* 34: 485–524.

Hart, Gillian. 2002. *Disabling Globalization: Places of Power in Post-Apartheid South Africa.* Berkeley, Calif.: University of California Press.

Hartman, Laura, Denis Arnold, and Sandra Waddock. 2003. "Rising Above Sweatshops: An Introduction to the Text and to the Issues." In *Rising Above Sweatshops: Innovative Approaches to Global Labor Challenges,* edited by Laura Hartman, Denis Arnold, and Richard Wokutch. Westport, Conn.: Praeger.

Hartman, Laura, Denis Arnold, and Richard Wokutch, editors. 2003. *Rising Above Sweatshops: Innovative Approaches to Global Labor Challenges.* Westport, Conn.: Praeger.

Held, David, and Mathias Koenig-Archibugi, editors. 2003. *Taming Globalization: Frontiers of Governance.* Cambridge: Polity Press.

Heller, Patrick. 1999. *The Labor of Development: Workers and the Transformation of Capitalism in Kerala, India.* Ithaca, N.Y.: Cornell University/ILR Press.

Herod, Andrew. 2001. *Labor Geographies: Workers and the Landscapes of Capitalism.* New York: Guilford Press.

Hilowitz, Janet. 1998. *Labeling Child Labor Products: A Preliminary Study.* Geneva: International Labor Organization. Accessed at http:/ /www.ilo.org /public/ english/standards/ipec/publ/policy/papers/ labelling/index.htm.

Hochschild, Adam. 2005. *Bury the Chains: Prophets and Rebels in the Fight to Free an Empire's Slaves.* New York: Houghton Mifflin.

Hoogvelt, Ankie, Christopher Candland, Denis McShane, Keramat Ali, Stephanie Barrientos, and Ngail-lim Sum. 1996. "Debate: International Labor Standards and Human Rights." *New Political Economy* 1(2): 259–82.

Howard, Allan. 1997. "Labor, History, and Sweatshops in the New Global Economy." In *No Sweat: Fashion, Free Trade, and the Rights of Garment Workers,* edited by Andrew Ross. London: Verso.

Howse, Robert. 1999. "The World Trade Organization and the Protection of Workers' Rights." *Journal of Small and Emerging Business Law* 3(1). Accessed at http://www.lclark.edu/org/jsebl/vol3nol.html.

Human Rights Watch. 2000. *Unfair Advantage: Workers' Freedom of Association in the United States Under International Human Rights Standards.* Accessed at http://www.hrw.org/reports/2000/uslabor/.

International Labor Organization. 1997. *World Labor Report, 1997–1998: Industrial Relations, Democracy, and Social Stability.* Geneva: ILO.

——. 1998a. *ILO Declaration on Fundamental Principles and Rights at Work.* Geneva: ILO (June 28).

——. 1998b. *Forced Labor in Myanmar (Burma).* Report of the Commission of Inquiry Appointed Under Article 26 of the Constitution of the International Labor Organization to Examine the Observance by Myanmar of the Forced Labor Convention, 1930 (no. 29). Geneva: ILO (July 2).

——. 2001. *Factory Improvement Program: Management and Corporate Citizenship Program.* Geneva: ILO.

——. 2003. *Employment and Social Policy in Respect of Export Processing Zones.* Governing Body, GB 286/ ESP /3. Geneva: ILO (March).

——. 2004. *Child Labor: A Textbook for University Students.* Accessed at www.ilo.org/public/english/stand-ards/ipec/publ/download/pol_textbook _2004.pdf, October 11, 2004.

——. 2006. *The End of Child Labor: Within Reach.* Report of the director-general to the ninety-fifth session of the International Labor Conference. Geneva: ILO.

International Labor Rights Fund. 1996. *Rugmark After One Year.* Washington: ILRF (October). Accessed at http://www.laborrights.org, May 10, 2006.

——. 2004. "Petition to Review Guatemala's Country Eligibility Under the Generalized System of Preferences (GSP) for Violation of Internationally Recognized Workers' Rights." Presented to the chairman of the GSP Subcommittee, Office of the U.S. Trade Representative, December 13, 2004. Accessed at http://www.laborrights.org, June 7, 2005.

Jasper, James. 1997. *The Art of Moral Protest: Culture, Biography, and Creativity in Social Movements.* Chicago, University of Chicago Press.

Jenkins, Rhys. 2002. "Political Economy of Codes of Conduct." In *Corporate Responsibility and Labor Rights: Codes of Conduct in the Global Economy,* edited by Rhys Jenkins, Ruth Pearson, and Gill Seyfang. London: Earthscan.

Jenkins, Rhys, Ruth Pearson, and Gill Seyfang, editors. 2002. *Corporate Responsibility and Labor Rights: Codes of Conduct in the Global Economy.* London: Earth-scan.

Jessup, David, and Michael Gordon. 2000. "Organizing in Export-Processing Zones: The Bibong Experience in the Dominican Republic." In *Transnational Cooperation Among Labor Unions,* edited by Michael Gordon and Lowell Turner. Ithaca, N.Y.: Cornell University/ILR Press.

Joffe, Hillary. 1989. "The Policy of South Africa's Trade Unions Towards Sanctions and Disinvestment." In *Sanctions Against Apartheid,* edited by Mark Orkin. Cape Town, South Africa: David Philips.

Jonas, Susanne. 2000. *Of Centaurs and Doves: Guatemala's Peace Process.* Boulder, Colo.: Westview Press.

Juarez Nunez, Huberto. 2002. *Rebelion en el Greenfield.* Puebla, Mexico: Benemerita Universidad Autortoma de Puebla, DirecciOn General de Fomento Editorial/AFL-CIO.

Juarez Nunez, Huberto, and Steve Babson, eds. 1998. *Confronting Change: Auto Labor and Lean Production in North America.* Detroit, Mich.: Wayne State University /Benernerita Universidad AutOnoma de Puebla.

Juyal, B. N. 1987. *Child Labor and Exploitation in the Carpet Industry.* New Delhi: Indian Social Institute.

Kabeer, Naila. 2003. "Deprivation, Discrimination, and Delivery: Competing Explanations for Child Labor and Educational Failure in South Asia." In *Child Labor and the Right to Education in South Asia: Needs Versus Rights?* edited by Naila Kabeer, Geetha B. Namissan, and Ramya Subrahmanian. New Delhi: Sage Publications.

Kabeer, Naila, Geetha B. Namissan, and Ramya Subrahmanian 2003a. "Needs Versus Rights? Child Labor, Social Exclusion, and the Challenge of Universalizing Primary Education." In *Child Labor and the Right to Education in South Asia: Needs Versus Rights?* edited by Naila Kabeer, Geetha B. Namissan, and Ramya Subrahmanian. New Delhi: Sage Publications.

——, editors. 2003b. *Child Labor and the Right to Education in South Asia: Needs Versus Rights?* New Delhi: Sage Publications.

Kaempfer, William, James Lehman, and Anton Lowenberg. 1987. "Divestment, Investment Sanctions, and Disinvestment: An Evaluation of Anti-apartheid Policy Instruments." *International Organization* 41 (3, Summer): 457–73.

Kahn, E. J., Jr. 1979. "Annals of International Trade: A Very Emotive Issue." *The New Yorker* (May 14): 117–53.

Kanbargi, Ramesh. 1988. "Child Labor in India: The Carpet Industry of Varanasi." In *Combating Child Labor,* edited by Assefa Baquele and Jo Boyden. Geneva: ILO.

Kaplinsky, Raphael. 1993. "Export-Processing Zones in the Dominican Republic: Transforming Manufactures into Commodities." *World Development* 21(11): 1851–65.

— 1995. "Technique and Management: The Spread of Japanese Management Techniques to Developing Countries." *World Development* 23(1): 57–71.

—. 2005. *Globalization, Poverty, and Inequality.* Cambridge: Polity Press.

Kapstein, Ethan. 1999. *Sharing the Wealth: Workers and the World Economy.* New York: Norton.

Kebschull, Dietrich. 1999. "Philosophy and Achievements of the 'Rugmark' Labeling Approach." In *Against Child Labor: Indian and International Dimensions and Strategies,* edited by Klaus Voll. New Delhi: Mosaic Books.

Keck, Margaret, and Kathryn Sikkink. 1998. *Activists Beyond Borders: Advocacy Networks in Transnational Politics.* Ithaca, N.Y.: Cornell University Press.

Kenny, Bridget. 2004. "Divisions of Labor, Experiences of Class: Changing Collective Identities of East Rand Food Retail Sector Workers Through South Africa's Democratic Transition." PhD dissertation, University of Wisconsin at Madison.

Khagram, Sanjay, James V. Riker, and Kathryn Sikkink. 2002. *Restructuring World Politics: Transnational Social Movements, Networks, and Norms.* Minneapolis, Minn.: University of Minnesota Press.

Khan, Shamshad. 1999. "Community Participation Eliminates Child Labor." In *Against Child Labor: Indian and International Dimensions and Strategies,* edited by Klaus Voll. New Delhi: Mosaic Books.

Khor, Martin. 1994. "The World Trade Organization, Labor Standards, and Trade Protectionism." *Third World Resurgence* 45: 30–34.

Kidder, Thalia. 2002. "Networks in Transnational Labor Organizing." In *Restructuring World Politics: Transnational Social Movements, Networks, and Norms,* edited by Sanjeev Khagram, James V. Riker, and Kathryn Sikkink. Minneapolis, Minn.: University of Minnesota Press.

Klein, Naomi. 2002. *No Logo,* 2nd ed. London: Picador Press.

Klotz, Audie. 1995. "Norms Reconstituting Interests: Global Racial Equality and U.S. Sanctions Against South Africa." *International Organization* 49(3, Summer): 451–78.

Koo, Hagen. 2001. *Korean Workers: The Culture and Politics of Class Formation.* Ithaca, N.Y.: Cornell University/ILR Press.

Kreamer, Christopher. 2002. *The Carpet Wars.* New York: HarperCollins.

Krupat, Kitty. 1997. "From War Zone to Free Trade Zone: A History of the National Labor Committee." In *No Sweat: Fashion, Free Trade, and the Rights of Garment Workers,* edited by Andrew Ross. London: Verso.

Labour File. 2005. "Assault on Honda Workers: A Citizens' Committee Inquiry Report." *Labour File* (September).

Langille, Brian. 1999. "The ILO and the New Economy: Recent Developments." *International Journal of Comparative Labor Law and Industrial Relations* 15(3): 229–58.

Lavalette, Michael. 1999a. "The Changing Form of Child Labor Circa 1880–1918: The Growth of 'Out of School Work.'" In *A Thing of the Past? Child Labor in Britain in the Nineteenth and Twentieth Century,* edited by Michael Lavalette. Liverpool: Liverpool University Press.

—, editor. 1999b. *A Thing of the Past? Child Labor in Britain in the Nineteenth and Twentieth Century.* Liverpool: Liverpool University Press.

Leary, Virginia A. 1996. "The Paradox of Workers' Rights as Human Rights." In *Human Rights, Labor Rights, and International Trade,* edited by Lance Compa and Stephen Diamond. Philadelphia, Pa.: University of Pennsylvania Press.

Lee, Ching Kwan. 1998. *Gender and the South China Miracle: Two Worlds of Factory Women.* Berkeley, Calif.: University of California Press.

Levy, Margaret, and April Linton. 2003. "Fair Trade: A Cup at a Time?" *Politics and Society* 31(3): 407–32.

Lieten, G. K. 2002. "Child Labor in India: Disentangling Essence and Solutions." *Economic and Political Weekly* (December 28): 5190–95.

Lipietz, Alain. 1987. *Mirages and Miracles: The Crisis in Global Fordism.* Translated by David Macey. London: Verso.

London, Jonathan. 2003. "The Economic Context: Grounding Discussions of Economic Change and Labor in Developing Countries." In *Rising Above Sweatshops: Innovative Approaches to Global Labor Challenges,* edited by Laura Hartman, Denis Arnold, and Richard Wokutch. Westport, Conn.: Praeger.

Malhotra, Vinod. 1996. "Indian Carpet Industry: Prospects and Perspectives." In *Carpet Industry: Prospects and Perspectives,* edited by B. Bhattacharyya and L. Sahoo. New Delhi: Indian Institute of Foreign Trade/Global Business Press.

Malkki, Liisa. 1994. "Citizens of Humanity." *Diaspora* 3(1): 41–68.

Mamic, Ivanka. 2004. *Implementing Codes of Conduct: How Businesses Manage Social Performance in Global Supply Chains.* Geneva: International Labor Organization/Greenleaf Publishing.

Mannon, Susan. 2003. "Our Daily Bread: Constructing Households, Constructing Labor Markets." PhD dissertation, University of Wisconsin at Madison.

Marshall, T. H. 1950/1992. "Citizenship and Social Class." In *Citizenship and Social Class,* edited by T. H. Marshall and Tom Bottomore. London: Pluto Press.

Marzullo, Sal. 1987a. "Corporations: Catalyst for Change." In *The South African Quagmire,* edited by Prakash Sethi. Cambridge, Mass.: Ballinger Press.

—. 1987b. "American Business in South Africa: The Hard Choices." In *Business and Society,* edited by Prakash Sethi and Cecilia M. Falbe. Washington: Lexington Books.

Massie, Robert Kinloch. 1997. *Loosing the Bonds: The United States and South Africa in the Apartheid Years.* New York: Doubleday.

McCann, Michael W. 1994. *Rights at Work: Pay Equity Reform and the Politics of Legal Mobilization.* Chicago, Ill.: University of Chicago Press.

McKay, Stephen C. 2006. *Satanic Mills or Silicon Islands: The Politics of High-Tech Production in the Philippines.* Ithaca, N.Y.: Cornell University/ILR Press. McMichael, Philip. 2000. *Development and Social Change,* 2nd ed. Thousand Oaks, Calif.: Pine Forge Press/Sage Publications.

Milkman, Ruth. 1997. *Farewell to the Factory: Auto Workers in the Late Twentieth Century.* Berkeley, Calif.: University of California Press.

—. 2006. L.A. *Story: Immigrant Workers and the Future of the U.S. Labor Movement.* New York: Russell Sage Foundation.

Milkman, Ruth, and Kim Voss, editors. 2004. *Rebuilding Labor: Organizing and Organizers in the New Union Movement.* Ithaca, N.Y.: Cornell University/ILR Press.

Mishra, G. P., and P. N. Pande. 1996. *Child Labor in Carpet Industry.* New Delhi: A.P.H. Publishing Co.

Mishra, Lakshmidhar. 2000. *Child Labor in India.* Oxford: Oxford University Press.

Mitchell, John, editor. 1998. *Companies in a World of Conflict: NGOs, Sanctions, and Corporate Responsibility.* London: Earthscan Publications/Royal Institute of International Affairs.

Montero, David. 2006. "Nike's Dilemma: Is Doing the Right Thing Wrong?" *Christian Science Monitor,* December 22, 2006.

Moody, Kim. 1997. *Workers in a Lean World: Unions in the International Economy.* London: Verso.

Moran, Theodore. 2002. *Beyond Sweatshops: Foreign Direct Investment and Globalization in Developing Countries.* Washington: Brookings Institution Press.

Morano, Roy. 1982. *The Protestant Challenge to Corporate America: Issues of Corporate Social Responsibility.* Ann Arbor, Mich.: University of Michigan Research Press.

Murillo, M. Victoria, and Andrew Schrank. 2005. "With a Little Help from My Friends: Partisan Politics, Transnational Alliances, and Labor Rights in Latin America." *Comparative Political Sciences* (38)8: 971–99.

Murray, Jill. 2003. "The Global Context: Multinational Enterprises, Labor Standards, and Regulation." In *Rising Above Sweatshops: Innovative Approaches to Global Labor Challenges,* edited by Laura Hartman, Denis Arnold, and Richard Wokutch. Westport, Conn.: Praeger.

Murray, Lauren. 1995. "Unraveling Employment Trends in Textiles and Apparel." *Monthly Labor Review* 118(8, August). Accessed at http://www.bls.gov/opub/mlr/1995/08art6abs.htm.

Mutersbaugh, Tad. 2002. "The Number Is the Beast: A Political Economy of Organic-Coffee Certification and Producer Unionism." *Environment and Planning* 34: 1165–84.

Myers, William. 2001. "The Right Rights? Child Labor in a Globalizing World." *Annals of the American Academy of Political and Social Sciences* (May): 38–55.

Nadvi, Khalid, with Sajid Kazmi. 2001. "Global Standards and Local Responses." Paper for the Institute for Developmental Studies workshop "The Impact of Global and Local Governance on Industrial Upgrading." Brighton, February 13–17.

Narayan, Ashok. 1988. "Child Labor Policies and Programs. The Indian Experience." In *Combating Child Labor,* edited by Assefa Baquele and Jo Boyden. Geneva: International Labor Organization.

National Resource Center on Child Labor. 2001. *Child Labor in India: An Overview,* revised 2nd edition. New Delhi: V. V. Giri National Labor Institute/ILO-IPEC (International Program on the Elimination of Child Labor).

Nelson, Lisa. 2000. "Who Speaks for the Trees? Consideration for Any Transnational Code." In *Global Codes of Conduct: An Idea Whose Time Has Come,* edited by Oliver F. Williams. Notre Dame, Ind.: University of Notre Dame Press.

Ness, Immanuel. 2003. "Globalization and Worker Organization in New York's Garment Industry." In *Sweatshop USA: The American Sweatshop in Historical and Global Perspective,* edited by Daniel Bender and Richard Greenwald. New York: Routledge Press.

Nike. 2006. "Nike Ends Orders with Soccer Ball Manufacturer." Press release, November 20, 2006. Accessed at http://www.nike.com/nikebiz/news/ pressrelease.jhtml?year=2006&month=11&letter=l, January 11, 2007.

Nimtz, August. 2002. "Marx and Engels: The Prototypical Transnational Actors." In *Restructuring World Politics: Transnational Social Movements, Networks, and Norms,* edited by Sanjeev Khagram, James V. Riker, and Kathryn Sikkink. Minneapolis, Minn.: University of Minnesota Press.

Nutter, Steve. 1997. "The Structure and Growth of the Los Angeles Garment Industry." In *No Sweat: Fashion, Free Trade and the Rights of Garment Workers,* edited by Andrew Ross. London: Verso Press.

Olsen, Elizabeth. 2002. "United Nations: Labor Monitor to Go to Myanmar." *New York Times,* March 23.

Ong, Aihwa. 1987. *Spirits of Resistance and Capitalist Discipline: Factory Women in Malaysia.* Albany, N.Y.: State University of New York Press.

Organization of American States (OAS). Inter-American Commission on Human Rights. 2001. *Fifth Report on the Situation of Human Rights in Guatemala.* Washington: OAS General Secretariat.

Orkin, Mark. 1987. *Divestment, the Struggle and the Future: What Black South Africans Really Think.* Johannesburg: Ravan Press.

—, ed. 1989. *Sanctions Against Apartheid.* Cape Town: David Philips.

O'Rourke, Dara. 2000. "Monitoring the Monitors: A Critique of PricewaterhouseCoopers Labor Monitoring," September 28. Accessed at nature.berkeley.edu/orourke/PDF/pwc.pdf.

—. 2003. "Outsourcing Regulation: Analyzing Nongovernmental Systems of Labor Standards and Monitoring." *Policy Studies Journal* 31(1): 1–29.

—. 2004. *Community-Driven Regulation: Balancing Development and the Environment in Vietnam.* Cambridge, Mass.: MIT Press.

Oxfam. 2004. *Trading Away Our Rights: Women Working in Global Supply Chains.* Oxford: Oxfam. Accessed at http://www.oxfam.org.uk/what_we_do/ issues/ trade/trading_rights.htm.

Paige, Jeffrey. 1997. *Coffee and Power: Revolution and the Rise of Democracy in Central America.* Cambridge, Mass.: Harvard University Press.

Paul, Karen. 1987. "The Inadequacy of Sullivan Reporting." In *The South African Quagmire,* edited by Prakash Sethi. Cambridge, Mass.: Ballinger Press.

—. 1991. "U.S. Companies in South Africa." In *Up Against the Corporate Wall: Modern Corporations and Social Issues of the Nineties.* Edited by S. Prakash Sethi and Paul Steidlmeier. Englewood Cliffs, N.J.: Prentice Hall.

Picciotto, Sol. 2002. "Reconceptualizing Regulation in the Era of Globalization." *Journal of Law and Society* 29(1, March): 1–11.

Piore, Michael J., and Andrew Schrank. 2006. "Trading Up: An Embryonic Model for Easing the Human Costs of Free Markets." *Boston Review* (September-October). Accessed at http://bostonreview.net/ BR31.5/pioreschrank.html.

Piven, Frances Fox, and Richard Cloward. 1977. *Poor People's Movements: Why They Succeed, How They Fail.* New York : Pantheon Books.

Plankey-Videla, Nancy. 2004. "It Cuts Both Ways: The Unintended Consequences of Lean Production in a Mexican Garment Factory." PhD diss., University of Wisconsin at Madison.

Polanyi, Karl. 1944/2001. *The Great Transformation: The Political and Economic Origins of Our Time.* Foreword by Joseph Stiglitz, introduction by Fred Block. Boston, Mass.: Beacon Press.

Posner, Michael, and Justine Nolan. 2003. "Can Codes of Conduct Play a Role in Promoting Workers' Rights?" In *International Labor Standards: Globalization, Trade, and Public Policy,* edited by Robert Flanagan and William B. Gould IV. Stanford, Calif.: Stanford University Press.

Posthuma, Anne. 1995. "Japanese Techniques in Africa? Human Resources and Industrial Restructuring in Zimbabwe." *World Development* 23(1): 103–16.

Prasad, Monica, Howard Kimeldorf, Rachel Meyer, and Ian Robinson. 2004. "Consumers of the World Unite: A Market-Based Response to Sweatshops." *Labor Studies Journal* (Fall): 57–79.

Proper, Carl. 1997. "New York: Defending the Union Contract." In *No Sweat: Fashion, Free Trade, and the Rights of Garment Workers,* edited by Andrew Ross. London: Verso Press.

Puri, Lakshmi. 1996. "Market Access Challenges for Indian Exporters in the Post-Uruguayan Round." In *Carpet Industry: Prospects and Perspectives,* edited by B. Bhattacharyya and L. Sahoo. New Delhi: Indian Institute of Foreign Trade/Global Business Press.

Raworth, Kate. 2004. "When Buying Clothes, Measure Their Ethics for a Good Fit." *Guardian Weekly* (March 11–17): 23.

Reich, Robert. 1997. *Locked in the Cabinet.* New York: Alfred A. Knopf.

Relly, Gavin. 1986. "The Costs of Disinvestment." *Foreign Policy* 63 (Summer): 131–46.

Rivoli, Pietra. 2005. *The Travels of a T-Shirt in the Global Economy: An Economist Examines the Markets, Power, and Politics of World Trade.* New York: John Wiley and Sons.

Robinson, William. 2003. *Transnational Conflicts: Central America, Social Change, and Globalization.* London: Verso Press.

Rodman, Kenneth. 1994. "Public and Private Sanctions Against South Africa." *Political Science Quarterly* 109(2, Summer): 313–34.

Rodriguez-Garavito, Cesar. 2005a. "Global Governance and Labor Rights: Codes of Conduct and Anti-Sweatshop Struggles in Global Apparel Factories in Mexico and Guatemala." *Politics and Society* 33 (2, June): 203–33.

— 2005b. "Nike's Law: The Anti-Sweatshop Movement, Transnational Corporations, and the Struggle over International Labor Rights in the Americas." In *Law and Globalization from Below: Towards a Cosmopolitan Legality,* edited by Boaventura de Sousa Santos and Cesar Rodriguez-Garavito. Cambridge: Cambridge University Press.

—. 2007. "Sewing Resistance: Global Production, Transnational Organizing, and Global Governance in the U.S.-Caribbean Basin Apparel Industry (1990–2005)." PhD dissertation, University of Wisconsin at Madison.

Rodrik, Dani. 1999. "Democracies Pay Higher Wages." *Quarterly Journal of Economics* 114(3, August): 707–38.

Rosen, Ellen. 2002. *Making Sweatshops: The Globalization of the U.S. Apparel Industry.* Berkeley, Calif.: University of California Press.

Ross, Andrew, ed. 1997. *No Sweat: Fashion, Free Trade, and the Rights of Garment Workers.* London: Verso Press.

—. 2003. "The Rise of the Second Anti-Sweatshop Movement." In *Sweatshop USA: The American Sweatshop in Historical and Global Perspective,* edited by Daniel Bender and Richard Greenwald. New York: Routledge.

Ross, Robert. 2004. *Slaves to Fashion: Poverty and Abuse in the New Sweatshops.* Ann Arbor, Mich.: University of Michigan Press.

Rudra, Nita. 2005. "Are Workers in the Developing World Winners or Losers in the Current Era of Globalization?" *Studies in Comparative International Development* 40(3, Fall): 24–64.

Rueschemeyer, Dietrich, Evelyne Huber Stephens, and John D. Stephens. 1992. *Capitalist Development and Democracy.* Chicago, Ill.: University of Chicago Press.

Ruggie, John Gerard. 1998. *Constructing the World Polity: Essays on International Institutionalization.* New York: Routledge.

—. 2003. "Taking Embedded Liberalism Global: The Corporate Connection." In *Taming Globalization: Frontiers of Governance,* edited by David Held and Mathias Koenig-Archibugi. Cambridge: Polity Press.

Ryan, Missy. 2000. "Child Labor as an Issue Comes of Age." *National Journal* 32(18, April 29): 1367–8.

Sampson, Anthony. 1987. *Black and Gold: Tycoons, Revolutions, and Apartheid*. London: Hodder and Stoughton.

Santoro, Michael. 2003. "Philosophy Applied I: How Nongovernmental and Multinational Enterprises Can Work Together to Protect Global Labor Rights." In *Rising Above Sweatshops: Innovative Approaches to Global Labor Challenges*, edited by Laura Hartman, Denis Arnold, and Richard Wokutch. Westport, Conn.: Praeger.

Santos, Boaventura de Sousa, and Cesar Rodriguez-Garavito, editors. 2005. *Law and Counter-Hegemonic Globalization: Toward a Cosmopolitan Legality*. Cambridge: Cambridge University Press.

Satyarthi, Kailash. 1994. "The Tragedy of Child Labor." Interview in *Multinational Monitor* 16(10, October 1994). Accessed at http://www.multinational monitor.org/hyper/issues/1994/10/mm109407. html, May 13, 2006.

Schlesinger, Stephen, and Stephen 'Kinzer. 1982. *Bitter Fruit: The Untold Story of the American Coup in Guatemala*. New York: Doubleday.

Schmidt, Elizabeth. 1980. *Decoding Corporate Camouflage: U.S. Business Support for Apartheid*. Washington: Institute for Policy Studies.

Schoenberger, Karl. 2000. *Levi's Children: Coming to Terms with Human Rights in the Global Marketplace*. New York: Atlantic Monthly Press.

Schrage, Elliot. 2004. *Promoting International Worker Rights Through Private Voluntary Initiatives: Public Relations or Public Policy?* Iowa City, Iowa: University of Illinois Center for Human Rights.

Schrank, Andrew. 2005. "Professionalization and Probity in the Patrimonial State: Labor Law Enforcement in the Dominican Republic." Paper presented to the MIT/Sloan IWER (Institute for Work and Employment Research) seminar series, Cambridge, Mass., February 8, 2005.

—. 2006. "Labor Standards and Human Resources: A Natural Experiment in an Unlikely Laboratory." Paper presented to the Latin American Studies Association meetings, Puerto Rico, March 2006.

Seccombe, Wally. 1993. *Weathering the Storm: Working-Class Families from the Industrial Revolution to the Fertility Decline*. London: Verso.

Seidman, Ann, and Neva Seidman. 1977. *South Africa and U.S. Multinational Corporations*. Westport, Conn.: Lawrence Hill and Co.

Seidman, Gay. 1994. *Manufacturing Militance: Workers' Movements in Brazil and South Africa, 1970–1985*. Berkeley, Calif.: University of California Press.

Sekar, Helen. 2001. "The Child Labour (Prohibition and Regulation) Act, 1986, and its Implementation." In National Resource Center on Child Labor, *Child Labor in India: An Overview*, revised 2nd edition. New Delhi: V. V. Girl National Labour Institute with ILO-IPEC.

Sethi, S. Prakash. 2000. "Gaps in Research in the Formulation, Implementation, and Effectiveness Measurement of International Codes of Conduct." In *Global Codes of Conduct: An Idea Whose Time Has Come*, edited by Oliver F. Williams. Notre Dame, Ind.: University of Notre Dame Press.

Sethi, S. Prakash, and Cecilia M. Falbe, editors. 1987. *Business and Society*. Washington: Lexington Books.

Sethi, S. Prakash, and Paul Steidlmeier, editors. 1991. *Up Against the Corporate Wall: Modern Corporations and Social Issues of the Nineties*. Englewood Cliffs, N.J.: Prentice-Hall.

Sethi, S. Prakash, and Oliver F. Williams. 2000. *Economic Imperatives and Ethical Values in Global Business: The South African Experience and International Codes Today*. Boston, Mass.: Kluwer Academic Press.

Shafir, Gershon. 2004. "Citizenship and Human Rights in an Era of Globalization." In *People Out of Place*, edited by Alyson Brysk and Gershon Shafir. New York: Routledge.

Shaiken, Harley. 1995. "Lean Production in a Mexican Context." In *Lean Work: Empowerment and Exploitation in the Global Auto Industry*. Detroit, Mich.: Wayne State University Press.

Shamir, Ronen. 2004. "The De-Radicalization of Corporate Social Responsibility." *Critical Sociology* 30(3): 670–89.

Sharma, Alakh. 2002. "Impact of Social Labeling on Child Labor in the Carpet Industry." *Economic and Political Weekly* (December 28): 5198–204.

Sharma, Mukul, and Tarun Bose. 1997. "Indian Carpet with a Smiling Face." *Labor File* 3(1 and 2, January and February): 5–15.

Shaw, Terri. 2002. "Child Labor Worries." *Newsday*, April 4.

Sikkink, Kathryn. 1993. "Human Rights, Principled Issue-Networks, and Sovereignty in Latin America." *International Organization* 47(3, Summer): 411–41.

—. 2002. "Restructuring World Politics: The Limits and Asymmetries of Soft Power." In *Restructuring World Politics: Transnational Social Movements, Networks, and Norms,* edited by Sanjeev Khagram, James V. Riker, and Kathryn Sikkink. Minneapolis, Minn.: University of Minnesota Press.

Silver, Beverly J. 2003. *Forces of Labor: Workers' Movements and Globalization Since 1870.* Cambridge: Cambridge University Press.

Silverman, Victor. 2000. *Imagining Internationalism in American and British Labor, 1939–1949.* Urbana, Ill.: University of Illinois Press.

Singh, Ruma Gosh, Nikhil Raj, and Helen R. Sekar. 2002. *Hard Labour at a Tender Age: Child Labour in the Home-Based Industries in the Wake of Legislation.* New Delhi: V.V. Girl National Labour Institute.

Slaughter, Anne-Marie. 2004. *A New World Order.* Princeton, N.J.: Princeton University Press.

Smith, Jackie, and Hank Johnston, editors. 2002. *Globalization and Resistance: Transnational Dimensions of Social Movements.* New York: Rowman and Littlefield.

Somers, Peggy. 1993. "Citizenship and the Place of the Public Sphere: Law, Community, and Political Culture in the Transition to Democracy." *American Sociological Review* 58(5): 587–620.

—. 1999. "The Privatization of Citizenship: How to Unthink a Knowledge Culture." In *Beyond the Cultural Turn: New Directions in the Study of Society and Culture,* edited by Victoria E. Bonnell and Lynn Hunt. Berkeley, Calif.: University of California Press.

—. 2005. "Citizenship Troubles: Genealogies of Struggle for the Soul of the Social." In *Remaking Modernity: Politics, History, and Sociology,* edited by Julia Adams, Elisabeth Clemens, and Ann Shola Orloff. Durham, NC.: Duke University Press.

Southall, Roger, editor. 1988. *Trade Unionism and the New Industrialization of the Third World.* London: Zed Press.

Spalding, Hobart. 1988. "U.S. Labor Intervention in Latin America: The Case of the American Institute for Free Labor Development." In *Trade Unionism and the New Industrialization of the Third World,* edited by Roger Southall. London: Zed Press.

Spence, J. E. 1998. "South Africa: A Case Study in Human Rights and Sanctions." In *Companies in a World of Conflict: NGOs, Sanctions, and Corporate Responsibility,* edited by John Mitchell. London: Earthscan Publications/Royal Institute of International Affairs.

Srivastava, Ravi, and Nikhil Raj. 2000. *Children of Carpet Looms: A Study of Home-Based Production of Carpet in Uttar Pradesh.* New Delhi: V. V. National Girl Labor Institute.

—. 2002. "Knots that Tie Up Children in Mirzapur: A Study of Child Labour in the Carpet Industry of Uttar Pradesh." In *Hard Labour at a Tender Age: Child Labour in the Home-Based Industries in the Wake of Legislation,* edited by Ruma Gosh Singh, Nikhil Raj, and Helen Sekar. New Delhi: V.V. Giri National Labour Institute.

Stallings, Barbara. 1995. "The New International Context of Development." In *Global Change, Regional Response: The New International Context of Development,* edited by Barbara Stallings. Cambridge: Cambridge University Press.

Stiglitz, Joseph. 2003. *Globalization and Its Discontents,* 2nd ed. New York: Norton.

Stillerman, Joel. 2003. "Transnational Activist Networks and the Emergence of Labor Internationalism in the NAFTA Countries." *Social Science History* 27(4, Winter): 577–601.

Stone, Philip. 1994. "Exit or Voice? Lessons from Companies in South Africa." In *Ethics and Economic Affairs,* edited by Alan Lewis and Karl-Erik Warneryd. New York: Routledge.

Su, Julie. 1997. "El Monte Thai Garment Workers: Slave Sweatshops." In *No Sweat: Fashion, Free Trade, and the Rights of Garment Workers,* edited by Andrew Ross. London: Verso Press.

Talbot, John. 2004. *Grounds for Agreement: The Political Economy of the Coffee Commodity Chain.* Lanham, Md.: Rowman and Littlefield.

Tarrow, Sidney. 2005. *The New Transnational Activist.* New York: Cambridge University Press.

Tegmo-Reddy, Leyla. 1996. "The ILO and Child Labor (with Special Reference to Child Labor in the Indian Carpet Industry)." In *The Indian Carpet Industry: Evolving Concerns, Prospects, and Strategies,* edited by B. Bhattacharyya and L. Sahoo. New Delhi: Indian Institute of Foreign Trade/Global Business Press.

Tendler, Judith. 2002. "Small Firms, the Informal Sector, and the Devil's Deal." *IDS Bulletin* 33: 3.

Thompson, E. P. 1963. *The Making of the English Working Class*. New York: Vintage Press.

—. 1975. *Whigs and Hunters: The Origins of the Black Act*. New York: Pantheon Press.

Thorat, Sukhadeo K. 1999. "Poverty, Caste, and Child Labor in India: The Plight of Dalit and Adivasi Children." In *Against Child Labor: Indian and International Dimensions and Strategies,* edited by Klaus Voll. New Delhi: Mosaic Books.

University of Maryland. Program on International Policy Attitudes (PIPA). 2000. *Americans on Globalization: A Study of Public Attitudes* (March). Accessed at "Americans and the World," http://www.americans-world.org/digest/ global_issues/intertrade/laborstandards.cfm.

U.S. Department of Labor. Office of Public Affairs (OPA). 1998. "Statement of U.S. Labor Secretary Alexis M. Herman on the Apparel Industry Partnership." Press release, November 3, 1998. Accessed at http://www.dol .gov/opa/media/press/opa/archive/opa98440.htm, November 13, 2006.

Voll, Klaus, editor. 1999. *Against Child Labor: Indian and International Dimensions and Strategies.* New Delhi: Mosaic Books.

Von Holdt, Karl. 2000. "From the Politics of Resistance to the Politics of Reconstruction? The Union and Ungovernability in the Workplace." In *Trade Unions and Democratization in South Africa, 1985–1997,* edited by Glenn Adler and Eddie Webster. New York: St. Martin's Press.

Waddock, Sandra. 2002. *Leading Corporate Citizens: Vision, Values, Value-Added*. New York: McGraw-Hill.

Warren, Kay. 1998. *Indigenous Movements and Their Critics: Pan-Mayan Activism in Guatemala*. Princeton, N.J.: Princeton University Press.

Wazir, Rekha. 2002. "'No to Child Labor, Yes to Education': Unfolding of a Grassroots Movement in Andhra Pradesh." *Economic and Political Weekly* (December 28): 5225–9.

Webster, Eddie, and Glenn Adler. 2000. "Consolidating Democracy in a Liberalizing World: Trade Unions and Democratization in South Africa." In *Trade Unions and Democratization in South Africa, 1985–1997,* edited by Glenn Adler and Eddie Webster. New York: St. Martin's Press.

Weedon, Reid. 1987. "The Evolution of Sullivan Principle Compliance." In *The South African Quagmire,* edited by Prakash Sethi. Cambridge, Mass.: Ballinger Press.

Weisband, Edward. 2000. "Discursive Multilateralism: Global Benchmarks, Shame, and Learning in the ILO Labor Standards Monitoring Regime." *International Studies Quarterly* 44: 643–66.

Wells, Don. 1998. "Building Transnational Coordinative Unionism." In *Confronting Change: Auto Labor and Lean Production in North America,* edited by Huberto Juarez Ntifiez and Steve Babson. Detroit, Mich.: Wayne State University /Benemerita Universidad Autonoma de Puebla.

Whittaker, Alan, ed. 1988. *India's Carpet Boys: A Pattern of Slavery*. London: Anti-Slavery Society.

Wiener, Myron. 1991. *The Child and the State in India: Child Labor and Education Policy in Comparative Perspective*. Princeton, N.J.: Princeton University Press.

Wilking, Lou. 1987. "Should U.S. Corporations Abandon South Africa?" In *The South African Quagmire,* edited by Prakash Sethi. Cambridge, Mass.: Ballinger Press.

Williams, Heather. 2003. "Of Labor Tragedy and Legal Farce: The Han Young Factory Struggle in Tijuana, Mexico." *Social Science History* 27(4): 525–50.

Williams, Oliver F. 2000a. "A Lesson from the Sullivan Principles: The Rewards for Being Proactive." In *Global Codes of Conduct: An Idea Whose Time Has Come,* edited by Oliver Williams. Notre Dame, Ind.: University of Notre Dame Press.

—, editor. 2000b. *Global Codes of Conduct: An Idea Whose Time Has Come*. Notre Dame, Ind.: University of Notre Dame Press.

Wolensky, Kenneth, Robert Wolensky, and Nicole Wolensky. 2002. *Fighting for the Union Label: The Women's Garment Industry and the ILGWU in Pennsylvania*. University Park, Pa.: Pennsylvania State University Press.

World Bank. 1996. *World Development Report 1995: Workers in an Integrating World*. Oxford: Oxford University Press/ World Bank.

World Trade Organization. 1996. "Draft Singapore Ministerial Conference." Ministerial Conference, December 9–13, Singapore. Accessed at http:/ /www .wto.org/English/thewto_e/minist_e/wtodoc_e.html, May 15, 2007.

Selected Websites

Rugmark Foundation: www.rugmark.org
Nepal Rugmark Foundation: www.nepalrugmark.org
Comision para la Verificacion de Codigos de Conducta (COVERCO): http:// www.coverco.org.gt
International Labor Organization, «Export-Processing Zones, by Sector»: http:// www.ilo.org/public/english/dialogue/sector/themes/epz/stats.htm

Government Documents

India, Government of, Ministry of Textiles. Carpet Export Promotion Council. 2002. "Note on Kaleen Labeling System" (mimeo). New Delhi: Government of India.
Ministry of Textiles. 2002. "Note on Child Labor in the Carpet Industry" (mimeo). New Delhi: Government of India (October).
United Nations System's Operation in India. 1998. "Position Paper on Child Labor." New Delhi: International Labor Organization area office for India and Bhutan on behalf of the UN System in India.

Interviews

Jane Bennett, Johannesburg, March 2004.
David Fig, Johannesburg, May 2004.
Hewlett-Packard spokesperson, Davis, Calif., May 1985. Neva Makgetla, Johannesburg, March 2004.
Scott Nova, San Francisco, Calif., August 2004.

Interviews in New Delhi and Agra

Swami Agnivesh. 7 Jantar Mantar Rd., New Delhi, January 8, 2003. Praveen Bansal, Bansal Carpets, Agra, January 11, 2003.
T. S. Chadha, executive director, Carpet Export Promotion Council, New Delhi, January 10, 2003.
K. Chandramouli, joint secretary to the Ministry of Labor, New Delhi, January 13, 2003.
Dr. Mohatir Dubey, president, Council for Social and Economic Development. Offices of the council, New Delhi, January 7, 2003.
John P. John, New Delhi, January 9, 2003.
Tinoo Joshi, development commissioner (handicrafts), Ministry of Textiles. New Delhi, January 8, 2003.
Amargit Kaur, New Delhi, January 9, 2003.
Dr. Dietrich Kebschull, director, Indo-German Export Promotion Council (IGEP). New Delhi, January 7, 2003.
S. B. Mohaptra, secretary to the Government of India, Ministry of Textiles, New Delhi, January 8, 2003.
Gerry Pinto, UNICEF, New Delhi. January 13, 2003.
Sharda Subramaniam, deputy director, ludo-German Export Promotion Council. Offices of the IGEP, German House, New Delhi, January 7, 2003.

Interviews in Guatemala

Alejandro Argueta, adviser to the Labor Ministry, Guatemala City, January 2005. Irene Barrientos, international affairs coordinator, Unsitragua (Union Sindical de Trabajadores de Guatemala), Guatemala City, May 2003.
Rodolfo Batres, manager of investment in Guatemala, Ministry of Economy, Guatemala City, January 2005.
Lucy Bautista, monitor for COVERCO, Guatemala City, May 2003.

Cesar Castillo, Vice-Ministry of Labor and Social Prevision, Guatemala City, January 2005.

Ricardo Changala, United Nations Verification Mission (MINIGUA). May 2003. ChoiSim/Simatex workers collective interviews, Villa Nueva, May 22, 2003. Sonia Figuero, director of Social Prevision, Ministry of Labor. January 2005. Homero Fuentes, coordinador, COVERCO, Guatemala City, 2003 to 2006. Cesar Gatica, labor inspector, Social Prevision, Ministry of Labor, Guatemala City, May 22, 2006.

Eda Gaviola and Floridalma Contreras, activists with CALDH (Centro de Accion Legal y Derechos Humanos), Programa de Derechos de las Mujeres, Guatemala City, May 2003.

Teresa Guillermo, VESTEX (Comision de Vestuarios y Textiles), Guatemala City, May 2003.

Carlos E. De Icaza, International Affairs, Regional Program of Labor Market Modernization, SIECA (Secretaria de Integracion Econemica de Centroamericana (Secretary for Central American Economic Integration), Guatemala City, January 2005.

Carlos Enrique Mancilla Garcia, CUSG (Confederacion de Unidad Sindical de Guatemala), Guatemala City, May 2003.

Jose David Morales, general secretary, FESTRAS (Federacion Sindical de Trabajadores de la Alimentacion Agro-Industria y Similares de Guatemala), Guatemala City, May 2003.

Jose Luis Morales Perez, labor inspector, Social Prevision, Ministry of Labor, Guatemala City, May 22–23, 2006.

Abby Najera interviews, Guatemala City, May 2003, January 2005, May 2006. Robert Perillo, U.S./Labor Education in the Americas Project, Guatemala City, May 2003.

Laura Podolsky, STITCH, Guatemala City, May 2003.

Guido Richi, Labor Commission, CACIF (Comite Coordinador de Asociaciones Agricolas, Comerciales, Industriales, y Financieras), Guatemala City, January 2005.

Dennis A. Smith, president, COVERCO, Guatemala City, May 2003.

Roberto Tobar and Wendy Tobar, COVERCO, Guatemala City, January 2005. Victor Hugo Toledo, congressman and chair of Comisi6n de Prevision y Seguridad Social, Guatemala Congress, Guatemala City, January 2005.

Gabriel Zelada Ortiz, CEADEL (Centro de Estudios y Apoyo al Desarrollo Local) , Guatemala City, May 2003.

PART IV

HUMAN RIGHTS

CHAPTER EIGHT

The Power of Norms versus the Norms of Power: Transnational Civil Society and Human Rights

Thomas Risse

Source: Ann M. Florini (ed.) *The Third Force: The Rise of Transnational Civil Society* (2000) 177–209 © 2000 Japan Center for International Exchange and Carnegie Endowment for International Peace—Reproduced with permission.

Dictators on the Run?

In October 1998, a Spanish judge requested that Britain arrest and extradite to Spain the former Chilean dictator General Augusto Pinochet to stand trial for genocide, torture, and executions. During the 1970s, Pinochet had been responsible for some of the worst human rights abuses in the history of his country. When Chile returned to democracy in 1990, few perpetrators of human rights abuses were brought to justice. General Pinochet became a member for life of the Chilean Senate, enjoying diplomatic immunity as a former head of state. But are torture and genocide part of the job description for heads of states? The British lord judges who adjudicated the Spanish extradition request judged that Pinochet could be held accountable for torture and other abuses, but only those committed after Britain had ratified the United Nations (UN) Anti-Torture Convention.

In May 1998, Indonesia's President Suharto was forced to resign after more than thirty years of ruling his country. Most observers agreed that the Asian financial crisis, with its disastrous consequences for the Indonesian population, caused Suharto's loss of power. Widespread riots and looting, attacks on the economically powerful Chinese minority, and a crime rate that has spiraled out of control seem to corroborate this analysis. A closer look at the events in Indonesia reveals, however, that Suharto's resignation was only the culmination of a longer chain of events. East Timorese human rights activists had at least as much to do with Suharto's loss of power as brokers on Wall Street did.

What do Pinochet's arrest in London and Suharto's resignation in Jakarta portend? Are dictators on the run worldwide? Are human rights norms finally gaining ground against the interests of the powerful? And if changes really are occurring, who is responsible?

Even a superficial look at the annual reports of Amnesty International and other human rights organizations reveals that torture, disappearances, mass killings, and other atrocities have not yet substantially decreased worldwide. Although governments and other state agents may be less likely to commit human rights violations, there is an alarming rise of atrocities against human beings by nongovernmental groups such as terrorists, guerrilla movements, paramilitary and private security forces, and the like.

Nevertheless, real progress has occurred. States that want to be members of international society "in good standing" increasingly realize that they have to respect basic human rights and meet some minimum standards of behavior toward their citizens. Even China's leaders, not generally known for their concern about the rights of their citizens, recently asked the Japanese and German governments to advise them how to institute the rule of law. Fifty years after the UN General Assembly adopted the Universal Declaration of Human Rights, these norms have become standards of acceptable behavior in international society. Dictators can no longer claim "interference in internal affairs" when confronted with gross violations of human rights. This is a profound change in the underlying principles of international society.

And that progress is overwhelmingly due to the efforts of transnational civil society. Pinochet's arrest and Suharto's resignation would not have been possible without the decade-long struggles and the transnational mobilization of human rights activists around the globe and in the countries concerned. The norms these activists have created increasingly circumscribe the power of governments and have profoundly transformed our understanding of national sovereignty. International nongovernmental organizations (INGOs), churches, trade unions, and political foundations were all crucial in accomplishing two tasks. First, they helped to establish human rights standards firmly in international law and to create monitoring institutions such as the UN Commission for Human Rights. Second, they linked up with groups in the domestic civil societies of many norms-violating states to help bring about change in human rights behavior.

This chapter traces the evolution of transnational civil society in the human rights sector. It shows how the increased sophistication of international human rights law and international institutions and the growth of transnational civil society in this area went hand in hand. It also analyzes the effects of these transnational activities "on the ground," that is, achieving government compliance with human rights standards. The chapter concludes by evaluating the overall record of transnational civil society in the human rights area and laying out future challenges.

The chapter concentrates on a subset of international human rights norms, namely, civil and political rights enshrined in the 1976 Covenant for Civil and Political Rights, in particular the "freedom from" norms (freedom from torture, from detention without trial, from disappearances, and so forth). This focus is purely practical, with no implications that such rights are more important than other widely recognized rights such as social or economic ones. Rather, progress (or failure) regarding norm compliance is more easily measurable when it comes to these rights. Moreover, the mechanisms and dynamics of transnational mobilization identified in this chapter may well be generalizable across other human rights.

International Human Rights and the Mobilization of Transnational Civil Society

INGOs have long mobilized for human rights. Centuries before terms like "transnational civil society" entered the language of social scientists and political practitioners, similar movements were already active across societies.[1] Anglo-American campaigns to abolish slavery in the United States and to prohibit the international slave trade from the late eighteenth to mid-nineteenth centuries are among the earliest. The Anti-Slavery Society, founded in 1839, was probably the oldest human rights INGO.[2] From 1874 to 1911, Western missionaries, Victorian ladies in Great Britain, and Chinese reformers joined forces in the Natural Foot Society to fight the practice of foot binding in Imperial China. There is even a predecessor to recent campaigns against female genital mutilation (female circumcision). In the 1920s, the Church of Scotland Missionary Society led a transnational campaign against female circumcision among the Kikuyus in Kenya.

But these isolated campaigns do not compare either in quantity or in quality with what happened after World War II. Transnational civil society in the human rights area today encompasses not only a much larger variety of INGOs, such as Amnesty International, Human Rights Watch, and the International Commission of Jurists, but also churches, trade unions, peace movements, and foundations such as the Ford Foundation and the German Friedrich Ebert and Konrad Adenauer Foundations. Although the latter are not solely human rights groups, they often engage in promoting international human rights.

Starting near the end of World War II, these groups began to shape a broad range of human rights norms. At the Dumbarton Oaks conference in 1944, followed by the San Francisco conference that founded the United Nations in 1945, NGO lobbying was crucial in securing the inclusion of human rights in various articles of the UN Charter. NGO lobbyists worked hard to ensure that the UN Charter would contain provisions setting up a human rights commission, which was then specifically mandated in the charter. This Commission on Human Rights drafted the Universal Declaration of Human Rights, which the UN General Assembly adopted in December 1948.[3] INGO input in this "Magna Charta of Human Rights" was significant.

These documents, however, were essentially nonbinding declarations of intent. Few intergovernmental organizations (IGOs) specifically worked in this area, so no binding agreements were negotiated. The same holds true for regional agreements and organizations to protect human rights—with the significant exception of Western Europe, where the binding European Convention on Human Rights (including a Human Rights Court) came into force in 1953. In Latin America, the Organization of American States (OAS) established the Inter-American Commission on Human Rights in 1959, but this organization got legal "teeth" only when the American Convention on Human Rights went into force twenty years later. At the time, the INGO sector focusing exclusively on human rights was equally limited. In 1953, for example, only thirty-three human rights INGOs existed worldwide.[4]

In 1961, however, Peter Benenson, a British lawyer, and two colleagues founded Amnesty International. Benenson had read a newspaper article about two Portuguese who had been imprisoned because of a dinner conversation criticizing the Salazar dictatorship. He decided that something ought to be done to help these "prisoners of conscience." On May 28, 1961, the London-based Observer published his article "The Foreign Prisoner," which other newspapers around the world picked up immediately. Amnesty International was born. The organization quickly spread from Britain to the Federal Republic of Germany and then on to other Western European countries and the United States. In 1977, when Amnesty received the Nobel Peace Prize, it had 168,000 members in 107 countries. These members were mostly organized in local groups. Each would "adopt" three political prisoners, one each in a Western democratic, a communist, and a Third World country; and work for their release. This principle of balanced neutrality toward the various types of political regimes served to quickly establish the moral authority of Amnesty, together with its meticulous research and information-gathering activities.[5]

From the early 1970s on, the activities of transnational civil society in the human rights area grew dramatically. Seventy-nine human rights INGOS were active worldwide by 1983; this number more than doubled to 168 by 1993.[6] By 1999, Amnesty International alone had more than a million members in more than 160 states, even though half of its membership is concentrated in three countries, the United Kingdom, Germany, and the United States.[7] There are some 5,300 local Amnesty groups in more than ninety countries registered with the International Secretariat in London.

This explosion of activities emerged out of particular transnational campaigns against repressive regimes during the 1970s. Four such campaigns stand out. First, the Greek coup d'etat in 1967 gave rise to human rights campaigns, particularly in Europe. When reports of widespread atrocities in Greek prisons became known, Amnesty International and others launched their first transnational campaign against torture, setting in motion a process that eventually led to the Anti-Torture Convention (see below).

Second, the repressive regime of Augusto Pinochet following his putsch against the democratically elected President Salvador Allende in 1973 led to the rise of a tremendous number of transnational activities, particularly in the United States, where the Nixon administration had actively supported Allende's overthrow. From 1974 to 1976, the U.S. section of Amnesty expanded from 3,000 to 50,000 members. Human rights organizations emerged everywhere in Latin America.[8]

Third, the antiapartheid campaign against South Africa spawned a vast number of transnational efforts.[9] The Soweto massacre in June 1976, during which police killed sixty-nine students during a demonstration, led to an international outcry against the apartheid regime. The antiapartheid movement soon became one of the most powerful campaigns in transnational civil society. Its claims resonated particularly well with and were able to "transnationalize" the demands of the civil rights movement in the United States of the 1960s.

The repressive regimes in these three regions of the world, which gave rise to the mobilization of so many people, did not commit particularly awesome crimes against humanity, at least as compared with other oppressive governments. At about the same time during the 1970s, Uganda's dictator Idi Amin ordered the systematic killing of supporters and tribal kinsmen of his predecessor, Milton Obote. He nearly committed a genocide against his own people—resulting in far less international mobilization. What Greece, Chile, and South Africa had in common, though, is the fact that the repressive regimes had either replaced democratic governments or—as in the case of South Africa—claimed to be a liberal democracy even though political rights were confined to the white minority. Thus, it was the gap between proclaimed liberal values and actual behavior that mobilized transnational civil society.

Last but not least came the 1975 Helsinki Final Act of the Conference on Security and Cooperation in Europe (CSCE). On Western European insistence, over the objections of both the United States and the Soviet Union, it included a human rights provision. The Helsinki human rights standard provided dissidents in communist Eastern Europe and the Soviet Union with a powerful tool against their regimes and had a dramatic effect on the rise of dissident movements in Eastern Europe and the former Soviet Union. Soviet and East European citizens learned quickly about the content of the Helsinki agreement through word of mouth, samizdat publications, and Western media. In May 1976, Soviet dissidents founded the Helsinki Watch Group; the Charter 77 movement was born in Czechoslovakia on January 1, 1977. Each of these and other groups legitimized their demands through reference to the Helsinki human rights document that their communist governments had signed. They then linked up with human rights organizations in Western states and in transnational civil society and provided them with regular updates on repression in the Soviet Union and Eastern Europe. As a result, human rights concerns became a regular feature of the CSCE follow-on meetings in Belgrade (1977–78) and Madrid (1980–83). Thus, the "Helsinki effect" led to substantial human rights mobilization in Eastern Europe, and this mobilization contributed significantly to the fall of the Berlin Wall and the end of the Cold War in 1989.[10]

The ordeal of the dissident groups in Eastern Europe and the Soviet Union also led in 1978 to the creation of Helsinki Watch, an American NGO. Arthur Goldberg, former Supreme Court justice and U.S. representative at one of the CSCE follow-on conferences, was concerned about the limited media coverage of human rights violations in the communist bloc and convinced the Ford Foundation to become active in this area. The president of the Ford Foundation approached Robert Bernstein, an activist among American publishers, to start a human rights campaign focusing on communist Eastern Europe and the Soviet Union. Bernstein founded Helsinki Watch in the United States—alluding to the Moscow group with the same name. Although Helsinki Watch originated from the initiative of a U.S. government official, it quickly asserted its independence. In 1981, Bernstein founded America Watch to investigate human rights abuses by right-wing dictatorships in Latin America that were supported by the Reagan administration. Over the next years, Bernstein and others created more regional "watchdog" organizations, such as Africa Watch and Asia Watch. Ten years later, Human Rights Watch (HRW) became the umbrella organization of the regional watchdogs and a main competitor as well as ally of Amnesty International among human rights INGOs. Although HRW originated as a US.-based organization, it mushroomed into a truly global INGO during the 1990s.[11]

At the same time that transnational civil society was mobilizing in these campaigns, it was also benefiting from the emergence of international legal standards that went beyond the broad goals of the Universal Declaration. In 1976, the Covenant for Civil and Political Rights, as well as the Covenant for Economic and Social Rights went into force. During the same year, the New York-based UN Human Rights Committee started its activities.

The strengthening of the international legal framework for human rights protection directly affected the growth of INGOs and other groups operating in transnational civil society. It did so through the authority of international law as opposed to just moral convictions. There is quite a difference between, say, arguing that female circumcision constitutes an immoral atrocity against human dignity and the right to one's own sexuality, on the one hand, and being able to pinpoint an international legal prohibition against genital mutilation, on the other. In the latter case, advocacy groups not only have a moral case against the particular human rights violation; they can also argue that the norm violator puts itself outside the community of civilized nations and often is violating standards it has agreed to.

The other side of this coin concerns the influence of transnational civil society on the creation of these norms themselves. As argued earlier, INGO activities during the 1940s had a significant impact on the UN Charter and the Universal Declaration of Human Rights. In the absence of sustained campaigns and lobbying efforts by INGOs and particular individuals, probably not a single human right would have been written into international law. The history of the 1984 UN Convention against Torture and Other Cruel, Inhuman, or Degrading Treatment or Punishment provides an instructive example.[12] It began with the 1967 Greek colonels' putsch against the democratically elected government in Athens. Amnesty International, together with several Scandinavian countries, accused the junta of torture and other violations of human rights and brought the case to the attention of the European Human Rights Convention and its organs. At the time, this convention contained the only legally binding provision against torture worldwide. The Greek case triggered worldwide protests, as a result of which Amnesty International decided to launch a global campaign against torture in 1972. Sweden, the Netherlands, Austria, Costa Rica, and others then used the Amnesty campaign to raise the issue of torture in the UN General Assembly one year later. The Chilean coup d'etat only added oil to the fire of the antitorture campaign. In 1974, the General Assembly mandated that experts begin working on a declaration against torture.

Amnesty and other INGOs started petition campaigns and mobilized public opinion to influence the attitude of their national governments. Amnesty's peculiar structure of national sections together with an international secretariat was helpful in organizing this campaign. The experts' draft, considerably influenced by lawyers working for Amnesty, became the basis for negotiations in the UN Human Rights Commission on an antitorture convention.

Various governments, including the Netherlands, France, and Australia, rejected some of the legally binding provisions as intrusions into their national sovereignty. At this point, Amnesty and other INGOs not only worked closely with the UN Human Rights Commission to influence the drafting of the convention but also increasingly lobbied national governments. This campaign concentrated on the weakest link in the chain of Western resistance to the convention—the Netherlands. Amnesty's ability to act both globally as an INGO and simultaneously through its national chapters greatly facilitated carrying out parallel global and national campaigns. When the Dutch government changed its position in 1980, Amnesty successfully persuaded the French and Australian governments to change course too. In December 1984, ten years after its first activities on the issue, the UN General Assembly passed the Anti-Torture Convention. It went into force in 1987.[13]

This case in many ways typifies how transnational civil society goes about creating international norms. First, Amnesty International and other groups were decisive in putting the question of torture on the international agenda. Such agenda setting is quite common. Recent examples concern the rights of indigenous peoples and women's rights.[14]

Second, nongovernmental actors participated in the negotiations and working groups drafting the international agreements, both indirectly as members of expert groups and directly as members of official national delegations. In other words, transnational civil society is involved in treaty making. In this role, INGOs are not necessarily opposing national governments. Rather, groups of states are closely cooperating with INGOs and relying on their expertise and knowledge. In the case of the Anti-Torture Convention, national governments such as Sweden worked closely with Amnesty and aligned with INGOs against other groups of states.

Third, transnational civil society does not operate solely within the frameworks provided by international organizations such as the UN. Rather, the effectiveness of human rights INGOS depends on their grounding in domestic civil societies. The successful conclusion of the Anti-Torture Convention was possible because Amnesty and other INGOS sat in the negotiating chambers and, at the same time, their activists lobbied local, regional, and national communities to become active toward their national governments.

Finally, the case demonstrates the .power resources available to transnational civil society. By any material standard, transnational civil society is weak. There is no antitorture army and no wealthy human rights multinational corporation. Amnesty, the giant among the human rights INGOs, has an annual budget of about $29 million.[15] A survey of NGOs working in the human rights area identified financial limitations as by far the most significant organizational obstacle facing transnational civil society in this area.[16] The mean annual budget of human rights NGOs was $ 1.6 million, with a huge gap between the annual revenues of Northern and Southern NGOs (average income of the latter was $400,000).

The influence of transnational civil society in the human rights area stems from the power of moral authority and legitimacy, on the one hand, and the accepted claim to authoritative knowledge, on the other. These two aspects—moral authority and knowledge—go together and cannot be separated.

Moral authority is directly related to the claim by transnational civil society that it somehow represents the "public interest" or the "common good" rather than private interests. This is a crucial condition. INGOs can quickly lose their credibility if they become identified with some special economic or political interests. It took HRW quite a while, for instance, to lose its initial reputation as an instrument of U.S. human rights policy. The ability to act as credible speakers for the oppressed with no other concern than to promote their inalienable rights is what makes the transnational human rights organizations so powerful, even if compared with and pitched against major states or private firms.

This rather idealist picture must be tempered somewhat. Human rights belong to the core identity of the community of liberal and democratic states, which also happen to be the most powerful states in terms of economic and other resources. Although human rights INGOs do not simply represent Western interests (they have been fighting Western policies for too long for such a claim to be credible), their moral authority is not totally disconnected from political, economic, and even military power in the global system.

Even so, moral authority by itself does not explain the impact of transnational civil society in human rights. It goes hand in hand with a widely accepted claim to knowledge. Today, Amnesty International, HRW, and the Lawyers Committee for Human Rights *define* what constitutes a human rights violation. Other groups, INGOs, and even states might provide the information and disseminate it. But only if Amnesty, HRW, or the Lawyers Committee "approves" of this information as being correct does this constitute a human rights violation in the eyes of the international community. Many Western governments, including the United States and Germany, often use information provided by Amnesty or HRW almost verbatim when they write their own human rights reports.[17]

The authoritative claim to knowledge enjoyed by INGOs today did not fall from heaven. Very strict information-gathering rules were necessary to establish such credibility. Amnesty International, for example, uses only information that at least three independent sources have corroborated. Moreover, while information gathering itself may be decentralized, Amnesty headquarters in London strictly controls the spread of news about particular rights violations in a given country. HRW uses similar rules of information gathering, but its use of the information in particular campaigns appears to be more strategic and more strongly geared toward raising media attention.

INGOs can then use their moral authority and their information to convince other actors— particularly governments and international organizations, but also the general public in many countries—that they have an obligation to act. When dealing with Western states, they usually remind these governments that liberal democracies, by definition, are supposed to be concerned with protecting human rights and the rule of law. In a liberal democratic state, why would a government place national sovereignty, economic gains, or strategic interests over human rights? Shaming strategies are used to highlight the gap between a country's proclaimed liberal identity, on the one hand, and its unwillingness to conduct its foreign policy accordingly, on the other.[18]

INGOs also rely on shaming when dealing with human rights-violating governments. Shaming in such a case serves the purpose of putting the government on notice that its actions place it outside the international community. In the South African case, for example, the transnational campaign against apartheid portrayed the country as a pariah state outside the community of "civilized" nations.[19] Some repressive governments might not care. Others, however, are deeply offended, because they want to belong to the "civilized community" of states. In many cases, leaders of countries care what leaders of other countries think of them. Shaming implies a process of persuasion, since it convinces leaders that their behavior is inconsistent with an identity to which they aspire. When transnational civil society accused Moroccan King Hassan II of serious human rights abuses in 1990, for example, he felt insulted, since the national identity of Morocco was at stake: "Our history, thanks to the creative spirit which illustrates a large contribution to the sciences, the arts, to civilization, and to the law, shows that our country has always seen itself as living in a civilized society next to the developed states and nations."[20]

Ultimately, then, human rights norms, and the transnational civil society agents that promote those norms, have become such powerful devices in international relations because they help define a category of states—"liberal states." Sovereignty has always depended on mutual recognition. Now, to be recognized as a state in good standing is moving beyond the old standard of effective and exclusive control of territory. In some cases, these liberal "clubs" are quite specific—in the case of the European Union, for example, only democratic states with good human rights records can join the club. In the inter-American system, such norms are just now emerging. The OAS Managua Declaration of 1993, for example, includes explicit statements about what kind of states are welcome in the club. The OAS members declare "the need to consolidate, as part of the cultural identity of each nation in the Hemisphere, democratic structures and systems which encourage freedom and social justice, safeguard human rights, and favor progress."[21]

Norm Spirals and Boomerangs: The Domestic Impact of Transnational Civil Society

Is the international human rights talk just cheap talk? What about the continual atrocities and human rights violations all over the world, as reported in the yearly statements of Amnesty International, the U.S. Department of State, and other monitoring institutions? What about the contribution of transnational civil society and its norm-creating activities on the ground, that is, in the domestic implementation of human rights standards?[22]

To estimate that impact, the study on which this chapter is based looked at paired cases of countries with serious human rights situations from five regions of the world—northern Africa, sub-Saharan Africa, Southeast Asia, Latin America, and Eastern Europe. In addition to the well-publicized "success stories" such as Chile, South Africa, the Philippines, Poland, and the former Czechoslovakia, we examined a series of more obscure and apparently intractable cases such as Guatemala, Kenya, Uganda, Morocco, Tunisia, and Indonesia. We explored the influence that transnational mobilization and campaigns had in a wide variety of states with very different cultures and institutions. On the basis of these country cases, we developed a dynamic model of human rights changes that links international law and the mobilization efforts of transnational civil society to opposition and dissident activities in the domestic societies of norm-violating countries.

Various studies on the impact of human rights norms in Latin America have emphasized how domestic and transnational social movements have united to bring pressure "from above" and "from below" to compel governments to abide by human rights standards. Margaret Keck and Kathryn Sikkink referred to this process as the "boomerang effect."[23] A boomerang pattern of influence exists when domestic groups in a repressive state bypass their government and directly search out international allies to bring pressure on their states from outside. National opposition groups, NGOS, and social movements link with foreign members of the transnational network, which then convince international organizations, donor institutions, or great powers to put pressure on norm-violating states. Transnationally operating INGOs provide access, leverage, information, and often money to struggling domestic groups. International contacts "amplify" the demands of domestic groups, pry open space for new issues, and then echo these demands back into the domestic arena.

To understand the full dynamics of transnational civil society in ensuring the implementation of human rights, we have to go beyond this boomerang model, which shows static snapshots of the linkages among local and transnational actors. In reality, the evolution of human rights practices resembles not a single boomerang throw but a whole spiral of boomerangs repeatedly crossing national borders. This dynamic approach reveals how governments are likely to respond to transnational pressures, what can be expected at various stages, and, most important, why transnational civil society is essential to bringing about change in national human rights practices. In short, the spiral keeps spiraling only if transnational civil society makes it happen.

The spiral is a dance with many partners: transnational civil society (composed of INGOs, churches, trade unions, political foundations, and the like) loosely connected to officials working for intergovernmental organizations or for national governments. The international institutions are primarily the human rights bodies of the UN and the various human rights treaties that have been drafted and ratified under UN auspices, but they also include some regional institutions, such as the Inter-American Commission and Court of Human Rights.

Phase 1: Repression and Activation of Transnational Civil Society

The spiral starts with a repressive situation in some country—the target. Struggles over political power are almost always the main reason for human rights abuses by repressive governments. In the Philippines, for example, President Marcos proclaimed martial law in 1972 to get rid of domestic armed opposition. Tens of thousands of Filipinos were arrested and tortured.[24] In Indonesia (1965), Morocco (1971–72), and Kenya (1982), repressive regimes committed human rights abuses to fight off coups d'etat. The levels of repression vary greatly among countries, from extreme repression bordering on genocide (as in the cases of Uganda and Guatemala) to much lower levels of repression (as in the case of Tunisia).[25] This phase of repression might last for decades, since many oppressive states never make it onto the agenda of transnational civil society. Unfortunately, the degree of repression may even determine whether transnational INGOs can acquire information about human rights conditions in a country. When the genocide in Rwanda took place in 1994, for example, information gathering was next to impossible, since all humanitarian organizations had fled. In the case of the Chilean coup d'etat in 1973, however, it took Amnesty International and the International Commission of Jurists just three days to send a cable to the OAS's Inter-American Commission on Human Rights requesting its intervention.[26] In Indonesia, a small legal foundation started operating in 1971 and then began exchanging information with Amnesty, the International Commission of Jurists, and others, thus throwing a first boomerang and linking with transnational civil society.[27] At this stage, transnational mobilization is a necessary condition for moving the process further.

Phase 2: Norms Denial

The second phase of the spiral puts the norm-violating state on the international agenda, almost always through the efforts of transnational civil society. Human rights violations in South Africa during the 1960s and 1970s, and in Chile and the Philippines during the 1970s, created an environment in which such consciousness-raising could take place and were thus crucial for the emergence of transnational civil society in the human rights area. These transnational groups could then be reactivated during the early 1980s, when they started lobbying Western powers and international organizations. Even in Poland and Czechoslovakia, where repression under communism had always been a concern for Western governments, it was transnational pressure that put human rights on the Western agenda in the late 1970s.[28] Helsinki Watch, among others, amplified the concerns of dissidents in Eastern Europe and the Soviet Union toward Western public opinion.

The initial activation of transnational civil society often results from a particularly awful violation of human rights, such as a massacre. When news about systematic torture and the disappearance of many opposition leaders reached the West after Pinochet's coup in 1973, transnational civil society quickly mobilized.[29] INGOs usually compile and disseminate information about human rights practices, often with the cooperation of human rights organizations in the repressive state. In the Chilean case, for example, the Catholic Church and its Vicariate of Solidarity provided the crucial link between national human rights organizations and transnational civil society. The transnational groups then start lobbying intergovernmental human rights organizations as well as Western states, where they target both public opinion and national governments. These lobbying activities might lead to some pressure on the repressive government to improve its human rights conditions.

Norm violators almost always react by denying the initial charges of human rights abuses. Denial goes further than simply objecting to particular accusations. The norm-violating government claims that the criticism constitutes an illegitimate intervention in the internal affairs of the country. For years, the communist regimes in Eastern Europe argued that Western accusations of human rights abuses constituted an intervention in internal affairs, even after the Helsinki accords had come into effect.[30] The government may even succeed in mobilizing some nationalist sentiment against foreign intervention and criticism. Kenya's Arap Moi and Indonesia's Suharto used similar anticolonial rhetoric to reject charges of human rights violations made by Amnesty International. As a quasi-official Indonesian statement put it in 1978, "Amnesty still suffers from a 'moral arrogance' of the West which has been deplored by the Third World at large . . . [A]ll their efforts and objectives will be just counterproductive."[31]

Thus, the first boomerang throw often appears to be counterproductive, because it allows the repressive regime to solidify domestic support. The presence of a significant armed insurgent movement can dramatically extend this stage by heightening domestic perceptions of threat and fear. Any success of insurgent movements appears to validate the government's claim that the order or the very integrity of the nation is at stake, and it isolates domestic human rights organizations and international pressures by identifying these groups as conscious or unconscious accomplices of terrorism. But governments that publicly deny the authority of international human rights law as interference in internal affairs are at least implicitly aware that they face a problem in terms of their international reputation.

The denial stage can last for quite a long time. Some repressive governments care little about international pressures. They might also kill off or buy off the domestic opposition while it is still too weak to mount a major challenge to the regime. Therefore, the transition to the third phase constitutes the biggest challenge. This transition depends primarily on the strength of transnational mobilization in conjunction with the vulnerability of the norm-violating government to international pressures.[32] Almost all human rights campaigns involve particular kinds of material pressures, for example, when foreign aid becomes conditional on human rights performance. But the vulnerability of repressive governments may also come from a country's tradition of accepting normative commitments. Chile's Pinochet, for example, never denied the validity of international human rights norms. Given Chile's democratic tradition, he could not simply claim the principle of noninterference. Pinochet even accepted visits by the Inter-American Commission on Human Rights and by Amnesty International, while he continued to torture political prisoners.[33]

In the Indonesian case, the local Catholic church gathered most of the information on human rights abuses in East Timor and disseminated it abroad via organizations such as Pax Christi (a Catholic peace movement) and Asia Watch. This information then reached various UN bodies as well as the Non-Aligned Movement. At the same time, transnational civil society managed to activate members of the U.S. Congress and the European Parliament on the situation in Indonesia. When the UN Commission on Human Rights started criticizing the Indonesian government in the mid-1980s, the government responded by opening the previously closed province to outside observers. This tactical concession backfired, because more information about human rights abuses reached the international community, and transnational civil society disseminated it widely. The turning point was reached in 1991. When the UN special rapporteur on torture visited Dili, East Timor, he witnessed a massacre of civilians who had peacefully demonstrated against the regime. The Dili massacre, immediately reported by the international media, mobilized transnational civil society in a comprehensive way against human rights abuses of the Suharto regime. International and domestic NGOS now changed course and brought together the previously unrelated activities of the East Timorese networks and human rights groups in Indonesia proper. Responding to INGO pressure, Canada, Denmark, and the Netherlands froze their economic aid to Indonesia, while the United States, Japan, and the World Bank threatened to do so. The international reaction to the Dili massacre moved Indonesia toward the next phase in the process.[34]

Phase 3: Tactical Concessions

If transnational civil society manages to escalate the pressures, the norm-violating state is likely to seek to pacify international criticism. At this point, the repressive government makes concessions to regain military or economic assistance or to lessen international isolation.

Although the government might then temporarily improve the situation—for example, by releasing prisoners—human rights conditions do not improve all that much. The more sustained period of international concerns, however, allows the initial "rally around the flag" effect to wear off. The minor improvements give the repressed domestic opposition new courage and space to mount its own campaign of criticism against the government.

In case after case, transnational pressure turns out to be the single most important cause of change toward initial concessions by the norm-violating government, even more important than pressure from other governments. In some cases—Indonesia, Kenya, Guatemala, Chile, and (to a lesser extent) the Philippines—the advocacy coalitions managed to convince some Western governments to institute sanctions, which can help but are not always needed. In the South African case, which entered the tactical concessions stage after the Soweto massacre in 1976, international sanctions emerged only gradually in response to the massacre and were not fully effective until the mid-1980s.[35]

Developments in Indonesia provide a good example of the dynamics of this phase.[36] In response to the international outcry following the 1991 Dili massacre, President Suharto speedily appointed a National Investigating Commission, which, surprisingly, issued a rather critical report of the events. This concession accomplished its goal in the sense that foreign donors resumed economic aid to Indonesia. But Suharto was no longer in control of the situation. INGOs worked hard to bring together the previously disconnected domestic human rights groups in East Timor and in Indonesia proper. They did so by convincing East Timorese leaders that they should focus on human rights violations rather than the question of self-determination. In the early 1990s, "human rights" proved to be an effective rallying cry, both unifying the domestic opposition and ensuring broader international support for its goals. The Indonesian opposition then used human rights violations in East Timor to criticize repressive practices of the Suharto regime in general. As East Timorese opposition leader and 1996 Nobel Peace Prize winner Jose Ramos-Horta put it, "the fate of East Timor and the democracy movement in Indonesia are intimately linked, each supports the other. . . . The more pressure that is focused on Suharto about East Timor, the more space there is for the opposition to push for change in Indonesia."[37] Suharto's tactical concessions opened political space for civil society in Indonesia to mobilize. In 1992, and again with the help of resources provided by transnational civil society, activists founded independent trade unions, an association of journalists, and new political parties tolerated by the regime. In 1993, the (International) Lawyers' Committee for Human Rights published a special report on Indonesia, "Broken Laws, Broken Bodies," condemning the widespread practices of torture. In March of the same year, the UN Human Rights Commission adopted a critical resolution that was supported by the U.S. government. In response to the increasing domestic and transnational pressures, and anticipating criticism of his country at the upcoming World Conference on Human Rights in Vienna, Suharto instituted a national human rights commission in 1993 that published rather critical reports. This move, of course, legitimized human rights claims of the opposition even further. In 1996, the human rights causes in East Timor and Indonesia in general gained further international legitimacy when

Ramos-Horta and Bishop Ximenes Belo received the Nobel Peace Price. By then, transnational civil society mobilization had succeeded in changing Indonesia's international image from that of a stable and reliable power in East Asia to that of a corrupt and oppressive dictatorship.

Yet human rights conditions in Indonesia did not improve. On the contrary, the Suharto government combined tactical concessions to relieve the pressure with continual crackdowns against the opposition. But the regime had long since lost control over the domestic situation, which became obvious when the economic crisis hit the country in late 1997. Since transnational civil society and the domestic opposition had successfully damaged Suharto's reputation—pointing to the lack of public accountability, systematic human rights violations, and widespread corruption—the crisis gained a different meaning than in Thailand or South Korea. It served as a catalyst for change, and mass protests ultimately led to Suharto's resignation in June 1998. Although the political situation in Indonesia is far from stable, it is quite remarkable that President Jusuf Habibie, Suharto's successor, continued on the path to establish the rule of law in the country. The fierce power struggle between the Indonesian military and the civilian leadership is far from over and has resulted in atrocious human rights abuses in East Timor (which is now de facto an international protectorate) and elsewhere in the country. Yet Indonesia's new president, Abdurrahman Wahid, has proceeded with the human rights policies of his predecessor.

There is remarkable similarity between the processes of change in Indonesia and events in totally different corners of the world during the phase of tactical concessions. Morocco, Kenya, South Africa, Guatemala, Chile, the Philippines, Poland, and former Czechoslovakia all experienced stages whereby transnational and domestic civil society aligned and put the repressive regimes under increasing pressure. Almost always, norm-violating governments responded with a combination of tactical concessions and continued repression. Almost always, they lost control over the domestic situation. They then faced two choices: change or run. Among the eleven countries investigated for this study, only the late Moroccan king picked the first choice and embarked on a process of sustained political liberalization. Today, the Islamic monarchy of Morocco is the most liberal state in the Maghreb region. In most other cases, human rights violators eventually had to go (though sometimes through negotiated transitions), as in South Africa, many Latin American countries, and Eastern Europe.

The most important effect of transnational mobilization against a determined government is not so much to change the behavior of the government but to facilitate social mobilization in the domestic arena of the repressive state. The focus of activities is now likely to shift from the transnational to the domestic level. Transnational mobilization in this stage empowers and legitimates the demands of the domestic opposition. It also protects the physical safety of many activists on the ground. It accomplishes these goals by:

- Spreading information about the domestic situation in the country around the globe.
- Lobbying key Western governments, parliaments, and international organizations to toughen their stance toward the norm-violating government.
- Providing financial resources and training in human rights issues to domestic NGOs and other opposition groups.
- Confronting the norm-violating government in a continuous debate regarding its human rights practices.

This is the most precarious phase of the spiral model. It moves the process forward toward enduring change in human rights conditions only if domestic opposition and civil society are able to use the boomerang provided by the transnational coalitions to mobilize inside the country. If a government responds with unrelenting repression of activists, it can temporarily break the upward spiral process. At the beginning of phase 3, the domestic human rights movements are often small and dependent on a handful of key leaders. Arresting or killing these leaders decapitates the movement, and the resulting fear paralyzes it. This is what happened during the 1989 demonstrations in Tiananmen Square in Beijing. But the additional repression is costly to the government in terms of its domestic legitimacy, and it may validate international criticism by revealing more clearly the coercive power of the state.

If the cycle is not delayed, the domestic opposition is likely to gain strength. The fully mobilized domestic NGO networks, linked to the global human rights coalitions, can be activated at any time. Toward the end of the tactical concession phase, norm-violating governments are no longer in control of the domestic situation.

Phase 4: Prescriptive Status

We reach the fourth phase of the spiral if and when national governments completely accept the moral validity of human rights norms and start institutionalizing the norms in the domestic legal context. The binding nature of human rights norms is no longer controversial, even if the actual behavior continues violating the rules. The process by which human rights ideas gain prescriptive status is decisive for their sustained impact on political and social change. Governments accept the validity of human rights norms if and when:

- They ratify the various international human rights conventions, including the optional protocols.
- They institutionalize the norms in the constitution or domestic law.
- They create an independent commission or provide some mechanism for individual citizens to complain about human rights violations.
- They publicly acknowledge the validity of the human rights norms irrespective of the (domestic or international) audience, no longer denounce criticism as interference in internal affairs, and engage in a dialogue with their critics.

Governments reach this stage after they have been confronted by fully mobilized domestic opposition groups and transnational INGO coalitions. At this point, either liberalization from above or a regime change is likely to occur. The move toward enduring human rights improvements in Poland, Czechoslovakia, South Africa, Chile, Guatemala, the Philippines, Indonesia, and Morocco resulted from the pressures of a full-fledged and well-organized domestic opposition linked with transnational civil society. In the cases of South Africa, Chile, Guatemala, the Philippines, and Indonesia, Western powers and major allies of the respective states finally joined the INGOs in their opposition against the norm-violating regimes and helped to move them "over the top." But they almost always followed rather than led the opposition. The Reagan administration ceased supporting the Marcos regime only when it had convinced itself that Marcos would be toppled anyway. The same holds true for the Clinton administration's decision ten years later to stop cooperating with Suharto one day before he resigned.[38] In other words, it is the interaction between transnational civil society and domestic opposition groups that brings countries to the phase of prescriptive status, rather than the (usually minimal) pressures exerted by Western governments or international organizations.

Uganda, the Philippines, and South Africa reached full prescriptive status immediately after the regime change, when the new governments began ratifying international agreements, institutionalizing them into domestic law, and fully embracing human rights norms in their communicative behavior. In Uganda, for example, the National Resistance Movement under the leadership of Yoweri Museveni took over power and ousted the Obote regime in 1986.[39] The new government immediately ratified the various international human rights conventions and transposed its provisions into domestic law, particularly the prohibition against torture. The government also established two procedures for individual complaints by citizens. In 1995, the new constitution instituted the Uganda Human Rights Commission with far-reaching legal competences. It has regularly issued reports on the Ugandan human rights situation that criticized the government. In 1997 alone, the commission dealt with more than 350 individual complaints.

Ratification of this or that international human rights agreement may constitute a tactical concession rather than the full acceptance of its precise normative content. Nevertheless, empirical case studies provide ample evidence that the acceptance of international norms through treaty ratification is not inconsequential. Governments entangle themselves in an international and domestic legal process that they subsequently find harder and harder to escape. The Helsinki human rights norm and its consequences for domestic change in Eastern Europe are a particularly striking example.[40] This process of rhetorical "self-entrapment" usually begins when a government is forced to make tactical concessions. Over time, however, a true dialogue frequently develops about concrete improvements in human rights conditions on the ground involving transnational civil society; international organizations, domestic groups, and the government of the target state.

The notion of prescriptive status describes developments in individual countries. But if prescriptive status were the result of primarily domestic factors, one would expect human rights norms to achieve this status in different countries at different times. Yet, in most of the countries we investigated, governments accepted the validity of international human rights norms around the same period—in the decade from 1985 to 1995. These countries are so different with regard to other aspects of their domestic politics, institutions, and socioeconomic conditions that the convergence around this period is puzzling, unless we incorporate global developments. There is no obvious reason why this happened at this time—the basic norms in the Universal Declaration of Human Rights and the main international institution, the UN Human Rights Commission, have been around since 1948, and the main treaties have been in force since 1976. The end of the Cold War might provide an explanation. But it is itself part of the story of the "power of norms," since the Helsinki human rights provision played a substantial part in ending communist rule in Eastern Europe and the former Soviet Union.[41] Another possible explanation is that all pieces of the domestic-transnational spiral model need to be firmly in place so that the international norm can have domestic effects on the ground. Not until the mid-1980s were all the components of this international and transnational structure fully formed, with the growing number of human rights treaties, international organizations, and INGOs; increased funding by political foundations for human rights work; and key countries now including human rights in their bilateral and multilateral foreign policies.

Phase 5: Rule-Consistent Behavior

Once human rights attain this prescriptive status, there is still a major role for transnational civil society in ensuring that deeds match words. Governments might accept human rights norms but still continue to torture prisoners or detain people without trial and the like. Sometimes, national governments are not fully in control of their police and military forces, which commit the human rights violations. The Ugandan, Philippine, and Indonesian cases are instructive.[42] Political violence escalated in the Philippines in the late 1980s, and counterinsurgency operations by the army led to increasing human rights abuses. Human rights conditions in the Philippines saw real improvement only after 1992, when the government negotiated peace agreements with various rebel groups.

In the Ugandan case, guerrilla activities in the north of the country have hindered the sustained improvement of human rights conditions.[43] Despite a consistent commitment to human rights by the new government under Yoweri Museveni, the police and the military continued to abuse human rights. While most of transnational civil society lost interest in the case, Amnesty International engaged the government in a continuous dialogue that included missions to Uganda and detailed proposals on how to improve prison conditions. Since the mid-1990s, international human rights organizations have increasingly focused on abuses and repression by Sudan-based rebel groups that conducted a systematic "war against children." UNICEF and other organizations, including the U.S. government, started paying attention to the situation in northern Uganda. This has become a rather peculiar case, whereby transnational civil society, Western states, and international organizations side with the government, which has proved its commitment to human rights, against guerrilla groups known for their widespread atrocities.

It is crucial for this phase that the domestic-transnational coalitions keep up the pressure in order to achieve sustainable improvements in human rights conditions. The particular difficulty in this phase is that gross violations of fundamental human rights actually decrease, so international attention declines, too. Although some INGOs try to keep the spotlight on actual behavior, international institutions and Western states are sometimes satisfied when rulers merely say the right things. This is particularly problematic when there has been a regime change, bringing into power a coalition that includes human rights activists. Nevertheless, conditions will improve in a sustainable way only when transnational civil society and domestic groups continually push national governments to live up to their claims. Only then can the final stage in the spiral model be reached, whereby governments comply with international human rights norms in a habitual way and the rule of law enforces compliance.

This does happen. Each of the seven countries included in our sample that reached full prescriptive status also experienced a subsequent, sustained, and drastic improvement in human rights conditions. Poland, Czechoslovakia, South Africa, Chile, Uganda, the Philippines, and Guatemala all matched words with deeds eventually.

Evaluation and Future Challenges

The Power of Transnational Civil Society

Transnational civil society has affected human rights at both the global and the national levels. At the global level, it has contributed in three ways. First, transnational civil society originally put human rights on the international agenda and kept it there. Thanks to the activities of INGOS lobbying international organizations, national governments, and domestic civil society, human rights are among the most densely regulated international norms. Second, transnational civil society provides credible information to the global community about human rights violations in various corners of the world. Third, thanks to transnational civil society lobbying national governments and mobilizing public opinion, many Western governments and international organizations such as the World Bank have incorporated human rights into their foreign policies or operational guidelines. Foreign offices all over the world have now instituted human rights desks and special human rights officers to monitor the issues and collaborate with transnational civil society.

As to improving human rights conditions on the ground, transnational civil society serves three purposes:

1. It puts repressive governments on the international agenda and raises moral consciousness.
2. It empowers and legitimates the claims of domestic opposition groups against their norm-violating governments, and it partially protects the physical integrity of such groups from repression.
3. It challenges norm-violating governments by creating a trans-national structure pressuring such regimes simultaneously from above and from below.

In sum, transnational civil society has established the power of norms against the norms of power. This does not mean that INGOs always win their struggles against norm violators (consider the People's Republic of China, Colombia, and Myanmar). In some cases, it has taken decades to achieve substantial human rights improvements. But the world would have far fewer established international human rights norms, and probably far fewer improvements in human rights practices in many countries, were it not for the constant efforts of activists in transnational civil society.

The Sustainability of INGO Power: Lessons

Although the activities of transnational civil society are necessary to bring about a sustained improvement in human rights conditions on the ground, there are limits to their influence. First, INGOs need to link up with domestic civil society in norm-violating states in order to be effective. "Free-floating" pressure is unlikely to bring about change. The stronger the links between transnational civil society and fully mobilized domestic opposition groups and social movements, the more likely it is that repressive governments will be forced to change course. Second, the spiral takes time to develop the necessary momentum. In cases such as South Africa and Indonesia, transnational pressure had to be sustained for several decades.

Third, transnational civil society needs the cooperation of states and national governments. To create robust and specific human rights standards, INGOs must convince enough states that international law needs to be strengthened. Sometimes, they do this by directly lobbying national governments. Sometimes, they change human rights policies of states by mobilizing domestic public opinion. Transnational civil society also needs states for the effective improvement of human rights conditions on the ground. Only states are able to guarantee the rule of law, and the rule of law is a necessary condition for the improvement of human rights on the ground. This presents a dilemma. On the one hand, the repressive state apparatus needs to be weakened in order to bring about human rights change in the first place and create political space for civil society to flourish. On the other hand, transition governments frequently lack the capacity to control their own repressive apparatus and enforce the rule of law.

Fourth, difficult challenges lie ahead. The most serious of these concerns human rights violations in situations of civil war and the like, where legitimate authorities with a monopoly on the use of force—that is, "states"—no longer exist. In Rwanda, Burundi, Liberia, Uganda, and Colombia, it is no longer national governments that commit the worst human rights violations but private armies, guerrilla troops, mercenaries paid by cartels of drug dealers, and others. The spiral model and the boomerang effect do not operate in these cases. International pressures and sanctions rarely work, since many of these groups are vulnerable to neither moral nor material pressures.

Fifth, this chapter concentrated on civil and political rights, which can be guaranteed only by states implementing the rule of law. When it comes to social and economic rights, however, states are often not the appropriate targets for INGO activities. Rather, private actors such as multinational corporations and domestic firms may become the targets of mobilization. Most recently, for example, INGOs have started targeting multinational corporations to prevent them from exploiting child labor. Campaigns against the Nike and Nestle corporations are cases in point. These campaigns have resulted in innovative agreements involving INGOs, states or international organizations, and private corporations to ban child labor. This example points toward a fruitful avenue of future activities, particularly in the area of social and economic rights—the underdeveloped agenda of the human rights area.

Another challenge concerns the links between transnational civil society and domestic civil societies, particularly nationally operating NGOs. In many countries, NGOs have become so dependent on external funding and other resources provided by the transnational community, such as foundations, that they tend to lose their domestic base. According to a worldwide survey of human rights NGOs, 60 percent of them relied on foundation grants, while more than 50 percent received funding from national governments or international organizations.[44] Of course, in the early phases of the spiral, external support is often needed to enable domestic NGOs to mount a challenge to their governments at all. But INGOs and political foundations need to be sensitive that they do not create new structures of dependency, this time between transnational and domestic civil societies. In the case of Kenya, for example, competition for funding increased among local NGOs when a growing number of international human rights organizations targeted the country during the late 1980s and early 1990s.[45]

These remarks finally lead to the question of how desirable the power of transnational civil society is in the human rights area. Of course, one can hardly argue against the role of transnational civil society in documenting gross human rights abuses and in condemning as well as preventing torture in many regions of the world. Yet questions of legitimacy and democratic accountability of transnational civil society arise as its activities touch on highly controversial questions of economic and political rights. Take the most recent example of the failed meeting of the World Trade Organization (WTO) in Seattle. Many human rights INGOs mobilized against the WTO's millennium round alongside environmental groups and (American) trade unions. Yet the relationship between free trade and human rights improvements is far from clear. It is at least an unsettled question whether opening up a country's economy to the outside world might also enable the domestic-transnational linkages necessary to unfold the dynamics of the spiral model. Many countries in the developing world have started to resent the unholy alliance of Western protectionist sectors (business and labor alike) with human rights advocacy coalitions. The latter need to be aware that their moral authority and knowledge as prime sources of normative power can easily be captured by private interests, even if these interests are highly legitimate (such as labor).

Notes

1. Margaret Keck and Kathryn Sikkink, *Activists Beyond Borders: Transnational Advocacy Networks in International Politics* (Ithaca, N.Y.: Cornell University Press, 1998), chap. 2.
2. William Korey, *NGOs and the Universal Declaration of Human Rights: "A Curious Grapevine"* (New York: St. Martin's Press, 1998), pp. 117–19.

3. For details, see Keck and Sikkink, *Activists Beyond Borders*, pp. 84–86; Korey, *NGOs and the Universal Declaration*, chap. I; John P. Humphrey, *Human Rights and the United Nations: A Great Adventure* (Dobbs Ferry, NY: Transnational Publishers, 1984).
4. Data in Keck and Sikkink, *Activists Beyond Borders*, p. ii; Jackie Smith, "Characteristics of the Modern Transnational Social Movement Sector," in *Transnational Social Movements and Global Politics: Solidarity Beyond the State*, ed. J. Smith et al. (Syracuse, NY: Syracuse University Press, 1997), p. 47.
5. Korey, *NGOs and the Universal Declaration*, chap. 7.
6. Keck and Sikkink, *Activists Beyond Borders*, p. 11.
7. According to Korey, *NGOs and the Universal Declaration*, pp. 301–2; for data, see http://www.amnesty.de/facts
8. Keck and Sikkink, *Activists Beyond Borders*, p. 90.
9. David Black, "The Long and Winding Road: International Norms and Domestic Political Change in South Africa," in *The Power of Human Rights: International Norms and Domestic Change*, ed. Thomas Risse et al. (Cambridge: Cambridge University Press, 1999), pp. 78–508; Audie Klotz, *Norms in International Relations: The Struggle Against Apartheid* (Ithaca, NY: Cornell University Press, 1995).
10. Daniel C. Thomas, *The Helsinki Effect* (Princeton, NJ: Princeton University Press, forthcoming).
11. Korey, NGOs and the Universal Declaration, pp. 237–39, chap. 14.
12. Hans-Peter Schmitz, "Nichtregierungsorganisationen and internationale Menschenrechtspolitik" *Comparativ* 7 (1997); Virginia Leary, "A New Role for Non-Governmental Organizations in Human Rights: A Case Study of Non-Governmental Participation in the Development of International Norms on Torture," in UN *Law/ Fundamental* Rights: *Two Topics in International Law*, ed. A. Cassese (Alphen as den Rijn: Sijthoff & Noordhoff, 1979), pp. 197–210; Korey, *NGOs and the Universal Declaration*, pp. 171–80.
13. The United States declared a reservation against the Anti-Torture Convention because of its position on the death penalty.
14. Korey, *NGOs and the Universal Declaration*, chap. 12; Alison Brysk, *From Tribal Village to Global Village: Indian Rights and International Relations in Latin America* (Stanford, Calif.: Stanford University Press, 2000).
15. 1998 figure; see http://www.amnestyde/facts.
16. Jackie Smith et al., "Globalizing Human Rights: The Work of Transnational Human Rights NGOS in the 1990s," *Human Rights Quarterly* 20, no. 2 (1998): 392.
17. Of course, when it comes to strategically important countries such as the People's Republic of China, Western states rarely quote human rights INGOs anymore.
18. On these and other "strategic constructions," see Keck and Sikkink, *Activists Beyond Borders*; Martha Finnemore and Kathryn Sikkink, "International Norm Dynamics and Political Change," *International Organization* 52, no. 4 (1998): 887–917.
19. Black, "Long and Winding Road"; Klotz, *Norms in International Relations*.
20. Quoted from Sieglinde Granzer, "Staatliche Menschenrechtsdiskurse in Marokko," manuscript, European University Institute, Florence, 1998.
21. Viron P. Vaky and Heraldo Munoz, *The Future of the Organization of American States* (New York: Twentieth Century Fund, 1993), p. 111.
22. This section reports results from a German-American research project that systematically investigated the domestic impact of international human rights norms (see Risse et al., *Power of Human Rights*). This part of the chapter draws on Thomas Risse and Stephen C. Ropp, "International Human RightsNorms and Domestic Change: Conclusions," in

Power of Human Rights, pp. 234–78 along with Thomas Risse and Kathryn Sikkink, "The Socialization of Human Rights Norms into Domestic Practices: Introduction," in *Power of Human Rights*, pp. 1–38.

23. Keck and Sikkink, *Activists Beyond Borders;* Alison Brysk, "From Above and Below: Social Movements, the International System, and HumanRights in Argen- tina," *Comparative Political Studies* 26, no. 3 (1993): 259–85; Brysk, *From Tribal Village.*

24. Anja Jetschke, in "Linking the Unlinkable? International Norms and Nationalism Indonesia and the Philippines," in Risse et al., *Power of Human Rights*, pp. 134–71.

25. Sieglinde Gilmer, "Changing Discourse: Transnational Advocacy Networks in Tunisia and Morocco," in Risse et al., Power *of Human Rights,* pp. 109–33.

26. Stephen C. Ropp and Kathryn Sikkink, "International Norms and Domestic Politics in Chile and Guatemala," in Risse et al., *Power of Human Rights*, p. 175.

27. Jetschke, "Linking the Unlinkable," p. 140.

28. Daniel C. Thomas, "The Helsinki Accords and Political Change in Eastern Europe," in Risse et al., *Power of Human Rights*, pp. 205–33; Thomas, *Helsinki Effect.*

29. Ropp and Sikkink, "International Norms."

30. Thomas, "Helsinki Accords."

31. Quoted fromJetschke, "Linking the Unlinkable," p. 141.

32. See Keck and Sikkink, *Activists Beyond Borders;* Kathryn Sikkink, "Human Rights, Principled Issue Networks, and Sovereignty in Latin America," *International Organization* 47, no. 3 (1993): 411–41.

33. Ropp and Sikkink, "International Norms," p. 179.

34. Jetschke, "Linking the Unlinkable," pp. 146–47, 155–56.

35. Black, "Long and Winding Road."

36. See Jetschke, "Linking the Unlinkable," pp. 155–62.

37. Quoted fromJetschke, "Linking the Unlinkable," p. 156.

38. Jetschke, "Linking the Unlinkable."

39. Hans-Peter Schmitz, "Transnational Activism and Political Change in Kenya and Uganda," in Risse et al., *Power of Human Rights*, pp. 39–77.

40. See Thomas, "Helsinki Accords"; Thomas, *Helsinki Effect.*

41. Thomas, *Helsinki Effect.*

42. Schmitz, "Transnational Activism"; Jetschke, "Linking the Unlinkable," pp. 162–65.

43. Schmitz, "Transnational Activism," pp. 67–71.

44. Smith et al., "Globalizing Human Rights," p. 410.

45. Schmitz, "Transnational Activism," p. 76.

CHAPTER NINE

Civil Society and the International Criminal Court[*]

Johan D. van der Vyver

Source: *Journal of Human Rights* (2003) 2:3, 425–439 © 2003 Taylor & Francis—Reproduced with permission.

Introduction

From 15 June to 17 July 1998, the United Nations Diplomatic Conference of Plenipotentiaries was held in Rome, Italy, with a view to 'finalizing and adopting a convention on the establishment of an international criminal court'.[1] The Conference culminated in the approval, by majority vote, of the text of the Statute of the International Criminal Court (ICC Statute). The 60th ratification of the ICC Statute required for the International Criminal Court (ICC) to become a reality was deposited with the Secretary-General of the United Nations on 11 April 2002 and the ICC was officially established 1 July 2002.

The proceedings in Rome were preceded by deliberations at the United Nations headquarters in New York of an *Ad Hoc* Committee (Gilmore 1995, Broomhall 1997), and subsequently of a Preparatory Committee (PrepCom).[2] The PrepCom completed its official business on 3 April 1998. It forwarded to Rome a 173-page *Draft Statute*, containing 116 articles and with approximately 1700 'brackets' indicating areas of disagreement.[3] At the Rome Conference, about 200 additional proposals were submitted in writing and numerous others derived from corridor discussions and informal negotiations (Kaul 1998, Lee 1999, Kirsch 1999).

Participation in the PrepCom[4] and in the Rome Conference[5] was open to all Member States of the United Nations and members of specialized agencies and of the International Atomic Energy Agency. In moulding the ICC Statute, the official delegations received invaluable support, and often trend-setting directions, from representatives of civil society. This essay will evaluate the role of NGOs. The first section records the establishment of the NGO Coalition for an International Criminal Court (CICC) and outlines in general terms its role in the proceedings that culminated in the successful conclusion of the Rome Conference. The second section singles out the successes of the Women's Caucus within the CICC with a view to illustrating the positive contributions that emanated from the tireless efforts of the NGOs in New York and in Rome. The third section looks at the ongoing role of civil society in laying the groundwork for the establishment and functioning of the ICC.

Formation and Functioning of the NGO Forum for an International Criminal Court

The NGO community has come to play a vital role within the domain of human rights promotion and protection. Its functions in this regard include the following:

- creating an awareness, through the dissemination of information and education, of human rights values;[6]
- developing norms and a general conceptual framework for human rights activities (in his powerful dissent in the Advisory Opinion of the International Court of Justice regarding the *Legality of the Threat or Use of Nuclear Weapons*, Judge Weeramantry paid special tribute to 'the wide variety of groups that have exerted themselves in the anti-nuclear cause—environmentalists, professional groups of doctors, lawyers, scientists, performers and artists, parliamentarians, women's groups, students' federations. . . . They come from every region and every country') (Weeramantry 1996);[7]
- coordinating human rights activities within the national or international arena;[8]
- promoting a particular human rights agenda through extensive lobbying with state representatives in norm-creating institutions or conferences;[9]
- gathering and disseminating information on human rights violations through fact-finding missions to, or national representative bodies within, the human rights trouble spots of the world;[10]
- submitting complaints of human rights violations to government institutions or to the enforcement agencies within the United Nations system of human rights protection;[11]
- affording publicity to instances of human rights violations as a means of persuading those responsible for such violations to desist from their repressive policies and conduct;[12]
- bringing pressure to bear on governments or government officials guilty of repression or human rights violations.[13]

International human rights organizations active in performing these activities have indeed contributed much to the development of human rights norms, the cultivation of a human rights awareness, and condemnation of human rights abuses. However, they have mostly done so individually. Concerted efforts within the human rights community have been few and far between.

Prior to Rome, the contribution of civil society to the outcome of norm-creating international conferences for the promotion or protection of human rights have, for that reason, not been particularly spectacular. In fact, the behavior of a cross-section of NGO representatives at the United Nations Conference on Human Rights of 1993 in Vienna was at times quite disgusting. One is reminded, for example, of one occasion when a section of the NGOs, led by a Latin American contingent, shouted down President Jimmy Carter and would not allow him to address the NGO Forum (as he had been invited to do).

Perhaps the greatest shortcoming on those occasions of the past was proper coordination of the activities of the NGOs which, in ever increasing numbers, descended on the major international events, as well as a general lack of discipline within their ranks. For those seriously engaged in completing the work of a conference, the NGOs quite often represented a certain nuisance value; they came to be perceived as a kind of conference hazard, and their interventions were at times barely tolerated.

Rome was to change all of this; for that the World Federalist Movement and the New York based Executive Director of its International Secretariat, William Pace, must be given credit

(Benedetti and Washburn 1999: 8–8, 22).[14] There were indeed earlier attempts at coordinating the input of civil society in international norm-creating conferences (Cohen 1990), but never on the scale and with the level of success achieved by the World Federalist Movement for purposes of establishing an international criminal court.[15]

On 25 February 1995, when the Ad Hoc Committee for an International Criminal Court was about to commence its initial deliberations, the World Federalist Movement convened a meeting of interested NGOs at its offces in New York with a view to coordinating the efforts of civil society to promote the establishment of the ICC. From this meeting emerged the creation of the NGO Coalition for an International Criminal Court (CICC), with Bill Pace as its convener (Pace and Thieroff 1999). The objectives of the CICC were defined as follows:

> The main purpose of the NGO Coalition for an International Criminal Court is to advocate the creation of an effective and just International Criminal Court. The Coalition brings together a broad-based network of NGOs and international law experts to develop strategies on substantive legal and political issues relating to the proposed statute. A key goal is to foster awareness and support among a wide range of civil society organizations: human rights, international law, judicial, humanitarian, religious, peace, women's, parliamentarian and others. To these ends, we engage in the following activities:

> Convene the Coalition and its working groups, such as the *ad hoc* Tribunal/ICC funding working group, information/media working group, and a working group on US strategies.

> Maintain a World Wide Web page, international computer conferences and listserv email lists to facilitate the exchange of NGO and expert documentation and information concerning the *ad hoc* Tribunals and the ICC negotiations and to foster discussion and debate about substantive issues arising from the negotiations for establishing a permanent International Criminal Court.

> Facilitate meetings between the Coalition and representatives of governments, UN officials and others involved in the ICC negotiations.

> Promote education and awareness of the ICC proposals and negotiations at relevant public and professional conferences—including UN conferences, committee, commission and preparatory meetings.

> Produce newsletters, media advisories, reviews and papers on the developments and negotiations.

The CICC lived up to all of these objectives. Fanny Benedetti and John Ashburn demonstrated how the CICC, through networking, disseminating of information and building coalitions, 'developed an increasingly powerful role in the development of the draft statute' (Benedetti and Washburn 1999: 22). Leila Sadat and Richard Carden maintained that adoption of the ICC Statute by the Diplomatic Conference in Rome can at least in part be attributed to 'the enormous lobbying and informational efforts of the NGOs, which conducted a tireless campaign in support of the Court' (Sadat and Carden 2000: 385). Mahmoush Arsanjani observed that through their intense lobbying NGOs played a signifcant role in the negotiating process in New York and in Rome (Arsanjani 1999: 23, Scheffer 1999: 1617, Lee 1999: 14, 37, Streians 1999: 385 note 94, 387, Pace and Thieroff 1999: 351, Slade and Clark 1999: 424, Bos 1999: 469–470).

During the early phases of the work of the Ad Hoc Committee and the Preparatory Committee, and particularly at intermittent meetings of the Sixth Committee of the General Assembly dealing with reports of those committees, NGO participation were at times confined to a faithful few (Benedetti and Washburn 1999: 21). During the final phases of the pre-Rome deliberations, the numbers of active participants in the CICC increased dramatically, and in the end, altogether 134 NGOs (represented by approximately 235 activists) were accredited by the Secretary-General's office to participate in the Rome Conference. They represented a wide range of regional and thematic interests, including human rights, international law, women's rights, children's rights, victims' rights, the right of the accused to a proper defense and the due process of law, peace and disarmament, humanitarian relief, and religion and faith. At a pre-conference general strategy meeting, a number of task groups, each with its own individual coordinator, were established, with William Pace taking on the responsibilities of Overall Coalition Strategy. This was extremely important for the organized and properly coordinated functioning of the CICC. Throughout the proceedings, William Pace acted as spokesperson and negotiator of the CICC in its dealings with the conference administrators. He also secured the proper and disciplined conduct of NGO participants. Through his interventions on behalf of, and instructions to, NGO representatives, the indulgence of the conference organizers and administrators remained secured—which in turn facilitated the free and orderly participation of the NGOs through attendance at conference proceedings, lobbying, distribution of written communications and regular meetings with government delegations.

NGOs were permitted to speak in the plenary sessions of the Rome Conference. Those that in the first week availed themselves of this opportunity included the World Federalist Movement (Pace 1998), The Brazilian Movement for Human Rights (Klich 1998), the International Commission of Jurists (Rishmawi 1998), REDRESS (concerned with victims' rights) (Rishmawi 1998), the CICC Caucus on Children's Rights (Boenders 1998), the International Centre for Human Rights and Democratic Development (Almeida 1998), the International Federation of Human Rights (Baudouin 1998), the European Law Students' Association (ELSA 1998), the Transnational Radical Party (Busdachin 1998), Human Rights Watch (Roth 1998, 24 and 26 June) and Parliamentarians for Global Action (Poptodorova 1998). William Pace, on behalf of the CICC, and Pierre Sané, Secretary-General of Amnesty International, made statements in the closing plenary session of the Rome Conference.

Individual NGO representatives were allocated to a number of teams, chaired in each instance by a designated coordinator and responsible for monitoring the debates and engaging in discussions and negotiations with government representatives in regard to a particular section of the proposed ICC Statute. Those teams included the Definitions Team, the State Consent Team, the Trigger Mechanisms and Admissibility Team, the General Principles Team, the Composition Team, the Investigation Team, the Trial, Appeal and Review Team, the Penalties Team, the Cooperation and National Security Team, the Enforcement Team, the Financing and Assembly of States Parties Team, and the Final Clauses Team. NGO participants further-more constituted different thematic caucuses, such as the Women's Caucus and the Caucus on Children's Rights, as well as regional caucuses, such as the ones for Africa and for Latin America. A Faith Caucus, which had already been active in New York, was reconvened in Rome during the course of the conference. The teams and caucuses from time to time submitted in-house reports reflecting developments and state positions pertinent to the subject-matter of their mandate.

The CICC held regular meetings to discuss developments that emerged from the conference proceedings, to plan strategies for the promotion of a strong, independent and effective tribunal, and to meet formally with different government delegations. The issues to be raised with government delegations were carefully considered, and persons were selected beforehand to put those matters to the delegation concerned. Several NGOs distributed position papers to promote those aspects of the ICC Statute that came within their particular field of interests or to challenge unacceptable positions advocated by particular delegations.

There were indeed also disagreements among NGO representatives. For example, the Real Women of Canada would have nothing of the proscription of 'forced pregnancies' for fear that it might be taken to legitimize abortions on demand. By and large, though, it could rightly be said that 'the NGOs present . . . [were] united in their support for a successful completion of these negotiations on the establishment of a permanent International Criminal Court' (CICC 1998).

On the third day of the conference, the proceedings in the plenary session were disrupted by a demonstration of Mothers of Plaza de Mayo while Justice Minister Raúl Ocampo of Argentina had the floor. The Mothers protested the disappearance of approximately 30,000 political prisoners in Argentina in the period 1976 to 1983. The demonstrators was forcibly removed from the premises of the Food and Agricultural Organization (FAO)—the venue of the Rome Conference—and strict precautions were subsequently taken to prevent the conference forum from being used for political demonstrations. The conference administration thereafter (for a time) strictly applied a daily admission card system, which limited the number of NGO representatives admitted to conference chambers (according to the available seating), and entrusted the CICC administrators with the task of distributing the admission cards to its members only. William Pace appealed to NGO representatives to play it by the rules—which they did—so that the strict control measures could again be relaxed—which they soon were. After the Argentina incident, demonstrations (mostly in support of the ICC) were confined to the sidewalk adjacent to the entrance to the FAO premises.

A most unfortunate incident happened during a session of the Working Group on Applicable Law while the gender issue was under consideration: the Chair, Per Saland of Sweden, suddenly decreed that the proceedings be converted into 'informal discussions' and ordered the NGO representatives, on that account, to leave the room. The only explanation given (in retrospect) for this extraordinary ruling was that '[t]he atmosphere became so intense' that the Chairman was requested by several delegates to take this course (Saland 1999).[16]

The NGO participants included many dignitaries, such as Bejamin F. Ferencz (in New York and in Rome), former prosecutor at the Nuremberg Tribunal, and William J. Butler (in Rome), President of the American Association of the International Commission of Jurists and in the period 1975–90 Chairman of the Executive Committee of the International Commission of Jurists. Richard Goldstone, a Justice in the South African Constitutional Court and former prosecutor in the International Criminal Tribunal for the Former Yugoslavia and the International Tribunal for Rwanda, also put in a brief appearance, and held a press conference, in Rome. Civil society was indeed also represented as advisers to, or members of, the official delegations of many states, including those of Canada, Australia, Bosnia and Herzegovina, Denmark and Germany.

Academics who served as official delegates included Prof. Gerhard Hafner, Director of the Institute for International Law and International Relations of the University of Vienna (Austria), Prof. M. Cherif Bassiouni, Professor of Law in De Paul University, Chicago (Egypt and Chair of the Drafting Committee in Rome), Prof. Roger Clark of Rutgers University in Camden, New Jersey (Samoa), Prof. Theo van Boven, Professor of International Law in Maastricht University (The Netherlands), Prof. Medard Rwelamira, Professor of Law in the University of the Western Cape (South Africa), and Dr Aziz Chukri, Professor of International Law in the University of Damascus (Syrian Arab Republic).

The reciprocation of civil society and government representation contributed greatly to the interchange of information and the unrestrained exchange of communications between official delegations and the CICC. It was not uncommon for government representatives to call on NGO lobbyists to promote a particular point of view, and for members of the CICC to urge government representatives of Like-Minded States to push for the inclusion of certain provisions in the ICC Statute. No one in the end denied that the NGOs played a vital and positive role in securing the successful completion of the work of the Rome Conference, and indeed in facilitating the adoption of a Statute conducive to the creation of a strong, effective and independent criminal tribunal.

Recording the outcome of proceedings of the Preparatory Committee in New York, Christopher Hall thus mentioned the 'constructive working relationship' between government representatives and NGOs, and expressed the opinion that NGO recommendations had a significant impact on proposals advanced by government representatives concerning the text of the ICC Statute (Hall 1998a: 125, 1998b: 339). Subsequent to the Rome Conference, Secretary-General of the United Nations Kofi Annan, speaking at the World Conference of Civil Society in Montreal, Canada, spoke of 'the new functional diplomacy' of NGOs that had resulted in the success of the Land Mines Convention and the Rome Conference, and expressed the opinion that a partnership between civil society and the United Nations 'is no longer an option but a necessity' (Annan 1999). In his key-note address of 23 May 2000 to the United Nations Millennium Forum, the Secretary-General again praised NGOs for their efforts to promote the establishment of an international criminal court, saying:

> Surely such worldwide alliances among like-minded NGOs, which have already proved so successful on issues like . . . the International Criminal Court, are the shape of things to come—on a much wider scale and on a more continuous basis. They make you an effective force for dealing with governments, and with us in the United Nations; they allow you to expand your capabilities and your reach. I hope they will enable you to make a real difference on many broad issues in the future.

A reference to reports prepared by teams of the CICC may here be singled out to illustrate the role of NGOs in the final outcome of the Statute. As indicated earlier, members of the CICC, divided into different (thematic) teams, monitored proceedings in the plenary sessions, Working Groups and the Committee of the Whole, and recorded country positions on different sections of the Draft Statute. This information was most helpful in the planning and execution of country-specific lobbying targets and strategies. The country positions on the most crucial and controversial components of the Statute were also reduced to statistical data. Although the details and statistical breakdown of country positions were initially intended for internal edification of and use by the CICC only, it was decided to publish those reflecting the debate in the Committee of the Whole on the *Bureau Proposal* of 10 July (Bureau Proposal 1998, NGO Coalition 1998, 13 and 15 July).

A *Discussion Paper* of 6 July (Discussion Paper 1998) and the *Bureau Proposal* were working papers prepared by the Conference Bureau in an attempt to clarify the myriad positions that remained current at the late stages of the Rome Conference, and to confine the options on vital issues that remained in contention, in 'an effort to break the logjam' which had persisted in the conference discussions and negotiations (Kirsch and Holmes 1999: 5). It was rumored at the time that the Bureau was contemplating the sacrifice, for the sake of 'general agreement', of important provisions with substantial majority support. There is reason to believe that the statistical information distributed by the CICC influenced the Bureau in the drafting of the (generally commendable) compromise proposal, which finally came to be accepted as the ICC Statute. A member of the German delegation described publication of those details as 'valuable and consequential' (*wertvoll und weiterführend*), particularly since it restored complete clarity to everyone regarding the main lines of thinking at the Conference in support of the ICC (Kaul 1998: 127).

Successes of the Women's Caucus

It is in a sense quite unfair to single out the achievements of a particular task group within the CICC. Every group had something to show for its efforts. However, if one must designate one of the task groups to illustrate the contributions of the NGO community in the refinement of the

ICC Statute, the Women's Caucus will evidently be the one. It introduced, and most competently lobbied for, the inclusion in the ICC Statute of several matters (Sellers and Okuizumi 1997: 73–80, Erb 1998: 424–434) and was successful in almost all of its endeavors. (Moshan 1998: 176–178), listing the 'victories' of the Women's Caucus.

Following publication of the Bureau's *Discussion Paper* of 6 July 1998, the Women's Caucus issued a Position Paper outlining the 'essential components of gender justice':

1. Judges and prosecutors must include people with expertise in sexual and gender violence and must reflect a balance of men and women.
2. The Victim and Witness Unit must be placed in the Registry with authority to protect, counsel and assist witnesses throughout the proceedings and after testifying.
3. The Statute must be interpreted and applied consistent with international human rights law including the prohibition on adverse distinction founded on gender, age, race and other similar criteria.
4. The jurisdiction of the court must include sexual and gender crimes including forced pregnancy as a war crime and crime against humanity.
5. The threshold for crimes against humanity must contemplate either widespread or systematic commission of crimes consistent with customary international law.
6. Persecution based on gender must be retained undiluted and persecution against the other similar grounds should not depend on their being 'universally recognized.'
7. The protection of witnesses must be fully protected at all stages and by all organs of the Court.
8. Reparations, including restitution, compensation and rehabilitation, must be made available to victims, who should have the right to participate before the Court (Women's Caucus 1998).

Perhaps the greatest achievement of the Rome Conference was its positive response to the women's caucus in the NGO Coalition to afford concrete substance to crimes against women (Streains 1999: 360–361). As one analyst (a member of the Australian delegation in Rome) has observed:

> The criminalization of violent sexual and gender-directed acts in the [ICC] Statute . . . , while not without precedent, represents a significant step forward in the international community's treatment of these crimes. (Streains 1999: 357)

In the past, such crimes were committed quite blatantly and with almost complete impunity as an instrument of, or a kind of free-for-all activity in times of, armed conflict (Reynolds 1998: 358, Streains 1999: 358). 'Around the world', said Kathleen Barry, 'prostitution is considered a necessary and even patriotic service to "our boys in uniform" ' (Barry 1979: 59). Prior to the Rome Conference, international humanitarian law addressed these offences in fairly general terms—mostly under the rubric of an affront against personal honor and dignity (Streains 1999: 362)—and perhaps for that reason, quite ineffectively. Fionnuala Ni Aolain speaks of 'the low status for sexual violations within the hierarchy of humanitarian law offences' (Aolain 1997: 888). Cate Streains (1999: 390) referred to the 'traditional marginalization' of gender-specific crimes under international law'.

The successes of the Women's Caucus included the insertion in the definition of crimes against humanity of '[r]ape, sexual slavery, enforced prostitution, forced pregnancy, enforced sterilization, or any other form of sexual violence of comparable gravity',[17] and similar proscriptions in the definition of war crimes in the case of international armed conflict,[18] as well as armed conflict not of an international character.[19] At least as far as war crimes were concerned, these offences could have been covered under the general rubric of outrages against personal dignity or humiliating treatment. Mentioning, on the contrary, gender-specific crimes as a distinct category of war crimes, and according to them a separate place in the list of such crimes, represented a major achievement of the Women's Caucus.[20]

The concept of 'gender' features in the Statute in several of its provisions, including, in the definition of crimes against humanity, the condemnation of '[p]ersecution against any identifiable group or collectivity on ... gender ... grounds that are universally recognized as impermissible under international law, in connection with any act referred to in this paragraph or any crime within the jurisdiction of the Court',[21] and in a clause requiring the applicable law in any particular case to be interpreted 'consistent with internationally recognized human rights, and ... without adverse distinction founded on grounds such as gender ...'.[22]

The reference to 'gender' in the latter provision was hotly debated in the Working Group and was initially opposed by delegations as far apart as the United Kingdom, the Holy See and Egypt. The UK opined that the non-discrimination part of the interpretation clause was already included in the directive founded on 'internationally recognized human rights' and was therefore tautological; the Holy See thought that the provision could implicate the institution of single-sex schools within the Roman Catholic education system; and Egypt (and other Arab States) maintained that the word 'gender' cannot be translated into Arabic. At least one Eastern European delegation also noted that 'gender' might be taken to afford protection to homosexuals (which that delegation thought would be a bad thing). What was not expressly stated, but which might have prompted some of these reservations, is the fact that Roman Catholicism and Islam discriminate against women. Be that as it might, the problem was resolved, at least to satisfy some of the Arab states, by inserting in the text a definition of 'gender' that restricts the meaning of that term to 'the two sexes, male and female, within the context of society'.[23]

The definition of 'gender' leaves much to be desired. Why not clearly state the obvious, namely that gender denotes the role attributed to persons in society by virtue of their sex-related attributes? In his report on the Beijing Conference, the Secretary-General of the United Nations more precisely defined the concept of 'gender' for UN purposes:

Gender analysis is done in order to examine similarities and differences in roles and responsibilities between women and men without direct reference to biology, but rather to the behaviour patterns expected from women and men and their cultural reinforcement. These roles are usually specific to a given area and time, that is, since gender roles are contingent on the social and economic context, they can vary according to the specific context and can change over time. In terms of the use of language, the word 'sex' is used to refer to physical and biological characteristics of women and men, while gender is used to refer to the explanations for observed differences between women and men based on socially assigned roles. (UN Secretary General 1996: para. 9)

The phrase 'in the context of society' in the ICC definition of 'gender' was intended to denote the sociological dimension of gender, while the second sentence was intended to exclude sexual orientation from the definition's enclave (Streains 1999: 374). That, according to Cate Streains (the coordinator on gender issues at the Rome Conference), was the only definition Arab States and some other delegations were willing to accept (Streains 1999: 374–375). As such, the definition represents 'a delicate, hard-fought compromise among delegations' (Streains 1999: 371); or, again, 'the culmination of hard-fought negotiations that managed to produce language acceptable to delegations on both sides of the debate' (Streains 1999: 374).

Basing the gender issue on the biologically defined male/female divide is in itself problematic. One has to be sensitive, namely, to the station in life not only of male and female but also of persons with, biologically, sexually ambiguous qualities, such as congenital adrenal hyperplasia (CAH),[24] the androgen insensitivity syndrome (AIS),[25] or those of the hermaphrodite.[26] It has been established that approximately 1.75% of newborn babies present some ambiguity as to sex. Their disposition in life is a gender issue but cannot be regulated on the based of the male–female divide. Coupling the definition of 'gender' to that divide would therefore leave such persons out in the cold.

The Women's Caucus was also decidedly influential in upholding the interests of women in the composition of the ICC and its organs (Streains 1999: 379–382). States Parties are instructed, when selecting judges for the Court, to take into account, *inter alia*, '[a] fair representation of female judges',[27] as well as 'the need to include judges with legal expertise on specific issues, including . . . violence against women and children'.[28] These gender-related considerations also have to be taken into account when the Prosecutor and Registrar appoint staff to their respective offices,[29] and the Prosecutor is furthermore instructed to appoint advisors with legal expertise in gender and sexual violence and violence against children.[30]

The ICC Statute furthermore sanctioned special precautions for the protection of female victims and witnesses. For example, the Prosecutor is instructed to take appropriate measures to ensure the effective investigation and prosecution of crimes and must, in doing so, 'respect the personal circumstances of victims and witnesses, including age, gender . . . and health', taking into account the nature of the crime, 'in particular where it involves sexual violence, gender violence or violence against children'.[31]

A similar duty rest with the Court – that is, all organs of the Court at all stages of the proceedings – to protect the safety, physical well-being, dignity and privacy of victims and witnesses, with special regard for all relevant factors, 'including age, gender . . . and health', as well as the nature of the crime, 'in particular, but not limited to, where the crime involves sexual or gender violence or violence against children'.[32] Provision is made for part of the proceedings to be conducted behind closed doors or the presentation of evidence by electronic or other special means, and it is provided that such measures 'shall be implemented in the case of a victim of sexual violence or a child who is a victim or a witness, unless otherwise ordered by the Court, having regard to all the circumstances, particularly the views of the victim or witness'.[33]

According to the coordinator of gender issues, Cate Streains of Australia, several NGOs, notably the Victims Rights' Caucus and the Women's Caucus, played a vital role in the negotiations that culminated in these latter provisions (Article 68) being included in the Statute (Streains 1999: 387). In the Islamic world, a stigma attaches to the victims of rape, and for that reason a number of Muslim States, led by Syria, wanted all trials involving sexual violence to be held in camera. These sentiments had to be counterbalanced by the need to comply with the wishes that a victim of sexual violence might entertain to testify in public. The compromise is reflected in Article 68(2): as a rule, trials involving sexual violence must be held in camera, but the Court is given a discretion to rule otherwise, taking into account in particular the views of the victim or witness (Streains 1999: 389).

The *Rules of Procedure and Evidence* (RPE) adopted by the Assembly of States Parties in September 2002 elaborated in several of its provisions similar gender-related interests. The Registrar is instructed to take gender-specific measures to facilitate the participation of victims of sexual violence in all stages of the proceedings (RPE: Rule 16(1)(d)); the Victims and Witnesses Unit 'may include, as appropriate' persons with expertise in gender and cultural diversity (RPE: Rule 19e), and must take gender-sensitive measures to facilitate the testimony of victims of sexual violence at all stages of the proceedings (RPE: Rule 17(2)(b)(iii)); the Victims and Witnesses Unit must further make available to the Court and the parties training in sexual violence (RPE: Rule 17(2)(a)(iv)), and must ensure training of its own staff with respect to victims' and witnesses security, integrity and dignity in the context, *inter alia*, of gender and cultural sensitivity (RPE: Rule 18(d)).

The *Rules of Procedure and Evidence* also entail principles of evidence in cases of sexual violence, discarding unbecoming means of establishing supposed consent of the victim, such as (i) taking as evidence of consent, words and conduct of a victim uttered or engaged in under force, threat of force, coercion, or in a coercive environment that undermines the victim's ability to give voluntary and genuine consent, (ii) inferring consent from words or conduct of a victim in circumstances where the victim is incapable of giving consent, and (iii) assuming consent by reason of the victim's silence or lack of resistance (RPE: Rule 70(a)–(c)). The *Rules of Procedure and Evidence* also renders inadmissible evidence of the prior or subsequent sexual conduct of a victim witness (RPE: Rule 71), and instructs the Court not to draw conclusions as to the credibility, character or predisposition to sexual availability of a victim or witness based on the sexual nature of his or her prior or subsequent conduct (RPE: Rule 70(d)).

These provisions did not simply emerge out of the blue: they are the result of intense reflections and deliberations within the Women's Caucus and persistent advocacy by its members of an ethos of gender equality and of gender specificity of the crimes within the jurisdiction of the ICC.

Continuing Pertinence of NGO Participation

The CICC continued to operate, and to do so with distinction, at proceedings of the (post-Rome) Preparatory Commission (Kaul 1998: 3233). It remained particularly vigilant regarding efforts by the United States to exploit the *Rules of Procedure and Evidence*, the *Rules of Procedure of the Assembly of States Parties*, and the relationship agreement between the United Nations and the ICC for the purpose of the primary objective of shielding US citizens from the exercise of ICC jurisdiction. In several position papers and circular letters the CICC analyzed the US proposals, highlighted their incompatibility with the ICC Statute, and alerted governments to their destructive consequences.

One of the landmark initiatives of civil society that is currently coming to fruition is the establishment of an International Bar Association for potential practitioners in the ICC. The Montréal-based International Criminal Defence Attorneys Associated and its President, Elise Groulx, deserve special mention for having taken the lead in this initiative. A meeting organized by the *Ordre des Avocats à la Cour de Paris* took place in Paris, France on 6–7 December 2002 to make it happen, and a further meeting was held in Montreal in June 2002. The International Criminal Bar held its first General Assembly in Berlin on 21–22 March 2003. An important primary function of the International Criminal Bar will be the drafting of rules of professional conduct. The *Rules of Procedure and Evidence* provide that a Code of Professional Conduct for defense counsel is to be drawn up by the Presidency on the basis of a proposal made by the Registrar (RPE: Rule 8). In composing those recommendations, the Registrar is required to consult, as appropriate, any independent representative body of counsel or legal association, including any such body whose establishment may be facilitated by the Assembly of States Parties (RPE: Rule 20(3)). The purpose of the Montréal/Paris initiative is, in part, to have something on the table that can be presented to the Registrar when the time comes and which will have emerged from the practicing lawyers themselves.

Due entirely to the positive role of civil society in New York and in Rome, drafters of the ICC Statute finally envisioned a continuing role for NGOs in the functioning of the Court. The *Rules of Procedure and Evidence* expressly recognize the role of NGOs in proceedings of the ICC. Included in the functions of the Victims and Witnesses Unit, for example, is its duty, in consultation with the Office of the Prosecutor, to make recommendations for elaborating a code of conduct that will emphasize 'the vital nature of security and confidentiality for . . . non-governmental organizations acting at the request of the Court . . . ' (RPE: Rule 17(2)(a)(v)). The Chamber of the Court may at any stage of the proceedings invite a State, organization or person to submit, in writing or orally, any observation on any issue that the Chamber may deem appropriate (RPE: Rule 103(1)).

It is to be hoped that the initiatives of the World Federalist Movement and its New York Director, and—emanating from those initiatives—the example of NGO participation in the proceedings in New York and in Rome for the establishment of the ICC, will remain the model for civil society to follow at similar future events. Fanny Benedetti and John Washburn sounded an optimistic note in this regard:

> The NGO coalition served as a formidable, disciplined, and omnipresent ally for the bureau, the Like-Minded Group, and the Secretariat. Its actions set a new standard and precedent for NGO effectiveness, both at further conferences and almost certainly in the General Assembly and elsewhere in the UN. Because the coalition's solidarity accommodated a considerable range of specific positions within a general commitment to the international criminal court, this kind of NGO mobilization may recur more readily than any other feature of the CICC. In particular, NGOs demonstrated that they could deal expertly and responsibly with the sorts of questions in the domain of peace and security that the international criminal court will affect and confront. (Benedetti and Washburn 1999: 33–34)

Notes

*   This essay is dedicated as a special tribute to Bill Pace, New York Executive Director of the World Federalist Movement, whose initiative and leadership was the driving force behind the extraordinary achievements of the NGO community in making its voice heard, and more often than not acted upon, in the deliberations that culminated in the successful conclusion of the Rome Conference.
1. General Assembly Resolution 52/160 (1997).
2. Prepcom Meetings; see Highet *et al.* (1997), Hall (1998a, 1998b), Benedetti and Washburn (1999).
3. PreCom Meetings; see Stevens (1998).
4. General Assembly Resolution 50/46 (1995).
5. General Assembly Resolution 52/160 (1997).
6. Steiner (1991: 45) emphasizes the commitment of NGOs to 'the central importance of wide-spread education in human rights to realization of their long-run goals'.
7. See Falk (1997: 342), where he refers to that case to confirm 'transnational initiatives to the process of international lawmaking' (p. 335), noting that 'stimulus for lawmaking with respect to nuclear weaponry originated in global civil society'. Anderson (2000) emphasizes the positive contribution of NGOs to the success of the Ottawa Conference for the banning of landmines.
8. Cohen (1990) outlines attempts of NGOs to coordinate their activities at the Rights of the Child Conference.
9. Cynthia Cohen in this context refers to the role of NGOs 'to advise, to assist, and to inspire' (Cohen 1990: 146). Mawlawi highlights the role of NGOs in international conflict resolution.

10. Steiner (1991: at 30) notes that national NGOs are better suited than their international counterparts to address human rights violations of particular individuals and to report such abuses; and as to the monitoring function of NGOs. See also Cohen (1990: 41–44).

11. See, for example, Weissbrodt (1988), highlighting attempts of NGOs such as Americas Watch, Amnesty International and the International Commission of Jurists to apply human rights law and humanitarian law in periods of armed conflict, and in the same context and including situations of foreign occupation, Steiner (1991: 56–59).

12. Steiner refers to NGOs (of First World countries) as 'monitors, objective investigators applying the consensual norms of the human rights movement to the facts found' and depicts those NGOs as 'defenders of legality' (Steiner 1991: 19 and 41, referring to 'investigating, reporting and related activities' of NGOs). See further, Neier (1990), emphasizing the recording of human rights violations in India by NGOs such as Human Rights Watch and the Committee to Protect Journalists.

13. Steiner (1991: 37), speaks of 'the arrest of ongoing violations of a systematic character'.

14. A special tribute should be given, too, to the late Bettina Pruckmayr, Director of the ICC Program of the World Federalist Association during the time of the Ad Hoc Committee, and who was brutally murdered in Washington DC on 16 December 1995.

15. As to the positive contributions of the NGOs in proceedings that attended the establishment of an international criminal court, see in general Kaul (1998: 127, 129); Benedetti and Washburn (1999: 21–23, 32, 33–34), King and Theofrastous (1999), Sadat (2000), Brown (2000), Chayes and Slaughter (2000), and Kaul (2001).

16. Per Saland was the Chairman who made that particular ruling. This writer observed that an NGO representative seemingly became so carried away with the debate that he uttered sounds—probably inadvertently—applauding (or perhaps denouncing) a statement that was made by one of the official delegates. The person concerned subsequently stated that he was only coughing, and the CICC was informed that the spontaneous response (or coughing) of the NGO representative was not the reason for the decision to continue the discussions in the absence of NGO observers.

17. ICC Statute (1998), article 7(1)(g).

18. ICC Statute (1998), article 8(2) (b) (xxii).

19. ICC Statute 1998, article 8(2) (c)(vi).

20. Streains (1999: 364), Moshan (1998: 176–177 and 180–181), making the same point in the context of crimes against humanity.

21. ICC Statute (1998), article 7(1)(h).

22. ICC Statute (1998), art. 21(3).

23. ICC Statute 1998, article 7(3): 'For the purpose of this Statute, it is understood that the term "gender" refers to the two sexes, male and female, within the context of society. The term "gender" does not indicate any meaning different from the above.'

24. Persons with classical CAH are born with masculine-appearing external genitals but with female internal organs, and they usually also have high levels of the male sex hormone, testosterone, in their blood.

25. The child with classical AIS is born with male (XY) sex chromosomes, but the male genital development of the external genitals continues along female lines, and at the same time, the development of the female internal organs is suppressed. The person with AIS therefore has genitals that are completely female, but internally there are testes instead of a uterus and ovaries.

26. The hermaphrodite is a person born with ovary and testicle tissue. The genitalia can vary from completely male or female to a combination of both.

27. ICC Statute (1998), article 36(8)(a)(iii).
28. ICC Statute (1998), article 36(8)(b).
29. ICC Statute (1998), article 44(2), read with art. 36(8).
30. ICC Statute (1998), article 42(9).
31. ICC Statute (1998), article 54(1)(b).
32. ICC Statute (1998), article 68(1).
33. ICC Statute (1998), article 68(2).

References

ALMEIDA, I. (22 June 1998) *CICC Monitor*, 6; also in: *Terra Viva*, 6, middle pp.

ANDERSON, K. (2000) The Ottawa Convention Banning Landmines, the role of international non-governmental organizations and the idea of international civil society. *European Journal of International Law*, 11, 91–112.

ANNAN, K. (1999) Les ONG et les Nations Unies Veulent Travailler Ensemble (Montreal: Agence France Presse: Informations Generales).

AOLAIN, F. N. (1997) Radical rules: the effects of evidential and procedural rules on the regulation of sexual violence in war. *Alabama Law Review*, 60, 883–888.

ARSANJANI, M. H. (1999) The Rome Statute of the International Criminal Court. *American Journal of International Law*, 93, 22–23.

BARRY, K. (1979) *Female Sexual Slavery* (Englewood Cliffs, NJ: Prentice-Hall).

BAUDOUIN, P. (1998, 22 June) Speech. Reprinted in *CICC Monitor*, as well as in *Terra Viva*, 6, middle pp.

BENEDETTI, F. and WASHBURN, J. (1999) Drafting of the International Criminal Court Treaty: two years to Rome and an afterword on the Rome Diplomatic Conference. *Global Governance*, 5, 1–21.

BOENDERS, E. (1998, 19 June) Speech. Reprinted in *CICC Monitor*, 5, 4; also in *Terra Viva*, 5, middle pp.

BOS, A. (1999) The International Criminal Court: a perspective. In R.S. Lee (ed.) *The International Criminal Court: The Making of the Rome Statute: Issues, Negotiations, Results* (The Hague/London/Boston: Kluwer Law International), 469–470.

BROOMHALL, B. (1997) Looking forward to the establishment of an international criminal court: between state consent and the rule of law. *Criminal Law Forum*, 8, 317–322.

BROWN, B. S. (2000) The Statute of the ICC: past, present, and future. In S. B. Sewall and C. Kaysen (eds) *The United States and the International Criminal Court* (Lanham/Boulder/New York/Oxford: Rowman & Littlefield), 61–65.

BUREAU PROPOSAL (1998, 10 July) UN Document, A/CONF.183/C.1 /L.59.

BUSDACHIN, M. (1998, 24 June) Speech. Reprinted in *CICC Monitor*, 8, 1 reprinted in *Terra Viva*, 8, middle pp.

CHAYES, A. and SLAUGHTER, A.-M. (2000) The ICC and the future of the global legal system. In S. B. Sewall and C. Kaysen (eds) *The United States and the International Criminal Court* (Lanham/Boulder/New York/Oxford: Rowman & Littlefield), 241–297.

CICC (1998, 15 June) Welcome speech. *Terra Viva*, 1, 5.

COHEN, C. P. (1990) The role of nongovernmental organizations in the drafting of the Convention on the Rights of the Child. *Human Rights Quarterly*, 12, 137–141.

DISCUSSION PAPER (1998, 6 July) UN Document A/CONF.183/C.1 /L.53.

ELSA (1998, 22 June) Speech. Reprinted in *CICC Monitor*, 6, 4; also in *Terra Viva*, 6, middle pp.

ERB, N. E. (1998) Gender-based crimes under the draft statute for the permanent international criminal court. *Columbia Human Rights Review*, 29, 401–434.

FALK, R. (1997) The nuclear weapons advisory opinion and the new jurisprudence of global civil society. *Transnational Law and Contemporary Problems*, 7, 333–342.

GENERAL ASSEMBLY (1995, 11 December) Resolution 50/46, para. 5. UN Document A/Res/50/46, at 307, para. 5.

GENERAL ASSEMBLY (1997, 15 December) Resolution 52/160, Annex UN Document A/52/49, at 384, para. 3.

GILMORE, W. G. (1995) The proposed international criminal court: recent developments. *Transnational Law and Contemporary Problems*, 5, 263–285.

HALL, C. K. (1998a) The Third and Fourth Sessions of the UN Preparatory Commission on the Establishment of an International Criminal Court. *American Journal of International Law*, 92, 124.

HALL, C. K. (1998b) The Fifth Session of the UN Preparatory Commission on the Establishment of an International Criminal Court. *American Journal of International Law*, 92, 331–339.

HIGHET, K., BEKKER, P. H. F. and ALFORD, R. P. (1997) International courts and tribunals. *International Lawyer*, 31, 599–610.

KAUL, H.-P. (1998) Durchbruch in Rom: Der Vertrag caber den Internationalen Strafgerichtshof. *Vereinte Nationen*, 46, 125–127.

KAUL, H.-P. (2001) The continuing struggle on the jurisdiction of the international criminal court. In H. Fisher, C. Kreß and S. R. Linder (eds) *International and National Prosecution of Crimes under International Law: Current Developments* (Berlin: Arno Spitz), 22–30.

KING, H. T. and THEOFRASTOUS, T. C. (1999) From Nuremberg to Rome: a step backward for US foreign policy. *Case Western Journal of International Law*, 31, 47–97.

KIRSCH, P. (1999) The development of the Rome Statute. In R. S. Lee (ed.) *The International Criminal Court: The Making of the Rome Statute: Issues, Negotiations, Results* (The Hague/London/Boston: Kluwer Law International), 451–452.

KIRSCH, P. and HOLMES, J. T. (1999) The Rome Conference on an International Criminal Court: the negotiations process. *American Journal of International Law*, 93, 2–5.

KLICH, O. (1998, 17 June) Reprinted in *CICC Monitor*, 3, 1; also in *Terra Viva*, 3, middle pp.

LEE, R. S. (1999) Introduction. In R. S. Lee (ed.) *The International Criminal Court: The Making of the Rome Statute: Issues, Negotiations, Results* (The Hague/London/Boston: Kluwer Law International).

MAWLAWI, F. (1993) New conflicts, new challenges: the evolutionary role for non-governmental actors. *International Affairs*, 46(2), 391.

MCKAY, F. (1998, 19 June) Speech. Reprinted in *CICC Monitor*, 5, also in *Terra Viva*, 5, middle pp. AD HOC COMMITTEE (1995, 14–25 August, 3–13 April etc.) UN Headquarters in New York.

MOSHAN, B. S. (1998) Women, war and words: the gender component of the permanent international criminal courts definition of crimes against humanity. *Fordham International Law Journal*, 22, 154–178.

NEIER, A. (1990) Transitions in the midst of crisis: the role of the non-governmental organization. *American University Journal of International Law and Policy*, 5, 970.

NGO COALITION (1998, 13 July) The numbers: NGO Coalition Special Report on Country Positions. *CICC Monitor*, 21, 1; also in *Terra Viva*, 23, middle pp.

NGO COALITION (1998, 15 July) The virtual vote. *CICC Monitor*, 23, 1; also in *Terra Viva*, 23, middle pp.

PACE, W. R. (1998, 16 June), Speech. In *CICC Monitor*, 2, 1; also in *Terra Viva*, 2, middle pp.

PACE, W. R. and THIEROFF, M. (1999) Participation of non-governmental organizations. In R. S. Lee (ed.) *The International Criminal Court: The Making of the Rome Statute: Issues, Negotiations, Results* (The Hague/London/Boston: Kluwer Law International), 391.

POPTODOROVA, E. (1998, 25 June) Speech. Reprinted in *CICC* Monitor, 9; also in *Terra Viva*, 9, middle pp. PREPCOM (Various dates) Meetings: 25 March–12 April 1996, 12–30 August 1996, 11–21 February 1997, 4–15 August 1997, 1–12 December 1997, 6 March–3 April 1998, UN Headquarters, New York.

PREPCOM (1998, 14 April) Report of the Preparatory Committee on the Establishment of an International Criminal Court, UN Document A/CONF.183/2/Add.1.

PREPCOM (2000, 12 July) Report of the Preparatory Commission for the International Criminal Court: Finalized Draft Text of the Rules of Procedure and Evidence, Rule 16(1)(d), UN Document PCNICC/2000/INF/3/ Add. 1.

REYNOLDS, S. (1998) Deterring and preventing rape and sexual slavery during periods of armed conflict. *Law and Inequality Journal*, 16, 601–606.

RISHMAWI, M. (1998, 18 June) Speech. Reprinted in *CICC* Monitor, 4; also in *Terra Viva*, 4, middle pp.

ROTH, K. (1998, 24 June) Speech. Reprinted in *CICC Monitor*, 8, 4; also in *Terra Viva*, 8, middle pp.

ROTH, K. (1998, 26 June) *CICC Monitor*, 10, 4; also in *Terra Viva*, 10, middle pp.

SADAT, L. N. (2000) The evolution of the ICC: from The Hague to Rome and back again. In S. B. Sewall and C. Kaysen (eds) *The United States and the International Criminal Court* (Lanham/Boulder/New York/Oxford: Rowman & Littlefield), 32.

SADAT, L. N. and CARDEN, S. R. (2000) The new international criminal court: an uneasy revolution. *Georgetown Law Journal*, 88, 381–385.

SALAND, P. (1999) International criminal law principles. In R. S. Lee (ed.) *The International Criminal Court: The Making of the Rome Statute: Issues, Negotiations, Results* (The Hague/London/Boston: Kluwer Law International), 189–216.

SCHEFFER, D. J. (1999) The United States and the International Criminal Court. *American Journal of International Law*, 93, 12–17.

SELLERS, P. V. and OKUIZUMI, K. (1997) International prosecution of sexual assaults. *Transnational Law and Contemporary Problems*, 7, 45–80.

SLADE, T. N. and CLARK, R. S. (1999) Preamble and final clauses. In R. S. Lee (ed.) *The International Criminal Court: The Making of the Rome Statute: Issues, Negotiations, Results* (The Hague/London/ Boston: Kluwer Law International), 421–424.

STATUTE OF THE INTERNATIONAL CRIMINAL COURT (1998, 17 July) UN Document A/CONF.183/9; also in *International Legal Materials* (1998) 37, 1002.

STEINER, H. J. (1991) *Diverse Patterns: Non-Governmental Organizations and the Human Rights Movement* (Cambridge, MA: Harvard Law School Human Rights Program and Human Rights Internship), 45–49.

STEVENS, L. L. (1998) Toward a permanent international criminal court. *European Journal of Crime, Criminal Law and Criminal Justice*, 6, 236–247.

STREAINS, C. (1999) Gender issues. In R. S. Lee (ed.) *The International Criminal Court: The Making of the Rome Statute: Issues, Negotiations, Results* (The Hague/London/Boston: Kluwer Law International), 357, 360, 362, 371, 374, 375, 379–392, 385, 387, 389.

UN SECRETARY GENERAL (1996, 3 September) Implementation of the Fourth World Conference on Women. UN Document A/51/322, para. 9.

WEERAMANTRY, C. (1996, 8 July) Advisory opinion. *International Court of Justice* 225–552 (para. IX.1); also 533–534 (para. VI.3).

WEISSBRODT, D. (1988) The role of international organizations in the implementation of human rights and humanitarian law in situations of armed conflict. *Vanderbilt Journal of Transnational Law*, 21, 313.

WOMENS CAUCUS (9 July 1998) Calls upon delegates: resist the attack on gender justice. *CICC Monitor*, 19, 2; also in *Terra Viva*, 19, middle pp.

CHAPTER TEN

Human Rights NGOs: A Critical Evaluation

Makau Mutua

Source: 'Human Rights International NGOs: A Critical Evaluation' in Claude E. Welch, Jr. (ed.) *NGOs and Human Rights: Promise and Performance* (2001) 151–163 © 2001 University of Pennsylvania Press—Reprinted with permission.

The human rights movement can be seen in variety of guises. It can be seen as a movement for international justice or as a cultural project for "civilizing savage" cultures. In this chapter, I discuss a part of that movement as a crusade for a political project. International nongovernmental human rights organizations (INGOs), the small and elite collection of human rights groups based in the most powerful cultural and political capitals of the West, have arguably been the most influential component of the human rights movement. They have led the promotion and "universalization" of human rights norms, even though the formal creation and promotion of human rights law is carried out by collections of states—the so-called international community—acting in concert and separately within and outside the ambit of the United Nations. Indeed, INGOs have been the human rights movement's prime engine of growth. INGOs seek to enforce the application of human rights norms internationally, particularly toward repressive states in the South, in areas formerly colonized by the West. In this chapter, I call INGOs conventional doctrinalists because they are marked by a heavy and almost exclusive reliance on positive law in treaties and other sources of international law.

INGOs are ideological analogues, both in theory and in method, of the traditional civil rights organizations that preceded them in the West. The American Civil Liberties Union (ACLU), one of the most influential civil rights organizations in the United States, is a classic example of a Western civil rights organization.[1] Two other equally important domestic civil rights organizations in the United States are the National Association for the Advancement of Colored People (NAACP)[2] and the NAACP Legal Defense and Educational Fund (LDF).[3] Although these organizations are called civil rights groups by Americans, they are in reality human rights organizations. The historical origin of the distinction between a "civil rights" group and a "human rights" group in the United States remains unclear. The primary difference is that Western human rights groups focus on abusive practices and traditions in what they see as relatively repressive, "backward" foreign countries and cultures, while the agenda of civil rights groups concentrates on domestic issues. Thus, although groups such as Human Rights Watch publish reports on human rights abuses in the United States, the focus of their activity is the human rights problems or abuses of other countries.

The half-dozen leading human rights organizations, the prototypical conventional doctrinalists, have arisen in the West over the last half century with the express intent of promoting

certain basic Western liberal values—now dubbed human rights—throughout the world, especially the non-Western world. These INGOs were the brainchildren of prominent Western civil
rights advocates, lawyers, and private citizens.

The International League for the Rights of Man, now the International League for Human
Rights (ILHR), is the oldest such organization, founded in New York in 1942.[4] At various times
it has focused on victims of torture, religious intolerance, the rights of human rights monitors
at its affiliates abroad, the reunification of Eastern Europeans with relatives in the West during
the Cold War, and the human rights treaty state reporting system within the United Nations,
and it even got interested in anticolonial struggles in Africa and Asia.[5] Roger Baldwin, the
founder of the ACLU, also founded the ILHR.[6] The ILHR itself was responsible for establishing
in New York the Lawyers Committee for International Human Rights, now known as the
Lawyers Committee for Human Rights (LCHR), another of the more important Western
INGOs, in 1975. The LCHR claims to promote the human rights standards contained in the
International Bill of Rights.[7] The New York-based Human Rights Watch, discussed in earlier
chapters, has developed into the most dominant American INGO working to expose violations
of basic liberal freedoms. The last major American INGO is the Washington D.C.-based
International Human Rights Law Group, which was established by the Procedural Aspects of
International Law Institute, a private American organization that explores issues in international law.[8] Some American domestic civil rights NGOs are acutely aware of their pioneering
role in the creation of similar organizations abroad.[9] Until recently, and to a large extent even
today, none of these American INGOs focused on human rights issues in the United States,
except to seek the reform of U.S. foreign policy and American compliance with aspects of
refugee law.[10]

The two other leading INGOs are located in Europe, in the United Kingdom and Switzerland.
The Geneva-based International Commission of Jurists (ICJ) was "founded in 1952 to promote
the 'rule of law'"[11] throughout the world."[12] The ICJ has been accused of being a tool of the
West in the Cold War, spending considerable resources exposing the failures of Soviet bloc and
one-party states.[13] Today, however, it is regarded as a bona fide INGO, concerned with rule of
law questions in the South and other issues.

Lastly, the London-based Amnesty International (AI), the most powerful human rights
INGO, is today synonymous with the human rights movement and has inspired the creation of
many similar human rights groups around the world. It was launched by Peter Benenson, a
British lawyer, writing in the May 28, 1961, issues of the *Observer* and *Le Monde*. Benenson's
article, "Forgotten Prisoners," urged moral outrage and appeals for amnesty for individuals who
were imprisoned, tortured, or executed because of their political opinions or religion.[14] The
recipient of the 1977 Nobel Peace Prize, AI claims that its object is "to contribute to the observance throughout the world of human rights as set out in the Universal Declaration of Human
Rights" through campaigns to free prisoners of conscience; to ensure fair trials within a reasonable time for political prisoners; to abolish the death penalty, torture, and other cruel treatment
of prisoners; and to end extrajudicial executions and disappearances. In the last few years,
AI has done substantial work in the West, including exposés of police brutality and the application of the death penalty in the United States.

Social Support and Political Bias

Some structural factors provide evidence of the ideological orientation of INGOs. They concern
the sources of their moral, financial, and social support. The founding fathers of major INGOs—
they have all been white males—were Westerners who either worked on or had an interest in

domestic civil and political rights issues; they sought the reform of governmental laws, policies, and processes to bring about compliance with American and European conceptions of liberal democracy and equal protection. Although the founders of the INGOs did not explicitly state their "mission" as a crusade for the globalization of these values, they nevertheless crafted organizational mandates that promoted liberal ideals and norms. In any case, the key international human rights instruments such as the Universal Declaration of Human Rights (UDHR) and the International Covenant on Civil and Political Rights (ICCPR) pierced the sovereign veil for the purposes of protecting and promoting human rights. The mandates of INGOs are lifted, almost verbatim, from such instruments. AI also deploys jurisprudential arguments developed in the context of Western liberal democracy to cast the death penalty as the "ultimate form of cruel, inhuman and degrading punishment."[15]

The pool for the social support of INGOs has therefore come from the private, nongovernmental, and civil society segments of the industrial democracies: prominent lawyers, academics at leading universities, the business and entertainment elite, and other professionals. In the United States, these circles are drawn from the liberal establishment; the overwhelming majority vote for and support the Democratic Party and its politics and are opposed to the Republican Party. The board of directors of Human Rights Watch, for example, counts among its members such luminaries as Robert Bernstein, formerly the top executive at Random House; Robert Joffe, the managing partner at Cravath, Swaine and Moore; Jack Greenberg, the former director-counsel at LDF and professor of law at Columbia University; and Alice Henkin, an important human rights advocate and spouse of the acclaimed professor of international law Louis Henkin. The board of directors of the Lawyers Committee for Human Rights includes its chair, Norman Dorsen, the prominent New York University law professor, former ACLU president, and First Amendment expert; Louis Henkin; Sigourney Weaver, the actress; Kerry Kennedy Cuomo, the founder of the Robert F. Kennedy Memorial Center for Human Rights, named for her father; Marvin Frankel, formerly the chairman of the board and a named partner in a major New York City law firm; and Tom Bernstein, the committee's president, a senior business executive, and son of Robert Bernstein. The board of directors of the International Human Rights Law Group is composed of similar personalities. These boards are predominantly white and male and almost completely American; some, such as those of the Lawyers Committee or HRW, typically have one or several African Americans or a member of another nonwhite minority.

The boards of the European-based INGOs, the ICJ and AI, tend to differ, somewhat, from American INGOs, although they too are dominated by Westerners, Western-trained academics, professionals, and policy makers, or non-Westerners whose world-view is predominantly Western. Thus, even these Asians and Africans—who, though nonwhite, nevertheless "think white" or "European"—champion, usually uncritically, the universalization of the human rights corpus and liberal democracy. In 1997, for example, the seven members of the executive committee of the ICJ included a British lawyer, a Dutch law professor, a Peruvian (a Westerner), and four establishment figures from India, Ghana, Cape Verde, and Jordan. The non-Westerners in the group were prominent legal professionals steeped in either the common law or the civil law traditions. AI's International Executive Committee, its principal policy-making organ, is arguably more global looking—it includes a number of members from the South—although it too has historically been dominated by Westerners.[16] The staffs of all the major INGOs, including AI's headquarters in London, are similarly dominated by Westerners, although both AI and the ICJ now have African heads.[17] The selection of the boards and staffs of INGOs seems designed to guard against individuals, even if they are Westerners, who may question the utility or appropriateness of the conventional doctrinalist approach. This vetting perpetuates their narrow mandates and contradicts the implied and stated norms of diversity and equality, the raison d'etre for the existence of these organizations.[18]

The relationship between social, financial, and other material support provides further evidence of the political character of INGOs. Except for AI, which relies heavily on membership dues, most INGOs are funded by a combination of foundation grants, private donations, corporations, businesses, and governments. While most do not accept government funds, some, among them the ICJ and the International Human Rights Law Group, have accepted financial support from governmental sources such as the United States Agency for International Development (USAID) and its Canadian and Nordic counterparts.[19] Those who reject government funds cite concerns for their independence of action and thought. It seems fair to conclude that to be considered for acceptance financial support must come from an industrial democracy with a commitment to promoting human rights abroad; presumably, support from Saudi Arabia or the Democratic Republic of the Congo, clearly authoritarian states, would be unacceptable.

The value of the board of directors is critical for groups that rely on private funding. Those networks and associations signify an INGO's reputation and acceptability by political and business elites. In the past decade, some INGOs, especially those based in the United States, have devised a fund-raising gimmick. At an annual dinner they present an award to a noted activist from a repressive country in the South or to a Westerner with superstar quality, such as Senator Edward Kennedy or George Soros, the philanthropist, and invite well-to-do, if not wealthy, citizens, corporations, law firms, and foundations to "buy a table," a euphemism by which it is meant an invitee purchases the right to the dinner by reserving a table for a certain number of guests for a substantial donation. This tapestry of social and business ties, drawn from leading Americans who believe in liberal values and their internationalization through the human rights regime, underlines the agenda of INGOs.[20]

Mandates of INGOs

Substantively, conventional doctrinalists stress a narrow range of civil and political rights, as is reflected by the mandates of leading INGOs like Amnesty International and Human Rights Watch. Throughout the Cold War period, INGOs concentrated their attention on the exposure of violations of what they deemed "core" rights in Soviet bloc countries, Africa, Asia, and Latin America. In a reflection of this ideological bias, INGOs mirrored the position of the industrial democracies and generally assumed an unsympathetic and, at times, hostile posture towards calls for the expansion of their mandates to include economic and social rights?[21]

In the last few years since the collapse of the Soviet bloc, however, several INGOs have started to talk about the "indivisibility" of rights; a few now talk about their belief in the equality of the International Covenant on Economic, Social, and Cultural Rights (ICESCR) and the International Covenant on Civil and Political Rights (ICCPR), although their rhetoric has not been matched by action and practice. Many, in particular Human Rights Watch, for a long time remained hostile, however, to the recognition of economic and social rights as rights. HRW, which considered such rights violations "misfortunes," instead advanced its own nebulous interpretation of "indivisible human rights," which related civil and political rights to survival, subsistence, and poverty, "assertions" of good that it did not explicitly call rights?[22] It argued that subsistence and survival are dependent on civil and political rights, especially those related to democratic accountability.[23] According to this view, civil and political rights belong to the first rank because the realization of other sets of concerns or rights, however they are termed, depend on them.[24]

In September 1996, however, Human Rights Watch abandoned its long-standing opposition to the advocacy of economic and social rights.[25] It passed a highly restrictive and qualified policy—effective January 1997—to investigate, document, and promote compliance with the

ICESCR. Under the terms of the new policy, HRW's work on the ICESCR will be limited to two situations: where protection of the ICESCR right is "necessary to remedy a substantial violation of an ICCPR right," and where "the violation of an ICESCR right is the direct and immediate product of a substantial violation of an ICCPR right." Furthermore, HRW will intervene to protect ICESCR rights only where the violation is a "direct product of state action, whether by commission or omission"; where the "principle applied in articulating an ICESCR right is one of general applicability"; and where "there is a clear, reasonable and practical remedy that HRW can advocate to address the ICESCR violation."

While an important step by HRW, this policy statement can be seen as a continuation of the history of skepticism toward economic and social rights HRW has long demonstrated; it sees economic and social rights only as an appendage of civil and political rights. Its construction seems to condition ICESCR rights on ICCPR rights—in other words, economic and social rights do not exist outside the realm of civil and political rights. Thus, one interpretation of the HRW policy could be that civil and political rights are the fundamental, primary rights without which other rights are less meaningful and unattainable. The policy also continues HRW's stress on state-related violations, an orientation that does not place emphasis on important violators, such as businesses and international corporations. What is important about the policy, however, is the commitment by the largest and most influential American INGO to begin advocacy of economic and social rights. No other major INGO has gone that far in its practical work. Experimental for the first year, the policy now appears to be part of HRW's mandate, although it remains marginal to its work.[26]

Steiner has described the character of INGOs succinctly:

> The term "First World" NGOs both signifies an organization's geographical base and typifies certain kinds of mandates, functions, and ideological orientations. It describes such related characteristics as a concentration on civil and political rights, a commitment to fair (due) process, an individualistic rather than group or community orientation in rights advocacy, and a belief in a pluralist society functioning within a framework of rules impartially applied to protect individuals against state interference. *In a nutshell, "First World" NGOs means those committed to traditional Western liberal values associated with the origins of the human rights movement.* Many of these NGOs work exclusively within their home countries, but the "First World" category also includes most of the powerful international NGOs that investigate events primarily in the Third World.[27]

Traditionally, the work of INGOs has typically involved investigation,[28] reporting,[29] and advocacy.[30] Investigation usually takes place in a Third World country, while reporting and advocacy aim at reforming policies of industrial democracies and intergovernmental agencies to trigger bilateral and multilateral action against the repressive state. Some INGOs now go beyond this denunciatory framework and work to foster and strengthen processes and institutions—rule of law, laws and constitutions, judiciaries, legislatures, and electoral machineries—that ensure the protection of civil and political rights.[31] Although the ideological commitment of these INGOs seems clear through their mandates and work, they nevertheless cast themselves as nonideological. For example, Amnesty International refused to condemn apartheid as a political system or to adopt Nelson Mandela, the century's most prominent prisoner, as a prisoner of conscience. They perceive themselves as politically neutral modern-day abolitionists whose only purpose is to identify "evil" and root it out. Steiner again notes that "although committed to civil-political rights and in this sense taking clear moral and political positions, First World NGOs prefer to characterize themselves as above the play of partisan politics and political parties, and in this sense as apolitical . . . . Their primary self-image is that of monitors, objective investigators applying the consensual norms of the human rights movement to the facts found. They are defenders of legality."[32]

Thus, although INGOs are "political" organizations that work to vindicate political and moral principles that shape the basic characteristics of a state, they consciously present themselves as disinterested in the political character of a state. When HRW asserts that it "addresses the human rights practices of governments of all political stripes, of all geopolitical alignments, and of all ethnic and religious persuasions," it is anticipating charges that it is pro-Western, procapitalist, and unsympathetic to Islamic and other non-Western religious and political traditions. The first two charges could have been fatal to a group's credibility at the height of the Cold War. In reality, however, INGOs have been highly partial: their work has historically concentrated on those countries that have not attained the stable and functioning democracies of the West, the standard for liberal democracy. Target states have included the Soviet bloc and virtually the entire South, where undemocratic or repressive one-party states and military dictatorships have thrived.

The content of the work of INGOs reveals their partiality as well. The typical INGO report is a catalogue of abuses committed by a government against liberal values. As Steiner notes, "given the ideological commitments of these NGOs, their investigative work naturally concentrates on matters such as governmental abuses of rights to personal security, discrimination, and basic political rights. By habit or established practice, NGOs' reports stress the nature and number of violations, rather than explore the socioeconomic and other factors that underlie them."[33]

Reports further document the abridgement of the freedoms of speech and association, violations of due process, and various forms of discrimination. Many INGOs fear that explaining why abuses occur may justify them or give credence to the claims of some governments that civil and political rights violations take place because of underdevelopment. Such an argument, if accepted, would destroy the abolitionists' mission by delaying, perhaps indefinitely, the urgency of complying with human rights standards. Abolitionists fear that this argument would allow governments to continue repressive policies while escaping their obligations under human rights law. INGOs thus demand the immediate protection and respect of civil and political rights regardless of the level of development of the offending state. By taking cover behind the international human rights instruments, INGOs are able to fight for liberal values without appearing partisan, biased, or ideological.

Law versus Politics

Conventional doctrinalists also perpetuate the appearance of objectivity by explicitly distinguishing themselves from agencies, communities, and government programs that promote democracy and democratization. The democracy and human rights communities see themselves in different lights.[34] The first is made up of individuals and institutions devoted to "democracy assistance programs" abroad, while the second is primarily composed of INGOs. The human rights community has created a law-versus politics dichotomy through which it presents itself as the guardian of international law, in this case human rights law, as opposed to the promoter of the more elusive concept of democracy, which it sees as a political ideology.[35] A complex web of reasons, motivations, and contradictions permeates this distinction.

The seeds of the dichotomy are related to the attempt by the human rights community not to side with the two protagonists of the Cold War, and in particular Ronald Reagan's crusade against communism and his efforts to pave the way for democracy and free markets across the globe. The human rights community, whose activists and leaders are mostly Democrats or sympathetic to the Democratic Party, in the case of the United States, or Social Democrats and Labor Party sympathizers in Europe—liberals or those to the left of center in Western political jargon—viewed with alarm Reagan's and Margaret Thatcher's push for free markets and support for any pro-Western government, notwithstanding its human rights record. This hostility was exacerbated by the Reagan administration's attempts to reverse the rhetorical prominence that the Carter administration had given to human rights in American foreign policy. Although INGOs delighted in Reagan's opposition to communist rule within the Soviet bloc—their own human rights reports on Soviet bloc countries were scathing—they sought "impartiality" and a "principled" use by the administration of human rights as a tool of foreign policy. INGOs also feared that "democracy programs" would focus only on elections without entrenching basic civil and political rights.[36] In addition, INGOs believed that the focus on democracy blurred the focus on violators and dulled the clarity of physical violations of rights.

The differentiation between democratic and free-market crusades and human rights had another advantage: Western governments and human rights groups could play "good cop, bad cop" roles in the spread of Western liberal values. While the West in bilateral agreements and projects opened up previously closed or repressive one-party societies to markets and "encouraged" democratization, human rights groups would be unrelenting in their assault on the same government for violating civil and political rights. Ordinarily, staffs of INGOs consulted extensively with the State Department or relevant foreign ministry, Western diplomats[37] in the "repressive" state, and elements of the United Nations charged with human rights oversight, such as the Commission on Human Rights, the Committee Against Torture, and the Human Rights Committee.

Other factors indicate the commitment of INGOs to liberal democracy as a political project. At least one American NGO, the Lawyers Committee for Civil Rights Under Law, a domestic NGO with an INGO dimension, expressly linked the survival of its international operations to the "attainment" of democracy by, for example, shutting down its Southern Africa Project after the 1994 South African elections. Some INGO reports explicitly lament the failure of democratic reform.[38] They defend and seek to immortalize prodemocracy activists in repressive states.[39] At least one former leader of an INGO recognizes that the distinction made between democracy and human rights is a facade:

> This determination to establish impartiality in the face of human rights violations under different political systems led Amnesty International to shun the rhetorical identification of human rights with democracy. But in fact the struggle against violations, committed mostly by undemocratic authoritarian governments, was closely bound up with the struggle for democracy. Thousands of prisoners of conscience for whom Amnesty International worked in its first three decades were political activists challenging the denial of their rights to freedom of expression and association.[40]

Conclusion

In the past decade, some INGOs have started seeking the deployment of the resources of other institutions, in addition to those of the United Nations, in their advocacy for liberal values. The Lawyers Committee for Human Rights, for example, has instituted a project that explores ways of encouraging international financial institutions such as the World Bank to build human rights concerns into their policies.[41] Perhaps INGOs should openly acknowledge the inescapable and intrinsic linkage between human rights and democracy, a fact consciously recognized by quasi-governmental agencies in the North.[42]

The facade of neutrality, the fiction that INGOs do not seek the establishment of a particular political system, in this case, a liberal democracy, must be abandoned immediately. No one should be expected to believe that the scheme of rights promoted by INGOs does not seek to replicate a vision of society based on the industrial democracies of the North. Only after openly conceding that INGOs indeed have a specific political agenda can discussions be had about the wisdom, problems, and implications for the advocacy of such values. And only then can conversations about the postliberal society start in earnest.

Notes

1. Initially founded in 1920 to advocate the rights of conscientious objectors, the ACLU sees itself as the "guardian of the Bill of Rights which guarantees fundamental civil liberties to all of us." These rights include the freedoms of speech, press, and religion (First Amendment); freedom from abuses by the police, domestic spying, and other illegal intelligence activities (Fourth Amendment); equal treatment and fair play (Fifth Amendment); fair trial (Sixth Amendment); prohibition against cruel and unusual punishment (Eighth Amendment); and privacy and personal autonomy (Fourth, Fifth, and Ninth Amendments). See Laurie S. Wiseberg and Hazel Sirett, eds., *North American Human Rights Directory* (Garrett Park, Md.: Garrett Park Press, 1984), p. 19.
2. The NAACP, the oldest U.S. civil rights organization, was founded in 1909 to seek equal treatment—the removal of racial discrimination in areas such as voting, employment, housing, business, courts, and transportation—for African Americans through peaceful reform. See ibid., p. 161.
3. Although today the LDF and the NAACP are separate legal entities, the LDF was founded in 1939 as the legal arm of the NAACP. It has initiated legal action in courts to challenge discrimination and promote equality in schools, jobs, the electoral system, land use, and other services and areas. Ibid., p. 159.
4. See Wiseberg and Sirett, eds., *North American Human Rights Directory*, p. 135.
5. Ibid. The ILHR was also involved, albeit paternalistically, in anticolonial struggles in Africa and Asia, particularly in South-West Africa, now Namibia. See William Korey, *NGOs and the Universal Declaration of Human Rights: "A Curious Grapevine"* (New York: St. Martin's Press, 1998), p. 101.
6. See Rita McWilliams, "Who Watched Americas Watch?" *National Interest* 19 (1990), pp. 45, 53, Jerome Shestack, a prominent American lawyer who long served as the president of the ILHR and is the organization's current honorary chair, was replaced in May 1996 by Scott Horton, a partner in a New York law firm. Telephone interview with the ILHR, September 13, 1996.
7. On the mandate of the LCHR, see Lawyers Committee for Human Rights, *Critique: Review of the Department of State Country Reports on Human Rights Practices for 1990* (New York: Lawyers Committee for Human Rights, 1991), back leaf.
8. See Wiseberg and Sirett, eds., *North American Human Rights Directory*, p. 133. The institute itself was established in 1965 and has devoted considerable resources to the promotion of the idea of human rights. Richard Lillich, its former president, is a professor of law at the University of Virginia School of Law and one of the leading writers on human rights.
9. At a 1992 LDF symposium of public interest law NGOs from around the world, Julius Chambers, then director-counsel of the LDF, recalled how Thurgood Marshall, his most celebrated predecessor, had in 1959 helped write the Kenya Constitution, and had helped to endow it with doctrines of due process, equality, and justice. Chambers also remembered how Jack Greenberg, another predecessor, had laid the groundwork for the Legal Resource Centre of South Africa, one of that country's leading public interest law firms under apartheid. Instructively, he noted that he did not view the symposium "primarily as an occasion for the LDF to *teach* others." See National Association

for the Advancement of Colored People Legal Defense and Educational Fund, *Public Interest Law around the World: Report of a Symposium held at Columbia University in May 1991 with Descriptions of Participating Legal Organizations from Twenty Countries* (New York: Columbia Human Rights Law Review, 1992), p. 1; emphasis added. Noting the progress made in establishing human rights NGOs around the world and arguing for the removal of restrictions on NGOs to allow them to operate more freely, see also Lawyers Committee for Human Rights, *The Establishment of the Right of Non-Governmental Groups to Operate* (New York: Lawyers Committee for Human Rights, 1993).

10. American INGOs argue, with some justification, that there is a glut of civil rights organizations addressing civil (human) rights problems in the United States. They therefore *see* little purpose in duplicating the excellent work of local NGOs. This posture is self-defeating in several respects. First, charges of "imperialism" undercut the effectiveness of American INGOs, even with some of their kindred spirits in the South and the former Soviet bloc. Secondly, domestic American NGOs remain unaware of the uses of the international rights regime and the solidarity of advocates elsewhere, facts which conspired to delay the ratification by the United States of major international human rights treaties. The absence of domestic U.S. NGOs from the international human rights movement served, among other things, to delegitimize the movement in the eyes of other cultures. Nevertheless, in a rare effort, Human Rights Watch and the ACLU in 1993 produced a report on human rights abuses in the United States. See Human Rights Watch and American Civil Liberties Union, *Human Rights Violations in the United States* (New York: Human Rights Watch and American Civil Liberties Union, 1993). Two things were unusual about the effort: first, that an American INGO produced a human rights report on the United States, and second, that it did so in collaboration with a domestic American NGO. In a rare call, Dorothy Thomas, formerly the director of the Human Rights Watch Women's Project, urged the use of international human rights norms in protecting human rights in the United States. Dorothy Q. Thomas, 'Advancing Rights Protection in the United States: An Internationalized Advocacy Strategy," *Harvard Human Rights Journal* 9 (1996), pp. 15–26. Amnesty International also launched an extensive campaign on human rights in the United States in 1998.

11. This term is commonly understood to describe a state that is accountable to the governed through the application of fair and just laws enforced by an independent and impartial judiciary. See Andrea J. Hanneman, "Independence and Group Rights in the Baltics: A Double Minority Problem," *Virginia Journal of International Law* 35 (1995), pp. 485, 523: "The extent to which a society protects human rights in general and minority rights in particular has been called the 'litmus test of liberty and the rule of law'"; citing Ralf Dahrendorf, "Minority Rights and Minority Rule," in Ben Whitaker, ed., *Minorities: A Question of Human Rights?* (New York: Pergamon Press, 1984), p. 79. For a history of the ICJ, see Howard B. Tolley, Jr., *Global Advocates for Human Rights: The International Commission of Jurists* (Philadelphia: University of Pennsylvania Press, 1994).

12. Laurie S. Wiseberg and Hazel Sirett, eds., *Human Rights Directory: Western Europe* (Washington, D.C.: Human Rights Internet, 1982), p. 216.

13. See Issa G. Shivji, *The Concept of Human Rights in Africa* (London: Codesria, 1989), p. 34. At its inception, the ICJ was funded in part by covert CIA funds. "It followed an essentially American set of priorities in its early years, then expanded and became less politically partial." Claude E. Welch, Jr., *Protecting Human Rights in Africa: Roles and Strategies gf Non-Governmental Organizations* (Philadelphia: University of Pennsylvania Press, 1995), p. 163.

14. See Ian Martin, *The New World Order: Opportunity or Threat for Human Rights?* (Cambridge, Mass.: Harvard Law School Human Rights Program, 1993), pp. 4–5. From 1986 to 1992, Martin was the secretary-general of Amnesty International. Benenson's article accompanied photos of six political prisoners: three were imprisoned in Romania, Hungary, and Czechoslovakia; the

other three were a Greek communist and unionist imprisoned in Greece, an Angolan doctor and poet incarcerated by the Portuguese colonial rulers in Angola, and the Rev. Ashton Jones, an American who had repeatedly been beaten and jailed in Louisiana and Texas for advocating the civil rights of black Americans. Ibid. Although AI now focuses most of its attention on Africa, Central America, and South America, the trigger for its creation was, ironically, the official conduct of Soviet bloc and Western governments, including the United States.

15. Ibid., p. 21. In addition, AI attacks the "arbitrary and irrevocable nature of the death penalty," its use as a "tool of political repression," and its disproportionate imposition on "the poor and the powerless." It disagrees with the argument that the death penalty has a deterrent effect on crime. Ibid.

16. See Henry J. Steiner, *Diverse Partners: Non-Governmental Organizations in the Human Rights Movement: The Report of a Retreat of Human Rights Activists* (Cambridge, Mass.: Harvard Law School Human Rights Program and Human Rights Internet, 1991), pp. 61–64.

17. Ibid. Pierre Sane, a Senegalese, became AI's first non-European secretary-general in October 1992. Adama Dieng, also a Senegalese, became the secretary-general of the ICJ in 1991. Although both AI and the ICJ accepted non-Western heads, the choices were more "safe" and less radical than they initially appeared. Sane came from the International Development Research Centre, a Canadian development aid organization, for which he had worked since 1978, Dieng was working for the ICJ before his appointment. Both were nationals of Senegal, with a reputation in the West as a stable formal democracy, and one of the most Francophilic countries in Africa.

18. When INGOs engage Southerners, it is ordinarily for area-specific responsibilities, usually their native region. For example, Africa Watch, the division of Human Rights Watch that addresses sub-Saharan African human rights problems, has been headed by Africans since its founding in 1988. Similarly, Americas Watch has been headed by Latin Americans virtually since its inception in 1981. This author, an African, was in 1989–91 the director of the Africa Project at the Lawyers Committee for Human Rights, having succeeded Rakiya Omaar, another African. This ghettoization—conscious or not—seeks to legitimize the organization in the particular region while retaining its commitment to Western liberal values. It also pigeonholes non-Westerners as capable of addressing issues in only their native region and incapable of dealing with questions from other regions. In effect, these hiring patterns leave the impression that only Westerners have the ability to develop a universal outlook.

19. In 1993 this author led a USAID-funded "rule of law" study mission to Ethiopia for the International Human Rights Law Group and wrote a report on the mission's findings. International Human Rights Law Group, *Ethiopia in Transition*.

20. In 1986, for example, the Lawyers Committee for Human Rights honored President Corazon Aquino of the Philippines for "her achievement in leading the people of her nation to peacefully reclaim democracy." See Lawyers Committee for Human Rights, *Tenth Anniversary Annual Report* (New York: Lawyers Committee for Human Rights, 1988). In 1987, it honored Robert Bernstein, senior executive at Random House and the founder of Human Rights Watch. NBC news anchor Tom Brokaw was the master of ceremonies at the 600-guest event which attracted prominent businessmen and lawyers. Ibid.

21. See Aryeh Neier, "Human Rights," in Joel Krieger, William A. Joseph, James A. Paul, et al., eds., *The Oxford Companion to Politics of the World* (New York: Oxford University Press, 1993), pp. 401, 403.

22. See Human Rights Watch, *Indivisible Rights: The Relationship of Political and Civil Rights to Survival, Subsistence and Poverty* (New York: Human Rights Watch, 1992). In 1993, Neier, the former executive director of HRW, expressed his opposition to the deployment of rights rhetoric to economic and social concerns: "When it comes to the question of what are called economic rights, I'm on the side of the spectrum which feels that the attempt to describe economic

concerns as rights is misguided. I think that when one expresses this opinion, it is often thought that one is denigrating the significance of economic misery and inequities. I would like not to be accused of that. I regard economic equity and economic misery as matters of enormous significance. I just don't think that it's useful to define them in terms of rights." Aryeh Neier, "Remarks to East Asian Legal Studies & Human Rights Program Symposium, Harvard Law School, May 8, 1993," in *Human Rights and Foreign Policy: A Symposium* (Cambridge, Mass.: Harvard Law School Human Rights Program, 1994), p. 16. For a critique of NGOs and their restrictive mandates, see James Gathii and Celestine Nyamu, "Note, Reflections on United States-based Human Rights NGOs' Work on Africa," *Harvard Human Rights Journal* 9 (1996), p. 291.

23. See Human Rights Watch, *Indivisible Rights*. One of the most coherent rationalizations of the opposition to economic and social rights was expressed in a meeting of American INGOs: "One participant felt strongly that it would be detrimental for U.S. human rights NGOs to espouse the idea of economic, social and cultural rights. Although they refer to important issues, they concern distributive justice rather than corrective justice, like civil and political rights. But distributive justice is a matter of policy, rather than principles; and human rights NGOs must deal with principles, not policies. Otherwise, their credibility will be damaged. Supporting economic demands will only undermine the ability of NGOs to promote civil and political rights, which are indispensable." M. Rodriguez Bustelo and Philip Alston, unpublished report of a conference held at Arden House, 1986, p. 26; quoted in Philip Alston, "U.S. Ratification of the Covenant on Economic, Social and Cultural Rights: The Need for an Entirely New Strategy," *American Journal of International Law* 84 (1990), p. 390, n. 107. The credibility of American INGOs to which the speaker referred was unlikely to be credibility among those whose economic and social rights are denied. It seems fair to suppose that the concern here was the reputation of NGOs with the governments of industrial democracies and the elites who support the INGO community.

24. Human Rights Watch, *Indivisible Rights*, pp. vi–vii.

25. Human Rights Watch, "Human Rights Watch's Proposed Interim Policy on Economic, Social, and Cultural Rights," internal document, September 30, 1996. All quotations in this paragraph are from this document.

26. Ibid. HRW has been reluctant to expand this mandate to cover more ICESCR rights for a number of reasons, including the lack of adequate human resources. Kenneth Roth, executive director, Human Rights Watch, telephone interview with author October 8, 1996. See generally, Human Rights Watch, *Human Rights Watch World Report 1999* (New York: Human Rights Watch, 1999).

27. Steiner, *Diverse Partners*, p. 19; emphasis added.

28. An investigation, known as human rights fact-finding mission, is conducted by the staffs of INGOs who typically spend anywhere from several days to a number of weeks in a Third World country interviewing victims of repression, government officials, local activists, local media, and academics. See, generally, Diane F. Orentlicher, "Bearing Witness: The Art and Science of Human Rights Fact-Finding," *Harvard Human Rights Journal* 3 (1990), p. 83.

29. Reporting involves compiling data and information from the fact-finding mission and correlating them to human rights standards to bring out discrepancies and disseminating the results through reports or other media. This method is also called "shaming" because it spotlights the offending state to the international community. See, e.g., Lawyers Committee for Human Rights, *Zimbabwe: Wages of War: A Report on Human Rights* (New York: Lawyers Committee for Human Rights, 1986); Human Rights Watch, *World Report 1995*.

30. This includes lobbying governments and international institutions to use their leverage to alleviate violations.

31. For example, according to its statute, Amnesty International works to "promote as appears appropriate the adoption of constitutions, conventions, treaties and other measures which guarantee

the rights contained in the provisions referred to in Article 1 hereof." Amnesty International, *Report,* appendix 2, p. 333. The International Human Rights Law Group undertakes rule of law assessments which aim at identifying institutional weaknesses and proposing structural reforms. See, generally, International Human Rights Law Group, *Ethiopia in Transition.*

32. Steiner, *Diverse Partners,* p. 19.

33. Ibid.

34. For a comprehensive journalistic account of the differences between the two communities, see Thomas Carothers, "Democracy and Human Rights: Policy Allies or Rivals?" *Washington Quarterly* 17 (1994), p. 109.

35. Ibid., p. 111.

36. See Lawyers Committee for Human Rights, *United States Draft Human Rights Action Plan,* p. 4.

37. Meetings at the request of INGOs with State Department officials responsible for policies in particular countries are indispensable to INGOs, whose clout often comes from their association with rich and powerful Western states. Ordinarily, INGO fact-finding missions also meet with Western diplomats to raise concerns and seek inside information about political issues in the country.

38. See, e.g., Amnesty International USA, *Zaire: Violence Against Democracy* (New York: Amnesty International USA, 1993), p. 23; Africa Watch, *Zaire: Two Years Without a Transition* (Washington, D.C.: Africa Watch, 1992), pp. 45–46.

39. The Robert F. Kennedy Memorial Center for Human Rights, for example, has often given its annual award to prodemocracy activists, including Gibson Kamau Kuria of Kenya, a leading figure in the struggle to end repressive one-party rule by introducing multiparty democracy in his country. See Robert F. Kennedy Memorial Center for Human Rights, *Justice Enjoined: The State of the Judiciary in Kenya* (Washington, D.C.: Robert F. Kennedy Memorial Center for Human Rights, 1992); Makau Mutua, *Confronting the Past: Accountability for Human Rights Violations in Malawi* (Washington, D.C.: Robert F. Kennedy Memorial Center for Human Rights, 1994).

40. Martin, *The New World Order,* p. 6.

41. See Lawyers Committee for Human Rights, *The World Bank: Governance and Human Rights* (New York: Lawyers Committee for Human Rights, 1993), pp. 2–3.

42. David Gillies, *Human Rights, Democracy and "Good Governance": Stretching the World Bank's Policy Frontiers* (Montreal: International Centre for Human Rights and Democratic Development, 1993).

PART V

WOMEN'S RIGHTS

CHAPTER ELEVEN

The Global Women's Movement: Origins, Issues and Strategies

Peggy Antrobus

Source: Peggy Antrobus *The Global Women's Movement: Origins, Issues and Strategies* (2004) 9–27, 109–136 © 2004 ZED Books—Reproduced with permission.

I. The Global Women's Movement: Definitions and Origins

The authors of this Kenya case study describe a process which is common to many of us as we are called on to consider the question of whether there is a women's movement. This chapter attempts to answer the questions: Is there a global women's movement? How can we understand such a movement? How can it be defined, and what are its characteristics? My conclusion is that there is a global women's movement. It is different from other social movements and can be defined by diversity, its feminist politics and perspectives, its global reach and its methods of organizing.

Personal reflection

When we were first approached about writing on the women's movement in Kenya, one question emerged in both of our minds: Is there a women's movement in Kenya? When we considered this, we simultaneously answered, 'No'. After more reflection, we began to ask, 'If there is no women's movement, what is this intense activity going on around us of women's group meetings, workshops, seminars, and even individual women agitating for women's rights in the courts, in the media and even on the streets? (*Wilhelmina Oduol and Wanjiku Mukabi Kabira*).[1]

Definitions

In her book, commissioned by the Ford Foundation as a contribution to the events surrounding the Fourth World Conference on Women held in Beijing in September 1995, Amrita Basu put together a collection of writings documenting the manifestations of feminist politics through local struggles which shape and are shaped by feminism. She defines women's movements as comprising 'a range of struggles by women against gender inequality'. The seventeen case studies, from as many countries or regions, describe and analyse a rich diversity of experience, grounded in specific local struggles.[2]

Many authors admit that this movement does not conform to conventional definitions of a 'movement', lacking as it does common objectives, continuity, unity and coordination. Yet this should not surprise us, nor should it be taken as a sign of deficiency. Women's movements are, after all, different from all other social movements in that they are crosscutting, ask different questions, and often seek goals that challenge conventional definitions of where we want to go.[3] Only a few activists take the view that the objectives of the women's movement are similar to those of labour, human rights and student groups, which seek justice for their members. Many see the objectives of women's groups as broader, seeking changes in relationships that are more varied and complex. At the same time it is sometimes difficult to identify clear objectives; worse, the objectives articulated by some groups seem to contradict those of others. The following quotes from the Nigerian case study illustrate the problem:

> The Nigerian women's movement is an unarmed movement. It is non-confrontational. It is a movement for the progressive upliftment of women for motherhood, nationhood and development.[4]

And again:

> When African women demand equality, we are only asking for our rights not to be tampered with, and the removal of laws that oppress and dehumanize women. We are not asking for equality with our husbands. We accept them as the bosses and heads of the family.[5]

The confusion and contradictions captured in these statements reflect the complexity of a movement that is caught in the tension between what is possible and what is dreamed of, between short-term goals and long-term visions, between expediency and risk-taking, pragmatism and surrender, between the practical and the strategic. Most of all, there is understandable ambivalence surrounding challenging and confronting relationships that are intimate and deeply felt. But the confusion also reflects a lack of clarity about definitions of what groups might be considered part of a 'women's movement'.

Many activists, including Nigerian activists who identify themselves with a women's movement, would question definitions of the objectives of their movement in terms of the 'upliftment of women for motherhood, nationhood and development'. They would argue that this instrumentalizes women, while being in complete accord with patriarchal definitions of women's traditional role.

It seems to me that the continuing confusion about what defines women's movements relates not so much to the fact that this movement does not conform to a conventional definition of a movement, but rather to lack of clarity about objectives in contexts that differ widely.

One way of clarifying these apparent contradictions is to recognize two mutually reinforcing tendencies within women's movements—one focused on gender identity (identity politics) and the other concerned with a larger project for social transformation.[6] There are two entry points to concerns about a larger social project. One is recognition of the centrality of the care and nurture of human beings to the larger social project, and that to address this, given the primacy of women's gendered role in this area, requires addressing gender relations in all the complex interplay of their economic, social, political, cultural and personal dimensions. It also involves locating gender inequality within other forms of inequality that shape and often exacerbate it.

Another entry point is recognition that women cannot be separated from the larger context of their lived experience and that this includes considerations of class, race/ethnicity and geographic location, among other factors. This means that the struggle for women's agency must include engagement in struggles against sources of women's oppression that extend beyond gender.

The larger social project would therefore include transforming social institutions, practices and beliefs so that they address gender relations along with other oppressive relationships, not simply seeking a better place within existing institutions and structures. For this reason, women's movements in countries where the majority of women are marginalized by class, race or ethnicity must be concerned with the larger social project. This is often a point of tension between women's movements in the context of North–South relations, as well as in the context of struggles against oppression on the basis of class, race and ethnicity.

I believe that confusion about definitions of women's movements is also caused by failure to make distinctions between women's organizations as part of a wide spectrum of nongovernmental organizations (NGOs) or civil society organizations (CSOs), and those that might be better understood as part of a politically oriented social movement.

Similarly, the term 'women's movements' is sometimes used interchangeably with 'feminist movements', an error that confuses and misrepresents both feminism and the broad spectrum of women's organizations.

In the final analysis, it seems to me that the identification of feminist politics as the engine of women's movements may help to clarify some of the confusion around women's organizing in the period covered by this book, as well as to focus the answer to the central question: Can women's movements make a difference in the struggle for equity, democracy and sustainability in today's globalized economy? It is the combination of struggles for gender justice with those for economic justice and democracy that enables women's movements to make a difference to the larger social project for transformation of systems and relationships.

An important segment of women's movements is composed of the associations that work to incorporate a feminist perspective into their theoretical, analytical, professional and political work. In academia, most disciplines now have feminist associations—Anthropology, Economics, Political, Social and Natural Sciences and Theology, among others. Moreover, within these disciplines—whether women are organized into feminist associations or not—women in the academies are doing important theoretical and empirical work that deepens our understanding of women's realities and produces the analyses and insights that strengthen the work of activists.

In the professions there are also women's associations—doctors, nurses, midwives, social workers, teachers, lawyers, bankers etc.—that are challenging patriarchal patterns and relationships, raising new questions and changing the practices and methods by which their professions operate.

Many women's organizations, even those that focus on traditional concerns of home and family, are nevertheless important participants in women's movements. Among these are grassroots women's organizations of various kinds—Women's Institutes, Federations of Women, the YWCA, and many worldwide organizations identified with strong advocacy on behalf of women's rights, although they may not describe themselves as feminist.[7]

Finally, a definition of a women's movement must include those individual women who would never join an organization, nor define themselves as feminists, but whose lives and actions nevertheless serve to advance the liberation of women in their community and beyond.

All of these women must be seen as part of, or at least contributing to, women's movements. They are all part of the diversity and richness of a movement that seeks change in the relationships of superiority and inferiority, domination and subordination between women and men in a patriarchal world.

The following statements summarize my own views on women's movements:

- A women's movement is a *political* movement—part of the broad array of social movements concerned with changing social conditions, rather than part of a network of women's organizations (although many women's organizations may be part of a women's movement).
- A women's movement is grounded in an understanding of women's relations to *social conditions*—an understanding of gender as an important relationship within the broad structure of social relationships of class, race and ethnicity, age and location.
- A women's movement is a *process*, discontinuous, flexible, responding to specific conditions of perceived gender inequality or gender-related injustice. Its focal points may be in women's organizations, but it embraces individual women in various locations who identify with the goals of feminism at a particular point in time.
- Awareness and *rejection of patriarchal privilege* and control are central to the politics of women's movements.
- In most instances, the 'movement' is born at the moments in which individual women become aware of *their separateness as women*, their alienation, marginalization, isolation or even abandonment within a broader movement for social justice or social change. In other words, women's struggle for agency within the broader struggle is the catalyst for women's movements.

Bell Hooks describes this process of *conscientization* thus:

Our search leads us back to where it all began, to that moment when an individual woman . . . who may have thought she was all alone, began a feminist uprising, began to name her practice, indeed began to formulate theory from lived experience.[8]

Women from across the world who identify themselves as part of an international and global women's movement are to be found participating in international meetings organized by feminist associations, networks and organizations such as the International Inter-disciplinary Congress, the Association for Women's Rights and Development (AWID) and UN conferences.[9] They celebrate annual special 'days' such as International Women's Day (IWD) on 8 March and International Day Against Violence Against Women on 25 November. They are in constant communication with each other through the Internet, where they sign petitions and statements in solidarity with women around the world, formulate strategies and organize campaigns and meetings.

The movement has important resources:

- resource centres such as the International Women's Tribune Centre (IWTC), set up following the 1975 International Women's Year (IWY) Conference in Mexico City;
- media, such as feminist radio stations like the Costa Rica-based FIRE (Feminist International Radio Endeavor); news services like WINGS (Women's International News Gathering Service) and Women's Feature Services (WFS), supported initially by UNESCO;
- websites (see p. 189–90);
- publishers and women's presses;

- artists and artistes—filmmakers, musicians, dancers, painters, writers, poets and playwrights;
- women's funds started by individual philanthropists and organizations that support women's projects, organizations and networks.

Characteristics

Diversity Experience of the past thirty years points to the pitfall of starting with an assumption of a 'global sisterhood', especially when that 'sisterhood' is defined by a privileged minority. The emergence of a global movement has indeed depended on the emergence of new and different voices challenging hegemonic tendencies and claiming their own voice and space, and the acceptance of differences within the movements.

Diversity is now recognized as perhaps the most important characteristic of women's movements. Nevertheless, many of the tensions among women in their movements can be related to differences of race/ethnicity, nationality/ culture and class, although, as Audre Lorde points out:

[I]t is not those differences between us that are separating us. It is rather our refusal to recognize [them] and to examine the distortions which result from our misnaming them and their effects upon human behaviour and expectation.[10]

She also reminds us, 'There is no such thing as a single-issue struggle because we do not live single-issue lives.'[11] Women under stand that each of us has multiple identities and that at any point in time one or other may be more important than others. Insistence on focusing on gender in isolation from issues like race, ethnicity and class has often been more divisive than the inclusion of these issues in the agendas of the various movements. It is indeed impossible and even counterproductive to separate the varied forms of oppression because of the systemic links between them. Thus in many countries of the South women have had to confront colonialism, imperialism or racism before they could confront patriarchy.

Feminist politics It may be useful to identify feminism as a specific politics, grounded in a consciousness of all the sources of women's subordination, and with a commitment to challenge and change the relationships and structures which perpetuate women's subordinate position, in solidarity with other women. The consciousness of sexism and sexist oppression is the essence of feminist politics, and it is this politics that energizes women's movements, whether or not the word 'feminist' is used. It is possible then to identify feminist politics as a specific element within a broader universe of women's organizations, women's movements and other social movements.

Feminists have worked with and within other social movements—especially those on peace, racism, the environment, indigenous peoples and the poor. These initiatives have served both to broaden and redefine the issues of concern to women, as well as to refocus the agendas of these movements.

In addition, there are feminists within institutions and agencies who recognize the ways in which the ideology of patriarchy constrains and diminishes the achievement of laudable goals and objectives, and who engage in the struggle to challenge it.

Feminist politics can also be identified within bureaucratic initiatives and institutional arrangements established for the improvement of the condition and position of women, enabling them to contribute to the movement for gender justice. These include women's bureaus, desks, commissions, special units and gender focal points within mainstream institutions.

Global reach Our understanding of the diversity within women's movements that has led us to speak more often of a multiplicity of 'movements' would lead many to question the concept of a single global women's movement. However, I would argue, as others have done, that despite the rich diversity of experience, grounded in specific local struggles, women have been able to transcend these to become a movement of global proportions, with a global agenda and perspective.

Here I want to distinguish between an international women's movement and a global women's movement.[12] Although, as Uta Ruppert has pointed out, local or national women's movements have never viewed their activities as 'simply crossing the borders of nation states',[13] I would conceptualize an 'international' movement as one in which the national and cultural differences between women were recognizable and paramount. Indeed, this was characteristic of women's movements at the international level in the mid-1970s, at the launching of the UN Decade for Women (1975–85), and to some extent throughout most of the Decade. However, as women established their separate identities along the prevailing axes of North–South, East–West, they discovered commonalities that moved them increasingly towards greater coherence and even common positions in the policy debates around issues of environment, poverty, violence and human rights. At the same time, as these issues became increasingly 'global' (as reflected in the themes and agendas of the global conferences of the 1990s), women's movements converged in these global arenas to negotiate and articulate common agendas and positions. As Ruppert puts it:

> The political process of international women's movements has been shaped by the insight that international politics does not simply take place at the inter-nation-state level, but also encompasses multicentric and multilevel processes. Thus the movement's multidimensional political understanding, which is sensitive to differences, almost predestined it to become the most global of social movements of the 1990s.[14]

She goes on to identify:

> [A] second component . . . essential for the women's movement to become an effective global actor, [which] was the movement's shift toward aiming for 'globality' as a main objective. Even though there has never been an explicit discourse along these lines, the movement's political practice suggests a conceptual differentiation between three different political approaches on the global level: criticizing and combating globalization as a neo-liberal paradigm; utilizing global politics, or rather global governance, as tools for governance under the conditions of globalization; and specifically creating 'globality',[15] which the women's movement has aimed for and worked towards as an important factor in women's global politics.[16]

Methods of organizing It is widely understood that a characteristic of a global women's movement is the linking of local to global, the particularities of local experience and struggles to, as Ruppert says, 'the political creation and establishment of global norms for world development and global ethics for industrial production, such as (social and gender) justice, sustainability and peace, based on the creation of globally valid fundamental human rights'.[17] However, few have related this to the particular methods of feminist organizing.

Although, as Ruppert rightly states, this practice has not been the subject of an explicit discourse, it has nevertheless been based on conscious decisions to involve women from different backgrounds and regions in the search for 'globality'. These decisions have been the result of an understanding of the ways in which global events, trends and policies impact on local experience, and in particular on the experiences of poor women in the global South.

While Ruppert and others cite women's organizing around the 1992 UN Conference on Environment and Development (UNCED) and the 1993 International Conference on Human Rights as the first signs of this kind of organizing, I would refer to the experience of the network of Third World women, DAWN, in their preparations for the Forum of the 1985 Third World Conference on Women. It was here that a conscious attempt was made to bring together local and regional experiences as the beginning of a process for the preparation of a platform document for a global event.

I speak more about this experience in Chapters 3, 4 and 5; here I merely want to use it to illustrate the feminist methodology used for the 'globalizing' of frameworks around economics, environment and rights. The starting point was a meeting at which women were invited to reflect on their experience of development over the course of the Decade for Women—from the perspective of poor women living in the economic South. In this way the final document reflected regional differences, even as it reached for a framework that revealed the linkages between these experiences. This process—which starts with testifying to local, regional, or even individual experiences ('telling our stories', 'speaking our truths'), leading to the negotiation of differences and finally to the articulation of a position that attempts to generalize, synthesize or 'globalize' the diversity of experience—was repeated in the processes leading to the global conferences on environment, human rights and population. Chapter 6 focuses on the processes around these events.

This methodology, clearly related to that of feminist consciousness-raising and Freirian *conscientization*[18] (combining reflection on personal experience with socio-political analysis to construct and generate global advocacy) has been a powerful tool for the global women's movement. Like *conscientization*, which takes specific realities 'on the ground' as the basis for social analysis that can lead to action, it is a *praxis* (process of reflection and action) that has helped to mobilize women to challenge neo-liberal and fundamentalist state policies at national and global levels. This praxis has also been a powerful tool in feminist theorizing.

To drive home one of the differences between international women's movements and a global women's movement, I want to compare this feminist method of globalizing to the process of regional meetings and consultations used by the UN in the preparation of their international conferences. The documents that feed into and emerge from these processes have to be screened and sanctioned by governments and, by their very nature, are limited in the degree to which they are able to reflect the realities of women. While the plans and platforms of action that emerge from the conferences contain many recommendations and resolutions that accord with the advocacy of women's movements, they often lack the coherence and clarity of the platforms produced by a movement unrestrained by the conventions of international diplomacy. Moreover, without the vigilance and political activism of women's movements, especially at local or national, but also at global, levels, these recommendations are meaningless to women.

This brings me to another aspect of the links between global and local—the ways in which local actors organize to defend themselves against global threats. Recognizing the relationship between global trends and local realities, women are organizing around the defence of their bodies, their livelihoods and their communities.[19] The word 'glocality' has been coined to highlight the ways in which global trends affect local experience. This recognition of a 'politics of place' poses new challenges to a global women's movement. While organizing in the defence of 'place' has the potential to be the most powerful and effective form of organizing,[20] local groups clearly need information and analysis on the broader policy frameworks that are affecting their lives. A global women's movement also needs links to this level of organizing to retain its relevance and to legitimize its advocacy.

The global women's movement is very aware that action at global level must have resonance at local, national and regional levels if it is to be meaningful to women. In this sense we need to see the global women's movement as made up of many interlocking networks. Many of the global networks have worked to strengthen their links to activities at regional, national and local levels.

A second method of organizing, which is also a strategy, is networking. Some may say that women's movements invented networking! Networking is the method used to make the vertical (local–global) as well as the horizontal (inter-regional as well as issue-specific) links that generate the analysis and the organizing underlying global action.

A third is the linking of the personal to the political, the ways in which gender identification and recognition of common experience can short-circuit difference to create a sense of solidarity. This often makes it easier for women who are strangers to each other to work together.

Symbols and Images

In the final analysis, words may not be enough to enable us to understand the complexity of a global women's movement made up of such a diversity of movements. In thinking about this book, I have often been struck by the ways in which images and symbols capture the shape and structure of a global women's movement. The images and symbols that come to mind are those of the spiral, the wheel, the pyramid, the web and the patchwork quilt.

A spiral is an open-ended circle. As an adjective it is a 'winding about a centre in an enlarging or decreasing continuous cone'. As a noun, 'a plane or three-dimensional spiral curve' (*Concise Oxford Dictionary*, 1990). In both cases it captures images of continuity and change, depth and expansion—something that is identifiable yet varied.

Inuit story-telling takes the form of a spiral, a three-dimensional curve that winds about centre in an enlarging continuous curve that allows the story-teller to start at any point and move backwards and forwards as appropriate. The story has no end. A spiral is open-ended, continuous, ever enlarging our understanding of events, our perspectives. The global women's movement can be thought of as a spiral, a process that starts at the centre (rather than at the beginning of a line) and works its way outwards, turning, arriving at what might appear to be the same point, but in reality at an expanded understanding of the same event.

A spiral is also dialectic, allowing for the organic growth of a movement of women organizing—a movement in a state of on-going evolution as consciousness expands in the process of exchanges between women, taking us backwards (to rethink and reevaluate old positions) and forwards (to new areas of awareness).

As a number of interlocking networks, a global women's movement might also be likened to pyramids, webs and wheels. In a study of two campaigns, the campaign against breast-milk substitutes in Ghana, and against child labour in the carpet industry in India, the New Economics Foundation (NEF) identified three structures for organizing constructive collaboration: the pyramid, the wheel, and the web. Pyramids have a coordinating secretariat who disseminates information through the campaign; wheels have one or more focal points for information exchange, but information also flows directly among the members; in the web, no focal point exist, so information flows to and from all the members in roughly equal quantities.[21]

The pyramid, the wheel and the web underline the fluidity of the global women's movement, comprised as it is of interlocking networks that come together as appropriate, even as each continues to focus on its specific area of interest.

Gita Sen's description of the Three Waves of the Women's Movement

The first wave had three distinct sources. One source was in the colonized countries with the emergence of social reform movements that had as their primary focus the transformation of cultural practices affecting civil laws, marriage, and family life. While these reform attempts mobilized possibly as many or more men as women, they were an important early strand in the transformation of social discourse and practice affecting gender relations. A second source was the major debate within the social democratic and communist organizations of the late nineteenth and early twentieth centuries, which then carried forward into the debates in the Soviet Union on the 'woman question'. This strand of debate was the most explicit about the connections between the institutions of private property, the control over material assets, and women–men relations within families and society. A third source was the liberal strand that combined the struggle for the vote with the struggle to legalize contraception; this strand existed mainly, though by no means exclusively, in Europe and North America.

The movement can also be understood as a patchwork quilt, full of colour and different patterns, discontinuous and defying description, but none the less an identifiable entity made up of units that have their own integrity. A quilt, an art form peculiarly developed by women, uses whatever material is available to make something both beautiful and functional. It represents ingenuity, creativity, caring and comfort. A global women's movement can have no better symbol as it seeks to create a world in which people might find beauty, comfort and security.

Origins

Since the concept of a global women's movement conceals the actors who make it possible, I turn now to consider some of the contexts that energized the local struggles out of which a global movement was formed. Reference is often made to 'three waves' of the women's movement: the first wave of the late 19th–early 20th century, the second covering the mid-20th century, and

The second wave, in the mid-twentieth century, was dominated by struggles against colonial domination, in which women were present in large numbers. Their experiences in these struggles shaped their attitudes to global economic and political inequality, even though specific issues of gender justice took a back seat at this time. Many women also went through the experience of being in the thick of anti-colonial struggles and then being marginalized in the postcolonial era.

The third wave, that we understand as the modern women's movement, had its roots in the social and political ferment of the 1960s, like so many other social movements of the later twentieth century. The anti-imperialist and anti-Vietnam War movements, civil rights struggles, challenges to social and sexual mores and behaviour, and above all the rising up of young people, brewed a potent mixture from which emerged many of the social movements of the succeeding decades worldwide. What was specific to the women's movement among these was its call for recognition of the personal as political.[22]

the third, the late 20th century. Although these waves are often depicted as distinct, it is instructive to look at the connections between them because, as Gita Sen points out:

> They delineate in an early form potential strengths as well as tensions that characterize the international women's movement right until today. The presence of multiple strands from early on has made for a movement that is broad and capable of addressing a wide range of issues. But the potential tensions between prioritizing economic issues (such as control over resources and property) or women's personal autonomy or bodily integrity existed then and continue to exist now.[23]

Conclusion

It is clear that, despite the lack of clear and common objectives, continuity, unity and coordination—characteristics that would make a women's movement identifiable with other social movements—there is nevertheless an identifiable movement enriched by its diversity and complexity, sustained by the depth of its passions and enduring commitment to its causes, and strengthened by the apparent lack of coordination and spontaneity of its strategizing.

Varied experiences highlight the complexity of women's struggles, the interplay between race, class and gender and the need to distinguish between the material and the ideological relations of gender.[24]

There are many roads to the awareness that manifests as involvement in a women's organization or identification as part of a women's movement. There are still more steps towards a feminist consciousness, which would transform involvement in a women's organization into a political struggle for gender equity and equality, often within a broader project for social transformation. Many of the women involved in women's organizations, or movements, were influenced by leftist politics, and discovered their own marginalization within the processes of these struggles. Others began the journey to feminist consciousness through personal experiences; still others through their work experience. A characteristic of many of those involved in women's movements is the process of personal transformation which they undergo as they become aware of gender subordination. At the same time, this essentially individualistic experience seems to engender a connection to the wider universe of injustice in a way that leads to a better understanding of the link between different forms of oppression and builds life-long commitments to the struggle against injustice.

Given these histories, there is no doubt that there is a global women's movement, recognizable in its understanding of how 'common difference'[25] links us all in a political struggle for recognition and redistributive justice. Its difference from other social movements lies not only in the absence of homogeneity and its lack of common objectives, continuity, unity and coordination, but in the value it places on diversity, its commitment to solidarity with women everywhere, its feminist politics and its methods of organizing.

II. Political Strategies and Dynamics of Women's Organizing and Feminist Activism

Women engaged in organizing and acting for change regarding the conditions and position of women employ a variety of strategies that range from reformist to revolutionary. All strategies may be valid in specific circumstances and for particular purposes. This chapter looks critically at the political strategies and political dynamics of women's organizations and feminist activism in organizing for change towards a more equitable and humane world. In analysing these strategies, I consider the lessons learned from the experience of the 1990s, and identify some of the tensions, shortcomings and limitations of the global movement.

I shall argue that, despite limitations, the strategies used by women in their organizing offer new and more varied possibilities for effective action. I will also argue that these forms of organizing draw strength from, and are specifically related to, the feminist politics and praxis used by leadership, and that this leadership is key to the achievement of the goals of women's movements.

Although I divide the strategies into three categories, activist, institutional and crosscutting, they often overlap, or get applied at different stages of struggles. In the first category I would list consciousness-raising groups, women's circles, coalition and alliance-building, global conferences and campaigns. In the second, research, analysis and advocacy, mainstreaming, monitoring and accountability. In the third, analysis, advocacy and networking, that cuts across the other two, often linking them.

Activist Strategies

In my own analysis of women's organizing I have identified six 'spaces': consciousness-raising groups, women's circles, caucuses, coalitions, conferences and campaigns. I sometimes think of these as forming a continuum starting with the smallest most intimate group and extending to the mass campaign. Like a pebble dropped in water, the individual experience extends to progressively larger circles, incorporating or being incorporated by, increasing diversity, until in the campaign the individual may find herself part of a mass movement of people who often have conflicting interests.

Consciousness-raising groups Feminist consciousness-raising is an important first step towards the identification and 'naming' of female subordination. Without this, activism can remain abstract, a purely intellectual notion of 'oppression' that fails to translate into lived experience and serious commitment to challenge female subordination. Although consciousness-raising is associated with 'white, middle-class housewives' in North America and Europe, it is far more widespread than that; for example, it was the basis of the 'speak bitterness' campaigns in China, out of which emerged challenges to foot binding and concubinage.

Consciousness-raising is experiential learning: through reflection on the personal experience of gender-based oppression, women can gain a deeper understanding of the experience of other forms of oppression based on class, race, ethnicity, culture and international relations. The process of consciousness-raising is an important tool in feminist organizing: making the link between one's own experience and the experience of others based on other categories of exclusion can be a powerful analytical tool, a stimulus to action that benefits oneself and others. Indeed, it is precisely because women of every class, race, ethnic group and country can identify with the experience of structured exclusion, marginalization and alienation within patriarchal society, that they can identify with the exclusion, marginalization and alienation of others on the basis of class, race/ethnicity, culture, religion, geographic location, age, physical ability, etc.

In the 1960s, breaking the silence of bourgeois and marital 'respectability', middle-class women shared experiences of oppression, exclusion and alienation to discover that they were not alone. This generated the analysis, consciousness and energy necessary to make change in their own lives. Many went on to become active in the women's liberation movement. However, what was lacking in this process, for women from North America and Europe, was an analysis of the links to other forms of oppression. A more holistic analysis of the links between the multi-layered sources of women's oppression in specific situations can help strengthen women's movements in their search for justice for everyone. In this way, identity politics can lead to the larger feminist social project.

Women's circles Women's circles are the spaces in which most organizing starts. The circle is made up of a group of close friends or colleagues, who share a common political philosophy and agenda. Women engaged in political action in the area of social change towards gender justice need a safe space with like-minded sisters in which to hone their analysis and develop strategies; a space in which there is sufficient trust to encourage honesty and critical thinking.[26] These small groups may be formalized as committees or working groups, meeting on an on-going basis to analyse and strategize. They may also be ad hoc, formed as caucuses within the context of conferences or campaigns.

Caucuses The women's caucuses inititated by the Women's Environment and Development Organization (WEDO) within the framework of UN conferences have become institutionalized. Although the analysis of options that informs the positions taken and strategies used by women at these conferences is often formulated in informal meetings of feminists (women's circles), the women's caucuses are the public spaces in which strategies for lobbying governments are negotiated. Under the leadership[27] of WEDO, women participating in UN conferences developed caucusing to a fine art, expanding the space for NGOs at the UN.

Preparations for the women's caucus included detailed analysis of conference documents and the drafting of amendments to the texts. Throughout the 1990s, WEDO circulated these documents to partner networks and individual women. At the same time, other networks, such as those on women's human rights and DAWN (Development Alternatives with Women for a New Era), would be involved in their own preparatory analyses of the documents as well as of the political context for the negotiations. Meetings of preparatory committees, PrepComs, provided opportunities for refining and testing alternative texts and, most importantly, for assessing allies and antagonists.

Women's caucuses are now a standard part of most international meetings, and are spaces in which newcomers and individual women can link their lobbying efforts to those more experienced in these activities. They are also unparalleled spaces for education, analysis, solidarity and movement building.

Coalition and alliance building Coalition and alliance building (national, regional, global/North–South, within and outside the movement) has been an important strategy for the global movement. The understanding of the linkages between the social, political, economic and cultural concerns of women, along with an analysis that links women's experience at the personal and micro level of the community to the common policy framework of neo-liberalism, has facilitated and encouraged the formation of alliances and coalitions, as shown in Chapter 6. For this reason, there has been more coherence and convergence in women's organizing than in that of other social movements. For example, during the conferences of the 1990s, women's networks concerned with the environment worked with those concerned with population, reproductive rights and development. The 'networking of networks' that was noted at the second World Social Forum in Porto Alegre (2002) was pioneered, tested and honed by women's movements at local and global levels during the global conferences of the 1990s.

Coalitions and alliances may be formed with other women's networks, as well as with NGOs working on common issues. However, while coalition and alliance building between women's groups and networks enriches the alliance or coalition by broadening the scope of the analysis and advocacy, that between women and other NGOs brings a perspective which may entail complex negotiations of the differences between the parties before the alliance or coalition can be effective in carrying out the task for which it was formed.

As DAWN has found in its work on environmental issues, women's perspectives can often be very different from those of NGOs, even those NGOs in which there are large numbers of women. An analysis that starts from the daily experience of poor women is one that rejects dualisms of personal and political, private and public, etc. A good example of this was given in the previous chapter in relation to DAWN's analysis on the environment. Mainstream environmental groups seldom start from this place, nor do they give the attention that feminists do to the links between women's needs and concerns and those expressed in their advocacy.

On the other hand, alliances and coalitions between women's networks have enriched advocacy and expanded outreach. Thus the women's human rights networks have linked with women's networks on reproductive health, or on economic issues, in order to underscore the indivisibility of women's human rights and emphasize the interconnectedness of the civil, political, social, economic and cultural dimensions of all human rights.

The use of women's experiences as a starting point for analysis is what makes the difference between the work of women in mainstream NGOs (where women's ideas and experiences are often marginalized) and their work with other women. The adoption of this starting point is basically an adaptation of the methodology of consciousness-raising.

Global conferences

UN Conferences

A great deal has been said about UN conferences in Chapters 4 and 6. I include them here to complete the list, to make some general observations, and specifically to consider the UN conference as a strategy for facilitating consensus at the global level around international norms, standards and accountability.

Global conferences have provided an important space for women's organizing, linking the work of movements at local levels to that at the global level. But what is often missed, when the spotlight is shone on the global arena, is the amount of preparatory work that goes into it. Indeed, without this preparatory work at local level, and again within the caucuses formed around the arena of global events, global conferences are little more than theatre. UN conferences are clearly unparalleled in the opportunities they provide for education, networking and movement building. Without them it is difficult to imagine how a global women's movement might have emerged, or manifested itself.

UN conferences have served women well, but they have also been frustrating experiences for many activists. The formality of these intergovernmental meetings, the often meaningless rhetoric, and the dynamic of political forces and geopolitical realities that often have little to do with the issues at hand, have led many women to question their value beyond a certain point. For the global women's movement they have been the arena in which great gains have been made in terms of articulating and advancing women's agendas, but they have also been spaces in which women have had to contend with the political realities of North–South divisions and the

The purposes served by UN conferences

I can think of three; there are undoubtedly more.

Educational. There is nothing like an international conference for raising awareness, generating knowledge and developing skills in advocacy, lobbying and negotiating. Many of the educational experiences take place on the fringe of the conference, in the panels and workshops organized by conference organizers, NGOs and women's organizations on related topics, and in the caucuses and corridors as much as in the conference rooms. Perhaps more in these other spaces than in the conference rooms, where official propaganda and geopolitical considerations often prevail.

Political. Conferences provide opportunities for negotiating the international norms and standards that set the framework for negotiation at local levels and for holding governments and international agencies accountable. They also provide unique opportunities for the networking, alliance and coalition building that create political capital for the movements.

Social. The social aspects of movement building cannot be ignored. Effective political action depends on good interpersonal relations and trust. The relationships developed and reinforced by the series of UN conferences spanning over thirty-five years have made it possible for women to continue to work together on movement building. Conferences build the social capital without which political action cannot be sustained.

manipulations of fundamentalist forces, as well as with the failure of their governments to honour commitments and agreements made in their own countries.

Increasingly, women engaged in these conferences have faced criticism from colleagues in the movement over the amount of time spent in these spaces against the needs of local movements, as well as in relation to the limited impact that international agreements have at local level in many instances. After all these years of UN meetings and events, women are questioning the value of further conferences. In the first instance, many women feel that there are enough programmes and platforms of action, resolutions and mandates to provide a basis for all the work that can be undertaken for decades to come: action on implementation, rather than more words, is what is required at this stage.

In addition to this, in recent years, with the strengthening of the fundamentalist backlash against women's advancement, women have had to struggle to maintain the ground gained in previous UN conferences. The five-year reviews of the International Conference on Population and Development (ICPD) and the Beijing conference have shown that UN conferences also provide opportunities for manoeuvre by forces opposed to women's advancement in order to reverse hard-won gains.

There is currently a debate about the value of holding another World Conference on Women in 2005.[28] This conference was proposed as an occasion for noting progress on the implementation of the programme of action from the Fourth World Conference, but the current views of some women's organizations and networks and the withdrawal of certain critical networks from the process make it unlikely, although there will be a review of the Beijing Platform in 2005 by the UN Commission on the Status of Women (CSW).

Despite these concerns, there is no doubt about the value of conferences for networking and for expanding the movements at local and global levels. My own assessment is that, while the UN remains an important space for interacting with governments and the UN system itself, and for educational purposes, its political importance for women and for other social movements is less-ened as it forms closer alliances with the International Financial Institutions and the corporate sector. It should be abundantly clear by this time that the UN is unlikely to do the kind of sharp analysis and critique of the neo-liberal agenda that would give hope for change. Without an anal-ysis that acknowledges the extent to which the power imbalance inherent in neo-liberalism stands as an obstacle to the achievement of the laudable goals of UN conferences, there is no basis for hope that these will be achieved.

Other (Non-UN) Conferences

Women have their own conferences. Before, and beyond, the UN Decade for Women, women from around the world had met around a variety of issues related to their rights. Among the major international women's conferences today are those organized by the Association for Women's Rights and Development (AWID) and the Women's International Inter-discipline Congress. While they do not have the resources and visibility of UN conferences, they provide opportunities for women to meet around their own agendas, produce clearer analyses and strengthen their movements.

Beyond women's conferences is the World Social Forum (WSF), the meeting place of the new social movement for global justice. Since its inception in 2000, this movement has been gaining in strength and visibility, fuelled by the continuing injustices of North–South relations, the collusion of international institutions in this, and corporate-led globalization. The WSF has now become the most important space for the mobilization of resistance to the relentless push for extension of the neo-liberal agenda. The global women's movement is part of this larger movement, although much more work needs to be done to realize any real partnership between the male-led organizations and networks and women's networks. In any event, beyond the mobilization against corporate-led globalization, and now the war in Iraq, and opportunities for networking, the campaigns of the movement for global justice, and the organization of the WSF itself, do not allow for the kind of communication and negotiations needed if the global women's movement is to have any real influence in these spaces. These issues will be addressed more fully in the next chapter.

Women's campaigns It can be argued that women's movements have achieved more from cam-paigns—especially those organized by networks with strong links between movements at local level and initiatives at global level—than they have from conferences. Particularly effective have been the global campaigns around women's human rights and against violence against women. However, campaigns around local issues have been easier to organize and more effective in achieving their objectives. Examples are the campaign against genital mutilation in parts of Africa, against dowry deaths in India, for the extension of reproductive rights in parts of Latin America, and, of course, the ongoing campaign against violence against women.

A good example of a global campaign is the Global Campaign for Women's Human Rights (GCWHR), referred to in Chapter 6 (see also below). Of special note here are the role played by other spaces—the women's circle and the caucus—and the importance of coalition building as well. The strategic planning institute in support of the GCWHR was in a sense a 'women's circle' which facilitated the formulation of strategies for linking the daily experiences of women at local levels to the global campaign.

Conclusions on activist strategies I want to end this section by commenting on the unevenness of the experience of women's organizing over the past twenty-five years. Although these comments relate to the strategies of local movements rather than to the global movement, they remind us of the diversity of the local experiences in which the global is grounded.

What is the Global Campaign for Women's Human Rights?

The GCWHR is a loose coalition of groups and individuals worldwide, formed in preparation for the UN Conference on Human Rights held in Vienna in 1993. Since the initial call for the conference did not mention women or recognize any gender-specific aspects of human rights in its proposed agenda, this became a natural vehicle for women's activities. One of the early actions of the campaign was a petition launched in 1991 that called on the Vienna conference to 'comprehensively address women's human rights at every level of its proceedings' and recognize 'gender violence, a universal phenomenon which takes many forms across culture, race, and class . . . as a violation of human right requiring immediate action'. A global leadership petition, distributed by the Center for Women's Global Leadership (CWGL) and the International Women's Tribune Centre (IWTC), was circulated through dozens of women's networks and taken up by women at all levels to further their organizing efforts. The petition had been launched at the first annual campaign of Sixteen Days of Activism Against Gender Violence, a global umbrella for local activities that promote public awareness about gender-based violence as a human rights concern. Groups participating in the campaign select their own objectives and determine their own local activities, within a larger global effort with some common themes. The campaign grew steadily during the 1990s, involving groups in over a hundred countries in events including hearings, demonstrations, media campaigns, cultural festivals and candlelight vigils. Many of its activities also mobilized women to participate in the UN world conferences. Since 1995, it has campaigned for implementation of the promises made to women in the various conference documents as well as in UN treaties such as the Convention on the Elimination of All Forms of Discrimination Against Women (CEDAW). The success of the global campaign was rooted in the activities of national and regional women's groups, who defined the important issues in their countries as they focused attention on the world conferences.

As part of this process CWGL held a strategic planning institute to coordinate plans for Vienna with women from around the world who had been active regionally. This meeting, in Geneva in April 1993, worked on lobbying strategies for the conference, including further development of recommendations on women's human rights; built on regional proposals, and served as the final international preparatory meeting. Institute attendees also began preparations for a Global Tribunal on Violations of Women's Human Rights that would give vivid personal expression to the consequences of such violations. Participants would provide graphic demonstration of how being female can be life-threatening, discussing such abuses as torture, terrorism and slavery, connecting human rights abuse in the family, war crimes against women, violations of women's bodily integrity, socio-economic violations, and political persecution and discrimination.[29]

- Despite the range of issues around which women have organized over the past twenty-five years, the *most effective organizing* has occurred around issues relating to violence against women, sexual and reproductive health and rights, and livelihood/ environmental issues such as access to land, forests and water. These are issues that link gender justice to economic justice.

- Although the women's movement has been active, in alliances and coalitions with other social movements and groups, in organizing efforts around citizenship and constitutional change (Latin America, South Africa, Fiji); structural adjustment and debt (Latin America, Africa, the Caribbean); poverty and landlessness (Asia); militarism (Pacific), it has been *less successful* in having its specific, gendered issues addressed in these broader struggles.

- Women's activism has been stronger in some regions and countries than in others. For example, the women's movement in the Caribbean seems dormant when compared with that in Latin America. However, differences in culture and political structures determine the nature of women's organizing at local level.
- Although organizing at the global level is important in terms of setting international standards and programmes of action, meaningful changes in women's lives depend on the extent to which these are translated into *local organizing*.

At the same time there are paradoxes that caution against reaching simple conclusions. Here are a few.

- Within the Caribbean some of the best examples of policies that come closest to women's agendas in the areas of health (including abortion), education, civil rights and economic empowerment occur in a country (Barbados) where the movement is *apparently weak* (especially when compared with other countries such as Jamaica and Trinidad).
- In some countries, *the church and the family* represent spaces from which women draw strength. It has been noted that in Czechoslovakia, especially during communism, the family was indeed one of the spaces within which women experienced a measure of liberation. In the Caribbean also, where the patriarchal family is weak, the family and the household constitute such a space: the extended family tends to include a number of independent women, and this is a major source of support for women and children, especially for women without male support.
- In the base communities of Latin America, the *Roman Catholic Church* showed that it could be a *liberating force* for women; many women find their faith a source of strength and empowerment.
- In countries without democratic institutions, or where women's rights are curtailed, *global action* may be the most effective means of guaranteeing women's rights or security at local level.

Where is the rage? There is another issue to be addressed before moving on to consider institutional strategies, and that is the criticism that women's movements have lost their political edge. I think this sometimes comes from judging women's movements by the expectations of models of left-wing politics. The issue might be posed this way: there is passion in this movement, but where is the rage? Women's revolutionary action seems to be different from that of men, grounded in a socialization that constructs women as less violent, more accommodating, than men. However, although women's political activism may be less violent than that of their brothers in struggle, their actions are no less revolutionary. How else does one describe a campaign to stop men who beat women by picketing their homes, or to get men to support their children by shaming them in their work-place, or to stop bulldozers by hugging trees, or confront the military by daily marches in the public square?

These strategies are designed for very specific locations. At the global level the protests rely on linking struggles around the world, from International Women's Day (8 March) to the Sixteen Days Against Gender Violence (10–25 November). They also rely on campaigns and symbols that are outrageous, like the campaign led by Latin American women at the most recent World Social Forum (2003), against 'fundamentalisms . . . all of them'—a campaign that juxtaposes pictures of Bush, Bin Laden, Saddam Hussein and the Pope.

The strengthening of women's movements in the 1980s in the context of the UN Decade for Women, the opening up of democratic space in the countries of Latin America and mobilizations there around feminist critiques of IMF-inspired structural adjustment policies, the triumph of neo-liberalism in the 1990s, and globalization since the mid-1990s, have opened the way to what some have termed *discursive democracy*—a concept that champions an active and informed citizenry, engaged in policy discourse to challenge and seek change in the status quo. While this engagement with policy-making processes has also carried the risk of co-optation,[30] it would be fair to say that the gains in terms of democracy have been considerable. Engagement in UN debates, as well as in those on debt and structural adjustment and globalization, have made women at all levels more knowledgeable about the political economy of neo-liberalism, a subject to which women had not paid much attention hitherto.

As we seek transformations of power, the most revolutionary approach for women's movements may be to reject male definitions of power and revolution.

Institutional Strategies

Since the 1990s, within the processes of the global conferences, the emerging global women's movement has created links between public discourse—which takes place in civil society—and the policy discourse that takes place among technocrats and political elites within systems of governance. Local women's movements linked to a global movement have engaged in policy dialogues, often without sacrificing their political legitimacy. It was through interaction between feminist activists (experts in their own right) and mainstream 'experts' (who may also be feminists) that activists often changed the terms of the debate on issues like human rights and reproductive rights. This also led to more direct engagement of feminist activists in bureaucratic processes such as mainstreaming and monitoring government policies and programmes to ensure accountability.

Mainstreaming The strategy of mainstreaming—integrating new frameworks, agendas, findings and strategies into mainstream policies, programmes and projects—has been used increasingly for advancing women's concerns. Institutions that have set up special programmes for women, or adopted UN mandates, especially favour this strategy. The Women/Gender and Development (W/GD) programmes of UN agencies, the World Bank, and bilateral aid agencies, have all supported mainstreaming. Some women's organizations and activist networks have also adopted mainstreaming strategies as they focus on the implementation of the various plans and programmes of action.

However, the effectiveness of this strategy has been mixed. Working to mainstream women's concerns leads inevitably to a degree of bureaucratization that depoliticizes, and can therefore weaken the effectiveness of the effort. Mainstreaming can, perhaps, be most effective when combined with mechanisms for independent monitoring by political groups working outside the institutions concerned.[31] At worst, it can lead to the disappearance of the focus on women, rendering them once again 'invisible', and distract from contradictory policies, covering up the absence of real change and a lack of political will. In instances where rhetoric about 'gender equity' becomes a tool of public relations, it can lead to justifiable cynicism.

For example, the gender mainstreaming strategies of many multilateral agencies, such as the UN and the World Bank, as well as bilateral aid agencies, include impressive gender assessment checklists, guidelines and gender impact assessments to be applied to all programmes and policies. However, these are often contradicted by policy frameworks that undermine and jeopardize the goals, objectives and values of the strategies. Thus the World Bank's Country Gender Assessment is intended

> to be used in dialogue with borrower governments to identify priority gender-responsive policies and interventions in high-impact sectors important for poverty reduction, economic

growth and sustainable development [and in] the reform of institutions to establish equal rights and opportunities for women and men; fostering economic development to strengthen incentives for more equal resources and participation; and taking active measures to redress persistent disparities in command over resources and political voice.

But the Bank continues to push policies which directly contradict these laudable objectives. The fundamental contradiction between policies that favour the interests of multinational corporations and those that favour the poor and marginalized has yet to be addressed by international institutions. Many activists are therefore justifiably critical of mainstreaming policies that deny political realities, and many from the global women's movement have come away from interactions with these institutions with feelings of disappointment and betrayal. When it comes to issues of gender equity, the limitations of purely 'technical-professional' approaches are all too clear.

Monitoring and accountability In the wake of UN conferences, monitoring governments and other institutions and holding them to account for the implementation of resolutions, recommendations and international conventions have become important strategies for change. Having fought for these provisions in international fora, feminist activists at local levels have tried to use them to legitimize and give strength to their advocacy. However, it is important to recognize that, in many cases, governments sign on to resolutions, programmes of action and even conventions that they have no intention of implementing. Feminist activists understand this and know that while international instruments provide political and normative guidelines, they must be 'domesticated'—translated into local realities and made meaningful to local movements—if they are to be meaningful for women in the country. Feminist activists have given a great deal of thought to how this might be done, and some interesting mechanisms have been devised.[32]

Crosscutting Strategies

Research, analysis and advocacy From the mid-1970s, research has been an important strategy for the movement. As mentioned in Chapter 4, the research generated by the UN Decade for Women served to make women's realities visible, while also revealing the links between the social relations of gender and the political, economic, social and cultural structures that marginalize and jeopardize whole communities and groups of people. Research and analysis have been the basis of advocacy, which to some extent has been effective in changing laws as well as some practices and attitudes.

However, postmodernist scholars and others have challenged the research on 'Third World women' carried out early in the Decade for Women. They argue, with some truth, that there was a tendency to present 'Third World women' as a category, a homogeneous 'powerless' group often located as implicit victims of particular socio-economic systems. This would be a fair criticism of research on women from Third World countries that denied the specificity of the varied and complex experiences of women in these countries. This is particularly important if research is to form the basis for policy change or direct political action, especially action by groups marginalized by race/ethnicity, class and location. However, starting with the challenge by African researchers in the African Association for Women and Development at the end of the 1970s to Western hegemony in the area of research on women, many scholar-activists have corrected this shortcoming, and in the process have produced a body of work that has informed political strategies and shaped advocacy since the mid-1980s. Following the path set by DAWN, the analysis produced by many global women's networks today is built on the differences between women of different regions, cultures, political orientations, racial and ethnic groups. Moreover, efforts are made to present an analysis 'from the perspective of the most marginalized groups', even if the researchers are not representative of this class or race.

In terms of political strategy it might be useful to distinguish between research and analysis that has supported reform and that which suggests the need for more radical change. The keys to differences in research methodologies and findings have been the theoretical and conceptual frameworks used, and the purpose for which the research is produced. These determine not only the questions asked but the relationships between different data sets. We have seen the same researcher produce very different analyses and conclusions according to the frameworks used. Thus, research and analysis carried out by Third World scholars like those involved in the DAWN collective can be contrasted with that carried out by scholars from similar backgrounds, as individuals, for institutions such as the World Bank, the UN and even independent research centres.

There is also a better understanding of the distinction to be made between research carried out for the purpose of advocacy and that carried out for the purpose of scholarship. When research is linked to advocacy, or policy, the questions must be determined by the needs of those who would use the research.[33]

In many instances research has been central to raising awareness, a process critical for launching or strengthening women's organizing. In many countries, commissions on the status of women led to institutional change, while research centres and women's studies programmes within the academy made important contributions to the promotion of feminist perspectives or the sensitization of the state to women's concerns.

Another important distinction must be made between different methodologies. It is fairly well accepted now that participatory methodologies are most appropriate for research intended to produce social change. Here the research process is as important as the output. Indeed, the gap between research and action can be reduced considerably by the use of participatory methodologies, which generate new knowledge as well as new consciousness of the contradictions and social relations of power; both are required for the promotion of social change.

Networking Networking has been one of the commonest strategies used by women's movements at all levels. It might be said that it is through networking that the global women's movement emerged: networking brought women together in formal and informal ways, around conferences and campaigns and outside these spaces, and helped the process of discovering 'common differences' on which solidarity was built.

Since 1975, and in the context of the UN Decade for Women, a number of women's networks emerged at all levels—local, national, regional and international (see list on pp. 189–90). Some have focused on single issues or specific activities; others are more general. The global women's movement, as represented by these networks, might also be conceptualized as an on-going campaign for women's rights and empowerment.

Approaches to Social Change

In relation to women's organizing for change, it is useful to think of a 'typology of social change efforts based on an analysis of their divergent root assumptions about value and the nature of reality rather than a categorization of their various activities'.[34] Three perspectives of social change can be identified: the professional-technical, the political and the counter-cultural, each leading to different strategies, methodologies and types of leadership. While it is clear, as is the case with all attempts at categorizing, that reality is more complex than theoretical formulations suggest, making distinctions between different perspectives and understanding their association with different paradigms help us analyse the different approaches used by the global women's movement and aid our understanding of what is needed if this movement is to contribute to the movement for global justice.

The global ideological and policy framework is presently dominated by professional-technical perspectives. Given the concentration of power in the hands of a global elite, there seems little chance that this approach, by itself, can achieve either broad-based socio-economic improvement for the majority, or the more specific goals embodied in the women's agendas negotiated at various UN conferences. Women's movements have, by definition, used the political approach. However, what has been significant, in the context of the global conferences, is the way in which traditional political approaches have been combined with professional-technical approaches. I would argue that what is needed now is some greater, more explicit, integration of counter-cultural[35] approaches with the professional-technical and political approaches adopted by the global women's movement to date.

To be sure, there are women and women's groups who have used a counter-cultural approach in their organizing,[36] especially at local levels. Some are part of the global women's movement as I have defined it. They may be largely marginalized, and yet they have a great deal to offer the more politically oriented movement. At the same time, for these counter-cultural groups, organizing autonomously, the adoption of professional-technical and political approaches could strengthen their efforts towards social change. At local levels it is particularly important for politically oriented women's movements to build alliances with these groups, since they enrich our understanding of a different kind of power—power within—a power that is often missing in mainstream women's movements, but one that is essential. In my view, all three are required for the changes that women seek, because of the systemic linkages between economic, social, cultural and political structures. But a counter-cultural approach is more than one approach among three. Using a definition[37] of culture as 'the particular ways in which a social group lives out and makes sense of its "given" circumstances and conditions of life', or as a 'system through which . . . a social order is communicated, reproduced, experienced and explored', we have recognized that those whose advocacy challenges norms and attitudes deeply embedded in patriarchal culture face a particularly difficult task.

During the past twenty-five years of advocacy on behalf of women's rights within the UN and other international agencies and institutions as well as at local level in relation to the state, the strongest resistance to change has been in relation to gender equity. Moreover, this is an area of advocacy that most states are unwilling to press on others: governments and international institutions have no difficulty pressing conditionalities in relation to economic and social policies, but when it comes to gender they hold back, talking about 'policies that are consistent with national laws and traditions'. Patriarchs do not challenge other patriarchs. VeneKlasen, quoted in Miller (2001), reinforces this:

It is not just the externally enforced social roles and expectations that perpetuate women's subordination and male superiority, it is the insidious way that culture shapes a man's psyche about 'proper' gender roles and the way it forms a woman's sense of self to ensure that she is often her best keeper. This is true in industrialized countries of the North—where the conflicting images of glamour and domestic nurturer set impossible standards for the ordinary woman to achieve—as much as it is true in nations of the South, where many woman cannot dream of leaving their home or participating in public life, let alone have aspirations for the future. The role that culture plays in perpetuating inferiority and the imbalance of power is profoundly political.

Summarizing Chesler's and Crowfoot's approaches to social change

The *professional-technical* approach is ostensibly the conventional, mainstream approach to development and social change in Western democracies. It is based on the assumption that 'only a certain class (race and gender as well) has the intellectual expertise to make decisions for the rest of society. In general these are people, whether local or foreign, who have been educated according to the dominant ideology and who subscribe to its values and dictates. This kind of hegemony is the more difficult to break because it is backed up by an economic system which is strongly entrenched and reinforced by the benefits it brings to those in power and by the interdependence of social, cultural, political and economic relations and moral obligations' (p. 81).

This perspective falls within a paradigm, or world view, that considers society, and most of its organizations and institutions, to be basically sound, needing only to manage change better, to be more transparent, accountable, and less 'corrupt'.

The *political approach*, which recognizes the role power relations play in decision-making, may also go to the other extreme of denying the value of sound professional input in the change process. Nevertheless, it comes closer to reality and provides a better basis for planning strategies for change, especially in relation to women in patriarchal societies. The political approach acknowledges that society is made up of different groups 'each defined by the uniquely shared interests of its members, each with different and often competing interests or goals'. These groups may be based on race, ethnicity, class, gender or location, and there are usually imbalances of power between them and the dominant group.

Crowfoot and Chesler say, 'This approach recognises the inevitability of conflict between the groups since, when commodities such as material goods, information, technical skill, respect, status and so on are perceived as scarce, groups will compete for their control. This is where the state needs to intervene in order to guarantee an equitable distribution of goods and resources. However, if those who operate the apparatus of the state are themselves beneficiaries of the system they will tend to opt for stability rather than equality in regulating the relations among groups and between groups and resources. The result is a high concentration of power in the hands of a few people or a few interest groups . . . The change process is initiated when this is understood and people are willing to deal with these differences in the interest of the common good' (pp. 83–4).

This approach accords with the 'conflict' or 'alternative' paradigm. It is not an approach that is often acknowledged by those in control. Yet failure to acknowledge that people of different classes, races, ethnic groups, genders and location etc. can have appreciably different interests from those in power may be the single most significant obstacle to change in today's world, where power is so concentrated in the hands of an international elite. This denial of the political imbalances and conflicting interests inherent in the assumptions underlying neo-liberal policy agendas, from those of structural adjustment to the trade agreements enforced by the WTO, explains the difficulties NGOs have had in making the case for global justice.

More importantly, this approach requires women's movements to pay more attention to issues of race/ ethnicity, class and location.

The *counter-cultural approach* is the most neglected, but of critical importance for women and other marginalized groups. This approach is based on 'affirming the culture and values of the society. It is suspicious of over technocratic and over bureaucratic approaches and concepts of progress', since these are considered to lead to a marginalization of local or indigenous knowledge, a decrease of initiative, creativity and individuality, and to inhibiting the individual from realizing his or her full human potential. This perspective places emphasis on individual change—in personal values, life styles and relationships with others, and emphasizes communal organizations as the building and rebuilding blocks of a new unalienating society.

Adapted from Crowfoot and Chesler (1992)

What this means is that women engaged in organizing for social change need a closer examination of power to assist in devising and selecting the strategies that might be most effective. Specifically, more attention has to be paid to the invisible power that operates to make advocacy on behalf of gender equity particularly difficult. This includes the internalization of 'the underlying ideology of female inferiority, which is disguised in an idealised image of women as perfect wife and mother'.[38]

Analysis of Power

Advocacy on behalf of women's agency and rights is by definition political, yet many advocates for gender equity proceed on the assumption that the asymmetry of gender relations can be sidestepped. Too often advocacy addresses itself to power structures that are visible and formal, and takes the form of the presentation of 'rational' arguments. This ignores the fact that resistance is deeply embedded in the culture of patriarchy. To address this, other less traditional kinds of action are needed. A more careful analysis of power would provide clues to a wider range of strategies. As Foucault and others remind us, power is not monolithic, and is always subject to contestation. There are also different kinds of power—power over others, power with others, inner power, and power to do and act together. 'Power over' is what immediately comes to mind when one thinks of power. It is embodied in the visible power structure of the society—the state. Within institutions like the family, this kind of power is exercised by the head of the household—usually a man, but by women when they are in charge.

Writing about women's empowerment, some feminists (Batliwala and others) often emphasize the other types of power—power with, power within and power to act. These types of power 'expand the possibility to create more symmetrical, equitable relationships of power between and within people and groups and to foster human agency—the ability to act and change the world'.[39] Women's movements need to focus on these types of power, in addition to the more obvious power structure.

In addition, it is important to recognize that women, like men, have a range of identities and characteristics, and these can also be taken into account in determining strategies. Thus, while women who have a certain status and credibility within the power structure because of class, race/ethnicity, education, occupation, age and so on may have more success, they may also be constrained by these same factors from pursuing less 'acceptable' strategies. Solidarity among women activists can lead to a creative and effective mix of 'insider-outsider' strategies.

Solidarity among women across common divides of class, race/ethnicity, etc., allows them to draw on the power of collective action—'power with'—that can be effective precisely because of the diversity of those involved. This is a particular strength of women's movements, and more attention needs to be paid to it.

An even more important source of power is 'power within'. A few years ago, in a discussion about 'empowerment' (sources of power), grassroots women in the Caribbean mentioned spirituality and sexuality. They made it clear that they were not referring to either religion (which they described as 'disempowering'), or sexual activity (which they felt could be distracting or oppressive). Spirituality and sexuality are sources of power that lie deep within women and are not frequently discussed. A counter-cultural approach would validate these sources of power. Women's circles and consciousness-raising processes provide spaces for this and should be recognized as important elements in women's organizing.

When confronting the formal power structure, women activists, especially those who are labelled 'feminist', need to recognize that they face a particular kind of resistance, which is cultural. The fact that the man or woman an activist is addressing does not acknowledge this simply underlines the power of patriarchy. The advocate assumes the person she is addressing is 'rational' and can be persuaded by the strength of her data and the logic of her argument. She needs to understand that this is far from the case. In the first instance because she is female, second because she is feminist, and third because of the nature of her advocacy, her advocacy is seldom taken seriously. Her presence, her politics and the content of her advocacy are all mediated by the culture of the person she is addressing. To this person she is 'unrealistic', 'illogical', 'irrational', 'hysterical', 'dangerous'—all because she dares to question the underlying assumptions of patriarchal culture. In this context, the nurturing of 'power within' to strengthen women's power to take action is critically important.

Equally important is that women who dare to act on behalf of women's agency be supported by others. Collective action by women from a variety of backgrounds can be powerful indeed. These kinds of power draw on the particular strengths of women's movements; I define these as counter-cultural approaches—countering the culture of patriarchy.

Lessons Learned

Reflecting on the strategies used by the global women's movement in the past thirty years, I would underline the following lessons.

- *The most effective strategies are those that combine political with professional and counter-cultural approaches*, i.e. paying attention to *cultural* elements through spiritual growth, consciousness-raising/ conscientization, solidarity and networking; political elements such as lobbying, advocacy, caucusing, coalition-alliance building including using insider/ outsider approaches; and technical-professional elements i.e. sound research and analysis.
- *Multiple strategies are often necessary.* These include the following:
  - *insider/outsider approaches*: critical engagement with the state while being accountable to the women's movement;
  - *between sectors*: e.g. health, education and women's/gender affairs in relation to HIV-AIDS, or health, welfare, housing and legal affairs in relation to domestic violence – in each case with links to women's movements;
- linking local to global: although some strategies may have been initiated at the global level, organizing must ultimately return to the *local level* if change is to be meaningful to women in these countries. Similarly, the most effective organizing at global level has been that which links with efforts at local level;
  - *at local level*, strategies that link literacy or popular education with research and advocacy, in a dynamic interplay, have the most meaning for the grassroots and are the most likely to lead to empowerment and change in democratic societies;
- *research methodologies must be appropriate to the task*: if the purpose of the research is to inform advocacy, the key questions must be generated by activists, not researchers; if the purpose is empowerment, the methodology must be participatory;
- advocacy must be based on *sound research and analysis, and grounded in women's realities*;
- *advocacy is more difficult when powerful interests are threatened*, be they economic, political or ideological; therefore it must be informed by a *more careful analysis of power*: an understanding of the difference between visible power and invisible power, and the role of ideology in disempowering women;
- *alliances must be built with those mainstream NGOs that share the values of social justice.* However, we must start with leadership that acknowledges the importance of gender equity, winning allies before attempting to influence the larger group. This involves identifying and making alliances with men who are supportive of feminist leadership. Change for women requires change in the behaviour of men, and we need to recognize that there are men who

identify with our agenda and see feminist analysis and women's agency as keys to the kind of personal and social transformation required to bring about the 'better' world they too seek. At the same time, however . . .

- o   alliance and coalition building must start with women before reaching out to the wider civil society, otherwise women advocating change may find themselves isolated from or de-legitimized by other associations of women.
- o   Feminist leadership is key.

Notes

1. In Basu (1995), p. 187.
2. See also Bonnie G. Smith's book, *Global Feminisms Since 1945*, published in 2000.
3. An ancient saying attributed to the Chinese states: 'If you don't change direction, you will end up where you're headed.' Where most conventional social movements are headed is still towards a place where the male is considered the definition of the human being.
4. Interview with representatives of the National Commission for Women, Abuja, 2 February 1993, Basu (1995), p. 211.
5. Interview with Obiageli Nwankwo, project coordinator, International Federation of Women Lawyers, Enugu, 1993, Basu (1995), p. 212.
6. I am grateful to Gita Sen for this analysis, which is developed in a chapter on 'The Politics of the International Women's Movement' in the book *Claiming Global Power: Transnational Civil Society and Global Governance*, edited by Srilatha Batliwala and David Brown, to be published by Kumarian Press.
7. However, there may be self-defined feminists among their members.
8. hooks (1994), p. 75.
9. Although UN conferences are also attended by women and organizations that are opposed to advances in women's human rights, as was seen at the Five-Year Review of the Fourth World Conference on Women, when the call went out from right-wing religion-based organizations for women to come to New York to 'defend' women against that 'dangerous' document, the Beijing Plan of Action.
10. Lorde (1984), p. 115.
11. Ibid., p. 138.
12. In thinking about this distinction I have found Uta Ruppert's analysis (Braig and Wolte 2002: 147–54) extremely helpful.
13. Ibid., p. 148.
14. Ibid., p. 149.
15. Ruppert defines 'globality' as 'everything global politics or global governance should be based on or directly accompanied by' (ibid., p. 151).
16. Ibid., p. 151.
17. Ibid.
18. The combination of consciousness and action, 'praxis', introduced by the Brazilian educator, Paolo Freire, to enable oppressed groups to gain an understanding of the forces impinging on their world, the sources of their oppression.
19. *Journal of the Society for International Development* (SID) on 'The Politics of Place', 2001.
20. Examples abound. The work of the Chipko movement and of the Self-Employed Women's Association (India) (SEWA) immediately come to mind because they have been so well documented; however there are examples of this kind of organizing in every region. The most recent was the action of local women in Nigeria to challenge the Shell oil company.

21. Jennifer Chapman (2001), 'What Makes International Campaigns Effective? Lessons from India and Ghana', in Edwards and Gaventa, pp. 263–4.
22. See chapter on 'The Politics of the International Women's Movement' in Srilatha Batliwala and David Brown's book cited in note 6, above.
23. Ibid.
24. Eudine Barriteau makes this distinction to show that while advances in women's material needs (practical gender interests) might be met within a policy framework of social equity based on race and class, the ideological relations of gender could cause men to resent and resist advances in terms of women's strategic gender interests.
25. Moharty and Alexander (1997). The term 'common difference' is the title of Gloria Joseph's book, and is associated with Chandra Moharty's writings.
26. In a sense, the steering committees or global networks like DAWN, the WICEJ, etc., are spaces where this kind of work takes place at a global level.
27. Under the leadership of the charismatic former US congresswoman, Bella Abzug, WEDO was established in the context of the preparations for UNCED. It later carved a niche for itself at the UN as the convenor of an increasingly effective women's caucus throughout the UN conferences of the 1990s.
28. See discussions on the websites of AWID, DAWN, and the proceedings of the 2003–04 Commission on the Status of Women.
29. Bunch and Reilly (1994).
30. A current (2004) example of this is in Haiti, where a wide range of civil society organizations have mobilized to oust the democratically elected President. I discuss this in greater detail in the Epilogue.
31. An example of this is the provision made by the Division for the Advancement of Women for independent reports on the implementation of CEDAW.
32. Brazil, for instance, has developed a framework for monitoring the implementation of the Programme of Action from ICPD.
33. In the International Gender and Trade Network this is well understood. Of course, as in the case of DAWN, the involvement of women who are both researchers and activists helps.
34. J. E. Crowfoot and M. A. Chesler (1974) 'Contemporary Perspectives on Planned Social Change: A Comparison', *Journal of Applied Behavioural Science*, 10 (3), pp. 278–303.
35. Alda Facio argues for the creation of a feminist counterculture 'from the arts, technologies, sciences, languages, symbols and myths from our true internal selves in connection with all other beings'. Her argument for a feminist spirituality and the use of consciousness-raising towards a feminist 'ultra-consciousness' (as distinct from a feminist consciousness) also resonate with my views expressed here and in Chapter 9. 'A feminist ultra-consciousness would allow us not only to see sexism in societal structures but also how sexism operates within us and how it is linked to all other forms of oppression.' See her chapter in Kerr et al. (2004).
36. These would include women's movements that focus on spirituality or the Goddess or Mother Nature. See chapter by Alda Facio cited above.
37. Quoted in Miller (2001).
38. Oxfam UK, quoted in Miller (2001), p. 3.
39. Quoted in Miller (2001), pp. 4–5.

References

Basu, Amrita (ed.) (1995) *The Challenge of Local Feminisms: Women's Movements in Global Perspective*, Boulder, CO: Westview Press.

Batiliwala, Srilatha, and David Brown (eds), *Claiming Global Power: Transnational Civil Society and Global Governance*, Massachusetts: ICumarian Press.

Berta, Rosalie (1985) *No Immediate Danger: Prognosis for a Radioactive Earth*, London: Women's Press.

Bhavnani, Kum-Kum, John Foran and Priya Kurian (2003) *Feminist Futures: Re-imagining Women, Culture and Development*, London: Zed Books.

Braig, Marianne and S. Wolte (eds) (2002) *Common Ground or Mutual Exclusion? Women's Movements and International Relations*, London: Zed Books.

Bunch, Charlotte (1987) *Passionate Politics: Essays 1968-1986, Feminist Theory in Action*, New York St Martin's Press.

Bunch, Charlotte and N. Reilly (1994) *Detnanding Accountability: The Global Campaign and Vienna Tribunal for Women's Human Rights*, New Brunswick, NJ: Center for Women's Global Leadership.

Chesler, M. and J. Crowfoot (1992) *Visioning Change*, Michigan: University of Michigan.

Correa, Sonia, with Rebecca Reichmann (1994) *Population and Reproductive Rights: Feminist Perspectives from the South*, London: Zed Books.

Edwards, Michael and John Gaventa (2001) *Global Citizen Action*, Boulder CO: Lynne Reinner Publishers.

Edwards, Michael and Gita Sen (2000) 'NGOs, Social Change and the Transformation of Human Relationships: A 21st Century Civic Agenda', *Third World* Quarterly, 21(4): 605-16.

Fraser, S. Arvonne (1987) *The UN Decade for Women: Documents And Dialogue*, Boulder, CO, and London: Westview Press.

Hooks, Bell (1994) *Teaching to Transgress*, London: Routledge.

Kerr, Joanna, Ellen Sprenger and Alison Symington (eds) (2004) *The Future of Women's Rights*, London: Zed Books.

Lorde, Audre (1984, 11th printing 1996) *Sister Outsider: Essays and Speeches by Audre Lord*, Freedom, CA: Crossing Press.

Miles, Angela (1996) *Integrative Feminisms: Building Global Visions 1960s–1990s*, New York and London: Routledge.

Miller, Valerie (2001) 'On Politics, Power and People: Lessons from Gender Advocacy Action and Analysis', Paper presented at On Democracy and Active Citizen Engagement: Best Practices in Advocacy and Networking, Symposium, August, Coady International Institute, St Francis Xavier University Antigonish, Nova Scotia.

Mohanty, Chandra Talpade, Ann Russo and Lourdes Torres (eds) (1991) *Categories of Struggle: Third World Women and the Politics of Feminism*, Bloomington, IN: Indiana University Press.

Mohanty, Chandra Talpade and M. Jacqui Alexander (eds) (1997) *Feminist Genealogies, Colonial Legacies, Democratic Futures*, New York and London: Routledge.

Morgan, Robin (1984) *Sisterhood is Global: The International Women's Movement Anthology*, New York Anchor Books Oxfam.

— (2003) Gender and Development: *Women Reinventing Globalization*, May, 11(1).

Petchesky, Rosalind Pollack (2003) *Global Prescriptions: Gendering Health and Human Rights*, London: Zed Books.

Sen, Gita and C. Grown (1976) *Development, Crises and Alternative Visions: Third World Women's Perspectives*, New York: Monthly Review Press.

Shiva, Vandana (1992) *Staying Alive: Women, Ecology and Development*, London: Zed Books.

Smith, Bonnie G. (ed.) (2000) *Global Feminisms Since 1945*, New York and London: Routledge.

Society for International Development (SID) Journal (2001) *Development*, special issue on 'On the Politics of Place', Rome: SID

Suares Toro, Maria (2000) *Women's Voices on Fire – Feminist International Radio Endeavor*, Austin, TX: Anomaly Press.

Taylor, Viviene (2000) *Marketization of Governance*, London: Zed Books.

Waring, Marilyn (1952) *If Women Counted: A New Feminist Economics*, San Francisco, CA: Harper and Row.

CHAPTER TWELVE

Contesting Women's Rights: Charting the Emergence of a Transnational Conservative Counter-network

Louise Chappell

Source: *Global Society* (2006) 20:4, 491–520 © 2006 Taylor & Francis—Reproduced with permission.

"The unholy alliance formed by the Holy See, Iran, Algeria, Nicaragua, Syria, Libya, Morocco and Pakistan has attempted to hold to ransom women's human rights."[1]

"During the 90's, at the international level, an unholy alliance of the Vatican, Muslim fundamentalists, the US right wing, and occasionally others united to fight particularly against women's reproductive and sexual rights".[2]

"The usual suspects—the unholy alliance of Pakistan, Egypt, Sudan, Iran, US, Holy See, plus Costa Rica, Dominican Republic and Ecuador, strongly opposed any language using a rights-based approach to sexuality".[3]

As the above statements indicate, a view abounds among human rights activists and academics that there exists an *unholy alliance* working within the United Nations (UN) system to contest, undermine, and, if possible, reverse the efforts of women's rights advocates to pursue gender equality internationally. The so-called alliance is considered unholy for two reasons: its members include actors—such as the USA and other states, including those from the middle-east—who take a conservative and patriarchal position on women but differ on other fundamental matters of international politics; and because it includes representatives of two of the worlds major religious blocs—Christianity and Islam—who have diametrically opposing views on many issues. As feminists have pointed out,[4] this alliance presents a challenge to the widely held conception advanced most notably by Samuel Huntington[5] that there exists a 'clash of civilisations' between the Confucian-Islamic East and the Christian West.

If this alliance does exist then it has profound significance for debates concerning the current state of international politics. However, before a conversation can start about the ramifications of such an alliance, it first needs to be asked: How organized and coordinated are those pursuing an anti-women's rights agenda? How successful have these actors been in challenging women's rights claims? What evidence is there that a transnational conservative patriarchal counter-movement or network exists?

The social movement (SM) literature provides a lens to consider these questions and to ask an additional, theoretical question: how well does the existing literature on social movements help explain the emergence of forces to counter women's rights? Two strands of the SM literature are especially relevant here: that of transnational social movements (TSMs) and networks;[6] and of the interaction between movements and counter-movements.[7] This paper employs three central concepts from this literature—political opportunities, framing and mobilizing structures—to see what explanatory power each has for assessing the appearance and influence of the so-called 'unholy alliance' internationally.

The argument here also contributes to the literature on the transnational women's rights movement (TWM). There is now a burgeoning literature which addresses the emergence and intervention of the TWM internationally, including at UN conferences.[8] Much of this research mentions the appearance of the 'unholy alliance', but its existence is usually asserted rather than proved. Very little information is given about the factors leading to its emergence and only minimal discussion is provided about its coherence, features, or relative success. Friedman[9] is an exception here, giving some attention to the rise of a counter-movement in the face of the successful women's movement at UN conferences. However, the main focus of her analysis remains on the TWM and not its opponents. Further important feminist work has recently begun to emerge on the role of religious forces internationally and their relationship to the mobilisation of the TWM. The work in the edited collection by Bayes and Tohidi[10] is useful for drawing out the links between religious forces at the Beijing Conference, but because it is grounded in theories of globalisation and modernity, it is less useful for considering the significance of these developments for theorizing social movements. Further, Buss and Herman[11] provide an excellent account of the influence of the Christian Right at the UN (CR UN), but their work does not seek to explore the links between Christian and non-Christian organisations. Other accounts of the influence of religious forces at the UN are important—for example Neale's[12] work on the Cairo Conference and Buss[13] on Beijing—but because they focus only on a single site of contention, this research does not allow for an assessment of whether or how the so-called alliance has developed over time.

The central argument of this article is that over the past decade, a very loosely structured transnational conservative patriarchal network (TCPN) has emerged at UN human rights conferences to counter the efforts of women's rights activists. The actors who have worked together against the TWM share a *conservative* and *patriarchal* point of view on gender issues which come together under a rhetorical 'pro-family' frame. Here the term conservative is taken to mean a commitment to preserving traditional relations between men and women; this entails viewing women as different to men, and as nurturers, firmly rooted in heterosexual family relationships. Patriarchy, is used here is to refer to a form of power used by men to subject and oppress women. In particular, it is refers to the underlying belief that women have a subordinate role to men within the public sphere and that their autonomy within the private sphere should be contained so as to maintain traditional family forms. Patriarchy is a concept often seen by contemporary feminists as being too monolithic to be useful in explaining the complexity of gender relations, but it is nevertheless is a useful concept for examining the views of international conservative actors. This is because these actors rely explicitly or implicitly on this concept of power to shape their understanding of the relationship between men and women.

Those who can be identified as part of the conservative network include a number of governments who, in the contemporary period at least, uphold fundamentalist religious beliefs. This encompasses governments from Iran, Egypt and Libya and increasingly the US. It also includes state-like actors such as the Vatican as well as non-government organisations, mostly from the Christian right.[14] In particular, these groups include members of what Herman and Buss define as the Christian Right United Nations (CR UN) which includes a range of religious groups, with otherwise diverse ideological and theological positions, primarily from North America such as: the Catholic Family and Rights Institute (C-FAM), Focus on the Family, the Family Research Council, National Right to Life, Concerned Wo-men of America, REAL

Women and the World Movement of Mothers. These CR UN groups have formed coalitions 'around an orthodox Christian vision and a defense of the traditional nuclear family formation.'[15]

Measuring the influence of the network requires rethinking the usual standards of success. Unlike other rights groups whose success is measured in positive terms, the measure here is the extent to which conservative actors have been able to defend the *status quo* by blocking text from inclusion in these documents. Using this yardstick, it is argued that that they have achieved some important victories, including the exclusion of rights related to reproduction and sexuality from UN conference documents. Counter activists have also kept feminists in a defensive position in regards to women's rights, making it difficult for these more 'progressive' forces to pursue an expansive agenda internationally.

Research Design and Method

Recent international United Nations conferences are the key sites for exploring the existence, activities and influence of the conservative patriarchal network. The analysis considers key conferences starting with the 1994 Cairo International Conference on Population and Development (ICPD), when opposition forces became increasingly obvious and organized. It also includes the 1995 Fourth World Conference on Women (FWCW) in Beijing, and the two follow up Beijing conferences held in New York in 2000 and 2005 (commonly referred to as the Beijing +5 and Beijing +10). The 1998 Rome Conference to establish the International Criminal Court is also included in the analysis given the significant debates around gender issues and the evidence of conservative patriarchal rights activists at that conference.

These conferences, and not other international institutions, such as the UN General Assembly or the Committee of the Convention for the Elimination of All Forms of Discrimination against Women, were selected as the sites for studying the emergence of a counter network because they have become the key international sites where contentious politics around women's rights takes place. They provide the most important structured venue for representatives of international agencies, transnational civil society and governments to meet, formulate, express and contest views on women's rights. While government delegates are the official actors at the conferences, non-government actors are also very much involved in the proceedings. Some NGOs receive official accreditation to take part in the conferences as observers, while others engage less directly by raising issues through UN sponsored parallel NGO conferences.[16] Both as official and unofficial actors, NGOs are able to wield influence with government delegations. Kardam's assessment of government and NGO relations at the Beijing Conference can be held equally for all the conferences under review:

> In some cases government delegations incorporated language suggested by NGOs directly and on others they consulted with NGOs to shape their positions on issues . . . by working with members of official delegations and by rallying public opinion, NGOs helped to craft much of the language adopted in many of these forums.[17]

There also exists a third category of actor participating in these events—'state-like' actors. The most notable of these in the UN setting is the Vatican through its official diplomatic body, the Holy See. While the Vatican has not been granted full state-status at the UN it is a permanent non-state observer enabling it to participate, but not vote, in all UN proceedings.[18] Other groups with permanent non-observer status relevant to the following discussion include the Organisation of the Islamic Conference (OIC) and the League of Arab States—both of which have periodically used their position to lobby against the extension of women's rights.

These conferences are also important because their formal outcomes—the conference documents—contribute directly to the ongoing framing and articulation of women's rights internationally. The documents produced at these conferences—such as the Cairo *Programme of Action*;[19] the *Beijing Declaration and the Platform for Action* (BPFA)[20]—are the battleground over which the framing of women's rights is fought. Going into these conferences, governments have already agreed on certain text and have 'bracketed' other more controversial segments for discussion on the floor and behind the scenes during the proceedings. The final language to emerge in these documents is significant because although it does not hold any formal legal weight, it signifies which frames and which framers have been (un)successful in the battle to define the meaning of women's rights. It also has normative authority; it is the articulation of international values and goals around issues of gender equality which forms the foundation for 'soft' international law on women's rights.[21] In relation to the *Rome Statute of the International Criminal Court* and its subsidiary documents, the *Rules of Evidence and Procedure* and *Elements of Crimes*, language holds even more significance. Because these documents form the basis for the operation of the International Criminal Court, the provisions are part of 'hard' international law[22] and justiciable in both international and domestic courts.

In order to understand the political opportunity structure available to counter-women's rights activists and their mobilizing structures, I undertook an extensive search of secondary literature as well as primary web-based sources from the UN, media and actor organisations. The latter category included documents from the Vatican, and Pro-family and Islamic organisations relating to each conference under review. Through an analysis of these sources I was able to compare how the TWM and counter activists perceived and responded to these events. These sources were also used to decipher the linkages between conservative patriarchal actors overtime both at and in-between UN meetings so as to attempt to gauge the extent to which they have taken on a network-like structure. A content analysis of the official documents from each of the conferences was undertaken to help determine how women's rights were framed by counter activists. This involved a careful reading of both the outcome document, and any formal reservations made to it. Because the counter-movement is involved in attempting to block new rights provisions from being included in these outcome documents, these formal texts alone could not demonstrate the success or failure of their counter-framing efforts. Therefore, additional primary and secondary documents were consulted to determine the nature and success of the frames used by counter activists.

Defining Transnational Social Actors and Counter-networks

In an important synthesis of the literature on transnational politics and social movements, Sidney Tarrow[23] identifies a number of weaknesses in current analyses. One of the problems he highlights is the lack of rigor in distinguishing between different types of transnational actors. As he notes, social movement scholars have been better at describing the activities of these actors than conceptualizing them in analytical terms.[24] He attempts to rectify this problem by clarifying and differentiating between the terms 'social movements', International Non-government Organisations (INGOs) and Transnational Advocacy Networks (TANs). Tarrow defines TSMs as:

> Socially mobilized groups with constituents in at least two states, engaged in *sustained contentious* interaction with power holders in at least one state other than their own, or against an international institution, or a multinational economic actor[25] (emphasis added).

TSMs differ from INGOs in terms of their behaviour. INGOs "engage in *routine* transactions with the *same kinds* of actors and provide *services* to citizens of other states"[26] (emphasis added).

In other words, INGOs are not necessarily involved in contentious action and the actors involved tend to be more alike than in the broader category of TSM. The final category is the TAN. According to Tarrow, TANs are not alternatives to TSMs or INGOS, but can contain them. The TAN concept is most fully developed in the work of Keck and Sikkink.[27] For these authors a TAN "includes those relevant actors working internationally on an issue, who are bound together by shared values, a common discourse, and dense exchanges of information and services".[28]

Different relationships exist between state and non-state actors in each of these categories. TSMs are usually working against rather than aligning with state actors while INGOs seek to maintain their integrity and independence by steering away from official government relationships even if they happen to agree with official policies. However, some of the TSM literature sees this boundary between government and non-government actors as being less distinct. For Rucht, a complex web of alliance exists between state and non-state actors, especially when non-government representatives are included on state delegations to international conferences.[29] The line between the state and non-state actors in relation to TANs is also seen to be blurred. As Tarrow[30] and Keck and Sikkink[31] note, transnational network structures are able to contain governmental agents in either their official or unofficial capacities. The concept of a TAN is useful in this analysis where, as is detailed below, state and non-state actors have worked in unison to oppose the TWM.

A second problem Tarrow raises is that recent studies of transnational contentious politics has been overly focused on 'good movements' such as the peace and human rights movements.[32] As a result, there is little known about the emergence, behaviour and success of those opposing progressive causes transnationally.[33] This problem is not so apparent at the domestic level. Over the years, some important analyses of domestic counter-movements have been undertaken. The work of Zald and Useem,[34] Meyer and Staggenborg[35] and McCright and Dunlap[36] in particular has contributed to a conceptualisation of the relationship between movements and counter-movements at the level of the state.

The key point about a counter-movement is its negative stance. As Zald and Useem note: "a counter-movement is the mobilisation of sentiments initiated to some degree in *opposition* to a movement" (emphasis in original).[37] For Meyer and Staggenborg counter-movements are:

> networks of individuals and organisations that share many of the same objects of concerns as the social movements that they *oppose*. They make competing claims on the state on matters of policy and politics and vie for attention from the mass media and broader public (emphasis added).[38]

While early literature in the area tended to see all counter-movements as reactionary in nature,[39] more recent work has moved away from this position. Rejecting the progressive/conservative dichotomy in relation to social change, more recent literature emphasizes the crucial characteristic of counter-movements to be their *oppositional* relationship to another movement.[40]

While it is theoretically possible that 'progressive' counter-movements exist, there is nevertheless a fundamental conservative aspect to their character—that is, the objective of these movements is to maintain the *status quo*.[41] This point is made by McCright and Dunlap[42] who argue that counter-movements are engaged in three levels of activities each of which is aimed at *preventing* change. These activities involve: first, preventing issues from becoming defined as problems in the first place—an act they term "the social construction of non-problematicity"; second, if a problem has been defined, preventing it from being put on the political agenda; and third, if it has made it on to the agenda, neutralizing it through what they term "consciousness-lowering" activities.[43] Instead of counting success in terms of effecting change, the measure of counter-movements is their ability to prevent their opponents' frames from being recognized or demands from being met. The extent to which these features of domestic counter-movements also apply to those operating at the transnational level will be considered in the following discussion.

Political Opportunities, Mobilizing Structures and Framing

Three central concepts are used in the SM literature to explain the emergence, activities and success of social movements. The first is *the political opportunity structure* (POS) which refers to the "consistent—but not necessarily formal or permanent—dimensions of the political environment that provide incentives for collective action by affecting people's expectations for success or failure".[44] Such structures provide external resources for actors to pursue their agendas and can include formal elements such as voting rules and institutional arrangements and informal elements, including the normative and cultural context.[45]

The second concept is *mobilizing structures* which are "those collective vehicles, informal as well as formal, through which people mobilize and engage in collective action".[46] These structures include the tactical repertoires and social movement organisation forms through which actors aggregate their demands. Movements tend to adopt tactics and structures appropriate to the particular context of venue in which they are operating—the tactics will be more or less confrontational and more or less decentralized depending upon the arena in which they are engaged.

Framing is the third concept used in the social movement literature which is relevant to this study. Frames are "the conscious strategic efforts by groups of people to fashion shared understandings of the world and of themselves that legitimate and motivate collective action".[47] They are, as Campbell notes: "metaphors, symbols and cognitive cues that cast issues in a particular light and suggest possible ways to respond to these issues".[48] Frames are shaped by and mediate between both the POS and mobilizing structures of movements.[49] The importance of framing to social movement emergence and success has been noted for domestic level movements[50] and also transnational networks. For example, Keck and Sikkink[51] explain that in order to influence change at the international level, TANs rely heavily on symbolic politics and in doing so carefully frame issues in ways that will attract attention. Dealing in the realm of ideas and values, they often frame their demands in a symbolic as opposed to a strictly rationalist way, and in simple terms that suggest there are right and wrong answers to complex moral and political issues. Using moral leverage, TANs seek to persuade powerful actors at both the domestic and international level first, a problem exists which needs attending to, then, that parties can be identified who are responsible for the problem and finally, that they have credible solutions to the problem.[52]

The counter-movement literature also emphasizes the importance of each of these three concepts for understanding oppositional actors, but with some important differences. In the next section of the paper, each concept is considered from a counter-movement perspective and discussed in terms of its relevance to the emergence, strategies and success of counter activism in relation to the transnational women's movement.

The Political Opportunity Structure and Counter Activists

The emergence of a counter-movement is just as likely to be influenced by political opportunity structures as an originating movement. However, as Meyer and Staggenborg[53] note, the nature of the POS influencing counter-movements can be quite different to those of originating movements. They indicate three conditions that promote the rise in domestic level counter-movements: 1. The originating movement shows signs of success; 2. Interests of some population are threatened by movement goals; and 3. Political allies are available to aid oppositional mobi-lisation. It is generally accepted in the literature that only movements that are successful will generate counter-movements.[54] In other words, somewhat ironically, the rise of a successful movement promotes a positive POS for the emergence of its opponent. As Zald and Useem note: "A movement's success demonstrates to a counter-movement's constituency the benefits of collective action".[55] Moreover, the greater the degree to which a movement is able to exploit or create critical events which alter the prevailing political opportunity structure, the more likely it will be that counter-movements will mobilize to advance their own causes.[56] But, as Meyer and Staggenborg[57] note, in order for a counter movement to emerge the gains of the originating movement must not be decisive; there must be further room for maneuver, or else there would be no point in putting any effort into a counter mobilisation. To what extent does each of these factors also apply to emergence of the counter activists who are the focus of this paper?

The argument that successful originating movements spur the development of a counter-movement appears to hold in the case of the TWM and its opponents. The TWM, which arose from a long tradition of women's organizing, has grown dramatically in the past 30 years with thousands of women from across all races, regions, religions and socio-economic groups com-ing together to pursue a similar set of gender equality goals.[58] The emergence of the TWM since the 1970s can be seen to have been heavily influenced by the prevailing political opportunity structure especially the critical events of the UN sponsored Mexico, Copenhagen, Nairobi and Beijing International Women's Conferences which provided venues for women from across the world to meet and discuss issues and strategies. The International Decade for Women which commenced with the Mexico Conference in 1975 helped provide a focus for lobbying both nationally and internationally and saw additional resources flow to activists in the movement. The development of the Convention to Eliminate All forms of Discrimination against Women (CEDAW), which was an outcome of the 1980 Copenhagen Conference, gave further impetus to activists to organize to pressure governments and international institutions on women's issues.[59]

The TWM has had a relatively high degree of success in terms of advancing its international agenda. As Friedman[60] and Chen[61] argue, its most significant advance has been its ability to 'gender the agenda'. This gendering is most obvious in UN documents, especially the BPFA, which have come to reflect key concepts advanced by TWM such as reproductive rights, the priority of women's rights over and above those of religious and cultural practices which dis-criminate against women; as well as the articulation of gender justice principles such as recog-nizing sexual assault rape as war crimes and crimes against humanity.[62] (However, as discussed below, it would be wrong to assume that this agenda has the support of all members of the TWM or has been established without debate and strong differences of opinion). Further, TWM efforts have not only helped to increase global awareness about women's rights issues, but also altered national and international discursive, procedural and policy responses to the problem of vio-lence against women along the lines suggested by activists.[63] Success has also come in the form of international cultural changes, including the TWM's ability to enact a different feminist form of politics in new international spaces.[64]

Having noted these advances, it is also true to say that in no sense can the TWM claim to have had such decisive victories that their interventions can be considered to be secure or permanent. Documents to come out of the conferences can be re-opened for negation and new political spaces quickly closed. The gender provisions of the Rome Statute which have become part of hard international law could probably be considered the closest thing to a definitive victory, but even in this case, there is no guarantee that these principles will be upheld in prac-tice, at the international or national level.[65] There is no doubt that TWM has challenged long accepted social values and that this has been reflected in a more gendered international agenda, as reflected in international documents, but in ways which can be challenged. The combination of these factors points to an environment ripe for the emergence of a campaign to counter TWM efforts.

The point made by Meyer and Staggenborg[66] about the importance for counter movements of critical events where their opponents achieve a degree of success, but not a decisive victory, is very relevant to the case of conservative patriarchal activists. Before the emergence of the TWM, and even after its initial forays into the international sphere, no prominent alternative voices were obvious. This began to change around 1993 spurred by the Vienna Conference on Human Rights where the tribunal on women's rights drew international attention to the issues of women's equality and violence. A year later at the IPDC in Cairo, activists opposing the agenda being advanced by the TWM became more prominent, preparing for conference debates and engaging in pre-conference caucusing and lobbying.[67]

The success of the TWM at Cairo and again at the 1995 Beijing FWCW led to a belief by many counter activists that that so-called 'radical feminists' had 'hijacked' the UN and had come to believe that "international politics is their domain".[68] Moreover, conference documents, such as the BPFA, were perceived to be "radical and dangerous".[69] These views, coupled with the ability of counter activists to make some small yet significant inroads at Beijing in 1995 including blocking the inclusion of sexuality rights in outcome documents[70] (see full discussion below) gave added impetus to better organisation between conservative actors to their continued orientation toward UN events.

Another element of the POS identified by Meyer and Staggenborg[71] as necessary for the emergence of a counter-movement is that the interests of some segments of the population are threatened by the movement's goals. When making this argument these authors stress that "the likelihood that opposition to a movement will take the form of a sustained counter-movement is directly related to the oppositions' ability to portray the conflict as one that entails *larger value cleavages in society*" (emphasis added).[72] This argument is highly relevant to the emergence of conservative counter activists. It would be difficult to find a set of issues more morally contentious than those with which the TWM and the conservative activists are engaged. Questions about what constitutes a family and the meaning of gender, equality and sexuality as well as those related to reproduction and abortion are at the core of the debate between these oppositional forces. The discussion below on the framing contests between these two groups illustrates the extent to which counter activists have emphasized the importance of family values in order to sustain its arguments and activities overtime. Suffice to say here that this condition for the emergence of a counter-movement has been amply met in this case.

The final point made by Meyer and Staggenborg regarding the POS necessary for the emergence of a counter-movement is the presence or absence of elite support.[73] Their domestic level analysis points to the importance of government and non-government allies, such as the business community or religious leaders. Utilizing a POS approach for understanding Women's Rights and NGOs at the UN, Joachim[74] suggests other allies also exist at the international level including government representatives from individual states, UN officers and the media.

In explaining the emergence of a transnational conservative counter network, the role of supportive governments cannot be underestimated. Although there have been some variations according to the UN conference and the issue at hand, at each of these critical events, counter activists have been able to rely on official government representatives to support their views. An analysis of the outcome documents and their reservations for each UN conference under review show that government representatives from Egypt, Libya, Iran and Pakistan, have been constant vocal critics of the TWM. They have been joined from time to time by governments from some South American countries with a strong Catholic heritage—Argentina, El Salvador, Nicaragua and Guatemala—as well as Ireland, and other countries with governments with a strong, (and largely conservative) Islamic orientation including Kuwait, Malaysia, Syria, the United Arab Emirates and Yemen. In addition to these governments, state-like actors, especially the Vatican through its diplomatic mission of the Holy See, and to a lesser extent, the OIC, the League of Arab States and the G-77[75] have played a leading role in challenging the frames of the transnational women's movement.

The election in 2000 of the conservative Republican Bush administration in the United States (US) provided an additional ally for counter activists. Unlike the previous Democrat administration, which had often been a supporter of the TWM in UN debates,[76] the incoming administration threw its weight behind efforts to wind back provisions related to international women's rights, especially in relation to reproduction. The intervention of the US at UN conferences post 2001—including Beijing+10, Cairo + 10 and on international AIDS policy and on children's issues—saw official US delegates, many with links to Christian Right groups, advance arguments which clearly echoed those of other counter activists.[77]

The Beijing +10 meeting in February and March 2005 was a test of the importance of the US to conservative patriarchal actors as it was the first specific women's rights event since the election of the Bush administration. Counter activists were not to be disappointed, with the US playing the leading role in efforts to thwart the extension of women's rights. In the first week, the 5 person delegation, all with links to the Republican party and many with links to pro-life organisations,[78] attempted to reopen and amend the BPFA to include the statement that the document does not confer any "international legal rights or legally binding obligations on states under international law".[79] The US found support for its view from the Vatican, CR UN groups and with other governments including Egypt, Qatar, Cost Rica, Nicaragua and Panama.[80] However, the overwhelming majority of government representatives at the meeting did not support the US position, with many upset by both its heavy-handed tactics and suggested amendments.[81] In the event the US withdrew its motion. Although this move was read by some members of the TWM as victory for women's rights,[82] others were more circumspect. The US opposition to the extension of reproductive and sexuality based rights remains firm and fits neatly with the views expressed by other counter activists.[83] While the US may change its controversial strategic approach to affecting change, under the current administration, it is unlikely to alter its policy stance on these issues, leaving the door open for further conflict between oppositional groups at future UN conferences.

The three elements identified by Meyer and Staggenborg[84] as providing a favourable opportunity structure for the emergence of a counter-movement are all relevant to the case of counter women's rights activists. Conservative forces emerged in response to an existing vibrant women's movement, they have engaged on issues that are highly value-laden and have been able to develop links with important allies. Their actions also confirm Joachim's argument about the importance of government allies in the international arena. The impact of the support of a conservative US government on other counter activists has only just begun to resonate but given its authority in world affairs, it is likely the US will provide a crucial future ally for those wishing to counter the TWM.

Mobilizing Structures and Counter Activists

Mobilizing structures are another important aspect of the development of any social movement or network, including those aimed at opposing originating movements. According to the literature, counter-movements tend to 'follow' the initial movement into a particular arena to contest their frames.[85] Sharing a venue with their opponents, counter-movements also adopt tactics and structures which take advantage of the POS that operates within a particular context. To the extent that the venue provides a similar POS for both sides, the counter-movement will tend overtime to develop isomorphic structures and select parallel tactics to that of the initiating movement.[86] To what extent have TWM and conservative forces followed this pattern?

TWM has taken on a diffuse network structure with different sections focusing on different issues such as economic development, violence against women and women and health, or on different geographic regions.[87] Although the movement is dispersed, it maintains sustained interpersonal relations—facilitated through mail, email, telephone and fax and personal encounters.[88] Over time, with a better understanding of the workings of the UN system and conferences, there have been noted improvements in the way the movement organizes itself at these meetings and a greater effort put into developing appropriate strategies to lobby states and UN officials.[89] As Razavi notes:[90]

> At recent global conferences, one could not help but notice the growth of an astute and regionally diverse cadre of advocates skilled in navigating the murky waters of global and regional policy and in moving through circuitous corridors of influence.

The main tactics and strategies of the TWM have tended to shy away from direct action, especially in its violent form. Although rallies, sit-ins and the like have been held at UN conferences to draw attention to specific issues—such as at the rally at the 1993 Vienna Conference on Human rights to draw attention to the use of rape as a weapon of war—the central focus of TWM activists has been lobbying, advocacy and information dissemination. The adage of 'engaging early and often' is one taken seriously by the TWM. The movement has been innovative in its selection of advocacy tools such as establishing 'women's tribunals' at mainstream UN conferences to highlight specific women's rights abuses.[91] Activists have developed a range of skills to advance their aims including in undertaking research, writing (alternative) policy documents, directly lobbying governments to adopt new policy positions, preparing press releases and reporting UN events through women's organisations websites and newsletters.[92] At the recent Beijing +10 conference, women's activists broke with the usual decorum shown at UN conferences to jeer and boo US and Vatican representatives who were seeking to reopen and weaken the language of the BPFA.[93]

Counter activists can be seen to have followed the TWM in adopting a loose network structure. The network contains the two features emphasized in Keck and Sikkink's work: sharing values and information exchange.[94] A common thread linking government, state-like and non-state representatives is that they have a foundation in fundamentalist religious doctrine—both Christian and Islamic. They are fundamentalist in that their "objectives are conservative, in the sense of trying to restore a real or imagined past against the encroachment of a perceived enemy".[95] This is not to argue that a religious network exists internationally. To do so would elide important differences and suggest a consensus within and between these religions on essential questions related to sex and gender which does not exist.[96] Rather, the actors who have worked together against the TWM are those who use religious arguments to advance a particular conservative and patriarchal point of view on gender issues (see further discussion on framing below). Counter activists not only share core values but also information. Exchange of information occurs through a range of means. Web-based resources have been developed by different segments of the movement and are especially advanced for CR UN—for instance the *Focus on the Family* e-newsletter and the Canadian *pro-life Lifesite* web portal. At times conservative activists have organized their own UN specific publications. For instance, at Beijing +5 the conservative Catholic C-FAM organisation published the daily newsletter *Vivant!* which reported on the efforts of all conservative patriarchal activists at the event.[97] However, by contrast, there does not appear to be the same information hubs used by the TWM, such as those maintained by the Global Campaign for Women's Rights and other organisations.[98]

Face-to-face information exchange between counter activists appears initially to have occurred in an informal and *ad hoc* way: members came together at UN conferences, but little effort was made to co-ordinate their efforts at other times. At the Cairo and Beijing conferences for instance, the Vatican, CR UN NGOs and states including Iran, Egypt and Libya were engaged in pre-conference caucusing.[99] According to Buss and Herman[100] the Beijing +5 conference was somewhat of a turning point for better co-ordination between network members. In their view:

> The CR UN . . . 'stormed' the Beijing +5 process, sending nearly four hundred delegates with the apparent intent of ensuring a disruptive CR UN attendance at every meeting. More important, the CR UN appeared to have successfully followed through plans to mobilize sympathetic state governments into a single, conservative religious voice.[101]

Links made at UN conferences have led conservative forces to organize outside these events. In 1995 a Catholic-Muslim commission was established to engage in an interfaith dialogue which met on at least three occasions to identify common issues.[102] An important event was the World Congress of Families II, held in 1999 in Geneva and organized by the pro-family Howard Center at Brigham Young University, Utah and the NGO, Family Voice. The conference, aimed at "defending the family and guiding public policy", was attended by representatives of a diverse range of CR UN groups, the Vatican, Catholic and Muslim-based states including Nicaragua, Argentina and Egypt as well as OIC representatives.[103] Mirroring UN events, the conference produced an outcome document entitled the Geneva Declaration which provided a conservative patriarchal view on marriage, children, sexuality, the sanctity of human life, economics and government.[104] According to Buss and Herman the event was significant because it: "played educative, political and mobilizing roles, acting as a forum for sharing information, providing an interface for CR UN intellectuals and grassroots activists, and beginning the process of . . . strengthening the monotheistic coalition".[105] Another meeting between conservative activists occurred just prior to the Beijing +5 meeting. A pro-family seminar which dealt with women's rights issues entitled "Church, Synagogue, Mosque: Solutions for the Modern Family" was held at UN headquarters and co-sponsored by the Vatican, the Catholic Family and Human Rights Institute, the OIC, Argentina and Nicaragua.[106]

Both CR UN groups as well as key conservative governments have made statements about the importance of each for the other in their efforts to advance a common pro-family agenda at the UN. Asked about allies for his cause, Austin Ruse, the director of C-FAM has stated:

> The Muslims have been true blue. They are undivided and strong enough to stand up to the pressure of the US and UN. We have also gotten good support from Latin America but some Latin American countries have fought us all the way. The only consistent support has come from the Muslims.[107]

OIC representative Mokhtar Lamani has also advanced the view that a partnership exists between governments from some Islamic based governments, CR UN NGOs and the US. In his view, "The main issue that brings us together is defending family values, the natural family" and notes with agreement the emphasis that the US Republican administration puts on these issues.[108]

In terms of tactics, conservative patriarchal actors initially followed those of the TWM. NGOs, especially CR UN members, as well as the Vatican have engaged in lobbying governments to support their position and attempted to convince them to include sympathetic individuals on official delegations. For instance, the Vatican successfully pressured Latin American governments including Argentina and Nicaragua to include conservative Catholics on their Beijing delegations.[109] Like the TWM, counter activists have also used imaginative tactics to draw attention to their cause. Prior to the Beijing Conference, Pope John Paul II[110] issued a letter to the women of the world drawing their attention to the limitation of rights speak and the need to uphold women's traditional roles. At Beijing +5 members of the CR UN, who claimed to have support of a number of conservative Islamic-based governments, walked around the UN wearing bright red motherhood buttons. According to the lobby, the buttons were aimed at "drawing attention of delegates to the failure of the Beijing document to affirm motherhood as a legitimate choice for women" and to combat "the radical feminist agenda to restrict the freedom of women by pushing them out of the home and into the work force".[111]

Some of the tactics used by counter activists have been more direct and disruptive. According to Austin Ruse, at the preparatory committee leading to Beijing +5:

> . . . we broke all the rules of UN lobbying . . . we had our people fan out across the floor of the conference and we placed this letter in the hand of every delegate. Something like pandemonium ensued.[112]

At Beijing +5 Ruse noted that his team was "in a tiny conference room leaning over the backs of diplomats, assisting in the drafting of the conference document".[113] Other tactics used by counter activists have included the pro-conservative World Youth Alliance sitting in and disturbing meetings at UN conferences as well some members engaging in more intimidating activities. According to a TWM activist, during Beijing +5 "monks and friars surrounded one of my staff . . . and prayed over her".[114]

The hypothesis posed in domestic-level analyses about counter-movements mirroring the mobilizing structures of the originating movement appears to hold in this transnational level case study. After counter activists followed the TWN into the UN arena, they gradually adopted a loose network structure based on shared values and information exchange. The links between members of the network have grown over time through events held within and outside UN venues. The tactics have also followed along the lines of those used by the TWM, with a reliance on lobbying and advocacy work. However, recent events suggest that the tactics of each network are becoming gradually more disruptive with both sides demonstrating a willingness to ignore established norms of behaviour at the UN as the battle over women's rights issues intensifies.

Framing and Counter Activists

Framing is the third concept used in the SM literature relevant to the development and activities of movements and counter-movements. In advancing collective frames in pursuit of a particular goal, a movement can provoke counter-framing contests[115] or become involved in what McCright and Dunlap call 'diversionary framing'—an attempt to draw attention away from the goals of the originating movement and remove them from the agenda.[116] The more successful a movement is in having their frames taken seriously, the more likelihood there is of counter frames being developed.[117] The emergence of counter frames complicates the environment for the initiating movement as it forces it to decide between the sometimes incompatible goals of framing its claims to respond to the opposition or to appeal to longtime supporters.[118] To the extent that a movement concentrates on the former, it may come to rely on a master frame which elides intra-movement differences but which is successful in offsetting the impact of its opponent's frames.

The TWM has used a variety of frames to advance its agenda. Gender equality, gender justice, domestic violence, women and development, the need to balance work and family, anti-discrimination against homosexuals, and reproductive rights are some of the primary frames that have been used to capture the demands of the women's movement.[119] With increasing frequency, one or more of these micro-frames have been subsumed under the master-frame of "Women's Rights as Human Rights"[120]—a frame first employed by the TWM at the 1993 Vienna Conference.

The increased use by the TWM of the women's rights master frame can be explained by a number of factors. First, it has allowed TWM members to overcome differences and achieve a degree of consensus. As the TWM has grown over time—both in terms of its numbers and interests—it has become increasingly more difficult to manage intra-movement differences and conflict.[121] Women from different regions have varying economic, cultural and social priorities which have sometimes conflicted with some of the micro-frames: Indigenous women have challenged the emphasis on pro-choice when their population is under threat; many Latin American women who have successfully used the frame of mother citizens are uncomfortable with Western feminists lack of emphasis on mothering; women from poorer countries want a greater emphasis on economic goals rather than the civil and political rights focus of many Western activists; Lesbian women feel altogether ignored. To a certain extent, the over-arching "Women's Rights as Human Rights" frame has been broad enough to embrace a growing diversity of views without imposing particular priorities on the activists themselves. There are still those within the TWM who have difficulty with the frame, seeing human rights as too limited a concept to address systems of structural economic and patriarchal disadvantage.[122] But it has nevertheless been important strategically. As Bunch et al note,[123] the use of a human rights frame has provided "[a] unifying value system and legitimacy" to the TWM.

Arguably, the use of this meta-frame has also been strategically necessary because of the growing influence of conservative counter activists. The ability of these counter forces to lobby to block the expansion of a women's rights agenda at UN conferences, discussed below, has forced TWM activists to find common ideas through which they can stake their claims. Although the result has been a shaky consensus, one that ignores important differences between the actors,[124] it has nevertheless enabled the TWM to present a coherent position at key international events to effect change on broadly agreed objectives.

Counter activists have entered into to a framing contest with the TWM. They have engaged in a campaign to directly challenge dominant frames in areas which could be considered TWM turf—such as in the in the areas of gender, equality, difference and reproduction—as well as in the areas of sovereignty and western liberalism. These actors have been strategic in the way they have developed their counter frames: they have not used a negative anti-women's rights discourse, but have utilized more positive 'pro-family' language. The pro-family frame can be seen to be the meta-frame of counter activists under which a range of other micro frames fit. Despite the positive casting of their agenda, the pro-family frame is not progressive in the sense of social change but has both conservative and patriarchal foundations. It is used to endorse a set of practices including heterosexual marriage, and the role of women as mothers and dependents within a hierarchical family structure.

Counter Frames on Gender, Sexuality, Equality and Reproduction

One of the core contested areas between the TWM and counter activists has been defining gender. Whereas feminists involved in the TWM would argue that the term can be understood as a social construct, conservative actors argue that it can only ever be understood in *biological* terms. The Holy See advanced this view in its reservations to the BPFA:

> The term 'gender' is understood as grounded in biological sexual identity, male or female . . . [it] thus excludes dubious interpretations based on world views which assert that sexual identity can be adapted indefinitely to suit new and different purposes.[125]

When the issue of gender was raised again at the Rome Conference for the ICC, the Holy See restated its position and was supported by a group of Arab League countries including Syria, United Arab Emirates and Qatar.[126] Members of the CR UN clearly support the emphasis on biologically rather than socially constructed differences between men and women. According to James Dobson, leading UN CR activist, the social construction of gender is problematic because it:

> . . . give[s] members of the human family five genders from which to choose instead of two . . . a person can decide whether to be male, female, homosexual, lesbian or transgendered. Some may want to try all five in time.[127]

The interpretation of gender as a biological fact rather than as a social construct is part of the effort of counter activists to block any expansion of gay rights—an area around which there has been a high degree of consensus between them.[128] Opposition by these actors to homosexuality in general and lesbianism in particular was clearly apparent at the Beijing and Beijing +5 conferences, where the Holy See together with UN CR groups and representatives of conservative Islamic-based governments together advanced an anti-homosexual agenda.[129] The Vatican made its views clear at Beijing when it stated it: "cannot accept ambiguous terminology concerning unqualified control over sexuality and fertility, particularly as it could be interpreted as a societal endorsement of . . . homosexuality".[130] Official delegates from Iran, Egypt, Malaysia and Morocco also opposed any inclusion of sexual orientation in the BPFA.[131] Sexual orientation was also a key issue at the Rome Conference and the ICC Prepcoms when the Holy See aligned with Islamic Arab representatives to argue against allowing sexual orientation to be included as a ground for discrimination.[132] Counter activists share the view that to give women sexual freedom would promote homosexuality among women and allow for sex outside conjugal relations. If women should take up the opportunity to live in non-traditional relationships, it would directly challenge the family, the realm in which women naturally exist.

Counter activists have also advanced a common view on another aspect of women's sexuality, the right of women to enjoy sexual autonomy. Lobbying before the Cairo conference, the Holy See working with Egypt and Libya, opposed the inclusion in the *Programme of Action* any reference to women's sexual freedom.[133] The inclusion in the *Beijing Platform for Action* of paragraphs 96, which deals with reproductive and sexual health, and paragraph 97, on sexual autonomy prompted extensive opposition and received more reservations than any other in the document including from the Holy See and the governments of Iran, Pakistan and Libya. At the Beijing +5 conference the Holy See with Iran and the CR UN worked unsuccessfully to proscribe women's right to control their sexuality by lobbying to have reference to it removed from the text of the final conference document.[134] Efforts to curb the extension of rights in the area of sexuality can be seen to fit neatly under a pro-family meta frame where the only acceptable expression of sexuality is confined to heterosexual relations between husband and wife.

At UN Conferences from Cairo onwards, counter activists have pursued alternative notions of equality to those advanced by the TWM; one that has been centered on the notion of an essential difference between men and women. Iran's statement on equality at Beijing reflects the general position of conservative forces:

> The concept of equality in our interpretation takes into account the fact that although women are equal in their human rights and dignity with men, their different roles and responsibilities underlie the need for an equitable system of rights where particular priorities and requirements of the woman in her multiple roles are accounted for.[135]

The Holy See "considers women and men as being of equal dignity in all areas of life, but without this always implying an equality of roles and functions".[136] In its view, sameness with men "would only impoverish women, and all of society, by deforming or losing the unique richness . . . of femininity".[137] The view that men and women have different roles fits neatly with a pro-family view which asserts that the natural place for a woman is in the family—and not the economy—where she carries out her primary role as nurturer.[138]

Frames related to reproduction which conflict with those presented by the TWM but which fit within a pro-family frame have also been developed by counter activists. At the Cairo conference the Vatican and the representatives of some Islamic-based government campaigned to have the international community reject the notion of reproductive rights and strongly opposed the terminology used in the chapter on *Reproductive Rights and Reproductive Health* which recognises *inter alia* abortion as a legitimate dimension of population policy.[139] A similar position was put at Beijing and Beijing +5 by the Vatican and UN CR groups and states including Iran who lobbied strenuously to dilute the language on abortion and reproduction.[140] At Beijing +10, when the US entered into the debate on reproduction, it made clear its opposition to abortion and restated its "ABC" reproductive health policy health—Abstinence, Be Faithful, and Correct and Consistent condom use where appropriate.[141] The US response at this conference was largely consistent with the views that had been put by CR UN NGOs and the Vatican on the issue since the time of the Cairo conference. To give women the right to control their child bearing capacity would not only conflict with important religious and moral reasoning on the right to life but could result in promiscuousness in sexual relations—an outcome which could only accelerate the demise of the traditional family.

Sovereignty and human rights

Aside from shared concerns about specific women's rights, conservative counter activists have advanced a common frame on state sovereignty. Their position has been to defend sovereignty in the face of the expansion of international human rights norms, especially where they are seen to conflict with traditional cultural and religious practices. The Holy See has invoked state sovereignty arguments as a defence in its efforts to limit the effect of expanded international norms surrounding reproductive rights on domestic-level anti-abortion legislation. Its position in this regard was made obvious in its effort to block the inclusion of the crime of forced pregnancy in the Rome Statute on the basis that it would weaken anti-abortion laws.[142] The concern of the Vatican on this matter has been mirrored by a range of conservative Islamic-based governments. At the Cairo Conference, Jordan stated that it would apply the agreement on population and development "within a framework of Islamic Sharia and our ethical values, as well as the laws that shape our behaviour".[143] This statement was typical of others made at the conference by Kuwait, the United Arab Emirates, Syria and Yemen. At Beijing, Egypt made clear that its compliance with the *Platform for Action* "will be conditional on complete respect for the rights of national sovereignty and various moral and religious values".[144]Iran, Iraq, Libya, Morocco and Tunisia made similar reservations to the document.[145]

Related to the concern about protecting state sovereignty, counter activists have also critiqued the underlying western bias of the human rights discourse promoted in international fora. Most particularly, they have been critical of the emphasis on individuals as rights bearing subjects. Such an emphasis, in their view, debases the notion of rights because it is founded on western liberalism and ignores the possibility of group rights, especially the rights of religions and cultures, to collectively defend their beliefs and practices. In the letter sent by John Paul II prior to the Cairo Conference, he condemned the draft *Programme for Action* on the basis that it promoted an individualistic lifestyle that was completely incompatible with marriage.[146] Later the Holy See argued that the *Beijing Platform for Action (BPFA)* "seems to want to impose a Western model of feminism that does not take due account of the values of women in the large majority of the world's countries".[147] It also made reservations about the excessive individualism of the final document.[148] Its position aligns closely with that of many Islamic states at Beijing, who joined with the Vatican in opposing the reproductive health section of the BPFA unless it contained a special qualification to subordinate the text on reproductive rights to cultural and religious values.[149]

Conservative actors have used the pro-family meta frame in their battle for moral supremacy internationally. This frame has enabled them to cast their claims—which are essentially negative in character in the sense of wanting to stop social progress—in a positive light. It has also enabled them to attack the TWM as anti-family and therefore, in a sense, unnatural. This meta frame, like the one used by the TWM, also has the additional benefit of enhancing mobilisation, as it brings together a diversity of actors—including conservative Christian and Islamic activists who otherwise hold vastly different world views.[150]

The Influence of Counter Activists

Much of the domestic social movement literature measures success of social movements in terms of their ability to change attitudes, behaviour and policies. Studies of transnational movements also emphasize the view that "change equals success". The work of Keck and Sikkink[151] is notable in this regard. In their view, the ultimate aim of Transnational Advocacy Networks is to influence state behaviour but they chose to do this through working at the international level. In what they call the *boomerang effect*, they describe how actors, faced with blockages to change at the domestic level, make links with like-minded activists in the international realm, and work through international fora to encourage (or shame) domestic governments to change their policies and practices.[152] Such measures of success are not appropriate to counter movements. As noted at the outset, the primary aim of counter-movements is to defend the *status quo* and therefore to block change.[153] Thus any evaluation of the success of counter activists must be based on their ability to prevent their opponents' frames from being recognized or demands from being met: in other words, their ability to ensure that the "boomerang does not fly". Using this negative measure of success, it is possible to argue that the conservative counter activists who are the subject of this study have had some significant accomplishments. Their success fits into three categories: 1) an ability to influence the outcome documents of the UN conferences; 2) an ability to influence conference proceedings and 3) an ability to influence the work of their TWM opponents.

Influence on Conference Documents

The documents to emerge from the Cairo, Beijing and Beijing +5 conferences as well as the Rome Statute and associated ICC documents reflect the influence of the counter activists.

Their most obvious influence is the large number of reservations made to each of the UN conference documents by conservative government representatives. These reservations weaken the impact of these documents in terms of building international norms and for the incorporation of these rights at the domestic level. They also leave open for future contestation many women's rights claims. These actors have also been successful in restricting the language used in an outcome document and/or to prevent the inclusion of more progressive text. The treatment of gender, sexuality and reproduction in the outcome documents reflects these trends.

The *Beijing Platform for Action* as well as the *Rome Statute* show the hallmarks of the influence of conservative groups in relation to the language on gender and equality. In the BPFW, the term gender was left undefined, but the document included a statement that "there was no indication that any new meaning or connotation of the term [gender], different from accepted prior usage, was intended".[154] The purpose of this caveat was to ensure that the BPFA was not read to include a socially constructed view of men and women.[155] At the Rome conference, the debate on the meaning of the term gender was strongly divided between those wanting to include or exclude a social constructivist approach. The final text of the ICC Statute was an attempt to reach some compromise: "it is understood the term 'gender' refers to the two sexes, male and female, within the context of society. The term 'gender' does not indicate any meaning from the above".[156] According to a feminist ICC delegate, the reference to the "two sexes" reflects the position of the Vatican and some states with conservative Islamic governments: they had lobbied for this wording with the objective of excluding sexual orientation from being read into the definition.[157]

At Beijing, counter activists were successful in ensuring that any reference to sexuality or sexual orientation was excluded from the final document. Such reference had been made in the draft *Platform for Action* but at the conference the text was dropped as a compromise with conservative forces.[158] Feminist advocates who had hoped that by the Beijing +5 conference the environment would be more conducive to the international recognition of rights based on sexual orientation were to be disappointed. The threat by conservative forces to reject the report in its entirety should sexual orientation be included was taken seriously by conference delegates. In the end all references to sexual orientation were removed from the final document.[159]

Counter activists have also succeeded in limiting the language around reproductive rights. At the ICPD in Cairo, the most significant influence of the conservative groups on the final document related to the language on abortion. After much debate the Holy See together with some Islamic states were successful in blocking the inclusion of abortion as a family planning device and were able to ensure access to safe abortion was not mentioned as a right in relation to reproductive health.[160] At the Beijing conference, both pro and anti-abortion activists agreed that the conservative forces were successful in holding back attempts to embrace more liberal language on abortion and reproductive rights more generally.[161] As was noted earlier, at an ICC Prepcom, counter activists were again successful in adding a rider to the definition of forced pregnancy to ensure that it could not be interpreted as diluting the application of anti-abortion laws at the national level.[162]

Influence on Proceedings

Aside from influencing international texts in significant ways, conservative forces have also been successful in influencing the nature of the proceedings at each of the conferences under review. Again their effect has essentially been a negative one; they have frustrated, blocked and slowed down conference procedures on matters that women's activists consider important. Whether this has been a conscious strategy on the part of these actors is debatable. Nevertheless, the result has been that counter activists have used up limited time at these forums for dealing with other issues and addressing the agenda of the TWM.

Time and again participants at each of these conferences have commented on the fact that the Vatican primarily, but often in combination with certain Islamic-based governments and UN CR partners, has slowed down discussions by forcing issues onto the agenda, especially around reproduction and particularly on abortion. At Cairo, according to Neale:

> [t]he Holy See, with relatively little assistance from its allies, was able to monopolize the conference agenda and to some extent the media . . . [in its view] the Holy See was not only spiritually empowered but also morally and ethically bound to redirect the conference's course of action, particularly surrounding abortion.[163]

At this conference the entire first week was taken up by the question of abortion, raised by the Holy See, instead of addressing the wide range of population questions that were up for debate. Also at the Beijing +5 conference, pro-choice participants commented that the conservative groups were seen to be stalling on key issues on abortion and sexual orientation.[164] The point being, in their view: "to chip away at the Beijing Platform's principles".[165] The conference ran longer than expected because of these contentious issues around reproductive rights and as a result of the impact of counter activists came to be known by some TWM activists as "Beijing minus 5".[166]

At the Rome Conference, some delegates were critical of the Holy See's intervention on the question of forced pregnancy as they saw this as an excuse by them to get abortion on the agenda. As the Women's Caucus for Gender Justice (WCGJ) noted in relation to this debate:

> It is difficult to understand how the debate about the crime of enforced pregnancy has become a debate about abortion. National laws which criminalize the termination of pregnancy are not violations under international law and thus would not come within the ICC's jurisdiction . . . [167]

Once the issue of abortion was opened up, it made the discussion on forced pregnancy the most contentious and drawn-out debate at the Rome conference.[168] The US now appears to have joined with other conservative actors in using abortion to shape proceedings. According to a journalist covering the 2005 Beijing +10 conference, there was a widespread view that Bush administration was "using the international women's rights forum to advance their own religious conservative agenda and using the abortion language as a stalling tactic to prevent the conference from moving forward".[169]

Influence on the Transnational Women's Movement

Counter activists present two key problems for the TWM. The emphasis on differences between men and women espoused by conservatives is not so far removed from the view of some feminists who also seek to celebrate women's difference; particularly their reproductive and mothering roles. Moreover, the way in which the Holy See and some Islamic-based governments critique the so-called western individualistic approach to rights reinforces existing tensions between transnational gender advocates about how to address differences between women across religions and cultures.[170] In sum, these counter activists have demonstrated an ability to unsettle and destabilise an already fragile feminist coalition.

The collective view of rights used by many counter activists has placed the TWM in a defensive position. Otto emphasises this point in relation to the experience at Beijing. In her view:

> Although, at one level, the contestation in Beijing between feminist and anti-feminist perspectives resulted in a hard-won reaffirmation of previously agreed 'equality' commitments

by states, at another level the outcomes represented few, if any advances for women. And the many reservations lodged by dissenting states indicate the continuing competence of fundamentalist forces and the ongoing precariousness of even small advances made in the name of formal equality.[171]

A similar argument can be made about developments at the Beijing +5 and especially the recent Beijing+10 Conference; at these events the TWM was locked into maintaining what had already been achieved within the confines of formal equality, rather than pursuing more expansive goals, including those to address difference between women.

One final element of the success of counter activists relates to their ability to create an environment in which the TWM has become wary of even using UN events as an arena to advance their views. After the ability of the TCPN to disrupt events and threatened to water-down text at Beijing +5, members of the TWM began discussing the need to revise its strategies. In 2004, TWM groups argued against any high level UN meeting to mark the 10 year anniversary of Beijing because of "the rise of religious fundamentalism . . . and the internationalisation of political conservatism"[172] which would allow governments to back out of previous commitments and ultimately wind back women's rights;[173] One key international women's NGO, DAWN, summed up the position of many of its allies when it stated:[174] "For the sake of our hard won gains. No official negations of any kind!". In some respects the TWM got their wish— Beijing +10 was a relatively low level diplomatic event, a special session of the Commission on the Status of Women rather than a General Assembly sponsored conference. But this outcome was a pyrrhic victory for the TWM. Prior to Beijing +10, it was agreed by all involved—the UN, government representatives and NGOS—that the BPFA would not be re-opened for discussion nor a new statement on women's rights constructed. Instead the meeting had the more modest aim of assessing the implementation of some of the less contentious aspects of the existing document. The Beijing *status quo* remained in tact: conservative forces did not get to wind back women's rights any further, but nor did the TWM have the opportunity to advance its claims.

Conclusions

TWM activists are right to argue that an alliance of otherwise unlikely partners is operating at the transnational level. As this paper has demonstrated, a range of conservative patriarchal activists—both state and non-state based—have followed the TWM into the UN arena taking advantage of the positive opportunity structures provided by its international conferences. Through these conferences, these counter activists have become better organized, developing new information channels and structures. Links between conservative patriarchal activists have become more than a coincidental confluence of views which arise from time to time at UN meetings. Coordinated efforts to advance common counter-frames to those of the TWM mean that these actors can be conceived of as a network—a transnational conservative patriarchal network (TCPN). While there is some fluidity in the network depending on issues, there have been core members including CR UN NGOs, the Vatican and certain governments with a conservative religious outlook who have co-operated before, during and after UN conferences to push forward a 'pro-family' agenda. The efforts of the TCPN have been successful in a negative sense: blocking text from conference documents, delaying proceedings, highlighting tensions within the TWM and perhaps ultimately, undermining the political opportunity structure for TWM activists in the UN arena.

The development of the TCPN confirms a number of recent arguments about social movements. It highlights the importance of Tarrow's[175] point that to date too much of this literature, especially that concerning transnational movements, has been focused on good movements rather their opponents. As a result, theoretical arguments about the aims and influence of transnational networks are skewed toward groups that seek to progress issues, not those who work to defend the *status quo* or regress issues. The work on counter-movements, most of which to date considers domestic level actors has proven to be very useful to this study. Zald and Usmeem[176] and Meyer and Staggenborg's[177] prediction that counter-movements arise when the originating movement shows signs of success and the interests of some population being threatened by movement goals holds in relation to this case. Equally relevant are the arguments that counter-movements develop isomorphic structures, similar tactics and engage in counter framing contests.

An issue emerging in this study of the TCPN, but which is overlooked in domestic level counter movement analysis, is the significance of government actors. As has been seen, conservative religious-based governments such as including Iran, Libya, Egypt and more recently the US, have demonstrated strong support for the views of non-government conservative patriarchal activists. Indeed, it is hard to imagine that CR UN NGOs would ever have achieved such influence in terms of conference documents and proceedings without the willingness of these parties to lobby for changes to texts before each conference and to support the demands of NGOs during conference proceedings. For this reason, it may be more precise to see these governments and state-like actors not just as allies, but as actual members of the network. This raises a more general point made by Tarrow[178] amongst others about the importance of the ongoing salience of state sovereignty in international politics, even in the face of strong globalizing pressures, to transnational social movements. As this study has shown, governments respond to NGO pressure but they themselves continue to be the key actors in international affairs.

Internationally over the past decade, a conservative patriarchal pro-family agenda has challenged women's rights. In this sense, the TCPN has been an effective counter force to the TWM. The TWM has been left in a precarious position, forcing it to become in a sense a conservative actor defending the 'Beijing status quo'. However, although the TWM is currently operating in defensive mode, the contest between these oppositional forces is far from over. After being shadowed by TCPN actors for some time, the TWM can now learn from counter-actors—both in terms of working more closely with supportive states and finding new morally persuasive frames through which to state its claims—which may help it to reassert its influence and push forward an emancipatory international agenda on women's rights.

Abbreviations

BPFA	Beijing Platform for Action
C-FAM	Catholic Family and Rights Institute
CR UN	Christian Right at the United Nations
DAWN	Development Alternatives with Women for a New Era
FWCW	Fourth World Conference on Women
ICPD	International Conference on Population Development
INGO	International Non-Governmental Organisation
NGO	Non-Government Organisation
OIC	Organisation of the Islamic Conference
POS	Political Opportunity Structure
SM	Social Movement
TAN	Transnational Advocacy Networks
TCPN	Transnational Conservative Patriarchal Network

TSM   Transnational Social Movement
TWM   Transnational Women's Movement
WCGJ   Women's Caucus for Gender Justice

Notes

1. Amnesty International, "Beijing +5 No Going Back On Women's Human Rights", Press Release (2000). (9 September 2005), available:<http://www.aworc.org/bpfa/ngo/ungass/amnesty.html>
2. Bunch, Charlotte Peggy Antrobus, Samantha Frost and Niamh Reilly, "International Networking for Women's Human Rights", in Michale Edwards and John Gaventa (eds.), *Global Citizen Action* (Boulder: Lynee Rienner Publishers, 2001).
3. Ana Elena Obando, "More News from the 61ˢᵗ Session of the Commission on Human Rights (CHR)", (2005). (9 September 2005), Available: <http://www.whrnet.org/docs/issue-hrc_session_1.html>
4. See Jane H. Bayes and Nayereh Tohidi (eds.), *Globalization, gender and religion: The Politics of Women's Rights in Catholic and Muslim Countries* (Basingstoke: Palgrave, 2001).
5. Samuel Huntington, "The clash of civilisations", *Foreign Affairs*, Vol. 72, No. 3 (1993), pp. 22–49.
6. Sidney Tarrow, "Transnational Politics: Contention and Institutions in International Politics", *Annual Review of Political Science*, Vol. 4 (2001), pp. 1–20; Margaret Keck and Kathryn Sikkink, *Activists Beyond Borders: Advocacy Networks in International Politics* (Ithaca: Cornell University Press, 1998); Doug McAdam, John D. McCarthy and Meyer N. Zald, *Comparative Perspectives on Social Movements: Political Opportunities, Mobilizing Structures and Cultural Frames* (Cambridge: Cambridge University Press, 1996).
7. Mayer N. Zald and Bert Useem.. "Movement and Counter-movement Interaction: Mobilization, Tactics and State Involvement", in Mayer N. Zald and John D. McCarthy (eds.), *Social Movements in and Organizational Society: collected essays* (New Brunswick: Transaction Publishers, 1987); David Meyer and Suzanne Staggenborg, "Movements, Counter-movements and the Structure of Political Opportunity", *American Journal of Sociology*, Vol. 101, No. 6 (1996), pp. 1628–60; Aaron M. McCright and Riley E. Dunlap, "Defeating Kyoto: The Conservative Movement's Impact on U.S. Climate Change Policy", *Social Problems*, Vol. 50, No. 3 (2003), pp. 348–373.
8. For instance see Valentine M. Moghadam, *Globalizing Women: Transnational Feminist Networks* (Baltimore: Johns Hopkins University Press, 2005); Nuket Kardam, "The Emerging Global Gender Equality Regime from Neoliberal and Constructivist Perspectives in International Relations", *International Feminist Journal of Politics* (2004), pp. 85–109; Elisabeth Jay Friedman, "Gendering the Agenda: The Impact of the Transnational Women's Rights Movement at the UN Conferences of the 1990s", *Women's Studies International Forum*, Vol. 26, No. 4 (2003), pp. 313–331; Jutta Joachim "Framing and Seizing Opportunities: The UN, NGOs, and Women's Rights", *International Studies Quarterly*, Vol. 47 (2003), pp. 247–274; Bunch et. al., op. cit.; Lois West, "The United Nations Women's Conferences and Feminist Politics" in Mary K. Meyer and Elisabeth Prugl (eds.) *Gender and Politics in Global Governance* (Lanham, Maryland: Rowman Littlefield, 1999); Keck and Sikkink, op. cit.; Martha Alter Chen, "Engendering World Conferences: The International Women's Movement and the UN", in T.G. Weisse and L. Gordenker (eds.), *NGOs, the UN and Global Governances* (Boulder, Colarado: Lynne Reimer, 1996).
9. Friedman, op. cit.

10. Bayes and Tohidi (eds.), op. cit.
11. Doris Buss and Did Herman, *Globalizing Family Values: The Christian Right in International Politics* (Minneapolis: University of Minnesota Press, 2003).
12. Palena R. Neale, "The bodies of Christ as international bodies: the Holy See, wom(b)an and the Cairo Conference", *Review of International Studies*, Vol. 24 (1998), pp. 101–18.
13. Doris Buss, "Robes, Relics and Rights: The Vatican and the Beijing Conference on Women", *Social and Legal Studies*, Vol. 7, No. 3 (1998), pp. 339–363.
14. Buss and Herman, op. cit.
15. Ibid., p. xviii.
16. The NGO conference sponsored by the UN which ran parallel to the Beijing conference was attended by over 30,000 people, while 3,000 gained official accreditation to attend the FWCW. Friedman, op. cit., p. 313.
17. Kardam, op. cit., p. 94.
18. The status of the Holy See as a permanent non-state observer at these conferences is highly controversial. Its status has been recently challenged by a coalition of women's religious and reproductive rights NGOS known as *Seechange*, which has petitioned the UN to remove the special status of the Church. In its view, the status gives the Holy See an unfair advantage compared to other NGOs and religions groups, enabling it to benefit from the consensus voting system of the UN and exert a degree of influence far beyond its authority. Catholics for a Free Choice (CFFC) "International Campaign Calls in to Question Vatican's Seat at UN", Press Release (1999). (2 February 2004), Available: <www.cath4choice/nobandwidth/English/new/pressrelease/internationalcampa>
19. United Nations, *Report of the International Conference on Population and Development: Programme of Action*, UN Document: A/Conf.171/13 (New York: UN Department of Public Information, 1994).
20. United Nations, *Platform for Action, Fourth World Conference on Women*, UN Document No. A/CONF.177/20 (New York: UN Department of Public Information, 1995).
21. See Buss, op. cit., p. 342.
22. *Soft* international law refers to non-legally binding instruments that nevertheless create expectations about future action. *Hard* law relates to binding legal obligations on states such as international treaties. Hilary Charlesworth and Christine Chinkin, *The boundaries of international law: a feminist analysis* (Manchester: Manchester University Press, 2000), p. 66. In relation to women's rights, *soft* law has been developed through the documents to emerge from the international women's conferences. Examples of *hard* law are the Convention on the Elimination of All Forms of Discrimination against Women (CEDAW) and the Rome Statute of the International Criminal Court.
23. Tarrow, "Transnational Politics: Contention and Institutions in International Politics", op. cit.
24. Ibid., p. 10.
25. Ibid., p. 11.
26. Ibid., p. 12.
27. Keck and Sikkink, op. cit.
28. Ibid., p. 2.
29. Dieter Rucht, "The Transnationalization of Social Movements: Trends, Causes, Problems", in Donatella della Porta, Hanspeter Kriesi and Dieter Rucht (eds.), *Social Movements in a Globalizing World* (Basingstoke: Macmillan, 1999), pp. 210 and 212.
30. Tarrow, "Transnational Politics: Contention and Institutions in International Politics", op. cit., p. 13.
31. Keck and Sikkink, op. cit., p. 9.

32. Tarrow, "Transnational Politics: Contention and Institutions in International Politics", op. cit., p. 13.
33. Ibid., p. 10.
34. Zald and Useem, op. cit.
35. Meyer and Staggenborg, op. cit.
36. McCright and Dunlap, op. cit.
37. Zald and Useem, op. cit., p. 249.
38. Meyer and Staggenborg, op. cit., p. 1632.
39. See Mottl in Meyer and Staggenborg, op. cit., p. 1631.
40. Meyer and Staggenborg, op. cit., p. 1632.
41. McCright and Dunlap, op. cit.
42. Ibid.
43. Ibid., pp. 351–2.
44. Sidney Tarrow, *Power in movement: social movements and contentious politics*, 2nd ed. (Cambridge: Cambridge University Press, 1998), pp. 76–7.
45. Joachim, op. cit., p. 251.
46. McAdam et. al., op. cit., p. 3.
47. Snow in McAdam et al, op. cit., p. 6.
48. John L. Campbell "Where do we stand: Common Mechanisms in Organizations and Social Movement Research", in Gerald F. Davis, Doug McAdam, W. Richard Scott and Mayer N. Zald, (eds.), *Social Movements and Organization Theory* (Cambridge: Cambridge University Press, 2005), p. 48.
49. Joachim, op. cit., p. 252; McAdam et. al., op. cit., p. 5.
50. For instance see the case studies in David et. al. (2005); McAdam et. al., op. cit.
51. Keck and Sikkink, op. cit.
52. Ibid., p. 19.
53. Meyer and Staggenborg, op. cit.
54. Meyer and Staggenborg, op. cit.; Tarrow *Power in movement: social movements and contentious politics*, op. cit.; Zald and Useem, op. cit.
55. Zald and Useem, op. cit., p.254.
56. Meyer and Staggenborg, op. cit., p. 1638.
57. Ibid., p. 1636.
58. Moghadam, op. cit.; Bunch et. al., op. cit.
59. Kardam, op. cit.
60. Friedman, op. cit., p. 313.
61. Chen, op. cit.
62. See Moghadam, op. cit., p. 12.
63. See Keck and Sikkink, op. cit.
64. West, op. cit., p. 191.
65. See Louise Chappell, "Women's Rights and Religious Opposition: the Politics of Gender at the International Criminal Court", in Yasmeen Abu-Laban (ed.) *Gendering the Nation State: Canadian Comparative Perspectives* (Vancouver: University of British Columbia Press, 2008).
66. Meyer and Staggenborg, op. cit.
67. Neale, op. cit.
68. LifeSite Daily news, "Beijing +5 Prepcom Final Report", 3 April 2000. Accessed at http://www.lifesite.net/ldn/2000/apr/000403a.html on 20 January 2004.
69. Ruse in Jennifer Butler, "300 religious Right Participants Attend Beijing Prepcom", (2000), p. 1. (2 September 2005), Available: <http://www.globalpolicy.org/ngos/00deb/beij5-2htm>

70. Dianne Otto, "Holding Up Half the Sky, But for Whose benefit?: A Critical Analysis of the Fourth World Conference on Women", *The Australian Feminist Law Journal*, Vol. 6 (1996), pp. 7–28.
71. Meyer and Staggenborg, op. cit.
72. Ibid., p. 1639.
73. Ibid., p. 1642.
74. Joachim, op. cit., p. 252.
75. The G-77 is the largest Third World coalition in the United Nations. It provides the means for the developing world to articulate and promote its collective economic interests and enhance its joint negotiating capacity on all major international economic issues in the United Nations system, and promote economic and technical cooperation among developing countries. Many Islamic countries who have played a prominent role in UN conference debates on women's issues are members of the G-77 including Egypt, Morocco, Iran, Kuwait, Malaysia and Libya.
76. Amy J. Higer, "International Women's Activism and the 1994 Cairo Population Conference", in Mary K. Meyer and Elisabeth Prugl (eds.), *Gender and Politics in Global Governance*, (Lanham, Maryland: Rowman Littlefield, 1999), p. 136.
77. Colum Lynch, "Islamic Bloc, Christian Rights Team Up to Lobby UN", *Washington Post*, June 17 2002, A. 1.
78. Allison Stevens, "U.S. Engages in Tug-of-War at Beijing Plus 10", *WeNews* (2005). (19 August 2005), Available: <http://www.womensenews.org/article.cfm/dyn/aid/2211>
79. Ellen Sauerbury, "United States Mission to the United Nations", Press Release USUN #39 (05), March 4 2005. (19 August 2005) Available: <http://www.un.int.usa/05print_039.htm>
80. Deborah Zabarenko "US draws jeers for abortion comments at UN", *Reuters News*, 5 March 2005.
81. See Mary-Ann Stephenson, "Bush versus Women's Rights", *Mail and Guardian Online*, 15 March 2005. (19 August 2005) Available: <http://global.factiva.com.exproxy.library.usyd.edu.au/en/arch/display.asp>; Warren Hoge, "Panel Backs Women's Rights After U.S. Drops Abortion Issue", *The New York Times*, 5 March 2005, p. 5.
82. Stephenson, op. cit.
83. Sauerbury, op. cit.
84. Meyer and Staggenborg, op. cit.
85. Ibid., p. 1649.
86. Ibid., pp. 1649–50.
87. Bunch et al 2001, 377.
88. Friedman, op. cit., p. 314; West, op. cit., p. 192.
89. Joachim, op. cit., p. 269.
90. Razavi in Kardam, op. cit., p. 93.
91. Bunch et. al., op. cit., p. 375.
92. Kardam 2004, 94; Bunch et al 2001
93. Press Trust of India, "UN Women's conference reaffirms Beijing action plan", *Asia Pulse* (2005). (26 August 2005) <http://0global.factiva.com.opac.library.usyd.edu.au/en.arch/print_results.asp>
94. Keck and Sikkink, op. cit., p. 9.
95. Rosalind Pollack Petchesky, *Global Prescriptions: Gendering Health and Human Rights*, (London: Zed Books, 2003), p. 36.
96. In no sense does this paper suggest that either all Christian or Islamic activists fit within a conservative patriarchal paradigm. In Catholic, Protestant and Islamic traditions an

array of alternative positions exist to challenge these views and much work, especially
by feminist religious practitioners, has been undertaken to highlight the extent to which
religious texts have been distorted to suit patriarchal political objectives. For Catholicism
see Neale, op. cit.; Frances Kissling "From Cairo to Beijing and Beyond", *Conscience*, (1995).
(15 July 2004) Available: <http://www.catholicsforchoice.org/articles/roadlong.asp>. For
Islam see Azizah Al-Hibri, "Islam, Law and Custom: redefining Muslim Women's Rights",
American University Journal of International Law and Policy, Vol. 12 (1997), pp. 1–44; Lisa
Hajjar, "Religion, State Power , and Domestic Violence in Muslim Societies: A Framework
for Comparative Analysis", *Law and Social Inquiry*, (2004), pp. 1–38; Nayereh Tohidi,
"Women's Rights in the Muslim World: The Universal-Particular Interplay" *HAWWA*,
Vol 1, No. 2 (2003), pp. 152–188.

97. Butler, op cit., p.10.
98. See Bunch et. al., op. cit., for details.
99. For Cairo see Neale, op. cit.; Jyoti Shankar Singh, *Creating a New Consensus on Population: The International Conference on Population and Development* (UK: Earthscan, 1998); for Beijing see Center for Reproductive Rights, "Five Year Review of the Beijing Fourth World Conference on Women", Briefing Paper, (2000). (3 February 2004), Available at: http:www.crlp.org/ww_adv_beijing.html; Kissling, op. cit.; Sabina Lauber, "Where to Now? International Women's Rights", *Alternative Law Journal*, Vol 26, No. 1, (2001), p. 18; Otto, op. cit., p. 16.
100. Buss and Herman, op. cit.
101. Ibid., p. 101.
102. Catholic World News, *"Catholic-Islamic Dialogue Continues", (1997)*. (2 September 2005). Available: <https://cwnews.com/news/viewstory.cfm?recnum=5330ambridge>
103. Buss and Herman, op. cit.; Butler, op. cit., pp. 5 and 18; World Congress of Families, "Geneva Declaration", (1999). (30 September 2005), Available: <www.worldcongress.org/WCF2/wcf2_declaration.htm>
104. World Congress of Families, op. cit.
105. Buss and Herman, op. cit., pp. 80–1.
106. Religion Counts, *Religion and Public Policy at the UN*, (Mount Vernon: Religion Counts, 2002), p. 9.
107. Austin Ruse in Clare MacDonnell, "A Catholic Voice In the Wilderness of the UN" *CatholicHerald.com*, (1999). (2 September 2005), Available: <www.catholicherald.com/articles/00articles/ruse.htm>
108. Lynch, op. cit.
109. Laura Guzman Stein, "The Politics of Implementing Women's Rights in Catholic Countries of Latin America" in Jane H. Bayes and Nayereh Tohidi (eds), op. cit.
110. Pope John Paul II, "Letter of Pope John Paul II to Women", (1995). (20 September 2005), Available: <http://www.vatican.va/holy_father/john_pail_ii/letters/documents/hf_jp_ii_let_29061995_women_en.html>
111. LifeSite Daily news, op cit.
112. Ruse in Butler, op. cit., p. 6.
113. Ruse in Lynch, op. cit.
114. Anonymous in Religion Counts, op. cit., p. 10.
115. Friedman, op. cit., p. 15.
116. McCright and Dunlap, op. cit., p. 351.
117. McAdam et. al., op. cit., p. 17.
118. Meyer and Staggenborg, op. cit., p. 1652.
119. Friedman, op. cit., p. 318.

120. Keck and Sikkink, op. cit., p. 184.
121. See for instance Joachim, op. cit., pp. 262 and 265; Bunch et. al., op. cit.
122. See Keck and Sikkink, op. cit., p. 184.
123. Bunch et. al., op. cit., p. 381.
124. See Friedman, op. cit.
125. UN, Platform for Action, Fourth World Conference on Women, op. cit., Reservations, para. 11.
126. Rhonda Copelon, "Gender Crimes as War Crimes: Integrating Crimes against Women into International Law", *McGill Law Journal*, Vol. 46 (2000), p. 236; Barbara C. Bedont, "Gender-Specific Provisions in the Statute of the ICC" in F. Lattanzi and W. Schabas (eds.), *Essays on the Rome Statute of the ICC*, (Naples: Editorial Scientifica, (1999). Fn. 15 (14 June 2004), Available: <http://iccwomen.addr.com/recourses/genderprovs.html>
127. James Dobson in Buss and Herman, op. cit., p. 113.
128. Buss, op. cit., p. 269; Copelon, op. cit.
129. Lauber, op. cit., p. 18; Otto, op. cit., p. 26.
130. UN, Platform for Action, Fourth World Conference on Women, op. cit., Reservations, para. 11.
131. Kissling, op. cit.
132. See Bedont, op. cit., p. 4; Copelon, op. cit., p. 236; Pam Spees, "Women's Advocacy in the Creation of the International Criminal Court: changing the landscapes of justice and power", *Signs*, Vol. 28, No. 4, (2003), p.1253.
133. Neale, op. cit., p. 118.
134. Buss and Herman, op. cit.
135. United Nations, *Platform for Action, Fourth World Conference on Women*, op. cit., Reservations, para. 14.
136. Holy See in Buss, op. cit., p. 347.
137. Pope John Paul II, op. cit.
138. For CR UN views on this see Buss and Herman, op. cit., p. 102.
139. Sajeda Amit and Sara Hossain, "Women's Reproductive Rights and the Politics of Fundamentalism: A view from Bangladesh", *American University Law Review*, Vol. 44, (1994–5), p. 1337; United Nations, *Report of the International Conference on Population and Development: Programme of Action*, op. cit.,. Reservations paragraph 27.
140. See Center for Reproductive Rights, op. cit.; Lauber, op. cit., p. 18; Otto, op. cit., p. 16.
141. Sauerbury, op. cit.
142. Holy See, "Intervention of the Holy See Diplomatic Conference of Plenipotentiaries on the Establishment of An International Criminal Court, Working Group on War Crimes" (1998). (14 June 2004), Available: <http://147.222.27.5/people.dewolf/hs.html>; H.E. Mons. Jean-Louis Tauran, "The Defence of Life in the Context of International Policies and Norms", (2004). (3 February 2004), Available: <file://C:Docume1~\ADMINI~ENT\Locals~Temp\triIIAOF.htm>; C-Fam, "Radical Feminists Laud International Criminal Court", (2000). (3 February 2004), Available: <http://www.lifesite.net/ldn/2000/mar/00030905.html>
143. United Nations, Report of the International Conference on Population and Development: Programme of Action, op. cit., Reservations paragraph 11.
144. United Nations, Platform for Action, Fourth World Conference on Women, op. cit., Reservations, para. 8.
145. See United Nations, Platform for Action, Fourth World Conference on Women, op. cit., Reservations.
146. Neale, op. cit., p. 110.
147. Navarro-Valls in Kissling, op. cit.

148. See United Nations, *Platform for Action, Fourth World Conference on Women*, op. cit., Reservations, para 11; Mary Ann Glendon, "Holy See Statement to the Fourth World Conference on Women", 5 September 1995. (13 July 2004), Available: <http://www.un/ org.esa.gopher-data/conf/fwcw/conf/gov/950905214652.txt>

149. Kissling, op. cit.

150. Bayes and Tohidi, op. cit., p. 3; Buss and Herman, op. cit.

151. Keck and Sikkink, op. cit.

152. Ibid., pp. 13–14.

153. McCright and Dunlap, op. cit.

154. United Nations, *Platform for Action, Fourth World Conference on Women*, op. cit.

155. See Otto, op. cit., p. 12.

156. *Rome Statute of the International Criminal Court*, (1998), UN Doc. A/Conf. 183/9. Article 7(3) (1 October 2003), Available: <http:///www.un.org.icc/statute/romefra.htm>

157. Copelon, op. cit., p. 237.

158. See Buss, op. cit., p. 248; Otto, op. cit., pp. 25–6.

159. Lauber, op. cit., p. 18.

160. Center for Reproductive Rights, op. cit.; Kissling, op. cit.

161. See Kissling, op. cit.; Tom Minnery, "Focus on the Family" Press Statement, *C-Fam*. Accessed at http:www.c-fam.org/holysee/voicesoftruth.html#9 on 1 November 2003.

162. See Copelon, op. cit.; Bedont, op. cit.

163. Neale, op. cit., p. 117.

164. See Neale, op. cit., p. 117; Anne Shepherd, "Abortion Debate Deferred as More Voices Join the Vatican" Press Release, *Women's Feature Service*, (1994). (23 July 2004) Available: < http: www.iisd.ca/Cairo/wfsabort.txt

165. See Center for Reproductive Rights, op. cit.

166. Asa Frostfeldt, "Beijing Plus Five – Much Work Left to Be Done", *Human Rights Databank* Vol. 7 (2000), pp. 2&3. (26 January 2004), Available: <http://64.26.129.97/tribune/ viewArticle.asp?ID=2568>

167. Women's Caucus for Gender Justice, "The Crime of Forced Pregnancy", (1998). (2 October 2002), Available: <http://www.iccwomen.org/icc/iccpc/rome>

168. See Bedont, op. cit.; Copelon, op. cit.

169. Stevens, op. cit.

170. For a discussion see Manisha. Desai, "Transnational Solidarity: Women's Agency, Structural Adjustment and Globalization", in Nancy A. Naples and Manisha Desai (eds.), *Women's Activism and Globalization: Linking Local Struggles and Transnational Politics* (New York: Routledge, 2002), p. 28.

171. Otto, op. cit., pp. 27–8.

172. Network of Women Parliamentarians of the America, "The Tenth Anniversary of the Beijing Conference and the Possible Holding of the Fifth World Conference on Women" (2004). (1 October 2005), Available: <http://www.copa.qc.ca/Anglais/Femmesang/ Brasilia-2004–03/F-RES-Beijing-10e%20anniversaire-a.pdf>

173. Asian Women in development (AWID), "The 5th World Conference/Beijing +10 Debate" (2005). (26 August 2005), Available: <http://www.awid.org/go.php?stid=613>

174. Development Alternatives with Women for a New Era (DAWN), "Dawn Says No to Negotiations", *DAWN Inform* (2003). (9 October 2005), Available: <http://www. dawn.org.fj/global/globalisation/linkagesproject/institute2003/prelimreaderdocs/ notonegs.doc>

175. Tarrow "Transnational Politics: Contention and Institutions in International Politics", op. cit.
176. Zald and Usmeem, op. cit.
177. Meyer and Staggenborg, op. cit.
178. Tarrow "Transnational Politics: Contention and Institutions in International Politics", op. cit.

PART VI

ENVIRONMENT

CHAPTER THIRTEEN

Spinning the Green Web: Transnational Environmentalism

Wendy E. F. Torrance and Andrew W. Torrance

Source: Srilatha Batliwala and L. David Brown (eds) *Transnational Civil Society: An Introduction* (2006) 101–123 © 2006 Kumarian Press—Reproduced with permission.

Introduction

The three and a half decades between 1957 and 1992 have been called the "formative years of the global environmental era."[1] The period began with the International Geophysical Year (IGY) in 1957, which witnessed a remarkable collaboration between scientists around the globe to produce baseline data on the state of the Earth, including its oceans and atmosphere, as well as its sun. By the time of the United Nations Conference on Environment and Development (UNCED) in 1992, scientists had been joined by official national delegates from countries around the world, including the largest gathering of heads of State ever assembled in one place, all of whom attended for the purpose of negotiating agreements to embody basic principles governing responsible care of the Earth's environment. Beyond the official UNCED participants was a vast penumbra of nongovernmental organizations (NGO), there to champion the interests and groups purportedly underrepresented by the official delegates. These two years serve as useful bookends to a watershed period during which awareness of the effect of human activities on the planet pierced public consciousness worldwide, and the number and scope of international environmental agreements grew at a prodigious rate.[2]

A number of factors have together pushed environmental issues onto the international agenda. Chief among these have been the marked growth in international scientific collaboration (begun during the IGY), which has often generated quality information about the Earth's condition, and an explosion in the number of nongovernmental organizations operating or collaborating on environmental issues whose causes or effects cross national boundaries. Together, these factors have highlighted the gravity of such international environmental issues as acid rain, the depleting ozone layer, global climate change, and loss of biodiversity in the minds of citizens around the world.

This chapter first traces the history of transnational environmentalism. A detailed analysis of two important environmental concerns then highlights the activities of transnational civil society as well as the nature of their role as agenda setters, information providers, and advocates for solutions to these problems. The chapter concludes with an assessment of the fundamental importance of transnational activism in spreading awareness of the impact of human activity on the health of the Earth, and the challenges that activists face in the pursuit of this goal.

History

Transnational environmentalism has used every kind of transnational activity to draw attention to its issues. Science and scientists have played a prominent role in the early history of environmental networks, as they continue to do in existing networks and negotiations on environmental concerns. Nongovernmental organizations, networks, and coalitions have galvanized the public, the media, and governments on numerous environmental issues. The activities of the United Nations and other institutions such as the World Trade Organization have provided important focal points for the development of international networks. And, though themselves largely the result of transnational activity, international conferences and negotiations have also contributed greatly to fostering further transnational connections.

Scientific networks were the first important transnational networks, and their influence remains strong to this day. These "epistemic communities,"[3] whose scientific results are often the first to reveal environmental problems, are credited with helping to raise a number of environmental issues to the international agenda by bringing them to the attention of governments and the public.[4]

The International Council of Scientific Unions (ICSU), whose origins date back to 1919, is an important example of an early transnational network. Over the years, the ICSU has succeeded in attracting funding from its members' home governments, creating a transnational environmental effort spanning sixty-seven participating countries. Most significantly, the ICSU helped to accumulate the data and interpretive knowledge upon which many subsequent actions in global environmental protection were built. The IGY was one of the ICSU's early programs, and its success illustrated the importance of a collaborative and interdisciplinary approach to the gathering of scientific information. The ICSU was largely responsible for building and encouraging transnational networks on environmental issues, while the IGY stimulated research that might not otherwise have been conducted by enabling extensive cooperation among scientists and generating enthusiasm for a wide range of scientific studies on the state of the Earth.[5] Along with the ICSU, the International Union for the Conservation of Nature and Natural Resources (IUCN) and the Friends of the Earth (FOE) were active participants at the 1972 United Nations Conference on Human Development, commonly known as the Stockholm Conference in recognition of its host city. Both organizations are part of what the IUCN, a transnational network of NGOs, calls a "green web" of partnerships on environmental issues.[6]

Early international cooperation on environmental issues did not attract widespread attention from other nongovernmental actors, though naturalists and conservationists were active in seeking agreements to protect certain aspects of it—for instance, wildlife.[7] Nongovernmental organizations made their presence felt for the first time at the Stockholm Conference by being "involved in the preparations for Stockholm [and sending] official observers to the Conference."[8] This conference was a watershed event in the development of international environmental politics. Where the IGY had laid the foundation for international exchange of scientific information on the state of the environment, the Stockholm Conference now spurred an era of greater political awareness of international environmental issues.

The Stockholm Conference produced a strong legacy of collective action. Of the 463 international environmental treaties negotiated over the past 120 years, the vast majority—roughly two-thirds of the total—date from after the Stockholm Conference.[9] This conference articulated a plan of action for the environment and also established the United Nations Environment

Programme (UNEP), a new UN agency intended to serve henceforth as the primary focal point for coordinating international responses to environmental issues. The formation of many national environmental ministries or agencies also dates from this time.[10]

During the Stockholm Conference, an official parallel conference called the Environment Forum was set up as a venue where NGOs could discuss issues of common concern.[11] The Environment Forum also arranged "lectures, exhibits, parades, and engaged in other attention-gathering activities, which were covered in the world press."[12] NGOs cooperated with each other to start *ECO*, a daily report on the proceedings of the conference that was distributed to NGOs and government delegates. Today, *ECO* still serves as an important means of communication between networks of environmental NGOs and delegates at international environmental negotiations. Since Stockholm, parallel conferences have become a common feature of international conferences, environmental or otherwise.

Influences and Changing Agendas

The rise in international cooperation on the environment has occurred alongside the growth of myriad transnational connections between scientists, governments and their agencies, businesses, NGOs dealing with other issues, and individual citizens. Scientists and NGOs, and, later, governments played key roles in encouraging the earliest of these connections. Businesses and individual citizens have since followed suit, and have been of influence themselves.

Environmental awareness grew during the 1970s mainly in the developed countries, where issues like those raised by Rachel Carson in *Silent Spring* and a focus on local concerns involving pollution, wildlife, and nuclear power spawned domestic environmental regulation. This new awareness of environmental issues spurred a growth in environmental organizations. These groups were initially focused on local and "visible" environmental problems, including "cleaner rivers, less air pollution, the closing down of a nuclear plant or polluting factory."[13]

ECO: An Example of Transnational Environmentalism

Since its debut at the Stockholm Conference in 1972, *ECO* has sought to provide participants of climate conferences with updates on the negotiations and the issues affecting them. As well as being distributed to the press, delegates, and NGOs by hand every morning, fast electronic distribution by fax and e-mail makes it possible to distribute *ECO* to a large unseen audience around the world. Fax copies are sent daily to six distribution nodes in Australia, Brazil, Belgium, Kenya, the United Kingdom, and the United States, from where they are faxed on in turn to other organizations, newspapers, national government representatives, and decision makers. It is also faxed directly to twenty-five World Wide Fund for Nature (WWF) organizations.

The 1980s saw a significant rise in awareness of a wide range of environmental issues among the media and the public, and during this period transnational environmentalism grew by leaps and bounds. Environmental organizations, particularly those in the developed countries, began to focus their attention on global environmental issues such as acid rain, the depletion of the ozone layer, and global warming; trans-boundary issues such as trade in hazardous waste; and threats to endangered species worldwide.

Scientific networks, organizational alliances, and other coordinated organizational movements helped to propel environmental issues onto the international agenda during this period.

By identifying problems that merited attention and urgent action, transnational alliances and scientific and other nongovernmental networks played an important role in highlighting the beleaguered state of the environment. Transnational alliances in many cases also provided other services: they contributed to the development of policy recommendations, identified stakeholders, and highlighted how policy change benefited, or at least lessened the damage to, the environment. These services often assisted in the formation and cohesion of coalitions of countries by helping them achieve a consensus on issues, with high attendant informational benefits.[14] Large transnational environmental organizations (WWF, Greenpeace, and IUCN, for example) developed strategies for spreading environmental concerns worldwide and played a crucial role in promoting transnational coalitions and networks.

By the 1980s, the environmental movement had spread to the developing countries as well, and with this came an understanding of the close ties between the environment and social development, and political and economic opportunity, particular to the Third World. *Our Common Future*, a report published by the World Commission on Environment and Development (created in 1983 and popularly known as the Brundtland Commission) drew direct connections between environmental and developmental issues, citing for the first time the need for "sustainable development" as a goal for the international community.[15]

The tremendous rise in media, public, and government attention on environmental issues culminated in 1992, when the international community gathered in Rio de Janeiro for the United Nations Conference on Environment and Development. Generally referred to as the Earth Summit, this meeting attracted over one hundred heads of State and more than fifteen hundred accredited NGOs. The culmination of a five-year preparatory process, the Earth Summit achieved five international agreements: the Framework Convention on Climate Change (FCCC), the Convention on Biological Diversity (CBD), a declaration on sustainable development entitled Agenda 21, the Rio Declaration on Environment and Development, and an effort to address forest resources in the Forest Principles.

The Earth Summit was a momentous event for environmental organizations worldwide. The NGOs actively participated at all levels throughout the preparatory process and indeed the entire duration of the conference, speaking and submitting written statements at the various forums. Furthermore, many of them served on national delegations to the conference, as governments valued them as an important source of information and experience.

This level of participation was greater than that at any previous international conference.[16] Transnational environmentalism had not up till then taken the form of a vast coordinated movement; the activities of the NGOs at the Earth Summit arguably represented a unique moment for transnational environmentalism, and the enthusiasm and idealism this generated continued to resonate for some time there-after, fueling hope that the environment would receive greater attention worldwide. A large number of NGOs also came together at the Global Forum, the parallel NGO conference, and produced "people's treaties": thirty-nine alternative treaties in nine different issue areas ranging from consumption and poverty to marine and biodiversity protection. The NGOs declared that:

> We, the people of the world, will mobilize the forces of transnational civil society behind a widely shared agenda that bonds our many social movements in pursuit of just, sustainable, and participatory human societies. In so doing, we are forging our own instruments and processes for redefining the nature and meaning of human progress and for transforming those institutions that no longer respond to our needs.[17]

The Earth Summit brought together diverse environmental organizations with concerns ranging from development to the rights of indigenous people and women. Agenda 21, a major component of government resolutions at the Earth Summit, also reflected a broader environmental agenda. Women's organizations mobilized in advance of the Earth Summit and developed the Women's Action Agenda 21. They successfully lobbied for the recognition of the role of women in the environmental arena and the importance of their participation in achieving the aims of the Earth Summit. Chapter 24 of the Rio Declaration directly addresses the role of women in sustainable development.

The decade since the Earth Summit has witnessed a marked deceleration in environmental achievements at the international level. After the great promise of the 1980s, "both public attention to global environmental risks and the rate of production of new international conventions [has] dropped off from its Rio peak."[18] There have been notable achievements, such as the 1997 Kyoto Protocol of the Framework Convention on Climate Change aimed at reducing emissions contributing to global climate change, but, in the main, many of the issues raised at Rio have remained unaddressed, particularly those concerned with ensuring that economic development is environmentally sustainable.

In 2002, the United Nations again sponsored a major meeting of governmental and nongovernmental representatives at the World Summit on Sustainable Development in Johannesburg, South Africa, to review and revise the issues raised in the Agenda 21. The Johannesburg Conference attempted to develop plans of action to alleviate poverty worldwide while promoting environmentally sustainable development practices,[19] but did not generate the same degree of enthusiasm or commitment. It is too early to judge the success of the Johannesburg Conference in attempting to revive some of the goals of the Earth Summit; however, it did mark a new high-water mark in participation by business interests, such as Alcan and HSBC, much to the dismay of some environmental NGOs, who saw these interests as potential competitors for influence and direct opponents to their environmental aims.[20]

The Problems of Definition and Structure

Environmental issues vary a great deal. The problems may be local (drinking water contamination), trans-boundary (air pollution), or truly global (ozone depletion). They may involve just two countries or fifty. They may involve use of common resources (fisheries) or private land (biodiversity), or renewable (timber) and nonrenewable (oil) resources. The issues may be those of preservation (whaling agreements), conservation (debt-for-nature swaps),[21] sustainability, or development. They may be issues primarily for developed countries (acid rain) or those that largely concern developing countries (tropical deforestation). Governments, NGOs, or industry may spearhead solutions to problems. Environmental issues may be presented in ethical terms—harm to nature or humans—or as problems that involve market failure or economic disincentives. This great variation in the environmental ambit gives rise to different constellations of interests, and means that one environmental perspective and an accompanying unified movement are unlikely to arise. Moreover, as one scholar of global environmental movements has observed, the diversity of circumstances between the liberal, developed democracies and the developing countries means that environmental concerns and discourses are unlikely to be "universally appropriate or accepted."[22] As discussed below, a developing country's environmental concerns are more likely to be rooted in local needs, and those related to economic development and sustainability, rather than in the conservation ideals that drove early environmental action in the West. In addition, conflicts have emerged between developed and developing countries over the responsibility for solving existing environmental problems, funding the implementation of obligations, and even the relative importance of particular environmental issues.

Transnational coordination and cooperation can be divided into three broad categories: transnational networks, coalitions, and movements. Transnational networks are common in the international environmental arena, coalitions less so, and movements characterized by mass mobilization and coordinated tactics even rarer. Scientific and advocacy networks are easily identified in a wide range of issues, and many effective transnational coalitions have emerged in a number of issue areas. However, the great variation in environmental concerns, along with a fundamental division in outlook between the developing and developed countries, has prevented a unified environmental movement from emerging. Nevertheless, transnational organizations have been important contributors to the success of various campaigns in developing countries. Local environmental organizations pair with transnational organizations (such as Greenpeace or WWF) to bring issues to the global stage. An example of this is the reform of funding considerations by the World Bank for development projects: in the late 1980s, for example, a transnational campaign halted a development project in Brazil's rainforest and brought environmental and social considerations into the World Bank's decision-making process. Transnational coalitions "clos[ed] the circle between the highest levels of public international finance, the Brazilian national government, and local concerns. It was a novel form of international political action, linking formerly isolated constituencies."[23]

The Role of Nongovernmental Organizations

While IUCN and FOE were joined by nearly two hundred NGOs at Stockholm, nearly fifteen hundred NGOs were accredited to the Earth Summit at Rio de Janeiro in 1992.[24] These and other NGOs have over the years engaged with growing frequency in transnational campaigns to raise awareness of environmental issues worldwide, lobby governments, and provide information and expertise on international environmental issues to governments, international institutions, and the public. Their participation in international environmental negotiations as well as their contribution to the implementation and monitoring of international environmental agreements is now well documented.[25]

Though it is difficult to measure the magnitude and form of their influence, NGOs are certainly considered to have played an important role in raising a general awareness of international environmental issues and persuading governments to negotiate agreements and protocols to address these concerns. Several major transnational organizations have been crucial to the dissemination of environmental concerns and action. The IUCN, FOE, the WWF, and Greenpeace have grown into large and wealthy organizations with a truly global reach. These organizations form important constituent parts of the green web, whose aim is to influence the opinions and actions of governments, international institutions, the public, and even other NGOs.

The structures and strategies of these NGOs shed some light on the roles and influences these organizations have had on international environmental issues, and explicate the array of organizations, strategies, and tactics that shape the broad outlines of environmental transnationalism. These organizations (along with many others) have contributed to the spread of environmental awareness worldwide through a variety of strategies. The IUCN exercises its influence most notably through its dissemination of high-quality information about the state of the Earth's environment, and through its direct involvement in implementing conservation plans rather than through coordinated tactics or social mobilization. The work of its largest commission, the Species Survival Commission, has contributed immensely to international conservation efforts. For example, the IUCN maintains a "Red List" of threatened species of living organisms, which has long been an essential reference both for governments and NGOs involved in the conservation of biodiversity. The IUCN has also been active in a wide range of other environmental issues of international importance, including climate change, trade in endangered species, and sustainable development.

Greenpeace engages in direct action worldwide, using its members to protest against what they perceive to be objectionable practices by blocking whaling vessels, hanging banners on prominent buildings, chaining themselves to trees, and other such maneuvers. The aim of these highly publicized actions is to "induce people to engage in ... environmentally sound practices."[26] In addition to influencing the cessation of nuclear testing in Alaska and French Polynesia, Green-peace has been actively involved in campaigns to end whaling and the indiscriminate dumping of toxic waste as well as in highlighting the hazards of acid rain, ozone depletion, and climate change.

FOE's strategy is to focus its attention on the activities of States in the international arena in an effort to make them "more accountable to environmental protection." FOE lobbies governments and tries to "corner states into environmentally sound behavior."[27] It does this by working at the local level (by persuading local municipalities to adopt Earth-friendly policies) while simultaneously applying pressure at the national level through international organizations (by participating in delegations to environmental negotiations). It also monitors whether States are complying with the international agreements signed by them, and generates potentially embarrassing publicity in the event of a State's noncompliance. FOE's sphere of activity has included transnational campaigns to pressure States to comply with the International Convention for the Regulation of Whaling, restrictions in the emission of chemicals that cause acid rain and ozone depletion, and protection of tropical rainforests. It has also organized networks of NGOs to lobby against multilateral banks, including the World Bank and the International Monetary Fund, organizations long seen as ignoring the environmental consequences of development projects.[28]

The WWF has always focused its efforts on the preservation of biodiversity. Its initiatives have included protecting tropical forests, promoting the establishment of marine sanctuaries, and protecting flora and fauna on the verge of extinction, such as its own symbol, the giant panda. Its strategies tend to be less confrontational than those of Greenpeace or FOE; rather than criticize the international trade system as a whole, the WWF has long supported working within that system to minimize its effects on biodiversity. To that end, is has been a strong proponent of TRAFFIC (Trade Records Analysis of Fauna and Flora in Commerce), a body created by the IUCN to monitor trade in endangered species and the products derived from these.[29] By focusing campaigns around "charismatic mega-fauna" like tigers, elephants, sea turtles, and whales, it has pioneered effective techniques for raising public awareness of, and money for, conservation issues. In recent years, the WWF campaigns have extended into additional environmental issues such as ozone depletion and climate change.

While environmental activism originated almost exclusively in the developed world, there is now increasing participation in local and transnational environmentalism from the developing world, and particularly in Latin America and Asia.[30] Alliances with large transnational environmental organizations have helped in the development and propagation of environmental groups in this region. Their campaigns are generally not limited to conservation or preservation concerns, and often encompass wider issues such as demands for social justice or economic reforms. They attract their supporters from rural areas and include young people, and particularly women.[31] The presence of Third World environmental organizations in the international arena has helped to reinforce the focus on sustainable development, explore funding mechanisms for developing nations, and, interestingly, to bring environmental concerns back to the local level by putting developing-country concerns for clean water, sanitation, and food also on the international agenda.

Ozone Depletion

Scientific collaborations to study the problem of ozone depletion accelerated in the 1980s with the discovery in 1985 of the ozone hole above the Antarctic. As scientific consensus began to coalesce around the severity of the damage being done to the ozone layer, the transnational network of scientists originally formed just to study the phenomenon began to expand its role into a crucial disseminator of scientific information.

Networks of scientists were able to provide not only critically important scientific theories and empirical discoveries but also to achieve scientific consensus: "The best scientists and the most advanced technological resources had to be brought together in a cooperative effort to build an international scientific consensus."[32]

Transnational coalitions of environmental organizations also played a role in mobilizing interest and action on the ozone issue. Environmental organizations in the United States swung into action from the early 1980s on, with the crucial support of industry and the US government.[33] Since European environmental organizations were showing little interest at the time the "[US] State Department encouraged American environmental organizations to motivate their European counterparts to offset the influence of industry."[34] Greenpeace and FOE, so often adversarial in their relationships with the US government, were especially effective in alerting European environmental organizations to the threat of ozone depletion. By 1988, British environmental organizations were not only mobilizing public support but were also pressing for parliamentary hearings to discuss the threat.[35] In September 1987, twenty-four countries, along with the Commission of the European Communities, signed the Montreal Protocol on Substances That Deplete the Ozone Layer.

Climate Change

Although extensive scientific observation of the earth's climate began after the 1952 IGY, and crucial observations of atmospheric CO_2 began in 1958, not until the mid-1980s did fears over changing climate patterns explode onto the international environment agenda. In 1985, relying for their material on a scientific assessment of global climate change authored by the SCOPE (Scientific Committee on Problems of the Environment) committee of the ICSU, a group of scientists at an international gathering in Villach, Austria, determined that "substantial warming" of the Earth's surface was likely to occur as a result of significant increases in the concentration of CO_2 in the atmosphere. It further noted that these increases "were attributable to human activities," and noted that the problem of "global warming" merited urgent international political attention.[36]

Acting as a transnational coalition, this group drew considerable attention to issues of global climate change in policy-making circles by conveying its conclusions to home governments, and urging governments worldwide to heed its warnings. It stressed the need for dissemination of information about greenhouse gases (i.e., gases such as CO_2 that can cause global warming) and called for further scientific research into the issue. The 1988 Toronto Conference on the Changing Atmosphere gathered together scientists and government delegates to discuss the evidence for global climate change and what actions could be taken to reverse it. This conference prompted the establishment of the Intergovernmental Panel on Climate Change (IPCC), consisting of a group of about three hundred climate scientists from around the world who were given the task of

⇨

reviewing and disseminating scientific information on global climate change. In addition, the governments of many industrialized countries represented at the Toronto Conference voluntarily committed themselves to reducing their emissions of greenhouse gases by 20 percent by 2005. The text of the Framework Convention for Climate Change was adopted in 1992, and the Convention itself entered into force on March 21, 1994. The Kyoto Protocol of 1997 established specific, binding targets for reductions in emissions of greenhouse gases.

Two Case Studies: Ozone Depletion and Climate Change

An analysis of two major international environmental issues illustrates the achievements and limitations of the roles of transnational networks, coalitions, and movements. Epistemic communities, which fall within the category of transnational networks, have been instrumental in catalyzing action on these two environmental issues. Networks of scientists were integral to developing agendas, providing essential information to countries and NGOs involved in negotiations, and suggesting remedies to the underlying environmental problems. Supported as they were by these networks, environmental NGOs were able to close the circle on ozone depletion by spurring agreement on the means of reducing emissions of ozone-destroying substances.

The case of ozone depletion is one that also highlights the importance of the influence of governments and industry in moving the issue forward. Success in this case may not be entirely ascribed to the role of transnational environmentalism. It is axiomatic that economic considerations play a crucial role in whether and to what extent industry and governments support environmental issues. In this case, it was in the interests of a US industrial giant, DuPont, to promote international limits on chlorofluorocarbons (CFC), the ozone-destroying substance present in widely used products like refrigerators and aerosol cans; they were already facing a domestic ban in the United States and held a significant lead in the development of CFC substitutes. While scientific consensus and transnational civil society concerns may have been a condition precedent to the Vienna Agreement in 1985 and the Montreal Protocol in 1987, the strong support of industry and the US government contributed significantly to these agreements becoming a reality.

The process has been similar for global climate change, but the outcome not nearly as successful. Transnational environmentalism has been present in the case of climate change, but limits on the development of a consensus, and the activity of significant industry interests against action to reduce carbon dioxide (CO_2), have contributed to a slower progress. The effort to prevent or reduce global climate change has become a highly contentious international environmental issue.

As awareness of the dangers of climate change spread in the wake of the Toronto Conference of 1988, many environmental NGOs and industry groups readied their strategies to deal with the problem. By 1990, eighty-eight NGOs were in attendance at the second World Climate Conference in Geneva, held to pave the way for an international climate change treaty.[37] By 1991, FOE had developed a strong campaign to combat global climate change. Greenpeace also pursued several simultaneous climate change strategies: First, it attempted to mobilize countries predicted to suffer the worst damage from global warming, especially low-elevation island States at risk from rising sea levels, and African States at risk from accelerated desertification. Second, it sought to politicize the issue among citizens and governments of the industrialized countries that formed the Organization for Economic Cooperation and Development (OECD). Third, by attempting to interpret scientific information itself so as to highlight the possible adverse effects of climate change and the "high-risk side of science," it tried to highlight the immediacy of the problem in contrast to the more neutral and balanced analysis of the IPCC.[38] In 1995, Greenpeace International alone spent USD 4.35 million on its climate campaign, making it the third most expensive protest campaign after antinuclear and disarmament issues.[39]

The Toronto Conference catalyzed the formation of the Climate Action Network (CAN), a transnational network of environmental NGOs. CAN is an important example of such a network and thus merits detailed attention. CAN was created in March 1989 with the purpose of strengthen[ing] communication and co-ordination with respect to:

1. information exchanges on science, policy, and events such as intergovernmental meetings concerning the greenhouse effect;
2. attendance at and preparation for relevant intergovernment and other meetings, including prior circulation of draft position-statements;
3. facilitating national effort through the sharing of expertise and information between network members; and
4. stimulating joint or simultaneous actions where appropriate.[40]

Originally established by twenty NGOs, CAN now has a membership of 287 NGOs and regional offices in Africa, Europe, Latin America, North America, South Asia, and Southeast Asia.[41] CAN has assumed the role of an umbrella organization for NGOs concerned with the climate change issue: the founders of CAN describe it as a "transnational system of information, communication, and coordination. "[42]

The similarities and differences between the two campaigns against ozone depletion and climate change are instructive. Especially during the early years of climate change as an international environmental issue, NGOs from developed countries (developed NGOs) largely viewed participation by NGOs from developing countries (developing NGOs) as a useful reinforcement to their demands on governments in their own industrialized countries. Such cooperation was seen as helpful because it demonstrated worldwide support for reductions of greenhouse gas emissions. However, the presence of these developing NGOs may have actually complicated rather than aided the effectiveness of the developed NGOs' message on this issue, because a schism soon emerged between the goals pursued by these two types of NGOs. Rather than being confronted by a united NGO position on global climate change, country representatives heard instead a cacophony of positions, wherein aims often differed from region to region. This stood in stark contrast to the relatively united stand articulated by transnational networks of climate scientists such as the IPCC.

Although NGOs did manage to champion a set of expectations and goals that came to dominate rhetoric about the overall targets for reductions in emissions of CO2, they achieved few consensus positions. The areas in which NGOs had the most difficulty in reaching unanimity often involved national policy choices that would have imposed significant costs or benefits on particular countries, regions, or interest groups within them. Even today, a consensus among NGOs on certain issues at the international level may be impossible: "NGOs from different parts of the world will always hold different views and different predilections for action based on their own individual and national interests."[43] Often, there is no concord even among NGOs within the same country. These constraints on the development of a universal agreement limit the extent of the transnationality of their message as well as the extent to which CAN could be considered anything more than a transnational network.[44] In contrast, ozone depletion was an issue in which the scientific evidence was relatively clear, and the solution uncontroversial.

Attempts to bring about legislation to retard climate change were also limited by interests that mobilized against elements of the climate agreement. The Global Climate Coalition (GCC), an organization of private companies and business/trade associations representing more than 230,000 firms (many from the fossil-fuel industry), was established in 1989 to coordinate participation by business interests in the science and policy debates on climate change. The GCC then represented industry at Rio, and spent USD 13 million in an advertising campaign to oppose the Framework Convention on Climate Change. Again in contrast, influential industrial actors, such as DuPont, supported international action to ban ozone-depleting substances, in part because they already faced domestic regulation and desired a level playing field internationally.

Challenges

As noted above, international interest in environmental issues seems to have peaked in the 1990s; little progress towards concrete international action has been made in the years since the Earth Summit. The United States has recently sought to roll back its obligations to the Montreal Protocol, and has refused to sign the Kyoto Protocol (though Russia has ratified it, bringing it into effect in spite of US hesitation). Current international priorities center around security issues; these developments in domestic and international politics mean that it will be difficult to introduce or keep environmental issues on the international agenda.

Scientific inquiry will be crucial to the future of transnational environmental action, as scientific evidence that human activity has an effect on the environment has, time and again, spurred international agreement. In a number of issue areas, scientific networks have been even more important than those concerned with advocacy: the Intergovernmental Panel on Climate Change has helped to clarify the importance of international agreement to reduce CO_2 emissions, for example. Future research may reveal evidence of environmental fragility that is too compelling to ignore. Anti-environmental interests have already mobilized in a number of issue areas. Such activity might be expected to increase as environmental considerations become increasingly influential. To combat this, transnational organizations will need to broaden and deepen their own transnational networks, and more effectively bridge internal divides—such as those between Northern and Southern perspectives on environmental priorities. They will also have to work with business and other interests to incorporate environmental concerns into business practices. This is not as difficult as it seems: despite strong and deep opposition from the fossil-fuel industry to acknowledge that climate change was an issue of real concern, concern for the environment has penetrated several companies. British Petroleum (BP), for example, has turned its attention to the development of cleaner fuel and has sought to reduce emissions in its own operations; "Beyond Petroleum" is its slogan in television advertisements. In 1998, BP joined the World Resources Institute in an initiative to combat climate change.[45] As seen from the ozone-depletion case, alliances between business and environmental organizations may serve to advance environmental aims in the future.

In an international climate that may be less hospitable to environmental issues in and of themselves, linkages between the environment and other issues have also become very important. Environmental side-agreements and provisions for environmental protection have been integrated into international agreements, particularly those concerning trade. This may be a fruitful way to ensure that the environment does not disappear from the international agenda. The North American Free Trade Agreement, as well as the European Union and the World Trade Organization, all provide for overseeing mechanisms and cooperation for addressing environmental concerns. At another level, however, these institutions also present challenges for transnational environmentalism as their missions are not primarily environmental; critics fear that the pursuit of global free trade will have environmental consequences, and tensions have developed when environmental considerations have clashed with the ideals of barrier-free trade. The WTO (and its predecessor GATT) have ruled against environmental concerns in two well-known cases.[46] Whether environmental considerations will ever prevail remains to be seen.

Conclusion

Consciousness of international environmental issues has increased markedly among both governments and their citizens over the last quarter of a century. In large part, this reflects the political globalism practiced by transnational networks of scientists such as the ICSU, and by NGOs such as WWF, Greenpeace, and FOE, that has lifted environmental issues to the top of the international agenda by mobilizing both the citizenry and high-level officials in nations around the world.

There is little doubt that vast transnational networks have contributed in myriad ways to species conservation, biodiversity protection, pollution prevention, and the ecological health and integrity of the Earth. Transnational networks and the communication they foster have served to provide information to citizens, organizations, and governments worldwide on the full range of environmental issues. This green web has supplied information and inspired action: in some instances, transnational networks and coalitions, by bringing unified pressure for environmental action to bear, have been able to change the practices of government, industry, and international institutions. As the current crop of international environmental issues continues to evolve and new issues arise, the participation of transnational networks and coalitions will likely continue to increase.

Notes

1. The Social Learning Group, *Learning to Manage Global Environmental Risks*, 2 vols. (Cambridge, MA: MIT Press, 2001), 1:3.
2. Multilateral treaties that could be broadly construed as environmental, in the sense that they dealt with transnational efforts to manage or protect wildlife, date as far back as the 1880s (for example, the Regulation of Salmon Fishery in the Rhine River Basin [Berlin], 1885) . Several treaties were signed before 1945, including the Convention for the Protection of Birds Useful to Agriculture (Paris, 1902); North Pacific Fur Seal Treaty (1911); Convention for the Regulation of Whaling (Geneva, 1931); Convention Relative to the Preservation of Fauna and Flora in Their Natural State (London, 1933).
3. This term was articulated for environmental politics by Peter Haas in *Saving the Mediterranean* (New York: Columbia University Press, 1990), 18. See chap. 2 in particular.
4. The Social Learning Group has documented the pioneering role of science in highlighting international environmental issues. It tracked the coverage of three atmospheric areas of concern—acid rain, ozone depletion, and climate change—in *Nature*, a leading international scientific journal, and Reuters World Newswire. Coverage of all three issues peaked in scientific circles prior to the same concerns being voiced in the popular press. Social Learning Group, *Learning to Manage Global Environmental Risks*, 1:27.
5. Currently known as the International Council for Science, ICSU has over one hundred constituent members, including individual scientific unions and other scientific organizations. Academy of Sciences, www.nas.edu/history/igy/ (accessed January 7, 2004); J. Eric Smith, "The Role of Special Purpose and Nongovernmental Organizations in the Environmental Crisis," *International Organization* 26, no. 2 (1972): 308.

6. International Union for the Conservation of Nature, "Welcome to IUCN—World Conservation Union," www.iucn.org/about/index.htm (accessed September 1, 2004).

7. Margaret E. Keck and Kathryn Sikkink, *Activists beyond Borders: Advocacy Networks in International Politics* (Ithaca, NY: Cornell University Press, 1998), 122.

8. Anne Thompson Feraru, "Transnational Political Interests and the Global Environment," *International Organization* 28, no. 1 (1974): 32.

9. Program of the Center for International Earth Science Information Network (the Socioeconomic Data and Applications Center, database 1885–2004), www.ciesin.columbia. edu/ (accessed September 1, 2004).

10. Michael Grubb, Matthias Koch, Abby Munson, Francis Sullivan, and Koy Thomson, *The Earth Summit Agreements: A Guide and Assessment* (London: Earthscan, 1993) .

11. Two unofficial parallel conferences were also set up: the Peoples Forum and Dai Dong. These were more radical in nature than the Environment Forum, and were inspired, in part, by opposition to the Vietnam War. See P. Haas, M. Levy, and T. Parson, "Appraising the Earth Summit: How Should We Judge UNCED's Success?" *Environment* 34, no. 8 (1992): 6–11, 26–33.

12. Feraru, "Transnational Political Interests," 48.

13. Hein-Anton van der Heijden, "Environmental Movements, Ecological Modernisation and Political Opportunity Structures," in *Environmental Movements: Local, National and Global*, ed. Christopher Rootes, 199–221 (London and Portland, OR: Frank Cass, 1999), 202.

14. There are many accounts of the role of transnational environmentalism in influencing local practice, government policies, and international agreements. See, for instance, M. Finger, "The Ivory Trade Ban: NGOs and International Conservation," in *Environmental NGOs in World Politics: Linking the Local and the Global*, ed. T. Princen and M. Finger, 121–59 (London: Routledge, 1994), for an account on the ivory trade; Keck and Sikkink, *Activists beyond Borders*, for tropical deforestation; B. Rich, *Mortgaging the Earth: The World Bank, Environmental Impoverishment, and the Crisis of Development* (Boston: Beacon Press, 1994), for World Bank reform; M. J. Peterson, "Whalers, Cetologists, Environmentalists, and the International Management of Whaling," *International Organization* 46, no. 1 (1992): 147–86, for whaling; and J. P. Manno, "Advocacy and Diplomacy: NGOs and the Great Lakes H2O Quality Agreement," in *Environmental NGOs in World Politics: Linking the Local and the Global*, ed. T. Princen and M. Finger, 69–120 (London: Routledge, 1994), for trans-boundary air pollution.

15. G. Brundtland, ed., *Our Common Future: The World Commission on Environment and Development* (Oxford: Oxford University Press, 1987), 16.

16. Grubb et al., *The Earth Summit Agreements*, 44.

17. The NGO Alternative Treaties, "People's Earth Declaration," article 23, habitat.igc.org/ treaties/ (accessed November 14, 2004).

18. Social Learning Group, *Learning to Manage*, 1:25.

19. United Nations Johannesburg Summit 2002, www.johannesburgsummit.org/html/basic_ info/basicinfo.html (accessed November 14, 2004).

20. "The Bubble-and-Squeak Summit," *The Economist*, September 4, 2002.

21. An example of a debt-for-nature swap is the purchase by a nongovernmental organization of discounted foreign debt followed by the forgiveness of that debt in exchange for conservation activity.

22. Christopher Rootes, "Environmental Movements from the Local to the Global," in *Environmental Movements: Local, National and Global*, ed. Christopher Rootes, 1–12 (London and Portland, OR: Frank Cass, 1999), 6.

23. Rich, *Mortgaging the Earth*, 132.
24. A. Doherty, "The Role of Nongovernmental Organizations in UNCED," in *Negotiating International Regimes: Lessons Learned from the United Nations Conference on Environment and Development*, ed. Bertram I. Spector, Gunnar Sjostedt, and I. William Zartman, 199–218 (London: Graham and Trotman, 1994), 199.
25. See, among many others, Princen and Finger, *Environmental NGOs in World Politics*; and K. Raustiala, "States, NGOs, and International Environmental Institutions," *International Studies Quarterly* 41, no. 4 (1997): 719–40.
26. P. Wapner, *Environmental Activism and World Civic Politics* (Albany: State University of New York Press, 1996), 14.
27. Ibid., 15, 126.
28. Ibid., 118; Also see Robert Lamb, *Promising the Earth* (London and New York: Routledge, 1996), 134.
29. World Wide Fund for Nature, www.panda.org/about_wwf/ who_we_are/history/ seventies.cfm (accessed November 14, 2004).
30. Jeff Haynes, "Power, Politics and Environmental Movements in the Third World," in *Environmental Movements: Local, National and Global*, ed. Christopher Rootes, 222–42 (London and Portland, OR: Frank Cass, 1999), 223.
31. Ibid., 223.
32. Richard Benedick, *Ozone Diplomacy: New Directions in Safeguarding the Planet* (Cambridge, MA: Harvard University Press, 1991), 5.
33. This support resulted from the development of competitive alternatives to CFCs by an American company, DuPont, whose interests the US government wished to promote. See Scott Barrett, *Environment and Statecraft: The Strategy of Environmental Treaty-Making* (Oxford: Oxford University Press, 2003), 234–35.
34. Benedick, *Ozone Diplomacy*, 27.
35. Ibid., 114.
36. International Council of Scientific Unions, United Nations Environment Programme and World Meteorological Organization, *Report of the International Conference on the Assessment of the Role of Carbon Dioxide and of Other Greenhouse Gases in Climate Variations and Associated Impacts*, WMO document no. 661 (Geneva: WMO, 1986).
37. J. Jaeger and H. L. Ferguson, eds., *Climate Change: Science, Impacts and Policy: Proceedings of the Second World Climate Conference* (Cambridge: Cambridge University Press, 1990).
38. Bill Hare, Greenpeace International policy director, interview with Wendy E. Franz, February 27, 1997, Bonn; Greenpeace International, *Climate Campaign Archives 1990–1997*. Notes on file with the authors.
39. Greenpeace International, *Annual Report*, 1995.
40. Climate Action Network Charter, working document, dated March 12, 1989.
41. Climate Action Network, "What Does CAN Hope to Achieve," www.climatenework.org/ pages/aboutCANInt.html (accessed November 13, 2004).
42. A. Roncerel and Navroz Dubash, "Needs, Challenges and Opportunities for Environmental Action: The Case of Climate Action Network," paper presented at a workshop on *The New Europe Conference: Opportunities for Foundations*, Paris, July 9, 1992.
43. A. Rahman and A. Roncerel, "A View from the Ground Up," in *Negotiating Climate Change: The Inside Story of the Rio Convention*, ed. Irving M. Mintzer and J. Amber Leonard, 239–72 (Cambridge: Cambridge University Press, 1994), 248.
44. Wendy E. Franz, *Changing the Climate? Non-State Actors in International Environmental Politics* (doctoral dissertation, Harvard University, 2000).

45. British Petroleum, "Environment and Society," www.bp.com (accessed September 1, 2004).

46. United States Restrictions on Imports of Tuna, August 16, 1991, GATT BISD (39th Supp.) at 1SS (1993), 30 ILM 1594 (1991) [commonly known as Tuna/Dolphin I]; and GATT Dispute Settlement Panel Report on United States' Restrictions on Imports of Tuna, 33 ILM 839 (1994) [commonly known as Tuna/Dolphin II].

CHAPTER FOURTEEN

Transnational Policy Networks and the Role of Advocacy Scientists: From Ozone Layer Protection to Climate Change

Reiner Grundmann

Source: Frank Biermann, Rainer Brohm and Klaus Dingwerth (eds) *Proceedings of the 2001 Berlin Conference on the Human Dimensions of Global Environmental Change "Global Environmental Change and the Nation State"* (Potsdam Institute for Climate Impact Research: 2002) 405–414 © 2002 Reiner Grundmann—Reproduced with permission.

International regulations for the protection of the ozone layer seem to be effective. The Montreal Protocol (MP) is a much celebrated success story in international environmental policy making, and rightly so. The Montreal Protocol served as a role model and trigger for the climate change dispute. Regarding the environmental threat posed by climate change and ozone depletion and their public perception, it has been observed that 'the ozone hole has arrived as a concept in the US public's consciousness, but the greenhouse effect is entering primarily as a subset of the ozone hole phenomenon, the closest model available[1] (Kempton et al. 1995). But so far, climate change negotiations have not quite moved onto a similar path of successful environmental governance. To be sure, the failure of reaching an agreement in The Hague in November 2000 was followed by a compromise in Bonn in July 2001 and further progress in Marrakech. However, the fact that the United States has withdrawn from the Kyoto Protocol highlights the serious obstacles that climate change policy faces. Comparing the landmark agreement of the Montreal Protocol with the Kyoto Process, the latter pales in effectiveness.[2] What are the reasons? There is a preliminary and obvious answer. As one commentator put it, 'perhaps one reason why expectations were so high [in the climate change case] is the success of negotiating the Montreal Protocol . . . Environmental NGOs and negotiators moved from ozone to climate change, many of them expecting the second shot to be much like the first one' (Ted Hanisch quoted in Rowlands 1995: 259). But is that all one can say?

From Kyoto to The Hague: Deadlock

After the 1992 Framework Convention on Climate Change (FCCC) was passed in Rio, it took several years before the international community agreed in 1997 to a protocol of binding measures in Kyoto. In the protocol, the industrialised nations pledged that they would by 2008–2012 reduce their emissions of greenhouse gases by 5% based on 1990 levels. The countries with the highest emissions committed themselves to a reduction of 6–8%. This was a starting point which, however, does not yet come close to the range of reductions which would have to be put in place if climate change were to be prevented. According to scientists working with the IPCC, carbon dioxide emissions would have to be cut by more than 60% in order to stabilise climate on present-day levels (Houghton et al. 1990; Wuebbles and Rosenberg 1998).

In the run-up to the Kyoto Protocol the participants found themselves in a deadlock: on the one side were countries willing to take action, on the other were countries against. Among the first group was the EU, among the second countries like the US, Canada, Australia, and Japan (later known as the 'umbrella group') but also developing countries. The opponents of strict regulations used scientific uncertainty as an argument to legitimise their reluctance [2] In Kyoto, a compromise was reached which mandated targets and timetables, leaving the implementation (including "flexible mechanisms") to further talks. In the run-up to the talks in The Hague, the EU and the umbrella group found themselves in a different kind of deadlock (with the developing world standing aside, for the time being): both disagreed about the extent to which flexible mechanisms should be allowed to reduce emissions. At The Hague, EU countries and the United States did not seem to disagree heavily over the reality of human-made climate change and the need of mitigation, but over the best way to achieve this goal, or—to stick with the official language—to maintain the 'integrity of the Kyoto protocol'.[3] The EU accused the umbrella group, especially the United States and Canada, of trying to exploit loopholes. The positions were not based on different scientific models or different orientations in principle: both sides agreed that something had to be done in order to mitigate climate change. It was a matter of agreeing on the appropriate measures where the conflicts arose.[4] Interestingly, the advocates of the environment were divided (as was industry) with some US environmentalists supporting flexible mechanisms (such as carbon trading and reforestation) proposed by their government.[5] On the other side there were more radical environmentalists supporting the position of EU countries who suspected the United States to aim at a cheap deal.

Over the course of the last decade, the US reluctance has wavered between a principled objection to a climate treaty as such and an acceptance of it provided that the perceived burden on the US economy was kept at a moderate level. Presidents Bush Sr. and Jr. exemplify the first position, the Clinton administration the second. Clinton and Gore were expressing clear endorsement of the IPCC recommendations.[6] The problem was that they were held hostage by the US Senate that made it clear before Kyoto that they would not agree to binding greenhouse gas (GFIG) reductions and subsequently did not ratify the Kyoto protocol (Harrison 2000). Therefore, the reluctant approach shown in Kyoto and the insistence on flexible mechanisms by the US delegation in The Hague reflects the fact that the US representatives (the official delegation, but also some environmentalists) think it is in the best interest of their country to use flexible mechanisms because they are cheaper and impose a lighter burden upon the US economy. They fear that a more rigorous approach would meet stiff domestic resistance. The leader of the US delegation in The Hague, Loy, put it this way: 'Nations can only negotiate abroad what they believe they can ratify at home' (The Washington Post 26 November 2000). This raises the question of why the US (at least from a European perspective)[7] was and still is less prepared to commit itself to stringent goals compared to the EU (Grubb 1999; Harrison 2000).

An obvious answer to this is the fact that US citizens have become accustomed to a lifestyle much more energy intensive compared to the rest of the world. Given the contemporary technostructure (fossil-fuel intense), this translates into higher levels of fuel consumption. In fact, per capita emissions of carbon dioxide are among the highest in the US—they are almost five times the global average (only Luxembourg and three small oil-producing countries exceed US per capita carbon emissions).

It would therefore require regulatory efforts on the part of the US government in order to increase energy efficiency. Such measures would probably include taxation which is not going to be very popular. This then raises the next question: why has the build up of public attention in the US been slow and weak? Here I will argue that in contrast to the ozone case, the advocates for regulation did not achieve what they aimed at.

The Role of Public Attention

In order to do so, I shall focus on the work of the IPCC and its effects on the policy process. The argument will be made that the architects of the IPCC may have drawn the wrong lessons from the ozone case. My starting point is a statement from the late Austrian diplomat and negotiator during the talks for the Montreal Protocol, Winfried Lang. He described the confrontation during these negotiations between the (then progressive) US delegation and the (then reluctant) European Community in the following way:

> During the negotiations on the ozone layer it was the US-delegation, which by means of continuous contacts with the media tried to build up a climate of public expectations which should induce still reluctant delegations (mainly those with EC-membership) to agree to substantial reductions of emissions. Further research will tell us, whether the relatively flexible stance finally adopted by the European Community was brought about by this manipulation of public opinion from the outside or rather by an internal process of rethinking threats and options. (Lang 1994: 175)

The roles have been reversed but we are watching the same play, aren't we? Not exactly, since the EC, for a long time, did not take a leadership role and did not do very much to build up a climate of public expectation. The expectations raised by the media in the ozone case have in fact been much higher in the US than in the EC countries. Taking the example of the German press, in the weeks before the Montreal Protocol was passed there were only two reports on the topic in the German press, compared to eight articles in the *New York Times* alone (Grundmann 2001). Let us see if this correlation between a country's active policy and high expectations in the relevant public sphere[8] also applies to the climate conferences.

Conducting an online database research in Lexis®—Nexis® Executive, I compared media attention about climate change in selected countries (see Table 14.1 for an overview). I limited the search to German, UK and US media attention.[9] The search was performed for the periods leading up to and including major international negotiations: Berlin, 7 March-8 April 1995; Kyoto, 15 November-15 December 1997; The Hague, 1–30 November 2000; Bonn, 1–31 July 2001.[10]

Comparing absolute numbers of media reports in these three countries, US news reports score very high, especially around the Kyoto meeting (see Table 14.1 (1)). However, the numbers of newspapers included in Lexis-Nexis vary across countries. Compared to German sources, US sources are represented at a much higher proportion (by a factor of 20). In order to avoid this imbalance, I calculated the relative values, dividing absolute numbers of news reports by the number of news outlets. Relative data reveal the paramount attention paid by Germany news outlets compared to both the UK and US. However, even this 'correction' of data has to be treated with caution. The Lexis-Nexis database seems to change over time, so it might not be internally consistent (see the Italian and Spanish data in Table 14.1 (1)). Apart from this, it is not clear how frequently the less important papers have reported on the issue. In order to avoid this problem, I reduced the number of press outlets to just one quality broad sheet in each country. Again it appears that the German media rates climate change more newsworthy than the other two countries. Taken together, there were 158 reports in the *FAZ*, 118 in the *FT*, and 83 in the *NYT*. German attention at the Berlin 1995 and Bonn 2001 conferences was far higher compared to the US and UK. Germany hosted these two international climate conferences and is also the home country to the UNFCCC secretariat (neither did the US nor the UK host an international climate conference during this period). Only in the case of the Kyoto and The Hague negotiations did *FAZ*, *FT* and *NYT* report on comparable levels.

If we look specifically at the reporting on these climate summits, and go back to total aggregated data, it emerges again that, apart from Kyoto, German attention was highest throughout. In contrast, US attention was low at the time of the Berlin conference, then rose for Kyoto, only to fall off for The Hague and Bonn. If we look at the establishment press, the *FAZ* dwarfs both *FT* and *NYT*—the *NYT* did not pay any attention to Bonn (for reasons of consistency I stuck to the search term "climate conference". The *NYT* did publish eight articles on Bonn, using the term "climate treaty").

Apart from the difference in media attention, there is a difference in lobbying activities. In the ozone case, advocates of strict regulations operating out of the US, developed an aggressive campaign at the international level via the network of US ambassadors. US scientists were sent to other countries in order to convince them that there was a scientific case for regulations. US environmental groups, in particular the NRDC, initiated activities in Europe and Japan corresponding to those of the local environmental groups, which had to this point remained largely passive. In Great Britain this was seen as interference in British internal affairs. As Richard Benedick observed: 'Not until early 1987 did the efforts of some US environmentalists in the United Kingdom begin to pay off in the form of television interviews, press articles, and parliamentary questions about the government's negative policy. Indeed, these US private citizens were so successful that Her Majesty's Government in April 1987 asked the US Department of State to restrain their activities' (Benedick 1991: 39).

Table 14.1 Media Reports

	Berlin 1995	Kyoto 1997	The Hague 2000	Bonn 2001
(1) European and US news reports on climate (major stories only). Search terms: "clima!" / "klima!"				
Dutch News	3	111	185	121
German News	297	259	539	727
Italian News	0	27	5	70
Spanish News	0	1	0	212
French News	108	154	334	264
UK News	114	277	279	167
Total European	522	829	1342	1561
US News	160	1640	427	562
(2) Relative values, selected countries only. Ratio of above data under (1) compared to number of news sources (28 German sources, 235 UK sources, and 438 US sources)				
German News	10.61	9.25	19.25	25.96
UK News	0.49	1.18	1.19	0.71
US News	0.37	3.74	0.97	1.28

(Continued)

Table 14.1 Cont'd

(3) News reports (major stories only) on "greenhouse" in UK News, US News, German News. Search terms: "greenhouse!"/"Treibhaus!"

German News	73	163	196	173
UK News	58	182	140	99
US News	70	727	219	190

(4) Relative values. Ratio of above data (3) compared to number of news sources (28 German sources, 235 UK sources, and 438 US sources)

German News	2.61	5.82	7.00	6.18
UK News	0.25	0.77	0.60	0.42
US News	0.16	1.66	0.50	0.43

(5) Establishment press on Climate Change. Search terms for NYT and FT: "greenhouse!" and place. Search term for FAZ: "Treibhaus!"

FAZ	39	50	22	47
FT	20	55	24	19
NYT	3	53	18	9

(6) News reports (major stories only) on climate conferences in UK News, US News, German News. Search terms: "climate conference"! "Klimakonferenz"

German News	102	89	196	62
UK News	25	23	38	6
US News	45	110	84	38

(7) Establishment press on Climate Conferences. Search terms: "climate conference"/"Klimakonferenz"

FAZ	31	41	13	33
FT	6	3	3	0
NYT	1	5	2	0

(8) Establishment press on Climate Conferences. Search terms: "climate treaty"! "Klimakonferenz"

FAZ	31	41	13	33
FT	0	1	0	2
NYT	0	8	8	8

All searches were limited to the following places and periods: Berlin, 7 March - 8 April 1995; Kyoto, 15 Nov-15 Dec 1997; The Hague, 1-30 Nov 2000; Bonn, 1-31 July 2001.

Source: Lexis®-Nexis® Executive [http:// web.lexis-nexis.com/ executive/1], accessed 3 September 2001

Nothing comparable has happened in the climate case.[11] The embassies seem to have kept quiet, there was no need felt to send scientists around the globe since the IPCC arguably was set up as a world-wide operation to achieve exactly this task. For historical reasons, it is obvious that Europe is ill prepared to take on a missionary role vis-à-vis the United States but has been used to accept the reverse. Moreover, there is a lack of European co-ordination during the negotiations. Whereas the US represents a coherent position in negotiations with the EU, the latter demonstrates the 'unwieldy (and introspective) morass of EU decision making' (Grubb 1999: 112). Last but not least, environmentalists thought that they were aiming for the same goals across the globe. Too much seemed to be taken for granted. The EC may have trusted the IPCC to do the job of getting everyone to agree to controls and therefore did not try to influence US policy from the outside. While the split in the ranks of the environmentalists is a recent (and maybe temporary) phenomenon and anyhow lies beyond the scope of this article, I shall focus on the role of the IPCC and show how the forging of a consensus among scientists was counterproductive.

Consensus as Priority

By institutionalising international scientific assessments, the architects of the IPCC drew what they think to be an essential lesson from the case of the ozone layer controversy.[12] They tried to arrive at a consensus view on the scientific aspects of global climate changes, thus forming an 'epistemic community' (Haas 1992).[13]

Apart from other leading scientists such as John Houghton and Bert Bolin, Robert Watson played a key role in this process. In the beginning of the 1980s he perceived that CFC regulations would be hampered by the existence of many differing ozone assessments. At the time there were six different reports on the state of knowledge on ozone. Operating under the assumption that scientific uncertainty would make regulations more difficult, this could only lead to confusion and, above all, it gave the opponents of regulations welcome arguments. These reports were commissioned by the European Community, NASA, NAS, UNEP, WMO, and the British government. As Watson told me,

> At that stage industry and other people were looking rather at the differences than at the commonalities of the different studies. So I tried to work with the international science community toward a single international assessment. (Author interview with Robert Watson, 21 November 1994)

Watson successfully led the international scientific community to write one single report. The first report was published in 1986 with several other reports following in 1988, 1989, 1991, and 1994. This reporting system provided a mechanism that allowed bringing together all relevant scientists and making them agree on a common position. While it is clear that these reports were used as scientific legitimisation for CFC controls, it is less from clear that they were the driving force. There is evidence that rising public concern created by a transnational network including advocacy scientists was much more important (Grundmann 2001).

The IPCC was founded in November 1988, sailing in the waves of enthusiasm created by the successful Montreal Protocol, by two UN bodies, UNEP and WMO. Its role is to review and assess the published scientific literature on climate change, its costs, impacts, and possible policy responses. It also plays a role in assessing scientific and technical issues for the UN Framework Convention on Climate Change (Shackley 1997). Therefore, the IPCC is modelled precisely after the WMO-UNEP assessment reports in the ozone case. In both cases, a standardisation and orchestration (Elzinga 1995) of scientific knowledge is seen as instrumental to get the right policy decisions. This follows a linear or 'technocratic' policy model according to which a scientific consensus can be transformed into political decisions.[14]

It has been remarked that insofar scientists adhere to this view, they must be regarded as rather naïve (Shackley and Skodvin 1995). Others have argued that the IPCC has primarily served the self-interest of the participating scientists in that they attracted huge funding resources and therefore stayed away from advocating specific policies (Boehmer-Christiansen 1995). To this, it has been replied that the avoidance of policy advocacy in IPCC reports is rooted in a desire to make the scientific information as effective as possible: 'For scientific information to be believed by the majority of participants in policy debates, it must be even-handed and not favour particular political or economic interests' (Moss 1995). Without doubt, the IPCC has succeeded in establishing a shared understanding of climate change that is accepted by many participants involved in building the climate change convention, although some powerful stakeholders seem unimpressed. But why has it been so difficult to implement the United Nations Framework Convention on Climate Change (UNFCCC) and the Kyoto Protocol?

The case of ozone layer protection was different in that there was, before the consensus assessment reports, strictly speaking, no epistemic community. From the beginning, a few advocacy scientists (like F. Sherwood Rowland, Mario Molina and, later, Paul Crutzen) dared to combine their scientific judgements with political recommendations or demands. Rowland was not afraid to demand first a ban on CFCs in spray cans and then, after the discovery of the ozone hole in 1985/86, a general ban. Moreover, it was he who coined the metaphor of the ozone hole. His credibility and that of other advocates grew as time passed, particularly after the onset of dramatic events in 1985 (the ozone hole). In the 1970s and the beginning of the 1980s, Rowland was considered an extremist by many colleagues (Roan 1989). In the case of climate change the role to be played by advocacy scientists was curbed by the deliberate creation of an epistemic community. To be sure, back in the 1980s, climate researchers Stephen Schneider and James Hansen distinguished themselves as advocates of a policy of prevention. At public hearings, they did not hesitate to describe current extreme climatic events as expressions of anthropogenic climate change (most famously by James Hansen in the heat wave of 1988)—for which they were much criticised (cf. Nance 1991). With the IPCC, this activity largely subsided.[15] Climatologists thereby gained an exciting, relatively well-funded international research field, but at a price: they did not move beyond the boundaries of the official consensus. This gave sceptics and outsiders the opportunity to question the available findings, which they did in public, primarily in the mass media (see Gelbspan 1997). So in the end, all attempts at reaching a consensus view notwithstanding, debate and controversy could not be avoided. As a result, in this game, the IPCC advocates of strong reduction goals ironically were disadvantaged since fierce enemies of regulation seemed to dominate the public debate where they were not attacked by equally adamant advocates of regulation but by a consensus view that expresses the least common denominator.[16]

There is an argument about the difference in both cases that pertains to the salience of the threat posed by the two cases. Ungar (2000) holds that the ozone case represents a 'hot crisis' which is perceived by the public to have direct effects on their lives, while in the case of climate change we only have long-term, abstract threats. However, as the preceding paragraph has shown, there have been several attempts to link extreme weather events to long-term climate change. It may be the case that after Hansen's 1988 statement and the formation of the IPCC, 'reputable scientists routinely claim that any extreme . . . weather season cannot be attributed to climate change. Whether intentional or not, this dissociation effect has been abetted by the media' (Ungar 2000: 308). In a different study on the US media, Ungar (1999) found no correlation between coverage of extreme weather events and stories on climate change. The picture in Europe is clearly different. In Germany, for example, the term climatic catastrophe is current in the mass media (Weingart et al. 2000: 269), and UK papers routinely link extreme weather events to climatic change. Incidentally, the flooding of large parts of England at the time when negotiators gathered in The Hague was very much used by the media to foster expectations for a successful outcome of the meeting. So there seems to be a difference between the US and parts of Europe (mainly Germany) regarding the public's perception of climate change as a 'hot crisis'.

The upshot of the argument so far is that it is not world-wide scientific consensus (or the lack of it), which explains the slow progress of the climate change policy but the (lack of) media attention in the US. From the argument put forward here it follows that the key variable in explaining the failure to agree to binding targets is the 'cool' US public (cf. Grubb 1999)[17] and the absence of advocates of a strong treaty who try to change this from outside. If there had been public concern about climate change in the US, the US delegation would have taken this into account at the negotiating table. To counterbalance public indifference to global climate change, a public discussion about all aspects would have been required. Recall the analysis provided by Lang according to which during the ozone negotiations 'it was the US delegation, which by means of continuous contacts with the media tried to build up a climate of public expectations which should induce still reluctant delegations . . . to agree to substantial reductions of emissions' (Lang 1994: 175). The consensus-driven IPCC has inhibited this, precisely because it was so successful at consensus building. The fact that everyone in The Hague agreed to the science did not mean that negotiating a treaty would be easier.

The case of climate change reveals the limits of the technocratic policy model, since reaching a common scientific judgement does not necessarily mean that the problem can be defined and solved in concert. Problem definition is a much broader concept than scientific description of a problem; the former contains essential elements of a pragmatic, practical, and political dimension, which the latter, as a rule, forgoes. Yet what is more, as we know from other examples, scientific knowledge (or the absence of it under conditions of uncertainty) has no direct bearing on policy outcomes. Ozone is an example where prudent political action was taken under uncertainty. In the 1970s, CFC regulations were taken on the basis of (disputed) model calculations. At the time of signature of the Montreal Protocol, no commonly accepted scientific explanation of the ozone hole was available. Conversely, in many cases no political action follows from conclusive scientific knowledge or consensus expert opinion because economic and political factors are much more influential. Policy makers make use of expert recommendations as they see fit. Are scientists deceiving themselves? They may, understandably, feel flattered by the role assigned to them and many environmentalists may think that the IPCC is essentially a 'good' thing. However, as some powerful players around the globe could not influence the composition of this expert body they sponsored contrarian scientists. In the end, even provided that well-meaning politicians were intending to bind themselves to the findings and recommendations of IPCC (which seems plausible if we follow Elzinga's analysis in terms of an 'orchestration of consensus'), the consensus was not all pervasive. It took only a few but powerful stakeholders to dominate US public opinion.[18] In sum, scientific consensus can hardly be seen as the driving force in the process of adopting environmental regulations. These will be the product of a political process in which the public (via the agenda setting function of the mass media) has much greater weight. The contrarians seem to have understood this much better than the architects of the IPCC.[19]

Conclusion: Ozone Simple, Climate Complex?

It would be foolish to downplay the differences of both cases. Both developed in historical time which is to say that many factors have changed since the signing of the Montreal Protocol, including the (lower) salience of environmental issues on the political agenda, the (self-) understanding of science and its accomplishments both among the public and the political system. However, both cases are path dependent and change our expectations as we move along in time. The fact that CFCs were the first class of industrially produced chemicals to be banned was unthinkable in the 1970s and 80s but now we seem to take it for granted. Therefore, the measures of success and failure may also shift in historical time. IPCC scientists concentrated their main activity on scientific scenarios which are supposed to prove beyond reasonable doubt that climate change is real, human made, happening now, and problematic. They have been largely successful in doing so, but did not convince some powerful stakeholders who block ambitious GHG reductions. At the same time, the IPCC could not quite keep up with the speed of the political process which—due to the influence of these powerful stakeholders—had moved in the direction of exploring a range of 'flexible measures'. The difficulty to develop reliable and agreed-upon indicators (and monitoring instruments) has led to a deadlock in The Hague which, for the time being, was resolved in Bonn. It is open to speculations how this issue will be resolved in future negotiations.

Popular explanations for the difference between the two cases either cite the greater size or complexity of the problem of climate change, or how 'simple' it was to solve the problem of the ozone layer. In retrospect it may seem so, in accordance with a functionalist logic that declares solved problems to be easily solved problems. Upon closer examination, the ozone case was anything but simple. For almost twenty years, producers of CFCs throughout the world resisted regulation, in part by means of the same arguments which are still heard in the case of climate: there were, they claimed, no cost-effective alternative technologies. Such technologies came onto the market after the producers were forced to forgo the use of CFCs. The anti-regulation position was still so strong in 1987 that six months before the signing of the Montreal Protocol, Lang, then chair of the international ozone negotiations, claimed that no more than 10 to 20% CFC reduction was feasible in the next decade (*New York Times*, 28 February 1987).[20]

It is sometimes also argued that the greater objective importance of greenhouse gases for the world economy makes it more difficult to curb them (compared to the relative small importance of CFCs). The decarbonisation of the world economy will amount to a radical restructuring of its technical infrastructure. However, from the fact that GHGs are more central to the economy it does not *immediately* follow that it is more difficult to reduce them. This is a matter of technical alternatives, political instruments, economic incentives, and public support (Hawken, Lovins and Lovins 1999; de Leo et al. 2001). To be sure, the more central a technology is, the more one should expect powerful actors to defend it. This is the case since the number of potential veto players is likely to increase. But there is a reverse side, too: as more technical and business opportunities arise, more new players will enter the game. Only if it could be shown that it is nearly impossible to power the carbon-based economy with alternative energy sources would the argument of 'objective importance' be convincing.

It is striking how often the argument of the greater size and complexity of the problem is advanced—but it applies mainly to the reluctant US policy, not across the board. Such attempts seem to forget that Europe is making good progress in substituting fossil fuels with renewable energy sources. This means that the size-and-complexity argument does not hold. We are led back to the major question, Why has the US been so reluctant in taking climate protection seriously?

There is some truth to the complexity thesis with regard to the structure of business in both fields. While Du Pont was the market leader, and its change of direction set off a chain reaction, this has not occurred in the climate case and it is doubtful if it can. Here, there is no dominant producer from whom all others take their cue. However, European oil companies such as BP and Shell have given up their obstructive role. For example, in May 1997, John Browne of BP announced that the company was in favour of gradual reductions in carbon dioxide emissions: 'The time to consider the policy dimensions of climate change is not when the link between greenhouse gases and climate change is conclusively proven, but when the possibility cannot be discounted and is taken seriously by the society of which we are part. We in BP have reached that point' (Browne 1997: 55). BP's declaration could in any case be seen as a sign that oil producers no longer see their future exclusively in terms of oil and thus trigger a bandwagon effect.

But the real important difference between the two cases is as follows. A strong, publicly visible, transnational policy network that alarmed the world public and advocated strict controls decided the ozone controversy. The advocates of regulation owned public credibility, the scarcest resource in such controversies. In the climate controversy, however, there were no vociferous advocacy scientists acting all the way through the debate. What is more, one of the early advocates seems to have mellowed down. In a way, the early institutionalisation of the epistemic community in the form of the IPCC suppressed any open controversy, including the creation of a 'climate of expectation' across territorial borders. In order to preserve a consensus (of which too much was expected politically), the scientific controversy was silenced. This gave outsiders the chance to make their name in media and effectively cast doubt on the consensus, albeit being condemned as essentially unscientific by the IPCC. If all conflicting opinions would have been openly aired, then the advocates' justification could have made their case for a serious commitment much better—assuming that their credibility had increased over the years.

The construction of the IPCC as an international epistemic community committed to a scientific consensus has proven, on this view, to be somewhat counterproductive. The drive to establish a scientific consensus robbed the controversy of an essential dynamic. The gain in public credibility of those advocating for climate protection, above all in the US, has not been sufficiently achieved in the climate debate. However, this would have been the essential requirement to influence the US position at international talks. This is a speculative lesson which follows from the above analysis. If plausible, it would put into question the main lesson drawn by the architects of the IPCC.

Notes

1. For the notion of regime effectiveness, see Miles et al. (2001).
2. In the US, groups such as the Global Climate Coalition, Citizens for a Sound Economy, Western Fuels Association or the American Petroleum Institute funded skeptical scientists who attacked findings of the intergovernmental panel on climate change, IPCC (see Balling 1992, Michaels et al. 1995; Singer 1996).
3. Before the start of the conference in The Hague, a consensus was reached on what previously was a contentious issue: whether climate change exists at all. Most players seemed to agree that the Earth is warming up and that this will eventually have negative impacts on ecosystems and society unless governments take action now to reduce emissions of carbon dioxide. It seems as if the US has now moved away from this consensus.
4. Ott (2001) has argued that the complexity of the issues on the negotiating table And a lack of leadership were to blame primarily for the breakdown in The Hague.
5. Eileen Claussen, president of the Pew Center on Global Climate Change said: 'In the long-term fight against global warming, we need every tool at our disposal . . . If we take carbon sequestration and market mechanisms out of the equation, or bog them down with such

overly restrictive rules that nobody uses them, then we are limiting our ability to meet our environmental objectives.' *(New York Times,* 26 November 2000).

6. In his address on July 3, 1997 to the United Nations General Assembly Special Session, President Clinton noted that 'the science is clear and compelling' and wanted the United States to take a strong leadership role on climate change. In the autumn of 1997, Clinton's administration also instigated a campaign to build public support for the Kyoto treaty (Krosnick et al. 2000).

7. Americans rightly point out that there is something hypocritical about the EU's position. The UK and Germany were the only two countries that made significant progress in reducing CO_2 emissions. This was largely the product of fortuitous circumstances (the shut down of mining in the UK and the breakdown of the East German economy after unification in 1990).

8. There is a difference between public opinion (as measured, e.g., through polls) and media attention (Gamson and Modigliani 1989). I chose to use the latter as an indicator of the agenda setting activities related to the policy process (cf. Baumgartner and Jones 1993; Mazur 1998; The Social Learning Group 2001). One reason for doing so is that elites listen more carefully to the published opinion as compared to the public opinion (they cannot ignore unpleasant news as easily as they can poll data). What is more, in most cases, media selection of issues predates public preoccupation. As eminent sociologist Luhmann noted, 'everything we know about our society, about the world we live in, we know from the mass media' (Luhmann 1996: 9). Mazur (1998: 459) asserts that `public worry and government action rise and fall with the quantity of news coverage'.

9. Including all European languages would have made the search too cumbersome. Instead, I focused attention on those countries which were allegedly taking a lead on climate change in Europe.

10. Due to a lack of German data for the year 1992 I did not include the Earth Summit in Rio. Lexis®-Nexis® Executive only provides data for the *Süddeutsche Zeitung.*

11. This could be one of the reasons why media attention on climate change stalled in the early 1990s. Mazur (1998) speculates about the reasons for this drop in media attention without mentioning this possibility.

12. As has been shown above, climate change assessments were already carried out since 1979. However, they have been largely confined to the US. It was only after the international conference in Villach (1985) that an international assessment process was established.

13. Haas (1992:187–8) defines an epistemic community as 'a knowledge-based network of specialists who share beliefs in cause-and-effect relations, validity tests, and underlying principled values and pursue common policy goals.'

14. Although government representatives nominate scientists to be represented in the IPCC and negotiate the wording of the executive summaries of the reports, this does not contradict the claim that IPCC follows a linear or technocratic model of policy consultancy. The fact that government representatives nominated the scientists they nominated suggests that they themselves intended to make global climate change into a political issue (O'Riordan et al. 1998: 369). This 'orchestration of consensus' did not, however, extend to those powerful stakeholders and parts of the American public who were hostile to climate change regulations.

15. What is more, Hansen (Hansen et al. 2000) recently has expressed some doubts: 'Dr. Hansen is considered the father of the theory of Man-made global warming due to his alarming testimony in 1988 before a United States Senate committee. Demonstrating a willingness to follow the evidence irrespective of where it may lead, he recently downplayed the

conventional wisdom, which he helped spawn, that CO_2 was the predominant "greenhouse gas".' *(United Press International,* 20 November 2000).

16. Just one example of how 'orchestration of consensus' works in practice. Late in 1999 when draft reports of the Third Assessment Report from Working Group II had leaked to the press; the co-chairs of Working Group III gave the following advice to lead authors for dealing with press inquiries about the draft WGIII report: 'the appropriate response is "no comment." Material in the draft report is embargoed from release to the press . . . For any author to comment to the press at this time beyond saying "no comment," could harm our credibility as objective assessors of scientific evidence. Until the review process is complete, any public comment on the content of the report or on press coverage of our activities can be interpreted as personal bias, and could be used by those who are looking for evidence to discredit our endeavors.' (Rob Swart, email to lead authors, 3 December 1999).

17. As indicated earlier, by public I mean mass media. However, there seems to be support for my argument also from poll data. Gallup's March 5–7, 2001 poll asked respondents to characterize the amount they worry about 13 different environmental issues as either 'a great deal,' a fair amount,' only a little' or 'not at all.' Only 33% of Americans told Gallup they personally worry about the 'greenhouse effect' or global warming a great deal. However, public concern over climate change has been waxing and waning over the years. The figures for previous years were: 35% in 1991, 24% in 1997, 28% in 1999 and 40% in 2000 (www. gallup.com/poll/releases/ pr010409.asp).

18. The *Seattle Weekly* (9 July 1997) described the process as follows: 'The Western Fuels Association's paeans to pollution, combined with strong-arm lobbying by oil industry groups such as the Global Climate Coalition and pseudo-scientific policy papers by conservative think tanks like the Marshall Institute, helped the administration derail international climate-change negotiations at the 1992 Earth Summit in Rio de Janeiro, Brazil. In the ensuing five years, under relentless fuel-industry pressure, negotiations have failed to produce any solid international commitments to fossil fuel reductions despite the increasingly grave warnings from the scientific community.'

19. An other example is the 'chapter 8 controversy' where contrarians accused two leading IPCC scientists, Ben Santer and Tom Wigley, to have altered parts of the IPCC's Second Assessment Report in order to make it sound more dramatic (Seitz 1996; Singer 1996). The fact that they could do so, no matter how unjustified their allegations were (cf. Edwards and Schneider 2001; Santer at al. 1996) vindicates the fragility of the IPCC construction. For the contrarians it was sufficient to publicly cast doubt on the integrity of the IPCC. Since the public is less interested in the technical details of scientific debates the contrarians scored points (mud always sticks').

20. It should be recalled that at the time, the idea of banning an entire class of industrially produced chemicals by means of international measures was completely outlandish. I am grateful to Konrad von Moltke for this suggestion.

References

Balling, R. 1992, *The Heated Debate.* San Francisco: Pacific Research Institute for Public Policy.

Baumgartner, F. and Jones, B.D. 1993, *Agendas and Instability in American Politics.* Chicago: University of Chicago Press.

Benedick, R. E. 1991, Ozone Diplomacy. New Directions in Safeguarding the Planet. Cambridge, MA: Harvard University Press.

Boehmer-Christiansen, S. 1994a, Global Climate Protection Policy: The Limits of scientific advice. Part 1, Global Environmental Change 4: 140–159.

Boehmer-Christiansen, S. 1994b, Global Climate Protection Policy: The Limits of scientific advice. Part 2, Global Environmental Change 4: 185–200.

Boehmer-Christiansen, S. 1995, A scientific agenda for climate policy? Nature 372 (1 December 1994), 400–2.

Browne, John: 1997, Climate Change: The New Agenda. In: A. Hoffman (ed.) Global Climate Change. San Francisco: The New Lexington Press.

Carmody, K. 1995, Environmental Journalism in an Age of Backlash, in Columbia Journalism Review, May-June: 40–45.

De Leo, G.A., Rizzi, L., Caizzi, A. and Gatto, M. 2001, Carbon emissions: The economic benefits of the Kyoto Protocol, Nature 413, 478–479.

Edwards, P. 1996, Global Comprehensive Models in Politics and Policymaking, Climatic Change 32: 149–161.

Edwards, P. 1999, Global Climate Science, Uncertainty and Politics: Data.laden Models, Model-Filtered Data, Science as Culture 8: 437–472.

Edwards, P. and Schneider, S., 2001, Governance and Peer-Review in Science-for-Policy: The Case of the IPCC Second Assessment Report, in C.A. Miller and P. Edwards (eds.) Changing the Atmosphere: Expert Knowledge and Environmental Governance. Cambridge: Cambridge University Press, 219–246.

Elzinga, A. 1995, Shaping World-wide Consensus: The Orchestration of Global Climate Change Research, in A. Elzinga and C. Lundstrom (eds.), Internationalism in Science. London: Taylor and Graham, 223–255.

Gamson, W. A. and Modigliani, A. 1989, Media Discourse and Public Opinion on Nuclear Power: A Constructionist Approach, in American Journal of Sociology 95: 1–37.

Gelbspan, R. 1997, The Heat is on. Reading, MA: Perseus.

Graedel, T. K and Crutzen, P.J. 1995, Atmosphere, Climate, and Change, New York: Scientific American Library.

Greenpeace: 2000, Should land-use change and forestry activities be included in the Clean Development Mechanism (CDM)? (August 2000) www.greenpeace.org/–climate/politics/ Iyonsink.html#_Toc489529294

Grubb, M., with Vrolijk, C. and Brack, D. 1999, The Kyoto Protocol. A Guide and Assessment. London: Earthscan.

Grundmann, R. 2001, Transnational Environmental Polity. Reconstrncting Ozone. London: Routledge.

Haas, P. M. 1992, Banning Chlorofluorocarbons: Epistemic Community Efforts to Protect Stratospheric Ozone. International Organization 46, 187–224.

Haas, P. M. 1993, Stratospheric Ozone: Regime Formation in Stages, in O. Young and G. Osherenko (eds.), Polar Politics, Creating International Environmental Regimes, Ithaca: Cornell University Press, 152–185.

Hansen J.E., Sato M., Lacis A., Ruedy R., Tegen I. and Matthews, E. 1998, Climate forcings in the Industrial era. Proceedings of the National Academy of Sciences of the United States of America 95: 12753–12758.

Harrison, N.E. 2000, From the Inside Out: Domestic Influences on Global Environmental Policy, in P. G. Harris (ed.) Climate Change and American Foreign Polity. New York: St Martin's Press, 89–109.

Hawken, P., Lovins, A. and Lovins, L. 1999, Natural Capitalism. London: Earthscan.

Houghton, J. T., Jenkins, G.J. and Ephraums, J.J. 1990, Climate Change: the IPCC scientific assessment. Cambridge: Cambridge University Press.

Houghton, J. T. et al., eds. 1996, *Climate Change 1995: The Science of Climate Change*. Cambridge, UK: Cambridge University Press.

Kempton, W., Boster, J. and Hartley, J. 1995, *Environmental Values in American Culture*. Cambridge, MA: MIT Press.

Krosnick, J.A., Holbrook, A.L. and Visser, P.S. 2000, The impact of the fall 1997 debate about global warming on American public opinion. *Public Understanding of Science* 9(3): 239–260.

Lang, W. 1994, Environmental Treatymaking: Lessons to be Learned for Controlling Pollution of Outer Space, in J. Simpson (ed.), Preservation for Near-Earth Space for Future Generations, Cambridge: Cambridge University Press, 165–179.

Luhmann, N. 1996, *Die Realitiit der Massenmedien*. Opladen, Westdeutscher Verlag.

Mazur, A. 1998, Global environmental Change in the News, *International Sociology* 13(4): 457–472.

Michaels, P.J. et al. 1995, Predicted and Observed Long Night and Day Temperature Trends, *Atmospheric Research* 37 N1–3:257–266.

Miles, E., Underdal, A, Andresen, S., Wettestad, Skjwrseth, J. and Carlin, EM, 2001, *Environmental Regime Effectiveness: Confronting Theory with Evidence*. Cambridge, MA: MIT Press.

Moss, R. 1995, The IPCC: policy relevant (not driven) scientific assessment. A comment on Sonja Boehmer-Christiansen's 'Global climate protection policy: the limits of scientific advice'. *Global Environmental Change* 5: 171–174.

Nance, J. 1991, *What Goes Up. The Global Assault on Our Atmosphere*. New York: William Morrow.

O'Riordan, T. et al., 1998: Institutional Frameworks for Political Action, in S. Reyner and E. Malone (eds) *Human Choice and Climate Change, Vol. 1: The Societal Framework*. Columbus, OH: Batelle Press, 345–439.

Ott, H.E. (forthcoming) The Bonn Agreement to the Kyoto Protocol—Paving the Way for Ratification, *International Environmental Agreements: Politics, Law and Economics* 1(4).

Ott, H.E. 2001, Climate Change: An important foreign policy issue, *International Affairs* 77(2): 277–296.

Prather,.M. J. and Watson, R.T. 1990, Stratospheric ozone depletion and future levels of atmospheric chlorine and bromine. *Nature*, 344, No. 6268, 729–34.

Rawls, J. 1971, *A Theory of Justice*, Oxford: Oxford University Press.

Roan, S. 1989, *Ozone Crisis. The 15-Year Evolution of a Sudden Global Emergency*. New York: Wiley.

Rowlands, I. H. 1995, *The Politics of Global Atmospheric Change*. Manchester and New York: Manchester University Press.

Santer, B. et al. 1996, Response to Wall Street Journal Editorial of June 12th, 1996 by Frederick Seitz, *Wall Street Journal*, (June 25).

Seitz, F. 1996, A Major Deception on Global Warming, *Wall Street Journal* (June 12).

Shackley, S. 1997, The Intergovernmental Panel on Climate Change: consensual knowledge and global politics, *Global Environmental Change* 7, 77–79.

Shackley, S. and Skodvin, T. 1995, IPCC gazing and the interpretative social sciences. A comment on Sonja BoehmerChristiansen's: 'Global climate protection policy: the limits of scientific advice', in: *Global Environmental Change* 5, 175–180.

Singer, F.S. 1996, Letter to the editor, *Wall Street Journal* (July 11).

The Social Learning Group 2001, Learning to Manage Global Environmental Risks. Volume 1: *A Comparative History of Social Responses to Climate Change, Ozone Depletion, and Acid Rain*; Volume 2: *A Functional Analysis of Social Responses to Climate Change, Ozone Depletion, and Acid Rain*. Cambridge, MA: The MIT Press.

Ungar, S. 1999, Is Strange Weather in the Air? A Study of U.S. National News Coverage of Extreme Weather Events, *Climatic Change* 41:133–50.

Ungar, S. 2000, Knowledge, ignorance and the popular culture: climate change versus the ozone hole, *Public Understanding of Science* 9:287–312.

Watson, R.T. et al. 2000, *IPCC Special Report: Land Use, Land Use Change, and Forestry.* Cambridge: Cambridge University Press.

Weingart, P., Engels, A., Pansegrau, P. 2000, Risks of communication: discourses on climate change in science, politics, and the mass media, *Public Understanding of Science* 9: 261–283.

Wuebbles, D. J. 1981, *The Relative Efficieng of a Number of Halo-carbons for Destroying Strato. ipheric Ozone.* Livermore, CA: Lawrence Livermore Laboratory.

Wuebbles, D. and Rosenberg, N. 1998, The Natural Science of Global Climate Change, in: S. Rayner/E.L. Malone (eds.) *Human Choice and Climate Change, Vol. 2: Resources and Technology.* Columbus, OH: Batelle Press, 1–78.

CHAPTER FIFTEEN

Challenging Global Warming as a Social Problem: An Analysis of the Conservative Movement's Counter-Claims

Aaron M. McCright and Riley E. Dunlap

Source: *Social Problems* (2000) 47:4, 499–522 © 2000 University of California Press—Reproduced with permission.

In the past decade global climate change became a widely accepted social problem. Also referred to as global warming or the anthropogenic greenhouse effect, global climate change is the discernible increase in mean global temperature resulting from the release of greenhouse gases produced by human activities. Awareness of this global threat reinforced public concern about environmental problems and thereby provided environmental activists, scientists, and policy-makers with new momentum in their efforts to promote environmental protection. Not surprisingly, opponents of these efforts mobilized in recent years to mount intense opposition to calls for major international action to prevent global warming, such as treaties designed to reduce carbon dioxide emissions (Gelbspan 1997; Brown, Jr. 1997). The purpose of this paper is to examine this growing opposition, which has heretofore been relatively ignored.

In particular, we will explore the role played by the American conservative movement in challenging the legitimacy of the climate change problem. It will be shown that core organizations in the conservative movement mobilized in recent years as a *countermovement* opposing the efforts of the environmental movement and its allies to establish the seriousness of global environmental problems. Specifically, we report the results of a content analysis of publications concerning climate change distributed via the Internet sites of key conservative think tanks, organizations that have influenced policy-making in areas ranging from health care to taxation. This analysis examines the nature of the counter-claims used by the conservative movement in its efforts to delegitimate the claim that global warming is a serious threat deserving governmental action. While there is a large body of literature on the role of framing in social movements and a rapidly growing body of literature on countermovements, there is as yet very little work on the framing processes of countermovements. Our analysis employs two existing typologies of counterrhetoric in an effort to demonstrate the utility of examining the framing processes employed by countermovements.

The existing body of social scientific literature on global warming has been dominated by a social constructionist approach (Dunlap and Catton 1994: 24; Rosa and Dietz 1998: 440), most particularly that of a social problems orientation to claims-making. After reviewing these studies, we turn to a brief theoretical discussion of the parallels and divergences between a social problems orientation and a social movements orientation, comparing their respective concepts of claims and frames. We argue that in order to understand the global warming controversy in the United States it is necessary to supplement the social problems' focus on claims-making with attention to framing processes and movement/countermovement interaction.

Legitimation of Global Warming as a Problem

In the early 1990s social scientists began to study how social and political forces facilitated the construction of global warming as a legitimate social problem requiring ameliorative action. In explaining the variation in public attention to the issue of global warming, most early studies in the social sciences either utilized Downs' (1972) issue-attention cycle or Hilgartner and Bosk's (1988) public arenas model. The more robust findings that emerged from these studies include the following. First, media coverage of global warming was minimal prior to 1988 (Miller, Boone, and Fowler 1990: 29; Mazur and Lee 1993: 695), but soon peaked between the middle of 1989 and early 1990 (Trumbo 1995: 31; Williams and Frey 1997: 289; McComas and Shanahan 1999: 43). Claims-makers were able to achieve this increased media attention to global warming for several reasons: (1) through its timely connection to more popular issues such as nuclear winter and ozone depletion (Mazur and Lee 1993: 709; Williams and Frey 1997: 291); (2) because of the extreme drought during the summer of 1988 (Ungar 1992: 491–492; Mazur and Lee 1993: 709); and (3) because of James Hansen's dramatic Senate testimony in June 1988 attributing the abnormally hot weather plaguing our nation to global warming (Miller, Boone, and Fowler 1990: 35; Mazur and Lee 1993: 698; Trumbo 1995: 25).

Early news stories on global warming relied heavily upon scientists as sources. Over time, however, economic and political specialists edged out scientific experts as the dominant sources in these news stories (Miller, Boone, and Fowler 1990: 34; Lichter and Lichter 1992: 3; Wilkins 1993: 78; Trumbo 1996: 277). With this shift in sources, the news media altered its focus from stories about global warming science to stories about policy debates regarding regulations and treaties (Lichter and Lichter 1992: 2; Trumbo 1995: 26). At the same time, counter-claims began to emerge with the growing concern over the economic costs of binding action and the ascent of the Bush administration (Mazur and Lee 1993: 699; Williams and Frey 1997: 298). In general, support for the reality of global warming was higher in news stories than in opinion-editorial articles, where the ideas of the few key scientists skeptical of global warming science flourished (Wilkins 1993: 79).

As the proponents of global warming theory eventually lost media dominance, the "skeptics" and politicians critical of the scientific evidence gained more visibility in the media (Lichter and Lichter 1992: 3; Wilkins 1993: 78; McComas and Shanahan 1999: 48). The prevalence of the "dueling scientists scenario," the tendency of most science-related news articles to cite scientists with opposing views, probably contributed to this shift in news coverage on global warming. Many researchers assert that the rising skepticism also reflected the entry of political sources, especially members of the Bush administration, into the media debate (Lichter and Lichter 1992: 3; Ungar 1992: 494; Trumbo 1995: 26; McComas and Shanahan 1999: 51; Nissani 1999: 36). Media attention eventually began to decrease after 1990 to levels lower than the peak coverage in 1989 but higher than the level prior to 1988 (Ungar 1992: 493; Williams and Frey 1997: 298), consistent with the latter stages of the public arenas model and the issue-attention cycle.

We believe that this existing sociological research on global warming from a social problems orientation has produced an inadequate understanding of the global warming controversy. Since most of the studies noted above ended in the early 1990s, concluding that global warming was completing the requisite stages of both the public arenas model and the issue-attention cycle, they are unable to shed light on more recent developments. Also, while the studies do track the claims regarding global warming via the media, they nevertheless fail to systematically address the historical context of the social actors involved in the problem definition process. Furthermore, the studies only occasionally acknowledge the existence of counter-claims, while never really dealing with the content or sources of these counter-claims. This is symptomatic of the more general asymmetric focus on the social construction of a condition's problematicity at the expense of ignoring what Freudenburg (2000) calls the social construction of its "non-problematicity."[1] In particular, Freudenburg argues that analyzing efforts to define issues as non-problematic provides insights into the use of power by dominant interests (also see Schnaiberg 1994: 39–42).

We think the dearth of work on the social construction of the *non*-problematicity of global warming limits our sociological understanding of the role of power in struggles to place global warming on the policy agenda. For instance, Ungar (1998) recently argued that the substantial controversy over global warming is due to it not being as marketable as the more successfully defined problem of ozone depletion, while the studies noted above claim global warming merely ran its course as a social problem and now competes with more pressing problems for attention. Unfortunately, these accounts fail to acknowledge the effects of the powerful opposition that has arisen to challenge the legitimacy of global warming. Thus, following Freudenburg (2000), we believe that an adequate account of a social problem's "career" should address efforts to construct its *non*-problematicity as well as those to construct its problematicity. To overcome the limitations of existing studies analyzing the construction of global warming as a problem, we shift to a social movements orientation and examine the framing activities of a counter-movement that challenges the legitimacy of global warming's problem status.

[. . .]

The Emergence of a Countermovement

According to Brulle (2000) and Switzer (1997) there has always been opposition to environ-mental movements and protection efforts in the United States, but this opposition "is more diverse than many observers have recognized" (Switzer 1997: xiii). The contemporary strands of the "green backlash" consist of industry opposition to environmental policy as well as "grass-roots" opposition as manifest in the wise-use movement, the county supremacy movement, and the property rights movement. Most of these segments tend to focus on local or regional issues, particularly challenging government restrictions on natural resource use. However, in the case of global environmental problems we see a new thrust of environmental opposition—the full-scale involvement of the conservative movement. So, while there has always been opposition to environmental movements and protection, the global frame of environmental problems is generating even more—especially from the mainstream conservative movement (Bruner and Oelschlaeger 1994; Beder 1997).

The global frame of environmental problems is the "schemata of interpretation" that ena-bles us to perceive that, for the first time in history, humans are disrupting the global ecosystem in ways that affect not only "environmental quality" but the current and future well-being of our species. This global frame is prominently reflected in the scientific establishment's wide-spread acknowledgement of global environmental change (GEC) and is clearly solidified in an official endorsement from the National Academy of Sciences (Silver with DeFries 1990). Because of this frame's considerable flexibility, numerous environmental problems, especially global warming, are increasingly interpreted as related instances of unprecedented human impact on global ecosystems.

Along with government and university scientists, particularly those involved with the Intergovernmental Panel on Climate Change (IPCC), environmental organizations such as the Natural Resources Defense Council played a major role in promoting specific claims about global warming since the late 1980s. In essence, these environmental proponents claim that increasing scientific evidence supports the idea that global warming is either occurring now or will occur in the near future. Further, they assert that global warming will negatively affect nearly every aspect of our lives, causing potentially momentous problems in the future. In addition, they argue that the actions needed to slow or halt global warming are beneficial overall since they will also help ameliorate other maladies such as resource depletion and pollution. Thus, they claim that we should act immediately to avoid future global crises. Over time, environmentalists promoting these claims have successfully mobilized to define global warming as a legitimate problem in need of amelioration (see, e.g., Schneider 1998). For example, in a 1992 national survey a majority of Americans not only saw global warming as a problem but also thought that it was already occurring (Dunlap 1998).

In this context, it is not surprising that the conservative movement turned its attention to global environmental change (GEC) and global warming in particular. Despite assertions that environmentalism represents a new ideology that is orthogonal to traditional liberalism-conservatism (e.g., Paehlke 1989), studies have consistently found conservatism to be negatively related to pro-environmental attitudes and actions among the general public and especially political elites such as members of Congress (Kamieniecki 1995). The reason is that pursuit of environmental protection often involves government action that is seen as threatening core elements of conservatism such as the primacy of individual freedom, private property rights, laissez-faire government, and promotion of free enterprise (e.g., Meyer 1964).

More broadly, conservatives often strongly defend a traditional frame about humans and nature that some have called the Dominant Social Paradigm (Dunlap and Van Liere 1984) and others have called Manifest Destiny (Brulle 2000). The Dominant Social Paradigm includes core elements of conservative ideology but also faith in science and technology, support for economic growth, faith in material abundance, and faith in future prosperity (Dunlap and Van Liere 1984). The discourse of Manifest Destiny stresses that human welfare is dependent upon unlimited access to abundant natural resources, development of these resources, and transformation of these resources into useful commodities through labor (Brulle 2000).

The degree to which contemporary conservatism's intense commitment to traditional American values influences its orientation toward environmentalism is reflected in a volume titled *American Values: An Environmental Vision* published by the conservative Environmental Policy Analysis Network. The introduction notes:

> Since the 1970s, American environmental policy has been based on the assumption that the federal government, through command-and-control laws and regulations imposed from Washington, D.C., is best suited to provide for the environment. However, this approach has trod on our traditional values, by limiting individual liberty, unconstitutionally expanding the reach of government, hindering free markets, and harming our economic prosperity. Also, command-and-control was often based on biased value judgments and politics rather than sound science, a key American value symbolized by our technological ingenuity and innovation. (Cohen, Milloy, and Zrake 1996: 1–2)

Given conservatism's historical unease with environmentalism and environmental protection, it should come as no surprise that the conservative movement would react negatively toward growing concern with global environmental problems such as climate change. The emergence of global warming and the possibility of large-scale social change resulting from efforts to ameliorate it are seen as far more threatening to American industry, prosperity, life-styles, and the entire "American way of life" than are traditional pollution control measures (e.g., Bailey 1993). Specifically, the characterization of global warming as a major problem and the consequent threat of an internationally binding treaty to curb carbon dioxide emissions are seen as a direct threat to sustained economic growth, the free market, national sovereignty, and the continued abolition of governmental regulations—key goals promoted by the conservative movement. Given the success of the conservative movement in other policy areas in recent years (Blumenthal 1986; Diamond 1995; Stefancic and Delgado 1996), it seems reasonable to expect the conservative movement would vigorously oppose internationally binding global warming policies by challenging environmental proponents' global frame and their specific claims about global warming.

By examining the specific counter-claims on global warming that are a part of the conservative movement's anti-environmental counter-frame, we build upon social movements research on countermovements and framing contests.[2] Mottl (1980: 620) defines a countermovement[3] as "a particular kind of protest movement which is a response to the social change advocated by an initial movement." Zald and Useem (1987: 254) remind us that "a countermovement is likely to emerge if the [original] movement appears to be accomplishing its goals." The theoretical need to examine the mobilization of a countermovement to better understand the ultimate outcome of the original change-oriented social movement was first noted conceptually by Vander Zanden (1958) and empirically supported more recently by Marshall (1985) and Voss (1996). Our position is that the mainstream conservative movement has taken on the character-istics of a countermovement in recent years in its opposition to the successful global thrust of the environmental movement. Thus, following Vander Zanden's advice, we examine the mobi-lization of this countermovement to better understand current debates over the status of global warming as a problem.

Among other types of interaction, movements and countermovements are "involved in framing contests attempting to persuade authorities and bystanders of the rightness of their cause" (Zald 1996: 269). While some attention has been given to defining and describing aspects of countermovements, as noted above, little research has been performed on countermovement framing processes, and those few existing studies are largely historical case studies sharing few theoretical links (e.g., Warnick 1977; Marshall 1985).[4] Benford and Snow (2000: 626) point out that countermovements "sometimes publicly challenge the [original] movement's diagnos-tic and prognostic framings." Noting again that frames are comprised of specific claims, we argue that such challenges are present in the counter-claims of a countermovement. To date, the most refined attempts to systematically establish typologies of "counterrhetoric" are by Hirschman (1991) and Ibarra and Kitsuse (1993)—the latter work coming from a social prob-lems perspective. We draw upon both works in the following analysis to illustrate how the con-servative movement challenges environmental proponents' diagnostic and prognostic frames about global warming.

The Study

This study systematically examines the nature of the conservative movement's counter-claims regarding global warming as contained in documents circulated by major conservative think tanks between 1990 and 1997. While performing this task, we are also providing needed balance to the social science literature on global environmental problems, which to date disproportion-ately analyzes and deconstructs the claims of environmental proponents. By examining the conservative movement's counter-claims, we are not only providing needed symmetry, but also shedding light on the conservative movement's efforts to construct the "*non*-problematicity" of global warming (Freudenburg 2000). In this section, we will first explain the process we used to identify our sample of documents and then briefly describe the coding procedures used in our content analysis.

[. . .]

Counter-Claims about Global Warming

Our thematic content analysis identifies three broad counter-claims through which the conservative movement challenges the legitimacy of global warming. Table 15.1 is a summary outline of these counter-claims.[5] First, the conservative movement criticizes the scientific evidence and general beliefs in support of the existence of anthropogenic global warming. That is, the countermovement argues that the problematic *condition* does not exist. Second, the movement emphasizes the potential benefits of global warming if it should occur. That is, the countermovement argues that the condition, if it should exist, would not be *problematic*. These two counter-claims specifically challenge environmental proponents' diagnostic framing of global warming as a problem.

Third, conservatives stress that taking any proposed internationally binding action would have numerous negative consequences. That is, the countermovement argues that solutions

Table 15.1 The Conservative Movement's Counter-Claims Regarding Global Warming

Theme	Description	N	%
Counter-Claim One	The evidentiary basis of global warming is weak and even wrong	159	71.0
1	The scientific evidence for global warming is highly uncertain	141	62.9
2	Mainstream climate research is "junk" science	30	13.4
3	The IPCC intentionally altered its reports to create a "scientific consensus" on global warming	16	7.1
4	Global warming is merely a myth or scare tactic produced and perpetuated by environmentalists and bureaucrats	41	18.3
5	Global warming is merely a political tool of the Clinton Administration	31	13.8
Counter-Claim Two	Global warming would be beneficial if it were to occur	30	13.4
1	Global warming would improve our quality of life	10	4.5
2	Global warming would improve our health	10	4.5
3	Global warming would improve our agriculture	20	8.9
Counter-Claim Three	Global warming policies would do more harm than good	139	62.1
1	Proposed action would harm the national economy	130	58.0
2	Proposed action would weaken national security	4	1.8
3	Proposed action would threaten national sovereignty	9	4.0
4	Proposed action would actually harm the environment	7	3.1

proposed by environmental proponents would be more detrimental than ameliorative. This counter-claim specifically challenges environmental proponents' prognostic framing of solutions to the global warming problem. Taken as a whole, these three counter-claims support the conservative movement's advocacy of inaction, thus undercutting the efficacy of environmental proponents' motivational framing to urge ameliorative collective action. Each of these three broad counter-claims is comprised of more specific themes. In the remainder of this section, we will describe each of these three counter-claims by providing illustrations of their constituent themes. For each data excerpt we present below, we identify the conservative think tank that circulated the publication.

Criticizing the Evidentiary Basis of Global Warming

The predominant counter-claim, found in 159 sampled documents (71.0%), attempts to discredit the scientific evidence for global warming and thereby undermine its credibility in the eyes of the public. In short, the five themes that comprise this counter-claim all debunk the evidentiary basis for global warming. One theme holds that the scientific evidence for the existence of anthropogenic global warming is characterized by substantial uncertainty and thus does not support environmental proponents' assertion that global warming is a serious problem. In the 141 documents displaying this theme, climate science is described with such words as "contradictory," "flawed," and "murky." With this characterization, some documents attack the claim that *any* consensus exists in the scientific community over the global warming issue. The following examples best illustrate this assertion.

> *There is no scientific "consensus" about the likelihood, extent, or even reality of human-induced global warming.* (National Center for Public Policy Research)

> *There is no scientific consensus that global warming is a problem or that humans are its cause.* (National Center for Policy Analysis)

Not only is there no scientific consensus about the existence of global warming according to these documents, but it is also strongly suggested that global warming is *definitely* not occurring. One document from the National Center for Public Policy Research proclaims, "Even if scientists haven't developed a consensus on global warming, the scientific data has: Global warming is not occurring." As the following excerpts indicate, all of this culminates in the assertion that climate scientists simply do not know much, if anything, about global warming.

> *A decade of focus on global warming and billions of dollars of research funds have still failed to establish that global warming is a significant problem.* (Competitive Enterprise Institute)

> *Scientists do not agree on man's effect on climate and it is unlikely that they will know the answer to this question anytime in the near future.* (Citizens for a Sound Economy Foundation)

In the words of a National Center for Policy Analysis publication, this theme proclaims that the scientific evidence for global warming is "uncertain at best, completely wrong at worst."

Another theme goes further by actually questioning the credibility of mainstream climate research. In thirty sampled documents (13.4%), the body of mainstream climate science research that provides evidence for environmental proponents is characterized by such terms as "junk science" and "tabloid science." In its *Issues '96: The Candidate's Briefing Book*, the Heritage Foundation declares that it is not clear whether a warming trend is occurring or would occur because "the climate models being used are biased in favor of warming." While some other publications also question the credibility of climate models, many others criticize climate scientists as well. This is illustrated in the following examples.

> *For all those who viewed the Union of Concerned Scientists' (UCS) recent foray into "sound science" as akin to Dr. Kevorkian opening a suicide prevention hotline comes this bit of confirmation: The Tucson, Arizona-based Doctors for Disaster Preparedness has obtained a tape of a media training teleconference for scientists hosted by the UCS that exposes the group's "Sound Science Initiative" as merely a tactical device to promote the global warming scare.* (National Center for Public Policy Research)

> *The balance of evidence—to use the U. N.'s lingo—now suggests that some scientists will do anything to ensure that their access to federal grants for global warming research continues. We must not place their greed above the needs of America's most disadvantaged citizens.* (National Center for Public Policy Research)

In short, this theme closely parallels Ibarra and Kitsuse's (1993) "counterrhetoric of insincerity," or the characterization of a claim as suspect because of a supposed hidden agenda on the part of the claims-makers. The characterization of mainstream climate research in general and global warming theory specifically as "junk science" has been particularly strategic in recent years as it accompanies the conservative movement's claim that it has aligned itself with "sound science."

A third theme, found in sixteen documents (7.1%), claims that the IPCC (Intergovernmental Panel on Climate Change) has intentionally "doctored" its reports to create a scientific consensus about global warming and suppress the contrary views of "skeptic" scientists. This public criticism of the IPCC is aimed at its very foundation as several of the documents claim that the entire peer-review process within the IPCC is motivated by political interests. Most of these documents focus on the alleged improprieties of the IPCC's (1996) *Climate Change 1995: The Science of Climate Change.*[6] The Marshall Institute is the most visible conservative think tank behind most of the allegations of wrongdoing by the IPCC. In an opinion-editorial essay discussing how the published version of the IPCC's 1996 study differs from the version approved by its contributing scientists, Frederick Seitz of the Marshall Institute declares that he has "never witnessed a more disturbing corruption of the peer-review process than the events that led to this IPCC report."

In a Marshall Institute report, leading "skeptic" scientist Patrick J. Michaels concludes, "The distorting bias lies right at the heart of the IPCC's process." Another Marshall Institute report claims, "The IPCC process is all about manufacturing . . . a consensus among researchers, and that makes sense if science is really about interests." In a *CEI Update* article, Competitive Enterprise Institute research associate James M. Sheehan declares, "What is clear is that the UN [IPCC] panel is so thoroughly politicized that its integrity and objectivity cannot be taken for granted." Clearly, this theme also parallels Ibarra and Kitsuse's "counterrhetoric of insincerity." It is interesting that no conservative document ever mentions any peer-reviewed social science articles also critical of the IPCC and government-funded research in general.[7]

Another theme, found in forty-one sampled documents (18.3%), is that global warming is merely a myth or a scare tactic produced and perpetuated by environmentalists and bureaucrats. Documents containing this theme basically assert that such parties rely upon imaginatively catastrophic scenarios to arouse support for their cause and justify any action that would maintain the security of their livelihoods. In short, the conservatives criticize what they perceive to be "doom and gloom" imagery. Phrases such as "doomsday crowd," "greenhouse alarmists," "millenarian doomsaying," "modern-day apocalyptics," and "prophets of doom" typify the manner through which the conservatives present this assertion.

In general, documents containing this theme tend to involve more name-calling than actual scientific discussion. As the following excerpts show, conservatives frame the global warming issue as an attempt on the part of "radical" environmentalists to "take over the world."

Radical environmentalism—which seeks to impose ever bigger government on society—has become the last refuge of many of the world's socialists. (National Center for Policy Analysis)

After the balloon bursts on global warming and it has been incorporated like overpopulation, resource depletion, biotech plagues, and the ozone hole into the conventional wisdom of doom, to what new doom will the environmental millenarians turn next? What new crisis can be conjured up and used to promote their sociopolitical engineering schemes while enhancing their power and influence over the world's governments? (Cato Institute)

Furthermore, several documents criticize the manner through which these "apocalyptic" environmentalists present their claims. As a Cato Institute publication declares, "Doomsayers indiscriminately latch onto and publicize just about any natural anomaly or local disaster as evidence to bolster their predictions of impending worldwide catastrophe."

A few documents specifically argue that money is the driving force behind the environmentalists' claims of global warming. In his well-known article in Cato Institute's *Regulation*, actually a reprinted speech underwritten by OPEC, leading "skeptic" scientist Richard Lindzen makes it clear that self-perpetuation is a major concern with environmental organizations and that "global warming has become one of the major battle cries in their fundraising efforts." As a whole, this theme is a good example of what Ibarra and Kitsuse (1993) refer to as the "counter-rhetoric of hysteria," or the dismissal of a claim because it is merely seen as a stereotypical expression from a hysterical social group. In this case, the conservatives dismiss global warming's problem status by characterizing it as a mere scare tactic of "radical environmentalists."

A final theme in this first counter-claim is that global warming is primarily a political tool of the Clinton Administration. The thirty-one documents (13.8%) espousing this theme assert that the Clinton Administration used the global warming issue as a way to gain more support and assert more control over the American people. Both a National Center for Policy Analysis policy brief and a Heritage Foundation backgrounder accuse the Clinton Administration of suppressing studies that lend support for those parties challenging a global warming treaty.

The scientific community's alleged widespread support for the administration's global warming agenda is more a reflection of the White House's public relations skills than real backing from the scientific community. (Heartland Institute)

Alarmists in the media and the Clinton administration clearly have decided that the best way to win the global warming debate is by shouting down the opposition and demonizing them in the eyes of the public. (Cato Institute)

Some documents specifically criticize the actions of Vice President Al Gore with regard to the global warming issue. The Competitive Enterprise Institute ran a bulletin from the Kyoto Conference in *CEI Update* criticizing the activities of the Vice-President, who is referred to as the "Chief Druid." In a Cato Institute essay, leading skeptic Patrick J. Michaels alleges that the Vice-President's recent activism regarding climate change is merely political posturing.

Other documents implicate the administration in a larger conspiracy. In a Heartland Institute newspaper article, James M. Sheehan, research associate at Competitive Enterprise Institute, proclaims that the Clinton administration's position and activities on global warming were heavily directed by environmental organizations. A Competitive Enterprise Institute policy study considers "Clinton-Gore, the United Nations, and the greenhouse lobby" to be one cohesive group acting in conspiracy on the global warming issue. Similar to the previous theme, this present theme also exemplifies Ibarra and Kitsuse's (1993) "counterrhetoric of insincerity."

Through each of these five themes, the conservative movement attempts to discredit the scientific evidence for global warming and thereby undermine its credibility in the eyes in the public. Thus, this first and fundamental counter-claim allows the conservative movement to challenge the scientific basis of global warming as a legitimate problem. This counter-claim is essential to the conservative movement's agenda since lay people and policy-makers must rely primarily upon science for evidence of global warming. By presenting this science as uncertain at best and completely wrong at worst, the conservative movement directly challenges the claim that global warming is a legitimate problem.

The Potential Benefits from Global Warming

Not only does the conservative movement argue that climate science cannot yet prove that global warming is occurring, but it uses a second counter-claim to proclaim the *benefits* of global warming should it actually occur. While only appearing in thirty of the sampled documents (13.4%), this counter-claim nevertheless is a crucial element of the conservative position. By challenging the allegedly pessimistic claims of environmentalists with an optimistic counter-claim, the conservatives are able to challenge further the claim that global warming is a *problem*. The following excerpts concisely illustrate this counter-claim.

> *Some research even suggests that a moderately warmer climate would be a far better one for humanity.* (Competitive Enterprise Institute; Heartland Institute)

> *On the whole, mankind should benefit from an upward tick in the thermometer.* (Hoover Institution)

It is especially important to note that this counter-claim is consistent with the previous one since it identifies benefits that are explicitly hypothetical. As one Hoover Institution publication states, "Global warming, if it were to occur, would probably benefit most Americans." Three themes constitute this counter-claim espousing the potential benefits of global warming.

One theme, found in ten documents (4.5%), specifically claims improvements in our quality of living should global warming occur.[8] Most documents having this theme mention improvements in our day-to-day lives, including such enhancements as lower heating bills and reduced transportation delays and accidents. These two selections nicely depict this theme.

> *Less cold weather would mean less snow shoveling, fewer days of driving on icy roads, lower heating bills, and reduced outlays for clothing.* (Hoover Institution)

> *Warmer weather means, if anything, fewer power outages and less frequent interruptions of wired communications.* (Hoover Institution)

Other documents make explicit reference to the probability of an expanding tourism market. One Hoover Institution publication declares, "New tourist opportunities might develop in Alaska, Northern Canada, and other locales at higher latitudes or in upper elevations."

Another theme, also found in ten documents, specifically states that global warming would improve our general health if it would occur. According to a Hoover Institution article, "If the IPCC is right and the globe does warm, history suggests that human health is likely to improve." Other documents claim that global warming would reduce the amount of disease and sickness in the world, thus saving a large number of people from impending death.

Global warming could save billions of people from malnutrition. (National Center for Public Policy Research)

A warmer climate would actually reduce disease and cut mortality. More people die of the cold than of the heat; more die in the winter than the summer. (Hoover Institution)

Global warming could save thousands of human lives. (National Center for Public Policy Research)

Interestingly, Hoover Institution fellow Thomas Gale Moore, author of the recent Cato Institute book *Climate of Fear* (1998), has written almost all the documents containing this theme as well as several containing the next one.

This counter-claim's final theme, found in twenty documents (8.9%), specifically claims that global warming would benefit agriculture. In general, global warming is seen as "an agricultural boon." The following two excerpts illustrate this assertion.

More carbon dioxide in the air would lead to more luxuriant plant growth and greater crop yields. The small increase in carbon dioxide experienced to date has probably advanced the much ballyhooed green revolution, with its striking increases in food production. (Heartland Institute)

The enrichment of the atmosphere with carbon dioxide will fertilize plants and make for more vigorous growth. (Hoover Institution)

This agricultural boon presumably would come about both by an increase in the amount of arable land and by an increase in agricultural productivity as the next two selections indicate.

Global warming would expand the world's agricultural belt. (Heritage Foundation)

Doubling carbon dioxide levels . . . may increase average crop yields by an estimated 33%. (Foundation for Research on Economics and the Environment)

Once again, all the documents exhibiting this counter-claim hold that global warming would offer ample benefits if it does occur. In fact, as noted earlier, most assert that the benefits would outweigh the costs. This counter-claim is essential to the conservative movement's position in two ways. First, by identifying hypothetical conditions, conservatives are further strengthening their position that global warming is not yet occurring and still might not occur in the future. Second, by identifying benefits that lay people and policy-makers can easily identify, they are able to problematize environmentalists' claims that global warming is a problem. The synthesis of the first two counter-claims provides the basis for the conservative movement's position on global warming—that is, global warming is not occurring, but if it should occur in the future it would not be a problem. These counter-claims provide a foundation for the final one.

The Harmful Effects of Proposed Action

The third counter-claim, which stresses the negative impacts of proposed international action, is found in 139 of the sampled documents (62.1%). This counter-claim is comprised of four specific themes that respectively assert that any proposed internationally binding action will be harmful to the national economy, national security, national sovereignty, and—quite ironically—the environment. On the whole, this counter-claim parallels a strategy identified by Ibarra and Kitsuse (1993) as the "counterrhetoric of the costs involved." This counter-claim argues that the proposed ameliorative treaties would cause more harm than would the threat of global warming. This counter-claim is also a prime example of how countermovements tend to invoke a reactionary rhetoric stressing futility and jeopardy (Hirschman 1991). Through this counter-claim, the conservative movement argues that proposed actions would waste time and resources and such actions could even make matters worse.

The first theme, found in 130 documents (58.0%), is that the proposed actions to ameliorate global warming will harm the national economy. These documents describe the potential impacts on the U. S. economy using such terms as "devastating" and "staggering." The following excerpts illustrate the general claim that our economy would suffer.

A binding U. N. Treaty will cripple our economy. (Competitive Enterprise Institute)

The implications of the proposed climate change commitments for the U. S. economy are grave. (National Center for Policy Analysis)

These documents particularly argue that the United States will be at a disadvantage in the global economy since developing countries will not be obligated to sign the proposed treaties to limit carbon dioxide emissions. Most of these publications make specific references to a loss of economic output or a decrease in economic growth as a result of the proposed binding action.

The national economy permanently would lose $3.3 trillion in output between 2001 and 2020. (Heritage Foundation)

Annual GDP levels are expected to fall between $200 to $300 billion. (Citizens for a Sound Economy Foundation)

The [Kyoto] treaty would cut economic growth by 50% by the year 2005. (Heartland Institute)

Moreover, these documents often identify more specific sectors or elements of the national economy that would suffer greatly. For instance, the conservative movement claims that proposed actions harm such generalized groups as the business community and industry, while also threatening the well-being of individual workers and consumers.

Another theme, found in only four documents (1.8%), asserts that proposed treaties will be a detriment to national security. Such a small number of documents is surprising given the conservative movement's emphasis on a strong national defense. Some examples are as follows.

The areas that will be at risk if we must reduce our military fossil fuel emissions are the readiness of our forces and the literal day-to-day ability to go fight the nation's wars if we have to. (National Center for Policy Analysis)

Opportunities for military espionage increase if international representatives are allowed to inspect U. S. planes, ships, and tanks to ensure that they meet emissions standards. (Heritage Foundation; National Center for Public Policy Research)

In sum, the conservative movement claims that proposed treaties jeopardize our military intelligence and readiness and thereby our national security.

A third theme, found in nine documents (4.0%), is that proposed treaties will threaten our national sovereignty. On the whole, the conservative movement claims that the United States will be turning over its sovereignty to powerful international bureaucrats who are "responsible neither to any nation nor to any individual." The following examples illustrate this theme.

One of the most disturbing aspects of this treaty is the threat to U. S. sovereignty. Is this country really ready and prepared to turn over its industry and responsibility for its manufacturing to multilateral international organizations with the power to close our own industries down? (Competitive Enterprise Institute)

When you subject American industry and business and jobs and all dynamics of our society, of our culture, of our country, of our government to international bodies with awesome power, the power to dictate industries being shut down, levying fines, we've crossed another line here . . . we have a major problem. (Heartland Institute)

This theme takes on further significance when one remembers that two themes within the first counter-claim implicate these same international bureaucrats as being party to a conspiracy to elevate global warming as a problem in need of a solution. This current theme complements these conspiratorial allegations by identifying what these "powerful interests" would allegedly control if any proposed treaty is accepted.

This counter-claim's final theme, found in seven documents (3.1%), ironically declares that the proposed treaties designed to ameliorate global warming will actually promote environmental degradation. The following examples illustrate this theme.

The treaty could actually cause environmental damage and could preclude efforts to continue environmental improvements not only in the developed world, but more importantly, in developing countries. (National Center for Policy Analysis)

To those who believe that industrial economies as we know them are at the root of all that is wrong with the world, curtailing industrial activity in the name of protecting public health and the environment makes certain sense. But the real consequence of this will be to harm public health and the environment. (Heartland Institute)

In examining how countermovements call for inaction, Hirschman (1991) argues that they invoke a rhetoric of reaction stressing jeopardy, the risk of losing achievements that we have already gained. This last theme runs parallel to Hirschman's (1991) argument by asserting that the environmental improvements of recent decades are at risk with any new treaty.

All of the themes in this counter-claim assert that there will definitely be harmful effects from any proposed treaty aimed at reducing carbon dioxide emissions. Proposed treaties are claimed to have harmful effects on most, if not all, sectors of the national economy, on national security, on national sovereignty, and on the environment. It is quite interesting that while the conservatives harshly criticize the apocalyptic imagery of environmentalists, they also rely strongly upon apocalyptic imagery of their own when discussing these purported harmful effects of taking action to halt global warming. The themes in this counter-claim are essential to the conservative movement's position since they emphasize the supposedly certain, harmful effects of policies to control global warming. Thus, the certainty of this counter-claim appears in stark opposition to the alleged uncertainty of the environmental proponents' claims.

Summary and Conclusion

In the past decade, the environmental movement successfully extended its mobilization to the international level by collaborating with scientists and policy-makers to bring several global environmental problems to the public's attention. Not surprisingly, those who oppose environmental protection efforts have begun to challenge the legitimacy of these problems. In this paper, we focus specifically on global climate change. Global warming was successfully defined as a social problem and placed on the policy agenda by the early 1990s, but its problem status was quickly challenged. While Brulle (2000) and Switzer (1997) identify several strands of "green backlash" in the United States, we argue that a new strand of environmental opposition—the conservative movement—is at the core of recent challenges to global environmental problems, particularly global warming.

It was noted earlier that much sociological research on GEC focuses on how various conditions such as global warming were successfully defined as social problems. This led some social scientists to "deconstruct" the claims of environmentalists and their scientific allies (e.g., Boehmer-Christiansen 1994a, 1994b; Taylor and Buttel 1992), and others to highlight the role of the media (e.g., Mazur and Lee 1993; Trumbo 1995, 1996; McComas and Shanahan 1999) or the unique characteristics of climate change relative to other problems (e.g., Ungar 1992, 1998) to account for the waxing and waning of global warming as a salient social problem. What is surprising, given sociology's sensitivity to power structures, is this literature's general neglect of organized opposition to the environmental lobby's framing of global warming as a serious problem. Specifically, social scientists paid little attention to the intense efforts of industry and the conservative movement to construct what Freudenburg (2000) calls the "*non*-problematicity" of global warming.

By focusing on the mobilization of the conservative movement into an effective counter-movement directly opposing environmental proponents' framing of global warming as a problem, our research is an effort to add needed balance to existing literature. Even though our study is limited to analyzing the content of the counter-claims used by the conservative movement to establish global warming's *non*-problematicity, it is a necessary first step in demonstrating that the controversy over global warming—and the resulting difficulty its advocates have in keeping it on the public agenda—is not simply a function of waning media attention, the ambiguities of climate change signals, or the complexities of climate science, but stems in large part from the concerted efforts of a powerful countermovement. Drawing upon recent social movements research on countermovements and frames, supplemented by work on counter-rhetoric, we provide insight into the sources and nature of the controversy over global warming and consequent difficulty in implementing policies to deal with it. The controversy is not an inevitable outcome of the issue-attention cycle or of the competitiveness of the public arena, but a direct function of the exercise of power by an influential countermovement.

Our research identifies three counter-claims through which the conservative movement challenged global warming's legitimacy as a social problem. First, conservatives claim that the evidentiary basis of global warming is weak, if not wrong. Second, conservatives argue that the net effect of global warming would be beneficial should it occur. Third, conservatives argue that the policies proposed to ameliorate the alleged global warming problem would do more harm than good. Briefly then, the conservative movement asserts that while the science of global warming is becoming more *uncertain*, the harmful effects of climate change policy are becoming more *certain*. This view, the essence of the conservative movement's position, is illustrated in the following excerpts.

While global warming is highly uncertain, the impacts of global warming policies are not. (Heartland Institute; Competitive Enterprise Institute)

The risks of climate change are speculative; those of climate change policy are all too real. (National Center for Public Policy Research)

The coupling of uncertain risks from global warming with certain economic risks from proposed action epitomizes the complementary relationships among these counter-claims. In total, these three counter-claims comprise the conservative movement's response to environmental proponents' call for ameliorative action. Consistent with both Hirschman's (1991) and Ibarra and Kitsuse's (1993) work on counterrhetorical strategies, we see that the conservative movement employs counter-claims that serve to block any proposed action on global warming that challenges its interests. Mottl (1980) identified this strategy as the defining trait of a countermovement. Not surprisingly, the conservative movement's challenge of global warming's problem status is consistent with the fundamental tenets of conservative ideology (Meyer 1964).

The counter-claims identified in this paper were highly visible and widely employed by conservative activists in an effort to halt United States' endorsement of the Kyoto Protocol in 1997. Almost 75% (166 of 224) of the sampled documents were written in 1997 alone, and most of these were published on the verge of the Kyoto Conference. Besides distributing documents on global warming, several conservative think tanks also sponsored press conferences and public speeches to promote their position. For instance, the National Center for Policy Analysis held a press conference on global warming for members of the House of Representatives on June 13, 1997, and the Competitive Enterprise Institute hosted a similar press conference at the National Press Club two days later. These two conservative think tanks then co-sponsored a press conference of the same nature for members of the Senate on September 29, 1997. Also, David Ridenour, Vice-President of the National Center for Public Policy Research, spoke at a rally against climate policy held on the West side of the U.S. Capitol Building on October 30, 1997. Furthermore, prior to and during the Kyoto Conference, several conservative think tanks sent representatives to Kyoto to promote their views to the media. Most prominently, the Competitive Enterprise Institute and the National Center for Public Policy Research published daily media bulletins. These and other examples of the conservative movement's heightened activities seem to indicate that the counter-claims identified in this paper have real-world practicality. As such, we expect to see the conservative movement heighten its mobilization efforts whenever the possibility increases that the United States will sign a climate treaty to reduce carbon dioxide emissions.

While our study provides insight into the nature of the conservative movement's counter-claims regarding global warming, future research is needed to examine the structure and operation of this countermovement with regard to global warming. Existing journalistic (Gelbspan 1997) and activist (Ozone Action 1996a, 1996b) analyses highlight the crucial roles of conservative foundations, conservative think tanks, and sympathetic "skeptic" scientists in debates over global warming, and it is time for in-depth sociological analyses of these phenomena as well. Future work on global warming and GEC in general needs to move beyond analyses of the claims of environmentalists and their scientific and policy allies to a consideration of the social forces opposing the "environmental lobby." Thus, we clearly need to pay more attention to the efforts of the conservative movement, and its industry allies, to mobilize an effective counter-movement dedicated to establishing the *non*-problematicity of global warming.

Notes

1. Freudenburg (2000: 106) uses the term problematicity to mean a condition's status as a legitimate social problem.
2. While we are only focusing on the counter-claims regarding climate change, it should be kept in mind that similar counter-claims exist regarding other global environmental problems such as ozone depletion, biodiversity loss, and tropical rainforest destruction (see, e.g., Brown, Jr. 1997).
3. See also Lo (1982), Zald and Useem (1987), and Meyer and Staggenborg (1996) for additional conceptualizations of countermovements.
4. See McCaffrey and Keys (2000) for a recent examination of how a movement reacts to a countermovement's challenge. Unfortunately, consistent with the authors' sole focus on the framing processes of the original social movement, they fail to systematically analyze the countermovement's counter-framing processes.
5. Our findings are similar to Schnaiberg's (1994: 39–42) more sweeping analysis of the nature of counter-claims promoted by capitalist producers when challenging environmentalists' claims. Schnaiberg argues that capitalist producers engage in "consciousness-lowering" activities that challenge environmentalists' claims that environmental problems are serious, are the products of the production system, and can be alleviated without unreasonable costs.
6. As a response to the critics of this series of events, Edwards and Schneider (1997) have clarified the IPCC peer review process and thereby disarmed many of the countermovement's allegations.
7. One such notable work is Sonja Boehmer-Christiansen's (1994a, 1994b) two-part article in *Global Environmental Change*. In this work, Boehmer-Christiansen argues that the IPCC is politically driven and more concerned with research funding than with research: "The primary interest of research is the creation of concern in order to demonstrate policy relevance and attract funding" (Boehmer-Christiansen 1994a: 141). Conservatives were either unaware of this work or simply chose not to use it for supporting evidence even when making the same argument.
8. This theme seems to indicate both a total lack of concern for ecological impacts and very little understanding of basic ecology.

References

Allen, Michael Patrick 1992 "Elite Social Movement Organizations and the State: The Rise of the Conservative Policy-Planning Network." *Research in Politics and Society* 4:87–109.

Babbie, Earl 1995 *The Practice of Social Research*. Seventh Edition. Belmont, CA: Wadsworth.

Bailey, Ronald. 1993 *Eco-Scam: The False Prophets of Ecological Apocalypse*. New York: St. Martin's Press.

Bash, Harry H. 1994 "Social Movements and Social Problems: Toward a Conceptual Rapprochement." *Research in Social Movements, Conflicts, and Change* 17:247–284.

— 1995 *Social Problems and Social Movements: An Exploration into the Sociological Construction of Alternative Realities*. Atlantic Highlands, NJ: Humanities Press.

Beder, Sharon 1997 *Global Spin: The Corporate Assault on Environmentalism*. White River Junction, VT: Chelsea Green Publishing Company.

Benford, Robert D., and David A. Snow 2000 "Framing Processes and Social Movements: An Overview and Assessment." *Annual Review of Sociology* 26:611–639.

Blumenthal, Sidney 1986 *The Rise of the Counter-Establishment: From Conservative Ideology to Political Power.* New York: Times Books.

Boehmer-Christiansen, Sonja 1994a "Global Climate Protection Policy: The Limits of Scientific Advice, Part 1." *Global Environmental Change* 4:140–159.

— 1994b "Global Climate Protection Policy: The Limits of Scientific Advice, Part 2." *Global Environmental Change* 4:185–200.

Brown, Jr., Rep. George E. 1997 "Environmental Science under Siege in the U.S. Congress." *Environment* 39:12–31.

Brulle, Robert J. 1994 "Power, Discourse, and Social Problems: Social Problems from a Rhetorical Perspective." *Perspectives on Social Problems* 5:95–121.

— 2000 *Agency, Democracy, and Nature: The U.S. Environmental Movement from a Critical Theory Perspective.* Cambridge, MA: MIT Press.

Bruner, Michael, and Max Oelschlaeger 1994 "Rhetoric, Environmentalism, and Environmental Ethics." *Environmental Ethics* 16: 377–396.

Burch, Philip H. 1997 *Reagan, Bush, and Right-Wing Politics, Volume I, The American Right-Wing Takes Command: Key Executive Appointments.* Greenwich, CT: JAI Press.

Cohen, Bonner R., Steven J. Milloy, and Steven J. Zrake, eds. 1996 *American Values: An Environmental Vision.* Washington, D.C.: Environmental Policy Analysis Network.

Diamond, Sara 1995 *Roads to Dominion: Right-Wing Movements and Political Power in the United States.* New York: Guilford Press.

Dolny, Michael 1996 "The Think Tank Spectrum." *Extra!* 5:21.

Dunlap, Riley E. 1998 "Lay Perceptions of Global Risk: Public Views of Global Warming in Cross-National Context." *International Sociology* 13:473–498.

Dunlap, Riley E., Chenyang Xiao, and Aaron M. McCright 2001 "Politics and Environment in America: Partisan and Ideological Cleavages in Public Support for Environmentalism." *Environmental Politics* 10(4):23–48.

Dunlap, Riley E., and Kent D. Van Liere 1984 "Commitment to the Dominant Social Paradigm and Concern for Environmental Quality." *Social Science Quarterly* 65:1013–1028.

Dunlap, Riley E., and William R. Catton, Jr. 1994 "Struggling with Human Exemptionalism: The Rise, Decline, and Revitalization of Environmental Sociology." *The American Sociologist* 25:5–30.

Edwards, Paul N., and Stephen H. Schneider 1997 "The 1995 IPCC Report: Broad Consensus or 'Scientific Cleansing'?" *Ecofable/Ecoscience* 1(1): 3–9.

Freudenburg, William R. 2000 "Social Constructions and Social Constrictions: Toward Analyzing the Social Construction of 'The Naturalized' as well as 'The Natural'." In *Environment and Global Modernity,* ed. Gert Spaargaren, Arthur P. J. Mol, and Frederick H. Buttel, 103–119. London: Sage.

Gelbspan, Ross 1997 *The Heat Is On: The High Stakes Battle over Earth's Threatened Climate.* Reading, MA: Addison-Wesley Publishing.

Hirschman, Albert 1991 *The Rhetoric of Reaction.* Cambridge: Harvard University Press.

Ibarra, Peter R., and John I. Kitsuse 1993 "Vernacular Constituents of Moral Discourse: An Interactionist Proposal for the Study of Social Problems." In *Constructionist Controversies: Issues in Social Problems Theory,* ed. Gale Miller and James Holstein, 21–54. New York: Aldine de Gruyter.

Kamieniecki, Sheldon 1995 "Political Parties and Environmental Policy." In *Environmental Politics and Policy,* ed. James P. Lester, 146–167. Durham, NC: Duke University Press.

Lichter, S. Robert, and Linda S. Lichter 1992 "The Great Greenhouse Debate: Media Coverage and Expert Opinion on Global Warming." *Media Monitor* 6(10):1–6.

Lo, Clarence Y. H. 1982 "Countermovements and Conservative Movements in the Contemporary U.S." *Annual Review of Sociology* 8:107–134.

Loseke, Donileen R. 1999 *Thinking About Social Problems: An Introduction to Constructionist Perspectives.* New York: Aldine de Gruyter.

Lukes, Steven 1974 *Power: A Radical View.* London: Macmillan Press.

Marshall, Susan E. 1985 "Ladies Against Women: Mobilization Dilemmas of Antifeminist Movements." *Social Problems* 32:348–362.

Mauss, Armand L. 1975 *Social Problems as Social Movements.* Philadelphia: Lippincott.

Mazur, Allan, and Jinling Lee 1993 "Sounding the Global Alarm: Environmental Issues in the US National News." *Social Studies of Science* 23:681–720.

McCaffrey, Dawn, and Jennifer Keys 2000 "Competitive Framing Processes in the Abortion Debate: Polarization-Vilification, Framing-Saving, and Frame Debunking." *The Sociological Quarterly* 41:41–61.

McComas, Katherine, and James Shanahan 1999 "Telling Stories about Global Climate Change: Measuring the Impact of Narratives on Issue Cycles." *Communication Research* 26(1):30–57.

Meyer, David S., and Suzanne Staggenborg 1996 "Movements, Countermovements, and the Structure of Political Opportunity." *American Journal of Sociology* 101:1628–1660.

Meyer, Frank S. 1964 "Consensus and Divergence." In *What is Conservatism?*, ed. Frank S. Meyer, 229–232. New York: Holt, Rinehart, and Winston.

Miller, Mark, Jeff Boone, and David Fowler 1990 "The Emergence of the Greenhouse Effect on the Issue Agenda: A News Stream Analysis." *News Computing Journal* 7:25–38.

Mottl, Tahi L. 1980 "The Analysis of Countermovements." *Social Problems* 27:620–635.

National Committee for Responsive Philanthropy 1997 *Moving a Policy Agenda: The Strategic Philanthropy of Conservative Foundations.* Washington, D.C.: National Committee for Responsive Philanthropy.

Nissani, Moti 1999 "Media Coverage of the Greenhouse Effect." *Population and Environment: A Journal of Interdisciplinary Studies* 21:27–43.

Ozone Action 1996a "Ties That Blind I: Case Studies of Corporate Influence on Climate Change Policy." *Ozone Action Report* Washington, D.C.

— 1996b "Ties That Blind II: Parading Opinion as Scientific Truth." *Ozone Action Report* Washington, D.C.

Paehlke, Robert C. 1989 *Environmentalism and the Future of Progressive Politics.* New Haven, CT: Yale University Press.

Peckham, Michael 1998 "New Dimensions of Social Movement/Countermovement Interaction: The Case of Scientology and its Internet Critics." *Canadian Journal of Sociology* 23:317–347.

People for the American Way 1997 *Buying a Movement: Right-Wing Foundations and American Politics.* Washington, D.C.: People for the American Way.

Rosa, Eugene A., and Thomas Dietz 1998 "Climate Change and Society: Speculation, Construction, and Scientific Investigation." *International Sociology* 13:421–455.

Schnaiberg, Allan 1994 "The Political Economy of Environmental Problems and Policies: Consciousness, Conflict, and Control Capacity." *Advances in Human Ecology* 3:23–64.

Schneider, Stephen H. 1998 *Laboratory Earth.* New York: Basic Books.

Silver, Cheryl Simon, with Ruth S. DeFries 1990 *One Earth/One Future: Our Changing Global Environment.* Washington, D.C.: National Academy Press.

Snow, David A., E. Burke Rochford, Jr., Steven K. Worden, and Robert D. Benford 1986 "Frame Alignment Processes, Micromobilization, and Movement Participation." *American Sociological Review* 51:464–481.

Snow, David A., and Robert D. Benford 1992 "Master Frames and Cycles of Protest." In *Frontiers in Social Movement Theory,* ed. Aldon Morris and Carol McClurg Mueller, 133–155. New Haven: Yale University Press.

Spector, Malcolm, and John I. Kitsuse 1977 *Constructing Social Problems.* Menlo Park, CA: Cummings Publishing Company.

Stefancic, Jean, and Richard Delgado 1996 *No Mercy: How Conservative Think Tanks and Foundations Changed America's Social Agenda.* Philadelphia: Temple University Press.

Switzer, Jacqueline Vaughn 1997 *Green Backlash: The History and Politics of Environmental Opposition in the U.S.* Boulder, CO: Lynne Rienner Publishers.

Taylor, Peter J., and Frederick H. Buttel 1992 "How Do We Know We Have Global Environmental Problems?: Science and the Globalization of Environmental Discourse." *Geoforum* 23:405–416.

Troyer, Ronald J. 1989 "Are Social Problems and Social Movements the Same Thing?" *Perspectives on Social Problems* 1:41–58.

Trumbo, Craig 1995 "Longitudinal Modeling of Public Issues: An Application of the Agenda-Setting Process to the Issue of Global Warming." *Journalism and Mass Communication Monographs* John Soloski, ed. No. 152.

— 1996 "Constructing Climate Change: Claims and Frames in U.S. News Coverage of an Environmental Issue." *Public Understanding of Science* 5:269–283.

Ungar, Sheldon 1992 "The Rise and (Relative) Decline of Global Warming as a Social Problem." *The Sociological Quarterly* 33:483–501.

— 1998 "Bringing the Issue Back In: Comparing the Marketability of the Ozone Hole and Global Warming." *Social Problems* 45:510–527.

Vander Zanden, James W. 1959 "Resistance and Social Movements." *Social Forces* 37:312–315.

Voss, Kim 1996 "The Collapse of a Social Movement: The Interplay of Mobilizing Structures. Framing, and Political Opportunities in the Knights of Labor." In *Comparative Perspectives on Social Movements*, ed. Doug McAdam, John D. McCarthy, and Mayer N. Zald, 277–258. New York: Cambridge University Press.

Warnick, Barbara 1977 "The Rhetoric of Conservative Resistance." *The Southern Speech Communication Journal* 42:256–273.

Wilkins, Lee 1993 "Between Facts and Values: Print Media Coverage of the Greenhouse Effect, 1987–1990." *Public Understanding of Science* 2:71–84.

Williams, Jerry 1998 "Knowledge, Consequences, and Experience: The Social Construction of Environmental Problems." *Sociological Inquiry* 68:476–497.

Williams Jerry, and R. Scott Frey 1997 "The Changing Status of Global Warming as a Social Problem: Competing Factors in Two Public Arenas." *Research in Community Sociology* 7:279–299.

Zald, Mayer N. 1996 "Culture, Ideology, and Strategic Framing." In *Comparative Perspectives on Social Movements: Political Opportunities, Mobilizing Structures, and Cultural Framings*, ed. Doug McAdam, John D. McCarthy, and Mayer N. Zald, 261–274. New York: Cambridge University Press.

Zald, Mayer N., and Bert Useem 1987 "Movement and Countermovement Interaction: Mobilization, Tactics, and State Involvement." In *Social Movements in an Organizational Society: Collected Essays*, ed. Mayer N. Zald and John D. McCarthy, 247–271. New Brunswick: Transaction Books.

PART VII

PEACE AND DISARMAMENT

CHAPTER SIXTEEN

Banning the Bomb

David Cortright

Source: David Cortright *Peace: A History of a Movements and Ideas* (2008) 126–54 © 2008 Cambridge University Press—Reproduced with permission.

With advent of the nuclear age the challenge of disarmament became enormously more urgent. At stake in the struggle to reduce armaments and prevent war was nothing less than *The Fate of the Earth*, as Jonathan Schell wrote, the very survival of human life.[1] Among the first to speak out against the new horror of self-destruction were the atomic scientists who built the bomb. Their efforts were followed in subsequent decades by waves of citizen activism in the late 1950s and early 1960s and then in the 1980s, which produced some of the largest mobilizations for peace in human history. These movements generated political pressure for arms control in the 1960s and 70s and for arms reduction at the end of the 1980s that brought an end to the cold war. They established a nuclear taboo in politics and culture that generated enduring pressure on the nuclear weapons states to reduce and deemphasize their reliance on nuclear weapons. This chapter summarizes the history of the struggle to ban the bomb and examines further implications of the relationship between disarmament and peace.

The Shock of Discovery

The explosion of the first atomic bomb at the Trinity site in New Mexico on 16 July 1945 had a transforming impact on the scientists and military officials who witnessed it. Robert Jungk observed in *Brighter Than a Thousand Suns* that many of those present—who otherwise professed no religious faith—"recounted their experiences in words derived from the linguistic fields of myth and theology." General Thomas Farrell, deputy director of the Manhattan Project, described the "strong, sustained, awesome roar which warned of doomsday and made us feel that we puny things were blasphemous to dare tamper with the forces heretofore reserved to the Almighty." J. Robert Oppenheimer, director of the Los Alamos scientists and a savant of Eastern religion, reflected on passages from the Bhagavad-Gita, the sacred Hindu epic:

> If the radiance of a thousand suns
> were to burst into the sky,
> that would be like
> the splendor of the Mighty One

As the sinister mushroom cloud rose in the distance, Oppenheimer was reminded of another line from the Gita: "I am become Death, the shatterer of worlds."

The bombings of Hiroshima and Nagasaki left many of the atomic scientists disturbed and bewildered. The scientists suddenly found themselves in an unprecedented and unaccustomed position of public acclaim. As Jungk writes, "the godlike magnitude of their performance had given them the standing of mythical figures. . . . They were called titans and compared with Prometheus."[2] Yet many felt uneasy about the destructive power their discoveries had unleashed. Some began to contemplate how they might put their new-found status to use in urging international control of atomic energy. A few expressed the cautious hope, as biophysicist Eugene Rabinowitch phrased it, "that the fate of Hiroshima and Nagasaki would cause [humankind] to turn a new leaf." Rabinowitch invited fellow scientists to be part of a "conspiracy to preserve our civilization by scaring [people] into rationality."[3]

It is one of history's supreme ironies that Einstein, the great pacifist, played a key role in urging the development of atomic weapons. Einstein's August 1939 letter to President Roosevelt recommending the development of a US nuclear program became the basis for the creation of the Project. At the end of the war Einstein regretted his action and felt that he and the atomic scientists who worked on the Manhattan Project had been deceived. He had supported the bomb only to guard against possible German development of such a weapon. He assumed that the United States would never use the bomb except to deter or retaliate against the use of such a weapon by another country. The bombing of a prostrate Japan on the verge of surrender was not what he had envisioned.

The feared German bomb never materialized. American military leaders had unequivocal proof well before the end of the war that Germany did not have a functioning atomic bomb program. When allied troops entered Germany after D-Day, a special intelligence unit code-named Alsos followed close behind to search for the suspected nuclear program. They tested Germany's rivers and found no evidence of the radionuclides that would signal the presence of uranium processing. They searched German-controlled research facilities in occupied France and Germany. They reviewed documents and interviewed scientists. They discovered that the German atomic research program was at least two years behind that of the United States, and that Germany possessed no factories for the production of enriched uranium or plutonium. By early 1945 it was clear that the dreaded German bomb did not exist.

[. . .]

Scientists Organize

One of the first scientists to sound the alarm about the danger of atomic weapons was Leo Szilard. As early as September 1942, Szilard drafted a memo outlining the ominous implications of the work upon which they were embarked. "We cannot have peace in a world in which various sovereign nations have atomic bombs in the possession of their armies."[4] At the Metallurgical Laboratory at the University of Chicago, where the first nuclear chain reaction took place in December 1942, a committee of atomic scientists began addressing the political problems of controlling and harnessing nuclear energy. The committee produced a 1944 report, "Prospectus on Nucleonics," which warned that attempts to achieve atomic supremacy could not bring lasting security. The report argued for the creation of "an international administration with police powers which can effectively control . . . the means of nucleonic warfare."[5]

In June 1945 the Chicago scientists produced a new report, largely written by Rabinowitch, which argued against the military use of the bomb against Japan. The report warned that there could be no effective defense against atomic weapons. It argued against bombing Japan because this could shatter the prospects for establishing the necessary degree of trust and mutual confidence to establish international control.

"If the United States were to be the first to release this new means of indiscriminate destruction upon mankind, she would sacrifice public support throughout the world, precipitate the race for armaments, and prejudice the possibility of reaching an international agreement on the future control of such weapons," the scientists wrote.[6] The report argued for a public demonstration of the new weapon in a desert or on a barren island. It urged American leaders to renounce the use of such weapons in the future and to join in the establishment of an international control mechanism.

When the government rejected the scientists' reports and proceeded with the bombings of Japan, the scientists joined together to form the Federation of Atomic Scientists, which soon changed its name to the Federation of American Scientists. Their mission was to enlighten the public about the new atomic danger and apply pressure on political leaders for international control. By early 1946 the FAS claimed seventeen local groups with nearly 3,000 members, including 90 percent of the scientists who had worked on the bomb. At the same time Rabinowitch and some of his colleagues in Chicago founded a new publication, the *Bulletin of Atomic Scientists*, which was to become, and remains today, the premier journal and most authoritative source of information on the state of the nuclear danger. Featuring the distinctive "doomsday clock," designed by Edward Teller, the *Bulletin* by mid-1947 had a circulation of 20,000, including scientists in seventeen countries. Szilard and Einstein organized the parallel Emergency Committee of Atomic Scientists, to help raise funds for the movement. Einstein served as chair of the committee, which was endorsed by other prominent scientists, including Hans Bethe and Linus Pauling. Szilard was the active force behind the Committee and played a crucial role in building the scientists movement.[7]

The atomic scientists' most urgent demand was for international control of atomic energy. For a brief time in early 1946 they helped to convince an otherwise skeptical US government to consider eliminating atomic weapons and establishing a system of international control of nuclear energy. When the bombs were dropped on Japan, President Truman had declared that Americans "must constitute ourselves trustees of this new force. . . . We thank God that it has come to us, instead of our enemies."[8] Within a few weeks, however, the administration began to consider a different approach. Future Secretary of State Dean Acheson drafted a message for the president in early October that declared "the hope of civilization lies in international arrangements looking, if possible, to the renunciation of the use and development of the atomic bomb."[9] In November US, British, and Canadian leaders issued a remarkable statement echoing many of the views of the scientists. There is no defense against atomic weapons, they declared, and no nation can maintain a monopoly on the new technology. The path to security lies in preventing war and establishing international control over this new power. The joint declaration of November 1945 was followed by the meeting of US, British, and Soviet foreign ministers on 27 December 1945, which supported the proposal for international control and called for the formation of an atomic energy commission under the authority of the United Nations. The very first resolution adopted by the UN General Assembly, meeting in London on 24 January 1946, called "for the elimination from national armaments of atomic weapons and of all other major weapons adaptable to mass destruction."[10] The resolution created a UN Atomic Energy Commission charged with developing immediate plans for: a) control of atomic energy to the extent necessary to ensure its use only for peaceful purposes; b) the elimination from national armaments of atomic weapons and of all other major weapons adaptable to mass destruction; and c) effective safeguards by way of inspection and other means to protect complying states against the hazards of violations and evasions.

To formulate the details of the nuclear control policy adopted at the UN, Truman appointed a special committee headed by Acheson, with significant input from David Lilienthal, director of the Tennessee Valley Authority. In March 1946 the committee presented one of the most far-reaching proposals of the nuclear era, which became known as the Acheson-Lilienthal plan. The proposal offered a formula for controlling atomic energy and preventing a nuclear arms race. It provided for the creation of an international body, an Atomic Development Authority, which would maintain a monopoly on the production of fissile materials and distribute them only in "denatured" form for peaceful purposes. The plan called for the elimination of atomic weapons then in existence (i.e. US weapons) and the creation of a system of international owner-ship and inspection to prevent the further development of such weapons and to guard against violations. Oppenheimer wrote that the report "proposes that in the field of atomic energy there be set up a world government, that in this field there be renunciation of national sovereignty." The plan contained, he believed, "new and healthy avenues of approach [for] the problem of preventing war."[11] It was a remarkable reflection of pacifist insight in the development of public policy.

The Baruch Plan

The success of the scientists and their allies was short-lived, however, for Truman soon appointed financier Bernard Baruch to serve as the US representative to the UN Atomic Energy Commission and gave him a free hand to formulate the specific proposal that would be presented to the United Nations. When Oppenheimer, Lilienthal, and other scientists learned of Baruch's appointment, they were deeply disappointed. Baruch was known as a self-promoter and a hard-liner who disdained the proposals of the scientists. Baruch's June 1946 address to the United Nations Atomic Energy Commission in New York began dramatically with an apocalyptic refer-ence: "We are here to make a choice between the quick and the dead." He spoke grandly of abolishing war, but the specific proposal he offered significantly diminished the prospects for creating a more secure world. The Baruch plan differed substantially from its predecessor. His plan called for a UN control body that would have the power to punish offending nations through enforceable sanctions, including military means. The destruction of existing [US] atomic weapons would come only at the end of the process, after the UN control body had con-ducted on-site inspections and had assured the dismantlement of all nuclear capabilities in other countries. The United States would have retained its monopoly on nuclear weapons until after the last stages of the disarmament process, when nuclear programs in other countries were dismantled. Soviet Foreign Minister Andrei Gromyko promptly dismissed the Baruch plan and proposed instead that the United States destroy its existing nuclear stockpiles first, before crea-tion of a system of international control. This was an equally one-sided proposal, from the opposite perspective, and would have allowed the Soviet Union to continue its rapidly develop-ing nuclear program while the United States disarmed unilaterally. The two nations entered an immediate stalemate, which persisted for decades.

During the cold war and afterwards, a kind of historical mythology developed around the Baruch Plan. Realists described Moscow's rejection of the plan as a sign of Soviet perfidy and a cause of the cold war. Arms controllers looked back upon the plan as a significant US initiative for the elimination of atomic weapons and international control of nuclear energy. Neither assumption was entirely correct. Stalin no doubt intended to pursue the development of nuclear weapons regardless of any diplomatic commitments, but the Baruch proposal was obviously one-sided. It was an assertion of unilateral US advantage, not a serious proposal for the elimina-tion of nuclear weapons or international control of atomic energy. From the very beginning of the atomic age, the United States insisted on retaining its nuclear weapons while demanding that other countries give up theirs. This has remained the basis of US nonproliferation policy to the present, and is a continuing obstacle to progress toward genuine disarmament.

Washington's declared intention to eliminate nuclear weapons might have been taken more seriously if the United States had not been at that very moment building additional bombs and preparing to begin nuclear testing on Bikini Atoll in the Pacific. On the very day Baruch spoke, the US Congress passed and President Truman signed a bill allowing the use of Navy ships as targets in the coming atomic tests.[12] Several Senators objected to the resolution and the tests, arguing that the US would be accused of double talk at the UN, but their concerns were swept aside. Two weeks later, on 1 July 1946, Test Able exploded over Bikini ending any further pretense of an American interest in eliminating nuclear weapons.

Meanwhile historical amnesia descended over the Acheson-Lilienthal plan and the first resolution of the United Nations that preceded it. Few historians acknowledged that for a few fleeting months in early 1946, the US government was committed to a plan for the elimination of nuclear weapons, and that the United States pledged to dismantle its existing nuclear capabilities in conjunction with the establishment of an international atomic control mechanism. The Acheson-Lilienthal plan had flaws, especially the lack of mechanisms for assuring international compliance, but it offered the promise of genuine diplomatic dialogue for the control of atomic weapons. The plan contained crucial provisions—a US commitment to eliminate its weapons in concert with the creation of an international control mechanism—that were then and remain today necessary foundations upon which to build international cooperation to prevent nuclear war.

In the wake of the collapse of the Baruch plan, and in the face of mounting hostility from an increasingly cold war-minded US government, the atomic scientists movement waned. The political atmosphere for nuclear disarmament became increasingly oppressive. Fear and distrust began to strain relations and friendships among the scientists. The anticommunist hysteria of the time was directed especially toward the foreign-born scientists who had helped to discover the secrets of the atom. More than half of those who were labeled communists during the congressional hearings of the early 1950s were physicists and mathematicians. Hundreds of scientists were mercilessly hounded and dismissed from their jobs. By 1951 the Emergency Committee of Atomic Scientists dissolved, and the Federation of American Scientists dwindled to just 1,000 members.[13] The *Bulletin of Atomic Scientists* lost subscribers, but it continued to publish, and persisted to become a vital voice of sanity in the succeeding waves of disarmament activism which emerged in the late 1950s and again in the 1980s.

For Nuclear Sanity

Disarmament activism revived in the late 1950s in parallel with the increase in nuclear weapons testing, especially H-bomb explosions, and the consequent rise of public concerns about radioactive fallout. In the years from 1945 through 1963, the United States and the Soviet Union conducted more than 550 nuclear tests, most of them in the atmosphere, including nearly 100 nuclear explosions at the Nevada test site. Radioactive debris from these explosions drifted over nearby towns, especially St. George, Utah, and was carried aloft over much of the country. Approximately 250,000 US soldiers participated in military maneuvers at the test site, exposing them to high levels of radioactivity. Many later suffered from leukemia and cancer. In the 1980s the survivors and their families formed the Atomic Veterans Association, which lobbied for and eventually won government compensation for the radiation-induced illnesses and premature deaths that resulted from their exposure. Fears of radioactive fallout and nuclear war increased not only in the United States but throughout the world.

One of the strongest voices against the worsening nuclear peril in the 1950s was that of British philosopher Bertrand Russell, a veteran pacifist who had opposed the Boer War, supported conscientious objectors during World War I, campaigned for peace during the interwar years, and endorsed the world federalist movement after World War II. In 1955 Russell joined with Einstein and other renowned international scientists in issuing an appeal for governments to acknowledge the suicidal nature of nuclear weapons and work for peace. In 1957 Linus Pauling issued a statement signed by 11,000 scientists, including 2,000 Americans, calling for a ban on atmospheric testing.[14] That same year atomic scientists from several countries, including the Soviet Union, gathered at a conference center in Pugwash, Nova Scotia for the start of annual meetings that provided a unique opportunity for dialogue between western scientists and their counterparts in the east. The Pugwash movement remains active today and in 1995 won the Nobel Prize for peace. Receiving the award for the scientists movement was Joseph Rotblat, the Polish-born physicist who had resigned from the Manhattan Project when he learned that the German bomb did not exist (he was the only scientist to do so) and who remained a stalwart campaigner for nuclear disarmament until his death in 2005 at age ninety-six.

It was during this time of nuclear awakening that two of the most important antinuclear organizations of the cold war era emerged, the Campaign for Nuclear Disarmament, CND, in Britain and the National Committee for a Sane Nuclear Policy, SANE, in the United States. CND debuted at a large public meeting at Central Hall, Westminster in February 1958. Addressing that inaugural meeting were Russell, Canon L. John Collins (the first chair of CND), playwright J. B. Priestley, former military commander Stephen King-Hall, Labour MP Michael Foot and historian A.J.P. Taylor. During 1958 and the years following CND flourished, drawing support from youth, the churches, and rank and file members of the Labour Party. By 1960 CND had more than 450 local groups. A CND demonstration that year in Trafalgar Square attracted more than 60,000 people, the largest public rally held in London in more than a hundred years.[15]

The National Committee for a Sane Nuclear Policy was formed in the United States in 1957. Founders included writer Norman Cousins, Clarence Pickett of the American Friends Service Committee, Norman Thomas of the Socialist Party, and Homer Jack, a Unitarian minister from Chicago. The name SANE was inspired by the work of the famed psychoanalyst and author Erich Fromm, whose book *The Sane Society* was highly influential at the time and who urged citizens to lift a "voice of sanity" against nuclear fear. SANE attracted the support of other peace groups and endorsements from prominent public figures, including Rev. Henry Emerson Fosdick, Paul Tillich, James Shotwell, Eleanor Roosevelt, and Cleveland Amory. Through a series of creative full-page ads in the *New York Times* (including one that featured Dr. Benjamin Spock worrying about the effects of fallout on children), SANE gained public attention and popular support. Within a year the organization had 150 local committees and some 25,000 members. Its most prominent chapter emerged in Hollywood, where actor Steve Allen gathered nearly 150 artists and entertainers to create the Hollywood for SANE committee.[16]

CND and SANE had many similarities (CND's newsletter was entitled *Sanity*), and they waxed and waned in parallel over the decades, as antinuclear activism rose in late 1950s and early 1960s, declined subsequently, and then rose to even greater heights in the late 1970s and early 1980s. The two groups differed in political approaches, however. CND from the outset was more explicit in supporting the demand for unilateral disarmament. In 1960 CND supporters mounted a successful effort to win official Labour Party endorsement of a resolution urging "the unilateral renunciation of the testing, manufacture, stockpiling and basing of all nuclear weapons in Great Britain."[17] The victory for unilateralism was short-lived, however, as the Labour Party reversed its position the following year. The CND program also included demands for multilateral objectives, such as a nuclear test ban treaty and the creation of nuclear-free zones, but the principle of unilateralism remained part of the CND program. Independent initiatives could stimulate mutual disarmament, CND leaders emphasized, by helping to reduce tensions and sparking a process of reciprocal reduction.

SANE's political program was more moderate than that of CND, focusing on an end to nuclear testing. SANE emphasized that its program was "not unilateralist," although it supported "political and military initiatives by the US to break the present impasse," which it hoped would encourage a "peace race" to replace the arms race. SANE's political methods focused on public education and political and legislative action aimed at decision makers in Washington. Although concentrating on testing issues, SANE also supported broader disarmament goals. A national conference in October 1959 adopted a program that included "comprehensive disarmament, a strong U.N. capable of enforcing world law, and the transition to a peacetime economy."[18]

Other disarmament groups formed at the time. In 1961 Dagmar Wilson joined with other women to create Women Strike for Peace, which consciously projected an image of "housewives" resisting nuclear destruction to save their children. In 1962 Leo Szilard founded the Council for a Livable World as a political action committee to support prodisarmament candidates. Throughout the United States and in many other countries, antinuclear activism increased. In Africa political leaders were outraged in 1960 when France detonated three nuclear bombs in the Sahara. Tanzania's Julius Nyerere decried the "humiliation under which we in Africa still labour . . . [when] a government can sit in Paris and decide what piece of Africa they are going to use for testing their hydrogen bomb!"[19] In Ghana the government froze French assets and Kwame Nkrumah threatened a mass nonviolent march into the testing zone.[20]

The Beginning of Arms Control

As the public outcry against radioactive fallout intensified in the early 1960s, government leaders were forced to respond. Political pressure for a test ban treaty was especially strong in Britain, where Prime Minister Harold Macmillan told President Kennedy that public pressures against testing were running high and that the British cabinet "wished for some new disarmament initiative to be taken and given wide publicity." The public clamor for an end to testing convinced US and Soviet leaders that, as Lawrence Wittner observed, "nuclear arms control measures made good politics."[21] A diplomatic breakthrough came in 1963, thanks partly to the intermediary role of SANE co-chair Norman Cousins, who met separately with Kennedy and Khrushchev to identify mutually acceptable terms. The resulting test ban treaty was a political landmark, the first nuclear disarmament agreement. It was also a triumph for public health and the environment, ending the radioactive poisoning of the earth's atmosphere. The treaty helped to reduce US-Soviet tensions, but it did not stop the arms race. Nuclear testing went underground and in fact accelerated. More nuclear explosions were conducted in the years after the test ban treaty than before. Nonetheless, the agreement was a beginning of the arms control process, and it established a precedent that eventually culminated in significant nuclear disarmament nearly three decades later. When the treaty was signed Kennedy expressed "deep gratification" to Cousins and other disarmament advocates for "mobilizing American public opinion in favor of a test-ban."[22]

The signing of the test ban treaty was a significant victory for the ban the bomb movement and gave a boost to the cause of nuclear pacifism. The weight of public pressure was a major factor in the political calculations of political leaders at the time. As Wittner wrote,

the antinuclear movement . . . constrained the major actors and helped shape the choices they made. . . . Antinuclear sentiment eased the dangerous international confrontation, slowed the nuclear arms race, and provided the basis for the unprecedented nuclear arms control agreements that were to follow.[23]

US, British, and Soviet leaders could not ignore the worldwide protest against radioactive fallout and the growing demands for a halt to nuclear testing. The cause of nuclear disarmament gained new legitimacy and public support. The cruciform symbol of CND "became as well known as the Union Jack," wrote Collins, and earned an enduring place in popular culture as the universal peace sign.[24] New organizations emerged and continued to function after the signing of the test ban treaty to carry on the fight for disarmament. The stage was set for the dramatic upsurge in disarmament activism that began fifteen years later.

Nuclear Pacifism in Japan

Opposition to nuclear weapons spread far beyond Europe and North America, as Wittner documented in his magisterial three-volume study on the world nuclear disarmament movement. Nowhere was support for the nuclear disarmament movement stronger or more persistent than in Japan, which has special authority and motivation on this issue as the only nation to suffer nuclear attack. The annual commemorative ceremonies at Hiroshima and Nagasaki became not only rituals for memorializing the dead but fervent pleas for nuclear disarmament and world peace. They affirmed a unique Japanese mission to work for the elimination of atomic weapons, and expressed the hope that the ordeal of those two cities might somehow be redeemed through a worldwide commitment to end war.[25]

Japanese antinuclear sentiment began to crystallize in 1954, when several Japanese fishermen aboard the ironically named *Lucky Dragon* were severely contaminated (one was killed) by radioactive fallout from a US nuclear test conducted at Bikini Atoll. The episode galvanized public opinion and sparked widespread antinuclear protest. Nearly 20 million signatures were collected on petitions calling for disarmament and an end to nuclear tests. Both the upper and lower chambers of parliament adopted unanimous resolutions calling for a ban on nuclear weapons. Most prefectural governments and some 250 municipalities passed similar resolutions.[26] For the first time in Japanese history, the peace movement gained widespread support and respectability within society and was able to influence government decision makers.

In the late 1950s, in response to the worldwide crisis over nuclear testing and radioactive fallout, the nuclear disarmament movement intensified. Gensuikyo, affiliated with the Socialist Party, became the leading force behind the mobilization of antinuclear sentiment and gained the endorsement of prominent Japanese leaders from all walks of life. In 1958 the famous social reformer Kagawa Toyohiko joined with Albert Schweitzer and Bertrand Russell in an open letter to world leaders urging a suspension of nuclear tests.[27] More than 1000 Japanese scientists signed Linus Pauling's petition against nuclear testing. Public opinion polls showed some 90 percent of the population opposed to nuclear testing and supporting a worldwide ban on nuclear weapons. The student federation Zengakuren organized hundreds of thousands of students to participate in public rallies and boycotts of classes. Protests were directed at both US and Soviet nuclear testing. Zengakuren activists unfurled a banner in Moscow's Red Square denouncing Soviet nuclear tests, and they organized massive rallies outside the Soviet Embassy in Tokyo.[28]

Antinuclear activism surged again in the 1980s. In preparation for the Second UN Special Session on Disarmament, which convened in New York in the spring of 1982, the major Japanese peace and disarmament groups joined together with a wide range of mainstream civil society groups to form the Japanese National Liaison Committee for Nuclear and General Disarmament. The Liaison Committee collected nearly 29 million signatures on a nuclear disarmament petition, which was presented to the United Nations in June 1982, at the time of the giant rally for disarmament in New York's Central Park that attracted nearly one million people. An anti-nuclear petition organized by the Union of New Religions was signed by more than 36 million people. Some 200,000 people participated in a disarmament rally in Hiroshima in March 1982, and 400,000 demonstrated in Tokyo in May of that year. More than 1,400 local governments passed resolutions urging the Japanese government to promote disarmament at the UN Special Session.[29]

The Rise of the Nuclear Freeze

The nuclear freeze and disarmament movements of the late 1970s and 1980s were a response to the accelerating nuclear buildup of the Soviet Union and the United States. The specific catalyst was the deployment by the Soviet Union of new intermediate range nuclear missiles (the SS 20) in eastern Europe in the late 1970s and the corresponding deployment by the United States in NATO countries of cruise and Pershing II missiles. The Soviet invasion of Afghanistan added to an already tense political climate and sparked a renewed cold war response in the United States which paved the way for the election of Ronald Reagan. Some European governments also hardened their policies toward the Soviet Union, although the people of Europe generally rejected the atmosphere of renewed cold war hostility.

Like the previous ban the bomb movement, the antinuclear campaigns of the late 1970s were rooted in environmental consciousness and growing public concerns about radiation and the fragility of nuclear technology. The accident at the Three Mile Island nuclear reactor in Pennsylvania in March 1979 gave a decisive boost to the antinuclear cause and accelerated the organizing that led to the nuclear weapons freeze campaign. In Germany the movement against nuclear power in the 1970s laid the foundation for the massive campaign against nuclear missiles in the 1980s. As public opposition to nuclear technology increased, a visceral fear of radiation spread throughout society. The "primitive fear" that Cousins had identified at the dawn of the atomic age reemerged and deepened.[30]

During the early 1980s nuclear fear reached unprecedented levels. Opinion surveys found a huge jump in the percentage of people fearing nuclear war. According to the Gallup poll of September 1981, 70 percent of Americans surveyed felt that nuclear war was a real possibility, and 30 percent felt that the chances of such a conflict were "good" or "certain."[31] In Europe the fear of nuclear war was even greater. The percentage of Europeans believing that nuclear war was "probable in the next 10 years" rose from just over 10 percent in 1977 to more than 30 percent in 1980. In West Germany, fear of nuclear war rose from 17 percent in July 1979 to a startling 48 percent in January 1980.[32] Daniel Yankelovich and John Doble wrote in *Foreign Affairs* that "a great change . . . has transformed the outlook of the American electorate," and the public is "determined to stop what they see as a drift toward nuclear confrontation."[33] This "sea change" was marked most significantly by widespread public doubt about the chances of surviving a nuclear war. Whereas in 1955, only 27 percent of the public thought humankind would be destroyed in an all-out nuclear war, thirty years later 89 percent agreed with that statement.

The new disarmament movements were also a response to the crisis in nuclear disarmament. The negotiated arms control agreements of the 1970s did not slow the arms race or reduce the nuclear danger but in fact allowed for the buildup of weapons on both sides. In the United States disarmament activists and liberal members of Congress grew increasingly frustrated with the Strategic Arms Limitation Treaty (SALT) process and began to search for a new approach that could reduce nuclear dangers and break the momentum of the continuing nuclear buildup. The idea of a US-Soviet nuclear freeze had been proposed in the early 1970s by Gerard Smith, chief US negotiator for the SALT I Treaty. The concept was raised again and developed in more detail by Richard Barnet of the Institute for Policy Studies in the spring 1979 issue of *Foreign Affairs*.[34] During the US Senate debate on the SALT II treaty that year, Senators Mark Hatfield and George McGovern introduced an amendment calling for a US-Soviet freeze on strategic nuclear weapons. These ideas soon crystallized into the proposal for a nuclear moratorium, which became the nuclear weapons freeze.

In 1980 Randall Forsberg, director of the Institute for Defense and Disarmament Studies in Massachusetts, issued the "Call to Halt the Arms Race." This was the founding manifesto of the nuclear weapons freeze campaign. Forsberg later published a feature article elaborating the rationale for a nuclear freeze in *Scientific American*.[35] The freeze proposal was breathtakingly simple yet profoundly significant in its political implications. It urged, the United States and the Soviet Union to accept an immediate, verifiable halt to the testing, production, and deployment of new nuclear weapons and their delivery systems.[36] This modest formulation became the basis for the nuclear weapons freeze campaign and sparked one of the largest peace mobilizations in American history.

The great political value of the freeze concept was its accessibility to the average citizen. It was "user friendly." Supporters did not need a Ph.D. in physics or a degree in international relations to understand and accept its logic. It was eagerly embraced by a public anxious for a way out of the worsening nuclear dilemma. The enormous popularity of nuclear disarmament in the 1980s transformed the politics of the nuclear debate. Previously an obscure and highly technical field reserved for experts, nearly all of them white males, nuclear policy-making now became the province of ordinary citizens. The debate over nuclear weapons and military strategy was radically democratized. The discussion of nuclear policy was removed from the cloistered board rooms of military strategists and taken to the city square. Ordinary citizens demanded a say in the most vital of all issues, the prevention of nuclear war and the survival of the human race. The antinuclear movements of Europe, although not adopting the nuclear freeze proposal per se, developed their own version of a demand for mutual disarmament. Their slogan was "no to SS-20s and cruise and Pershing missiles." This call for an end to nuclear deployments on both sides captured the essential symmetry of the freeze concept.

The demand for mutual disarmament by the Soviet Union and the United States was of profound political significance. Western peace advocates were able to transcend the limitations of previous campaigns that directed protests primarily against US nuclear weapons. By directing their political demands equally at Moscow and Washington, the disarmament activists of the 1980s dispelled the political stereotypes that had hindered earlier peace movements. They were able to overcome lingering suspicions from the early days of the cold war that disarmament activists were dupes of the Soviet Union. The demand for mutual disarmament enabled the peace movement to achieve a decisive breakthrough in political credibility.

God against the Bomb

One of the most distinctive features of the disarmament debate during the 1980s was the extensive involvement of the religious community. The engagement of the churches cast a "mantle of respectability" over the peace movement and gave new legitimacy to discussions of disarmament.[37] When religious leaders spoke out for reversal of the arms race, it became easier and more acceptable for others to express similar views. The backing of the religious community made peace a mainstream issue and gave credibility and momentum to the disarmament movement. The enhanced legitimacy arising from this support strengthened peace activism and helped to generate the political pressure that ultimately led to changes in nuclear policy.

Veteran religious peace activists like William Sloane Coffin Jr. and Jim Wallis played a decisive role in building the disarmament and nuclear freeze campaigns of the 1980s. As senior minister of New York's prestigious Riverside Church, Coffin initiated a disarmament program that reached thousands of clergy and laity across the United States. *Sojourners* editor Wallis was on the founding committee of the nuclear weapons freeze campaign. Along with Coffin he played an important role in articulating the moral and religious argument for disarmament. Religious peace organizations like Pax Christi, the Fellowship of Reconciliation, and the American Friends Service Committee were major players in the developing disarmament movement.

By far the most significant statement from American religious leaders during the 1980s was the pastoral letter of the US Catholic Conference of Bishops, *The Challenge of Peace: God's Promise and Our Response*, issued in May 1983. Written by Father J. Bryan Hehir for a committee of bishops chaired by Joseph Cardinal Bernardin of Chicago, with significant input from Bishop Thomas Gumbleton of Detroit, the Bishop's pastoral letter had a profound impact on public discourse. The letter from the normally conservative Catholic hierarchy challenged the very foundations of US nuclear policy and specifically opposed key elements of the Reagan administration's military buildup.

While avoiding the phrase "nuclear freeze," the bishops declared their support for "immediate bilateral agreements to halt the testing, production and deployment of nuclear weapons systems." They endorsed a policy of no first use and a comprehensive nuclear test ban treaty. The bishops condemned any initiation of nuclear war and opposed even retaliatory strikes that threaten innocent life. The logic of this position should have led the bishops to reject any possession of nuclear weapons and to oppose the doctrine of nuclear deterrence itself, since these are predicated on the threat of nuclear weapons use. The bishops chose instead to offer an interim "strictly conditioned" acceptance of nuclear deterrence, with the provision that "nuclear deterrence should be used as a step on the way toward progressive disarmament."[38] The influential Catholic journal *Commonweal* called the Catholic pastoral letter a "watershed event" not only for the church but for society as a whole.[39] George Kennan wrote in the *New York Times* that the bishops' letter was "the most profound and searching inquiry yet conducted by any responsible collective body into the relations of nuclear weaponry, and indeed of modern war in general."[40]

Many other religious bodies and church denominations issued statements condemning nuclear weapons during the 1980s. Most of the Protestant churches went further than the Catholic bishops in condemning the very existence of nuclear weapons. The uneasy acceptance of nuclear deterrence that had characterized the Protestant tradition prior to the 1980s gave way in many instances to explicit endorsement of disarmament. Not only the use but the very possession of nuclear weapons became unacceptable. The American Lutheran Church and the Lutheran Church of America passed resolutions urging the elimination of nuclear weapons. The executive ministers of the American Baptist Church called the existence of nuclear weapons and the willingness to use them "a direct affront to our Christian beliefs." At the World Council of Churches assembly in Vancouver in 1983, delegates proclaimed:

"We believe that the time has come when the churches must unequivocally declare that the production and deployment as well as the use of nuclear weapons are a crime against humanity and that such activities must be condemned on ethical and theological grounds."[41]

Many pastoral letters were issued during the 1980s but none was more far-reaching in its condemnation of nuclear policy than that of the United Methodist Church. The Methodist document, *In Defense of Creation*, went beyond the Catholic letter in a number of respects. It was more radical in its critique of nuclear policy and explicitly rejected not only the arms race but the whole concept of deterrence. Addressing the ambiguity left by their Catholic colleagues, the Methodist bishops declared that nuclear deterrence "must no longer receive the churches' blessing, even as a temporary warrant." The Methodist statement also addressed the economic consequences of the arms race: "Justice is forsaken in the squandering of wealth in the arms race while a holocaust of hunger, malnutrition, disease, and violent death is destroying the world's poorest peoples."[42] The Methodist bishops supported a comprehensive test ban, a ban on space weapons, and no first use of nuclear weapons.

The Jewish community also spoke out for disarmament in the 1980s. The Union of American Hebrew Congregations, led by rabbis Alexander Schindler and David Saperstein, was an early supporter of the nuclear weapons freeze proposal and sponsored local educational forums in synagogues and among community groups across the country. Even conservative Jewish groups spoke out against the nuclear threat. In April 1982, the Rabbinical Assembly of America issued a statement endorsing the nuclear freeze. In February 1983, the Synagogue Council of America, an umbrella group embracing all branches of Judaism, adopted a resolution urging that the United States and the Soviet Union "implement a bilateral mutual cessation of the production and deployment of nuclear weapons."[43]

The involvement of the religious community in the nuclear debate in the 1980s played a major role in generating public pressure and support for nuclear disarmament. The clergy who issued pastoral letters and declarations against the nuclear danger awakened public consciousness and encouraged citizen activism. This religious community involvement was decisive in shaping the political climate and building public support for peace and disarmament.

A Prairie Fire

The nuclear weapons freeze movement swept through the United States in the 1980s like the proverbial prairie fire. It began with a ballot initiative in western Massachusetts in the 1980 election. The proposal for a bilateral nuclear freeze was endorsed by 59 percent of voters in rural districts that went heavily for Ronald Reagan. The freeze proposal thus demonstrated its ability to win voter approval among conservatives as well as liberals. Hundreds of local town meetings in Vermont and other New England states subsequently voted to endorse the freeze. By 1982, the freeze had been endorsed by eleven state legislatures, more than 200 city councils, and forty county governments.[44] Support for the freeze poured in from prominent academic scholars and former government officials. More than 150 national organizations endorsed the freeze, including the U.S. Conference of Mayors, the Young Women's Christian Association, the American Nurses Association, and more than two dozen of the largest US trade unions.[45]

The most dramatic expressions of support for disarmament came in 1982. On June 12 nearly one million people marched to New York's Central Park to protest the nuclear arms race. It was the largest peace demonstration in US history. That year disarmament organizers and sympathetic public officials also placed the nuclear freeze proposition on the ballot in numerous locations. A quarter of the American electorate voted in what amounted to an informal national referendum on the nuclear arms race. It was the largest electoral mobilization for peace in US history. The vote in California was especially significant, not only because of the state's size and leadership in establishing national trends but because the White House mounted a major campaign of opposition. The freeze resolution won by a 52–48 margin in an election where Republicans swept statewide races. Nationwide the freeze resolution was approved in eight out of nine states and in many of the country's largest cities. Across the nation, 18 million Americans voted on the freeze, with 10.7 million, or 60 percent, voting in favor. As Representative

Ed Markey, the principal freeze leader in Congress, observed, "it was the closest our country has ever come to a national plebiscite on nuclear arms control." Disarmament activists translated their proposal for mutual disarmament into "political muscle at the ballot box, delivering to the White House a resounding vote of no-confidence in its nuclear buildup."[46]

Ferment in Europe

As the nuclear freeze campaign attracted growing support in the United States, an unprecedented wave of antinuclear activism spread across western Europe. The Soviet and NATO decisions to deploy new intermediate range nuclear missiles on the continent sparked the largest peace movement mobilization in modern European history. In the fall of 1981 and then again in October 1983, Europeans took to the streets by the millions to protest the nuclear arms race. Throughout western Europe, opposition to the new missiles reached enormous proportions, and the peace movement enjoyed unprecedented popularity. According to a 1982 poll, approval of the peace movement in the major NATO countries ranged from a low of 55 percent to a high of 81 percent. The result was intense political opposition to NATO and Soviet missiles, and powerful pressures not only against the intermediate range weapons but the entire cold war system of east-west nuclear competition.

In October 1981 more than 250,000 people gathered in Bonn, 100,000 marched in Brussels, 250,000 demonstrated in London, and half a million people took to the streets in several cities in Italy. A month later nearly 500,000 people jammed the streets of Amsterdam. A huge banner carried through the streets of Paris captured the message of the day: "Neither Pershings nor SS-20's."[47] In Milan a banner read "No to the Pentagon! No to the Kremlin!"[48] At nearly all of the rallies and mass demonstrations held that year and two years later in 1983, protesters called for the elimination of both Soviet and NATO nuclear weapons. The major organizations involved, such as the Interchurch Peace Council in the Netherlands and the Campaign for Nuclear Disarmament (CND) in Britain, criticized Soviet as well as NATO policy. To be sure, the emphasis was on western policy, since the demonstrators were citizens of NATO countries and were speaking primarily to their own governments, but Soviet policies were openly criticized as well.

One of the most significant antinuclear peace mobilizations of the 1980s was the women's peace camp at Greenham Common in Britain. In September 1981 members of the group "Women for Life on Earth" marched to the Greenham Common military base, which was scheduled to receive NATO missiles. The women decided to remain and kept up a continuous peace presence at the base for several years. The women's peace camp attracted significant media attention and prompted the creation of other long-term peace camps at more than a dozen sites in Britain and elsewhere in Europe. A similar camp was established in the United States at Rome Air Force base near Seneca, New York, site of the founding conference of the woman's suffrage movement more than a hundred years earlier. In December 1982 nearly 30,000 women representing various peace camps and other peace organizations descended upon Greenham Common for a major protest against nuclear weapons.[49] The encampment at Greenham Common became an inspiration to the antinuclear cause, especially to the women who played a leadership role in building the disarmament movement.

The culmination of the historic peace mobilization of the 1980s came in October 1983 when nearly 3 million people poured into the streets of cities all across western Europe to protest nuclear missile deployments and to demand an end to the arms race. In London more than 300,000 people assembled in Hyde Park for what the *New York Times* called the "the largest protest against nuclear weapons in British history."[50] Similar mobilizations of hundreds of thousands of people took place in Rome, Vienna, Brussels, Stockholm, Paris, Dublin, Copenhagen, and other cities.[51] The largest crowd assembled in The Hague, as nearly one million people filled the streets of the Dutch capital.[52] The biggest turnout of protesters occurred in West Germany, when on a single day, 400,000 marched in Bonn, 400,000 in Hamburg, 250,000 in Stuttgart, and 100,000 in West Berlin. In addition, more than 200,000 people participated in an extraordinary human chain that stretched continuously for sixty-four miles from the US Army headquarters in Stuttgart to the missile base at Neu Ulm.[53] The October 1983 demonstrations were the largest mobilization of peace sentiment in human history up to that time (the worldwide mobilization against war in Iraq in February 2003 was even larger).

Despite the massive outpouring of disarmament activism, NATO governments disregarded public opinion and proceeded with the deployment of cruise and Pershing intermediate range nuclear missiles. On the surface, it appeared that the peace movement had lost the battle against new nuclear weapons, and that all the massive mobilization of protest had been for naught. Yet the peace movement eventually prevailed in the larger political struggle against new nuclear weapons in Europe and the overall arms race. The Reagan administration responded to the antinuclear ferment in 1981 by proposing the "zero option" plan, which called for the elimination of all intermediate range nuclear weapons in Europe. Reagan supported the zero option, contrary to the advice of military officials, because it appealed to his desire to see nuclear weapons eliminated.[54] Some of his advisers saw political value in the proposal as a way of co-opting peace movement demands. A White House official told disarmament supporter Mary Kaldor, "We got the idea from your banners . . . the ones that say 'No cruise, No Pershing, No SS-20.'"[55] The White House fully expected that Brezhnev-era Soviet leaders would reject the plan, which they did. Even Mikhail Gorbachev was initially skeptical and tried to link Soviet acceptance of the plan to limits on the US Strategic Defense Initiative, which Reagan flatly refused. In 1987, Gorbachev unexpectedly dropped the demand for SDI linkage and accepted the zero option without conditions. NATO leaders had to accept the offer, despite serious misgivings from Henry Kissinger and other conservative leaders and former officials. In the end the peace position prevailed. Peace advocates crafted the message ("No to Soviet and NATO missiles") and created the antinuclear political climate that helped to produce the 1987 Intermediate-range Nuclear Forces (INF) treaty, which led to the ending of the cold war.

Who Won?

According to the conventional wisdom, the policies of peace-through-strength brought about the collapse of the Soviet Union. As Margaret Thatcher famously said "Ronald Reagan won the Cold War without firing a shot."[56] President George H.W. Bush made a similar claim in his State of the Union address in January 1992. It was the US military buildup, western officials declared, especially Reagan's cherished Strategic Defense Initiative, that broke the back of Soviet power and forced the Kremlin to sue for peace. This theory of cold war triumphalism has had an enduring impact on US strategic thinking, reinforcing the realist faith in the dominant influence of military power. American political leaders believe that more of the same— military buildups, wars of intervention, and coercive diplomacy—can bring further victories for western interests. This belief in the transformative effect of military might is at the core of political thinking in Washington and was part of the mentality that led to the war in Iraq. The consequences of misinterpreting history can be severe.

The cold war was ended not by military buildups but by Mikhail Gorbachev's "new thinking," which broke decisively with the logic of militarism, and by the pressures of disarmament activism, which created a political climate conducive to arms reduction and east-west understanding. Reagan deserved credit for accepting Soviet concessions and proposing sweeping nuclear reductions (including at Reykjavik the elimination of all nuclear weapons), but the leading role belonged to Gorbachev and to the people of Europe, west and east, who demanded political change. The Soviet system collapsed when millions of citizens and human rights campaigners in the east took to the streets in the historic "velvet revolution" of 1989. George Kennan described the triumphalist interpretation as "silly and childish." Military pressures from the west during the cold war were usually counterproductive and had the effect of reinforcing Soviet repression and militarism. "The general effect of cold war extremism was to delay rather than hasten the great change that overtook the Soviet Union at the end of the 1980's," Kennan observed.[57] As the Russian poet Yevgenii Yevtushenko put it, "your hardliners help our hardliners, and our hardliners help your hardliners."[58] The Soviet leaders responsible for changing Kremlin policy described the triumphalist interpretation as "absolute nonsense," according to Georgi Arbatov, and "a very big delusion," in the words of Gorbachev.[59] Alexander Yakovlev, the principal architect of perestroika, said that US hard-line policies "played no role. None. I can tell you with the fullest responsibility. Gorbachev and I were ready for changes in our policy regardless of whether the American President was Reagan, or . . . someone more liberal."[60] The pressures that brought change in the east came mainly from within, not without.

Missing from the conventional debates about who won the cold war is a recognition of the role of the peace movement. The first President Bush made a special point of attempting to dismiss the influence of antinuclear activism. On three occasions during the televised presidential and vice presidential debates of October 1992, Bush and his running mate, Dan Quayle, denounced the nuclear freeze movement. In fact, disarmament activism in the west played an important role in generating political pressures for an end to the cold war. Even before the advent of Gorbachev, the nuclear freeze movement began transforming the Reagan administration's approach to nuclear policy.[61] Arms control supporters in Congress forced the administration to adopt a more flexible negotiating approach toward the Soviet Union, and the White House began tailoring its rhetoric and declaratory policy to address the new climate of public opinion the movement helped to create. The decision to begin arms control negotiations (contrary to the administration's initial intentions), the shaping of the zero option and other bargaining positions at the Geneva talks, the stalemating of the MX missile program, the rejection of civil defense planning, the development of a formidable arms control lobby within Congress— all of these developments were the result of peace movement activism and occurred before Gorbachev came to power. Continued peace pressures placed constraints on the Strategic Defense Initiative, cut off funding for nuclear testing and restricted US military intervention in Central America. The global public mood in favor of disarmament provided encouragement for Gorbachev's initiatives and played a role in perhaps the most crucial Kremlin decision, de-linking the issue of intermediate-range missiles in Europe from the question of the Strategic Defense Initiative. As Gorbachev declared at a meeting of Soviet officials, "untying the package on the medium-range missiles . . . will be our response to the state of public opinion in the world."[62] This was the decisive step that opened the floodgates to negotiated arms reduction. The pressures generated by the disarmament movement pushed the political system toward nuclear restraint and helped to change the course of history.

[. . .]

Notes

1. Jonathan Schell, *The Fate of the Earth* (New York, Knopf, 1982).
2. Robert Jungk, *Brighter than a Thousand Suns: A Personal History of the Atomic Scientists* (New York: Harcourt Brace & Company, 1958), 201, 221–22.

3. Eugene Rabinowitch, "Five Years After," *Bulletin of the Atomic Scientists* VII, no. 1 (January 1951): 3.
4. Quoted in Lawrence S. Wittner, *One World or None: A History of the World Nuclear Disarmament Movement Through 1953*, vol. 1 of *The Struggle Against the Bomb* (Stanford: Stanford University Press, 1993), 20.
5. "Prospectus on Nucleonics (the Jeffries Report)," in *A Peril and a Hope: The Scientists' Movement in America: 1945–47*, ed. Alice Kimball Smith (Chicago: University of Chicago Press, 1965), 554.
6. James Franck, et al., "A Report to the Secretary of War (June 1945)," in *The Atomic Age: Scientists in National and World Affairs*, ed. Morton Grodzins and Eugene Rabinowitch, 19–27 (New York: Basic Books, 1963), 27.
7. Wittner, *One World or None*, 60–61.
8. Harry S. Truman, "Radio Report to the American People on the Potsdam Conference" (radio address, White House, Washington, D.C., 9 August 1945).
9. Quoted in Wittner, *One World or None*, 249.
10. United Nations General Assembly, *Establishment of a Commission to Deal with the Problems Raised by the Discovery of Atomic Energy*, 1 (I), London, 24 January 1946.
11. Quoted in Wittner, *One World or None*, 250–51.
12. Jonathan M. Weisgall, *Operation Crossroads: The Atomic Tests at Bikini Atoll* (Annapolis, Md.: Naval Institute Press, 1994), 101–03.
13. Wittner, *One World or None*, 266–67, 326.
14. Charles DeBenedetti, *The Peace Reform in American History* (Bloomington, Ind.: Indiana University Press, 1980), 160.
15. Lawrence S. Wittner, *Resisting the Bomb: A History of the World Nuclear Disarmament Movement, 1954–1970*, vol. 2 of *The Struggle Against the Bomb* (Stanford: Stanford University Press, 1997), 47, 185.
16. Milton S. Katz, *Ban the Bomb: A History of SANE, the Committee for a Sane Nuclear Policy, 1957–1985* (New York: Greenwood Press, 1986), 24, 42.
17. Quoted in Wittner, *Resisting the Bomb*, 186.
18. Quoted in Ibid., 247.
19. Julius K. Nyerere, *Freedom and Unity: Uhuru na umoja: A Selection from Writings and Speeches, 1952–65* (London: Oxford University Press, 1967), 69.
20. Kwame Nkrumah, *I Speak of Freedom: A Statement of African Ideology* (New York: Praeger, 1962), 214–215.
21. Wittner, *Resisting the Bomb*, 394–95, 415.
22. Quoted in Ibid., 418.
23. Ibid., 383.
24. Canon L. John Collins, *Faith Under Fire* (London: Leslie Frewin, 1966), 310.
25. Robert Kisala, *Prophets of Peace: Pacifism and Cultural Identity in Japan's New Religions* (Honolulu: University of Hawai'i Press, 1999), 175.
26. Mari Yamamoto, *Grassroots Pacifism in Post-war Japan: The Rebirth of a Nation* (London: RoutledgeCurzon, 2004), 167.
27. Robert Schildgen, *Toyohiko Kagawa: Apostle of Love and Social Justice* (Berkeley, Calif.: Centenary Books, 1988), 281.
28. Wittner, *Resisting the Bomb*, 42–43, 242–43.
29. Lawrence S. Wittner, *Toward Nuclear Abolition: A History of the World Nuclear Disarmament Movement, 1971 to the Present*, vol. 3 of *The Struggle Against the Bomb* (Stanford: Stanford University Press, 2003), 203–04.

30. Norman Cousins, *Modern Man is Obsolete* (New York: Viking Press, 1945), 7.
31. "Poll Finds 7 out of 10 Imagining Outbreak of Soviet Nuclear War," *Washington Post*, 27 September 1981, A17.
32. Thomas R. Rochon, *Mobilizing for Peace: The Antinuclear Movements in Western Europe* (Princeton, N.J.: Princeton University Press, 1988), 46–47.
33. Daniel Yankelovich and John Doble, "The Public Mood: Nuclear Weapons and the U.S.S.R.," *Foreign Affairs* 63, no. 1 (Fall 1984): 33–35.
34. Richard Barnet, "U.S.-Soviet Relations: The Need for a Comprehensive Approach," *Foreign Affairs* 57, no. 4 (Spring 1979): 779–795.
35. Randall Forsberg, "A Bilateral Nuclear-Weapon Freeze," *Scientific American* 247, no. 5 (November 1982): 52–61.
36. Pam Solo, *From Protest to Policy: Beyond the Freeze to Common Security* (Cambridge, Mass.: Ballinger Publishing, 1988), 45.
37. William Sloane Coffin, interview by the author, 3 December 1990.
38. National Conference of Catholic Bishops, *The Challenge of Peace: God's Promise and Our Response, A Pastoral Letter on War and Peace* (Washington, D.C.: United States Catholic Conference, 1983), 58–59.
39. "The Pastoral & The New Moment," *Commonweal* CX, no. 10 (20 May 1983): 291–92.
40. George F. Kennan, "The Bishops' Letter," *New York Times*, 1 May 1983, E21.
41. David Gill, ed., *Gathered for Life: Official Report, VI Assembly World Council of Churches* (Grand Rapids: Wm. B. Eerdmans, 1983), 137.
42. The United Methodist Council of Bishops, *In Defense of Creation: The Nuclear Crisis and a Just Peace* (Nashville, Tenn.: Graded Press, 1986), 48, 15.
43. L. Bruce van Voorst, "The Churches and Nuclear Deterrence," *Foreign Affairs* 61, no. 4 (Spring 1983): 845.
44. Neal R. Peirce and William R. Anderson, "Nuclear Freeze Proponents Mobilize on Local Referenda, House Elections," *National Journal* 14, no. 38 (18 September 1982): 1602–1605.
45. Solo, *From Protest to Policy*, 66.
46. Ed Markey, interview by the author, 28 August 1991.
47. Frank J. Prial, "50,000 March in Paris to Protest Weapons Buildup," *New York Times*, 26 October 1981, A11.
48. "100,000 in a Milan Peace March," *New York Times*, 1 November 1981, 6.
49. Alice Cook and Gwyn Kirk, *Greenham Women Everywhere: Dreams, Ideas and Actions from the Women's Peace Movement* (Cambridge, Mass.: South End Press, 1983), 32.
50. R.W. Apple, Jr., "Missile Protesters Jam Central London," *New York Times*, 23 October 1983, A16.
51. James A. Markham, "Vast Crowds hold Rallies in Europe against U.S. Arms," *New York Times*, 23 October 1983, A1; and Jon Nordheimer, "500,000 Join Dutch Antimissile Rally," *New York Times*, 30 October 1983, 3.
52. Rochon, *Mobilizing for Peace*, 6; and Maarten Huygen, "Dateline Holland: NATO's Pyrrhic Victory," *Foreign Affairs* 62 (12 November 1984): 176.
53. Rochon, *Mobilizing for Peace*, 6.
54. Paul Lettow, *Ronald Reagan and His Quest to Abolish Nuclear Weapons* (New York: Random House, 2005), 60.
55. Mary Kaldor, "'We Got the Idea from Your Banners'," *New Statesman* 113, no. 2920 (13 March 1987): 14–15.
56. Quoted in Dinesh D'Souza, "How Reagan Won the Cold War," *National Review* 49, no. 22 (24 November 1997): 38.

57. George Kennan, *At a Century's Ending: Reflections, 1982–1995* (New York: W.W. Norton, 1996), 185; George F. Kennan, "The G.O.P. Won the Cold War? Ridiculous.," *New York Times*, 28 October 1992.

58. *Moscow News*, 23–30 October 1988.

59. Georgi Arbatov, *The System: An Insider's Life in Soviet Politics* (New York: Random House, 1992); "A Very Big Delusion," *The New Yorker* 68, iss. 37, no. 2 (2 November 1992): 4.

60. Quoted in Wittner, *Toward Nuclear Abolition*, 487.

61. Ibid., 403, 446.

62. Quoted in Ibid., 397.

CHAPTER SEVENTEEN

The Ottawa Process: Nine-Day Wonder or a New Model for Disarmament Negotiations?

Maurice Bleicher

Source: *Disarmament Forum* (2000) 2, 69–77 © 2000 United Nations Institute for Disarmament Research (UNIDIR)—Reproduced with permission.

October 1996-December 1997. Fourteen months to negotiate and adopt a disarmament treaty which, fifteen months later, entered into force with 135 signatory states and 67 states parties.[1] Such dispatch, rare in disarmament matters, is only one of the unusual features of the Ottawa Convention on the prohibition of anti-personnel mines. The "Ottawa Process" which led to the adoption of the Convention was in fact a very special proceeding which overturned the established order of classical multilateralism. It challenged the preponderant role of states, the accepted negotiating forums for disarmament matters and the consensus rule. States espousing the traditional ways of conducting disarmament talks lined up against states and nongovernmental organizations (NGOs) advocating a new form of diplomacy.[2]

Given this new development, it may legitimately be asked what it was that made the procedure, in which few placed much hope, a success. It is also interesting to consider whether the innovative aspects of the Ottawa Process mark the beginnings of a new style of international disarmament negotiation or, less ambitiously, a return to nineteenth century negotiating practice. And one may wonder whether the model will be of lasting value and whether, for instance, it might serve in other areas of disarmament.

The Ottawa Process

Deeply concerned at the widespread injury to civilians caused by anti-personnel mines, France took the initiative in February 1993 of asking the Secretary-General of the United Nations to convene a review conference of the states parties to the Convention of 10 October 1980 prohibiting the use of certain conventional weapons (the CCW)[3] and, in particular, Protocol II thereto governing the use of "mines, booby-traps and other devices".[4]

On 3 May 1996, an amended Protocol II laying down stricter rules on the use of anti-personnel mines was adopted.[5] By then, a growing number of states believed that the only way to avoid the tragedy caused by anti-personnel mines was to ban them outright, not merely to restrict their use. Fifty states met in Ottawa between 3 and 5 October 1996 to mark a political commitment to the common position that anti-personnel mines should be banned, and to consider what form the future ban should take and where the negotiations should take place.

Some states, urged on by NGOs, argued that, in order to avoid the hitches that had been run into during the review talks on Protocol II to the 1980 Convention, they should break away from the traditional negotiating framework and rules, in particular the consensus rule.

It was at that first conference in Ottawa that the Canadian Foreign Minister, Lloyd Axworthy, challenged the international community to sign a treaty banning anti-personnel mines within fourteen months.

The target seemed utterly unrealistic in October 1996, yet it had been well and truly reached by December 1997,[6] with a Convention signed by 122 states—far more than the man who issued the challenge had hoped.

The challenge worked because a number of "ingredients" came together to help make it a success.

A Cause

In the first place, the Ottawa Process owes its success to a situation and a cause that were visible and palpably real in the public mind and the media.

It is estimated that there are some 110 million live anti-personnel mines still buried in about sixty different countries, long after the conflicts during which they were laid have ended.[7] Openly targeted against the general public, or used indiscriminately against military targets, civilian property and civilians, they kill or injure thousands of people every month. They also make large tracts of land uninhabitable and unsuitable for farming. Clearing them is a long, dangerous and expensive undertaking.

This "humanitarian disaster", as the former United Nations Secretary-General put it,[8] assumed unprecedented proportions beginning in the 1980s.

Mobilization of Public Opinion

Starting in 1991, NGOs active in the fields of development, human rights and humanitarian assistance mounted a campaign, aimed at international public opinion, to make people aware of the damage caused by anti-personnel mines. They called for a total ban on such instruments of war, believing that it was the only way to put an end to the disastrous humanitarian situation.[9]

The cause mobilized an impressive number of NGOs and increased international pressure for a ban on anti-personnel mines. The movement, launched by six NGOs in October 1992,[10] gave rise to the International Campaign to Ban Landmines (ICBL), which brought together nearly a thousand NGOs and won the Nobel Peace Prize in October 1997. By stirring up public opinion and lobbying states, the ICBL built up real pressure in favour of a total ban and swayed many states in their decisions.

The mobilization of public opinion by this NGO network with media support coincided with the determination of a hard core of states[11] to seize the initiative on this issue. These small and middle powers, advocates of humanist ideals and values, are also looking for a role on the international scene, and often take on initiatives and positions that allow them to act as significant international players. These initiatives generally relate to fields such as human rights, disarmament and peacekeeping.

But beyond the part played by these states, it was one man's initiative that made the Ottawa Process a success.

Axworthy's Strategy

Since taking up the post of Minister of Foreign Affairs, Lloyd Axworthy has promoted an international political strategy based on the notion of "human security".[12] Arguing that "the changing nature of violent conflict and intensifying globalization have increasingly put people at the centre of world affairs," he says that "the safety of the individual [. . .] has become both a new measure of global security and a new impetus for global action." He emphasizes the "need for a new approach to security" and remarks on the paradoxical situation in which "since the end of the Cold War, security for the majority of states has increased, while security for many of the world's people has declined." "Security between states remains a necessary condition for the security of people," but "national security is insufficient to guarantee people's security".

Giving substance to this concept of human security, the Canadian Minister has taken many initiatives in a vast range of fields, from environmental protection to human rights. He has tempered Canadian foreign policy with greater sensitivity to human rights issues (for example, isolating Nigeria), greater involvement in peace-keeping (Haiti and efforts to assemble a force in the Great Lakes region), and disarmament exercises (parliamentary debates on nuclear weapons).

Two recent sets of talks in which Canadian diplomacy has provided a driving force, the ban on anti-personnel mines and the establishment of the International Criminal Court, are described as examples of a new approach to security which takes "people as its point of reference, rather than focusing exclusively on the security of territory or govern ments."[13]

How the Process Was Handled

The way the initiative was handled was another factor that made for its success. A core group of states dealt with it, "locking out" any possibility of negotiation or amendment to a draft they themselves had put forward until the last minute. Only at the very last stage of the process were negotiations allowed to commence.[14]

The short period allowed for negotiations (three weeks), and the obligation to come up with a result (signing the Convention in December 1997), constrained participating states to stick close to the Austrian draft on which the negotiations were based.[15] For the most part, therefore, the amendments made to the draft were not substantive and all efforts by certain states to introduce wording mitigating a total ban ended in failure.

The way the process was handled also marked a departure from the traditional negotiating venues.

The Conference on Disarmament in Geneva, then known as the Committee on Disarmament, was described by the United Nations General Assembly at its first Special Session Devoted to Disarmament as the "single multilateral disarmament negotiating forum".[16] It was there or in its precursor bodies (Committee of 18, Conference of the Committee on Disarmament, Committee on Disarmament) that the basic international disarmament agreements were negotiated: the Non-Proliferation Treaty, the Sea-Bed Treaty, the Biological Weapons Convention, the Convention Prohibiting Hostile Use of Environmental Modification Techniques, the Chemical Weapons Convention and the Comprehensive Nuclear-Test-Ban Treaty.[17]

It was natural, then, that many states would look to the Conference on Disarmament to begin negotiating a ban on anti-personnel landmines. But the Conference faced opposition from three quarters: States opposed to any fresh ban on anti-personnel mines, some non-aligned states which considered that the Conference should not concern itself with conventional weapons but concentrate on nuclear disarmament, and the promoters of the Ottawa Process who regarded the Conference on Disarmament as a competing body.

The promoters of the Ottawa Process felt there was a danger that the prevailing consensus rule at Geneva and in other United Nations bodies and the pace of work at the United Nations would limit the scope of the future Convention and fail to match the urgency of banning anti-personnel mines. As Mario Bettati puts it, "this way of making haste slowly, so typical of international legal diplomacy, naturally arouses indignation in people whose emergency-dominated agendas demand swift action."[18]

It was for these reasons that the promoters of the Ottawa Process leant towards the convening of an ad hoc diplomatic conference of like-minded states. It was also for these reasons that they were able to reject the consensus rule and opt for a modified system where, in the absence of consensus, votes on matters of substance could be passed by a qualified majority.[19]

Innovation or Return to Past Practice?

The innovative character of the process stems essentially from the close cooperation and a new kind of association between states, international organizations and NGOs.

A New Kind of Association

NGOs are increasingly being associated with the preparations for and running of large multilateral events. Only 200 NGOs were represented at the San Francisco Conference in 1945; today, more than 1,600 have been accorded consultative status with the Economic and Social Council (ECOSOC) of the United Nations under Article 71 of the Charter.

NGOs have been particularly active at major conferences organized by the United Nations: the Rio Summit (1992), the International Conference on Population and Development (Cairo, 1994), the World Summit for Social Development (Copenhagen, 1995), the Fourth World Conference on Women (Beijing, 1995), the United Nations Conference on Human Settlements (Istanbul, 1996) and the World Food Summit (Rome, 1996).

There is already a symbiosis between states, international organizations and NGOs in, for example, the field of the environment. NGOs have come together with states, universities and research institutes within the International Union for Conservation of Nature and Natural Resources and play their full part at large international conferences.[20]

NGOs are also becoming increasingly involved in international criminal law. As Serge Sur points out, a feature of the Rome Conference which led, in July 1998, to the adoption of the convention establishing an international criminal court was "the influence exerted by many NGOs which, directly or indirectly, played a real part in the negotiations. [They invaded] some delegations, defining their positions and providing supporting arguments, sometimes even speaking on their behalf through the intermediary of members included on the states' official lists of representatives."[21]

Nuclear disarmament has prompted a great many campaigns and mobilized numerous NGOs (Greenpeace, International Physicians for the Prevention of Nuclear War—which won the Nobel Peace Prize in 1985, the Pugwash Conferences—which won the Nobel Peace Prize in 1995). NGOs were influential in the application to the International Court of Justice for an advisory opinion on the legality of the threat or use of nuclear weapons. They are even said to have been "largely responsible for the wording of many national statements".[22] The year 1997 saw discussions on the increased role that NGOs should be assigned in debates and negotiations on disarmament in various international forums (First Committee of the United Nations General Assembly, Disarmament Commission, Conference on Disarmament).

But it was really with the Ottawa Process that NGOs were drawn into the thick of disarmament negotiations. The NGOs of the ICBL were very closely associated with the whole of the Ottawa Process, from the production of different drafts of the Convention to the unfolding of the negotiations. The relationship between the states promoting the Ottawa Process and the

NGOs may be said to have worked both ways. The NGOs took advantage of the role offered to them to ensure that the Convention would indeed ban landmines outright, and the states relied on the NGOs to mobilize support, press for as many states as possible to join in the process, and provide "moral backing" for their initiative.

At the Ottawa Conference Kofi Annan, the Secretary-General of the United Nations, acknowledged that such a "union of governments, civil society and international organizations" was the "international community of the future". He also described the Ottawa Process as "a remarkable expression of the new diplomacy".[23] Jody Williams, ICBL Coordinator and 1997 Nobel Peace laureate, went further, describing the alliance of civil society and governments as a "superpower".[24] Lloyd Axworthy observed that international organizations and conferences had recently been opening up to non-governmental players. Civil society had demanded and obtained a seat at the table and it would now be necessary to come to terms with people power on the international stage.[25]

When the Nobel Peace Prize was awarded to the ICBL in Oslo on 10 December 1997, the Norwegian Deputy Minister for Foreign Affairs, Jan Egeland, said the process went to show that coalitions of NGOs and governments could work together to change international law more quickly and radically than traditional diplomacy.

The success of the Ottawa Process has, indeed, been ascribed in part to this new kind of collaboration among many parties.

Lloyd Axworthy remarked that states and NGOs, working as true partners, could arrive at results neither would have achieved on their own. He attributed the success of the Ottawa Process to the "new synergies" that had come about.[26] That view was shared by Steve Goose of the ICBL, who described the process as a rare occasion when governments had not only listened to civil society but worked with it.[27]

Humanitarian Motives

It is interesting to note that, unlike recent disarmament treaties, the Ottawa Convention is based on humanitarian principles. As Robert J. Mathews and Timothy L.H. McCormack remark,[28] humanitarian principles prompted the negotiation of bans or restrictions on weapons under international humanitarian law (the 1899 Hague Declaration prohibiting the use of asphyxiating gases, the 1925 Geneva Protocol, the 1980 Convention on Certain Conventional Weapons). As these agreements proved incapable of preventing the use of the weapons they were supposed to ban or restrict (chemical and biological weapons, anti-personnel mines) and the attendant human suffering, the international community turned to disarmament. Although the negotiations that led to the adoption of the 1972 Biological Weapons Convention and the 1993 Chemical Weapons Convention were originally prompted by humanitarian concerns (preventing the "excessive injuries" such weapons caused), these soon gave way to strategic non-proliferation considerations.

By contrast, the Ottawa Convention is a new departure in that it is based exclusively on humanitarian considerations and explicitly rules out any restriction or reservation entered to satisfy military objectives.

A Return to Past Practice

Despite these innovative features, it is reasonable to wonder whether the way in which the Ottawa Convention was negotiated was not, in some aspects, a return to past practice. Before international negotiating forums became institutionalized (the League of Nations and later the

United Nations), many negotiations were launched at the initiative of a state. This was especially true of the law of warfare: it was at Russia's initiative that the International Military Commission convened in St. Petersburg in 1868, leading to the adoption of the first international agreement regulating the methods and instruments of war. It was also Tsar Alexander II who called for the conference in Brussels that, in August 1874, drew up rules governing the conduct of hostilities and the treatment of persons in the power of the enemy. The First Hague Peace Conference, in 1899, was called by Tsar Nicolas II to "guarantee all peoples the blessing of true and lasting peace and, above all, to halt the progressive development of existing armaments".[29] The Second Hague Peace Conference, in 1907, was called jointly by the United States and Russia.

Furthermore, as Ken Rutherford points out,[30] in some ways the manner in which the negotiations on the Ottawa Convention were conducted resembles that of the 1899 and 1907 Hague Conventions.

The choice by the sponsors of the Ottawa Process of a swift negotiating path carries echoes of the short time limits set for the 1899 (18 May to 29 July) and 1907 (15 June to 18 October) Hague Conferences.

The abandonment of the consensus rule, one of the Ottawa Process sponsors' major demands, perhaps indicates a desire to return to pre-Cold War practice. The 1899 Hague Declarations, for example, were adopted by majority vote. Another similarity that Ken Rutherford mentions is the pointed opposition of the period's great powers to both the Hague and the Ottawa negotiations.[31] In 1899, the United Kingdom[32] and the United States refused to sign two of the three declarations adopted, while in 1997 the United States, powerless to induce the other delegations to accept its exceptions to the draft Convention, withdrew from the Oslo conference the day before it ended.

Nine-Day Wonder or New Model for Negotiations?

Thus the Ottawa Process displayed a number of features which together helped to make it a success. One must wonder whether this is a nine-day wonder or the harbinger and prototype of a new style of international negotiations on disarmament matters.

A number of people at the Ottawa Conference explicitly mentioned a future role in other disarmament-related topics. Lloyd Axworthy said that the Conference had opened up a new way of conducting international relations and that what held for anti-personnel mines should be true of all weapons of war.[33]

Cornelio Sommaruga, the President of the International Committee of the Red Cross, said that anti-personnel mines were only one aspect of ICRC's concerns. He also spoke of small arms, vast quantities of which were in circulation around the globe, and were regularly used in violation of international humanitarian law.[34] The Japanese Foreign Minister, Keizo Obuchi, also explicitly mentioned the problem of small arms.[35]

Since July 1998, several former sponsors of the Ottawa Process (such as Norway and Belgium) have sought to put the combat against the spread of small arms on the international agenda, organizing international meetings in conjunction with NGOs.[36] Paralleling these initiatives, nearly 200 NGOs have formed an "electronic coalition" and launched an Internet-based information campaign on the subject, The International Action Network on Small Arms.[37]

The campaign is overtly modelled on the Ottawa Process and hopes to be similarly successful. If it is to be so, the same factors will have to be brought into play. The problem will probably be to identify and shape a goal and solution. In the case of anti-personnel mines, that was easy—banning them—but this approach cannot readily be transposed to small arms.

When the ICBL was awarded the Nobel Peace Prize, the Chairman of the Nobel Committee, Professor Francis Sejersted, drew a parallel between the anti-landmine cause and the cause of nuclear disarmament, saying that the Ottawa Process, as a model for the future, could prove of decisive importance to the international effort for disarmament and peace. Some states, indeed, are tempted to transpose the Ottawa model to the question of nuclear weapons, even though conditions at present do not lend themselves to such an exercise and the parallel with anti-personnel mines is not easy to draw.

There is a danger that the deadlock in the Conference on Disarmament since 1997 will seriously compromise its credibility as a negotiating forum. Proponents of nuclear disarmament, deploring the lack of activity in the Conference, may be tempted to explore other avenues and call for the kind of large conference on the subject that was suggested by the non-aligned states at the Durban Summit,[38] or in resolution 53/77 Y adopted by the General Assembly of the United Nations on 4 December 1998. Such a move would clearly benefit from the precedent set by the Ottawa Process.

The process has thus moved into the "standard", reproducible range that can be applied to other questions relating to disarmament or the law governing armed conflicts, such as that of child soldiers. Some also regard it as a response to the weakness and deadlock found in the traditional multilateral negotiating forums.

The Alliance between States and NGOs

But it is in the verification of the Ottawa Convention that one key element of the process, the alliance between states and NGOs, is expected to play its greatest part.

Bob Lawson of the Canadian Ministry of Foreign Affairs said at the Ottawa Conference that an idea should be borrowed from human-rights procedures, where most of the information on compliance with international standards comes from NGOs. This system can be transposed to the verification of the Ottawa Convention. Collaboration with NGOs is needed to build up civil society's capacity to conduct such expert surveillance.[39]

The suggestion was enthusiastically taken up by the NGOs, which have recently set up a combined verification and warning mechanism.[40] This has led to an annual report (The Landmine Monitor) on implementation of the Convention in all its aspects (ban, demining, stockpile destruction, etc.).[41] Philippe Chabasse, the joint director of Handicap International, says he hopes to create a "surveillance and pressure network, a sort of Amnesty International on mines". Such a mechanism could help to perpetuate the partnership between governments and NGOs that made the Ottawa Process a success.

So a new kind of close cooperation between states and NGOs has emerged from the Ottawa Process. Some, like Serge Sur, may decry the "excessive prominence" accorded to NGOs, which are "developing a parallel diplomacy without any democratic foundation that interferes with relations among states".[42] There may be worries about the Conference on Disarmament's loss of credibility and paralysis since 1997. On the other hand there are grounds for believing, like Professor Bronislaw Geremek, the Polish Minister for Foreign Affairs, that "henceforth international security will be built more and more around the concept of international civil society in which, along with governments, international organizations, economic and financial institutions, an ever more prominent role will be played by citizens and their spokesmen—the non-governmental organizations."[43]

At this stage it is hard to determine how long the phenomenon will endure. It might, nevertheless, be the point at which civil society begins to play a genuine role in matters which have hitherto been exclusively official preserves, such as negotiations on disarmament.

Notes

1. The Ottawa Convention entered into force on 1 March 1999.
2. After the Convention entered into force, UNIDIR dedicated an issue of Disarmament Forum to various elements of the Ottawa Convention—such as the role of NGOs, landmine victims, verification, civil society's watchdog function, etc. See issue 4, 1999 of *Disarmament Forum*, "Framework for a Mine-Free World".
3. Convention on Prohibitions or Restrictions on the Use of Certain Conventional Weapons Which May Be Deemed to Be Excessively Injurious or to Have Indiscriminate Effects.
4. Letter dated 16 February 1993 from the Minister-delegate to the Minister for Foreign Affairs, Georges Kiejman, addressed to the Secretary-General of the United Nations.
5. Review Conference of the States Parties to the Convention on Prohibitions or Restrictions on the Use of Certain Conventional Weapons Which May Be Deemed to Be Excessively Injurious or to Have Indiscriminate Effects, final document, part I: CCW/CONF. I/16 (Part I).
6. Ottawa Land Mine Ban Signing Conference and Mine Action Forum, 2–4 December 1997.
7. United Nations, Assistance in mine clearance, report by the Secretary-General (A/49/357), 6 September 1994.
8. Boutros Boutros-Ghali, The Land Mine Crisis, *Foreign Affairs*, September/October 1994, pp. 8–14.
9. Internet site <www.icbl.org>
10. Human Rights Watch, Medico International, Mines Advisory Group, Handicap International, Physicians for Human Rights, Vietnam Veterans of America Foundation.
11. Canada, Belgium, Norway, Austria, South Africa.
12. Lloyd Axworthy, *Human Security: Safety for People in a Changing World*, Ottawa, Canadian Department of Foreign Affairs and International Trade, April 1999.
13. Ibid.
14. Diplomatic Conference on an International Total Ban on Anti-Personnel Land Mines, Oslo, 1–18 September 1997.
15. Draft dated 13 May 1997, reproduced at the Oslo Conference, document APL/CRP.3 of 1 September 1997.
16. New York, 23 May-30 June 1978.
17. The Comprehensive Nuclear-Test-Ban Treaty was negotiated in the Conference on Disarmament but adopted by the First Committee of the United Nations General Assembly.
18. Mario Bettati, Le droit d'ingérence, Paris, Odile Jacob, 1996, p. 11.
19. Rules of procedure of the Oslo Conference, APL/CRP. 2 dated 1 September 1997, articles 3347, 50.
20. Jean-Marc Lavieille, Droit international du désarmement et de la maîtrise des armements, Paris, L'Harmattan, 1997, p. 113.
21. Serge Sur, Vers une Cour pénale internationale : la Convention de Rome entre les ONG et le Conseil de Sécurité, Revue Générale de Droit International public, vol. 103/1999/1, pp. 29–45.
22. Serge Sur, ibid.
23. Speech to the Ottawa Convention signing ceremony, 3 December 1997.
24. Ibid.
25. Speech to the opening ceremony of the Ottawa Land Mine Ban Signing Conference and Mine Action Forum, 2 December 1997.
26. Ibid.

27. Ibid.
28. Robert J. Mathews and Timothy L.H. McCormack, The influence of humanitarian principles in the negotiation of arms control treaties, *International Review of the Red Cross*, vol. 81, no. 834, June 1999, pp. 331–52.
29. British Parliamentary papers, 1899, vol. CX, cited in Geoffrey Best, Peace conferences and the century of total war: the 1899 Hague Conference and what came after, *International Affairs*, vol. 75, no. 3, 1999, pp. 619–34.
30. Ken Rutherford, The Hague and Ottawa Conventions: a model for future weapon ban regimes? *The Nonproliferation Review*, Spring-Summer 1999, vol. 6, no. 3, pp. 36–50.
31. Ibid., pp. 44–45.
32. The United Kingdom refused to sign Declaration III banning dum-dum bullets, wishing to retain "the liberty of employing projectiles of sufficient efficacy against savage races". Statement by Sir John Ardagh, First Committee, fourth meeting, 23 June 1899. Cited in James Brown Scott, *The Reports of the Hague Conferences of 1899 and 1907*, Oxford, Clarendon Press, 1917, p. 286; and Ken Rutherford, The Hague and Ottawa Conventions: a model for future weapon ban regimes? *The Nonproliferation Review*, Spring-Summer 1999, vol. 6, no. 3, p. 40.
33. Op. cit., note 25.
34. Op. cit., note 23.
35. Ibid.
36. Oslo meeting on small arms, 13–14 July 1998; International Conference on Sustainable Disarmament for Sustainable Development, Brussels, 12–13 October 1998.
37. International Action Network on Small Arms, <www.iansa.org>
38. Twelfth Conference of Heads of State or Government of Non-Aligned Countries, September 1998.
39. Ottawa Land Mine Ban Signing Conference and Mine Action Forum, Round Table 9, Cooperative Compliance: Building Capacities to Monitor the Ban Treaty, 3 September 1997.
40. Landmine Monitor was created by the ICBL in Oslo, in June 1998. Its Core Group comprises Human Rights Watch, Handicap International, Kenya Coalition Against Landmines, Mines Action Canada and Norwegian People's Aid.
41. ICBL, *Landmine Monitor Report 1999: Toward a Mine-Free World*. The first edition was released at the First Meeting of the States Parties to the Convention, Maputo, 37 May 1999.
42. Serge Sur, op. cit., note 21.
43. Speech to the Conference on Disarmament, Geneva, 23 March 1999.

CHAPTER EIGHTEEN

Assessing the Small Arms Movement: The Trials and Tribulations of a Transnational Network

Suzette R. Grillot, Craig S. Stapley, and Molly E. Hanna

Source: *Contemporary Security Policy* (2006) 27:1, 60–84 © 2006 Taylor & Francis—Reproduced with permission.

Introduction

Like many other transnational concerns today, the issues associated with the global spread and availability of small arms have been the focus of international nongovernmental organization (NGO) attention. For nearly ten years, nongovernmental actors have raised concern about the increased accessibility of small arms and light weapons around the world.[1] By the late 1990s, hundreds of these nongovernmental actors began to coalesce together in an effort to enhance awareness, conduct research, and affect policy relevant to small arms issues. How did this NGO coalition emerge? How does it operate? How effective has it been? Where is it headed in the future? These are the questions we must ask ourselves in an effort to understand and perhaps enhance the small arms movement (SAM).[2]

To answer these questions we seek to assess the structure and activities of the SAM based on existing understandings of transnational social movements.[3] Doing so will help us identify the strengths and weaknesses of the SAM and offer some solutions for more effective operations. Moreover, there are a number of gaps in existing research that this study of the SAM will serve to fill. First, most studies of transnational social movement networks (TSMNs) focus extensively on non-military-security related issues such as the environment, human rights, women's issues, development, health or education. The creation and operation of organizations and networks that focus to a great extent on weapons issues, military practices, or violent conflict problems have been examined infrequently.[4] This project, therefore, contributes to existing literature by focusing on a TSMN that concentrates on weapons related issues.

Second, few studies emphasize the importance of movement structure. Early studies of transnational networks were heavily descriptive and emphasized the similarities among groups.[5] More recent studies have focused on the varying characteristics of organizational structures and the impact of such on movement success.[6] There remains, however, much room for improvement in our understanding of how and why structure affects impact. Moreover, to further strengthen our assessment of TSMN structure, we include a comparative analysis of the anti-personnel landmine movement (another weapon and security oriented network) in an effort to provide key distinctions between two rather differently structured TSMNs. The International

Campaign to Ban Landmines (ICBL), a collection of over 1,100 NGOs, achieved an international ban on the manufacture, transfer, use and deployment of anti-personnel landmines at about the same time that the SAM was getting started (1997).[7] According to those involved with the small arms movement from the beginning, the ICBL served as a very positive example of what non-governmental actors could achieve in international politics, motivating them to organize their efforts as the ICBL had done. It is important, therefore, to understand how the ICBL—a successful transnational social movement—affected the development of the SAM and whether that influence was appropriate.

Third, most of the academic literature on NGOs and TSMNs focuses on the value-based nature of such actors and does not emphasize the competitive, and sometimes cut-throat, environment in which NGOs and TSMNs exist and operate. Assumed to be organizations and movements centered on 'doing good' and affecting 'positive change', the literature tends to focus on the 'good' and 'positive' side of NGO and movement activities. Although struggles for resources, information, access, and visibility may be mentioned in NGO and network studies, they are usually addressed in the context of how these actors have been able to overcome such obstacles in order to achieve success.[8] Furthermore, NGO and TSMN literature is overwhelmingly focused on the success of such actors and does not well address failed attempts to do good and affect positive change. The factors that contribute to such failures, however, provide valuable lessons that should not be ignored. This study, therefore, highlights the entirety of the SAM—its efforts to 'do good' and the sometimes resulting negative outcomes.

Finally, very little scholarship on NGOs and TSMNs examines the effectiveness of such organizations and networks from the inside out.[9] Most studies explore the effectiveness of NGOs and TSMNs by studying their ability to affect change in their particular issue areas—how well they have influenced positions, policies, and prescriptions. Occasionally, however, it would be useful to take stock of a movement's activities and effectiveness as perceived by its participants and or stakeholders and those who have interacted with them—to determine from the inside out what can and should be changed and what can and should be maintained.[10] Critical evaluation, after all, is important for enhancing future work, and NGOs and movement networks often do not and cannot engage in such evaluative efforts given their daily activities in support of their mandates. In addition, inside out evaluations of movement activities may very well shed important light on academic understandings of NGO and TSMN action. For both practical and theoretical reasons, therefore, exposing the strengths and weaknesses of NGO and TSMN work from their own participants' perspectives, as well as from outside observers, is a necessary endeavor—and this study does just that.

Ultimately, this study addresses all of these gaps by focusing on the emergence, structure, and effectiveness of the SAM—a movement that has, according to many of its own participants, founders, and observers, struggled over its years of operation to achieve its objectives; and a movement that is, therefore, in dire need of evaluation in order to take stock and, hopefully, improve its operations. At the center of this movement is the International Action Network on Small Arms (IANSA). Many, but not all, of the organizations involved in the SAM are members of IANSA, which was created in the late 1990s to address and combat the problems associated with the widespread and unchecked proliferation, circulation, availability, use and misuse of small arms and light weapons worldwide.[11] Hundreds of NGOs and individuals are members of this network, and various other NGOs and individuals cooperate, collaborate, and partner with IANSA and its members.

IANSA has a number of goals. Overall, the network says it aims to:

reduce small arms violence by: raising awareness among policymakers, the public and the media about the global threat to human security caused by small arms; promote the work of

NGOs to prevent small arms proliferation through national and local legislation, regional agreements, public education and research; foster collaborative advocacy efforts, and provide a forum for NGOs to share experiences and build skills; establish regional and subject-specific small arms networks; [and] promote the voices of victims in regional and global policy discussions.[12]

According to many movement participants and outside observers, however, the network has only managed to make significant ground on its first goal of raising awareness, making rather minimal progress on the others. In fact, some members, participants, and observers claim the small arms movement, in general, and IANSA, in particular, has been a 'complete and abject failure' in achieving an effective web of interaction that contributes to positive outcomes in the field of small arms.[13] Why is this the case? How has the SAM evolved to such a point and where is it headed? These are the questions this study seeks to address.

This study, therefore, highlights and examines the SAM's structure, function, and operating environment. To do this, we look to existing material and documents about the SAM, but we also survey its participants, interview key players, and contribute personal experiences and observations. From here, we provide an overview of the transnational social movement network literature and its relevance to the small arms movement. Second, we outline the emergence, structure and operations of the small arms movement, comparing it to another TSMN, the International Campaign to Ban Landmines (ICBL). Third, we discuss the results of our surveys of and interviews with SAM network participants. Finally, we conclude with the implications and significance of our findings, offer recommendations for the movement's way forward, and make suggestions for future research.

Transnational Social Movement Networks

Although nongovernmental organizations have been involved in international politics for some time, they have grown in number and force only in recent years. A considerable amount of scholarship has focused on the role and significance of NGO actors in an effort to illuminate how and why they emerge, how and why they operate, and how and why they influence policy and behavior.[14] From a focus on individual nongovernmental organizations to groups of NGOs working in concert with state and/or non-state actors, research has highlighted the tremendous role that ideas, information, knowledge, and values play given the work in which NGOs engage.

What Are They?[15]

Many scholars have most recently focused on transnational social movement networks.[16] These studies focus on how and why NGOs work together in coalition to mobilize action on global issues of concern. Although TSMNs may include a host of different actors, NGOs tend to play the key role. Some movement networks have the purpose of knowledge creation,[17] while others focus on policy advocacy.[18] More recent analyses suggest that contemporary movement networks focus on direct action.[19] In any case, these actors contribute to a growth of global civil society and engage in activities that seek to bring about needed change within states and societies, as well as between states and societies.[20] These groups, therefore, are often assumed to be value-based—working to produce collective 'good' for often unseen and untold others. They are, in other words, considered to be global 'do-gooders.'[21]

How and why do TSMNs emerge and what do they do? Network studies tell us that these groups are set into motion when domestic NGOs have little or no access to state actors and, therefore, little or no ability to influence state decisions and actions. These groups 'bypass their state and directly search out international allies to try to bring pressure on their states from outside.'[22] Individual activists or 'political entrepreneurs' also create TSMNs 'when they believe that transnational networking will further their organizational missions—by sharing information, attaining greater visibility, gaining access to wider publics, multiplying channels of institutional access, and so forth.'[23] The 'growth of international contact' also explains how and why movement networks emerge. Opportunities for like-minded individuals and groups to network have grown substantially in the past several years. International meetings and conferences have greatly proliferated and have, therefore, enhanced the development of TSMNs.[24]

Functions and Effects

To achieve their goals, TSMNs seek to engage in what Keck and Sikkink call 'information,' 'symbolic,' 'leverage,' and 'accountability' politics. They collect and disseminate *information* in order to frame and raise the salience of the problem about which they are concerned. They give voice to those who do not have one by developing and sharing stories and testimonies for those for whom they advocate, using such stories as *symbols* for their work. They use *leverage* by persuading more powerful actors, such as particular states or international organizations, to join them in pressuring target actors. And finally, TSMNs seek to hold target actors *accountable* to the positions and pronouncements they express.[25]

Ultimately, TSMNs influence world politics in a number of ways.[26] First, networks create and draw attention to new issues and set agendas. In this process they heighten awareness via the media and encourage public meetings and hearings. Second, TSMNs affect the 'discursive positions' of governments and international organizations via persuasion. The third type of influence builds on network persuasion in that target actors may respond with a change in procedure—oftentimes leading to increased and direct contact with key members of a government or organization. This change provides movement networks the opportunity 'to move from outside to inside pressure strategies.'[27] Finally, networks may affect actual policy and behavioral changes in target states, organizations, or other actors, which may then spread to affect changes in other, perhaps peripherally targeted players.

There are, of course, certain factors that affect the impact of TSMNs. Earlier studies suggest that various characteristics inherent to the issue or the actor help us understand the extent to which TSMNs effectively influence outcomes. Some issues, for example, may be more easily framed and presented to target audiences than others. In fact, Keck and Sikkink suggest that networks have organized most effectively around issues that exhibit two particular characteristics: '(1) issues involving bodily harm to vulnerable individuals, especially when there is a short and clear causal chain (or story) assigning responsibility; and (2) issues involving legal equality of opportunity.'[28]

No matter how important the issue, or how strong a case can be made in its favor, target characteristics are also relevant in determining the impact of TSMNs. Specifically, '[t]arget actors must be vulnerable either to material incentives or to sanctions from outside actors, or they must be sensitive to pressure because of gaps between stated commitments and practice.'[29] Those countries that are most interested in belonging to a 'normative community of nations,' for example, may be more vulnerable or favorably disposed to TSMN pressures than other countries.[30]

First and Second Generation TSMNs

Network characteristics may also affect TSMN success. As stated earlier, many movement network studies tend to focus on the general characteristics that TSMNs share. A few recent studies, however, highlight differences among networks—particularly differences in structure—and how those differences may affect TSMN operations and impact.[31] W. Lance Bennett, for example, suggests that there are 'two eras of transnational activism.' Earlier eras were characterized by centralized, coordinated, hierarchical networks. These 'first generation' networks are NGO centered, focus on single issues, and aim to achieve policy changes from 'institutional targets,' such as governments. Today's movement networks, or 'second generation' TSMNs, are more decentralized, diverse, and leaderless. They exhibit more 'relaxed framing' and 'multiple identities.' They tend to focus on multiple issues, involve more bottom-up decision-making, and incorporate various campaigns that are not controlled by a central organization.[32]

Some argue that this shift from first to second generation networks is the result of technology and the advent of the Internet.[33] With the ability to communicate more broadly and include previously unheard voices from even distant and remote parts of the world, today's networks tend to reflect the diversity and inclusiveness that comes along with additional perspectives and viewpoints.[34] Moreover, such inclusion and enhancement of global participation affects demands for more 'democratic' decision-making, as opposed to more centralized, top-down management. The result, therefore, is transnational activity that incorporates wide participation and demonstrates a significant amount of tolerance within movements.[35]

Why does structure matter? Some suggest that this 'newer' form of network structure appears to ease tensions within social movements. While more centralized, hierarchical networks tend to necessarily exclude some voices and dictate action; these decentralized networks are inherently and purposefully inclusive, thereby decreasing and perhaps even preventing internal conflict. Some even argue that the 'multiplicity of reference bases' in today's movements enhances a 'sense of belonging to a movement.'[36] Such diversity may also lead to an effective 'division of labor' within a movement network so that the overall effort is more productive and ultimately more successful.[37]

Concerns have been raised, however, about the structure of this newer generation of networks. Questions have been asked about whether these loose, leaderless, diverse networks can produce the kind of dedication, concentration, and attention needed for movements to mobilize.[38] Bennett asks, for example, whether these networks are 'able to generate enough internal dialogue to achieve the message unity required to focus broader public discussion? Or do weak ties also produce a weakness of core ideas?'[39] Another concern raised about these more diffuse and diverse networks concerns the lack of leadership. Scholars suggest, for example, that for movement networks to be effective 'they need clear and strong leadership ensuring concerted advocacy.'[40] Moreover, these scholars argue that movement networks are much more likely to achieve success if their 'component groups share compatible goals; otherwise [they] will be split by internal dissent.'[41] From this perspective, the diverse nature of second-generation networks would be quite problematic.

Although some believe that this new generation of networks is more effective, there still remain questions about the challenges these movements face. As one study suggests, the choice of a particular organizational structure often means, 'choosing between a number of different dilemmas.'[42] How does structure specifically affect the work and impact of TSNMs? Unfortunately, few empirical studies answer this question for us. This study of the small arms movement, therefore, seeks to answer some of these questions as it focuses on how the movement network emerged, how it is structured, how it operates, what it has achieved, and where its participants say it should be headed.

The Small Arms Movement

Since the mid 1990s, a transnational effort to address the problems associated with small arms and light weapons has emerged. Nongovernmental actors have been involved, to varying degrees, in a number of small arms initiatives ranging from fact-finding missions, to weapons collection and destruction programs, to the establishment of best practices and codes-of-conduct, to interstate conventions focusing on illicit trafficking. Working either individually or collectively, what binds these actors together and moves them to act is their concern about small arms as a problem for human, national, and international security.

Origins

The Small Arms Movement's roots may be found in the publication of research on the issue in 1996.[43] By the latter half of 1997, the small arms movement started to emerge. In December of that year a meeting took place in Washington, which included representatives of 23 nongovernmental organizations working on the small arms issue. After this meeting, Ed Laurance (one of the leading 'political entrepreneurs' involved with establishing the SAM) founded and served as the administrator of the Preparatory Committee (Prepcom) for a Global Campaign on Small Arms and Light Weapons, which was created to develop an Internet database of information on small arms activities.[44] In 1998 there were four NGO meetings held to discuss the small arms issue, the last two of which took place in Canada and Brussels and set the stage for a transnational network dedicated to the issue of small arms. The meeting in Canada joined together 33 NGOs from 18 countries, forming the basis of the International Action Network on Small Arms. In Brussels, more than 100 organizations met to decide on IANSA's organizational structure and goals.[45]

This growth in international contact allowed network members to formally launch the International Action Network on Small Arms in May 1999 at The Hague, The Netherlands, with an overall objective of stemming the proliferation and misuse of small arms and light weapons in an effort to contribute to a more just and violence-free world, sustainable peace, development, human security, and respect for human rights.[46] The IANSA network has at its core common values concerning the problematic nature of small arms availability, transfer, and circulation—either from a demand or supply perspective. The IANSA founding document is laden with value statements regarding the human right to live in a secure environment characterized by peace, dignity, and humanity.[47] Moreover, participants in the SAM, most widely conceived, tend to reflect a general consensus that small arms are tools of death that fuel and increase the lethality of conflict and that such weaponry poses various challenges for development, security, peace, and justice.

Objectives

IANSA has a number of specific goals and objectives meant to address both weapons supply and demand. These include: (1) controlling legal transfers between states; (2) controlling the availability, use and storage of small arms within states; (3) preventing and combating illicit transfers; (4) collecting and removing surplus arms from both civil society and regions of conflict; (5) increasing transparency and accountability; (6) supporting research and information sharing; (7) reversing cultures of violence; (8) reforming the security sector; (9) creating norms of non-possession; (10) enhancing demobilization and reintegration programs; (11) halting the use of child combatants, combating impunity; and (12) tackling poverty and underdevelopment.[48]

To achieve its goals, IANSA members certainly seek to engage in 'information,' "symbolic,' 'leverage,' and 'accountability' politics. Regarding information, IANSA explicitly states that information is key to the network. Via its Founding Document, IANSA commits itself to gathering, sharing, and disseminating information at all levels. Its policy framework sets out a plan for supporting research and the sharing of information—and mentions that NGOs have a special role in independently collecting and interpreting reliable information. IANSA documents state that the network will identify research and evaluation needs, will encourage data collection and dissemination among its members, and will conduct research on little knows issues and in little known regions.[49] Moreover, information is viewed as instrumental in raising the profile of the network and its programs, and in building and supporting constituencies. This includes the drafting of 'culturally appropriate' messages, campaign materials, and slogans.[50]

Concerning symbolism, IANSA members utilize a number of symbols and symbolic events in achieving their objectives. The network encourages, for example, the use of particular individuals, such as former combatants, in educational efforts as they serve as symbols of the small arms problem.[51] Symbolic events such as weapons bonfires are important for the network. In fact, a 'Flame of Peace' kicked off the launching of IANSA in The Hague where dozens of 'donated small arms were burned in a bonfire as a symbol of IANSA participants' dedication to do their part to tackle the difficult task of actively addressing the tools of violence in today's conflicts.'[52] IANSA also focuses symbolically on the civilian victims of small arms and light weapons around the world. For example, network members often raise the fact that more than 40 Red Cross personnel were killed in the 1990s in Chechnya and Rwanda alone. This is astonishing when you compare that number with the 15 Red Cross volunteers who died in the line of duty between 1945 and 1990.[53]

As for leverage politics, IANSA's founding document states that it seeks to enlist 'respected and popular public figures to convey campaign messages.'[54] Acknowledging that well-known and identifiable people may affect the receptivity of the message by officials and the public, IANSA commits itself to leveraging its work by collaborating with more powerful actors. Linking with powerful actors such as governments and international organizations, however, may bear the most fruit, according to many IANSA members.[55] In fact, many participants actively seek out the support of some governments, many of which have funded and supported the small arms activities of such participants. Moreover, members have sought to establish strong ties with the United Nations, which has been extremely active on the issue of small arms proliferation and openly welcomed and applauded the creation of IANSA.[56]

Regarding attempts to hold targets accountable for their promises and actions, IANSA seeks to publicize discrepancies between target actor statements and practices and to highlight unacceptable behavior. The network commits itself to 'monitoring the international political and social context of small arms' by assessing national policies, evaluating state adherence to human rights standards, promoting nonproliferation norms and standards of behavior, and developing mechanisms for monitoring the implementation of local, national, regional, and international initiatives.[57] To further this commitment, IANSA compiles a database of news publications focusing on government action and misconduct related to small arms and publishes it on its website.

Accomplishments

Ultimately, IANSA and the SAM have achieved much over the past few years. Since its inception, the small arms issue has certainly been given more attention. There are more organizations and individuals working and concentrating on small arms problems. Regional networks have emerged in Central and South America, West Africa, South Asia, South East Asia, East and West Africa, and Western and Eastern Europe.[58] IANSA was intricately involved in the July 2001 UN meeting that led to the *Programme of Action to Prevent, Combat and Eradicate the Illicit Trade in Small Arms and Light Weapons in All its Aspects*. IANSA has also worked to include NGOs in subsequent UN meetings, giving a voice to NGOs from around the world.[59] IANSA also plays a central role in evaluating member country attempts to implement the 2001 agreement.[60] Moreover, IANSA has become involved in a coordinated campaign, the Control Arms campaign, with Amnesty International and Oxfam, in an effort to build support for an international Arms Trade Treaty that would 'ban arms transfers if they are likely to contribute to human rights violations or fuel conflict, or undermine development.'[61]

Most of the stated goals of IANSA and the SAM, however, have yet to be achieved. Of the twelve objectives outlined in IANSA documents (see above), the SAM has managed to make significant ground on only one item—the support of research and information sharing. The SAM, in general, and IANSA specifically, has been much less successful at addressing the bulk of what it has set out to achieve.

Explaining Relative Success: ICBL and IANSA

A natural comparison for IANSA and the SAM is the International Campaign to Ban Landmines. Founded in 1992 by six nongovernmental organizations, the ICBL quickly grew to approximately 1,100 organizations in more than 90 countries. By 1997, the network successfully achieved its major goal: an international treaty banning anti-personnel landmines. In the process, the ICBL won the Nobel Peace Prize for its efforts.[62] Subsequently, the ICBL became the benchmark by which other TSMNs are often measured. The achievements of IANSA and the SAM, for example, pale in comparison to those of the ICBL. Exploring the similarities and differences of these two movement networks may shed some light on why one has been more successful than the other.

Similarities

Like IANSA, the members of the ICBL shared some basic values. All saw the need for a complete ban on the production, transfer, and use of antipersonnel landmines and also agreed that current stockpiles must be destroyed. Furthermore, there was a shared commitment by ICBL's members regarding those that have been victimized by antipersonnel landmines. As a result, there has been a considerable effort aimed at educating people about the risks of mines—especially in mine-affected areas.[63]

Also like IANSA, the ICBL engaged in 'information,' 'symbolic,' 'leverage,' and 'accountability' activities. Information sharing is one of the foundational premises for the ICBL and has been an effective tool in controlling and shaping the discourse about landmines.[64] Landmine victims regularly served as symbols of the landmine problem in education and informational efforts.[65] Middle-power states, such as Canada, and high-profile celebrities, such as Princess Diana, were engaged by the ICBL and its member groups to leverage pressure on governments.[66] And the campaign shifted soon after 1997 to monitor the implementation of the Ban Treaty by publicizing the acts of states that are non-compliant.[67]

Because of these similarities, the ICBL provides a useful comparison for the SAM. Other reasons, however, also support the comparison of the two movement networks. First, the founders of the SAM were influenced and motivated by the success of the ICBL. Having witnessed ICBL activities, those involved in the earliest efforts to construct the small arms movement had in mind that they would pattern such behavior by creating an NGO network to address small arms issues.[68] Second, the ICBL is cited as the benchmark by which other such movements should be measured.[69] Third, and perhaps most significantly, however, the ICBL is useful for comparison in this case because it is important to understand what, if anything, IANSA and the SAM has, can, or should learn from other efforts.

Differences

Despite the above mentioned similarities, however, key distinctions between the ICBL and the SAM must be made—and it is these key differences that may help us understand why the ICBL is considered by most, if not all, analysts to be a shining example of network activity and why the SAM fails to measure up to that standard. First, what perhaps separates the small arms movement network from many other transnational movement networks, including the ICBL, is the sheer complexity with which it is dealing—the complexity of the problem and the complexity of the solutions (as evidenced by the 12 different and detailed goals that IANSA articulated). The small arms issue, after all, spans a number of concerns—from human rights, human security, conflict resolution, and disarmament, to development and public health, to global peace, justice, and law enforcement.[70] In fact, the small arms 'problem' is really a number of 'problems' that result mainly from one particular issue—the unchecked spread and misuse of these weapons.

As Keck and Sikkink remind us, those issues that involve 'bodily harm to vulnerable individuals' lend themselves more readily to successful network action—and the small arms issue certainly meets this criteria. In fact, the SAM has been most successful in highlighting the humanitarian impact of small arms and light weapons.[71] The small arms issue, however, struggles to meet other issue criteria, such as the establishment of a 'short and clear causal chain' and the involvement of concerns regarding 'legal equality of opportunity.'[72] Because small arms are sold, transferred, moved, and otherwise acquired in various (legal and illegal) ways—and because gun violence may be the result of a multitude of factors, such as instability, corruption, and poverty, as well as gun availability and build-up—constructing a causal chain that is 'short and clear' remains quite difficult. Moreover, the 'legal equality of opportunity' concern also remains rather problematic in that guns of many different varieties are considered legitimate possessions, as police forces, military personnel, and individuals around the world are legally allowed to own and use such weaponry. Some may argue that the massive availability of small arms may impinge on one's 'legal equality of opportunity' to live in a secure environment, but others argue that a legal opportunity to own and use firearms is and should be afforded to individuals, groups and governments for various reasons. Regarding the issue of small arms, therefore, there remains a competing view of what should be considered 'legal equality of opportunity'—and this proves problematic for the movement network.

Contrast the characteristics of the small arms issue with those concerning landmines. The success of the ICBL may largely be due, in other words, to the fact that anti-personnel landmines more easily meet these issue criteria. First, anti-personnel landmines clearly involve 'bodily harm to vulnerable individuals' as landmines, once deployed, are not able to distinguish between combatants and non-combatants. Second, because landmines, once deployed, do not move—and because there is significant evidence of their existence in large quantities and numerous injuries and deaths as a result—constructing a 'short and clear causal chain' regarding the impact of landmines is much more likely. And third, competing ideas regarding the 'legal equality of opportunity' were relatively weak. The argument that landmines greatly affected the lives and welfare of millions of people around the world seemingly outweighed any legal argument that governments, groups, and individuals have the legal right (based on equality of opportunity) to use such weapons. In fact, the argument may be more readily made that governments, groups, and individuals had the opportunity to choose other methods and other weapons to achieve their goals (whether it be self-defense or sport, for example)—and that these other choices were less indiscriminate.

Target characteristics also have an impact on network success. The targets of network activities must be vulnerable to sanctions or responsive to incentives for them to be affected by external pressure. In the case of landmines, the ICBL worked to develop a coalition of middle-power states that banned together with the NGO network to pressure other states to join the landmine treaty. Such a coalition has been much more problematic in the small arms area where many states, and even some previously involved in the landmine campaign, have strong incentives to manufacture, sell, and transfer such weapons. Moreover, because states are the primary users of landmines, state actors were the primary targets. The ICBL, therefore, did not have to concern itself with other actors. In the small arms area, however, the targets are many, as small arms issues are affected not only by states, but also by arms dealers, gun runners, insurgent groups, terrorists, and even individual citizens who seek gun ownership, among others. Such a plethora of targets, most of which are not vulnerable to sanctions or sensitive to pressure, enhances the complexity of the small arms issue.

Because of the complex and cross-cutting nature of the small arms issue, therefore, the movement and its network of actors that have emerged to address the issue is rather diverse—and is structured rather differently than the landmine network.[73] Human rights and humanitarian organizations, development and anti-poverty organizations, inter- and intra-national conflict prevention organizations, arms control organizations, regional organizations, public health organizations, gun control and anti-violence organizations, and law-enforcement organizations have joined IANSA and the small arms movement—all because they agree that the proliferation of small arms is a problem, but not necessarily because there is consensus among them about how to solve it.

First and Second Generation TSMNs: Spider-Webs and Honey-Combs

Ultimately, the many different groups involved in the small arms movement, with their many different mandates, have affected the way in which the network has taken shape. Specifically, because of the very diverse and inclusive nature of the SAM's membership (Table 18.1), and because of the numerous goals it has expressed, the network looks less like a web of NGOs than a honey-comb—each connected by some common idea but not at all focused on a particular or central goal. Despite the existence of the International Action Network on Small Arms, the SAM is relatively absent of leadership—by design. The participants in the small arms movement have numerous perspectives and various goals and cover a significant amount of territory around the world (more than 105 countries, two-thirds of which are in the southern hemisphere). Central leadership and common, collective goals are, therefore, rather problematic. IANSA does not speak for its members with any authority—instead serving a facilitating role as a 'network of networks' or 'movement of movements.' In fact, this structure certainly resembles the second-generation movement to which W. Lance Bennett refers.[74]

The membership of the ICBL, by contrast, also included a variation of organizations, but nearly half of the participants were from human rights and faith-based groups and were overwhelming located in the northern hemisphere (Table 18.2). The network, therefore, was less diverse and more centralized, sharing a common goal and reflecting a central leadership. More like a spider-web in structure, the ICBL was more focused and certainly resembles the first generation movement network described earlier.

We see, therefore, relatively different structures regarding IANSA and the ICBL—and we also see relatively different records of success. The first generation, centralized, focused network—the ICBL—sets itself apart as a shining example of TSMNs. The second generation, diffuse, diverse, leaderless network—IANSA—struggles to achieve its goals and has many critics—many of whom are members of the network. In fact, the very problems that second generation networks seek to avoid, according to the scholars noted above, seem to be affecting the viability of the small arms movement. Although participants in the small arms movement

Table 18.1 Typology of SAM Participants

Organization Type	Northern Hemisphere	Southern Hemisphere	TOTALS
Faith-Based	10	14	24
Education	6	11	17
Human Rights/Humanitarian	40	41	81
Economic, Social, Environmental, Development	12	36	48
Medical/Public Health	12	14	26
Democracy/Governance	14	26	40
Crime and Justice	4	11	15
Conflict Resolution, Peace and Security	39	53	92
Anti-Gun Violence/ Domestic Gun Control	9	17	26
International Disarmament/ Arms Control	28	14	42
Miscellaneous	8	5	13
TOTALS	182	242	424

Table 18.2 Typology of ICBL Organizations

Organization Type	Northern Hemisphere	Southern Hemisphere	TOTALS
Faith Based	254	34	288
Education	22	12	34
Human Rights/Humanitarian	187	77	264
Economic, Social, Environmental Development	85	45	130
Medical/Public Health	69	5	74
Democracy/Governance	23	10	33
Crime and Justice	14	5	19
Conflict Resolution, Peace and Security	106	24	130
Anti-Gun Violence/ Domestic Gun Control	21	34	55
International Disarmament/ Arms Control	23	4	27
Miscellaneous	30	47	77
TOTALS	834	297	1131

have been intricately involved in small arms activities at all levels and have achieved much, many participants and their targets have suggested that the movement has failed to develop a unified front and establish a cohesive approach. Some say this is inherent in the issue of small arms because it is so broad and diverse. Yet many others point to particular weaknesses within the movement. To determine more precisely how and why the small arms movement has struggled, we turned to the participants themselves for the answers.

An Internal Assessment of the Small Arms Movement: Participant Perspectives

Because of the many and divergent views that have often been expressed about the small arms movement, and because no internal, systematic assessment of the SAM has been attempted, we conducted an email survey of many organizations and individuals involved in the small arms movement from all around the world in order to achieve a broader understanding of perspectives within the movement. Our initial survey consisted of only three questions. First, we wanted to know what participants' perceptions were of the small arms movement (how effective they thought it to be). Second, we asked what the respondent's role or involvement was in the small arms movement. And third, we asked what the member thought the movement could do better or differently to enhance its ultimate success. Based on the response to that survey, we constructed a more structured questionnaire and conducted a second email survey.[75] In this survey, we wanted to get specific feedback about the positive contribution of IANSA, about the diffuse and decentralized structure of the movement and its network, about the inclusive or exclusive nature of the movement network, about the sense of community or solidarity among movement participants, about movement leadership, and about the environment in which participants must operate. All of these issues were raised by the majority of respondents in the first survey. We asked, therefore, for respondents to elaborate further on these issues in the second survey. To strengthen our survey data, we traveled to Washington, D.C., New York City, and London to conduct interviews with small arms NGO network members and movement participants, as well as UN and government officials who are involved in small arms activities. Our findings are as follows:

Sharing Information and Raising Awareness

Respondents to our survey and individuals we interviewed overwhelmingly agreed that the one shining success that the small arms movement has achieved is the sharing of information and raising awareness inside and out. IANSA was praised, in particular, for its efforts to enhance knowledge and communication among and between network members, as well as among and between members and target actors (mainly governments and international organizations). Since its inception, the small arms network has highlighted the various small arms problems in multiple international, regional, and national forums. The IANSA website serves, according to most, as an 'effective clearinghouse' for useful information related to small arms research and advocacy. Many respondents stated that this is IANSA's biggest strength and main contribution to the small arms movement. IANSA is not without its critics, however. Some respondents suggested that although the network 'used to be quite effective in sharing information, increasing knowledge and enhancing communication on the small arms issue,' today it is not as effective. WebPages are often out of date or inoperative, and the network has little capacity to share knowledge about all aspects of the small arms problem. Although the network is widely praised for its information sharing activities, many believe there is still room for improvement and that the movement network can do better to enhance information, awareness, and communication.

Collective Goals and Centralization

Our first survey indicated that many participants in the small arms movement found the lack of collective goals and strategies a problem for the work of the movement. We asked specifically about this issue in our second survey and during our interviews and found rather divergent results, perhaps reflecting the very diverse nature of the players within the movement. Several respondents and interviewees suggested that the small arms issue was 'too context and culturally specific to have a broad common project.' According to some, such 'national contexts and cultures are distinct and it would be counterproductive to standardize strategies.' These respondents, therefore, suggested small arms work should be locally oriented, making collective goals unnecessary.

A few respondents stated that there should be a middle-of-the-road approach—that participants in the small arms movement should develop a loose set of goals rather than have a single, collective goal or strategy. These participants were likely to suggest that the movement should 'harmonize, but not homogenize' efforts within the movement network. A slight majority of respondents, however, believe that the lack of collective action is the movement's greatest weakness. Members responded that 'those working on this issue would be more effective were they to pool their energies and work towards a common goal'—that the movement was 'held back by the lack of a clear and collective mandate'—and that 'within the network we must agree on a limited set of priorities [that] we can all work on together.'

Although not everyone agrees, the majority of survey and interview respondents suggested that the small arms movement requires greater centralization in order to be productive. It is the case, however, that these same respondents remain rather pessimistic about the likelihood or feasibility of such centralization. One participant stated, 'A united front in support of a few specific goals would enhance efficacy in pursuing them.' Another suggested, 'Centralized efforts are crucial for posing a united front.' Others said, 'The network needs a central goal that everyone can rally around' and highlighted the new Control Arms campaign, led by Amnesty International, Oxfam, and IANSA, as a prime example of centralized efforts around which others can organize their work.[76]

The Control Arms campaign and this idea of centralized efforts are not, however, without their critics. Some respondents suggested that central campaigns are problematic. 'The Oxfam campaign against all arms is creating problems [for] the majority of NGOs who fight small arms and light weapons because, in this struggle, we have allies within the military and within governments who will not favor a fight against all arms.' Moreover, some respondents were incredibly negative about centralized efforts suggesting that the movement is 'too diverse to centralize'—that 'although it may be useful, it would be difficult to impossible'—that 'it's too late to centralize small arms efforts'—and that such efforts would be a 'lost cause' given that they would be 'bogged down in rivalries.' Ultimately, one respondent stated, 'there is no unified front in the small arms arena, and many, many thousands of person-hours have been wasted already, trying to persuade disparate groups to follow an agreed plan.'

The Powerful Few

Survey respondents and interviewees overwhelmingly suggested that the small arms movement is dominated by only a few organizations—all of which are located in the developed North. Large, well-funded NGOs located primarily in Western Europe and the United States dominate small arms work. The 'usual suspects' were often mentioned by name in surveys and interviews and include such NGOs as Saferworld, Oxfam, Amnesty International, Small Arms Survey, International Alert, and Human Rights Watch. These organizations, as well as others in the western world, are acknowledged to have better resources, skills, and information, on the one hand, but are often charged with drowning out the voices of other actors, on the other hand. Most respondents were quite critical of the fact that such few organizations take center stage within the movement. One response, for example, suggested, 'Too many people sit in offices in London, Geneva, and New York. They should spend more time in Cape Town, Rio, and Manila.'

Another respondent stated, 'Northern NGOs impose their views and interests on southern NGOs.' Still another suggested that northern domination is to be expected 'because that is where the money is—and the network is less about norms and values than it is about money.' Overall, the majority of respondents acknowledged that the small arms movement is dominated by the powerful few, that most participants were under-represented and under-funded, that such a fact is 'inevitable,' and that 'there is nothing that can be done about it.'

The Need for Inclusiveness

Because the small arms movement is believed to be dominated by a few, western actors in the developed North, there is an overwhelming belief among respondents and interviewees that participants in the movement should do much more to include southern, non-western actors in the movement network. Ironically, the majority of IANSA's membership is southern—and this was done by design.[77] These actors, however, rarely have the funds and capacities necessary to engage in the work and attend the meetings that northern members do. Every respondent suggested, therefore, that in some way, southern actors should be included.

This will, of course, require resources—and nearly all respondents stated that more funding was needed in order to become a truly inclusive movement. In addition to funding, many respondents stated that northern participants should 'provide information, training, and exchange opportunities.' Others also suggested that northern actors 'must allow space for alternative views' and 'must not manipulate the positions of NGOs in the south to serve their needs.' Still others are even more critical of inclusive efforts, suggesting that southern participants 'need to prove they can do the job. They must earn respect because too many individuals and NGOs in developing nations have taken money from the north [and] then simply disappeared.' Moreover, another respondent suggested that inclusive efforts 'will only work if network NGOs are interested in working together—which, while in principle they all agree to do, in practice they often don't.'

Strengthening Solidarity

As with other problematic issues, participants in the small arms movement overwhelmingly responded that there should be a strengthened sense of solidarity within the movement, but few knew how to make that happen. Many respondents suggested that there is no 'sense of belonging' within the movement network and that this lack of solidarity negatively affects the movement's success. Some members believe that in order to strengthen the community there 'should be more timely and regular communication within the network'—that 'network members should listen to each other more'—that 'solidarity will be created by campaigning, campaigning, and more campaigning'—and that 'a feeling of solidarity will be enhanced by the sharing of stories in the sense that NGOs [would] see that their experiences are also felt in other regions.' There are those participants, however, that believe a sense of solidarity within the movement is 'impossible' and that efforts to enhance 'belonging' within the community would be a 'waste of time.'

Looking for Leadership

Although a few disagree, most survey respondents and interviewees suggested that leadership is lacking within the small arms movement. Most identify IANSA as the natural place to forge leadership, but that this has not happened and most likely will not. Moreover, many respondents stated that particular individuals within the movement prevent the emergence of an effective leader. One member in particular said, 'There appear to be some strong individual personalities who are more intent on promoting themselves or their country or their group than they are in working together with others.' Another said, 'IANSA did spend too much time bending over backward to accommodate particular individual personalities rather than solidifying leadership in the early days.' Another adds, 'IANSA hasn't yet figured out how to lead, although it would be the ideal leader' for the small arms movement. Many members believe there needs to be someone extremely visible leading the small arms charge, but that leaders ultimately have to emerge naturally. Some say that a particular state or an appointed NGO should lead the movement. Ultimately, what members do agree on is that leadership is lacking. How to solve the leadership problem—or whether it could be solved at all—is a matter that, like so many other issues, reflects the very diverse nature of the movement in that there appears to be little to no consensus.

A Competitive Environment

Perhaps the most consistent matter on which movement participants expressed their over-whelming concern was the competitive environment in which NGOs must operate. Nearly all respondents expressed some kind of distress regarding the negative effects of competition within the movement and among its participants. Members suggested that there is a 'constant and terrible fight for resources' that leads to 'divisions in the network.' One member stated that 'large organizations in particular, that control the lion's share of funding, not only compete but exercise considerable control over which of the smaller organizations get support and whose voices are heard.' Another said that within the small arms movement 'resources are scarce, information could be better shared, and competition for funding and grass-roots support tends to promote competition for territorial exclusivity and visibility.' Numerous members pointed to 'jealousies among member groups' as a key problem. 'Everyone is guarding their turf and competing for funding,' says one member—and this 'distracts everyone from their work' and 'holds us all back.'

A couple of members are quick to suggest that it is only a 'few bad apples' that create this competitive environment and 'spoil it for everyone.' A number of respondents also referred to 'favoritism' within the movement as only a few get the majority of the available resources and that these participants are reluctant to share. Some participants are accused of 'possessing a campaign' and being concerned more with 'the visibility of their work rather than the quality.' Many participants, therefore, knowing that they 'don't have any possibility of getting funds, respect, visibility, or access' must do their work 'the best they can, despite the serious obstacles.' Only one respondent highlighted the positive aspect of a competitive environment in that it enhances good work within the movement. Overwhelmingly, members are bothered by the competitive environment, but seem resigned to its existence. Not a single respondent or inter-viewee could suggest how to overcome it.

Conclusion

After our analysis of the SAM, we can offer a number of theoretical and practical findings. First, our results concerning the role and significance of information-sharing and awareness-raising within the small arms movement is consistent, but not entirely compatible, with theoretical expectations. Keck and Sikkink, as well as others, highlight the importance of discursive activities among and between network participants. In fact, such practices become the 'glue' that binds participants together.[78] In the case of the small arms movement, information-sharing and awareness-raising has certainly played a role—and most participants say this is the movement's greatest success. Such activities have not, however, served to solidify the movement network to a great degree as many participants still consider communication within the movement to be severely lacking.

Regarding collective goals, strategies, and the need for centralization, we see rather diverse results. Most research on transnational movement networks suggests that such actors are most effective if they are cohesive and focused.[79] Other research suggests that a lack of unity is not so damaging—that diversity and fragmentation energizes the movement.[80] What we see with the small arms movement is evidence to support both contentions. The movement has arguably, according to many of its participants, been ineffective in its ability to achieve much ground toward its goals and objectives—and the lack of collective goals and centralized efforts are often to blame. Others, however, find such diversity within the framework to be appropriate and inevitable—lending support to the notion that NGOs may be energized by the disparity. Conflict between the first- and second-generation structures seems to exist within the SAM as participants are not necessarily 'on the same page' regarding the collective needs of the movement. The SAM is, however, showing signs of collective action with the Control Arms campaign. Even this effort, however, has had to overcome serious obstacles. Originally an effort created by Amnesty International and Oxfam, the campaign excluded the central network actor, IANSA, until a later date as Amnesty and Oxfam members were reportedly reluctant to include the organization because of the fear that its 'incoherence would slow the campaign down.'[81] Despite this effort, it is clear that the small arms movement remains diffuse and decentralized, absent of collective goals and strategies. It is also clear that there is no consensus among the movement's participants as to the significance of such.

There is clearly a call among the movement's membership to become more inclusive and move away from the dominant role of the few within the movement network. Other studies have highlighted the difficulties of incorporating actors from both the north and south in transnational movement activities.[82] Ironically, founding members of IANSA and the small arms movement sought to be inclusive from the beginning[83]—and more than half of IANSA's current membership is from the southern hemisphere.[84] Nonetheless, southern members believe they are less involved, are least likely to be funded, and are, therefore, less likely to be heard.

Such splits within the movement network contribute to the lack of a sense of belonging and the lack of a feeling of cohesiveness.[85] As other scholars have suggested, networks are comprised of 'like-minded' individuals and groups that share common values and ideas. In the case of the small arms movement, however, the like-minded nature of its membership is rather minimal. Movement participants are bound together by the lowest common denominator—a fundamental concern about small arms. There exists a very weak sense of identity among participants and many say it is 'exhausting' to try and develop a stronger bond.[86]

Although some studies focus on the role of 'political entrepreneurs' in developing a transnational network, such individuals may or may not be leaders within network operations.[87] High profile spokespeople have been shown to be useful in bringing attention to network issues,[88] but skillful leadership, such as that provided by Nobel Prize winning Jody Williams for the ICBL, may be key—and participants in the small arms movement seem to agree. What remains problematic to many in the movement is the lack of leadership. Although IANSA has been identified as the natural source of leadership, this organization remains, according to its own membership and others, weak, under-funded, and incoherent.[89] Interviews with founding members revealed that early discussions about the formation of the small arms movement network were hampered by clashing interests in leadership—the problem being that a number of individuals 'wanted to be Jody Williams.'[90] Because too many leaders is as problematic as none at all, the small arms movement has struggled to identify who shall be sheep and who shall be shepherds—largely a result, according to movement participants, of the diverse and strong personalities that have been involved.

It has been highlighted in other studies that NGO network strategies are not terribly distinct from other materially motivated organizations such as businesses and for-profit enterprises.[91] What has not been well understood is the competitive nature within NGO networks.[92] This study demonstrates the pitfalls of competition among participants of a transnational social movement—particularly calling into question the theoretical argument that second-generation, honey-comb shaped networks ease tensions, promote cooperation, and quell conflict. Ill feelings and despair were evident in survey responses and individual interviews because of the competitive environment in which the participants were working. From our own experiences as researchers in the small arms area, we have witnessed territorial and protective activities regarding information-gathering and publishing, as well as the precarious ways in which movement NGOs interact with each other in order to facilitate individual, rather than collective, interests. Such competition is clearly damaging to the small arms movement as it inhibits cooperation and collective action and prevents solidarity and identity, thereby diminishing the overall force and effectiveness of the movement. Like with state actors who overcome the negative effects of international anarchy and seek the joint- rather than self-maximization of goals in order to further their national interests and solve common problems, so too must the participants in the small arms movement move toward jointly maximizing their self interests by minimizing the competition to which they all contribute. Otherwise, the impact of the movement will continue to be minimal.

As for the case of small arms, it is clear that after much hope in the 1990s for an effective transnational social movement, much frustration remains. The small arms issue is indeed a complex one—and the complexity has certainly affected the structure and operations of the network. The issue alone, however, cannot fully explain why the movement has not been as successful as hoped. Findings suggest that the incoherent, diffuse, decentralized nature of the movement, as well as personality, leadership, dominance, and competitive factors, together help us understand movement weaknesses, at a minimum, and failures, at a maximum. For those issues that have a more clear causal chain and more reachable and vulnerable targets, such as anti-personnel landmines, concerns about network structure are perhaps less important. For other issues that are more complex, diverse, and difficult, such as small arms, structure may matter more. And in the case of the SAM the negative effects are already taking their toll as a number of NGO and individual actors have decided to move on to other issues.[93]

What should the SAM do? We suggest that the participants within the SAM take stock of where they have come individually and collectively and assess whether they are likely to make more progress together or separately. Our study demonstrates that the movement may be better served if its participants strengthened their bonds and developed more collective goals. It may very well be the case that united the movement stands whereas divided it falls—and the participants should purposefully consider current structures and enhance their cooperative network. At a minimum, the SAM may continue down this path of token collective effort and negligible impact. The movement, however, has much more to offer—as evidenced by the ICBL example. Why not learn from those who have been most successful and consider adopting those practices and operations that have served others well? While second-generation structures may work for some, in other words, it appears that the SAM should consider enhancing its first-generation characteristics by altering its honey-comb shape and becoming more of a spider-web in structure and function. The alternative is greater diffusion and greater weakness—a result that does not well serve the purpose of addressing the serious problems associated with small arms.

This study has addressed a number of questions and filled a number of gaps in the existing literature, but many more remain. Avenues for future research include the exploration of (1) the conditions under which transnational social movement networks, in general, and the SAM, in particular, can overcome competition within their ranks; (2) the specific ways in which movement networks, such as the ICBL, achieve convergence and consensus; (3) the various structural forms movement networks take in order to produce the best outcomes under various circumstances; and (4) the reasons for why movement networks take on certain structures and functions across other cases. We still have much to learn about TSMNs—and the complex, problematic, and challenged networks, like the SAM, should, in particular, be better understood.

Notes

1. One of the first known nongovernmental commentaries on the issue of small arms was published in 1996. See Edward J. Laurance, *The New Field of Microdisarmament: Addressing the Proliferation and Buildup of Small Arms and Light Weapons* (Bonn, Germany: Bonn International Center for Conversion, September 1996).
2. To us, the small arms movement (SAM) refers to the collective of nongovernmental actors involved in highlighting the importance of and targeting specific action on small arms issues. This movement includes a host of policy, advocacy and research NGOs, individual experts, analysts, and academics. At the center of the movement is the International Action Network on Small Arms (IANSA), which consists of over 500 loosely connected NGOs and individuals involved in small arms research and/or advocacy. Although comprised of a large number of organizations, IANSA is only a part of the small arms movement and does not speak for all of its members with any authority. What binds these actors together and moves them to act is their concern about small arms as a problem for human, national, and international security.
3. For example, see Ann Florini, ed., *The Third Force: The Rise of Transnational Civil Society* (Tokyo and Washington: Japan Center for International Change and Carnegie Endowment for International Peace, 1999); Margaret Keck and Kathryn Sikkink, *Activists Beyond Borders: Advocacy Networks in Internaitonal Politics* (Ithaca: NY: Cornell University Press, 1998); Sanjeev Khagram, James V. Riker, and Kathryn Sikkink, eds., *Restructuring World Politics: Transnational Social Movements, Networks and Norms* (Minneapolis: University of Minnesota Press, 2002); Ann Marie Clark, *Diplomacy of Conscience: Amnesty International and Changing Human Rights Norms* (Princeton: Princeton University Press, 2001); Michael Edwards and David Hulme, eds., *Beyond the Magic Bullet: NGO Performance and Accountability in the Post-Cold War World* (West Hartford, CT: Kumarian Press, 1996); Craig Warkentin, *Reshaping World Politics: NGOs, the Internet, and Global Civil Society* (Lanham, MD: Roman and Littlefield Publishers, 2001); and Mari Fitzduff and Cheyanne Church, *NGOs at the Table: Strategies for Influencing Policies in Areas of Conflict* (Lanham, MD: Rowman and Littlefield Publishers, 2004).
4. For exceptions, see Fitzduff and Church, *NGOs at the Table*; and Richard Price, "Reversing the Gun Sights: Transnational Civil Society Targets Land Mines," *International Organization*, Vol. 52, No. 3 (Summer 1998), pp. 613–644.
5. See Keck and Sikkink 1998, for example.
6. See John Clark, "Introduction: Civil Society and Transnational Action," in John Clark, ed., *Globalizing Civic Engagement: Civil Society and Transnational Action* (London: Earthscan Publications, Ltd., 2003), pp. 1–28; and W. Lance Bennett, "Social Movements Beyond

Borders: Understanding Two Eras of Transnational Activism," in Donatella della Porta and Sidney Tarrow, eds., *Transnational protest and Global Activism* (Lanham, MD: Rowman and Littlefield, Inc., 2005), pp. 203–226. Jackie Smith and Joe Bandy also emphasize "the diversity of organizational structures" and their impact on the work of transnational coalitions. See Jackie Smith and Joe Bandy, "Introduction: Cooperation and Conflict in Transnational Protest," in Joe Bandy and Jackie Smith, eds., *Coalitions Across Borders: Transnational Protest and the Neoliberal Order* (Lanham, MD: Rowman and Littlefield, 2005), p. 9.

7. www.icbl.org/tools/faq/campaign/role. Accessed June 22, 2005.

8. A few network studies have highlighted the rational, instrumental and material strategies employed by NGO actors. See, for example, Alexander Cooley and James Ron, "The NGO Scramble: Organizational Insecurity and the Political Economy of Transnational Action," *International Security*, Vol. 27, No. 1 (Summer 2002), pp. 5–39; Susan K. Sell and Aseem Prakash, "Using Ideas Strategically: The Contest Between Business and NGO Networks in Intellectual Property Rights," *International Studies Quarterly*, Vol. 48 (2004), pp. 143–175; and Thomas J. Ward, *Development, Social Justice, and NGOs: The Political Economy of NGOs* (St. Paul, MN: Paragon House, 2000).

9. For exceptions, see Tadashi Yamamoto, *Emerging Civil Society in the Asia Pacific Community* (Singapore and Japan: Institute of Southeast Asian Studies and Japan Center for International Exchange, 1995); Donatella della Porta, "Multiple Belongings, Tolerant Identities and the Construction of 'Another Politics': Between the European Social Forum and the Local Social Fora," in Donatella della Porta and Sidney Tarrow, eds., *Transnational Protest and Global Activism* (Lanham, MD: Rowman and Littlefield, 2005), pp. 175–202; and Ken Rutherford, "The Hague and Ottawa Conventions: A Model for Future Weapons Prohibition Regimes," *The Nonproliferation Review*, Vol. 6, No. 3 (Spring/Summer 1999), pp. 36–50.

10. Michael Edwards and David Hume, *Beyond the Magic Bullet: NGO Accountability in the Post-Cold War World*, (West Hartford, Connecticut: Kumarian Press, 1996).

11. A United Nations 16-member Panel of Governmental Experts on Small Arms identifies small arms and light weapons as the following: assault rifles, pistols, sub-machine guns, light machine guns, mortars, portable anti-aircraft guns, grenade launchers, anti-tank missile and rocket systems, hand grenades and anti-personnel land mines. In other words, small and light arms are those weapon systems that can be carried and operated by a single individual or a small group of people working as a team. See the *Report of the Panel of Governmental Experts on Small Arms*, UN General Assembly document A/52/298, 27 August 1992, available at http://www.un.org/sc/committees/sanctions/a52298.pdf.

12. See details at http://www.iansa.org/about.htm.

13. Authors' interviews with movement participants, March 2003 and March 2005.

14. Early studies of NGO actors in world politics include: Kjell Skjelsbaek, "The Growth of International Nongovernmental Organization in the Twentieth Century," *International Organization*, Vol. 25, No. 3 (Summer 1971), pp. 420–442; Samuel P. Huntington, "Transnational Organizations in World Politics," *World Politics*, Vol. 25 (1973), pp. 333–368; Anne Thompson Feraru, "Transnational Political Interests and the Global Environment," *International Organization*, Vol. 28, No. 1 (Winter 1974), pp. 31–60; and Robert O. Keohane and Joseph S. Nye, *Transnational Relations and World Politics* (Cambridge: Harvard University Press, 1972). More contemporary studies include (in addition to those mentioned above) Elisabeth J. Friedman, *Sovereignty, Democracy, and Global Civil Society: State-Society Relations at UN World Vonferences* (Albany, NY: SUNY Press, 1995); Peter Willets, *Conscience of the World: The Influence of Non-Governmental Organizations in the U.N. System* (Washington, D.C.: Brookings Institution Press, 1996); Jackie Smith, *Transnational Social Movements and Global Politics: Solidarity Beyond the State* (Syracuse: Syracuse University

Press, 1997); Alison Van Rooy, *The Global Legitimacy Game: Civil Society, Globalization, and Protest* (New York: Palgrave Macmillan, 2004); Claude E. Welch, *NGOs and Human Rights: Promise and Performance* (Philadelphia: University of Pennsylvania Press, 2000); and Paul K. Wapner, *Environmental Activism and World Civic Politics* (Albany: SUNY Press, 1996).

15. We adopt the term transnational social movement network (TSMN) in order to encompass the entirety of the actors—policy, advocacy, and research organizations and individuals—involved in a particular transnational problem or issue. We rely on literature focusing on NGOs, transnational advocacy networks, and social movements to construct our understanding of a TSMN. See Ann Florini, ed., *The Third Force: The Rise of Transnational Civil Society* (Tokyo and Washington: Japan Center for International Change and Carnegie Endowment for International Peace, 1999); Margaret Keck and Kathryn Sikkink, *Activists Beyond Borders: Advocacy Networks in Internaitonal Politics* (Ithaca: NY: Cornell University Press, 1998); Sanjeev Khagram, James V. Riker, and Kathryn Sikkink, eds., *Restructuring World Politics: Transnational Social Movements, Networks and Norms* (Minneapolis: University of Minnesota Press, 2002); Donatella della Porta and Sidney Tarrow, eds., *Transnational Protest and Global Activism* (Lanham, MD: Rowman and Littlefield Publishers, Inc., 2005); W. Lance Bennett, "Social Movements Beyond Borders: Understanding Two Eras of Transnational Activism," in della Porta and Tarrow, eds., *Transnational Protest and Global Activism*, pp. 203–226; Jeff Goodwin and James M. Jasper, *The Social Movements Reader: Cases and Concepts* (Malden, MA: Blackwell Publishing, 2003); and Donatella della Porta and Mario Diani, *Social Movements: An Introduction*: Oxford: Blackwell Publishers, Ltd., 1999).

16. The focus on these NGO networks increased following the publication of Keck and Sikkink's, *Activists Beyond Borders* in 1998.

17. See Peter Haas, *Saving the Mediterranean: The Politics of International Environmental Cooperation* (New York: Columbia University Press, 1990); Peter M. Haas, "Do Regimes Matter? Epistemic Communities and Mediterranean Pollution Control," *International Organization*, Vol. 43, No. 3 (Summer 1998), pp. 377–403; Emanuel Adler, "The Emergence of Cooperation: National Epistemic Communities and the International Evolution of the Idea of Nuclear Arms Control," *International Organization*, Vol. 46, No. 1 (Winter 1992), pp. 101–145; James K. Sebenius, "Challenging Conventional Explanations of International Cooperation: negotiation Analysis and the Case of Epistemic Communities," *International Organization*, Vol. 46, No. 1 (Winter 1992), pp. 323–365; and Dave Toke, "Epistemic Communities and Environmental Groups," *Politics*, Vol. 19, No. 2 (1999), pp. 97–102.

18. See Keck and Sikkink, *Activists Beyond Borders*; Thomas Risse-Kappen, ed., *Bringing Transnational Relations Back In: Non-State Actors, Domestic Structures, and International Institutions* (Cambridge: Cambridge University Press, 1995); Michael Edwards and John Gaventa, eds., *Global Citizen Action* (Boulder, CO: Lynne Rienner Publishers, Inc., 2001); Robert Rohrschneider and Russell J. Dalton, "A Global Network? Transnational Cooperation Among Environmental Groups," *Journal of Politics*, Vol. 64, No. 2 (May 2002), pp. 5–39; and Michele M. Betsill and Harriet Bulkeley, "Transnational Networks and Global Environmental Governance: The Cities for Climate Protection Program," *International Studies Quarterly*, Vol. 48 (2004), pp. 471–493.

19. See John Clark, ed., *Globalizing Civic Engagement: Civil Society and Transnational Action*; and Donatella della Porta and Sidney Tarrow, eds., *Transnational Protest and Global Activism*.

20. For more on global civil society, see Ronnie D. Lipschutz, *Global Civil Society and Global Environmental Governance: The Politics of Nature from Place to Planet* (Albany: SUNY Press, 1996); Ronnie D. Lipschutz, "Reconstructing World Politics: The Emergence of Global Civil Society," *Millennium: Journal of International Studies*, Vol. 21, No. 3 (1992),

pp. 389–420; Paul Wapner, "Governance in Global Civil Society," in Oran R. Young, ed., *Global Governance: Drawing Insights from the Environmental Experience* (Cambridge: MIT Press, 1997); Jan Aart Scholte, "Civil Society and Democracy in Global Governance," *Global Governance*, Vol. 8 (2002), pp. 281–304; John Keane, *Global Civil Society?* (Cambridge, UK: Cambridge University Press, 2003); and Ann Marie Clark, Elisabeth J. Friedman, and Kathryn Hochstetler, "The Sovereign Limits of Global Civil Society: A Comparison of NGO Participation in Global UN Conferences on the Environment, Women, and Human Rights," *World Politics*, Vol. 51, No. 1 (October 1998), pp. 1–35.

21. We do not include in this analysis of TSMN those movement networks that use violence to achieve their goals—groups such as terrorist networks or other violent organizations.

22. Keck and Sikkink 1998, p. 12.

23. Keck and Sikkink define activists the same as Oliver and Marwell do: "people who care enough about some issue that they are prepared to incur significant costs and act to achieve their goals." See Pamela E. Oliver and Gerald Marwell, "Mobilizing Technologies for Collective Action," in Aldon D. Morris and Carol McClurg Mueller, eds., *Frontiers in Social Movement Theory* (New Haven: Yale University Press, 1992), p. 252; and Keck and Sikkink, *Activists Beyond Borders*, p. 14. Other scholars see these activists as no different than most political entrepreneurs who capitalize on opportunities to move forward their personal agendas. See, for example, Cooley and Ron, "The NGO Scramble."

24. Keck and Sikkink 1998, pp. 14–16.

25. Ibid, pp. 17–24.

26. Keck and Sikkink refer to "stages of impact" because they believe that the first two types of influence networks exhibit open up the process for affecting change via the last three types of influence. See p. 26.

27. Ibid.

28. Ibid., p. 27.

29. Ibid., On the importance of gaining the support of domestic groups within the target state, see Thomas Risse-Kappen, "Ideas Do Not Float Freely: Transnational Coalitions, Domestic Structures, and the End of the Cold War," *International Organization*, Vol. 48, No. 2 (Spring 1994); and Clark, Anne-Marie. "Non-Governmental Organizations and Their Influence on International Society," *Journal of International Affairs*, Vol. 48, No. 2 (1995), pp. 507–25.

30. Keck and Sikkink, *Activists Beyond Borders*, p. 29. For more on international communities of states and the impact of social interaction among nations, see Alexander Wendt, *Social Theory of International Politics* (Cambridge: Cambridge University Press, 1999); Martha Finnemore, *National Interests in International Society*, (Ithaca: Cornell University Press, 1996); and Peter J. Katzenstein, ed., *The Culture of National Security: Norms and Identity in World Politics* (New York: Columbia University Press, 1996).

31. See W. Lance Bennett, "Social Movements Beyond Borders: Understanding Two Eras of Transnational Activism," in Donatella della Porta and Sidney Tarrow, eds., *Transnational Protest and Global Activism*, pp. 203–226; Donatella della Porta, "Multiple Belongings, Tolerant Identities, and the Construction of 'Another Politics': Between the European Social Forum and the Local Social Fora," in Donatella della Porta and Sidney Tarrow, eds., *Transnational Protest and Global Activism*, pp. 175–202; and John Clark, "Introduction: Civil Societ and Transnational Action," in John Clark, ed., *Globalizing Civic Engagement: Civil Society and Transnational Action*, pp. 1–28.

32. W. Lance Bennett 2005, pp. 203–205.

33. Jody Williams attributes ICBL's success to the Internet and e-mail. Thomas L. Friedman, *Longitudes and Attitudes: Exploring the World After September 11.* (New York: Farrar, Straus, & Giroux, 2002).

34. John Clark and Nuno Themudo, "The Age of Protest: Internet-Based 'Dot Causes' and the 'Anti-Globalization' Movement," in John Clark, ed., *Globalizing Civic Engagement*, pp. 109–126.
35. Della Porta 2005.
36. Ibid., p. 187.
37. Della Porta and Diani 1999, p. 155.
38. See Bennett 2005, p. 208.
39. Ibid., p. 209.
40. Clark 2003, p. 19; and Clark and Themudo 2003, p. 114.
41. Clark and Themudo 2003, p. 124.
42. Della Porta and Diani 1999, p. 161.
43. See Edward Laurance, *The Field of Microdisarmament: Addressing the Proliferation and Buildup of Small Arms and Light Weapons* (Bonn, Germany: Bonn International Center for Conversion, September 1996).
44. See Keith Krause, "Multilateral Diplomacy, Norm Building and UN Conferences: The Case of Small Arms and Light Weapons," *Global Governance*, Vol. 8, No. 2, April-June 2002, pp. 247–263.
45. Ibid.
46. See IANSA's Founding Document (May 1999) at http://www.iansa.org/about/m1.htm. Also see http://www.iansa.org/about.htm for more on IANSA's purpose and objectives.
47. Ibid.
48. See specifics about each goal and objective in IANSA's Founding Document at http://www.iansa.org/about/m1.htm.
49. See IANSA's Founding Document, pp. 8–9.
50. Ibid., p. 9.
51. Ibid.
52. See IANSA website at http://www.iansa.org/mission/newspub/launch/hap.htm.
53. Jeffrey Boutwell and Michael T. Klare, "A Scourge of Small Arms," *Scientific American* (June 2000), p. 52. Also see personal interviews with IANSA founders and members, Washington, D.C., November 1999 and June 2000. For another mention of the murder of Red Cross workers, see Lumpe, "Curbing the Proliferation of Small Arms and Light Weapons," p. 152.
54. IANSA Founding Document, p. 9.
55. Personal interviews with IANSA members, Washington, D.C., November 1999 and June 2000. For more on the importance of government involvement on the issue and the positions of various states around the world, see Margherita Serafini, "Small Arms: The Emerging Coalition of States for the UN Conference in 2001," Program on Security and Development at the Monterey Institute of International Studies, found at http://www.iansa.org/documents/research/2000/2001db_paper.htm.
56. See the U.N. Press Release about IANSA and its briefing to the Coordinating Action on Small Arms (CASA), Press Release DC/2646 (May 28, 1999), available at http://www.un.org/News/Press/docs/1999/19990528.DC2646.html. For more on U.N. activities regarding small arms, see Ambassador Jayantha Dhanapala, "The UN's Role in Combating Small Arms Proliferation," in *Stopping the Spread of Small Arms*, pp. 10–12.
57. IANSA Founding Document, p. 10.
58. For specifics on the regional networks, see the IANSA Members page at http://www.iansa.org/about/members.htm.
59. Interview and correspondence with SAM network participant, March 2005 and July 2005.
60. For the text of the Programme of Action, see http://disarmament.un.org;8080/cab/poa/html. For IANSA's most recent evaluation of the implementation of the Programme of Action, see http://www.iansa.org/documents/2004/iansa_2004_wrap_up_revised.doc.

61. See details about the Control Arms campaign at http://www.controlarms.org. For the text of the Arms Trade Treaty, see http://www.iansa.org/documents/2004/att_0504.pdf.

62. For more information on the beginning of the ICBL and the campaign to ban landmines, see the ICBL website, www.icbl.org/problem/history.

63. One of the four goals that ICBL endorses is "Demining and risk education to safeguard lives and livelihoods." For more information on ICBL's goals, See the ICBL website http://www.icbl.org/tools/faq/campaign/what_is_icbl.

64. A more detailed explanation of ICBL's action plan for their informational, symbolic, leverage and accountability activities can be accessed at http://www.icbl.org/campaign/actionplan?eZSESSIDicbl=0c92726ddb20dd67e0203ef80e75205f . Also see author interviews with ICBL staff member (May 2002 and July 2005).

65. In a current description of ICBL's role in the campaign to ban landmines, ICBL explained that significant activities included information-sharing and symbolic activities such as, "Marking significant anniversaries through media work and public events" and "Research and production of the Landmine Monitor Report which monitors implementation of and compliance with the 1997 Mine Ban Treaty" as well as leverage activities such as, "Lobbying ahead of international fora for inclusion of the landmine issue e.g. Commonwealth, the Francophonie, the European Union". These activities are described at the ICBL website http://www.icbl.org/tools/faq/campaign/role.

66. *Journal of Mine Action* records the action of celebrities and their influence on the landmine issue in "Celebrities and Landmines," by Jenny Lange, Issue 6.1, April 2002.

67. See above note referencing http://www.icbl.org/tools/faq/campaign/role.

68. Numerous interviews with IANSA founders and SAM participants, 1999–present.

69. The Nobel committee described ICBL as, "a model for similar processes in the future, it could prove of decisive importance to the international effort for disarmament and peace."

70. See Stephan Brem and Ken Rutherford "Walking Together or Divided Agendas," *Security Dialogue* Vol. 32, No. 2 (June 2001), pp. 169–186.

71. Interviews with SAM participants and government officials, June 2004, March 2005, and June 2005. For more on the human impact of small arms, see Cate Buchanan and Robert Muggah, *No Relief: Surveying the Effects of Gun Violence on Humanitarian and Development Personnel* (Geneva: Small Arms Survey, 2005), available at http://www.smallarmssurvey.org/copublications/NoRelief.pdf,

72. Keck and Sikkink, p. 27.

73. Despite the positive lessons the small arms organizations and individuals learned from the success of the ICBL efforts, the small arms participants very purposefully structured their movement differently. Acknowledging the significant differences in issues and targets, the small arms people set out to create a different kind of network—one that was more inclusive and diverse. This may also be the result of tension that was briefly evident within the ICBL in the wake of the ban in 1997 and the Nobel Prize in 1998. In any case, there was a notable lack of communication between the ICBL and SAM people as the small arms participants sought their own path. See first author's interviews with ICBL and SAM participants, November 1999, May 2002, March 2005 and July 2005.

74. Bennet, 'Social Movements Beyond Borders'.

75. For our first survey we distributed 222 questionnaires by email to random SAM participants and received 28 completed questionnaires in return. Responses were received from 16 countries across 5 continents. 16 of the 28 surveys were from countries in the northern hemisphere and 12 were from the south. Our second survey was distributed randomly by email to 248 recipients. We received 31 complete responses from 22 countries. 20 responses

were from the north and 11 from the south. Between both our surveys, we received completed questionnaires from NGO actors from 32 different countries. Admittedly, however, our response rate of about 12% for both surveys is low—and those who responded are, of course, self-selecting in that they chose to share their thoughts while many others did not. Nonetheless, we believe that because our results are representative of many different organizations from several different countries across five continents we can make some general inferences from the survey findings.

76. For specifics on the Control Arms campaign, see http://www.controlarms.org.
77. Interviews with IANSA founding members revealed that they were very conscious of including NGOs from the southern hemisphere after southern NGOs were reportedly rather disgruntled about being marginalized during the campaign to ban landmines. See one author's interviews with movement participants, November 1999 and June 2000.
78. Keck and Sikkink, *Activists Beyond Borders*, pp. 10–18; and Betsill and Bulkeley, "Transnational Networks and Global Environmental Governance," p. 490.
79. See, for example, John Clark, *Democratizing Development: The Role of Voluntary Organizations* (West Hartford, CT: Kumarian Press, 1990), pp. 203–4.
80. See, for example, Rupert Taylor, *Creating a Better World: Interpreting Global Civil Society* (Bloomfield, CT: Kumarian Press, 2004), p. 9.
81. Authors' interviews with small arms movement participants, March 2005. Incidentally, the director of IANSA never made herself available for interviews with the authors. Repeated attempts to schedule meetings went unanswered or plans were canceled. Only one IANSA staff member responded to our email survey.
82. Rohrschneider and Dalton, "A Global Network? Transnational Cooperation Among Environmental Groups," p. 513; and Keck and Sikkink, *Activists Beyond Borders*, p. 197. Also see Sarah Gardner, "Major Themes in the Study of Grassroots Environmentalism in Developing Countries," *Journal of Third World Studies*, Vol. 12, No. 2 (1995), pp. 200–245; Hein-Andon Van der Heijden, "Environmental Movements, Ecological Modernization, and Political Opportunity Structures," *Environmental Politics*, Vol. 8, No. 1 (1999), pp. 199–221; and Smith and Bandy, "Introduction: Cooperation and Conflict in Transnational Protest," p. 7.
83. One author's interviews with movement participants, November 1999 and June 2000.
84. For a complete list of IANSA members, see http://www.iansa.org/about/members.htm.
85. On the importance of collective identity within transnational social movements, see Scott A. Hunt and Robert D. Benford, "Collective identity, Solidarity, and Commitment," in David A. Snow, Sarah A. Soule, and Hanspeter Kriesi, eds., *The Blackwell Companion to Social Movements* (Malden, MA: Blackwell Publishing, Inc., 2004), pp. 433–457; Smith and Bandy, "Introduction: Cooperation and Conflict in Transnational Protest," pp. 10–11; and Pauline P. Cullen, "Conflict and Cooperation within the Platform of European Social NGOs," in Bandy and Smith, eds., *Coalitions Across Borders*, pp. 84–85; and Bandy and Smith, "Factors Affecting Conflict and Cooperation in Transnational Movement Networks," in Bandy and Smith, eds., *Coalitions Across Borders*, p. 23.
86. Authors' interviews with small arms movement participants, March 2005.
87. Keck and Sikkink, *Activists Beyond Borders*, p. 14.
88. Price, "Reversing the Gun Sights," p. 621.
89. Authors' interviews with small arms movement participants, March 2005.
90. One author's interviews with small arms movement participants, November 1999 and June 2000.
91. Cooley and Ron, "The NGO Scramble;" and Sell and Prakash, "Using Ideas Strategically."

92. For examples, see Fitzduff and Church, *NGOs at the Table*; della Porta and Diani, *Social Movements*; and Jackie Smith, "Transnational Processes and Movement," in Snow, Soule, and Kriesi, eds., *The Blackwell Companion to Social Movements*, pp. 311–329.
93. Authors' interviews with small arms movement participants, March 2005.

PART VIII

SOCIAL JUSTICE AND DEMOCRACY

CHAPTER NINETEEN

Before Seattle: The Historical Roots of the Current Movement against Corporate-led Globalization

Robin Broad and Zahara Heckscher

Source: *Third World Quarterly* (2003) 24:4, 713–728 © 2003 Taylor & Francis—Reproduced with permission.

As an expert on transnational corporations bemoaned to one of the authors, the current movement to alter globalisation is 'a movement that does not . . . recognise its own history'.[1] The purpose of this article is to 'recognise' that history and to examine its relevance to the contemporary period and movement.

Economic integration through trade, investment and financial flows is not simply a phenomenon of the 1990s, even if that decade popularised the term economic 'globalisation'. Nor, this article argues, did resistance to this economic integration erupt only recently. By some accounts, the resistance appears to have grown magically from nothing to the 40 000–60 000 on the streets of Seattle. Indeed, thanks to widespread media coverage, the 1999 'Battle of Seattle' brought this resistance to living rooms around the world. But today's resistance and the alternative proposals have important roots and antecedents that not only precede Seattle and the 1990s; they also precede Ronald Reagan, Margaret Thatcher, Helmut Kohl and the neoliberal consensus (also known as the Washington Consensus) that came to monopolise economic development thinking and policy in the 1980s and 1990s.

To explore the historical roots of the movement against corporate globalisation, the article provides snapshots of three dynamic waves of enhanced economic integration that provoked transboundary resistance by civil society, by governments or both: 1) the period of European colonialism, with case studies of the anti-slave trade and the international workers' movements; 2) the early post-World War II period (1940s–60s), which saw the creation of public institutions to manage the world economy and also marked a period of vibrant debate over the role of developing countries in the economic order; and 3) the 1970s, when Southern governments banded together to establish alternative rules and institutions, and when popular resistance to different aspects of economic integration spread in many nations. These case studies will illustrate ways in which today's movement has important antecedents in past popular movements and debates. (Any one of these periods could—and should—be examined in more depth by others; our purpose here is explicitly to employ a broader sweep by combining them.)

For those who think that cross-border citizen movements to confront economic globalisation began in Seattle in 1999, this article is meant to offer another perspective. There are actually several hundred years of movements that, with varying degrees of success, made international linkages on specific issues related to economic integration. Today's movement can learn lessons from these earlier cross-border organising forays. In addition, the particularly rich period of cross-border organising in the 1970s is interesting for yet another reason. As we will detail below, there are some threads that tie today's movement directly to that period. Notable, for instance, is the fact that several leaders of the current movement cut their teeth on related scholarship and activism during the 1970s. Although their earlier work is not necessarily widely known by today's movement against corporate globalisation, these individuals carry links and lessons into their current work.

Origins of Global Integration and Resistance

Trade across borders is at least as ancient as the Book of Genesis, which tells of Joseph being sold by his brothers into slavery courtesy of 'a company of Ishmaelites [who] came from Gilead with their camels bearing spicery and balm and myrrh, going to carry it down to Egypt'.[2] Throughout the millennia, extensive regional trade took place on all continents, from the Chinese dynasties to the Roman Empire, from the complex society of Great Zimbabwe to the astonishing Aztec markets of Mexico.

Today's patterns of global exchange date back to the period of European colonialism that began in the late 15th century. Before then, most of the regions of the world were largely self-sufficient. But this changed over the next two to three centuries, as a few European powers built fleets and militaries and began to claim large parts of the rest of the world under their rule. During this early era of economic integration, the central driving force was colonialism. Once the colonisers took over a territory, they began to transform economic activity. Indeed, this was at least part of the colonisers' motivation. Listen to the words of Cecil Rhodes, British colonial founder of Rhodesia: 'We must find new lands from which we can easily obtain raw materials and at the same time exploit the cheap slave labour that is available from the natives of the colonies. The colonies would also provide a dumping ground for the surplus goods produced in our factories.'[3] Thus, local and regional trade gave way to global trade, as European colonialism spread to Africa, Asia and the Pacific, the Middle East, Latin America and the Caribbean.

Local economies were integrated into the global economy in ways that served the needs of the colonial powers over those of the colonies and the local populace. Library shelves are filled with volumes that detail this brutal creation of a 'colonial division of labour' and its winners and losers. Uruguayan Eduardo Galeano's *Open Veins of Latin America: Five Centuries of the Pillage of a Continent*, for example, chronicles rapacious colonialism in economic, social and environmental dimensions: 'Latin America is the region of open veins. Everything, from the discovery until our times, has always been transmuted into European—or later United States—capital, and as such has accumulated in distant centers of power. Everything: the soil, its fruits and its mineral-rich depths, the people and their capacity to work and to consume, natural resources and human resources.'[4] These and similar trade and investment patterns elsewhere were created to serve narrow economic and political interests, invariably sowing the seeds of resistance.

Just as the current system of international trade dates back hundreds of years, so does the resistance to exploitative forms of global integration. Many early expressions of resistance to European attempts at economic integration were individual and small-group acts of non-cooperation or sabotage. In virtually every society the Europeans colonised, people rose up to protest at the cruelty of slavery, theft of land, and plunder of resources. Some communities retreated into less accessible territories rather than submit to the devastation of European colonialism. Many captured Africans rebelled or committed suicide rather than become slaves.

Native Americans practised guerrilla warfare in thousands of incidents of armed rebellion. A few Europeans—including Columbus' outspoken contemporary and chronicler Bartolomé de Las Casas—used their power and privilege to protest against the worst abuses of the colonial trade and labour practices.[5]

Eventually, out of these isolated incidents, organised social movements developed in an attempt to counter or abolish perceived injustices of international trade in goods and labour. Most of these movements were local and national, but a few were transnational. It is the transnational movements that interest us here as the antecedents of today's international campaigns to alter corporate-driven economic globalisation. Consider two of the most dynamic examples of organised transnational resistance to economic integration between the 1780s and the early 1900s: the movement to abolish the slave trade and the First International Workingmen's Association.[6]

In the 1700s a movement against the Atlantic slave trade gained strength in Europe and North America.[7] At its peak, from 1787 to 1807, the movement was strongest in the UK. Numerous sectors of society were mobilised there—from the textile workers of Manchester to Methodist Church founder John Wesley, from artisans in small Scottish towns to wealthy businessmen in London, from rural housewives to prime ministers. But this was also an international movement that involved significant collaboration among civil society across continents—British, North American, French, and also people of African origin, including black sailors of various nationalities, sons of African royalty sent to Europe to round out their education, and free European and American blacks. Former slaves from the Americas also played an important role, for example Olaudah Equiano, whose autobiography was a bestseller in the 1790s.

In other contexts, some have argued that the anti-slave trade movement was the first modern social movement and the innovator of social-change methodologies used by virtually every social movement that followed.[8] Indeed, the tactics used by the campaign should sound surprisingly familiar to the organisers of and participants in the modern anti-corporate globalisation campaigns: popular theatre, speaking tours and rallies, political poetry, pins, letter-writing campaigns, direct lobbying, petitions, electoral politics, and commercial boycotts. International networking was essential to the success of the movement. For instance, former slaves from the USA conducted speaking tours in the UK, providing firsthand testimonies about the cruelties of the slave trade and bringing thousands of new supporters into the movement. British religious denominations shared their strategies with their counterparts in the USA, which helped to strengthen the North American movement. Indeed, the religious sector, with its often uncompromising moral core, formed the backbone of the movement on both continents.

The anti-slave-trade movement was certainly effective; not only was the slave trade banned in the UK and the USA, the English Navy was also used to intercept ships off the coast of Africa, search them, and send any Africans found onboard back to Africa. The banning of the slave trade also helped create momentum for the abolition of slavery itself. The movement thus permanently altered the rules of the global economy and set a precedent for social movements promoting the value of human rights above the value of commerce.[9]

In the case of the European workers and the First International Workingmen's Association, the same ideas of justice and equality that had spurred the antislave-trade movement also led to an international movement focused on the rights of workers in the economic integration of mid-19th century Europe. In the 1800s, as a result of the Industrial Revolution, an increasing number of Europeans worked in factories under dire conditions: excessive work hours, low wages, abusive bosses, and so on. Economic integration brought in new technologies that threatened jobs and foreign-made goods that threatened domestic production.[10] European labour unions, which had developed out of craftsmen's guilds, began using strikes, work slowdowns, and destruction of machinery to fight for better wages, better work conditions and protective tariffs. In England in the 1850s factory owners fought back by importing workers from poorer European countries to replace striking workers, including cigar-makers, tailors and builders.

In response, some European workers developed a strategy that combined international solidarity with self-interest. Their unions, along with their intellectual supporters and associations of non-unionised workers, formed the First International Workingmen's Association in 1864. The First International successfully intervened in 1866 to prevent the bosses of striking tailors in England from hiring strike-breakers from Belgium, France and Germany by convincing workers overseas not to become scabs. In 1867 a delegation of striking Parisian bronze workers visited London to seek support for their right to unionise; the First International subsequently sent financial support from British unions and contributed to the success of the Paris strike.

While the First International lasted only until 1872, it played a key role in the development of national labour unions and working-class consciousness in Europe. In turn, these new unions and new ideas made significant changes not only in labour conditions, but also in national policies, from freedom of speech laws to the extension of voting rights to people who did not own property. Many union activists, recognising parallels between the exploitation of workers in Europe and the enslavement of Africans in the Americas, also played a role in the eradication of slavery overseas, along with veterans of the anti-slave trade movement.[11] In short, like the current anti-corporate globalisation movement, the international workers' movement was a multi-issue movement that included domestic as well as global goals. And, while its effectiveness might not match that of the movement against global trade in slaves, it certainly laid down a yardstick against which subsequent international movements of and for workers have been and can continue to be measured.

Rebuilding the World Economy . . . and Restructuring

With that broad sweep of almost 500 years of economic integration and resistance before World War II, this section moves to the second of the dynamic waves of enhanced economic integration and resistance: the early postwar period. To understand this period, one must put centre stage the public and private institutions that set the rules for the post-World War II global economy.

The Depression years and the world war that ensued were crisis times for the global economy and economic integration—so trying that, while the war was still raging (indeed, before it was at all clear which side would be victorious), some of the leading economic thinkers from the richer countries (including Britain's renowned Lord John Maynard Keynes) began to exchange detailed plans for the public multilateral institutions that would manage the postwar world economy.

From these plans came the well known post-World War II triumvirate. In finance, the International Monetary Fund (IMF) was created to oversee an orderly exchange rate system and to provide short-term loans for countries which experienced unexpected shocks to their balance of payments. To stimulate production and the rebuilding of war-ravaged nations, the World Bank (officially the International Bank for Reconstruction and Development) was created to offer long-term, low-interest loans for the 'reconstruction' of Europe and the 'development' of the independent Third World countries. To complement these 'Bretton Woods twins', the General Agreement on Tariffs and Trade (GATT) was set up in 1948 to oversee the reduction of tariff barriers to trade in manufactured goods.[12]

In addition to gearing up production, finance and trade, these post-World War II public institutions created an atmosphere ideal for the growth and global spread of large private corporations, the twentieth century's version of the East India Company. As barriers to trade and investment fell in the decades following World War II, several hundred large private corporations began to weave certain parts of the globe together even more tightly than before the war through trade and investment flows.

The growth and influence of both 'multinational' corporations and the public 'multilateral' institutions over the development process elicited debate over other possible routes to development via economic integration. Although originally created to focus on economic growth and job creation, the multilateral economic institutions increasingly took a free-market focus, requiring borrowing developing countries to open up their economies to the world economy through liberalised trade and investment flows.

The controversy surrounding the free-market advice offered by these institutions fed into a debate about how developing countries should relate to the global economy. Likewise, the global expansion and enlargement of modern multinational corporations elicited a related debate over whether they should be allowed to move around the globe freely or whether there should be 'checks' placed on them (and who should and how to place those checks). As will be discussed in this section, the first of these debates influenced development thought and practice in the 1960s. The second, as we shall see in the next section, became more operative in the 1970s.

How developing countries should relate to the global economy was considered in Latin America as early as the late 1950s, with a Southern 'home-grown', influential critique and alternative economic integration programme: structuralism. The 'structuralists' sought to restructure developing countries' positions in the world economy. Their critique focused not on environmental or social and other distributional issues within a country, but rather on the question of why 'economic growth' via global economic integration was disproportionately benefiting richer 'core' countries at the expense of poorer 'periphery' ones and why the economic gap between the two appeared to be growing rather than shrinking. The answer, according to Argentine father of structuralism Raul Prebisch, was clear: as long as countries in the 'periphery' relied on commodity exports and manufactured imports (ie, as long as they were mired in the colonial division of labour), their economies would be exploited to the benefit of the 'core' countries. Indeed, Prebisch and others at the Chilean-based UN Economic Commission for Latin American and the Caribbean (set up in 1948) professed that the very development of the 'core' depended on the underdevelopment of the 'periphery'—to the extent that periphery countries were actually moving backwards economically as the value of their commodity exports fell relative to the value of their manufactured imports (or 'declining terms of trade').

To break out of this bind, Prebisch—along with fellow structuralists Celso Furtado and Hans Singer (among others)—instead suggested temporarily de-linking parts of an economy from the world economy to build up industrial capacity and internal markets through a concerted, multi-tiered plan of import-substitution industrialisation (ISI) geared to move a country into ever-higher value-added manufactured goods. Only when a country in the periphery had built up the capacity for industrial exports, according to Prebisch, could that country reinsert itself on an equal basis in the world economy.

This was more than an academic debate. Indeed, Prebisch and structuralism changed both national policies and the global debate. Prebisch became the first Secretary General of the United Nations Conference on Trade and Development (UNCTAD) after its creation in 1964. Prebisch's vision led Southern countries across the globe—from Brazil to the Philippines—to try import-substitution over the course of the 1950s and 1960s.[13] And it led to a much more vibrant period of divergent national development strategies that continued until the onset of the neoliberal Washington Consensus in the 1980s. Ironically, these ISI strategies were also important in that opponents termed them 'failures' in practice and used that assessment as a springboard for the neoliberal consensus of the 1980s and 1990s.[14]

The 1970s: Resistance to the Corporate 'Global Reach'

Despite the continuing vibrant development debate, the 1970s witnessed a significant increase in multinational/transnational corporations' 'global reach', as Richard Barnet and Ronald Müller so aptly phrased it in their best-selling book chronicling the expansion of these corporations and the transnational banks that funded them in the Third World.[15] With the rise of transnational corporations in the 1970s came increasing concern over TNCs' economic and political power *vis-à-vis* Third World governments.

A major scandal turned the US-headquartered International Telephone and Telegraph (ITT) into the poster child for these concerns. For those involved in this work in the 1970s, the backlash provoked by the ITT case stands out as a key moment of governmental and nongovernmental 'resistance' to unfettered global expansion. The ITT case, however, is far less known among more recent critics of corporate practices overseas and thus merits a summary here. In terms of the scandal itself, evidence surfaced in the early 1970s that ITT had offered funds to the US government to prevent the democratically elected, socialist government of Salvador Allende from taking power in Chile in 1970.

Using that incident as a starting point, the US Senate Subcommittee on Multinational Corporations of the Senate Foreign Relations Committee, under Senator Frank Church, convened a multi-year inquiry into 'Multinationals and United States Foreign Policy', interviewing dozens of expert witnesses to look at the power and practices of US corporations in the developing world. As Church stated in his opening statement to a 20 March 1973 hearing, the subcommittee was charged with moving beyond this one case study to 'undertake a broad examination of the role of multinational corporations . . . Do the activities of the multinational corporations advance the interests of the people of the United States taken as a whole? Are they exporting jobs which might otherwise be kept at home?'[16] Over the period from 1972 to 1976 the Church Subcommittee hearings covered corporate practices ranging from the 'ITT and Chile', to 'Multinational Petroleum Companies and Foreign Policy', to 'Political Contributions to Foreign Governments'. From that investigation came 17 riveting volumes that offer a more thorough examination of corporate practices overseas than any other inquiry of this (or perhaps any) era.

To say that Church and his staff trod on potentially controversial topics is to put it mildly. And, indeed, in 1976, as this era of willingness to criticise TNCs began to close, the Subcommittee was 'neutered' (in the words of its then staff director) by being converted into a Subcommittee on International Economic Policy.[17]

Outside the USA in the early to mid-1970s—energised by such public revelations of irresponsible TNC behaviour, educated by Raul Prebisch and his structuralist theory, and emboldened by the economic success in the early to mid-1970s of the oil-exporting nations belonging to the Organisation of Petroleum Exporting Countries (OPEC)—a number of Southern governments found a collective voice to demand a different set of rules for the world economy and its players. And so it was that structuralist theory was transformed into the core of the 'new international economic order' (NIEO) demands that Southern governments, ranging from those of Julius Nyerere in Tanzania to Ferdinand Marcos in the Philippines, brought to the United Nations in the early 1970s. Centred on proposals to raise and stabilise raw material prices (ie, to mediate the conundrum of declining terms of trade) and to increase Southern exports of manufactured goods (ie, to break out of the colonial division of labour), the NIEO focused on how to get the economic benefits from interaction with the world economy to the Southern nation state. In May 1974 the UN General Assembly 'solemnly proclaimed' a 'Declaration on the Establishment of a New International Economic Order'. This stated, among other things, that 'every country has the right' to 'control of the activities of transnational corporations', that 'a just and equitable relationship between the prices of raw materials, primary products, manufactured and semi-manufactured goods' needed to be established 'with the aim of improving [developing countries'] terms of trade which have continued to deteriorate' and that 'the whole international community' needed to increase its 'active assistance to developing countries'.[18]

Using the new pulpit and power afforded the South by OPEC's economic success, Southern governments succeeded in pushing the UN not only to pass the NIEO declaration but also to create a Commission on Transnational Corporations (UNCTC). For close to a decade and a half after its establishment in 1975, UNCTC oversaw an attempt (which eventually failed) to negotiate a UN Code of Conduct on Transnational Corporations, which spelled out norms for corporate 'rights' and 'responsibilities'. Included in the code's provisions, for example, is the requirement that 'corporations shall respect human rights and fundamental freedoms in the countries in which they operate. In their social and industrial relations, transnational corporations shall not discriminate on the basis of race, colour, sex, language, social, national and ethnic origin or political or other opinion'. So too, in this era of 1970s corporate exposés and vociferous Southern demands, did both the International Labour Organisation (ILO) and the Organisation of Economic Cooperation and Development (OECD) issue their own corporate codes of conduct, in 1977 and 1978 respectively. While providing important precedents in terms of language and reach, these codes were basically non-enforceable documents that most observers agree did little to effect change in corporate behaviour or public opinion.[19]

Thus far this section has chronicled an era in which governments, individually and collectively, attempted to reform the workings of the world economy and its key actors. But the 1970s also saw non-governmental actors push for change. Indeed, catalysed by the ITT scandal, the revelations of the Church Subcommittee and the new international economic order demands, citizen campaigns for more specific corporate codes grew rapidly across borders to challenge various corporate abuses: corporate support for apartheid, unethical marketing practices by infant formula corporations such as Nestlé, and exploitative marketing practices by global pesticide, alcohol and tobacco companies, to name a few of the key campaigns. Rather than delineating an overall code of conduct for corporate 'rights' and 'responsibilities' in the pattern of the UN code, these campaigns focused on specific instances of egregious corporate behaviour. While some of these campaigns were local and most were less grandiose than the UN code initiative, several were sophisticated global efforts that succeeded in fundamentally changing the public perception of infant-formula and other corporations, if not to alter the on-the-ground realities.[20]

The 1970s and Resistance to the World Bank and IMF

On a parallel front, governments and citizen groups began to focus on the World Bank, the IMF and other public institutions. On one hand, as seen in the previous section, Southern governments called, through their NIEO demands, for expanded governmental and multilateral assistance to poorer countries, ie, more aid. On the other hand, a series of exposés over the course of the 1970s began to suggest that aid, be it bilateral assistance from governments or multilateral assistance from the World Bank and IMF, often had more harmful than beneficial effects on supposed local beneficiaries. On the ground, of course, local people had been witness to the impact of these loans in previous decades, but the fact that this criticism became more global in the 1970s reflects both the era and the growth of these institutions over the 1970s. (The World Bank, for example, increased its lending more than 10-fold from 1968 to 1981.)[21]

In essence, these exposés said that when one analyses aid on the ground and listens to what local people have to say, one discovers that loans often coddle dictators and the well-off at the expense of the poor and a country's growth and development. According to these scholars and practitioners, by the 1970s most aid was invariably geared toward pushing a free-market development model that encouraged either 1) expansion of traditional primary-product exports (cementing a colonial division of labour); or 2) entry into labour-intensive, low-value added manufacturing exports such as apparel and electronics (creating what academics termed a 'new international division of labour'[22]). In the latter case, the critics claimed, what a great deal of donor money and concomitant advice promoted was not anything like the structuralist version of developing country industrialisation, but rather 'enclaves' of exploitative, import-dependent manufactured exports that gave the lion's share of the profits to TNCs for repatriation to their home countries. Furthermore, the exposés continued, aid was seldom grants but was typically loans for which repayment would burden vulnerable populations.

This literature combined critiques based in international political economic analysis with specific country and project case studies. Building on structural analysis, in part the literature deconstructed the kind of economic integration pushed by Northern assistance. By looking at who benefits and who loses within countries, however, these critiques went beyond an NIEO focus and, indeed, foreshadowed the focus of today's citizen backlash on specific sectors (labour and environment, or women and indigenous communities, for example) *within* North and South.

The initial 1970s exposés and critiques that were published in the North are perhaps the most direct forebears of today's movement versus the World Bank and IMF. The authors were mostly female and their books' titles summarise their pathbreaking theses. From Europe in 1971 came Teresa Hayter's *Aid as Imperialism* and in 1977 Susan George's *How the Other Half Dies*. In 1974 Cheryl Payer wrote one of the first critiques of the IMF in her illuminating work *The Debt Trap*. Through detailed country-specific case studies, Payer outlined the devastating impact of IMF policies on poorer nations, locking them into a development model based on debt, which subsequently forced them into more borrowing, more faulty development and more debt.[23]

One of the first critical, in-depth, book-length country case studies of World Bank lending was that of the Philippines (a World Bank 'country of concentration'[24] and one of its top 10 loan recipients at that time). Over the late 1970s to early 1980s Filipino scholar/activist Walden Bello and a group of his colleagues (including one of the present authors) amassed a wealth of evidence to provide a detailed case study of how World Bank aid bolstered dictator Ferdinand Marcos while restructuring the Philippine economy to serve the interests of global corporations and the global market. While research in the Philippines was crucial to this documentation, much of the evidence also come from 'confidential' documents supplied by increasingly disillusioned World Bank employees.[25]

When these exposés began to appear, their audience and the number of protesters in the North were still small. It was the impact of this World Bank lending on indigenous communities around the world that brought environmental issues into the critique and Northern environmentalists into the protests. One of the first large-scale infrastructure projects to jump from being protested against by indigenous, local inhabitants to capturing international attention was also in the Philippines: the Chico dam project in the north of the country. This project, partially funded in the initial stages by the World Bank, provoked local, national and international outcries by and on behalf of the indigenous communities in the Cordillera mountain region, whose ancestral land was to be inundated by the Chico dam project.

In fact, in 1975, some of the affected indigenous communities wrote to the then World Bank president Robert McNamara, beseeching him to stop the funding: 'We, the [indigenous] Bontocs and the Kalingas affected by the Chico River Basin Development Project, object most strongly to any assistance from the World Bank . . . to the Philippine government for this project.

The reason is simple: the project would wipe us out as a people! At least ten Kalinga settlements and six Bontoc settlements will be devastated as a result of this dam project.'[26]And five years later in Antwerp, Belgium, a so-called 'Permanent Peoples' Tribunal on the Philippines' not only rendered judgement on dictator Ferdinand Marcos but, upon hearing testimony from a local indigenous leader against the Chico dam project, also held that the multilateral financial institutions were culpable:

> the International Monetary Fund, the World Bank, and the Asian Development Bank . . . are playing a crucial role in sustaining, supporting and encouraging the Marcos regime, despite its commission of systematic state crimes, and [the Tribunal] calls upon these international financial institutions to terminate these relationships that abet the violation of the rights of peoples and are responsible for disrupting the life and threatening the very existence of such tribal peoples as the [indigenous] Igorot and Kalinga through their support for high-technology hydro-electric projects.[27]

The significance of both the local letter and the international verdict must be emphasised. Unlike the contemporary moment, this was before the days when a World Bank president received such complaints and criticisms regularly. For the local inhabitants the protests against the Chico dam were somewhat successful (the World Bank eventually pulled out of further funding), but extremely risky given the excesses of the Marcos dictatorship. As the testimony at the Tribunal detailed, several local inhabitants were killed, including the community's revered spokesperson Macli-ing Dulag.[28]

The major legacy of Chico, foreign-funded dam projects in India, and other huge infrastructure projects affecting indigenous communities and involving large-scale resettlement of local populations was the awakening of Northern environmental groups to the connections between the aid money and environmental degradation. Starting in the early to mid-1980s, major US-based environmental groups launched campaigns to reform the World Bank in terms of large infrastructure projects. Over the course of the 1980s, development and human rights advocates joined in—in some instances building on Hayter, Payer, Bello and other broader political economic critiques of the 1970s but more often not even aware of them. Indeed, it was not until the 1990s that the resistance grew to encompass more issues and an expanded lens of analysis. It built from a focus on specific projects to reinsert broader political economic critiques reminiscent of Bello, Payer and others, from a concern with environment and development in the 1980s to reinsert social justice, from a preoccupation with aid to include trade and investment, and from a focus on the World Bank to the IMF and then to the GATT's powerful successor, the World Trade Organization (WTO).

This overview of the 1970s resistance is important for another reason. Several of the leading spokespeople for and organisations in the current backlash to corporate globalisation began their work in different parts of the globe during the 1970s. Their thinking was, in part, shaped by this decade. Moreover, these leaders have personal and professional trajectories that are themselves cross-national. And most have actually known, if not worked with, each other over these 30 years, building ties of trust that transcend disagreements.

Take the case of Malaysian Martin Khor (Khor Kok Peng) of the Third World Network, who in the 1970s was active in building international consumer movements that helped push the NIEO agenda at the United Nations and other venues. From France came American-born Susan George, now a leader of the global ATTAC network and of the World Social Forum who, as previously noted, wrote her first bestseller, *How the Other Half Dies*, in the mid-1970s. Institute for Policy Studies co-founder Richard Barnet, who co-authored *Global Reach* during that same period, launched that institute into the centre of globalisation work for the ensuing three decades. And there is Walden Bello, a Filipino who had come to the USA for graduate studies and remained there in political exile during the Marcos years, now director of the Thailand-based Focus on the Global South. Bello began his investigations into the World Bank in the late 1970s as part of his scholarship and activism on both the Philippines and Chile.[29]

Each of these and several other of today's activists understands the power that citizen movements allied with sympathetic Third World governments can exercise. Each of these individuals, as well as other current activists with roots going back to the 1970s, provides not only continuity between the resistance of the 1970s and the resistance of today, but also a historical frame for the current processes of economic integration. And yet, while Bello *et al* appear to be respected as among the 'wise people' of today's movement, most protesters and observers do not know of their 1970s and 1980s work.

Concluding Reflections

As we move into the current period, we must not forget the threads that link what is new and innovative with what has been said and/or tried before. For example, one sub-sector of today's global backlash focuses on 'reshaping' or 'restructuring' the current rules and institutions of economic globalisation. These 'reshapers' have a constructive agenda centring on a range of proposals from the regulatory world of trade agreements to proposals that rely on voluntary corporate initiatives—notably codes of conduct for corporations, third-party certification initiatives and fair trade to ensure higher prices for commodities. Decades ago, the NIEO and UNCTAD proposals were in essence trying to *reshape* the rules of the world economy to increase the benefits of economic integration to Southern nation states in general—although the policies they promoted most benefited the elite. The Nestlé campaigners were also trying to *reshape*, but with a more targeted goal of protecting specific vulnerable populations within the South against Northern corporate power.

For most of today's *reshapers*, the goal is to ensure that globalisation's burden does not fall on workers, communities, the environment, women and other more marginalised sectors of society, while global corporations receive the lion's share of the benefits. But some of today's *reshape* initiatives, such as those focused on market-access via Northern trade liberalisation, bear noticeable similarities to certain of the NIEO demands.

Another sub-sector of today's backlash—often rooted in an environmental critique—is intent on rolling back certain aspects of globalisation (for example, halting the privatisation and export of bulk water or the patenting of indigenous rice seeds) and on slowing down other aspects (for example, reducing the flow of short-term and volatile speculative financial flows). Its constructive agenda prioritises invigorating local economies.[30] So too the 1970s had its *rollback* proponents, including Teresa Hayter and others who attacked the 'imperialist' aspects of foreign aid, as well as indigenous communities who fought the World Bank's funding of huge hydroelectric dams. Their agenda was to *stop* the aid and the projects.[31]

Indeed, the current global backlash against corporate-led globalisation has much to learn from the resistance to earlier forms of coercive economic integration that preceded it. This should be studied further; in some cases, the parallels to today's movements are striking. Take the earliest antecedents that this article has examined. Part of the success of movements like the ones that ended the Atlantic slave trade was the creative use of a broad array of tactics. As noted earlier, the tactics of the anti-slave trade movement and today's movement have pronounced similarities, especially in the way the creative arts were and are used to educate people. The Internet and list-serves play the same role as the thousands of anti-slave trade pamphlets and newsletters that reached the furthest outposts of England, Scotland, Ireland and Wales, as well as the USA and Canada. North–South alliances and multiracial coalitions are common now, as then. Now, as then, activists have had to confront racism within their movement.

Likewise, the workers' movement of the 1860s provides some parallels and some contrasts to union involvement in the globalisation movement of today. As did the First International, the labour movement today uses arguments of self-interest linked to solidarity to promote working-class involvement in anti-corporate globalisation. In both cases, intellectuals in union leadership have worked hard to challenge workers to move from protectionist, nationalist and/or xenophobic perspectives of 'my workplace' and 'my country' to 'our rights as workers everywhere' or what John Sweeney, head of the American Federation of Labor–Congress of International Organizations (AFL–CIO), terms a 'new internationalism'.[32] A dramatic change since the 1860s is the enhanced role of women and people of colour in unions as they join anti-corporate globalisation campaigns. Moreover, the development of vibrant trade unions in countries like South Africa lays the foundation for a different type of internationalism than that of the Europeans in the 1860s.

Beyond parallels and contrasts, there are important lessons for today. Effectiveness depends on creative ways to engage constituencies who have not yet been involved by reaching people where they are, as the anti-slave-trade movement reached people in pubs, at the theatre and during afternoon teas. Another of the anti-slavery movement's most important lessons is less obvious: to create institutional change, one must also engage with the system. Protest alone did not end the slave trade; work to change the laws was also imperative.

Indeed, the current movement would do well to study to the constellation of forces that successfully delivered change in the past. In most cases, fervent resistance from citizen movements was joined to sympathetic leaders in government. Today, movements to *rollback* and/or *reshape* corporate globalisation are strong in many countries and draw forces from many different segments of society. They have found allies in the parliaments of rich-country governments and, beginning in the 1999 anti-WTO protests in Seattle, they have found some allies among poor-country governments. The 2002 and 2003 elections of governments that reject the neoliberal agenda in Argentina, Brazil and Ecuador add strength to momentum for change and reform.

In sum, the anti-corporate globalisation activists, as they work to *reshape* or to *rollback* the WTO, IMF, World Bank, and other institutions of globalisation, should not think that they represent the spontaneous generation of a new protest phenomenon. Certainly, some aspects of the current movement are new—the use of the Internet for informing and organising, mass demonstrations of coordinated small groups, and a high degree of economic literacy. But the roots of the Seattle/Washington/Prague/Quebec/Johannesburg protests are deep. Changes in technology, innovative protest styles, information politics and analytical advances have been used for hundreds of years by activists seeking to oppose the devastating effects of economic integration on their communities and on communities in other countries and to provide alternatives. Conscious study of the precedents set by earlier activists—of the successes and failures of the past—can help today's movements become more vibrant and effective.

Too many contemporary analysts and activists treat the current cross-border movement to alter economic globalisation as something so new, so novel, so without precedent. As this article has argued, not only is this inaccurate but it also deprives today's movement of the various strategic and tactical insights that incorporating history affords.

The events in Seattle in late 1999 were, indeed, momentous. But they need to be understood as a new stage in a concatenation of historical processes and events, some of which are linked by direct threads, others of which are stitched together through more circuitous and longer historical trajectories.

Notes

* This article expands upon Robin Broad (ed), *Global Backlash: Citizen Initiatives for a Just World Economy*, Lanham, MD: Rowman & Littlefield, 2002. The authors would like to thank Robert Blecker, John Cavanagh, Maria Floro, Adam Hochschild, Joseph Horgan, Jerome Levinson, Michael Prokosch, Shahid Qadir, Richard Tucker, John Willoughby and two anonymous reviewers for commenting on earlier drafts of this article. Robin Broad would also like to thank the Ford Foundation and the Center of Concern for their support.

1. Harris Gleckman, personal communication, July 1999. Gleckman had been chief of the Environmental Unit at the now-defunct UN Center on Transnational Corporations.

2. Genesis 37: 25.

3. Quoted in 'The Uruguay Round: gunboat diplomacy by another name', editorial, *The Ecologist*, 20 (6), 1990, p 202.

4. Eduardo Galeano, *Open Veins of Latin America: Five Centuries of the Pillage of a Continent*, New York: Monthly Review Press, 1973, p 12.

5. Bartolomé de Las Casas, *In Defense of the Indians*, Dekalb, IL: Northern Illinois University Press, 1992.

6. This is adapted from Zahara Heckscher, 'Long before Seattle: historical resistance to economic globalization', in Robin Broad (ed), *Global Backlash: Citizen Initiatives for a Just World Economy*, Lanham, MD: Rowman & Littlefield, 2002, pp 86–91. See Heckscher for other case studies, including the Tupac Amaru II uprising in Peru, the campaign against the colonisation of the Congo, and the US-based anti-imperialist movement.

7. The main sources for the anti-slave trade movement examples are Seymour Drescher, 'Whose abolition? Popular pressure and the ending of the British slave trade', *Past and Present*, 143, 1944, pp 136–166; Roger Anstey, *The Atlantic Slave Trade and British Abolition 1760–1810*, NJ: Humanities Press, 1975; Clare Midgley, *Women Against Slavery: The British Campaigns, 1780–1840*, London: Routledge, 1992; Olaudah Equiano, *The Interesting Narrative of the Life of Olaudah Equiano, Written By Himself*, Boston, MA: Bedford Books, 1995 (first published 1789); JR Oldfield, *Popular Politics and British Anti-Slavery*, Manchester: Manchester University Press, 1995; Wylie Sypher, 'The African prince in London', *Journal of the History of Ideas*, 2 (2), 1941, pp 237–247; and Herbert Klein, *The Atlantic Slave Trade*, Cambridge: Cambridge University Press, 1999.

8. This analysis of the anti-slave trade movement as precursor to today's social movements was informed by Margaret Keck & Kathryn Sikkink, *Activists Without Borders*, Ithaca, NY: Cornell University Press, 1998.

9. See *ibid.*

10. It was in this context that Karl Marx wrote the Communist Manifesto. The examples of the European trade union internationalism in this section are from Susan Milner, *The Dilemmas of Internationalism*, New York: Berg, 1990; and Henry Collins & Chimen Abramsky, *Karl Marx and the British Labor Movement: Years of the First International*, New York: Macmillan, 1965.

11. Betty Fladeland, *Men and Brothers: Anglo-American Anti-Slavery Cooperation*, Urbana, IL: University of Illinois Press, 1972.

12. Note also that today's work on international 'labour rights' has its roots in this period. Indeed, the Havana Charter, the draft document for the ill-fated International Trade Organization (of which the GATT was supposed to be only one part) actually included a workers' rights clause. A small subset of what had been envisioned as an International Trade Organization, GATT was the least powerful of the trio and in 1995 was subsumed by a more powerful World Trade Organization which extended its domain to include agriculture and services, including investment.

13. Much of what Raul Prebisch wrote was published in the *CEPAL Review*, the publication of the UN Economic Commission for Latin American and the Caribbean (www.eclac.org) and of UNCTAD (www.unctad.org). Prebisch's seminal work is *The Economic Development of Latin America and Its Principle Problems*, New York: UN Department of Economic Affairs, 1950. Other key structuralist writing includes Hans Singer, 'The distribution of gains between investing and borrowing countries', *American Economic Review*, 40, 1950, pp 473–485; and Celso Furtado, *Development and Underdevelopment: A Structural View of the Problems of Developed and Underdeveloped Countries*, Berkeley, CA: University of California Press, 1967. For more on import substitution industrialisation to build up domestic manufacturing, see Albert Hirschman's *The Strategy of Economic Development*, New Haven, CT: Yale University Press, 1959.

14. See Robin Broad, 'The Washington Consensus meets the global backlash: the shifting debate over development in theory and practice', paper presented at the International Studies Association, Portland, OR, 28 February 2003.

15. Richard Barnet & Ronald Müller, *Global Reach: The Power of Multinational Corporations*, New York: Simon and Schuster, 1974. See also the pioneering work produced by Frederic F Clairmont for UNCTAD, including *The Marketing and Distribution System for Bananas*, Geneva: UNCTAD, 1973.

16. United States Senate, Committee on Foreign Relations, Subcommittee on Multinational Corporations, 'Opening statement by Senator Frank Church on Tuesday, March 20, 1973', *Multinational Corporations and United States Foreign Policy*, 93rd and 94th Congresses, Part 1: 'The International Telephone and Telegraph Company and Chile', 1970–71, pp 1–2.

17. Jerome Levinson to Robin Broad, email correspondence, 10 September 2001. Levinson thought the verb I had originally used—'disbanded'—was somewhat too tame.

18. United Nations General Assembly, 'Declaration on the Establishment of a New International Economic Order', Sixth Special Session, 1 May 1974, UN General Assembly Resolution 3201. Quotes are from the preamble and section 4(e). The NIEO declaration plus its attached 'programme of action' can be found in Karl P Savant & Joachim W Müller, *The Third World Without Superpowers*, second series, Vol 20, *The Collected Documents of the Group of 77*, New York: OCEANA Publications, 1995, pp 337–354.

19. The quotation is from Lance Compa & Tashia Hinchliffe-Darricarrere, 'Enforcing international labor rights through corporate codes of conduct', *Columbia Journal of Transnational Law*, 33 (663), 1995, p 670. See pp 670–671 for a summary of the OECD and ILO Codes. On the 1970s UN and other external codes of conduct, see also the work of Harris Gleckman (former chief of the UNCTC's Environmental Unit). Harris Gleckman & Riva Krut, *Business Regulation and Competition Policy: The Case for International Action*, London: Christian Aid, World Development Movement, and other NGOs, 1994.

20. See Robin Broad & John Cavanagh, 'The corporate accountability movement: lessons and opportunities', a study for the World Wildlife Federation's Project on International Financial Flows and the Environment, 30 July 1997; and Kathryn Sikkink, 'Codes of conduct for transnational corporations: the case of the WHO/UNICEF Code', *International Organization*, 40, 1986, pp 815–840.

21. See Barend A de Vries, *Remaking the World Bank*, Cabin John, MD: Seven Locks Press, 1987, pp 13–14; and Robin Broad, *Unequal Alliance: The World Bank, the International Monetary Fund, and the Philippines*, Berkeley, CA: University of California Press, 1988, chs 2 and 3. The latter originally appeared as Broad's doctoral dissertation (Princeton University, 1983).

22. On the new international division of labour, work by members of then West Germany's Max Planck Institute stands as a classic. Folker Fröbel, Jürgen Heinrichs & Otto Kreye, *The New International Division of Labour: Structural Unemployment in Industrialized Countries*

and Industrialization in Developing Countries, trans Pete Burgess, Cambridge: Cambridge University Press, 1980.

23. Teresa Hayter, *Aid as Imperialism*, London: Penguin Books, 1971; Cheryl Payer, *The Debt Trap: The IMF and the Third World*, New York: Monthly Review Press, 1974; and Susan George, *How the Other Half Dies*, Montclair, NJ: Allanheld, Osmun & Co, 1977.

24. Michael Gould, then the World Bank's Philippine division chief, in the confidential World Bank document, 'Philippines—Country Program Paper', Washington, DC, 26 March 1976, p 17.

25. This group of scholars and activists documented and analysed the Philippine–World Bank case study in two separate books: a collaborative effort by Walden Bello *et al*, *Development Debacle: The World Bank in the Philippines*, San Francisco, CA: Institute for Food and Development Policy, 1982; and Broad, *Unequal Alliance*.

26. The Bontoc and Kalinga delegates to the Vochong Conference on Development, 'Letter to Robert S McNamara, President, World Bank', 12 May 1975, reprinted in Vivencio R José (ed), *Mortgaging the Future: The World Bank and IMF in the Philippines*, Quezon City: Foundation for Nationalist Studies, 1982.

27. The proceedings and verdict are reproduced in Permanent Peoples' Tribunal on the Philippines, *Philippines: Repression and Resistance*, Utrecht: Philippines–European Solidarity Centre-Komite ng Sambayanang Pilipinos (PESC-KSP), 1980, p 278.

28. Wada Taw-il (pseudonym), 'We are to be sacrificed: indigenous peoples and dams', in *ibid*, pp 84–91.

29. See www.twnside.org.sg, www.attac.org, www.focusweb.org and www.ips-dc.org. See also the interview with Walden Bello, 'Pacific Panopticon', *New Left Review*, 16, 2002, pp. 68–85. See also note 30.

30. For more on alternatives and on the World Social Forum, see Teivo Teivainen, 'The World Social Forum and global democratisation: learning from Porto Alegre', *Third World Quarterly*, 23, 2002, pp 621–632; and John Cavanagh, Jerry Mander *et al*, *Alternatives to Economic Globalization: A Better World Is Possible*, San Francisco, CA: Berrett-Koehler, 2002.

31. For expansion on the differences and similarities between today's 'rollback' and 'reshape' proponents, see Broad, *Global Backlash*, Parts III–V.

32. John J Sweeney, 'The new internationalism', speech to the Council on Foreign Relations, New York, 1 April 1998, reproduced in Broad, *Global Backlash*, pp 47–50.

CHAPTER TWENTY

Reclaiming the Commons

Naomi Klein

Source: Transcript of a talk at the Center for Social Theory and Comparative History, UCLA, in April 2001. Published in Tom Mertes (ed.) *A Movement of Movements: Is Another World Really Possible?* (2004) 219–229

What is 'the anti-globalization movement'?[1] I put the phrase in quotemarks because I immediately have two doubts about it. Is it really a movement? If it is a movement, is it anti-globalization? Let me start with the first issue. We can easily convince ourselves it is a movement by talking it into existence at a forum like this—I spend far too much time at them—acting as if we can see it, hold it in our hands. Of course, we have seen it—and we know it's come back in Quebec, and on the US–Mexican border during the Summit of the Americas and the discussion for a hemispheric Free Trade Area. But then we leave rooms like this, go home, watch some TV, do a little shopping and any sense that it exists disappears, and we feel like maybe we're going nuts. Seattle—was that a movement or a collective hallucination? To most of us here, Seattle meant a kind of coming-out party for a global resistance movement, or the 'globalization of hope', as someone described it during the World Social Forum at Porto Alegre. But to everyone else Seattle still means limitless frothy coffee, Asian-fusion cuisine, e-commerce billionaires and sappy Meg Ryan movies. Or perhaps it is both, and one Seattle bred the other Seattle—and now they awkwardly coexist.

This movement we sometimes conjure into being goes by many names: anti-corporate, anti-capitalist, anti-free trade, anti-imperialist. Many say that it started in Seattle. Others maintain it began five hundred years ago—when colonialists first told indigenous peoples that they were going to have to do things differently if they were to 'develop' or be eligible for 'trade'. Others again say it began on 1 January 1994 when the Zapatistas launched their uprising with the words *Ya Basta!* on the night NAFTA became law in Mexico. It all depends on whom you ask. But I think it is more accurate to picture a movement of many movements—coalitions of coalitions. Thousands of groups today are all working against forces whose common thread is what might broadly be described as the privatization of every aspect of life, and the transformation of every activity and value into a commodity. We often speak of the privatization of education, of healthcare, of natural resources. But the process is much vaster. It includes the way powerful ideas are turned into advertising slogans and public streets into shopping malls; new generations being target-marketed at birth; schools being invaded by ads; basic human necessities like water being sold as commodities; basic labour rights being rolled back; genes are patented and designer babies loom; seeds are genetically altered and bought; politicians are bought and altered.

At the same time there are oppositional threads, taking form in many different campaigns and movements. The spirit they share is a radical reclaiming of the commons. As our communal spaces—town squares, streets, schools, farms, plants—are displaced by the ballooning marketplace, a spirit of resistance is taking hold around the world. People are reclaiming bits of nature and of culture, and saying 'this is going to be public space'. American students are kicking ads out of the classrooms. European environmentalists and ravers are throwing parties at busy intersections. Landless Thai peasants are planting organic vegetables on over-irrigated golf courses. Bolivian workers are reversing the privatization of their water supply. Outfits like Napster have been creating a kind of commons on the internet where kids can swap music with each other, rather than buying it from multinational record companies. Billboards have been liberated and independent media networks set up. Protests are multiplying. In Porto Alegre, during the World Social Forum, José Bové, often caricatured as only a hammer of McDonald's, travelled with local activists from the Movimento Sem Terra to a nearby Monsanto test site, where they destroyed three hectares of genetically modified soya beans. But the protest did not stop there. The MST has occupied the land and members are now planting their own organic crops on it, vowing to turn the farm into a model of sustainable agriculture. In short, activists aren't waiting for the revolution, they are acting right now, where they live, where they study, where they work, where they farm.

But some formal proposals are also emerging whose aim is to turn such radical reclamations of the commons into law. When NAFTA and the like were cooked up, there was much talk of adding on 'side agreements' to the free trade agenda, that were supposed to encompass the environment, labour and human rights. Now the fight-back is about taking them out. José Bové—along with the Via Campesina, a global association of small farmers—has launched a campaign to remove food safety and agricultural products from all trade agreements, under the slogan 'The World is Not for Sale'. They want to draw a line around the commons. Maude Barlow, director of the Council of Canadians, which has more members than most political parties in Canada, has argued that water isn't a private good and shouldn't be in any trade agreement. There is a lot of support for this idea, especially in Europe since the recent food scares. Typically these anti-privatization campaigns get under way on their own. But they also periodically converge—that's what happened in Seattle, Prague, Washington, Davos, Porto Alegre and Quebec.

What this means is that the discourse has shifted. During the battles against NAFTA, there emerged the first signs of a coalition between organized labour, environmentalists, farmers and consumer groups within the countries concerned. In Canada most of us felt we were fighting to keep something distinctive about our nation from 'Americanization'. In the United States, the talk was very protectionist: workers were worried that Mexicans would 'steal' away 'our' jobs and drive down 'our' environmental standards. All the while, the voices of Mexicans opposed to the deal were virtually off the public radar—yet these were the strongest voices of all. But only a few years later, the debate over trade has been transformed. The fight against globalization has morphed into a struggle against corporatization and, for some, against capitalism itself. It has also become a fight for democracy. Maude Barlow spearheaded the campaign against NAFTA in Canada twelve years ago. Since NAFTA became law, she's been working with organizers and activists from other countries, and anarchists suspicious of the state in her own country. She was once seen as very much the face of a Canadian nationalism. Today she has moved away from that discourse. 'I've changed', she says, 'I used to see this fight as saving a nation. Now I see it as saving democracy.' This is a cause that transcends nationality and state borders. The real news out of Seattle is that organizers around the world are beginning to see their local and national struggles—for better funded public schools, against union-busting and casualization, for family farms, and against the widening gap between rich and poor—through a global lens. That is the most significant shift we have seen in years.

How did this happen? Who or what convened this new international people's movement? Who sent out the memos? Who built these complex coalitions? It is tempting to pretend that someone did dream up a master plan for mobilization at Seattle. But I think it was much more a matter of large-scale coincidence. A lot of smaller groups organized to get themselves there and then found to their surprise just how broad and diverse a coalition they had become part of. Still, if there is one force we can thank for bringing this front into being, it is the multinational corporations. As one of the organizers of Reclaim the Streets has remarked, we should be grateful to the CEOs for helping us see the problems more quickly. Thanks to the sheer imperialist ambition of the corporate project at this moment in history—the boundless drive for profit, liberated by trade deregulation, and the wave of mergers and buy-outs, liberated by weakened anti-trust laws—multinationals have grown so blindingly rich, so vast in their holdings, so global in their reach, that they have created our coalitions for us.

Around the world, activists are piggy-backing on the ready-made infrastructures supplied by global corporations. This can mean cross-border unionization, but also cross-sector organizing—among workers, environmentalists, consumers, even prisoners, who may all have different relationships to one multinational. So you can build a single campaign or coalition around a single brand like General Electric. Thanks to Monsanto, farmers in India are working with environmentalists and consumers around the world to develop direct-action strategies that cut off genetically modified foods in the fields and in the supermarkets. Thanks to Shell Oil and Chevron, human rights activists in Nigeria, democrats in Europe, environmentalists in North America have united in a fight against the unsustainability of the oil industry. Thanks to the catering giant Sodexho-Marriott's decision to invest in Corrections Corporation of America, university students are able to protest against the exploding US for-profit prison industry simply by boycotting the food in their campus cafeteria. Other targets include pharmaceutical companies who are trying to inhibit the production and distribution of low-cost AIDS drugs, and fast-food chains. Recently, students and farm workers in Florida have joined forces around Taco Bell. In the St Petersburg area, field hands—many of them immigrants from Mexico—are paid an average $7,500 a year to pick tomatoes and onions. Due to a loophole in the law, they have no bargaining power: the farm bosses refuse even to talk with them about wages. When they started to look into who bought what they pick, they found that Taco Bell was the largest purchaser of the local tomatoes. So they launched the campaign *Yo No Quiero Taco Bell* together with students, to boycott Taco Bell on university campuses.

It is Nike, of course, that has most helped to pioneer this new brand of activist synergy. Students facing a corporate take-over of their campuses by the Nike swoosh have linked up with workers making its branded campus apparel, as well as with parents concerned at the commercialization of youth and church groups campaigning against child labour—all united by their different relationships to a common global enemy. Exposing the underbelly of high-gloss consumer brands has provided the early narratives of this movement, a sort of call-and-response to the very different narratives these companies tell every day about themselves through advertising and public relations. Citigroup offers another prime target, as North America's largest financial institution, with innumerable holdings, which deals with some of the worst corporate malefactors around. The campaign against it handily knits together dozens of issues—from clear-cut logging in California to oil-and-pipeline schemes in Chad and Cameroon. These projects are only a start. But they are creating a new sort of activist: 'Nike is a gateway drug', in the words of Oregon student activist Sarah Jacobson.

By focusing on corporations, organizers can demonstrate graphically how so many issues of social, ecological and economic justice are interconnected. No activist I've met believes that the world economy can be changed one corporation at a time, but the campaigns have opened a door into the arcane world of international trade and finance. Where they are leading is to the central institutions that write the rules of global commerce: the WTO, the IMF, the FTAA, and for some the market itself. Here too the unifying threat is privatization—the loss of the commons. The next round of WTO negotiations is designed to extend the reach of commodification still further. Through side agreements like GATS (General Agreement on Trade and Services) and TRIPS (Trade-Related Aspects of Intellectual Property Rights), the aim is to get still tougher protection of property rights on seeds and drug patents, and to marketize services like health care, education and water-supply.

The biggest challenge facing us is to distil all of this into a message that is widely accessible. Many campaigners understand the connexions binding together the various issues almost intuitively—much as Subcomandante Marcos says, 'Zapatismo isn't an ideology, it's an intuition.' But to outsiders, the mere scope of modern protests can be a bit mystifying. If you eavesdrop on the movement from the outside, which is what most people do, you are liable to hear what seems to be a cacophony of disjointed slogans, a jumbled laundry list of disparate grievances without clear goals. At the Democratic National Convention in Los Angeles last year, I remember being outside the Staples Centre during the Rage Against the Machine concert, just before I almost got shot, and thinking there were slogans for everything everywhere, to the point of absurdity.

This kind of impression is reinforced by the decentralized, non-hierarchical structure of the movement, which always disconcerts the traditional media. Well-organized press conferences are rare, there is no charismatic leadership, protests tend to pile on top of each other. Rather than forming a pyramid, as most movements do, with leaders up on top and followers down below, it looks more like an elaborate web. In part, this web-like structure is the result of internet-based organizing. But it is also a response to the very political realities that sparked the protests in the first place: the utter failure of traditional party politics. All over the world, citizens have worked to elect social democratic and workers' parties, only to watch them plead impotence in the face of market forces and IMF dictates. In these conditions, modern activists are not so naive as to believe change will come from electoral politics. That's why they are more interested in challenging the structures that make democracy toothless, like the IMF's structural adjustment policies, the WTO's ability to override national sovereignty, corrupt campaign financing, and so on. This is not just making a virtue of necessity. It responds at the ideological level to an understanding that globalization is in essence a crisis in representative democracy. What has caused this crisis? One of the basic reasons for it is the way power and decision-making has been handed along to points ever further away from citizens: from local to provincial, from provincial to national, from national to international institutions, that lack all transparency or accountability. What is the solution? To articulate an alternative, participatory democracy.

If you think about the nature of the complaints raised against the World Trade Organization, it is that governments around the world have embraced an economic model that involves much more than opening borders to goods and services. This is why it is not useful to use the language of anti-globalization. Most people do not really know what globalization is, and the term makes the movement extremely vulnerable to stock dismissals like: 'If you are against trade and globalization why do you drink coffee?' Whereas in reality the movement is a rejection of what is being bundled along with trade and so-called globalization—against the set of transformative political policies that every country in the world has been told they must accept in order to make themselves hospitable to investment. I call this package 'McGovernment'. This happy meal of cutting taxes, privatizing services, liberalizing regulations, busting unions—what is this diet in aid of? To remove anything standing in the way of the market. Let the free market roll, and every other problem will apparently be solved in the trickle down. This isn't about trade. It's about using trade to enforce the McGovernment recipe.

So the question we are asking today, in the run up to the FTAA, is not: are you for or against trade? The question is: do we have the right to negotiate the terms of our relationship to foreign capital and investment? Can we decide how we want to protect ourselves from the dangers inherent in deregulated markets—or do we have to contract out those decisions? These problems will become much more acute once we are in a recession, because during the economic boom so much has been destroyed of what was left of our social safety net. During a period of low unemployment, people did not worry much about that. They are likely to be much more concerned in the very near future. The most controversial issues facing the WTO are these questions about self-determination. For example, does Canada have the right to ban a harmful gasoline additive without being sued by a foreign chemical company? Not according to the WTO's ruling in favour of the Ethyl Corporation. Does Mexico have the right to deny a permit for a hazardous toxic-waste disposal site? Not according to Metalclad, the US company now suing the Mexican government for $16.7 million damages under NAFTA. Does France have the right to ban hormone-treated beef from entering the country? Not according to the United States, which retaliated by banning French imports like Roquefort cheese—prompting a cheese-maker called Bové to dismantle a McDonald's; Americans thought he just didn't like hamburgers. Does Argentina have to cut its public sector to qualify for foreign loans? Yes, according to the IMF—sparking general strikes against the social consequences. It's the same issue everywhere: trading away democracy in exchange for foreign capital.

On smaller scales, the same struggles for self-determination and sustainability are being waged against World Bank dams, clear-cut logging, cash-crop factory farming, and resource extraction on contested indigenous lands. Most people in these movements are not against trade or industrial development. What they are fighting for is the right of local communities to have a say in how their resources are used, to make sure that the people who live on the land benefit directly from its development. These campaigns are a response not to trade but to a trade-off that is now five hundred years old: the sacrifice of democratic control and self-determination to foreign investment and the panacea of economic growth. The challenge they now face is to shift a discourse around the vague notion of globalization into a specific debate about democracy. In a period of 'unprecedented prosperity', people were told they had no choice but to slash public spending, revoke labour laws, rescind environmental protections—deemed illegal trade barriers—defund schools, not build affordable housing. All this was necessary to make us trade-ready, investment-friendly, world-competitive. Imagine what joys await us during a recession.

We need to be able to show that globalization—this version of globalization—has been built on the back of local human welfare. Too often, these connexions between global and local are not made. Instead we sometimes seem to have two activist solitudes. On the one hand, there are the international anti-globalization activists who may be enjoying a triumphant mood, but seem to be fighting far-away issues, unconnected to people's day-to-day struggles. They are often seen as elitists: white middle-class kids with dreadlocks. On the other hand, there are community activists fighting daily struggles for survival, or for the preservation of the most elementary public services, who are often feeling burnt-out and demoralized. They are saying: what in the hell are you guys so excited about?

The only clear way forward is for these two forces to merge. What is now the anti-globalization movement must turn into thousands of local movements, fighting the way neoliberal politics are playing out on the ground: homelessness, wage stagnation, rent escalation, police violence, prison explosion, criminalization of migrant workers, and on and on. These are also struggles about all kinds of prosaic issues: the right to decide where the local garbage goes, to have good public schools, to be supplied with clean water. At the same time, the local movements fighting privatization and deregulation on the ground need to link their campaigns into one large global movement, which can show where their particular issues fit into an international economic agenda being enforced around the world. If that connexion isn't made, people will continue to be demoralized. What we need is to formulate a political framework that can both take on corporate power and control, and empower local organizing and self-determination. That has to be a framework that encourages, celebrates and fiercely protects the right to diversity: cultural diversity, ecological diversity, agricultural diversity—and yes, political diversity as well: different ways of doing politics. Communities must have the right to plan and manage their schools, their services, their natural settings, according to their own lights. Of course, this is only possible within a framework of national and international standards—of public education, fossil-fuel emissions, and so on. But the goal should not be better far-away rules and rulers, it should be close-up democracy on the ground.

The Zapatistas have a phrase for this. They call it 'one world with many worlds in it'. Some have criticized this as a New Age non-answer. They want a plan. 'We know what the market wants to do with those spaces, what do *you* want to do? Where's your scheme?' I think we shouldn't be afraid to say: 'That's not up to us'. We need to have some trust in people's ability to rule themselves, to make the decisions that are best for them. We need to show some humility where now there is so much arrogance and paternalism. To believe in human diversity and local democracy is anything but wishy-washy. Everything in McGovernment conspires against them. Neoliberal economics is biased at every level towards centralization, consolidation, homogenization. It is a war waged on diversity. Against it, we need a movement of radical change, committed to a single world with many worlds in it, that stands for 'the one no and the many yesses'.

Note

1. This is a transcript of a talk given at the Centre for Social Theory and Comparative History, UCLA in April 2001.

CHAPTER TWENTY-ONE

Creating Spaces for Global Democracy: The World Social Forum Process

Jackie Smith

Source: Jackie Smith *Social Movements for Global Democracy* (2008) 206–220 © 2008 John Hopkins University Press—Reproduced with permission.

Just as was true with the emergence of democratic national states, a more democratic global political order requires that citizens have spaces where they can freely interact with other citizens, debate and discuss public questions, and cultivate alliances. If democracy is a political system that treats all members equally, all groups must have the ability to articulate their interests and concerns and be heard by others in society. No political order whose legitimacy is based on democratic premises can survive for long without conscious attempts to cultivate spaces where open, mutually respectful, and equitable discourse can happen. But the global economic system described above is notoriously lacking in this regard. Global policy arenas are, as we have seen, dominated by government and corporate actors, and there are no formal structures to enable democratic input and accountability. Without attempts to democratize this illegitimate system of global governance, it will become more subject to violent resistance and dependent upon coercion to maintain itself.

The World Social Forum might be seen as a model for expanded citizen participation in the global polity. If political leaders respond to it in ways that encourage more interaction with the United Nations and other global institutions while supporting its autonomous and popular character, they might find a solution to the crisis of institutional legitimacy. The World Social Forum is a self-consciously global project, attempting to bring people from diverse countries and cultural traditions together to consider alternative visions of how the world might be organized and to take action to realize these visions. It is essentially a global public meeting, which serves three crucial functions to help construct a foundation for a more democratic global order. Specifically, it contributes to the development of global identities, the cultivation of shared understandings of the world's problems and their appropriate solutions, and the building of capacities for citizens groups to challenge existing global power relations.

The World Social Forum first met in Porto Alegre Brazil in 2001, with considerable support from Brazil's Worker's Party (*Partido Trabalhadores* or PT). A team of French and Brazilian activists tied to various national groups in Brazil and France, as well as the international group, ATTAC (the international alliance of citizens for a tax on international financial transactions) launched the idea for the World Social Forum (Schonleitner 2003). Glasius and Timms describe the WSF as "an idea waiting to happen" (Glasius 2006:191). Indeed, the initiative emerged at a crucial time when activists were debating the limitations of the strategy of "summit hopping," that is moving from city to city to confront policy makers at the sites of their international meetings. The ease with which a small number of militants or agents-provocateur could turn peaceful protests into scenes of vandalism and violence led many activists to seek other means of resisting neoliberal globalization. Given the nature of mainstream media in most countries, even very large and peaceful demonstrations were having limited effects on broader debates. Also, many—particularly those from the global South—found it difficult to maintain a consistently large presence at official meetings while also seeking to build local and national organizations to address both the causes and the effects of global neoliberal policies. And their sustained attention to global economic issues motivated them to develop more comprehensive thinking about how to struggle against the effects of neoliberalism.

When the invitation to participate in the World Social Forum came, it was a welcome opportunity to shift the network's energies in new directions. The fact that the event was scheduled at the same time as, but across the world from, the annual World Economic Forum meeting in Davos, Switzerland, dramatized this strategic break. The symbolic link to the World Economic Forum highlighted the claims of the democratic globalization network that the global economy must be embedded within and governed by a broader system of norms and social relations.[1] The geographic location of the WSF in the global South also made an important statement about its intention to challenge the global organization of power.

The first WSF was an overwhelming success: organizers initially expected a few thousand participants, but more than 15,000 people attended. The second meeting in 2002 attracted more than 60,000, and the following year (also in Porto Alegre) drew at least 100,000. The WSF tested its wings in 2004 by moving the site to Mumbai, India, where a more economically and ethnically diverse collection of more than 100,000 people gathered. It returned to the incubator of Porto Alegre again for its 2005 meeting, drawing more than 155,000 registered participants from 135 countries to participate in more than 2500 different sessions.

The extraordinary success of the WSF lies in the fact that it emerged from an extensive history of transnational activism that had built a foundation of network ties capable of spreading the word about the initiative and of providing resources and motivation for participants. Now the forum contributes to this organizing base by providing "a venue in which churches and anarchists, punks and farmers, trade-unionists and greens can explore issues of common concern, without having to create a new web" (Mertes 2004:244).

Youth have been an important element of the WSF from the beginning, even though they had to struggle to gain greater access to the WSF process. At the first WSF the youth camp was located far from the main Forum site, while by 2005, the camp, which housed an estimated 35,000 participants, was the focal point of the "WSF Territory" in Porto Alegre's riverfront area. Youth initiatives have influenced the WSF process significantly, and the persistence of youth activists has been a key factor in holding the International Council accountable to the values of participatory democracy and an explicit rejection of hierarchy. For instance, a youth-led direct action to protest the presence of a VIP lounge at the first WSF led organizers to abandon the practice of establishing exclusive spaces for politicians and other luminaries. And youth have been most vocal in demanding that the WSF process generate more in the way of actions. Indeed, a central part of the youth programs at social forums has included "action laboratories" where activists enact direct action tactics during the forum itself and reflect on the limits and possibilities of particular actions (Juris 2004).[2]

The WSF was somewhat novel in that it constituted an autonomous gathering of civil society actors rather than one specifically targeting a particular inter-governmental forum. However, it was by no means the first such autonomous gathering, and indeed it built upon pre-existing models to become what we might call a modular form of collective action (e.g., Tarrow, 1995). This helps explain why it generated such immediate and widespread support. For instance, the basic format of the forum itself resembles in many ways the civil society conferences that paralleled UN global conferences of the 1990s. It also mirrors a model forged by feminist activists in Latin America, who gathered in what they called *encuentros*. These meetings familiarized activists with a common model for dialogue and exchange (Sternbach et al. 1992).[3]

> Encuentros are critical spaces where Latin American feminist activists exchange ideas, discuss strategies, and imagine utopias among themselves, along with 'other' feminists who— although belonging to different countries, social classes, ethnic and racial groups, age groups, sexual preference, etc., with the most diverse personal-political trajectories and involved in the broadest array of political practices—share visions of the world and declare their political commitments to a wide gamut of feminist and social justice struggles. (Alvarez et al. 2003)

The *encuentro* as a form of action gained wider international attention when the Zapatistas called the First International *Encuentro* for Humanity and Against Neoliberalism in 1996 as part of their efforts to expand their own struggle against the global sources of their grievances (Alvarez et al. 2003; Chesters 2004).

While the *encuentro* and the civil society conferences that paralleled the UN global conferences provided familiar templates for action, the scheduling of the WSF alongside a global meeting like the World Economic Forum meant that it occurred at a time when activists would be habitually seeking to act together. These overlapping understandings and expectations, which result from the history of social movement activism in general and transnational activism in particular, facilitated the rapid spread of attention to the WSF process as well as local attempts to replicate the process. In particular, one could also say that the successful diffusion of the WSF process is related to the more general "transnational resonance" of Zapatismo (Khasnabish 2005). The WSF links itself to the Zapatista struggle in both its organizing methods as well as by adopting as its own Zapatista slogans such as "another world is possible," and "against neoliberalism and for humanity."

Although the size of the WSF prevents much of the intimate exchange and consensus-building that "*encuentro*" implies, it strives to remain an "open space" for activists to gather in large and small groups to exchange experiences, support each other's struggles, build transnational alliances, and coordinate strategies and actions. It explicitly rejects a representative role, and it makes no recommendations or formal statements on behalf of participants. It does require that participants adopt a general opposition to neoliberal globalization and a commitment to nonviolent struggle. These basic principles have allowed it to include many voices while minimizing major divisions and hierarchies.[4]

The substance of the WSF workshops and plenaries is understandably diverse. The WSF Charter of Principles specifies the broad definition of the aims of the WSF and principles for inclusion. Of course, the central elements of the Charter have generated debate, but there is broad acceptance of the notion that the Forum is a space for those working to oppose neoliberalism in its various forms and that it seeks only to promote those forms of actions that do not intentionally harm people.[5] The first WSF was largely an "anti-Davos" people's assembly. The second WSF encouraged more explicit searches for alternatives to neoliberal globalization, and subsequent meetings have sought to articulate concrete steps towards achieving these alternatives. More recent Forums have devoted extensive energy to questions about the connections between neoliberalism and the United States's militant and unilateralist foreign policy, while also broaching questions about what sorts of political institutions might help transform global relations (Adamovsky 2005). This latter, institutional question seems to have captured more focused attention in the WSF meetings of 2004 and 2005, although it is probably the least developed. Encompassed within this question are issues such as how the inter-governmental system might be democratized and made more effective, as well as how the WSF itself can be made more inclusive and responsive.

Struggles for Internal Democracy in the WSF

The leadership of the WSF consists of its International Council (IC), which invites diverse groups to its membership in an attempt to bring representative leadership to the WSF while insuring its continuity and basic principles. The IC is plagued by the constant tensions between the demands of organizing annual meetings for more than 100,000 people while maintaining self-consciously inclusive and decentralized decision making structures. It includes a wide range of organizations, and organizers explicitly seek to avoid exclusionary tendencies and to maximize space for expressions of diversity. However, the absence of a formal process designed to promote inclusive and non-hierarchical relations has generated the familiar "tyranny of structurelessness" (Freeman 1972).[6]

There will always be room for improvement with regard to representativeness and inclusion in the WSF, as is true with all representative structures. These two goals are in necessary tension, but WSF leaders may need to create a more explicit and formalized process for making collective decisions and statements in order to avoid exacerbating internal struggle while also creating de-facto, un-authorized leaders. As the size of the WSF expands, many are calling for new approaches to facilitating global dialogue on a more manageable scale. There is also much discussion about how the location of this global meeting privileges some voices over others. Tensions remain over whether Porto Alegre should hold a special status as the WSF's birthplace, and how much to risk the continuity of the Forum by moving it to locations that lack the physical and social infrastructures to support this immense gathering.

Another important challenge is the exclusion of activists who don't explicitly reject neoliberalism or the use of violence as a political tactic. Such exclusion is in tension with the broader democratic ideology of the movement as well as some activists' strategic thinking. While an expressed opposition to neoliberalism might be important for resisting attempts by the rival network to co-opt segments of the democratic globalization network, many activists wanting to attend the WSF may not have all the information they need to decide their position regarding global capitalism. Shouldn't the Forum be a space where people can learn diverse views before they come to such a position? Similarly, with regard to the use of violence, some groups challenge the idea that dialogue with groups that use violence should be banned by WSF rules. In particular, as divisions between Arab and Palestinian peoples and the west become more strained, some argue that nonviolent activists must engage efforts at dialogue with groups linked to violent struggles, even as they reject their tactics.[7]

The lack of a representative function of the WSF and the attempt by leaders to avoid making it a body that can speak on behalf of a global movement eliminates the possibility that the WSF could be used more effectively to mobilize activists around a shared global agenda. Moreover, there are tremendous pressures on activists to generate common statements, fueled in part by the mass media, which have complained about the failure of WSF organizers to provide a format that allows effective media coverage of the event. The mass media seeks spokespersons or leaders who can reflect the many common sentiments of the thousands of activists attending the Forums, and many participants also want this process to be used to more effectively demonstrate what Charles Tilly refers to as WUNC: their worthiness, unity, numbers, and commitment (2004:3–4). Clearly a WSF that could speak for its participants and mobilize around key concerns of the various movements represented there would benefit the struggle to make "another world" possible.

Localizing the WSF Process

While the debate about how to routinize the WSF and to insure that it attempts to be inclusive and open in its operations occupies considerable attention among some activists, there is little disagreement over the need to decentralize the efforts of the Forum and to maximize connections to local organizers. And many of the networks involved in the WSF process have simply made the practical decision to devote their energies to addressing this problem directly. People cannot be represented if they are not involved in the WSF process, and many have yet to learn of the WSF process. So activists at local, national, and regional levels have organized social forums in these more localized settings, and these efforts have helped to decentralize the WSF process overall. Similarly, the WSF's notion that "another world is possible," and that this movement is about creating that world, has come to permeate the discourse and focus the creative attention of activists around the world.

The 2005 WSF meeting was notable in that it reflected some decisive moves toward greater decentralization. Clearly there were always conscious efforts to prevent centralization among the leading players in the WSF process, and the ideology of openness and inclusion helped reinforce the legitimacy of those demanding more space for participation. But two important features of the 2005 WSF meeting helped create more structured possibilities for an even more open and participatory process.

First, the 2005 meeting helped strengthen efforts to mobilize social forums at regional and local levels by deciding to replace the global gathering in 2006 with a "polycentric" World Social Forum of interlinked regional social forums in Caracas (Venezuela), Karachi (Pakistan), and Bamako (Mali). This move is largely in response to the difficulties of managing such a large global meeting as well as a flowering of more localized attempts to mobilize people around the ideals of the world social forum. Between 2001 and 2004 Glasius and Timms identified a minimum of 166 local social forums (not counting at least 183 in Italy and a similarly large number in Greece), 58 national social forums, and 35 regional and thematic social forums all explicitly linked to the WSF process (2006: 198).[8] Clearly the World Social Forum process has captured the political imagination of activists. By encouraging activists to organize regional social forums, the International Council of the WSF hopes to reinforce the global process while also strengthening local organizing efforts.[9]

Second, in 2004 the IC reorganized its methodology for soliciting participation in the global WSF, eliminating centrally organized panels and facilitating the use of its website by groups working to develop integrated proposals for panels before the Forum and to disseminate proposals in its aftermath. While the process was far from perfect, and remains confusing and complex,[10] by all accounts it was successful in making the Forum more open and accessible and in helping encourage the emergence of leadership from more diverse locations (Albert 2003). Moreover, the process included efforts to generate from the huge variety of Forum events some movement towards common positions. Daily assemblies were scheduled in each of the eleven thematic spaces to allow participants to highlight common themes and programs for action. This helped to focus different groups on the task of developing joint programs even in the planning stages of the forum. These experiences at transnational collaboration will have long term effects on the capacities of the democratic globalization network. They will certainly inform subsequent campaigns, reinforce trust between diverse groups, and encourage activists to develop important skills in transnational organizing.

While the WSF marks an important milestone in the development of the struggle for alternatives to neoliberal globalization, it builds upon a much longer tradition of activism within a global context. And as this discussion shows, it has been propelled by both global and local leadership, and the debates and tensions between these have contributed much to the WSF's evolution. Over recent years, civil society meetings with a global perspective are becoming larger (55% had more than 10,000 participants), more coordinated across the globe, and are taking up a more diverse political agenda (Pianta and Silva 2003). The organizational data I reported in chapter six, as well as the work of Pianta and Silva show that more people are making conscious connections between economic issues and other demands such as democracy and peace. Pianta and Silva also report, based on their longitudinal survey of international groups attending different global civil society forums, that activist groups are becoming more outward-looking and they maintain a strong commitment to developing stronger and more diverse networks among global civil society organizations. The WSF process both reflects and contributes to this diversification and strengthening of global civil society networks.

The proliferation of local social forums demonstrates the power of the political imagination encouraged by the democratic globalization network as well as the capacities of the WSF process to integrate diverse groups. While many of these gatherings resemble those taking place long before the WSF was established, the WSF process allows people to imagine these kinds of events as part of a much bigger struggle. It encourages them to consider the linkages among diverse issues and campaigns and to feel themselves part of a much larger global effort. More importantly, the WSF process provides some of the few places where individuals can engage in global political deliberation and action, since global institutions lack formal mechanisms for promoting public engagement and participation.

Experiments in Global Democracy

Despite limitations to the WSF's representativeness and its failure to fully incorporate many of those most disadvantaged by neoliberal globalization, it remains without a doubt the most open and diverse space where global policy issues are considered. Even without formal designation as such, the WSF is a mechanism for helping people articulate and aggregate their demands for policy, and where activists can learn about each other's concerns while finding ways to improve communications. Thus, many observers have called it an "incubator" or a "laboratory" for global democracy. What is clear is that participants in the WSF process are helping articulate models of global participatory democracy that might contribute to a collective search for ideas about how to structure a more democratic global order (Juris 2005). As activists reflect on the process itself and seek to enhance its inclusiveness and representativeness, they are engaging in the essential steps of experimenting, refining, and elaborating plans for a more formal system for global democracy. More serious attention to how the WSF might relate to the broader multilateral system, however, might produce some important gains for global democracy.

Since the very origins of the United Nations, activists agitated for a "People's Assembly" or a "Global Parliament" to enhance the representativeness of the United Nations. These types of bodies would provide at least some formal mechanisms to link individuals and groups at local levels with global level political debates, strengthening the connective tissues between local and global politics. A key challenge, however, has been in determining how to create a globally representative body that is also manageable and politically relevant. Some have suggested that a global parliament select its members from elected national legislatures. Another is to model the European Parliament, where representatives are elected directly by voters. But clearly the major impediment to efforts to expand representation in global bodies is government opposition.

Governments prefer to maintain maximum control over decisions in international political arenas, and thus they have long resisted attempts to democratize these spaces. By giving the multilateral economic organizations the capacities to enforce their decisions while denying such capacities to the United Nations General Assembly and other more inclusive and democratic bodies, they have supported a global order based on coercion over one based on consent (Monbiot 2003). But as I have argued earlier, such an effort is inherently unstable, as it violates a fundamental premise of modern political institutions that states derive their authority from the consent of the governed. In the face of this contradiction, activists themselves are creating structures to enable popular participation even over government opposition. Many believe that by continuing to foster public debates and proposals for global policy, social movements will eventually force governments to formally accept some form of participation by globalized civil society (Falk and Strauss 2001; Monbiot 2003). Indeed, a recent report by the United Nations Secretariat recommends some concrete steps for enhancing civil society's role in the organization, and democratic globalizers might unite behind efforts to actualize some of the report's recommendations (United Nations 2004).

In short, the WSF process reflects the efforts of the democratic globalization network to create autonomous spaces in which people can be active politically. But as much of this book has emphasized, the Forum and other activities of the democratic globalization network go beyond purely political debates to promote efforts to better integrate the economy within society, challenging the (dys)functional boundaries between the UN and multilateral economic organizations (e.g., O'Brien 2002). Many commentators in the mainstream media and political circles have asked what critics of neoliberalism propose as alternatives to the current economic practices. The World Social Forum promotes the notion that "another world is possible" by creating places for people to discuss what such a vision might look like as well as to encourage and support the concrete steps needed to realize an alternative to a neoliberal world.

Cultivating Global Collective Identities

By creating opportunities for activists to come together with counterparts from diverse sectors and parts of the world, the WSF process not only contributes to the elaboration of new modes of democratic global governance, but it also helps develop the networks and the sense of global community needed for the practice of global democracy. A Zapatista slogan used frequently by those in the democratic globalization network says that this effort is "against neoliberalism and for humanity." This phrase conveys the idea that this movement encourages people to think of themselves as more than just citizens of a single country but as members of a global human community with many common values and concerns. Again borrowing from Zapatista writings that encourage values of equality and empathy, many WSF participants proclaim variations on the statement "we are all Zapatistas; we are all Subcomandante Marcos."[11] Every democracy requires that all of its members identify as part of a single community, and that every member recognizes and respects the rights of all other community members. Thus, a more democratic global polity requires that people think of themselves as part of a broader, human community. All movements engage in efforts to promote new collective identities, and these identities are negotiated and re-negotiated by activists themselves, as group members work in an ongoing way to define a collective "we" and its relation to opponents (Gamson 1991: 40–41; McAdam and Paulsen 1993; Polletta 2001; Melucci 1989; Rupp and Taylor 1999). In short, the WSF process creates a space that helps people overcome the geographic boundaries, limited shared experiences, cultural diversity, and high transaction costs that make it difficult to develop collective identities on a global scale.

Within the WSF, activists from more privileged backgrounds will frequently find themselves in dialogue (both face-to-face and indirect) with their organizational and activist counterparts from poor countries. They are also consistently challenged to consider how the WSF process and their own organizations might be excluding the voices of less privileged groups.

This culture of inclusion and tolerance is widespread among WSF activists, and it is linked to their shared aim of promoting participatory democracy, which encourages practices of mutual respect, openness, and commitment to inclusive decision making processes (della Porta 2005a; Polletta and Jasper 2001).

Amory Starr emphasizes the different role of identity in contemporary struggles against neoliberalism and those of earlier identity movements, arguing that "[t]he international invitation to be a Zapatista [. . .] is a moral solidarity around a political economic critique, not any kind of claim about interiority or essence" (Starr 2000:167). Indeed, observers of the WSF process have noted the presence of multiple or ambiguous identities among activists who cross geographic and ideological boundaries on a regular basis in spaces such as these. Della Porta, for instance, found that activists in various social forums adopted "flexible identities and multiple belongings," that enabled them to make sense of the complex issues and political processes in which they were engaged (della Porta et al. 2006). Juris found a tendency for activists to use different identities in strategic ways within the various spheres of activism in which they operated. Activists who are particularly skillful in this regard frequently serve as "network bridgers," or brokers, who are essential to building diverse coalitions among activists from such a wide variety of backgrounds (Juris 2004:45; see also contributions in Bandy and Smith 2005; Tarrow 2005). Thus, we see contemporary activists responding to the need for more expansive and inclusive identities as they seek to mobilize in a global context.

Although many activists will never have the chance to attend a global WSF meeting, the WSF process encourages local groups to identify with a global movement and connect to transnational networks. Regional and local social forums serve as focal points that help dramatize and clarify the connections among diverse local and global struggles, helping to cultivate an "imagined global community" with its own agenda and culture. For instance, U.S. activists targeting the nominating convention of the Democratic Party organized the "Boston Social Forum," to create space for U.S. activists to both discuss their varied concerns and policy interests while encouraging and enabling them to understand connections between their own local struggles and those of other activists from around the world. And New York activists have staged their own city-wide social forums, one of which coincided with the 2002 meeting of the World Economic Forum in New York. This created new opportunities for groups working on global issues to connect with more locally-oriented ones while encouraging local activists to see their problems and their struggles in global terms. These kinds of global identities and the related social forum culture are not likely to emerge from inter-governmental processes that are controlled by geographically defined states. Nor are they likely to disappear quickly, even if activists don't have regular opportunities to gather with their international counterparts. Together with the communication possibilities generated through the internet, local social forums contribute to the breadth, depth, and intensity of global activist networks.

Developing Shared Analyses

WSF events focus on particular, issue-specific campaigns around which activists hope to build broad transnational coalitions, they seek to explore the connections between different problems such as environmental degradation, poverty, and neoliberal globalization policies, and they focus on practical questions about how to build a global movement to advance the various needs and objectives expressed in the forum. Many sessions devote substantial amounts of time to the sharing of experiences and analyses. Here, activists learn about how neoliberal policies impact people in different countries, as well as how activists from diverse regions define what policy changes are needed. Such exchanges sensitize activists to the complexities of global interdependence, and they help them develop joint strategies that address the concerns of activists in the global North as well as the South. For instance, while many Northern groups initially sought to integrate labor and environmental agreements into global trade negotiations, conversations with Southern activists convinced many of the dangers of such policies, which would further weaken the political voice of Southern countries while strengthening international financial institutions (see, e.g., Khor 2000; Waterman 2005). Also, much of the activity around the creation of local and solidarity economies (more on this below) is informed by the analyses of global capitalism derived from dialogues among activists in different parts of the world economy.

The WSF process has also created an important transnational place for activists to explore the potentially contentious theme of the connections between neoliberal globalization and the systematic use of violence by governments.[12] While peace movements have long had transnational components, the history of peace activism has shown that national boundaries and ideologies can impede transnational solidarity, particularly in wartime (Chatfield 1992; Cortright and Pagnucco 1997; Wittner 1997). Attention to the connections between militarism and neoliberalism is not something that began after the attacks on the U.S. in 2001 and the subsequent U.S. invasions of Afghanistan and Iraq. Even before the WSF process began, these connections were part of activist discourse in places like the May 1999 Hague Appeal for Peace conference, where thousands of activists gathered months before the Seattle WTO protests to discuss, among other topics related to the theme of "peace is a human right," the connections between economic globalization and war. A significant number of sessions and organizational displays at the very first WSF focused on the connections between militarism and neoliberalism, and at that time particular attention was directed at the U.S. counter-narcotics operation called "Plan Colombia." Such connections are particularly obvious for Latin American activists, even if many Northern activists have differentiated these issues in their analyses and organizing strategies.

The WSF process helped generate a "General Assembly of the Global Antiwar Movement," which began in regional forums and convened at the 2004 WSF in Mumbai (Reitan Forthcoming). The Assembly provided spaces for antiwar activists around the world to exchange notes on their organizing experiences and to strategize for the future. Antiwar activists in the WSF helped launch the world's biggest demonstration against war on February 15, 2003, to protest the imminent U.S. invasion of Iraq. The WSF setting allows activists to develop shared understanding and mutual respect in a situation where the absence of direct communication could lead to suspicion and hostility. Activists from outside the U.S. have little opportunity to meet Americans who oppose official U.S. policy, but at the WSF, they meet in a context where they can develop trust and mutual support. For instance, a Costa Rican delegate at the 2004 WSF meeting argued, "We must coordinate with American [antiwar] movements, not let ourselves be seen as anti-American, and not be seen as violent." And in another panel, Achin Vanaik, a prominent Indian nuclear weapons expert and founder of the Coalition for Nuclear Disarmament and Peace called for international solidarity in the antiwar movement:

To beat U.S. imperialism we must help struggles and resistances develop within each country. And we must recognise and explain to the people that there is a direct connection between U.S. empire-building, war and globalisation. We are trying to change the relationships between the forces against the United States [policy] and thus strengthen and unite the move[ment].[13]

As a space where people come together around their identities as activists rather than as nationals of particular countries, the WSF helps activists generate new understandings of the structures against and within which they struggle. It also helps them identify the commonalities in their struggles while they work to understand the causes of the problems they face. In the process, it helps nurture bonds of mutual trust and solidarity as activists learn to appreciate the experiences, knowledge, and determination of their counterparts in different parts of the world.

Socialization for Struggle

A huge amount of energy at the World Social Forums is devoted to enhancing the capacities of groups to both oppose neoliberal globalization and promote alternative visions. Thus, organizations use the WSF as a setting for their own organizational or campaign meetings, piggybacking their efforts as they also did (and still do) during the United Nations conferences. By holding organizational meetings at the WSF, groups both conserve resources while improving their capacity to expand representation of their own members, since often they can obtain funding to bring members to a WSF meeting but cannot raise funds for internal organization-building. More importantly, though, meeting at the WSF allows groups to envision their work in a broader context, and to familiarize themselves with the work and discourses of other activists. This can promote the building of coalitions among groups working on similar themes while preventing redundancy and enhancing complementarities in transnational organizing work. This is essential network-building work.

In addition to helping organizations envision themselves as part of a broader political process, the WSF creates opportunities for individual activists to expand their awareness of the various struggles and analyses of different people around the world and to cultivate skills in the various tasks surrounding transnational social change work. In 2005, for instance, women's groups organized special orientation sessions to help acquaint activists with the WSF process and to guide them in making effective use of their time at the Forum. Groups leading particular campaigns also use the WSF process to help build broader awareness of and commitment to their programs. For instance, Amnesty International and collaborating organizations ran programs at both the European and World Social Forum on their initiative to promote norms for businesses within the United Nations, explaining the UN processes in which they were working and identifying particular ways that other groups could help support the initiative by, for instance, pressing their own governments at the times of key votes or by referring to the draft norms in their own legal or activist work.

Notes

1. For a more detailed history and analysis of the WSF process, see, e.g., Fisher and Ponniah (2003) Reitan (Forthcoming); Sen et al. (2003); Teiveinan (2002).
2. The direct action laboratories have also generated strong criticism even from youth activists themselves, since these sessions tend to draw those more concerned with doing civil disobedience than with serious reflection on the limitations of some tactics. For instance, a young observer at the European Social Forum in 2004 noted that actions aimed at promoting "free public transit" by evading payment for subway and bus fares were inappropriate for use in the smaller towns where many activists were based, and where bus drivers were familiar with riders than in large urban settings like London (Smith et al. 2004).
3. On the explicit connections between the *encuentro* form and the World Social Forums, see, e.g., Escobar (2003) Chesters (2004); Fisher and Ponniah (2003).
4. I do not want to suggest that tension is absent from this meeting. It is most certainly there, and there are wide disagreements over basic questions such as whether or not the forum

should make common statements and whether and how to involve governments, political parties, and private entities such as foundations and corporations. But these conflicts have not prevented the Forum from convening and providing space for participants to act on shared goals.

5. For a discussion of the debates surrounding these principles, see (Sen 2003; Patomäki and Teiveinan 2004).

6. Activists actively discuss this dilemma, and more than once I've heard people reference Freeman's article.

7. Walden Bello made this argument in a speech at the European Social Forum in London in the fall of 2004. Of course, such a position is problematic on many levels, not the least of which is that critics of the movement will use such contacts to discredit the entire movement. And in the context of the "global war on terror," such contacts are likely to bring repressive responses from nominally democratic governments.

8. Their counts excluded local social forums in Italy and Greece, where the numbers were too high to track reliably, and also excluded are those lacking an internet presence and that operate using non-west European languages.

9. Discussions at the WSF and at the European Social Forum revealed important strains over the difficulties of hosting very large meetings while also working to build local organizations and coalitions. However, many participants in these discussions did not want to abandon regular meetings at the broader, regional or global levels, for fear of losing the more outward-looking, global orientation to the forum process. The decision of the IC to devote one year to regional meetings and to return to a global meeting in 2007 may provide a good balance between these tensions.

10. I participated in the 2005 World Social Forum in Porto Alegre as a coordinator for a delegation from the international group, Sociologists Without Borders. In this capacity, I coordinated and registered our delegation through the WSF website, and consulted with other registered groups to develop a joint program for the actual WSF meeting. I learned to appreciate the difficulties involved in attempts to organize transnationally within the WSF process. One problem is the difficulty of developing a cross-nationally coherent scheme for classifying the various activities groups propose for the WSF. The WSF organizing team made considerable efforts to "map the terrain" of WSF events, identifying 11 "thematic spaces" that included, among others "autonomous thought," "defending diversity," "democratic alternatives," "peace, demilitarization and trade," etc. Many people I spoke with found the result of these efforts confusing and difficult to use. The main reason was the fact that they were not mutually exclusive, so it could be difficult to identify groups working on similar themes and to classify the proper location for reporting the proposals emerging from events in the WSF's "mural of proposals."

11. During the first WSF in Porto Alegre, French farmer-activist José Bové was arrested for "decontaminating" a genetically modified crop test plot. As the news of his arrest and imminent deportation was announced, organizers passed around stickers with the phrase "Somos todos José Bové," (We are all José Bové).

12. This includes not only international war-making but also internal repression and the expansion of what activists call the "prison industrial complex" of modern, neoliberal states.

13. Quoted in Hayden (2004).

References

Adamovsky, Ezequiel. 2005. "Beyond the World Social Forum: The Need for New Institutions." In Opendemocracy.net, vol. 2005.

Ahmadjian, Christina L., and Gregory E. Robbins. 2005. "A Clash of Capitalisms: Foreign Shareholders and Corporate Restructuring in 199os Japan." *American Sociological Review* 70:451–472.

Albert, Michael. 2003. "The WSF: Where to Now?" Pp. 323–328 in *Challenging Empires: The World Social Forum*, edited by J. Sen, A. Anand, A. Escobar, and P. Waterman. At vvvvw.choike.org/nuevo_eng/informes/1557.htird.

Alger, Chadwick F. 1963. "United Nations Participation as a Learning Experience." *Public Opinion Quarterly* 27:411–426.

Alston, Philip. 1992. "The Commission on Human Rights." Pp. 126–2m in *The United Nations and Human Rights: A Critical Appraisal*, edited by P. Alston. New York: Oxford University Press.

Alvarez, Sonia, Nalu Faria, and Miriam Nobre. 2003. "Another (also Feminist) World is Possible: Constructing Transnational Spaces and Global Alternatives from the Movements." Pp. 199–206 in *Challenging Empires: The World Social Forum*, edited by J. Sen, A. Anand, A. Escobar, and P. Waterman. At www.choike.org/nuevo_eng/informes/1557.html.

Amnesty International. 2004. "The UN Human Rights Norms For Business: Towards Legal Accountability." Amnesty International, London. At http://web.amnesty.org/library/pdf/IOR420022oo4ENGLISH/SFile/IOR4200204

Anand, Anita. 1999. "Global Meeting Place: United Nations' World Conferences and Civil Society." Pp. 65–108 in *Whose World Is It Anyway? Civil Society, the United Nations and the Multilateral Future*, edited by J. W. Foster and A. Anand. Ottawa: United Nations Association in Canada.

Anderson, Carol. 2003. *Eyes off the Prize: African-Americans and the Struggle for Human Rights, 1948–1954.* New York: Cambridge University Press.

Anheier, Helmut, and Hagai Katz. 2005. "Network Approaches to Global Civil Society." Pp. 206–221 in *Global Civil Society 2004/5*, edited by H. Anheier, M. Glasius, and M. Kaldor. London: Sage.

Arquilla, John, and David Ronfeldt, eds. 2005. *Networks and Netwars: The Future of Terror, Crime, and Militancy.* Santa Monica, CA: Rand Corporation.

Arrighi, Giovanni. 1999. "Globalization and Historical Macrosociology." Pp. 117–133 in *Sociology for the Twenty-First Century*, edited by J. L. Abu-Lughod. Chicago: University of Chicago Press.

Asia Pacific Resource Center. 1994. *The People vs. Global Capital: The G-7, TNCs, SAPs, and Human Rights-Report of the International People's Tribunal to Judge the G-7.* Tokyo: Asia Pacific Resource Center.

Atwood, David. 1997. "Mobilizing Around the United Nations Special Session on Disarmament." Pp. 141–158 in *Transnational Social Movements and Global Politics: Solidarity Beyond the State*, edited by J. Smith, C. Chatfield, and R. Pagnucco. Syracuse: Syracuse University Press.

Ayres, Jeffrey M. 1998. *Defying Conventional Wisdom: Political Movements and Popular Contention Against North American Free Trade.* Toronto: University of Toronto Press.

—. 2004. "Framing Collective Action Against Neoliberalism: The Case of the 'Anti-Globalization' Movement." *Journal of World Systems Research* 10:11–34.

Babb, Sarah. 2003. "The IMF in Sociological Perspective: A Tale of Organizational Slippage." *Studies in Comparative International Development* 38:3–27.

Babones, Salvatore J., and Jonathan H. Turner. 2003. "Global Inequality." Pp. 101–125 in *Handbook of Social Problems*, edited by G. Ritzer. Malden, MA: Blackwell.

Baiocchi, Gianpaolo. 2003. "Emergent Public Spheres: Talking Politics in Participatory Governance in Porto Alegre, Brazil." *American Sociological Review* 68:52–74.

—. 2004. "The Party and the Multitudes: Brazil's Worker's Party (PT) and the Challenges of Building a Just Social Order in the Globalizing Context." *Journal of World Systems Research* 10399–215.

Ball, Patrick. 2000. "State Terror, Constitutional Traditions, and National Human Rights Movements: A Cross-National Quantitative Comparison." Pp. 54–75 in *Globalizations and Social Movements: Culture, Power, and the Transnational Public Sphere*, edited by J. A. Guidry, M. D. Kennedy, and M. N. Zald. Ann Arbor. University of Michigan Press.

Bandy, Joe, and Jackie Smith. 2005. *Coalitions Across Borders: Transnational Protest and the Neoliberal Order.* Lanham, MD: Rowman & Littlefield.

Barbaro, Michael. 2005. "A New Weapon for Wal-Mart: A War Room." *New York Times,* r November. At www.wakeupwalmart.cominews/2005no5-nythtml.

Barber, Benjamin. 1995. *Jihad vs. Mc World.* New York: Random House.

Barlow, Maude, and Tony Clarke. 1998. *MAI: The Multilateral Agreement on Investment and the Threat to American Freedom.* New York: Stoddart.

Barnett, Antony. 2005. "The Man Who Fought for the Forgotten: Peter Benenson, 1921–2005, Founder of Amnesty International." In *Observer/UK*. London. 27 February. At obsenrer.guardian.co.uk/ulc_news/story/o,6903,4266,00.html.

Barnett, Michael, and Martha Finnemore. 1999. "The Politics, Power, and Pathologies of International Organizations." *International Organization* 53:699–732.

Barr, Bob. 2002. "Protecting National Sovereignty in an Era of National Meddling." *Harvard Journal on Legislation* 39(2):299–324.

Bechler, Rosemary. 2004. "Islam and Politics Don't Mix: Massoud Romdhani Interviewed." In *Open Democracy, vol.* 2004.

Bello, Walden. 1999. *Dark Victory: The United States and Global Poverty*. London: Pluto.

— 2000. "UNCTAD: Time to Lead, Time to Challenge the WTO." Pp. 163–174 in *Globalize This! The Battle Against the World Trade Organization and Corporate Rule*, edited by K. Danaher and R. Burbach. Monroe, ME: Common Courage.

— 2003. *Deglobalization: New Ideas for Running the World Economy*. London: Zed.

Benchmark. Environmental Consulting. 1996. "Democratic Global Civil Governance Report of the 1995 Benchmark Survey of NGOs." Royal Ministry of Foreign Affairs, Oslo.

Bendell, Jem. 2004. "Flags of Inconvenience? The Global Compact and the Future of the United Nations." Nottingham University Business School, Nottingham, UK. At www. globalpolicy.org/reform/business/2004/flags pdf.

Bennett, W. Lance. 2003. "Communicating Global Activism: Some Strengths and Vulnerabilities of Networked Politics." In *Cyberprotest: New Media, Citizens and Social Movements*, edited by W. van de Donk, B. D. Loader, P. G. Nixon, and D. Rucht. London: Routledge.

— 2004. "Branded Political Communication: Lifestyle Politics, Logo Campaigns, and the Rise of Global Citizenship." In *The Politics Behind Products: Using the Market as a Site for Ethics and Action*, edited by M. Micheletti, A. Follesdal, and D. Stolle. New Brunswick, NJ: Transaction.

—. 2005. "Social Movements Beyond Borders: Understanding Two Eras of Transnational Activism." Pp. 203–226 in *Ransnational Protest and Global Activism*, edited by D. della Porta and S. Tarrow. Lanham, MD: Rowman & Littlefield.

Bennis, Phyllis. 1997. *Calling the Shots: How Washington Dominates Today's UN*. New York: Olive Branch.

— 2006. *Challenging Empire: How People, Governments, and the UN Defy US Power*. Northampton, MA: Olive Branch.

Black, Richard. 2005. "Inuit Sue US over Climate Policy." *BBC News*, 8 December. At news.bbc.co.uk/2/hi/scienceinature/4511556.stm.

Bob, Clifford. 2004. "Contesting Transnationalism: Anti-NGO Mobilization and World Politics." Presented at the American Political Science Association Annual Meeting.

Boli, John. 1999. "Conclusion: World Authority Structures and Legitimation." Pp. 267–302 in *Constructing World Culture: International Nongovernmental Organizations Since 1875*, edited by J. Boli and G. M. Thomas. Stanford: Stanford University Press.

Boli, John, and George M. Thomas. 1999. *Constructing World Culture: International Nongovernmental Organizations Since 1875*. Stanford: Stanford University Press.

Bonacich, Edna, and Richard Applebaum. 2000. *Behind the Label: Inequality in the Los Angeles Apparel Industry*. Berkeley: University of California Press.

Boswell, Terry, and Christopher Chase-Dunn. 2000. *The Spiral of Capitalism and Socialism*. Boulder, CO: Lynne Rienner.

Boulding, Elise. 1990. *Building a Global Civic Culture*. Syracuse: Syracuse University Press. Brecher, Jeremy, Tim Costello, and Brendan Smith. 2000. *Globalization from Below The Power of Solidarity*. Cambridge, MA: South End.

Broad, Robin. 2006. "Research, Knowledge, & the Art of 'Paradigm Maintenance': The World Bank's Development Economics Vice-Presidency (DEC)." *Review of International Political Economy* 13:387–419.

Brooks, Ethel. 2005. "Transnational Campaigns Against Child Labor. The Garment Industry in Bangladesh." Pp. 121–140 in *Coalitions Across Borders: Transnational Protest and the Neoliberal Order*, edited by J. Bandy and J. Smith. Lanham, MD: Rowman & Littlefield.

Brune, Robert J., and J. Craig Jenkins. 2005. "Foundations and the Environmental Movement: Priorities, Strategies, and Impact." In *Foundations for Social Change: Critical Perspectives on Philanthropy and Popular Movements*, edited by D. Faber and D. McCarthy. Lanham, MD: Rowman & Littlefield.

Bruno, Kenny, and Joshua Karliner. 2002. Earthsummit.biz: The *Corporate Takeover of Sustainable Development*. Oakland: Food First.

Brysk, Allison. 2000. *From Tribal Village to Global Village: Indigenous Peoples' Struggles in Latin America*. Stanford: Stanford University Press.

Bunting, Madeleine. 2006. "Last Year, the Politics of Global Inequality Finally Came of Age." In *Guardian/UK*. At *www.guardian.co.uk/comment/story/o,,1676369,00.html.*

Burawoy, Michael. 2004. "The World Needs Public Sociology." *Sosiologisk tidsskrift* (Journal of Sociology, Norway). At *http://sociology.berkeley.edu/faculty/burawoy/burawoypdf* PS.Norway.pdf.

Buss, Doris, and Didi Herman. 2003. *Globalizing Family Values: The Christian Right in International Politics*. Minneapolis: University of Minnesota Press.

Byerly, Carolyn M. 2006. "Those Missing Media Voices." In TomPaine.com At www.tompaine.com/ articles/2006/11/20/those_missing_media_voices.php.

Campbell, John L. 2004. *Institutional Change and Globalization*. Princeton: Princeton University Press.

Castells, Manuel. 1996. *The Rise of the Network Society*. Cambridge: Blackwell.

Cavanagh, John, and Jerry Mander. 2004. *Alternatives to Economic Globalization: A Better World Is Possible*. 2nd ed. San Francisco: Berrett-Koehler.

Chabot, Sean. 2005. "Activism across Borders, Dialogue across Differences: A Freirean Reinvention of Scale Shift and Transnational Contention." Manuscript.

Charnovitz, Steve. 1997. "Two Centuries of Participation: NGOs and International Governance." *Michigan Journal of International Law* 18:183–286.

—. 2002. "Triangulating the World Trade Organization." *American Journal of International Law* 96:28–55.

Chase-Dunn, Christopher. 1998. *Global Formation,* Updated Edition. Boulder, CO: Row-man & Littlefield.

—. 2002. "Globalization from Below: Toward a Collectively Rational and Democratic Global Commonwealth." *The Annals of the American Academy of Political and Social Science* 581:48–61.

Chatfield, Charles. 1992. *The American Peace Movement: Ideals and Activism*. New York: Twayne.

—. 1997. "Intergovernmental and Nongovernmental Associations to 1945." Pp. 19–41 in *Transnational Social Movements and World Politics: Solidarity Beyond the State*, edited by J. Smith, C. Chatfield, and R. Pagnucco. Syracuse: Syracuse University Press.

—. 2007. "National Insecurity: From Dissent to Protest Against U.S. Foreign Policy." Pp. 456–516 in *The Long War: A New History of U.S. National Security Policy since World* War *II,* edited by A. J. Bacevich. New York: Columbia University Press.

Chesters, Graeme. 2004. "Global Complexity and Global Civil Society." *Voluntas: International Journal of Voluntary and Non-Profit Organizations* 15:323–342.

Chicago Council on Foreign Relations and Program on International Policy Attitudes. 2004. "The Hall of Mirrors: Perceptions and Misperceptions in the Congressional Foreign Policy Process." University of Maryland, College Park, MD.

Chua, Amy. 2003. *World on Fire: How Exporting Free Market Democracy Breeds Ethnic Hatred and Global Instability*. New York: Anchor.

Clark, Ann Marie. 2003. *Diplomacy of Conscience: Amnesty International and Changing Human Rights Norms*. Princeton: Princeton University Press.

Clark, John D. 2003. *Worlds Apart: Civil Society and the Battle for Ethical Globalization*. Bloomfield, CT: Kumarian.

Clayman, Stephen E., and Ann Reisner. 1998. "Editorial Conferences and Assessments of Newsworthiness." *American Sociological Review* 63:178–199.

Cobb, Roger, Jennie-Kieth Ross, and Marc Howard Ross. 1976. "Agenda Building as a Comparative Political Process." American *Political Science Review* 70:126–138.

Coleman, William D, and Tony Porter. 2000. "International Institutions, Globalization and Democracy: Assessing the Challenges." *Global Society* 14:377–398.

Coleman, William D., and Sarah Wayland. 2004. "Global Civil Society and Non-Territorial Governance: Some Empirical Reflections." *Global Governance* 12(4)523–526. Cortright, David. 1993. *Peace Works*. Boulder, CO: Westview.

Cortright, David, and Ron Pagnucco. 1997. "Limits to Transnationalism: The 1980s Freeze Campaign." Pp. 159–173 in *Solidarity Beyond the State: The Dynamics of Transnational Social Movements*, edited by J. Smith, C. Chatfield, and R. Pagnucco. Syracuse: Syracuse University Press.

Couch, Corm. 2004. *Post-Democracies*. Cambridge: Polity.

Cullen, Pauline. 2005. "Obstades to Transnational Cooperation in the European Social Policy Platform." Pp. 71–94 in *Coalitions Across Borders: Transnational Protest and the Neoliberal* Order, edited by J. Bandy and J. Smith. Lanham, MD: Rowman & Littlefield.

Daly, Herman E. 1996. *Beyond Growth: The Economics of Sustainable Development*. Boston: Beacon.

—. 2002. "Globalization versus Internationalization, and Four Economic Arguments for Why Internationalization is a Better Model for World Community." At www.bsos.umd.edu/socy/conference/newpapers/daly.rtf.

Davenport, Christian, Hank Johnston, and Carol Mueller. 2005. *Repression and Mobilization*. Minneapolis: University of Minnesota Press.

Davis, Gerald, Doug McAdam, W. Richard Scott, and Mayer Zald. zoos. *Social Movements and Organizational Theory*. New York: Cambridge University Press.

Dawkins, Kristin. 2003. *Global Governance*. Toronto: Seven Stories.

DeBenedetti, Charles. 1980. *Peace Reform in American History*. Bloomington: Indiana University Press.

Deen, Thalif. 2002. "US Dollars Yielded Unanimous UN Vote Against Iraq." *Inter Press Service*, is November. At *www.globalpolicy.org/securitylissues/iraq/attack/2992/midolkirs.htm*.

della Porta, Donatella. 2005. "Multiple Belongings, Tolerant Identities, and the Construction of 'Another Politics': Between the European Social Forum and the Local Social Flora." Pp. 175–202 in *Transnational Protest and Global Activism*, edited by D. della Porta and S. Tarrow. Lanham, MD: Rowman & Littlefield.

della Porta, Donatella, Massimiliano Andretta, Lorenzo Mosca, and Herbert Reiter. 2006. *Globalization from Below: Transnational Activists and Protest Networks*. Minneapolis: University of Minnesota Press.

della Porta, Donatella, and Herbert Reiter. Forthcoming. "The Policing of Transnational Protest: A Conclusion." In *Policing Transnational Protest in the Aftermath of the "Battle of Seattle,"* edited by D. Della Porta, A. Peterson, and H. Reiter. Lanham, MD: Rowman & Littlefield.

della Porta, Donatella, and Dieter Rucht. 1995. "Left-Libertarian Movements in Context: A Comparison of Italy and West Germany, 1965–1990." Pp. 229–272 in *The Politics of Social Protest: Comparative Perspectives on States and Social Movements*, edited by B. Klandermans and C. Jenkins. Minneapolis: University of Minnesota Press.

Diamond, Jared. 2005. *Collapse: How Civilizations Choose to Fail or Succeed*. New York: Penguin.

Diani, Mario. 2003. "Introduction: Social Movements, Contentious Actions, and Social Networks: 'From Metaphor to Substance?'" Pp. 1–19 in *Social Movements and Networks*, edited by M. Diani and D. McAdam. Oxford. Oxford University Press.

Diani, Mario, and Ivano Bison. 2004. "Organizations, Coalitions and Movements." *Theory and Society* 33:281–309.

DiMaggio, Paul J., and Walter W. Powell. 1991. "The Iron Cage Revisited: Institutional Isomorphism and Collective Rationality in Organization Fields." Pp. 63–82 in The *New Institutionalism in Organizational Analysis*, edited by W. W. Powell and P. J. DiMaggio. Chicago: University of Chicago Press.

Doherty, Brian, and Timothy Doyle. 2006. "Friends of the Earth International: Negotiating a Transnational Identity." *Environmental Politics* 15:860–880.

Domhoff, G. William. 1998. *Who Rules America: Power and Politics in the Year 2000*. Mountain View, CA: Mayfield.

Economist, The. 2000. "A Survey of the New Economy." *The Economist* (23 September)m-I9. Economy, Elizabeth C. 2004. *The River Runs Black: The Environmental Challenge to China's Future*. Ithaca: Cornell University Press.

Edwards, Bob, and Michael Foley. 1997. "Social Capital and the Political Economy of Our Dissent." *American Behavioral Scientist* 40:668–677.

Edwards, Bob, Michael Foley, and Mario Diani, eds. 2001. *Beyond Tocqueville: Social Capital in Comparative Perspective*. Lebanon, NH: University Press of New England.

Edwards, Bob, and John D. McCarthy. 2004. "Resources and Social Movement Mobilization." Pp. 116–551 in *Blackwell Companion to Social Movements*, edited by D. A. Snow, S. A. Soule, and H. Kriesi. New York: Blackwell.

Ellison, Katherine. 2002. "Kyoto, U.S.A.: Tackling Climate Change at the Local Level." Grist *Magazine: Environmental News and Analysis*, 31 July.

Epstein, Barbara. 1991. *Political Protest and Cultural Revolution: Nonviolent Direct Action in the* 1970s *and* 1980s. Berkeley University of California Press.

Ericson, Richard, and Aaron Doyle. 1999. "Globalization and the Policing of Protest The Case of APEC 1997." *British Journal of Sociology* 50:589–608.

Escobar, Arturo. 2003. "Other Worlds Are (Already) Possible: Self-Organisation, Complexity, and Post-Capitalist Cultures." Pp. 349–358 in *Challenging Empires: The World Social Forum,* edited by J. Sen, A. Anand, A. Escobar, and P. Waterman. At www.choike.org/ nuevo_eng/informes/1557.html.

Escobar, Arturo, and Sonia E. Alvarez. 1992. *The Making of Social Movements in Latin America: Identity, Strategy, and Democracy.* Boulder, CO: Westview.

Evans, Peter B. 1997. "The Eclipse of the State? Reflections on Stateness in an Era of Globalization." *World Politics* 50:62–87.

Evans, Robert. 2000. "UN: Report Calls WTO 'Nightmare.'" *Reuters,* is August. At http:// corpwatch.org/ article.php?ic1=659.

Evans, Susan M., and Harry C. Boyt. 1986. *Free Spaces: The Sources of Democratic Change in America.* New York: Harper & Row.

Faber, Daniel. 2005. "Building a Transnational Environmental Justice Movement: Obstacles and Opportunities in the Age of Globalization." Pp. 43–68 in *Coalitions Across Borders: Transnational Protest and the Neoliberal Order,* edited by J. Bandy and J. Smith. Lanham, MD: Rowman & Litdefield.

Falk, Richard 2005. "The World Speaks on Iraq." *The Nation, 1* August. At www.thenation.corn/ doc/2005080i/fallc.

Falk, Richard, and Andrew Strauss. 2001. "Toward Global Parliament." *Foreign Affairs* 80M:212–220.

Farrell, Mary, Bjorn Hettne, and Luk Langenhove. 2005. *Global Politics and Regionalism.* London: Pluto.

Ferree, Myra Marx. 2005. "Soft Repression: Ridicule, Stigma, and Silencing in Gender-Based Movements." Pp. 138–158 in *Mobilization and Repression,* edited by C. Davenport, H. Johnston, and C. Mueller. Minneapolis: University of Minnesota Press.

Ferree, Myra Marx, William A. Gamson, Jurgen Gerhards, and Dieter Rucht. 2002. *Shaping Abortion Discourse: Democracy and the Public Sphere in Germany and the United States.* New York: Cambridge University Press.

Ferree, Myra Marx, and Beth B. Hess. 1985. *Controversy and Coalition: The New Feminist Movement.* Boston. Twayne.

Ferree, Myra Marx, and Carol Mueller. 2004. "Feminism and the Womerfs Movement: A Global Perspective." Pp. 576–607 in *The Blackwell Companion to Social Movements,* edited by D. A. Snow, S. A. Soule, and H. Kriesi. New York: Blackwell.

Fetner, Tina. 2001. "Working Anita Bryant The Impact of Christian Antigay Activism on Lesbian and Gay Movement Claims." *Social Problems* 48:411–428.

—. Forthcoming. *Fighting the Right: How the Religious Right Changed Lesbian and Gay Activism.* Minneapolis: University of Minnesota Press.

Finnemore, Martha. 1996. *National Interests in International Society.* Ithaca: Cornell University Press.

Finnemore, Martha, and Kathryn Sikkink. 1998. "International Norm Dynamics and Political Change" *International Organization* 52:887–917.

Fisher, Dana R., Kevin Stanley, David Berman, and Gina Neff 2005. "How Do Organizations Matter? Mobilization and Support for Participants at Five Globalization Protests." *Social Problems* 52:102–121.

Fisher, William, and Thomas Ponniah, eds. 2003. *Another World Is Possible: Popular Alternatives to Globalization at the World Social Forum.* New York: Zed.

Flacks, Richard. 1988. *Making History: The* American *Left* and *the American Mind.* New York: Columbia University Press.

Florini, Ann. 2003. *The Coming Democracy: New Rules for* Running *a New World.* Washington, DC: Island.

Ford Foundation. 2004. "Close to Home: Case Studies of Human Rights Work in the United States."

Foster, John ,W. 1999. "Civil Society and Multilateral Theatres." Pp. 129–195 in *Whose World Is It Anyway? Civil Society, the United Nations, and the Multilateral Future,* edited by J. W. Foster and A. Anand. Ottawa: United Nations Association of Canada.

—2005. "The Trinational Alliance Against NAFTA: Sinews of Solidarity." Pp. 209–230 in *Coalitions Across Borders: Transnational Protest and the Neoliberal Order,* edited by J. Bandy and J. Smith. Lanham, MD: Rowman & Littlefield.

Foster, John W., and Anita Anand, eds. 1999. Whose World Is It Anyway? Civil Society, the United Nations, and the Multilateral Future. Ottawa: United Nations Association of Canada.

Fox, Jonathan. 2002. "Assessing Binational Civil Society Coalitions: Lessons from the Mexico-U.S. Experience." Pp. 341–417 in Cross-Border Dialogues: U.S.-Mexico Social Movement Networking, edited by D. Brooks and J. Fox. La Jolla, CA: Center for U.S.- Mexican Studies, University of California-San Diego.

Fox, Jonathan, and L. David Brown. 1998. The Struggle for Accountability: The World Bank, NGOs, and Grassroots Movements. Cambridge, MA: MIT Press.

Frank, Robert H. 2000. Luxury Fever. Princeton: Princeton University Press.

Freeman, Jo. 1972. "The Tyranny of Structurelessness." Pp. 285–299 in Radical Feminism, edited by A. Koedt, E. Levine, and A. Rapone. New York: Quadrangle.

Friedland, Roger, and Robert R. Alford. 1991. "Bringing Society Back In: Symbols, Practices, and Institutional Contradictions." Pp. 232–263 in The New Institutionalism in Organizational Analysis, edited by W. W. Powell and P. J. DiMaggio. Chicago: University of Chicago Press.

Friedman, Elisabeth Jay, Ann Marie Clark, and Kathryn Hochstetler. 2005. Sovereignty, Democracy, and Global Civil Society: State-Society Relations at the UN World Conferences. Albany: State University of New York Press.

Friends of the Earth International. 2004. "World Bank Spins Renewable Energy Conference." Press Release, 3 June . At www.foe.co.uk/resource/press_releases/world_bank _spins_renewable_03062004.html.

Frith, Maxine. 2005. "The Ethical Revolution Sweeping Through the World's Sweatshops." Independent, 16 April. At www.commondreams.org/headlineso5/0416-or.htin.

Gaer, Felice D. 1996. "Reality Check: Human Rights NGOs Confront Governments at the UN." Pp. 51–66 in NGOs, the UN, and Global Governance, edited by T. G. Weiss and L. Gordenker. Boulder, CO: Lynne Rienner.

Gamson, William A. 1991. "Commitment and Agency in Social Movements." Sociological Forum 6:27–50.

— 1992. Talking Politics. Cambridge: Cambridge University Press.

— 2004. "Bystanders, Public Opinion, and the Media." Pp. 242–261 in The Blackwell Companion to Social Movements, edited by D. A. Snow, S. A. Soule, and H. Kriesi. Oxford: Blackwell.

Gamson, William A., David Croteau, William Hoynes, and Theodore Sasson. 1992. "Media Images and the Social Construction of Reality." Annual Review of Sociology 18:373–393.

Gamson, William A., and David Meyer. 1996. "The Framing of Political Opportunity." Pp. 275–290 in Political Opportunities, Mobilizing Structures and Framing: Social Movement Dynamics in Cross-National Perspective, edited by D. McAdam, J McCarthy, and M. Zald. New York: Cambridge University Press.

Gamson, William A., and Antonio Modigliani. 1989. "Media Discourse and Public Opinion on Nuclear Power." American Journal of Sociology 95:1–37.

George, Jane. 2005. "ICC seeks legal ruling against U S on dimate change: ICC petition alleges violation of Inuit human rights." Nunatsiaq News, vol. 2006. At www.nunatsiaq.cominews/nunavut/51209_04.html.

Gerhards, Jurgen, and Dieter Rucht. 1992. "Mesomobilization Contexts: Organizing and Framing in Two Protest Campaigns in West Germany." American Journal of Sociology 98:555–596.

Gertz, Emily. 2005. "The Snow Must Go On: Inuit Fight Climate Change with Human-Rights Claim against U S" Grist Magazine: Environmental News and Commentary (Online), 26 July. At www.gristorginews/maindish/2005/07/26/gertz-inuit/index.html.

Giddens, Anthony. 1990. The Consequences of Modernity. Stanford: Stanford University Press.

Gillham, Patrick F. 2003. "Mobilizing for Global Justice: Social Movement Organization Involvement in Three Contentious Episodes, 1999–2001." Ph.D. Dissertation, University of Colorado, Boulder.

Glasius, Marlies. 2002. "Expertise in the Cause of Justice: Global Civil Society Influence on the Statute for an International Criminal Court." Pp. 137–169 in Global Civil Society Yearbook, 2002, edited by M. Glasius, M. Kaldor, and H. Anheier. Oxford: Oxford University Press.

Glasius, Marlies, and Mary Kaldor. 2002. "The State of Global Civil Society: Before and After September is." Pp. 3–34 in Global Civil Society Yearbook, 2002, edited by M. Glasius, M. Kaldor, and H. Anheier. Oxford: Oxford University Press.

Glasius, Marlies, and Jill Timms. 2006. "The Role of Social Forums in Global Civil Sodety: Radical Beacon or Strategic Infrastructure." Pp. 190–239 in Global Civil Society Yearbook 2005/6, edited by M. Glasius, M. Kaldor, and H. Anheier. Thousand Oaks, CA: Sage.

Goldman, Michael. 2005. Imperial Nature: The World Bank and Struggles for Social Justice in the Age of Globalization. New Haven: Yale University Press.

Goldstone, Jack A., ed. 2003. *States, Parties and Social Movements*. New York: Cambridge University Press.

Gowan, Peter 2004. "UN-U.S." In *Presentation at the European Social Forum*. London. Greenberg, Josh, and Graham Knight. 2004. "Framing Sweatshops: Nike, Global Production, and the American News Media." *Communication and Critical/Cultural Studies* 1:151–175.

Greenberg, Michael R., David B. Sachsman, Peter M. Sandman, and Kandice L. Salomone. 1989. "Risk, Drama and Geography in Coverage of Environmental Risk by Network TV." *Journalism* Quarterly 66:267–276.

Guardian, The. 2005. "Editorial: Climate Change US Grassroots Revolt," 17 May. At www. guardian.co.uk/ climatechange/story/o,12374,485651,00.html.

Guidry, John A. 2000. "The Useful State? Social Movements and the Citizenship of Children in Brazil." Pp. 147–180 in *Globalizations and Social Movements: Culture, Power, and the Transnational Public Sphere*, edited by J. A. Guidry, M. D. Kennedy, and M. N. Zald. Ann Arbor: University of Michigan Press.

Guidry, John A., Michael D. Kennedy, and Mayer N. Zald. 2000. "Globalizations and Social Movements: Introduction." Pp. 1–32 in *Globalizations and Social Movements: Culture, Power, and the Global Public Sphere*, edited by J. A. Guidry, M. D. Kennedy, and M. N. Zald. Ann Arbor: University of Michigan Press.

Haddon, Heather. 2000. "Poor People's Summit Grounds Global Community in NYC." Independent Media Center, New York, zo November. At http://projects.is.asu.edu/ pipermail/hpn/z000-November/oc1995. html.

Haines, Herbert. 1988. *Black Radicals and the Civil Rights Mainstream, 1954–1970*. Knoxville: University of Tennessee Press.

Halperin, Sandra, and Gordon Laxer. 2003. "Effective Resistance to Corporate Globalization." Pp. 1–23 in *Global Civil Society and Its Limits*, edited by G. Laxer and S. Halperin. New York: Palgrave Macmillan.

Hamm, Brigitte I. 2001. "A Human Rights Approach to Development." Human Rights Quarterly 23:1005–1031.

Hanagan, Michael. 2002. "Irish Transnational Social Movements, Migrants, and the State System." Pp. 53–74 in *Globalization and Resistance: Transnational Dimensions of Social Movements*, edited by J. Smith and H. Johnston. Boulder, CO: Rowman & Littlefield. Hannan, Michael T., and John Freeman. 1977. "The Population Ecology of Organizations." *American Journal of Sociology* 82:929–964.

Hardt, Michael. 2004. "Today's Bandung?" Pp. 230–236 in A Movement of Movements: Is Another World Really Possible? edited by T. Mertes. London: Verso.

Hayden, Tom. 2004. "Talking Back to the Global Establishment." *Alternet*, 18 January. At www.alternetorg/ story/r7593/.

Herman, Edward. 1995. Triumph of the Market: Essays on Economics, Politics, and the Media. Boston: South End.

Herman, Edward, and Noam Chomsky. 1988. *Manufacturing Consent*. New York: Pantheon. Hertz, Noreena. 2001. *The Silent Takeover: Global Capitalism and the Death of Democracy*. New York: The Free Press.

Hill, Tony. 2004. "Three Generations of UN-Civil Society Relations: A Quick Sketch." Civil Society Observer, April.

Hippler, Jochen. 1995. The Democratisation of Disempowerment: The Problem of Democracy in the Third World. East Haven, CT Pluto with Transnational Institute.

Hobbs, J., I. Khan, M. Posner, and K. Roth. 2003. "Letter to Louise Frechette raising concerns on UN Global Compact," 7 April. At http://web.amnesty.org/pages/ec_briefings _globaL7April03.

Hochschild, Adam. 1998. *King Leopold's Ghost*. New York: Houghton Mifflin.

Hoge, Warren. 2004. "Latin Americans Losing Hope in Democracy, Report Says." New York Times, 22 April, 3A.

Hutton, Will. 2003. A Declaration of Interdependence: Why America Should Join the World. New York: W. W. Norton.

Imig, Doug, and Sidney Tarrow. 2001. Contentious Europeans: Protest and Politics in an Integrating Europe Lanham, MD: Rowman & Littlefield.

Indigenous Peoples' Caucus. 2000. "Indigenous Peoples' Seattle Declaration." Pp. 85–91 in *Globalize This! The Battle Against the World Trade Organization and Corporate Rule*, edited by K. Danaher and R. Burbach. Monroe, ME: Common Courage.

International Forum on Globalization. 2002. Alternatives to Economic Globalization: A Better World Is Possible. New York: Berrett-Kohler.

International Network for Economic Social and Cultural Rights. 2005. "History of UN Norms for Business Campaign." At www.escr-netorg/EngGeneral/unnormstasp.

Inuit Circumpolar Conference-Canada. 2005. "Inuit Petition Inter-American Commission on Human Rights to Oppose Climate Change Caused by the United States of America." Vol. 2005.

Iyengar, Shanto. 1991. *Is Anyone Responsible? How Television Frames Political Issues*. Chicago: University of Chicago Press.

Jackson, Hunter. 2005. "The Blossoming of the Green Economy." Global Exchange Newsletter 64(3):3.

Jacobson, David, and Galya Benarieh Ruffer. 2003. "Courts Across Borders: The Implications of Judicial Agency for Human Rights and Democracy." *Human Rights Quarterly* 25:74–92.

Jawara, Fatoumata, and Aileen Kwa. 2003. *Behind the Scenes at the WTO: The Real World of International Trade Negotiations*. New York: Zed and Focus on the Global South. Jenkins, J. Craig, and Charles Perrow. 1977. "Insurgency of the Powerless: Farm Worker Movements." American Sociological Review 42:249–268.

Joachim, Jutta. 2003. "Framing Issues and Seizing Opportunities: The UN, NGOs and Women's Rights." *International Studies Quarterly* 47:247–274.

Johansen, Robert C. 2006. "The Impact of US Policy toward the International Criminal Court on the Prevention of Genocide, War Crimes, and Crimes Against Humanity." *Human Rights Quarterly* 28: 301–331.

Johnston, Josee, and Gordon Laxer. 2003. "Solidarity in the Age of Globalization: Lessons from the Anti-MAI and Zapatista Struggles." Theory and Society 32:39–91.

Jordan, Lisa, and Peter van Tuijl. 2000. "Political Responsibility in Transnational NGO Advocacy." World Development 28:2051–2065.

Juris, Jeffrey Scott. 2004. "Digital Age Activism: Anti-Corporate Globalization and the Cultural Politics of Transnational Networking." Ph.D. Dissertation, University of California-Berkeley.

—. 2008. *Networking Futures: The Movements Against Corporate Globalization*. Durham, NC: Duke University Press.

Kaldor, Mary. 2003. *Global Civil Society: An Answer to War*. Cambridge: Polity.

Karliner, Joshua. 1997. *The Corporate Planet: Ecology and Politics in the Age of Globalization*. San Francisco: Sierra Club.

Katz, Hagai, and Helmut Anheier. 2006. "Global Connectedness: The Structure of Trans-national NGO Networks." Pp. 240–265 in *Global Civil Society 2005/6*, edited by M. Glasius, M. Kaldor, and H. Anheier. London: Sage.

Keck, Margaret, and Kathryn Sikkink. 1998. *Activists Beyond Borders*. Ithaca: Cornell University Press.

Kelly, Dominic. 2005. "'Markets for a Better World?' Implications of the Public-Private Partnership Between the International Chamber of Commerce and the United Nations." International Studies Association Annual Meeting, Chicago, 22–24 February.

Kensington Welfare Rights Union Education Committee. 2002. "Why We're Fighting for Economic Human Rights." Independent Media Center, Philadelphia *(www.phillyimc.org)*, so April. At *www.nasw-pa.org/displaycommon.rn?an=rksubsrticlenbr=62* (Archived).

Kent, Deirdre. 2005. *Healthy Money Healthy Planet: Developing Sustainability Through New Money Systems*. Nelson, New Zealand: Craig Potton.

Keraghel, Chloe, and Jai Sen. 2004. "Explorations in Open Space: The World Social Forum and Cultures of Politics." *International Social Science Journal* 182:483–494. Khagram, Sanjeev. 2004. *Dams and Development: Transnational Struggles for Water and Power*. Ithaca Cornell University Press.

Khasnabish, Alex. 2004. "Globalizing Hope: The Resonance of Zapatismo and the Political Imagination(s) of Transnational Activism." Working Paper, Institute on Globalization and the Human Condition, McMaster University, Hamilton, Ontario. At http:// globalization.mcmaster.ca/wps/Khasnabish.pdf.

—. 2005. "'You Will No Longer Be You, Now You Are Us': Zapatismo, Transnational Activism, and the Political Imagination." Ph.D. Dissertation, McMaster University, Hamilton, Ontario.

Khor, Martin. 2000. "How the South is Getting a Raw Deal at the WTO." Pp. 7–53 in *Views from the South: The Effects of Globalization and the WTO on Third World Countries*, edited by S. Anderson. Chicago: Food First.

Kielbowicz, Richard B., and Clifford Scherer. 1986. "The Role of the Press in the Dynamics of Social Movements." Pp. 71–96 in *Research in Social Movements, Conflict and Change*, vol. 9, edited by L. Kriesberg. Greenwich, CT: JAI.

Kim, Sunhyuk, and Phillippe C. Schmitter. 2005. "The Experience of European Integration and Potential for Northeast Asian Integration." *Asian Perspective* 29:5–39. Kingdon, John W. 1984. *Agendas, Alternatives and Public Policies*. Boston: Little, Brown. Kingfisher, Catherine. 2003. *Western Welfare in Decline: Globalization and Women's Poverty*. Philadelphia: University of Pennsylvania Press.

Kitchelt, Herbert. 2003. "Landscapes of Political Interest Intermediation: Social Movements, Interest Groups, and Parties in the Early Twenty-First Century." Pp. 81–104 in *Social Movements and Democracy*, edited by P. Ibarra. New York: Palgrave Macmillan.

Klein, Naomi. 1999. *No Logo: Taking Aim at the Brand Name Bullies*. New York: Picador.

Kolb, Felix. 2005. "The Impact of Transnational Protest on Social Movement Organizations: Mass Media and the Making of ATTAC Germany." Pp. 95–119 in *Transnational Protest and Global Activism*, edited by D. della Porta and S. Tarrow. Lanham, MD: Row-man & Littlefield.

—. 2007. *Protest, Opportunities, and Mechanisms: A Theory of Social Movements and Political Change*. New York: Campus Verlag.

Koopmans, Ruud. 2005. "Repression and the Public Sphere: Discursive Opportunities for Repression against the Extreme Right in Germany in the 1990s." Pp. 159–188 in *Mobilization and Repression*, edited by C. Davenport, H. Johnston, and C. Mueller. Minneapolis: University of Minnesota Press.

Korten, David. 1996. *When Corporations Rule the World*. West Hartford: Kumarian.

—. 1997. "Memo to United Nations General Assembly President, Mr. Razali Ismail." People Centered Development Forum. At *www.pcdflorg/1997/UNfacs.htm*.

Korzeniewicz, Roberto Patricio, and Timothy P. Moran. 1997. "World Economic Trends in the Distribution of Income, 1965–1992." *American Journal of Sociology* 105:1000–1039.

Korzeniewicz, Roberto Patricio, and William C Smith. 2000. "Poverty, Inequality, and Growth in Latin America: Searching for the High Road to Globalization." *Latin American Research Review* 35(3)7–54.

—. 2001. "Protest and Collaboration: Transnational Civil Society Networks and the Politics of Summitry and Free Trade in the Americas." North-South Center, University of Miami, Miami.

Kriesberg, Louis. 1997. "Social Movements and Global Transformation." Pp. 3–18 in *Transnational Social Movements and World Politics: Solidarity Beyond the State*, edited by J. Smith, C. Chatfield, and R. Pagnucco. Syracuse: Syracuse University Press.

Kriesi, Hanspeter. 1996. "Organizational Development of New Social Movements in a Political Contexts." Pp. 152–184 in *Political Opportunities, Mobilizing Structures and Framing: Social Movement Dynamics in Cross-National Perspective*, edited by D. McAdam, J. McCarthy, and M. Zald. New York: Cambridge University Press.

— 2004. "Political Context and Opportunity." Pp. 67–90 in *The Blackwell Companion to Social Movements*, edited by D. A. Snow, S. A. Soule, and H. Kriesi. Oxford: Blackwell.

Kriesi, Hanspeter, Ruud Koopmans, Jan Willem Duyvendak, and Marco Giugni. 1995. *New Social Movements in Western Europe: A Comparative Analysis*. Minneapolis: University of Minnesota Press.

Krut, Riva. 1997. "Globalization and Civil Society: NGO Influence on International Decision Making." UN Research Institute for Social Development, Geneva.

Kunstler, James Howard. 1996. "Home from Nowhere." *Atlantic Monthly* 278(3):43–66.

Langman, Lauren. 2005. "From Virtual Public Spheres to Global Justice: A Critical Theory of Intemetworked Social Movements." *Sociological Theory* 23:42–74.

Laxer, Gordon, and Sandra Halperin. 2003. *Global Civil Society and Its Limits*. New York: Palgrave Macmillan.

Levy, Marc A., Robert O. Keohane, and Peter M. Haas. 1993. "Improving the Effectiveness of International Environmental Institutions." Pp. 397–426 in *Institutions for the Earth: Sources of Effective International Environmental Protection*, edited by P. Haas, R. Keohane, and M. Levy. Cambridge, MA: MIT Press.

Lichbach, Mark, and Paul Almeida. 2005. "Global Order and Local Resistance: The Neo-liberal Institutional Trilemma and the Battle of Seattle." Manuscript, University of California, Riverside.

Lichterman, Paul. 1995. "Piecing Together Multicultural Community: Cultural Differences in Community Building Among Grass-Roots Environmentalists." *Social Problems* 42:513–534.

—. 1996: *The Search for Political* Community: American *Activists Reinventing Commitment.* New York: Cambridge University Press.

Linz, Juan J., and Alfred Stepan. 1996. *Problems of Democratic Transition and Consolidation: Southern Europe, South America, and Post-Communist Europe.* Baltimore: Johns Hopkins University Press.

Lipsky, Michael. 1968. "Protest as a Political Resource." *American Political Science Review* 62:1144–1158.

Livezey, Lowell W. 1989. "U.S. Religious Organizations and the International Human Rights Movement." *Human Rights* Quarterly 1E14–81.

Luders, Joseph. 2003. "Countermovements, the State, and the Intensity of Racial Contention in the American South." Pp. 27–44 in *States, Parties and Social Movements,* edited by J. A. Goldstone. New York: Cambridge University Press.

MacDonald, Laura. 1997. *Supporting Civil Society: The Political Role of Non-Governmental Organizations in Central America.* New York: St. Martin's.

—. 2005. "Gendering Transnational Social Movement Analysis: Women's Groups Contest Free Trade in the Americas." Pp. 21–42 in *Coalitions Across Borders: Transnational Protest and the Neoliberal Order,* edited by J. Bandy and J. Smith. Lanham, MD: Rowman & Littlefield.

Malamud, Andres. 2004. "Regional Integration in Latin America: Comparative Theories and Institutions." *Sociologia-Problemas e Practices* 44:135–154.

Malhotra, Kamal, and others. 2003. *Making Global Trade Work for People.* London: Earth-scan in cooperation with the United Nations Development Program, Heinrich Boll Foundation, The Rockefeller Foundation, and The Wallace Fund.

Mander, Jerry, and Edward Goldsmith. 1996. *The Case Against the Global Economy and for a Turn Towards the Local.* San Francisco: Sierra Club.

Maney, Gregory M. 2001. "Rival Transnational Networks and Indigenous Rights: The San Blas Kuna in Panama and the Yanomami in Brazil." *Research in Social Movements, Conflicts and Change* 23:103–144.

Markoff, John. 1996. *Waves of Democracy: Social Movements and Political Change.* Thousand Oaks, CA: Pine Forge.

—. 1999. "Globalization and the Future of Democracy." *Journal of World-Systems Research* 5:242–262.

— 2001. "The Internet and Electronic Communications." Pp. 387–395 in *Encyclopedia of American Cultural and Intellectual History, vol.* 3, edited by M. K. Cayton and P. W. Williams. New York: Scribner's.

— 2004a. "Democracy." In *Encyclopedia of Social Theory,* volume II, edited by G. Ritzer. Thousand Oaks, CA: Sage.

—. 2004b "Who Will Construct the Global Order?" Pp. 19–36 in *Transnational Democracy,* edited by B. Williamson. London: Ashgate.

Markoff, John, and Veronica Montecinos. 1993. "The Ubiquitous Rise of Economists." *Journal of Public Policy* 13:37–68.

Marks, Gary, Liesbet Hooghe, and Kermit Blank. 1994. "European Integration and the State." American Political Science Association Meetings, New York, 1–3 September.

Martens, Jens. 2003. *Precarious "Partnerships": Six Problems of the Global Compact between Business and the UN.* New York: Global Policy Forum. At *www.globalpolicy.org/reform/ business/zoo4/o623partnerships.htm.*

Marullo, Sam, Ron Pagnucco, and Jackie Smith. 1996. "Frame Changes and Social Movement Contraction: U.S. Peace Movement Framing After the Cold War." *Sociological Inquiry* 66:1–28.

Massamba, Guy, Samuel M. Kariuld, and Stephen N. Ndegwa. 2004. "Globalization and Africa's Regional and Local Responses." *Journal of Asian and African Studies* 39:29–45.

Mayo, Marjorie. 2005. *Global Citizens: Social Movements* and *the Challenge of Globalization.* New York: Zed and Canadian Scholars' Press.

McAdam, Doug. 1982. *Political Process and the Development of Black Insurgency.* Chicago: University of Chicago Press.

—. 1988. *Freedom* Summer. New York: Oxford University Press.

McAdam, Doug, John D. McCarthy, and Mayer Zald, eds. 1996. *Comparative Perspectives on Social Movements: Political Opportunities, Mobilizing* Structures and *Cultural Framings.* New York: Cambridge University Press.

McAdam, Doug, and Ronnelle Paulsen. 1993. "Specifying the Relationship between Social Ties and Activism." *American Journal of Sociology* 99:640–667.

McAdam, Doug, and Dieter Rucht. 1993. "The Cross-National Diffusion of Movement Ideas." *The Annals of the American Academy of Political and Social Science* 528:56–74.

McAdam, Doug, Sidney Tarrow, and Charles Tilly. 2001. *Dynamics of Contention*. New York: Cambridge University Press.

McCarthy, John D. 1987. "Pro-Life and Pro-Choice Mobilization: Infrastructure Deficits and New Technologies." Pp. 49–66 in *Social Movements in an Organizational Society*, edited by M. Zald and J. D. McCarthy. New Brunswick, NJ: Transaction.

—. 1994. "The Interaction of Grass-roots Activists and State Actors in the Production of an Anti-Drunk Driving Media Attention Cycle." Pp. 133–167 in *New Social Movements: From Ideology to Identity*, edited by E. Larana, H. Johnston, and J. Gusfield Philadelphia: Temple University Press.

—. 1996. "Constraints and Opportunities in Adopting, Adapting and Inventing." Pp. 141–151 in *Comparative Perspectives on Social Movements: Political Opportunities, Mobilizing Structures and* Cultural *Framings*, edited by D. McAdam, J. McCarthy, and M. Zald. New York: Cambridge University Press.

McCarthy, John D., Clark McPhail, and Jackie Smith. 1996b. "Images of Protest: Selection Bias in Media Coverage of Washington, D.C. Demonstrations." *American Sociological Review* 61:478–499.

McCarthy, John D., Jackie Smith, and Mayer Zald. 1996a. "Accessing Media, Electoral and Government Agendas." Pp. 291–311 in *Comparative Perspectives on Social Movements: Political Opportunities, Mobilizing Structures and Cultural* Framings, edited by D. McAdam, J. McCarthy, and M. Zald New York: Cambridge University Press.

McCarthy, John D., and Mark Wolfson. 1992. "Consensus Movements, Conflict Movements, and the Cooptation of Civic and State Infrastructures." Pp. 273–300 in *Frontiers in Social Movement Theory*, edited by A. Morris and C. M. Mueller. New Haven, CT: Yale University Press.

McChesney, Robert W. 1999. *Rich Media, Poor Democracy: Communication Politics in Dubious Times.* Champaign-Urbana: University of Illinois Press.

McCright, Aaron, and Riley Dunlap. 2003. "Defeating Kyoto: The Conservative Movement's Impact on U.S. Climate Change Policy." *Social Problems* 50:348–373. McKenna, Brian. 2005. "Dow Chemical Buys Silence in Michigan." *Counterpunch*, 18 April 2005.

McMichael, Philip. 2003. *Development and Social Change: A Global Perspective*. 3rd ed. Thousand Oaks, CA: Pine Forge.

Meade, Geoff. 2005. " 'McLiber Campaigners Win Legal Aid Battle." *Independent*. UK. At http://news.independent.co.uk/europe/artidei1256.ece.

Mendez, Juan E., and Javier Mariezcurrena. 1999. "Accountability for Past Human Rights Violations: Contributions of the Inter-American Organs for Protection." *Social Justice* 26:84–107.

Mertes, Tom. 2004. *A Movement of Movements: Is Another World Really Possible?* London: Verso.

Meyer, David, and Suzanne Staggenborg. 1996. "Movements, Countermovements, and the Structure of Political Opportunity." *American Journal of Sociology* 101:1628–1660.

Meyer, John W., John Boli, George M. Thomas, and Francisco O. Ramirez. 1997. "World Society and the Nation-State." *American Journal of Sociology* 103:144–181.

Meyerson, Frederick A. B. 2002. "Burning the Bridge to the 21st Century: The End of the Era of Integrated Conferences?" *Population, Environmental Change and Security Newsletter (PECS)a*, 12.

Mills, C. Wright. 1956. *The Power Elite*. New York: Oxford University Press.

Minkoff, Debra C. 1995. *Organizing for Equality: The Evolution of Women's and Racial Ethnic Organizations in America, 1955–1985*. New Brunswick, NJ: Rutgers University Press. Minkoff, Debra C., and John D. McCarthy. 2005. "Reinvigorating the Study of Organizational Processes in Social Movements." *Mobilization* 10:401–421.

Moghadam, Valentine. 2000. "Transnational Feminist Networks: Collective Action in an Era of Globalization." *International Sociology* 15:57–85.

—. 2005. *Globalizing Women: Transnational Feminist Networks*. Baltimore: Johns Hopkins University Press.

Monbiot, George. 2003. *The Age of Consent: A Manifesto for a New World Order*. London: Harper Perennial.

Moody, Kim. 1997. *Workers in a Lean World: Unions in the International Economy*. New York: Verso.

Mooney, Chris. 2004. "Blinded by Science." *Columbia Journalism Review*. Vol. 6. At www.cjr.org/issues/2004/6/mooney-science.asp.

Morris, Douglas. 2004. "Globalization and Media Democracy: The Case of Indymedia." In *Shaping the Network Society: The New Role of Civil Society in Cyberspace,* edited by D. Schuler and P. Day. Cambridge, MA: MIT Press.

Munck, Ronaldo. 2002. *Globalization* and *Labour: The New* Great Transformation. London: Zed. Murphy, Gillian, and Margaret Levi. 2004. "Coalitions of Contention: The Case of the WTO Protests in Seattle." Seattle, WA.

Nanz, Patrizia, and Jens Steffek. 2004. "Global Governance, Participation and the Public Sphere." *Government and Opposition* 39:314–335.

Nelson, Paul. 1995. The *World Bank and Nongovernmental Organizations: The Limits of Apolitical Development.* New York: St. Martirfs.

— 2001. "Multilateral Development Banks, Transparency and Corporate Globalization." Presented at International Studies Association Annual Meeting, Chicago, 21–24 February.

Nepstad, Sharon Erickson. 2002. "Creating Transnational Solidarity: The Use of Narrative in the U.S.-Central America Peace Movement." Pp. 133–152 in *Globalization and Resistance: Transnational Dimensions of Social Movements,* edited by J. Smith and H. Johnston. Lanham, MD: Rowman & Littlefield.

Niman, Michael I. 2001. "Buy Nothing Day." Alternet, 12 November. At http://alternet.org/story/H9oi/.

Nimtz, August. 2002. "Marx and Engels: The Prototypical Transnational Actors." Pp. 245–268 in *Restructuring World Politics: The Power of Transnational Agency and Norms,* edited by S. Khagram, J. Riker, and K. Sikkink. Minneapolis: University of Minnesota Press.

Norris, Pippa. 2002. *Democratic Phoenix: Reinventing Political Activism.* New York: Cambridge University Press.

NYC Indymedia. 2000. "Report on New York City Poor People's Summit." November. New York Indymedia. At www.indymedia.nyc.org.

Nye, Joseph S., Jr. 2002. *The Paradox of American Power: Why the World's Only Superpower Can't Go It Alone.* New York: Oxford University Press.

Oberschall, Anthony. 1980. "Loosely Structured Collective Conflict: A Theory and an Application." *Research in Social Movements, Conflict and Change* 3:45–68.

O'Brien, Robert. 2002. "Organizational Politics, Multilateral Economic Organizations and Social Policy." *Global Social Policy* 2:141–161.

—. Forthcoming. *The Global Labour Movement.*

O'Brien, Robert, Anne Marie Goetz, Jan Aard Scholte, and Marc Williams, 2000. *Contesting Global Governance: Multilateral Economic Institutions and Global Social Movements.* New York: Cambridge University Press.

Oliver, Pamela E., and Hank Johnston. 2000. "What a Good Idea! Ideologies and Frames in Social Movement Research." *Mobilization: An International Journal* 5:37–54.

Olsen, Thomas. 2005. *International Zapatismo: The Construction of Solidarity in the Age of Globalization.* New York: Zed.

O'Neill, Kate. 2004. "Transnational Protest: States, Circuses, and Conflict at the Frontline of Global Politics." *International Studies Review* 6:233–251.

Ostry, Sylvia. 2007. "The World Trade Organization: System Under Stress." In *Globalisation and Autonomy,* edited by S. Bernstein. Vancouver: University of British Columbia Press.

Otto, Dianne. 1996. "Nongovernmental Organizations in the United Nations System: The Emerging Role of International Civil Society." *Human Rights Quarterly* 18:107–141.

Pagnucco, Ron, and Jackie Smith. 1993. "The Peace Movement and the Formulation of U.S. Foreign Policy." *Peace and Change* 18:157–181.

Paine, Ellen. 2000. "The Road to the Global Compact: Corporate Power and the Battle over Global Public Policy at The United Nations." Global Policy Forum. At www.globalpolicy.org/reform/papers/2000/road.htm.

Parsons, Craig. 2003. *A Certain Idea of Europe.* Ithaca: Cornell University Press.

Patomald, Heikki, and Teivo Teivainen. 2004. "The World Social Forum: An Open Space or a Movement of Movements?" *Theory, Culture at Society* 21:145–154.

Paul, James. 1999. "NGO Access at the UN." Vol. 2005. New York: Global Policy Forum. Paul, Scott. 2005. "Mayors Look to Youth and Forge Ahead." At www.itsgettinghotinhere.org/archives/so6.

Pauly, Louis. 1997. *Who Elected the Bankers? Surveillance and Control in the World Economy.* Ithaca: Cornell University Press.

Peet, Richard. 2003. *Unholy Trinity: The IMF, World Bank and WTO.* New York: Zed. Peoples' Global Action. 2000. "Worldwide Resistance Roundup: Newsletter 'Inspired by' Peoples' Global Action." London.

Peterson, Luke Eric. 2004. "Bilateral Investment Treaties and Development Policy-Making." International Institute for Sustainable Development and Swiss Agency for Development and Cooperation, Winnipeg. At www.iisd.org/publications/pub.aspx?id=658.

Pianta, Mario, and Federico Silva. 2003. "Parallel Summits of Global Civil Society: An Update." Pp. 387–394 in *Global Civil Society Yearbook, 2003,* edited by H. Anheier, M. Kaldor, and M. Glasius. London.

Podobnik, Bruce. 2005. "Resistance to Globalization: Cycles and Evolutions in the Globalization Protest Movement." Pp. 51–68 in *Transforming Globalization: Challenges and Opportunities in the Post 9/11 Era,* edited by B. Podobnik and T. Reifer. Boston: Brill. Polanyi, Karl. 1944. *The Great Transformation.* Boston: Beacon.

Polletta, Francesca. 2002. *Freedom is an Endless Meeting.* Chicago: University of Chicago Press. Polletta, Francesca, and James Jasper. 2001. "Collective Identity and Social Movements." *Annual Review of Sociology* 27:283–305.

Porter, Tony. 2005. *Globalization and Finance.* Malden, MA: Polity.

Powell, Walter W., and Paul J. DiMaggio. 1991. *The New Institutionalism in Organizational Analysis.* Chicago: University of Chicago Press.

Price, Richard. 1998. "Reversing the Gun Sights: Transnational Civil Society Targets Land Mines." *International Organization* 52:613–644.

Pring, George W., and Penelope Canan. 1996. *SLAPPs: Getting Sued for Speaking Out.* Philadelphia: Temple University Press.

Putnam, Robert D. 1992. *Making Democracy Work.* Cambridge: Cambridge University Press.

—. 1995. "Bowling Alone: America's Declining Social Capital." *Journal of Democracy* 6:65–78.

Rabkin, Jeremy. 2003. "Why The Left Dominates NGO Advocacy Networks." Presented at conference, "We're Not from the Government, but We're Here to Help You Nongovernmental Organizations: The Growing Power of an Unelected Few." Washington D.C.: American Enterprise Institute. At http://www.aeLorg/events/eventID.329,filter./ event_detail.asp#.

Radcliff, Benjamin, and Patricia Davis. 2000. "Labor Organization and Electoral Participation in Industrial Democracies." *American Journal of Political Science* 44:132–141.

Reimann, Kim D. 2002. "Building Networks from the Outside In: International Movements, Japanese NGOs, and the Kyoto Climate Change Conference." Pp. 173–189 in *Globalization and Resistance: Transnational Dimensions of Social Movements,* vol. 6, edited by J. Smith and H. Johnston. Lanham, MD: Rowman & Littlefield.

Reitan, Ruth. 2006. *Activism Goes Global: The Internationalization of Activism against Neoliberal Globalization and the Role of the World Social Forum in This Process.* London: Routledge.

—. 2007. "The Global Anti-War Network and the World Social Forum: A Study of Transnational Mobilization." Presented at the International Studies Association (ISA) Convention, Chicago, 28 February-3 March.

Renner, Michael. 2006. "Worldwide Mergers and Acquisitions 1980–1999." At www.globalpolicy.org/socecon/tncs/tables/mergdata.htm.

Revkin, Andrew C. 2005. "Youths Make Spirited Case at Climate Meeting." *New York Times,* 9 December. At www.nytimes.com/2005/12/09/international/americas/o9dimate.html ?ex=12917844008cen=b68ab 9co1737cof8&ei=5089&partner=rssyahoo8cemc=rss.

Rich, Bruce. 1994. *Mortgaging the Earth: The World Bank, Environmental Impoverishment and the Crisis of Development.* Boston: Beacon.

Riles, Annelise. 2001. *The Network Inside Out.* Ann Arbor. University of Michigan Press.

Risse, Thomas, Stephen C. Ropp, and Kathryn Sildcink. 1999. *The Power of Human Rights: International Norms and Domestic Change.* New York: Cambridge University Press.

Robinson, William. 1996. *Promoting Polyarchy: Globalization, U.S. Intervention and Hegemony.* Cambridge: Cambridge University Press.

— 2004. *A Theory of Global Capitalism.* Baltimore: Johns Hopkins University Press.

Rochon, Thomas. 1998. *Culture Moves: Ideas, Activism, and Changing Values*. Princeton: Princeton University Press.

Rootes, Christopher. 2002. "Global Visions: Global Civil Society and the Lessons of European Environmentalism." *Voluntas: International Journal of Voluntary and Nonprofit Organizations* 20: 411–429.

—. 2005. "A Limited Transnationalization? The British Environmental Movement." Pp. 21–43 in *Transnational Protest and Global Activism*, edited by D. della Porta and S. Tarrow. Lanham, MD: Rowman & Littlefield.

Rose, Fred. 2000. *Coalitions Across the Class Divide: Lessons from the Labor, Peace, and Environmental Movements*. Ithaca: Cornell University Press.

Rosenthal, Naomi, Meryl Fingrutd, Michele Ethier, Roberta Karant, and David McDonald. 5985. "Social Movements and Network Analysis: A Case Study of Nineteenth-Century Women's Reform in New York State." *American Journal of Sociology* 90:1022–1054.

Rothman, Franklin Daniel, and Pamela E. Oliver. 2002. "From Local to Global: The Anti-Dam Movement in Southern Brazil 1979–1992." Pp. 115–131 in *Globalization and Resistance: Transnational Dimensions of Social Movements*, edited by J. Smith and H. Johnston. Lanham, MD: Rowman & Littlefield.

Rucht, Dieter. 1996. "The Impact of National Contexts on Social Movement Structures: A Cross-Movement and Cross-National Comparison." Pp. 185–204 in *Political Opportunities*, Mobilizing Structures and Framing: *Social Movement Dynamics in Cross-National Perspective*, edited by D. McAdam, J. McCarthy, and M. Zald. New York Cambridge University Press.

—. 2000. "Distant Issue Movements in Germany: Empirical Description and The oretical Reflections." Pp. 76–107 in *Globalizations and Social Movements: Culture, Power, and the Transnational Public Sphere*, edited by J. A. Guidry, M. D. Kennedy, and M. N. Zald. Ann Arbor. University of Michigan Press.

— 2003. "Social Movements Challenging Neo-liberal Globalization." Pp. 211–227 in *Social Movements and Democracy*, edited by P. Ibarra. New York: Palgrave Macmillan.

—. 2004. "Movements, Allies, Adversaries, and Third Parties." Pp. 197–216 in *The Blackwell Companion to Social Movements*, edited by D. A. Snow, S. A. Soule, and H. Kriesi. Oxford: Blackwell.

Rudra, Nita. 2002. "Globalization and the Dedine of the Welfare State in Less-Developed Countries." *International Organization* 56:411–445.

Ruggie, John G. 2002. "The Theory and Practice of Learning Networks: Corporate Social Responsibility and the Global Compact." *Journal of Corporate Citizenship* (Spring): 27–36.

Rupert, Mark. 2000. *Ideologies of Globalization: Contending Visions of a New World Order*. New York: Routledge.

Rupp, Leila J. 1997. *Worlds of Women: The Making of an International Women's Movement*. Princeton: Princeton University Press.

Ryan, Charlotte. 1991. *Prime Time Activism*. Boston: South End.

Sands, Philippe. 2005. *Lawless World:* America *and the Making and Breaking of Global Rules-From F DR's Atlantic Charter to George W Bush's Illegal War*. New York: Viking. Sassen, Saskia. 1998. *Globalization and Its Discontents*. New York: The New Press.

Schell, Jonathan. 2005. "Faking Civil Society." *The Nation*, 25 April. At www.commondreams.org/views05/0407-2r.htm.

Schlosberg, Justin. 2006. "The Day the Music Failed: A Reflection on 6 Months after the Live8 Concerts, the Broken Promises and Bob's Unusual Silence." CommonDreams .org. At www.commondreams.org/views06/0105-35.htm.

Schonleitner, Gunther. 2003. "World Social Forum: Making Another World Possible?" Pp. 127–149 in *Globalizing Civic Engagement: Civil Society and Transnational Action*, edited by J. Clark. London: Earthscan.

Schor, Juliet B. 1993. *The Overworked American: The Unexpected Decline of Leisure*. New York: Basic.

—. 2004. *Born to Buy: The Commercialized Child and the New Consumer Culture*. New York: Scribner.

Schreinemacher, Elisabeth. 2005. "IPS Honours Anti-Poverty Alliance." Inter *Press Service News*, 8 December. At www.ipsnews.net.

Schroyer, Trent. 1997. A *World that Works: Building Blocks for a Just and Sustainable Society*. New York: Bootstrap.

Schulz, Markus S. 1998. "Collective Action Across Borders: Opportunity Structures, Network Capacities, and Communicative Praxis in the Age of Advanced Globalization." *Sociological Perspectives* 41:587–617.

Seidman Gay W. 2000. "Adjusting the Lens: What Do Globalizations, Transnationalism, and the Anti-apartheid Movement Mean for Social Movement Theory?" Pp. 339–358 in *Globalizations and Social Movements: Culture, Power, and the Transnational Public Sphere*, edited by J. A. Guidry, M. D. Kennedy, and M. N. Zald. Ann Arbor. University of Michigan Press.

—. 2004. "Deflated Citizenship: Labor Rights in a Global Era." Pp. 109–129 in *People Out of Place: Globalization, Human Rights, and the Citizenship Gap*, edited by A. Brysk and G. Shafir. New York: Routledge.

Sell, Susan K. 2003. *Private Power, Public Law The Globalization of Intellectual Property Rights*. Cambridge: Cambridge University Press.

Sen, Amartya. 1999. "Democracy as a Universal Value." *Journal of Democracy* 10:3–17.

Sen, Jai, Anita Anand, Arturo Escobar, and Peter Waterman. 2003. Challenging Empires: The World Social Forum. Third World Institute. At: www.choike.org.

Sengupta, Arjun. 2000. "Realizing the Right to Development." *Development and Change* 31:553–578.

Shiva, Vandana. 2000. "War Against Nature and the People of the South." Pp. 91–125 in *Views from the South: The Effects of Globalization and the WTO on Third World Countries*, edited by S. Anderson. Chicago: Food First.

—. 2005. *Earth Democracy: Justice, Sustainability, and Peace*. Boston: South End.

Sieg, Richard. 2007. At International Commission, Inuit Want To See Change in U.S. Policy on Global Warming." Vermont *Journal of Environmental Law* 8. At www.vjel.org/ news/NEWSio0058.html.

Silddrik, Kathryn. 1986. "Codes of Conduct for Transnational Corporations: The Case of the WHO/ UNICEF Code." *International Organization* 40:815–840.

Sklair, Leslie. 1997. "Social Movements for Global Capitalism: The Transnational Capitalist Class in Action." *Review of International Political Economy* 4:514–538.

—. 1999. "Competing Conceptions of Globalization." *Journal of World* Systems Research 5:143–162.

—. 2001. *The Transnational Capitalist Class*. Cambridge: Blackwell.

—. 2002. *Globalization and Its Alternatives*. New York: Oxford University Press.

Skogly, Sigrun. 1993. "Structural Adjustment and Development: Human Rights–An Agenda for Change?" Human *Rights Quarterly* 15:751.

Slaughter, Anne-Marie. 2004a. "Disaggregated Sovereignty: Towards the Public Accountability of Global Government Networks." *Government and Opposition* 39:159–190.

—. 2004b. A *New World Order*. Princeton: Princeton University Press.

Smith, Christian. 1996. *Resisting Reagan: The U.S. Central America Peace Movement*. Chicago: University of Chicago Press.

Smith, Jackie. 2000. "Framing the Nonproliferation Debate: Transnational Activism and International Nudear Weapons Negotiations." Pp. 55–82 in *Research in Social Movements, Conflict and Change*, vol. 22, edited by P. Coy. Greenwood, CT: JAI.

—. 2002. "Globalizing Resistance: The Battle of Seattle and the Future of Social Movements." Pp. 183–199 in *Globalization and Resistance: Transnational Dimensions of Social Movements*, edited by J. Smith and H. Johnston. Lanham, MD: Rowman & Littlefield.

—. 2004. "Exploring Connections between Global Integration and Political Mobilization." *Journal of World Systems Research* 10:255–285.

—. 2005. "Building Bridges or Building Walls? Explaining Regionalization among Transnational Social Movement Organizations." *Mobilization* 10:251–270.

Smith, Jackie, Charles Chatfield, and Ron Pagnucco, eds. 1997. *Transnational Social Movements and Global Politics: Solidarity Beyond the State*. Syracuse: Syracuse University Press.

Smith, Jackie, and Tina Fetner. 2007. "Structural Approaches in the Study of Social Movements." In *Handbook of Social Movements: Social Movements Across Disciplines*, edited by B. Klandermans and C. Roggeband. New York: Springer.

Smith, Jackie, Marina Karides, Marc Becker, Dorval Brunelle, Christopher Chase-Dunn, Dontatella della Porta, Rosalba Icaza, Jeffrey Juris, Lorenzo Mosca, Ellen Reese, Peter Jay Smith, and Rolando Vaszuer. 2008. *Global Democracy and the World Social Forums*. Boulder, CO: Paradigm.

Smith, Jackie, John McCarthy, Clark McPhail, and Boguslaw Augustin. 2001. "From Protest to Agenda-Building: Description Bias in Media Coverage of Protest Events in Washington, D.C." *Social Forces* 79:1397–1423.

Smithson, Shelley 2002. "Big Plan on Campus: Universities Combat Climate Change." Grist *Magazine: Environmental News and Commentary,* 31 July.

Snow, David, E. B. Rochford, S. Warden, and Robert Benford. 1986. "Frame Alignment Processes, Micromobilization and Movement Participation." *American Sociological Review* 51:273–286.

Snow, David A., Louis A. Zurcher, and Sheldon Ekland-Olson. 1980. "Social Networks and Social Movements: A Microstructural Approach to Differential Recruitment." *American Sociological Review* 45:787–801.

Snyder, Anna. 2003. *Setting the Agenda for Global Peace: Conflict and Consensus Building.* Burlington, VT: Ashgate.

Soros, George. 2002. *On Globalization.* New York: Public Affairs.

South Commission. 1989. *Redefining Wealth and Progress: The Caracas Report on Alternative Development Indicators.* New York: Bootstrap.

Starhawk. 2001. "Response to 'Manifest of Anti-capitalist Youth against the World Social Forum." Electronic Communication.

Stark, David, Balazs Vedres, and Laszlo Bruszt. 2005. "Global Links, Local Roots? Varieties of Transnationalization and Forms of Civic Integration." European University Institute, Florence, Italy.

Starr, Amory. 2000. *Naming the Enemy: Anti-Corporate Movements Confront Globalization.* New York: Zed.

Stearns, Linda Brewster, and Paul D. Almeida. 2004. "The Formation of State Actor-Social Movement Coalitions and Favorable Policy Outcomes." *Social Forces* 51:478–504.

Steinberg, Marc W. 1995. "The Roar of the Crowd: Repertoires of Discourse and Collective Action among the Spitalfields Silk Weavers in Nineteenth-Century London." Pp. 57–88 in *Repertoires and Cycles of Collective Action,* edited by M. Traugott. Durham: Duke University Press.

Sternbach, Nancy Saporta, Marysa Navarro-Aranguren, Patricia Chuchryk, and Sonia E. Alvarez. 1992. "Ferninisrns in Latin America: From Bogota to San Bernardo." Pp. 207–239 in *The Making of Social Movements in Latin America: Identity, Strategy, and Democracy,* edited by A. Escobar and S. E. Alvarez. Boulder, CO: Westview.

Stewart, Julie. 2004. "When Local Troubles Become Transnational: The Transformation of a Guatemalan Indigenous Rights Movement." *Mobilization* 9:259–278.

Stiglitz, Joseph. 2003. *Globalization and Its Discontents.* New York: W. W. Norton.

Structural Adjustment Participatory Review International Network (SAPRIN). 2002. "The Policy Roots of Economic Crisis and Poverty." Washington, DC: SAPRIN.

Subramaniam, Mangala, Manjusha Gupte, and Debarashmi Mita. 2003. "Local to Global: Transnational Networks and Indian Womeris Grassroots Organizing." *Mobilization* 8:335–352.

Swarts, Heidi J. 2003. "Setting the State's Agenda: Church-Based Community Organizations in American Urban Politics." Pp. 78–106 in *States, Parties and Social Movements,* edited by J. A. Goldstone. New York: Cambridge University Press.

Tarrow, Sidney. 1988. "National Politics and Collective Action." *Annual Review of Sociology* 14:421–440.

—. 1995. "Cydes of Collective Action: Between Moments of Madness and the Repertoire of Contention." Pp. 89–116 in *Repertoires and Cycles of Collective* Action, edited by M. Traugott. Durham: Duke University Press.

—. 2005. *The New* Transnational *Activism.* New York: Cambridge University Press.

Tavola Della Pace. 2005a. "Call for Global Day of Mobilisation against Poverty, War and Unilateralism." Call to mobilization on September 10, 2005, vol. 2005. At www.un-ngls.org/cso/cso6/appeal.htm.

— 2005b. "Reclaim Our UN." Porto Alegre, Brazil. At www.un-ngls.org/UN-reform-Tavola%2odella%20 pace%20-%20WSF%202005.doc.

Teivainen, Teivo. 2002. "The World Social Forum and Global Democratisation Learning from Porto Alegre." Third *World Quarterly* 23:621–632.

Tharoor, Shashi. 2001. "Are Human Rights Universal?" *New Internationalist,* March. At www.findartides. com/p/articles/mi_moJQP/is_332/aL30144069.

Tilly, Charles. 1978. *From Mobilization to Revolution.* Reading, MA: Addison Wesley.

—. 1984. "Social Movements and National Politics." Pp. 297–317 in *Statemaking and Social Movements: Essays in* History and *Theory,* edited by C. Bright and S. Harding Ann Arbor: University of Michigan Press.

—. 1990. *Coercion, Capital and European States, AD* 990–1990. Cambridge: Blackwell.

—. 1995. "Globalization Threatens Labor Rights." *International Labor* and *Working Class* History 47:1–23.

— 2004. *Social Movements, 1768–2004.* Boulder, CO: Paradigm.

ul Haq, Mahbub. 1989. "People in Development." Pp. 17–25 in *Redefining Wealth* and *Progress: The* Caracas *Report on* Alternative *Development Indicators,* edited by South Commission. New York: Bootstrap.

UN. 2004. "We the Peoples: Civil Society, the United Nations and Global Governance: Report of the Panel of Eminent Persons on United Nations-Civil Society Relations." UN Secretary General, New York.

UN Development Programme. 2000. *Human Development Report 2000: Overcoming Human Poverty.* New York: UNDP.

—. 2001. *Human Development Report* 2001: Making *New Technologies Work for* Human *Development.* New York: Oxford University Press.

—. 2002. *Human Development Report 2002: Deepening Democracy in a Fragmented World.* New York: Oxford University Press.

—. 2004. *Human Development Report 2004: Cultural Liberty in Today's Diverse World.* New York: Oxford University Press.

—. 2005. *Human Development Report 2005: International Cooperation at a Crossroads.* New York: Oxford University Press.

UN Food and Agriculture Organization. 2005. "State of Agricultural Commodity Markets." UN Food and Agriculture Organization, Rome.

Urquhart, Brian, and Erskine Childers. 1996. A *World in Need of Leadership: Tomorrow's United Nations.* Uppsala, Sweden: Dag Hammarskjold Foundation.

Vasi, Ion Bogdan. Forthcoming. "Thinking Globally, Planning Nationally, and Acting Locally: Institutional Spheres and the Diffusion of Environmental Practices."

Verba, Sidney, Kay Schlozman, and Henry Brady. 1995. *Voice and Equality: Civic Volunteerism in American Politics.* Cambridge, MA: Harvard University Press.

Wainwright, Hilary. 2003. *Reclaim the State: Adventures in Popular Democracy.* London: Verso, Transnational Institute.

Wallach, Lori, and Patrick Woodall. 2004. *Whose Trade Organization? A Comprehensive Guide to the* WTO. New York: The New Press.

Wallerstein, Immanuel. 1976. *The Modern World System.* New York: Academic. Wallerstein, Immanuel, ed. 2004. *The Modern World-system In The Longue Duree.* Boulder, CO: Paradigm.

Walton, John, and David Seddon. 1994. *Free Markets and Food Riots: The Politics of Global Adjustment.* Cambridge: Blackwell.

Wapner, Paul. 2002. "Defending Accountability in NGOs." *Chicago Journal of International Law* 3:197–205.

Waterman, Peter. 1998. *Globalization, Social Movements, and the New Internationalisms.* Washington, DC: Mansell.

—. 2001. *Globalization, Social Movements and the New Internationalism.* New York: Continuum.

—. 2005. "Talking across Difference in an Interconnected World of Labour." Pp. 141–162 in *Coalitions Across Borders: Transnational Protest and the Neoliberal* Order, edited by J. Bandy and J. Smith. Boulder, CO: Rowman & Littlefield.

Waterman, Peter, and Jill Timms. 2004. "Trade Union Internationalism and a Global Civil Society in the Making." Pp. 175–202 in *Global Civil Society 2004/5.* London: Sage.

Whitaker, Chico. 2005. "The World Social Forum: Towards a New Politics?" Presentation at World Social Forum panel, Porto Alegre, Brazil.

Wiest, Dawn, and Jackie Smith. 2007. "Explaining Participation in Regional Transnational Social Movement Organizations." *International Journal of Comparative Sociology* 48:137–166.

Willetts, Peter. 1989. "The Pattern of Conferences." Pp. 35–63 in *Global Issues in the United Nations Framework,* edited by P. Taylor and A. J. R. Groom. New York: St. Martirfs.

—. 1996. "Consultative Status for NGOs at the United Nations." Pp. 31–62 in *The Conscience of the World: The Influence of NGOs in the United Nations System,* edited by P. Willetts. London: C. Hurst.

— 2000. "From 'Consultative Arrangements' to 'Partnership': The Changing Status of NGOs in Diplomacy at the UN." *Global Governance* 6:191–213.

Wise, Timothy A., and Kevin P. Gallagher. 2006. "Doha Round and Developing Countries: Will the Doha Deal Do More Harm than Good?" Research and Information System for Developing Countries, New Delhi.

Wittner, Lawrence. 1997. *Resisting the Bomb: A History of the World Nuclear Disarmament Movement, 2954–1970.* Vol. 2. Stanford: Stanford University Press.

Wolf, Eric. 1982. *Europe* and *the People without History.* Berkeley: University of California Press.

Wolfson, Mark. 2001. *The Fight Against Big Tobacco: The Movement, the State, and the Public's Health.* Hawthorne, NY: Aldine de Gruyter.

Wood, Lesley Julia. 2004. "The Diffusion of Direct Action Tactics: From Seattle to Toronto and New York." Ph.D. Dissertation, Columbia University, New York.

—. 2005. "Bridging the Chasms: The Case of Peoples' Global Action." Pp. 95–119 in *Coalitions Across Borders: Transnational Protest and the Neoliberal Order,* edited by J. Bandy and J. Smith. Lanham, MD: Rowman & Littlefield.

World Commission on the Social Dimensions of Globalization. 2004. "A Fair Globalization: Creating Opportunities for All."

World Health Organization. 2000. "Tobacco Company Strategies to Undermine Tobacco Control Activities at the World Health Organisation." World Health Organization, Geneva. At wwvv.who.int/genevahearings/inquiryhtml.

Wuthnow, Robert. 1989. *Communities of Discourse: Ideology and Social Structure in the Reformation, the Enlightenment, and European Socialism.* Cambridge, MA: Harvard University Press.

—. 1998. *Loose Connections: Joining Together in America's Fragmented* Communities. Cambridge, MA: Harvard University Press.

Zald, Mayer, and John D. McCarthy. 1987. "Religious Groups as Crucibles of Social Movements." Pp. 67–95 in *Social Movements* in an *Organizational Society,* edited by M. Zald and J. D. McCarthy. New Brunswick, NJ: Transaction.

Zoelle, Diana, and, Jyl J. Josephson. 2005. "Making Democratic Space for Poor People: The Kensington Welfare Rights Union." Pp. 55–74 in *Beyond Global Arrogance: Trans-national Democracy and Social Movements,* edited by J. Leatherman and J. Webber. New York: Palgrave Macmillan.

CHAPTER TWENTY-TWO

Is Another World Possible? Problems and Shortcomings of the World Social Forum[*]

Owen Worth and Karen Buckley

Source: An earlier version of this article appeared in *Third World Quarterly*, see Owen Worth and Karen Buckley, 'The World Social Forum: postmodern prince or court jester?' *Third World Quarterly* 30 (4), 2009, pp 649–661.

In January 2001, the local government of Porto Alegre sponsored the first World Social Forum (WSF). Situated against the background of indigenous insurgencies led by Subcommandante Marcos in Mexico and public demonstrations against international financial institutions that culminated in Seattle 1999, the WSF was widely declared to provide a space for social forces pitted against neoliberal economic globalisation. The WSF, it was suggested, would profit from the momentum, energy and actions of a germinating movement for social justice while also representing a novel 'postmodern' strategic and methodological advance for the social forces of global resistance.

Largely backed by western-based non-governmental organisations (NGOs) rooted in the politics of social transformation, the gathering was initiated to provide a forum to reflect the innovations of the local branch (Porto Alegre) of the Workers Party, which had proposed social alternatives to local problems, and to suggest how progressive policy could be used as a counter to neoliberal economic globalisation. Since its inception, the WSF has increased in both its size and its 'inclusivity' and has led to the creation of regional forums—European Social Forum, Asian Social Forum, Boston Social Forum—that are based upon the objectives of the WSF. Subsequent annual forums have led to the belief that the WSF can be seen as the sum of the 'anti-globalisation' movement—or the Global Justice movement—whereby global civil society has reacted to the injustices that have resulted from the globalisation of economic neoliberalism. For activists and scholars the WSF has provided an 'open space' for contestation and dialogue, whereby a multitude of social movements, NGOs and grassroots, indigenous groups can formulate co-ordinating ideas and struggles.[1] Here an ethico-political counter-hegemonic movement that has multi-dimensional roots which include civil society activists, radical political parties and unions, environmentalists and religious representatives, has emerged to contest the economic principles of globalisation, and to promote the maxim of 'another world is possible'.

Yet, whilst the euphoria that surrounds the variety of sites of resistance may suggest that the forum provides a platform for this 'another world' to be imagined, the reality can also paint a different picture. Against the claims by its supporters that the WSF has provided a unique space for the construction of a counter-hegemonic movement able to facilitate the realisation, we argue that the WSF has largely failed in such a manoeuvre. Instead it has suffered from being a directionless series of events, whereby the working formula of 'open space' has led to the creation of nothing more of a 'talking shop', rather than any valid construction of counter-hegemony.[2]

At the same time, when the WSF has sought to mobilise ideas and concrete policies in order to formulate potential from such counter-hegemonic strategies, they have suffered from huge inconsistencies and contradictions that make them unsustainable. In addition, many key campaigners and speakers involved in the 'open' forums employ ideas and pursue objectives that are highly exclusive and elitist in both language and purpose.[3] We argue here that the WSF falls down in terms of its strategy, its elitism and its representation in a way that prevents it to be considered as a realistic organic body capable of realising or delivering a blueprint for 'another world'.

The WSF and Strategy

The question of strategy and objectives has been at the centre of debate since the inception of the WSF in 2001. This is partly to do with the origins of the Forum itself. Whilst in its 'recognised history' the WSF emerged from the events of Seattle, Washington, London, Quebec, and so forth,[4] its genesis emerged entirely from Brazil. Indeed out of the eight organisations that formed the initial Organizing Committee (OC), only one was linked towards an international campaign.[5] As such whilst the Forum has global reaches and is intended to facilitate the progressive objectives inherent within global civil society, its origins remain distinctly rooted within Brazil. The radical components that made up the local government in Porto Alegre were heavily involved in promoting and organising the first Forums and allowed Brazil's Worker's Party (*Partido dos Trabalhadores*, PT) a significant and unique role. Indeed, such was the national success of the first three Forums on the national persona that it was one of the contributing factors to the Presidential electoral success of the Worker's Party's first leader, Lula da Silva. Yet, the national-specific origins of the WSF are not seen as being a problem for its overall development as the sum of the reflection of global civil society. Indeed, the Forum's supporters point to the necessity of such a political support base for its development and expansion towards greater regional autonomy.[6] Also, whilst the early years may have had a distinctly Brazilian slant to it (which were still somewhat notable at the last meeting in Belem), the strategies and objectives put forward were distinctly international and pluralistic.

The edited volume by Fisher and Ponniah remains perhaps the most coherent account of what the WSF is building and how this might be achieved. Here, the editors attempt to demonstrate, using material bought up from the first three Porto Alegre Forums, that a coherent form of counter-hegemonic strategy is being fashioned, forged through the dichotomy between the local and the global. Along with general proposals for economic democratisation and wealth distribution and sustainability, the volume includes a variety of reflections and objectives to mobilise global civil society from contrasting geographical and societal perspectives. According to Fisher and Ponniah this demonstrates that the WSF structure is providing a diverse, yet viable framework for contesting the current economic world order. This is emphasised by their own account of counter-hegemony, which they believe requires the articulation of contrasting forms of resistance. Following Laclau and Mouffe's proposal of radical democracy, and in keeping with Gill's configuration of the post-modern prince, they argue that the only method for this to gain any momentum is through placing together the sum of its disparate parts, in order to create a coherent whole. They continue:

A counter-hegemonic discourse must have a common articulating thread that can weave together disparate movements by demonstrating that their particular long-term interests can be best served by pursuing a common project. It cannot accomplish this if it is simply a resistance discourse. A counter-hegemonic discourse encompasses a resistance discourse:

it constitutes a new form of radical subjectivity by demonstrating that what was previously construed as a neutral relation of subordination, simply as horizontal difference, is really a hierarchical relation of oppression. However, a counter-hegemonic discourse also demonstrated how that hierarchical relationship can be subverted, made horizontal, by pursuing a larger collective project.[7]

Whilst one can agree with Fisher and Ponniah in their understanding of the requirements of constructing counter-hegemony, their affirmation that the World Social Forum embraces such a condition is less convincing. For whilst the Fisher and Ponniah volume and WSF reports are presented to demonstrate that there are consistencies within such diversities,[8] the stark contradictions between these various parts cannot be overlooked. In a multi-thematic gathering of groups with diverse priorities, consensus in the form of a unified discourse is not easy to achieve. Inevitably, out of diversity arises conflict between, for example, labour unions and environmentalists, as labour calls for more growth and employment and environmentalists call for a reduction of growth and consumption.[9] There has been tension between the national-first strategy, traditionally drawn up by trade unions and the attempt to create a culture of international convergence. Furthermore, it has been noted by observers that despite involvement in the social forum, national trade unions have not changed their traditional nature, whilst international trade movements themselves have not been significantly involved from an early stage.[10]

The area where debates between radicals and reformers is perhaps most evident is over the current institutions of international capitalism and in particular whether to abolish or reform the World Trade Organisation (WTO), the IMF and the World Bank.[11] Thus reformists, who advocate dialogue and reform of these institutions, come into conflict with radicals who reject dialogue on the basis that this increases the legitimacy of international institutions and advocate that these institutions be abolished. Such divisions here are perhaps best noticed through the academics and NGO campaigners—to use Gramsci's term's 'traditional intellectuals'—formally presenting ideas and papers in centrally based panels and the more radical campaigners outside.

Contradictions over the boundaries of cultural space were perhaps best illustrated at the 2007 forum in Nairobi, where a far greater religious presence meant that western-inspired situationism that had long been a feature of anti-capitalist demonstrations in the industrial world,[12] clashed with Orthodox Church groups.[13] In addition, the sheer volume of contrasting panels and stalls that make up the Forum demonstrates a high degree of stark contradiction amongst its diversity that cannot merely be overlooked. For example panels based around human rights of the individual are placed alongside panels showcasing the development of Vietnamese socialism, whilst environmental groups are placed alongside those campaigning for oil sovereignty. Likewise, campaigns and stalls place national liberation movements alongside international socialist groups; faith-based organisations alongside eco-anarchists; NGOs alongside national and international political coalitions, held together by corporate catering and World Bank-sponsored bookshops. From this, one cannot ignore the words of José Fogaça, current anti-PT mayor of Porto Alegre, when dismissing the Forum as an 'ideological Disneyland'.[14] Indeed, Naomi Klein shared this observation to an extent, by stating that without any foundation for accountability and some form of direction, there is not much hope for the Forum to viably construct any form of 'alternative world'.[15]

The absence of meaningful strategic objectives on the part of the WSF has largely frustrated aspirations towards the creation of an open space beyond the celebration of festivals of ideas in its name. The closely adhered to charter guidelines ground the WSF as a non-deliberative space within which individuals cannot express positions on behalf of all participants and decisions cannot be taken by the Forum as a body. This allows the WSF to present itself as a neutral plain whereby participant organisations and movements can take decisions and issue declarations without requiring the authorisation of the Forum itself. It also represents, for Forum supporters, a break with the rigid dogmatic socialism of the past and an opportunity to underline the more novel and 'progressive' character of the Forum process. This has resulted, however, in a proliferation of calls from assemblies of social movements, 'walls of proposals' and more recent manifestos of social movements that exist in a vacuous open space undefined by specific strategic objectives. Numerous pronouncements by social movements are supplemented by, often lacklustre and overlapping, efforts to consolidate a virtual 'memory' of Forum events through documenting individual and group experiences and activities in the absence of formal Forum-led strategy.

The challenges of a non-deliberative WSF space are inherent instigators of debates centring on two proposals that aim towards politicising the WSF and facilitating the emergence of more concrete strategic objectives. The first of these, the Manifesto of Porto Alegre, aims to create points of convergence or a 'Consensus of Porto Alegre' focused on twelve proposals for creating 'another possible world'.[16] Many of the proposals focus upon issues of economic governance such as debt cancellation, equitable trade, international financial taxation, patenting and privatisation of common resources. These are accompanied by predictable 'progressive' proposals for increased social protection, measures to combat discrimination, an alternative development model and democratic control of natural resources. General critiques of the Manifesto pointed to the non-consultative manner in which it was drawn up and male gender bias not only in its content but also in its key signatories. More specifically, Chico Whitaker, prominent founder of the WSF and strong defender of the WSF as a neutral space that does not take positions or define political actions, saw the Manifesto as a violation of the principle of open space. The Manifesto, according to similar viewpoints, encroaches upon the radical and polemical capacity of the WSF as an open space, and represents a premature attempt to draw up a consensual political programme from an, as yet, ideologically diverse WSF process.[17] Rather, defenders of the WSF as an open space suggest that consensus and political clarity would organically evolve from political struggle implicit in the WSF process.

Meanwhile, the Bamako Appeal, would also represent a similarly contested, and foundering, attempt to develop a political programme for the WSF. Prepared in advance of the Bamako stage of the 2006 polycentric Forum, the Bamako Appeal hosts a greater number of signatories from individuals and collective entities than the 'Manifesto of 19'. Strategically the authors of the Bamako Appeal want to move the WSF from a place of dialogue to 'a base for coordinated anti-imperialist and pro-socialist action'.[18] According to the text of the Appeal it aims to contribute "to the emergence of a new popular and historical subject . . . one that is diverse, multipolar and from the people" thus turning people into "protagonists of their history". The rhetorical content of the Appeal images the Manifesto's focus on consensus-formation, internationalism and solidarity while also adding mechanisms through which goals may be achieved such as the formation of working groups or the development of databases to facilitate greater solidarity and sharing of information. Beyond improved rhetorical clarity and broader appeal the Bamako Appeal has not noticeably led to greater political co-ordination nor to the creation of a more effective 'historical subject'. Both the Manifesto of Porto Alegre and the Bamako Appeal contribute to the accumulation and celebration of ideas that the WSF as an open space represents. Less evident, however, is the emergence of substantive strategic objectives that can serve to guide these ideas towards a meaningful counter-hegemonic strategy.

The absence of forward-looking Forum-led strategy is reflected in the recent 'strategy-debate' launched at a WSF International Committee meeting in Abuja in 2008. The outcome reflects a general reluctance to adopt new strategic directions for the WSF particularly within the remit of Charter-bound provisions. While the meeting agreed on a schedule for future WSF events and the continuation of Global Days of Actions (GDA) an agreement was not reached on the form and periodicity of GDAs. The strategy debate included reflection on proposals for WSF-led political positions and calls for action such as the Manifesto and Bamako Appeal. It was reemphasised that while similar proposals constitute legitimate expressions of social movements they would not receive WSF authorisation. The Abuja meeting proposed the adoption of a document entitled 'Guiding Principles for holding WSF events' that would be drawn up to address 'controversial' issues concerning funding and participation by violent and reactionary groups that had persisted since the inauguration of the Forum. Initial drafts of the document and continued discussion on participation of heads of state at Forum events suggest that despite these efforts the ambiguities of 'open space' continue to persist.

Elitism

If the pursuit of 'open space' has led to several problems in terms of the construction of a viable blueprint of 'another world', then the exclusivity of the Forums' participants and its activities has added to these shortcomings. The charge of elitism is one that has been central to criticisms of the WSF since its inception, with claims that the agenda and alternative visions of the Forum have been generated by a small and distinct group, but that those participating in the events themselves are largely from a highly privileged background. For example, whilst a high number of participants may be local—that would tentatively suggest that attendance would feature a split across the social groups—at the 2005 WSF nearly 30 per cent of participants had postgraduate qualifications and well over 80 per cent had daily access to internet facilities.[19] Yet the make-up of the organising committee has often overshadowed this figure, by consistently organising itself around a highly elite body of intellectuals and NGO activists. At the WSF in Nairobi for example, discussions led by the organising committee were narrowly confined towards their respective interests, whilst other sessions appeared no more than academic panels.[20] As such it has become increasingly difficult for those without some knowledge of the academy to contribute.

This is not to say that this elitism has been formed unconsciously or that initiatives have not been made to address this trend. Indeed at the 2009 Belem WSF, attempts at solving the problems of diversity and lack of unity were addressed through the construction of 22 Assemblies aimed towards 'convergence'. Yet whilst the 22 groups themselves did represent the general themes associated with the WSF, their selection and nature still characterised very narrow forms of representation, reinforcing the academic/NGO hegemony at its organising core. As a result, rather than widening the social base of participation, one could observe that elitism has been maintained and strengthened through a new layer of organisation. Thus, in attempting to consciously address the growing representative gap within the forum, existing practices have tended to be reinforced.

In looking at the charges of elitism, one is reminded of David Chandler's critique of global civil society. For Chandler, the whole idea of global civil society is an imagined one whereby any alternative normative solution to counter neoliberal capitalism has been constructed around the interests of its components.[21] Thus, the so-called 'radical resistance from below' which the Forums claim to represent has not initiated a growth of progressive non-state actors with transformative potential, but has created a succession of NGOs which determine what is progressive and what is not. In other words, it is the elites within such organisations that have created the idea that these social alternatives are viable and provide greater democratic representation, which illustrates that at closer examination new forms of elitism are being created.[22] Further empirical studies on participation seem to back up this argument. Chase-Dunn and Reese's substantial study on participation at the WSF, concluded that there was a marked and growing

6

overrepresentation of NGOs, and a dominance of European and Latin American activists with a high level of education. As a result, as Biagiotti argues, the principles of openness allow those with the most powerful voices to use such privileged autonomy for their own purposes.[23]

The theme of elitism also applies to the funding of the Forums, which adds to the problems of accessibility to those organisations and individuals that lack appropriate funds. Funding was largely an issue that was discussed in depth at the first WSF when it became notable that there were links with the PT and that the emphasis of Brazilian based funding was substantially unproportionally weighted. The aims were thus to ultimately create a funding structure that did not benefit one regional voice or one better resourced over another. As a result, the organizing committee of the WSF decided to set up a wider International Committee (IC) that would structurally develop further processes. Yet despite this development that has allowed the Forum to devolve in order to provide separate issues to certain regions far more systematically, the question of funding has yet to be adequately resolved. In pursuing a solidarity-based system for funding, the WSF has operated a system whereby participants contribute according to the economic status of their region of origin. Yet, the amount requested for entrance to official Forum activities still prices all but the more substantial organisations and the more affluent individuals out of the process.

Like many of the issues with the WSF, the issue of funding was perhaps shown up the best at Nairobi. Possibly, because this was the first Forum held in a prominently peripheral country—as opposed to both India and Brazil where the emergence of 'a progressive middle class' has often been the catalyst for civil societal representation. However, in Nairobi, the general lack of representation from specifically local groups was recognisable at the Forum. Indeed, the pricing and admission in Nairobi was such that smaller local grassroots organisations were frozen out—to the extent that they formed alternative local meetings in another area of the city. In addition to the problems with accessibility the other area where funding has become an increasingly prominent issue is in the commercial sponsorship, and indeed on the continued dependency that the Forum has on funding from governments—however direct or indirect—foundations and the private sector. For Nairobi the event was one where smaller local businesses could compete their entrepreneurial skills with 'ethical multilaterals' and state-owned companies as the event became an opportunity for the national and local economy to boast its consumer and tourist based service industries. NGOs, on the other hand followed this entrepreneurial spirit by equally competing for their own expansion. One could have said that the event in 2007 was adding to the problems recognised by Klein in earlier events whereby 'fierce NGO brand wars were waged behind the scenes—about whose stars would get the most airtime, who would get access to the press and who would be seen as the true leaders of this movement'.[24]

In terms of private funding, The Ford Foundation, in particular has been a prominent financial contributor directly to the WSF and indirectly through participant organisations.[25] Thus while the 2004 Indian organising committee declined financial support from the Ford Foundation this did not prevent Ford grantees from attending. In this way foundations such as Ford, Rockefeller and Carnegie, widely viewed as carriers of American globalisation and foreign policy, become involved in the discourse of creating an alternative globalising project. This prompts criticism from the far left that continued dependency on external funding allows the WSF to resemble 'an international network of liberal-reformist globalisers'[26] working to maintain a dominant vision of global civil society through stifling direct action and promoting unfocused discussion and debate. The forum can be perceived as an intricate part of neoliberal governance, a 'legitimising tool' that can be used to carry though reformist aspects of neoliberal policy.[27]

If the WSF and its regional components were set up to recognise the emergence of critical global civil society and the sum of the anti-globalisation movement,[28] then the reality has been that it has not been activists and campaigners per se that are represented, but rather leading NGOs and academics. This, as Waterman suggested in his critique of the London European

Social Forum, has led to the exclusion of 'a broad range of libertarian—autonomist—anarchist and feminist groups,[29] of left or just liberal-democratic NGOs, of critically-minded intellectuals, artists and professionals, all unprepared to accept the domination of power (politics) and money (capital) that the organising committee represented'.[30] This is compounded by the 'gigantic gap between the bureaucratic organizers and those that participate in grassroots social movements'.[31] Whilst, the mandate of the IC and OC to speak on behalf of the disparate participants of the WSF has been largely addressed through attempts to effect a more representative re-composition of the IC and an expanded International Secretariat (IS), the larger query of the mandate of the WSF to speak on behalf of all those affected by globalisation remains to be addressed. It seems here that what instead is required is a rejection of the 'making' of transnational political subjects, in which through forging universal representation the WSF produces a 'mollifying consensus' on those left behind by global civil society.[32] Instead, the exclusive nature of the WSF serves to widen this gap and further isolate those who are constrained from participating on the grounds of finance, geography, discourse and education. Indeed if the IC is set to increase its organisational capacity, which the recent Abuja meeting seems to suggest, then one can also argue that rather than addressing the problem of representation, an even larger gap between organizers and movements might be established.

The WSF as Political Initiative

In this same way that the private sector and leading NGOs have looked at the WSF as a form of opportunism, then leading political figures and parties have also looked at it as an opportunity to mobilise support and international exposure. In the years since its inception, the WSF has attracted (amongst others) Lula da Silva, Hugo Chavez, Winnie Mandela, Kenneth Kaunda and Evo Morales whilst the regional forums have attracted figures such as Ralph Nader, Ken Livingstone and Gerry Adams. In addition to the PT in Brazil, the various social forums have had political input from such diverse bodies—amongst many others—as the Party of the European Left, the Vietnamese Communist Party, various official Green Parties and indirectly through many mainstream centre-left parties across Latin America and Europe. In terms of organisation, the involvement—however indirect—of political institutions has allowed the democratic arena of 'open space' become used for political campaigning.

There are a number of examples where political figures, parties and institutions can be seen as being guilty of such campaigning. The most obvious example here is local governmental involvement in Porto Alegre with the PT administration in the city. Yet the PT involvement in the fabric of the WSF does not merely stop with the promotion of progressive civil society, but with the backing of popular support for Lula. At both the Porto Alegre forums and in Mumbai and Nairobi, the PT funded panels and stalls served as useful propaganda for Lula. In the same vein, the involvement of the PSUV—the United Socialist Party of Venezuela—has similarly used the Forums to propel the success of Chavez. Indeed the latter included more blatant forms of populism whereby demonstrations organised by the party to embrace the cult of Chavez have been organised around the main arenas both in Caracus and in Nairobi. Whilst both Chavez and Lula have both made previous appearances at the Forums—the latter arguing that the WSF was one of 'the most important political events taking place each year in the world today'[33]—until 2009 they had not neglected the Davos Summit or World Economic Forum in the manner that the organising committee had ideally wished for. Indeed, paradoxically, Lula has repeatedly been seen as a rising star of free trade at Davos, giving rise to the opinion that the WEF is the place to do business, whilst the WSF is the place to mobilise the populist vote.

At the Belem Forum, this opportunism reached new levels when the five 'leftist' South American leaders (Lula, Morales, Chavez, Correa and Lugo) not only appeared on a central platform together, but symbolically stressed their choice of promoting regional unity at the WSF ahead of active participation at Davos. Citing the global credit crisis, they stated how the functions of the WSF in constructing alternatives provided further indication that the neoliberalism associated with Davos was decaying. Or as Chavez more poignantly put that one represented a 'world that was dying' and the other 'was that was being born'.[34] Yet, whilst the message and symbolism might have facilitated the spirit of the forum, their presence appeared to signify political campaigning rather than anything substantial. As before the leaders were accompanied by a band of supporters that maximised its location in the Amazon—and within close proximity to all five electorates—to their advantage, particular in light of the credit crisis and the potential of a wider Latin American response. In various ways, they also used Belem to further their respective brand of individual populism. This perhaps seen best with Lugo's homage to the spirit of 'Che' (Guevara) and Chavez's using his address to reiterate his now legendary condemnation of US Imperialism.[35]

As mentioned above, the issue of the heads of states was discussed at Abuja, but at Belem, it became obvious that the Forum would be used by regional leaders as a means of showing solidarity in light of the global financial crisis. Lula's discussion to 'shun Davos' for the WSF might have been presented as a symbolic act towards challenging global capitalism, yet his previous absences from forums outside of Brazil were not mentioned, nor indeed was the amount of respect he gained from the international economic community in previous years at Davos. If Chavez has used the Forums as a means of building on their cult following, and Lula on his political support within Brazil, then other groups have been guilty of either dominating the organisation of certain events or of using the events to promote specific causes. For example the Socialist Workers Party, often criticised for being dogmatic and sectarian in their outlook, heavily dominated many of the activities in the European Social Forums in London and Athens, whilst London also saw Ken Livingstone's mayoral administration become highly influential in its organisation, with aides such as Gerry Adams using a headline session—alongside Livingstone and others such as Susan George—on global inequality to outline Sinn Fein's political agenda, whilst many NGOs with close links to the administration gained significant coverage.

Thus whilst the WSF remains committed to non-governmental involvement and towards a new form of post-modernist, post-statist socialism,[36] the reality is that powerful figures, parties and regimes that have certain appeal to the 'international left' have used the Forums for popular, civil and electoral support. As a result, rather than constructing a vision for 'another world', what we see here can be best summed up through another Gramscian term—that of 'transformism' or *trasformismo*. This is seen as a strategy by the leading or ruling groups—or class—to co-opt potential alternative counter-hegemonic projects into their own wider political ideology. Through forming alliances with the global institutions which the Forum claims to oppose, the Forum has, in fact, as one critical group put it, 'adjusted itself to the new internationalised politics of capital'.[37] Defenders of open-space however argue that involvement of such dominant actors suggests that a political programme ought to emerge from struggle particularly from transnational sectoral forums, a stage which the ideologically diverse WSF cannot yet reach. Nonetheless this representation of the WSF locates its greatest—but as yet unrealised—potential in the linking of radical movements to create the twenty-first century's anti-capitalist 'manifesto'.[38] Such idealism however fails to account for the reality within the Forum itself, where a lack of direction and innovation makes the WSF prone to merely to fall into the hands of the centre-left populism of certain political leaders and parties.

Conclusion: 'Another World'?

Despite its obvious problems, many campaigners maintain that the WSF and its regional counterparts are already making important advances within global civil society. For them the WSF
has already facilitated three critical functions for global civil society: (a) a space both physical
and temporal to meet and network; (b) a retreat to gather energy and chart future directions; (c)
a site and a space to elaborate, discuss and debate an alternative world order.[39] Nonetheless, even
Bello admits there is not an 'insignificant truth' in the criticism of the WSF that it isn't anchored
in actual political struggle, has limited social impact and has failed to endorse any political or
other type of struggle. This throws open the question of what kind of movement has emerged
from the space that the WSF undoubtedly served to open up and suggests that we should focus
on the processes of social change by asking what is happening and how, rather than becoming
over-concerned with the direction of social change—the result of social resistance to globalisation. Again for those heavily involved in the WSF movement, such a space is progressively
moving towards one which has until now maintained a defensive role but is now developing into
an offensive position, that would allow the Forum to take advantage of the 'shifting power
equation'.[40] As a result this offensive can—within the next few decades—build towards the creation and the imagination or the possibility of 'another world' through either seeking to create a
'web of networks' that will progressively gain political and civil 'clout'[41] or using the WSF as an
instrument towards establishing a kind of a proto-political party or global political party that
allows new organic intellectuals to steer a new hegemony and leadership within civil society.[42]

   Yet, in truth these claims are nothing more than pipedreams, which as we have demonstrated here, only exist in the imagined realm of civil society. For all the rhetoric forwarded by
academics and activists, the WSF neither represents the sum of the anti-globalisation movement, nor presents us with any coherent counter position to contest the inequalities within
neoliberal economic globalisation. Discontent with globalisation is not merely played out
through different intellectual exchanges within the—hierarchal—realm of civil society, but
expressed through a variety of ideologies at different levels. Similarly, the anti-globalisation
movement is not merely played out through visionary procedures such as the WSF, but through
competing ideological practices, that are articulated in different forms.[43] Rather than attempt to
conceptualise or engage with such diversity, the WSF has occupied one element of this resistance, and has not been able to channel this into anything more than an open space for the convergence of progressive change. As a result, the WSF has turned itself into something of an elitist
post-modern playground, whereby prominent academics and established NGOs imagine alternative futures and speak on behalf of the subaltern classes. The paradox of the WSF is that whilst
futures and alternatives are being discussed inside the Forum, the local commercial economy of
the host locality often remains the one short-term winner, often joined by populist left-leaning
politicians, unless absent due to more meaningful commitments in Davos.

Notes

1. J Sen, 'The world social forum as an emergent learning process', *Futures*, 39(5), 2007,
   pp 505–522; S Tormey, *Anti-Capitalism: An Introduction*, London: One World, 2004; WSF,
   'World Social Forum Charter of Principles', 2002, at http://www.forumsocialmundial.org.
   br/main.php?id_menu=4&cd_language=2, accessed 9 April 2008.
2. M Engler, 'The last Porto Alegre. Discerning the state of the World Social Forum after five
   years', *Znet*, 14 February 2005, at http://www.zmag.org/content/print_article.cfm?itemID=

7247&sectionID=1, accessed 9 April 2008; O Worth & K Buckley, 'Social struggle or unholy alliance? A critique of Porto Alegre and the European Social Forum', paper presented at the International Studies Association Annual Convention, San Diego, March 2006.

3. I Biagiotti, 'The world social forums. A paradoxical application of participatory doctrine', *International Social Science Journal*, 56(4), 2004, pp 529–540.

4. W F Fisher & T Ponniah (eds) *Another World is Possible. Popular Alternatives to Globalization at the World Social Forum.* London and New York: Zed Books, 2003, pp 1–3.

5. The original organisations were the Brazilian Association of Non-Governmental Organisations (ABONG), ATTAC Brazil, the Brazilian Justice and Peace Commission (CSJP), The Brazilian Association for Entrepreneurs for Citizenship, The Brazilian Central Trade Union Federation, The Brazilian Institute for Social and Economic Studies (IBASE), the Social Network for Justice and Human Rights and the Landless Movement (MST). Out of these only ATTAC Brazil is distinctly international in organisation and principle.

6. F Whitaker, 'World Social Forum: origins and aims', 20 June 2004, at http://www2.forum-socialmundial.org.br/dinamic.php?pagina=origem_fsm_ing, accessed 9 April 2008.

7. Fisher & Ponniah, *Another World is Possible*, pp 12–13.

8. WSF, 'Report on the World Social Forum International Council meeting, Utrecht Holland from March 31st to April 2nd 2005', at http://www.forumsocialmundial.org.br/main.php?id_menu=3_2_2&cd_language=2, accessed 9 April 2008.

9. Fisher & Ponniah, *Another World is Possible*.

10. See K Foltz & S Moodliar, 'The Future of the world social forum process', *Znet*, 9 February 2005, at http://www.globalpolicy.org/ngos/advocacy/conf/2005/0209futurewsf.htm accessed 9 April 2008; P Waterman, 'The old and the new in the GJ&SM', *The Voice of the Turtle*, 21 January 2005, at http://voiceoftheturtle.org/show_printer.php?aid=425 accessed 9 April 2008.

11. Fisher & Ponniah, *Another World is Possible*.

12. O Worth & C Kuhling, 'Counter-hegemony, anti-globalisation and culture in International Political Economy', *Capital & Class*, 84, 2004, pp 31–42.

13. Perhaps the best demonstration of this at Nairobi concerned a sculpture depicting a pregnant woman on a crucifix that was placed inside the main entrance to the forum. According to one official WSF media source, the crucifix was designed to demonstrate the right and necessity to contraception, but religious groups and supporters condemned and 'misunderstood' the work. See WSF Nairobi, African Voice: 3, 2007.

14. M Engler, 'The last Porto Alegre'.

15. N Klein, *Fences and Windows. Dispatches from the Front Lines of the Globalisation Debate*, London: Flamingo Harper Collins, 2002.

16. B de Sousa Santos, *The Rise of the Global Left: The World Social Forum and Beyond*, London: Zed Books, 2006.

17. CACIM and CCS (2007) 'In defense of open space' *World Social Forum Session*, 23 Jan, Nairobi.

18. Sen, J and Kumar, M with Bond, P and Waterman, P (2007) *A Political Programme for the World Social Forum? Democracy, Substance and Debate in the Bamako Appeal and the Global Justice Movements. A Reader*, Indian Institute for Critical Action: CACIM/CCS.

19. B de Sousa Santos, Ibid.

20. For example, one of the committee members argued that the main positive of the WSF for him was not that it aimed to reduce global inequality or promote alternative worlds, but that it gave greater thought for his Master's Studies. Examples of more highbrow academic panels include the many on labour and globalisation. Bond, a keen supporter of the Forum,

gave a paper synthesising Luxemburg's capital accumulation thesis with Harvey's position on capital dispossession.

21. D Chandler, *Constructing Global Civil Society*, Basingstoke: Palgrave, 2004. Whilst Chandler is correct in his critique of the imagined discourse of global civil society, his critique falls down when he challenges the very nature of normativism, globalisation or indeed the processes of resistance and contestation. Here his account slides into a form of Nietzcherian nihilism, where the very fabric of norms, ideas and ethics seemed to be challenged.

22. Ibid.

23. I Biagiotti, 'The world social forums. A paradoxical application of participatory doctrine', *International Social Science Journal*, 56(4), 2004, pp 529–540.

24. N Klein, 'More democracy – not more political strongmen', *The Guardian*, 3 February 2003, at http://www.globalpolicy.org/ngos/advocacy/conf/2003/0203klein.htm, accessed 9 April 2008.

25. I Parmar, 'Anti-Americanism and major foundations' in *The rise of Anti-Americanism*, BO Connor & M Griffiths (eds), London: Routledge, 2006, pp 169–194. Also see an Open Democracy interview with L Jordan, 'The Ford Foundation and the World Social Forum', Open Democracy, 2004, at http://www.opendemocracy.net/globalization-world/article_1678.jsp. For information on grants see the Ford Foundation website at http://www.fordfound.org/, both accessed 9 April 2008.

26. Parmar, 'Anti-Americanism'.

27. Cf. C Armstrong, 'Global civil society and the question of global citizenship', *Voluntas*, 17, 2006, pp 349–357.

28. Fisher & Ponniah, *Another World is Possible*.

29. E Cruells 'European Social Forum: A huge lack of inclusiveness at the 2004 edition in London', *Les Pénélopes*, 2005, at http://www.penelopes.org/Anglais/xarticle.php3?id_article=1162, accessed 9 April 2008.

30. P Waterman, 'The old and the new in the GJ&SM', *The Voice of the Turtle*, 21 January 2005, at http://voiceoftheturtle.org/show_printer.php?aid=425, accessed 9 April 2008.

31. Independent Media, 'Report of the Sunday arrests and betrayal facilitated by official ESF', 18 October 2004, at http://www.indymedia.org.uk/en/regions/london/2004/10/299442.html?c=on, accessed 9 April 2008.

32. A Drainville, 'Quebec city 2001 or the making of transnational subjects', in *The Socialist Register 2002: A World of Contradictions*, L Panitch, & C Leys (eds), London: Merlin Press, 2001.

33. Engler, 'The last Porto Alegre'.

34. Rory Carroll, 'World Social Forum message to Davos: We told you so', *Guardian*, Friday 30th January, 2009

35. Ibid.

36. Fisher & Ponniah, *Another World is Possible*.

37. WOMBLES, 'Beyond ESF: A short analysis of the socio-political role of the WSF-ESF', 2006, at http://www.wombles.org.uk/article20060453.php, accessed 9 April 2008.

38. P Bond, 'From WSF 'NGO trade fair' to left politics?' *Znet*, 1 February 2007, at http://www.zmag.org/sustainers/content/2007–02/01bond.cfm, accessed 9 April 2008.

39. W Bello, 'The Forum at the crossroads', *Foreign Policy in Focus*, 4 May 2007, at http://www.fpif.org/fpiftxt/4196, accessed 9 April 2008.

40. I Wallerstein, 'The World Social Forum from defence to offence', *Agence Global*, 31 January 2007, at http://www.openspaceforum.net/twiki/tiki-read_article.php?articleId=328, accessed 9 April 2008.

41. Ibid.

42. K Sehm Patomaki & M Ulvila, (eds) Democratic politics globally—Elements for a dialogue on global political party formations. *Network Institute for Global Democratization (NIGD) Working Paper 1/2006.*

43. O Worth & C Kuhling, 'Counter-hegemony, anti-globalisation and culture in International Political Economy', *Capital & Class*, 84, 2004, pp 31–42; O Worth & J Abbott, 'Land of false hope? The contradictions of British opposition to globalization', *Globalizations*, 3(1), 2006, pp 49–65.

Notes on Authors

Peggy ANTROBUS is a founding member of many regional and international organizations including the Caribbean Association for Feminist Research and Action, the Caribbean Policy Development Centre, Development Alternatives with Women for a New Era, the network of Third World women, and the International Gender and Trade Network.

Maurice BLEICHER is a mission officer, Strategic Affairs Unit, in the French Ministry of Defence. He took part in the negotiations that led to the adoption of the Ottawa Convention on the prohibition of antipersonnel mines.

Robin BROAD is Professor of International Development at American University.

Karen BUCKLY is a teaching associate and doctoral candidate at the University of Limerick.

Louise CHAPPELL teaches at the University of New South Wales, Sydney Australia.

David CORTRIGHT is the Director of Policy Studies at the Kroc Institute for International Peace Studies at the University of Notre Dame and Chair of the Board of the Fourth Freedom Forum in Goshen, Indiana.

Huw T. DAVID is currently completing a doctorate in history at Lincoln College, University of Oxford.

Thomas Richard DAVIES is Lecturer in International Politics at City University, London. He has also been a Research Fellow at St Antony's College and a Lecturer at St Catherine's and New Colleges in the University of Oxford.

William E. DEMARS is Professor and Chair of the Department of Government at Wofford College in South Carolina.

Riley E. DUNLAP is Regents Professor of Sociology at Oklahoma State University. He has also served as Chair of the environmental sociology sections within the American Sociological Association, the Society for the Study of Social Problems, and the Rural Sociological Society.

Dan GALLIN is former secretary-general of the International Federation of Food, Agriculture, Hotel and Catering and Tobacco Workers' Unions and is currently director of the Global Labour Institute in Geneva.

Suzette GRILLOT is the Max and Heidi Berry Chair, Associate Director of International Programs, and Associate Professor of International and Area Studies at the University of Oklahoma.

Reiner GRUNDMANN was a consultant to the United Nations Global Public Policy Project. He teaches sociology within the School of Languages and Social Sciences and is course director of the new Masters degree in Social Research and Social Change.

Molly E. HANNA practices as a workers' compensation defense attorney representing insurance companies and self-insured employers in Oklahoma.

Zahara HECKSCHER is a writer and social justice organizer who has worked overseas, volunteering to plant fruit trees in rural Zambia and helping to build a medical clinic in Nicaragua.

Mary KALDOR is Professor of Global Governance at the London School of Economics, where she is also the Director of its Centre for the Study of Global Governance.

Margaret E. KECK is Professor of Political Science at the Johns Hopkins University.

Naomi KLEIN is a Canadian author and activist known for her political analyses and criticism of corporate globalization.

Aaron M. McCRIGHT is an Assistant Professor of Sociology in Lyman Briggs College and the Department of Sociology at Michigan State University.

Makau MUTUA is Dean, SUNY Distinguished Professor, and the Floyd H. & Hilda L. Hurst Faculty Scholar at Buffalo Law School, the State University of New York. He is also the Director of the Buffalo Human Rights Center.

Thomas RISSE currently acts as chair for "transnational relations, foreign- and security policy" at Otto-Suhr Institute for Political Science at Freie Universität Berlin.

Gay W. SEIDMAN is Professor of Sociology at the University of Wisconsin-Madison.

Kathryn SIKKINK is a Regents Professor and the McKnight Presidential Chair in Political Science at the University of Minnesota.

Jackie SMITH is associate professor of sociology and peace studies at the Kroc Institute for International Peace Studies at the University of Notre Dame.

Craig STAPLEY directs the Security Studies Master and Doctoral programs at Kansas State University.

Andrew W. TORRANCE teaches law at the University of Kansas School of Law.

Wendy E. F. TORRANCE is director, Entrepreneurship, at the Kauffman Foundation in Kansas City.

Johan van der VYVER is I.T. Cohen Professor of International Law and Human Rights at Emory University.

Owen WORTH is a lecturer in International Relations at the University of Limerick, Ireland.

Index

Abolition Act (1807) 57
abolitionism *see* anti-slavery movement, transatlantic
Aborigines Protection Society 64
abortion and Rome Conference 207
accountability politics 303, 306, 307
Acheson-Lilienthal plan 277
Ad Hoc Committee, for an International Criminal Court 134, 136
Adams, Gerry 382, 383
advocacy
    campaigns and 31–2
    of NGOs 10
    of women's movement 182, 183, 185–6
    see also transnational advocacy networks
Afghanistan 11, 281
African Association for Women and Development 181
Africa Watch 119
Agenda 21 224–5
Alagiah, George 12
Alexander, Tsar II 296
Algeria 79
Al Jazeera TV 19
Allende, Salvador 118
All India Trade Union Congress 78
Al-Quaeda 15
Alvarez, Sonia 349
American Association of the International Commission of Jurists 138
American Baptist Church 283
American Civil Liberties Union (ACLU) 149, 156n1
American Convention on Human Rights 117
American Enterprise Institute 10
American Federation of Labor (AFofL) 78
American Federation of Labor–Congress of International Organizations (AFL–CIO) 337
American Friends Service Committee 278, 283
American Lutheran Church 283
American Nurses Association 284

American Values: An Environmental Vision 254
America Watch 119
Amnesty International (AI) 10, 11, 115, 117, 118, 119–20, 121, 123, 124, 129, 150, 153, 312, 356
    International Executive Committee 151
Amory, Cleveland 278
anarcho-syndicalist unionism 78, 79
Anglicanism 49
Anglo-American campaigns *see* anti-slavery movement, transatlantic
Angola 12
Anheier, Helmut 35
Annan, Kofi 95, 139, 141, 295
anti-apartheid movement 118, 121
anti-capitalist movement, new 16–18
anti-globalization movement 341, 376
anti-personnel mines, prohibition of 291–7, 308
Anti-Slavery International 37–8
anti-slavery movement, transatlantic 47, 116
    abolitionism, expansion of 55
    abolitionism in Britain 52–5
    customs and traditions 50–1
    interaction with state 56–7
    Quakerism in Britain and America 49–50
    slavery and Quakers 51–1
Anti-Slavery Society 37–8, 59, 60, 62, 64, 116
anti-slave trade movement 329, 336
Anti-Torture Convention, UN 115, 118, 120
Antrobus, Peggy 163
Argentina 27, 78, 138, 197, 200, 201, 337, 345
Ashburn, John 136
Asian Social Forum 376
Asia Watch 119, 124
Association for Women's Rights and Development (AWID) 166, 177
Atomic Development Authority 276
Atomic Veterans Association 277
ATTAC network 335, 347
Australia 78, 119, 120, 138, 223, 237
Austria 39, 76, 119, 228

Axworthy, Lloyd 292–3, 295, 296
Ayres, Ian 94

Baldwin, Roger 150
Bamako Appeal 378
Bangladesh 11, 89
Bangladesh Rural Advancement Committee
    (BRAC) 10
Barlow, Maude 342
Barnet, Richard 282, 332
    Global Reach 335
al-Bashir, Omar 66
Bassiouni, Cherif 138
Basu, Amrita 163
Baumgartner, Frank R. 28
Beijing Conferences 192, 196, 206
Beijing +5 conference 199, 200, 201, 203, 204,
    207, 208
Beijing +10 conference 198, 199, 204, 208
Beijing Declaration and the Platform for
    Action (BPFA) 193, 196, 199, 203, 204,
    205, 206, 207
Beijing minus 5 207
Belem Forum 383
Belgium 223, 330, 335
Bello, Walden 334, 336
Benedetti, Fanny 136, 144
Benenson, Peter 117, 150
Benezet, Anthony 49, 53, 56
    Observations on the enslaving, importing
    and purchasing of negroes 54
    Some historical account of Guinea 55
    The case of our fellow creatures, the
    oppressed Africans 54, 56
Bennett, W. Lance 303, 304, 309
Bernardin, Joseph Cardinal 283
Bernstein, Robert 118, 119, 151
Bernstein, Tom 151
Bethe, Hans 275
Bill and Melinda Gates Foundation 65
Biological Weapons Convention (1972) 295
Black Box anarchists 17
Bleicher, Maurice 291
Boli, John 36
Bolin, Bert 241
Bolsheviks 76
bomb, banning of 273–87
    arms control, beginning of 279–80
    Baruch plan 276–7

Europe and 285–6
    nuclear freeze, rise of 281–2, 284
    nuclear pacifism in Japan 280–1
    for nuclear sanity 277–9
    religious community and 282–4
    support for nuclear freeze 284–5
boomerang effect 13, 27, 122, 205
Bosnia 65, 138
Boston Social Forum 376
Bové, José 342, 357n11
boycotts, consumer 86–8
Braithwaite, John 94
Brayton, Patience 56
Brazil 17, 27, 78, 223, 226, 331, 337, 341, 377,
    381, 383
The Brazilian Movement for Human
    Rights 137
Brent Spa 12
British and Foreign Anti-Slavery Society
    (1839) 37–8
British Anti-Slavery Society 59, 60, 62
British Petroleum (BP) 231, 245
Broad, Robin 327
Brooks, Ethel 89
Brundtland Commission see World
    Commission on Environment and
    Development
Buckley, Karen 376
Bulletin of Atomic Scientists 275, 277
Burma 20
Burundi 130
Bush, George H.W. 30, 286
Bush, George W. 65
Buss, Doris 200
Butler, William J. 138

Cairo Conference 193, 203, 204
Cairo International Conference on
    Population and Development (ICPD)
    (1994) 192, 206
Calhoun, Craig 32
Call to Halt the Arms Race manifesto 282
Campaign for Nuclear Disarmament
    (CND) 278, 280, 285
campaigns
    transnational 86–8
    and transnational advocacy networks
    31–2
    and women's movement 177

Canada 78, 124, 138, 139, 237, 305, 307, 342, 345
Cape Verde 151
Caribbean 179, 331
Carnegie Commissions 10
Carson, Rachel
    Silent Spring 223
Carter, Jimmy 135
Carter Center 65
Casement, Roger 64
Castells, Manuel 13
Catholic Family and Rights Institute (C-FAM) 191, 200
Catholic-Muslim commission (1995) 200
Cato Institute 259
caucuses, of women 174
CEI Update 258, 259
Center for Women's Global Leadership (CWGL) 178
Centre for Civil Society in India 10
certain conventional weapons (CCW) 291
Chabal, Patrick 11
Chabasse, Philippe 297
Chandhoke, Neera 19
Chandler, David 380, 386n21
Chappell, Louise 190
Charnowitz, Steve 8
Charter 77 movement 118
Chavez, Hugo 382, 383
Chemical Weapons Convention (1993) 295
Chevron 343
Chico River Basin Development Project 334-5
Chile 78, 115, 118, 122, 123, 124, 125, 126, 127, 129, 332, 336
China 42, 67, 84, 116, 127, 130, 173
Chinese anarchist groups 79
Chipko movement 188n20
chlorofluorocarbons (CFC) 229, 241, 242, 243, 244
Christian Right United Nations (CR UN) 191-2, 199, 200, 201, 203, 208
Chukri, Aziz 138
Church, Frank 332
Churchill, Winston 40
Church of Scotland Missionary Society 117
Citigroup 343
Citizens for a Sound Economy Foundation 257, 262

civil society 93
Clark, Roger 138
Clarkson, Thomas 57
Climate Action Network (CAN) 230
climate change 228-31
Clinton, Bill 65, 246n6, 259
coalition and alliance building, for global women's movement 174-5
Coalition for an International Criminal Court (CICC) 134, 138, 139, 143
    Caucus on Children's Rights 137
    objectives of 136
Coalition for Nuclear Disarmament and Peace 355
Code of Marketing for Breast-milk Substitutes 32
Coffin, William Sloane Jr. 283
cognitive frames, building 28-30
Cohen, Bonner 254
collective bargaining 91
Collins, Canon L. John 278, 280
Colombia 130
Collor de Mello, Fernando 30
Commission for the Protection of the Natives 64
Commission on Human Rights, UN 116, 117, 124
Committee for the Protection of Interests in Africa 64
Committee of the Convention for the Elimination of All Forms of Discrimination against Women 192
Commonweal 283
Communist Manifesto 75
community building groups (CBOs) 9, 10, 11
Competitive Enterprise Institute 257, 259, 260, 262, 263, 265
Concerned Women of America 191
Conference on Disarmament 293, 297
Conference on Security and Cooperation in Europe (CSCE) 118
conferences and women's movement 175-80
    non-UN 177-80
    UN 175-7
Congo Reform Association 64
Congo Reform Movement 59-67
Congress of Industrial Organizations (CIO) 78
conscientization 166, 169

consciousness-raising groups, feminist 173
conservative movement counter-claims *see*
   global warming
consumer boycotts 86–8
contentious politics 4
   transnational 194
Control Arms campaign 312
Convention on the Elimination of All Forms
   of Discrimination Against Women
   (CEDAW) 178, 196, 211*n*22
Copenhagen Conference (1980) 196
corporate-led globalization
   global integration and resistance origins
      and 328–30
   resistance to 332–3
   resistance to World Bank and IMF 333–6
   and women's movement 177
   world economy, rebuilding and
      restructuring and 330–1
corporate managers 82
corporate social responsibility 95
Corrections Corporation of America 343
Cortright, David 273
Costa Rica 119, 198
Council for a Livable World 279
Council of Canadians 342
counter activists
   and framing 201–5
   influence on conference documents 205–6
   influence on proceedings 206–7
   influence on transnational women's
      movement 207–8
   and mobilizing structure 198–201
   and political opportunity structure 195–8
counter-cultural approach, to social
   change 184
counter-cultural groups and women's
   movement 183
counter frames 201, 202
   on equality 204
   on gender 203
   on reproduction 204
   on sexuality 203
counter-hegemony 377–8
counter-movements 194–5, 196, 197, 198, 209
   emergence of 253–5
counterrhetoric of insincerity 251, 255, 258,
      259, 260
Cousins, Norman 278, 279, 281

Covenant on Civil and Political Rights
   (1976) 116, 119
Covenant on Economic and Social Rights
   (1976) 119
Cuomo, Kerry Kennedy 151
Czechoslovakia 118, 122, 123, 126, 127, 129, 179

da Silva, Lula 377, 382
Darfur movement 66
David, Huw T. 47
Davies, Thomas Richard 35
DAWN 169, 174, 175, 181, 208
Debs, Eugene Victor 78
Declaration for Humanity and Against
   Neo-Liberalism 17
Declaration on Fundamental Principles and
   Rights at Work 90
decolonization and transnational civil
   society 41
DeMars, William E. 59
Democratic Republic of the Congo 152
Denmark 124, 138, 196
De Waal, Alex 66
Des Forges, Alison 66
Dili massacre 124
discursive democracy 180
diversionary framing 201
diversity and women's movement 167
Doble, John 281
Dobson, James 203
Dominant Social Paradigm 254
Dominican Republic 84
Dorsen, Norman 151
Dumbarton Oaks conference 117
Dunlap, Riley E. 251
DuPont 229, 231
Durban Summit 297

Earth Summit 224–5, 226, 231, 247*n*18
ECO 223
Economic and Social Committee, UN 8
Economic and Social Council
   (ECOSOC) 294
economic restructuring 82
Ecuador 337
Edmundson, William 51
Egeland, Jan 295
Egypt 141, 191, 197, 198, 200, 203, 204, 209,
      213*n*75

Einstein, Albert 274, 275, 278
El Salvador 84, 197
electronic coalition 296
elitism 380–2
Emergency Committee of Atomic
  Scientists 275, 277
encuentros 349
Engels, Friedrich 75
Enlightenment philosophy 53
Environmental Policy Analysis Network 254
Environment Forum 223
epistemic communities 222, 229, 246n13
Ethical Trading Initiative 88
ethnicity, transnational 15–16
Ethyl Corporation 345
European Convention on Human Rights 117
European Human Rights Convention 119
European Law Students' Association 137
European Recovery Program 77
European Social Forum 357n9, 376, 383
European Trade Union Confederation
  (ETUC) 79
European Trade Union Federations
  (ETUF) 79
European Union (EU) 121, 231, 237, 241
European works councils (EWC) 80

Facio, Alda 188n35
Family Research Council 191
Farmer, Paul 65
fascism 76
Federation of American Scientists (FAS) 275,
  277
Fellowship of Reconciliation 283
feminist activists 181
feminist politics 167–8
feminist ultra-consciousness 188n35
Ferencz, Bejamin F. 138
fire-alarm approach 93
First Hague Peace Conference (1899) 296
First International 75, 78
First International Encuentro for Humanity
  and Against Neoliberalism 349
First International Workingmen's
  Association 329, 330, 337
First World NGOs 153–4
First World War 39
Fisher, Williams 377, 378
Focus on the Family 191

Fogaça, José 378
Foot, Michael 278
Ford Foundation 117, 118, 163, 381
Foreign Affairs 281, 282
Forsberg, Randall 282
Fosdick, Henry Emerson 278
Fothergill, John 54
Fothergill, Samuel 52, 53
Foundation for Research on Economics and
  the Environment 261
Fourth World Conference on Women
  (FWCW) (1995) 192, 197
Fowler, Alan 12
Fox, George 50, 51
frame alignment 28
frame resonance 28
Framework Convention on Climate Change
  (FCCC) 229, 231, 236, 241
framing 195
  and counter activists 201–5
France 17, 29, 53, 77, 79, 119, 120, 143, 279,
  330, 335, 345, 347
Frankel, Marvin 151
French colonies, trade union movement
  in 79
Freudenburg, William R. 253, 264
Friedrich Ebert Foundation 117
Friends of the Earth (FOE) 222, 226, 227,
  228, 229
Fromm, Erich
  The Sane Society 278
Fung, A. 95, 96
Furtado, Celso 331

G8 summit in Genoa, demonstrations at 17
G-77 198, 213n75
Galeano, Eduardo
  Open Veins of Latin America 328
Gallin, Dan 73
gender 206
  analysis 141
  and counter frames 203
General Agreement on Tariffs and Trade
  (GATT) 330, 338
General Assembly of the Global Antiwar
  Movement 355
General Electric 343
Geneva Declaration 200
Genoa Social Forum 17

Gensuikyo 280
Geographical Conference, of Leopold 62
George, Susan
    How the Other Half Dies 334, 335
Geremek, Bronislaw 297
Germany 39, 42, 63, 76, 78, 117, 121, 138, 239,
    243, 246n7, 274, 281, 330
Ghana 151, 170, 279
Glasius, Marlies 35
Global Call to Action against Poverty 41
Global Campaign for Women's Human
    Rights (GCWHR) 177, 178, 200
Global Campaign on Small Arms and Light
    Weapons 305
global civil networks see transnational civic
    networks
global civil society 4, 19–20, 94,
    critique of 380
    typology of actors of 5
    see also individual entries
Global Climate Coalition (GCC) 230–1
Global Compact 95–6
Global Days of Actions (GDA) 380
global environmental change (GEC) 254, 264
Global Exchange 88
Global Forum 224
global governance 92–7
globalization 41, 83, 89, 95, 177, 341–6
    see also individual entries
Global Justice movement 376
global politics 3
Global Tribunal on Violations of Women's
    Human Rights 178
global warming 251
    conservative movement's counter-
        claims 256
    countermovement, emergence of 253–5
    evidentiary basis of, criticizing 257–60
    harmful effects of proposed action
        against 262–4
    legitimation, as problem 252–3
    potential benefits from 260–1
    study 255–6
glocality 169
Goldberg, Arthur 118
Goldstone, Richard 138
Gorbachev, Mikhail 286, 287
Gore, Al 259
grassroots organisations (GROs) 9, 10, 11

Great Awakening 51
Great Depression 39
Greece 118
Greek coup d'etat 117–18
Greenberg, Jack 151
greenhouse effect 236
Greenpeace 11, 12, 30, 226, 227, 228, 229
Grillot, Suzette R. 300
Gromyko, Andrei 276
Groulx, Elise 143
Grundmann, Reiner 236
Guatemala 16, 122, 123, 125, 126, 127, 129, 197
Gumbleton, Thomas 283
Gymah-Boadi, E. 11

Habibie, Jusuf 126
Hafner, Gerhard 138
Hague Conference (2000) 236, 237, 243,
    286
Hague Peace Conferences (1899, 1907) 8, 38
Halliday, Fred 15
Handicap International 297
Hanna, Molly E. 300
hard international law 211n22
hate radio 18
Hatfield, Mark 282
Havana Charter 338n12
Hayter, Teresa 336
    Aid as Imperialism 334
Health Action International 27
Heartland Institute 259, 260, 261, 262, 263, 265
Heckscher, Zahara 327
Hehir, Father J. Bryan 283
Helsinki Agreement (1975) 13
Helsinki Final Act (1975) 118
Helsinki Watch 118, 119, 123
Helsinki Watch Group 118
Henkin, Alice 151
Henkin, Louis 151
Heritage Foundation 261, 262, 263
Herman, Did 200
Herzegovina 138
Hochschild, Adam 62
Holy See 141, 192, 198, 203, 204, 205, 206,
    207, 211n18
homosexuality, counter frames on 203
Hooks, Bell 166
Hoover Institution 260–1
Houghton, John 241

Howard, Michael 40
War and the Liberal Conscience 38
Howell, Jude 16
human rights
activists 85
and labor rights *see* labor rights, as human rights
NGOS 149–55
and transnational civil society *see under* transnational civil society
Human Rights Commission, UN 119–20, 125, 128
Human Rights Watch (HRW) 66, 83, 117, 119, 120, 121, 137, 149, 150, 151, 152, 154, 312
human security 292–3
Huntington, Samuel 190

imagined communities 18
In Defense of Creation 283
India 10, 78, 151, 170, 335, 343, 348, 381, 382
Indochina 79
Indonesia 79, 115, 122, 123, 124, 125, 127, 130
industrial production and new technologies 84
Industrial Workers of the World (IWW) 78
information politics 30–1, 303, 305–6, 307
Institute for Defense and Disarmament Studies 282
Institute for Policy Studies 282, 335
Interallied Federation of Ex-Servicemen 39
Inter-American Commission on Human Rights 27, 117, 123, 124
Interchurch Peace Council 285
intergovernmental organizations (IGOs) 117
Intergovernmental Panel on Climate Change (IPCC) 228–9, 230, 231, 237, 238, 241–2, 244, 245, 246n14, 254, 261
Climate Change 1995 258
International Action Network on Small Arms (IANSA) 296, 301–2, 305–7, 311, 313
differences with ICBL 308–9
leadership and 313–14
Programme of Action to Prevent, Combat and Eradicate the Illicit Trade in Small Arms and Light Weapons in All its Aspects 306
similarities with ICBL 7
International African Association 62
International Alert 312

International Alliance of Women (1902) 38
International Atomic Energy Agency 134
International Baby Food Action Network (IBFAN) 27, 32
International Bar Association 143
International Bill of Rights 150
International Campaign to Ban Landmines (ICBL) 292, 294, 297, 298, 322nn65, 73
differences with IANSA 308–9
similarities with IANSA 307
typology of organizations of *310*
International Centre for Human Rights and Democratic Development 137
International Chamber of Commerce 8
International Coalition for Development Action 27
International Commission of Jurists (ICJ) 117, 123, 137, 150, 152
International Commissions 9
International Committee of the Red Cross (ICRC) 296
International Confederation of Free Trade Unions (ICFTU) 77, 79
International Conference on Human Rights 169
International Congo Association 63
International Convention for the Regulation of Whaling 227
International Council (IC) 350, 351
International Council of Scientific Unions (ICSU) 222, 232n5
International Covenant on Civil and Political Rights (ICCPR) 151, 152
International Covenant on Economic, Social, and Cultural Rights (ICESCR) 152, 153
International Criminal Bar 143
International Criminal Court 66, 134, 192
NGO forum for 135–9
NGO participation, continuing pertinence of 143–4
Women's Caucus, success of 139–43
International Criminal Defence Attorneys Association 143
International Decade for Women (1975) 196
International Federation of Human Rights 137
International Federation of Trade Unions 39
International Federation of Trade Unions (IFTU) 75, 76, 77, 78

International Geophysical Year (IGY) 221, 222
International Human Rights Law Group 150,
    151, 152
International Inter-disciplinary
    Congress 166
international labor movement 73
    history 74–7
    worldwide 77–80
International Labor Organization (ILO) 8,
    76, 90, 333
International League for Human Rights
    (ILHR) 150, 156n5
International League for the Rights of Man
    (1922) 39
International Military Commission 296
International Monetary Fund (IMF) 227,
    330, 333–5
international non-governmental
    organizations (INGOs) 8, 20, 116, 122,
    149–50, 193–4
    American 157n10
    authoritative claim to knowledge by 121
    evolution of, since mid-nineteenth
        century 35–42
    and human rights 119, 120
    information dissemination by 123
    law versus politics and 154–5
    mandates of 152–4
    shaming and 121
    social support and political bias and 150–2
    sustainability of power of 130–1
International Order of Good Templars
    (1852) 38
International Peace Bureau (1891) 38
International Telephone and Telegraph
    (ITT) 332
International Trade Organization 338n12
international trade secretariats (ITS) 75
International Union for the Conservation of
    Nature and Natural Resources
    (IUCN) 222, 226–7, 294
International Women's Day 179
International Women's Tribune Centre
    (IWTC) 178
International Workingmen's Association
    (1864) 38
Iran 191, 197, 200, 203, 204, 205, 209, 213n75
Iraq 177, 205
Ireland 197

Iriye, Akira 38
Italy 39, 76, 78

Jack, Homer 278
Jacobson, Sarah 343
Japan 39, 42, 79, 125, 237, 239, 275, 280–1
Japanese National Liaison Committee for
    Nuclear and General
    Disarmament 280–1
Joffe, Robert 151
Johannesburg Conference 225
John Paul II, Pope 201, 205
Johns Hopkins Survey 9
Jones, Bryan D. 28
Jordan 19, 151, 204
Jospin, Lionel 18
Jubilee 2000 40, 41, 42
Jungk, Robert 273, 274

Kaldor, Mary 3, 35, 286
Kardam 192
Kaunda, Kenneth 382
Keck, Margaret E. 13, 24, 48, 57, 88, 122, 194,
    199, 205, 303
Kennan, George 283, 287
Kennedy, Edward 32
Kennedy, John F. 279
Kenya 117, 122, 123, 124, 125, 126, 131, 160,
    163, 196, 223, 380, 381, 382
Khor, Martin 335
Khrushchev, President 279
King-Hall, Stephen 278
Kissinger, Henry 286
Klein, Naomi 341, 378
Kohl, Helmut 327
Konrad Adenauer Foundation 117
Kosovo Commission 10
Kothari, Rajni 7
Kouchner, Bernard 17
Kristof, Nicholas 66, 67
Kuwait 198, 204, 213n75
Kyoto Protocol (1997) 225, 229, 231, 236–7, 265

Labor and Socialist International 76
labor rights, as human rights 81
    boycotts and 85–8
    campaigns and 88–92
    global governance 92–7
    national state, thinned 82–5

Lake, Anthony 66
Lamani, Mokhtar 200
Landmine Monitor 297, 322n65
Lang, Winfried 238
Latin America 26, 78, 117, 118, 119, 122, 179,
    227, 328, 331, 349
Laurance, Ed 305
Lawson, Bob 297
Lawyers' Committee for Human Rights
    (LCHR) 121, 125, 150, 151, 155
Lawyers Committee for Civil Rights Under
    Law 155
Lawyers Committee for International Human
    Rights see Lawyers' Committee for
    Human Rights (LCHR)
Le Monde 150
League of Arab States 192, 198
League of Nations 8, 39, 40
Legal Defense and Educational Fund
    (LDF) 149, 156n2
Leopold, King 59, 60, 61–3, 64
Lesseps, Viscount de 62
leverage politics 303, 306, 307
Liberia 130
Libya 19, 191, 197, 200, 203, 205, 209, 213n75
Like-Minded Group 144
Lilienthal, David 275, 276
Lindzen, Richard 259
Liverpool Dockers strike 17
Livingstone, David 59, 61, 66
    Missionary Travels and Researches in
        Southern Africa 60
Livingstone, Ken 382, 383
London Missionary Society 60
London Yearly Meeting 52, 53, 54, 56
Lorde, Audre 167
Lundestad, Geir 41
Lutheran Church of America 283

Macmillan, Harold 279
Magna Charta of Human Rights 117
mainstreaming strategy and women's
    movement 180–1
Malaysia 198, 203, 213n75
Mandela, Winnie 382
Manifest Destiny 254
Marcos, Ferdinand 123, 332, 334, 335, 376
Markey, Ed 285
Marshall Institute 258

Martin, Ian 155
Marx, Karl 75, 84
Mauritius 82
McCright, Aaron M. 251
McGovern, George 282
McGovernment 344, 346
McNamara, Robert 334
media, role of 18–20
media coverage
    and NGOs 12
    in network information politics 31
mediatique events 18
Metalclad 345
Methodism 49, 55, 56
Mexico 78, 196, 341, 345
Mexico Conference (1975) 196
Meyer, David 194, 195, 196, 197
Michaels, Patrick J. 258, 259
Millennium Development Goals, UN 65
Miller, Valerie 183
mobilizing structures 195
Moi, Arap 124
Monsanto 343
Montesquieu, Charles-Louis 54
    Enclopédie 53
    Esprit des Lois 53
Montreal Protocol (1987) 36, 228, 229, 231,
    236, 238, 243
Moore, Thomas Gale
    Climate of Fear 261
moral accountability 86, 88
moral authority 120–1
Morales, Evo 382
Morel, E. D. 59, 60, 63–5
Morocco 19, 122, 123, 127, 203, 205, 213n75
Mothers of Plaza 138
Müller, Ronald 332
multilateral environmental treaties 232n2
Munck, Roland 17
Museveni, Yoweri 128, 129
Mutua, Makau 149
mutual benefit NGOs 10
Myanmar 130

Nader, Ralph 382
NAFTA 342
National Association for the Advancement
    of Colored People (NAACP) 149,
    156n2

National Center for Policy Analysis 257, 259, 262, 263, 265
National Center for Public Policy Research 257, 258, 261, 263, 265
National Committee for Sane Nuclear Policy (SANE) 278, 279
National Investigating Commission 125
nationalists and fundamentalist movements, new 14–16
National Resistance Movement 128
National Right to Life 191
nation-state 38
Natural Foot Society 116
Natural Resources Defense Council 254
Nature 232n4
Neale, Palena R. 207
Nestle Kills Babies 29
the Netherlands 79, 119, 120, 125, 285, 305
network activism see anti-slavery movement, transatlantic
networking and women's movement 170, 182
New Economics Foundation (NEF) 170
new international economic order' (NIEO) 332, 333, 335, 336
new labour movement 17
new policy agenda 9
Newsweek 66
New York Herald 61
New York Times 66, 238, 239, 278, 283, 285
New Zealand 78
Nicaragua 197, 198, 200, 201
Nicolas, Tsar II 296
Nigeria 12, 164, 188n20, 343
Nike 343
Nkrumah, Kwame 279
Non-Aligned Movement 124
non-governmental development organizations (NGDOs) 12
non-governmental organisations (NGOs) 3–4, 7–12, 25, 30, 32, 186, 192, 200–1, 222, 224, 229, 292, 296
  continuing pertinence of participation of 143–4
  criticisms against 11–12
  differences among 10–11
  environmental 229, 230–1, 236
  forum, for International Criminal Court 135–9
  human rights 149–55
  and labor unions 93, 96
  lobbying 117
  Ottawa process and 294–5
  small arms movement and 312–13, 316
  and states, alliance between 297
  transnational environmentalism and 226–9
  and transnational social movement networks (TSMNs) 300–1, 302–4, 309–10
  as value-driven organizations 8, 12
non-party political process 7
nonprofits see non-governmental organisations (NGOs)
non-state actors 4
non-state transnational networks 94
North American Free Trade Agreement 231
Northern NGOs 10, 12
Norway 78
Nova, Scott 93
Nyerere, Julius 279, 332

OAS Managua Declaration (1993) 121
Obote, Milton 118
Observer 150
Obuchi, Keizo 296
Ocampo, Raúl 138
Offe, Claus 7
Oppenheimer, J. Robert 273, 276
orchestration of consensus 243, 246n14, 247n16
Ordre des Avocats à la Cour de Paris 143
Organisation of Petroleum Exporting Countries (OPEC) 332, 333
Organisation of the Islamic Conference (OIC) 192, 198
Organization for Economic Cooperation and Development (OECD) 229, 333
Organization of African Trade Union Unity (OATUU) 79
Organization of American States (OAS) 117
Organizing Committee (OC) 377
O'Rourke, Dara 93
Ottawa Landmines Convention (1997) 36
Ottawa process 291–7
  handling of 293–4
  humanitarian motives and 295
  negotiations and 296–7
  NGOs and 294–5
  state–NGO alliance and 297

Otto, Dianne 207
Oxfam 10, 88, 96, 312
ozone depletion 228, 229, 242–3

Pace, Bill 136, 144
Pace, William 135, 137, 138
Pakistan 197, 203
Panama 198
Parliamentarians for Global Action 137
patriarchy 191
patrimonial states and NGOs 11–12
Pauling, Linus 275, 278, 280
Pax Christi 124, 283
Payer, Cheryl
    The Debt Trap 334
Peace Corps 26
Pearce, Jenny 16
Permanent Peoples' Tribunal on the
    Philippines 335
Peron, General 78
Pesticides Action Network 27
Pew Center on Global Climate Change 245n5
Philadelphia Yearly Meeting 51, 52, 54
Philippines 84, 122, 123, 125, 126, 127, 128–9,
    331, 332, 334, 336
Pickett, Clarence 278
Pinochet, Augusto 115, 118, 124
Plan Colombia 355
Poland 122, 123, 126, 127, 129
political approach, to social change 184
political opportunity structure (POS) 195
    and counter activists 195–8
Ponniah, Thomas 377, 378
Portugal 39, 76, 78, 79
post-Fordism 84
Powell, Colin 65
Power, Samantha
    A Problem from Hell 66
praxis 169
Prebisch, Raúl 331
Prendergast, John 66
Preparatory Committee (PrepCom) 203, 305
    for International Criminal Court 134, 136
    for women's caucuses 174
Presbyterianism 49
Priestley, J. B. 278
private entertainment media 19
Procedural Aspects of International Law
    Institute 150

professional-technical approach, to social
    change 184
Programme of Action (Cairo) 193, 203, 205
Protocol II 291
public interest groups see non-governmental
    organisations (NGOs)
public service broadcasting 18–19
Pugwash movement 278, 294

Qatar 19, 198, 203
Quakerism in Britain and America 49–50
    customs and traditions 50–1
    parallel structures 50
    and slavery 51–2
Quayle, Dan 287

Rabbinical Assembly of America 284
Rabinowitch, Eugene 274, 274, 275
radical environmentalism 259
radio B92 19
Ramos-Horta, Jose 125, 126
Ratcheting Labor Standards (RLS) 95–6, 97
Razavi, Shahra 199
Reagan, Ronald 154, 155, 281, 286, 327
REAL Women 191–2
REAL Women of Canada 137
Reclaim the Streets 343
Red Army 76
Red International of Labor Unions (RILU) 76
REDRESS 137
regulation-by-monitoring 94
Reinsch, Paul S. 35, 38
repertoire, of social movements 4, 6
repressive regimes and human rights 118
resolution 53/77 Y 297
Reuters World Newswire 232n4
Rhodes, Cecil 328
Ridenour, David 265
Risse, Thomas 115
Rivoli, Pietra 88
Rome Conference 134, 137, 138, 139, 140,
    192, 203, 207, 294
Rome Statute of the International Criminal
    Court 193, 206, 211n22
Roosevelt, Eleanor 278
Rotblat, Joseph 278
Rousseau, J.
    Discours sur l'origine et les fondements de
    l'inégalité 53

Royal Geographical Society 60
Ruggie, John 96
Rules of Evidence and Procedure and
    Elements of Crimes 193
Rules of Procedure and Evidence (RPE) 142–4
runaway shop 82
Ruppert, Uta 168–9
Ruse, Austin 200, 201
Russell, Bertrand 277–8, 280
Russia 42, 76, 77, 296
Rwanda 65, 123, 130, 138
Rwelamira, Medard 138

Sachs, Jeffrey 65
Saferworld 312
Salamon, Lester 9
Saland, Per 138, 145*n*16
Sané, Pierre 137
San Francisco conference 117
Santoro, Michael 92
Saperstein, David 284
Saudi Arabia 15, 19, 152
Save the Children International Union
    (1920) 39
Schell, Jonathan
    The Fate of the Earth 273
Schindler, Alexander 284
Schweitzer, Albert 280
Scientific American 282
scientific networks 222, 226
SCOPE (Scientific Committee on Problems of
    the Environment) 228
Seattle Weekly 247*n*18
Second Hague Peace Conference (1907) 296
Second International 75, 78
Seechange 211*n*18
Seidman, Gay W. 81
Sejersted, Francis 297
Self-employed Women's Association
    (SEWA) 10, 188*n*20
self-entrapment 128
self-regulation 94
Sen, Gita 171, 172
Sen, Sun Yat 79
Senegal 158*n*17
Serbia 19
service provision, of NGOs 10
shaming 121, 159*n*29

Sharp, Granville 55, 56
Sheehan, James M. 258, 260
Shell Oil 343
Shotwell, James 278
Sierra Leone 13
Sikkink, Kathryn 13, 24, 48, 57, 88, 122, 194,
    199, 205, 303
Singer, Hans 331
Sixteen Days of Activism Against Gender
    Violence 178, 179
Slavery Abolition Act (1833) 48
small arms movement (SAM) 300
    accomplishments 306–7
    ICBL and IANSA, relative success
        of 307–10
    internal assessment of 311–14
    objectives of 305–6
    origins of 305
    participants, typology of *310*
    transnational social movement networks
        (TSMNs) and 302–4, 309–10
Small Arms Survey 312
Smith, Gerard 281
Smith, Jackie 40, 347
Snow, David 28
social change, Crowfoot's and Chesler's
    approaches to 184
social citizenship 84
social-democratic and communist labor
    movement
    cold war period 77
    interwar years 75–7
    Word War I origins 74–5
Socialist International 77
Social Learning Group 232*n*4
social movements 49, 190–1, 195, 198–201
    old and new 4–7, 5, 20
    taming of 3, 6, 7–8, 9, 12
    transnational 47
    see also individual entries
social networks 25–7
Society for the Abolition of the Slave
    Trade 56, 59
Society of Friends 49, 50
Sociologists Without Borders 357*n*10
Sodexho-Marriott 343
soft international law 211*n*22
Sojourners 283

solidarity 7, 67, 144, 166, 167, 170, 185, 337, 379
  consumer campaigns and 86
  funding and 381
  international labor 89
  international 355
  moral 354
  versus mutual benefit NGOs 10
  strengthening of 313
  trade union 75, 79
Sommaruga, Cornelio 296
South Africa 78, 118, 121, 122, 123, 125, 126, 127, 129, 130, 225
Southern NGOs 10
South Korea 126
sovereignty 61, 63
  and human rights 204–5
  national 116, 119, 121, 263, 276
Soviet Union 118, 119, 123, 128, 276, 277, 278, 281, 282, 285, 287
Soweto massacre 118
spaces, of women's organizing 173–5
Spain 39, 76, 78, 79
Species Survival Commission 226
Staggenborg, Suzanne 194, 195, 196, 197
Stamp Act (1765) 48
Stanley, Henry Morton 59, 60–1, 62, 63
Stapley, Craig S. 300
Star TV 19
Steiner, H. J. 153–4
Stockholm Conference on Environment and Development (1972) 8, 222–3
Stockholm Forum 223
Strategic Arms Limitation Treaty (SALT) 281
Strategic Defense Initiative 286, 287
Streains, Cate 140, 141–2
Sudan 66
Suharto, President 115, 124, 125, 126
Sweden 119, 120, 138
Sweeney, John 337
Switzerland 150, 348
symbolic politics 303, 306, 307
Synagogue Council of America 284
Syria 142, 198, 203, 204
Szilard, Leo 274, 275, 279

Taco Bell 343
taming, of social movements 3, 6, 7–8, 9, 12
Tanzania 279, 332

Tarrow, Sidney 6, 32nn1, 3, 193, 194
Taylor, A.J.P. 278
Tennessee Valley Authority 275
testimony 30
Thailand 126
Thatcher, Margaret 155, 286, 327
think tanks 9, 10
Third International 76
third way politicians 9, 17
Third World Action Group 29
Third World Conference on Women (1985) 169
Third World environmental organizations 227
Third World Network 335
Third World trade unions 79
Third World women 181
Thomas, George 36
Thomas, Norman 278
Tilak, Bal Gangadhar 78
Tillich, Paul 278
Tilly, Charles 4, 7, 350
Toronto Conference on the Changing Atmosphere (1988) 228, 229, 230
Torrance, Andrew W. 221
Torrance, Wendy E. F. 221
Toyohiko, Kagawa 280
Trade Records Analysis of Fauna and Flora in Commerce (TRAFFIC) 227
transformism 383
transnational activism 48, 86
  see also individual entries
transnational advocacy networks (TANs) 13–14, 24, 47, 205
  campaigns 31–2
  cognitive frames, building 28–30
  information politics 30–1
  political opportunity structure 27–8
  social networks and 25–7
transnational civic networks 13–14
transnational civil society 122
  defining and measuring of 35–7
  evolution of 37–41
  future of 41–2
  global economy and 37
  limits of 130–1
  mobilization of 116–22
  norms denial and 123–5

transnational civil society (*Cont'd*)
  political factors and 37
  power of 129–30
  prescriptive status 127–8
  repression and activation of 123
  rule-consistent behavior 128–9
  social factors and 37
  tactical concessions and 125–7
  technological developments and 37
transnational coalitions 47, 226, 228
transnational conservative patriarchal
  network (TCPN) 191, 208, 209
transnational corporations (TNC) 80
transnational environmentalism 221
  challenges 231–2
  definition and structure, problems
    of 225–6
  history of 222–3
  influences and changing agendas 223–5
  NGO role in 226–9
  ozone depletion and climate change, case
    studies of 229–31
transnational networks 226
transnational policy networks and advocacy
  scientists 236
  consensus as priority 241–3
  The Hague Conference 237
  Kyoto Protocol 236–7
  public attention, role of 238–41
Transnational Radical Party 137
transnational social actors (TSMs) 193–4
transnational social movement networks
  (TSMNs) 300–1, 319n15
  first and second generation 303–4, 309–10
  functions and effects of 303
transnational women's rights movement
  (TWM) 191, 196–7, 199, 200, 201, 202–3,
    206, 208
  influence of counter activists on 207–8
  see also women's movement, global
transnational social movements 47
Treaty of Paris (1783) 50
Treaty of Versailles 76
Truman, President 275, 277
Tunisia 19, 122, 123, 205

Uganda 122, 123, 127, 128, 129, 130
Uganda Human Rights Commission
  (1995) 128

umbrella group 237
UN Atomic Energy Commission 276
UN Code of Conduct on Transnational
  Corporations 333
UN Conference on Environment and
  Development (UNCED) 169
UN Convention against Torture and Other
  Cruel, Inhuman, or Degrading
  Treatment or Punishment (1984) 119
UN Decade for Women 168, 177, 179,
  181, 182
UN Human Rights Committee 119 (1976)
Union of American Hebrew
  Congregations 284
Union of Concerned Scientists' (UCS) 258
Union of New Religions 281
United Arab Emirates 198, 203, 204
United Farm Workers 86
United Kingdom 29, 48, 77, 78, 115, 117, 141,
  150, 223, 239, 246n7, 279, 285, 296
United Methodist Church 283–4
United Nations 352–3
United Nations' Women's Conference 13
United Nations Commission on
  Transnational Corporations
  (UNCTC) 333
United Nations Conference on Environment
  and Development (UNCED) 221, 224
United Nations Conference on Human Rights
  (1993) 135, 178
United Nations Conference on Trade and
  Development (UNCTAD) 331, 336
United Nations Diplomatic Conference of
  Plenipotentiaries 134
United Nations Environment Programme
  (UNEP) 223
United Socialist Party of Venezuela 382
United States 26, 38, 63, 73, 78, 83, 117, 118,
  121, 125, 151, 152, 198, 223, 228, 237, 239,
  241, 262–3, 275, 277, 281, 282, 296, 342,
  345, 355
United States Agency for International
  Development (USAID) 152
Universal Declaration of Human Rights
  (UDHR) 116, 117, 119, 128, 150
UN Special Session on Disarmament
  (1982) 280
US Catholic Conference of Bishops
  The Challenge of Peace 283

U.S. Conference of Mayors 284
Useem, Bert 194, 196, 255
US Senate Subcommittee on Multinational
    Corporations of the Senate Foreign
    Relations Committee 332

van der Vyver, Johan D. 134
Vanaik, Achin 355
Vanity Fair 65
velvet revolution (1989) 287
venue shopping 28
Verhofstadt, Guy 17
Via Campesina 342
Vicariate of Solidarity 123
Victims Rights' Caucus 142
Vienna Agreement (1985) 229
Vienna Conference on Human rights
    (1993) 197, 199
Vietnam 82
Vivant! 199

Wahabi 15
Wahid, Abdurrahman 126
Walker, Rob 6
Wallis, Jim 283
War on Want 29
Washburn, John 144
Washington Consensus 82, 327, 331
Watson, Robert 241
Weaver, Sigourney 151
WEDO 174
Wesley, John 48, 51
    Thoughts upon slavery 55
West, Benjamin 56
West African Mail 64
West African Missionary Association 64
Whitaker, Chico 378
Whitefield, George 51
Wilberforce, William 57, 64
Williams, Jody 295, 315
Wilson, Dagmar 279
Wittner, Lawrence 279–80
Women's Caucus for Gender Justice
    (WCGJ) 207
women's circles 174
Women's International Inter-discipline
    Congress 177
Women's International League for Peace and
    Freedom (WILPF) 8

women's movement, global 163
    activist strategies 173–80
    advocacy 182, 183, 185–6
    characteristics 167–70
    definitions 164–7
    institutional strategies 180–1
    networking 182
    origins 171–2
    power analysis 185–6
    research and analysis 182
    social change, approaches to 182–5
    symbols and images and 170–1
    three waves of 171
    see also transnational women's rights
        movement (TWM)
women's rights, contesting 190
    counter-movements 194–5
    framing and counter activists 201–5
    influence of counter activists 205–8
    mobilizing structures and counter
        activists 198–201
    political opportunity structure (POS) and
        counter activists 195–8
    research design and method 192–3
    transnational social actors 193–4
Women's Rights as Human Rights frame 202
Women for Life on Earth 285
Women Strike for Peace 279
Woolman, John 49, 53, 55
Worker's Party (*Partido Trabalhadores*) 347,
    376, 377, 382
Workers' Rights Consortium (WRC) 93
Working Group on Applicable Law 138
World Bank 29, 125, 226, 227, 330, 333–5
    Committee 9
    Country Gender Assessment 180–1
World Climate Conference (1990) 229
World Commission on Dams (WCD) 10
World Commission on Environment and
    Development
    Our Common Future 224
World Conference of Civil Society 139
World Conference on Human Rights 125
World Congress of Families II (1999) 200
World Council of Churches assembly 283
World Disarmament Conference (1932–3) 39
World Federalist Movement 135–6, 137, 144
World Federation of Trade Unions
    (WFTU) 77

World Movement of Mothers 192
World Resources Institute 231
World Social Forum (WSF) 16, 18, 42, 175,
   177, 179, 335, 341, 347, 376, 384
   Charter of Principles 349
   elitism and 380–2
   experiments in global democracy and 352–3
   global collective identity cultivation
      and 353–4
   International Committee 379–80, 381
   localizing the process of 351–2
   as political initiative 382–3
   shared analyses, developing 354–6
   socialization for struggle and 356
   and strategy 377–80
   struggle for internal democracy in 350
World Summit on Sustainable
   Development 225
World Trade Organization (WTO) 90, 231,
   232, 344, 345

World Wide Fund for Nature (WWF) 226,
   227
World Youth Alliance 201
Worth, Owen 376

Ximenes Belo 126

Yakovlev, Alexander 287
Yankelovich, Daniel 281
Yemen 198, 204
Yevtushenko, Yevgenii 287
Young Women's Christian Association 284
Yugoslavia 138

Zald, Meyer 194, 196, 255
Zambia 78
Zapatistas 17, 344, 346, 349, 353
Zee TV 19
Zengakuren 280
Zimbabwe 20